The Very Best
Baby Name
Book
in the whole wide world

The Very Best Baby Name Book

in the whole wide world

Bruce Lansky

Meadowbrook Press

Distributed by Simon & Schuster
New York

Distributed in the UK by
Chris Lloyd Sales and Marketing

Acknowledgments

The list of names and their images is derived from *The Baby Name Survey Book* by Bruce Lansky and Barry Sinrod. Copyright © 1998 by Meadowbrook Press.

The most popular name lists were derived from a survey conducted by the Social Security Administration.

Some of the material in "Fascinating Facts about Names" comes from "The Names People Play," by Frank Remington. It originally appeared in the November 1969 issue of *Today's Health*. Used with permission.

Some of the names and occupations of persons listed in "The Name's the Game" are reprinted from *Remarkable Names of Real People*, compiled and annotated by John Train, illustrated by Pierre Le-Tan. Copyright © 1977 by John Train. Used with permission of Clarkson N. Potter.

Dick Crouser's contributions to "Fascinating Facts about Names" are used with permission.

Dick Neff's contributions to "Fascinating Facts about Names" first appeared in the January 8, 1968, and April 1, 1968, issues of *Advertising Age*. Copyright © 1968 by Crain Communications, Inc. Used with permission.

Library of Congress Cataloging in Publication Data

Lansky, Bruce.
    [Best baby name book in the whole wide world]
    The very best baby name book in the whole wide world/by Bruce Lansky.
        p. cm.
    ISBN 0-88166-479-0 (Meadowbrook). — ISBN 0-684-02873-5 (Simon & Schuster)
    1. Names, Personal—Dictionaries.   I. Title.
    CS2377.L36   2004
    929.4'4—dc22   2004017145

First edition published 1979. Revised editions published 1984, 1995, 2003, 2004.
© 1979, 1984, 1995, 2003, 2004 by Bruce Lansky

Published by Meadowbrook Press, 5451 Smetana Drive, Minnetonka, MN 55343

BOOK TRADE DISTRIBUTION by Simon & Schuster, a division of Simon and Schuster, Inc., 1230 Avenue of the Americas, New York, NY 10020

08 07 06 05 04   10 9 8 7 6 5 4 3 2 1

Printed in the United States of America

Editors: Megan McGinnis, Kelsey Anderson, Angela Wiechmann, Joseph Gredler
Production Manager: Paul Woods
Cover design: Lynn Johnston, Luke Pegoraro, Cathleen Casey, Linda Norton, Tamara Peterson
Cover Illustrations: Lynn Johnston

Contents

15 Things to Consider
When Naming Your Baby

1. Namesakes

Exact reproductions of a person's name, even if it is followed by Jr. or II, are often confusing to everyone involved. Parents frequently vary the middle name of a son who carries his father's first and last names, and then call the son by his middle name to distinguish him from his father; but the potential for confusion still exists. What's worse, the child never gets the satisfaction of having a name and a clear identity of his own.

Namesakes can also lead to unfortunate name choices. Somehow the name Mildred just doesn't seem to fit a little girl comfortably, even though it fits eighty-year-old Aunt Mildred perfectly. Generally, make sure that a namesake's name is one you'd choose on its own merits, quite apart from the good feelings you have for the person you're complimenting this way.

2. Nationality

If you choose a "foreign-sounding" name, be sure it's not unpronounceable or unspellable, or the name will be a burden to your child. Combinations of names from different countries, like Francois Finklebaum or Marco Mazarowski, may provoke smiles. So if you want to combine names with different ethnic roots, try them out on lots of people before making a final decision.

3. Religion

To some parents it is important to follow religious traditions in naming a baby. Roman Catholics have traditionally chosen saints' names, sometimes using Mary as a first name for each daughter and pairing it with different middle names: Mary Rose, Mary Margaret, and so on. Jews traditionally choose Old Testament names, often the name of a deceased relative, while Protestants choose both Old and New Testament names. Muslims turn to the Koran and the names of Mohammed and his family as traditional sources of names.

4. Gender

There are two opposing lines of thought on names that can be given to boys and girls alike, whether they are changeable ones like Carol/Carroll, Leslie/Lesley, and Claire/Clair or the truly unisex names like Robin, Chris, and Terry. Some parents feel that a unisex name allows them to pick a name with certainty before the baby's sex is known and that such names "type" children in gender roles and expectations less than traditional boy names and girl names do. Others argue that it's unfair and psychologically harmful to require a child to explain which sex he or she is. (Remember the song "A Boy Named Sue"?) Finally, boys may feel more threatened or insulted when they are presumed to be girls than girls may when they're taken to be boys.

5. Number of Names

No law requires a person to have three names, though most forms provide spaces for a first name, middle initial or name, and surname. When choosing a name for your child, you have several options: a first and last name; a first and last name and only a middle initial (Harry S. Truman's S is just an S); initials for both first and middle names; or several middle names. Keep your child's lifelong use of the name in mind when you do something unusual—four middle names are going to cause space problems for your child every time he or she fills out a form!

6. Sounds

The combination of letters in a person's name can make saying the name easier or harder. Alliteration, as in Tina Turner or Pat Paulsen, is fine, but such rhymes as Tyrone Cohn or Alice Palace invite teasing. Joke names, punning names, and other displays of your wit may sound funny, but living with such a name is no laughing matter.

7. Rhythms

Most naming specialists agree that unequal numbers of syllables create pleasing rhythms. Such names as Dwight David Eisenhower or Molly Melinda Grooms fit this pattern. When first and last names have equal numbers of syllables, a middle name with a different number creates a nice effect, as in Albert Anthony Cleveland or Gail Canova Pons. Single-syllable names can be especially forceful if each name has a rather long sound, as in Mark Twain or Charles Rath.

8. Pronunciation

Nobody likes having his or her name constantly mispronounced. If you pick an unusual name, such as Jésus or Genviève (hay-soos and zhan-vee-ev), don't expect people to pronounce it correctly. Other names with high mispronunciation potential are names that have more than one common pronunciation, as in Alicia (does the second syllable rhyme with fish or leash?) or Shana (does the name rhyme with Anna or Dana?). And if you choose a unique pronunciation of

a name (for example, pronouncing Nina like Dinah), don't expect many people to get it right.

9. Spelling

In his poem *Don Juan,* Lord Byron writes, "Thrice happy he whose name has been well spelt," and it's true that you feel a special kind of irritation when your name gets misspelled.

Ordinary spellings have the force of common sense behind them. On the other hand, a new or unusual spelling can revitalize an old name. If the name Ethel only reminds you of Ethel Mertz in the old *I Love Lucy* show, but your mate is crazy about having a daughter with that name, perhaps Ethelle will be a happy substitute. However, some people think it's silly to vary from "traditional" spellings of names and are prejudiced against any Thom, Dik, or Hari.

10. Popularity

Some names are so popular, you shouldn't be surprised to find more than one child with that name in your child's classroom. A child with a very popular name may feel that he or she must "share" it with others, while a child with a very uncommon name is likely to feel that it is uniquely his or hers. However, a child with a popular name may be accepted by peers more easily than a child with a very uncommon name, which may be perceived as weird.

11. Uniqueness

Did you ever try to look in the phone book for the telephone number of someone called John Smith? You wouldn't be able to find it without also knowing the address. To avoid confusion, many people with common last names choose distinctive first and/or middle names for their children. However, a highly unusual name, such as Teague or Hestia, could be an even greater disservice to your child than Michael or Emily.

12. Stereotypes

Most names call to mind physical or personality traits that often stem from a well-known namesake, real or fictional. Some names—Adolf and Judas, for instance—may never outlive the terrible associations they receive from a single person who bore them. Because the image of a name will affect its owner's self-image as well as the way he or she is perceived by others, consider what associations come to mind as you make your selections.

13. Initials

Folk wisdom has it that a person whose initials spell a word—any word—is destined to be successful in life. But it can be irksome, even embarrassing, to have *DUD* or *HAG* stamped on your suitcases and jewelry. So be sure your child's initials spell "happy" words— or none at all—to avoid these problems.

14. Nicknames

Most names have shortened or familiar forms that are used during childhood or at different stages of life. For example, Michael might be called Mikey as a child, Mike as a teenager, and Michael on his college application. So if you don't want your daughter to be called Sam, don't name her Samantha.

If you are thinking of giving your child a nickname as a legal name, remember that Trisha may grow weary of explaining that her full name is not Patricia. And consider the fact that names that sound cute for a child, as in Missy and Timmy, could prove embarrassing later in life. Can you picture Grandma Missy and Grandpa Timmy?

15. Meanings

Most people don't know the meanings of their names—first, middle, or last. But most names do have meanings, and you should at least find out what your favorite choices mean before giving them to your child. A name that means something funny or embarrassing probably won't overshadow your child's life, but if you have to choose between two names that are equally attractive to you, meanings may help tip the balance.

The Most Popular Names
from 1900 to 2003

The popularity of names, like the length of hemlines and the width of ties, is subject to change every year. The changes become even more noticeable when you think about the changes in name "fashions" over longer periods.

Think about the names of your grandparents and famous entertainers of their generation: Debbie Reynolds, Troy Donahue, Doris Day, Rock Hudson, and Patti Page—none of their first names is in the list of top 100 names.

Popular entertainers of the 1960s included Annette Funicello, Frankie Avalon, Jerry Lee Lewis, Elvis Presley, and Audrey Hepburn—none of their first names is in the list of top 100 names either.

It seems that in every decade a new group of names rises in popularity, as names associated with a previous generation of babies decline. So, it is wise to consider whether a name's popularity is rising, declining, or holding steady.

To help you assess name popularity trends, we are presenting the most recently available top 100 names given to baby boys and girls. The rankings are derived from a survey of all new births nationwide, conducted by the Social Security Administration.

Alternate spellings of each name are treated as separate names. For example, Sarah and Sara are ranked separately.

As you refer to the following data, remember that the popularity issue cuts two ways: 1) Psychologists say a child with a common or popular name seems to have better odds of success in life than a child with an uncommon name. 2) A child whose name is at the top of the popularity poll may not feel as unique and special as a child whose name is less common.

The 100 Most Popular Girls' Names in 2003

1. Emily	26. Hailey	51. Makayla	76. Autumn
2. Emma	27. Jasmine	52. Faith	77. Lillian
3. Madison	28. Rachel	53. Amanda	78. Audrey
4. Hannah	29. Morgan	54. Kaylee	79. Ariana
5. Olivia	30. Megan	55. Jenna	80. Jada
6. Abigail	31. Jennifer	56. Andrea	81. Erin
7. Alexis	32. Kaitlyn	57. Trinity	82. Isabel
8. Ashley	33. Julia	58. Zoe	83. Leah
9. Elizabeth	34. Haley	59. Katelyn	84. Danielle
10. Samantha	35. Mia	60. Madeline	85. Maya
11. Isabella	36. Katherine	61. Mary	86. Arianna
12. Sarah	37. Destiny	62. Michelle	87. Gabriela
13. Grace	38. Alexandra	63. Kimberly	88. Jocelyn
14. Alyssa	39. Nicole	64. Rebecca	89. Evelyn
15. Lauren	40. Maria	65. Sara	90. Avery
16. Kayla	41. Ava	66. Alexa	91. Aaliyah
17. Brianna	42. Savannah	67. Caroline	92. Leslie
18. Jessica	43. Brooke	68. Gabrielle	93. Sofia
19. Taylor	44. Ella	69. Lily	94. Melanie
20. Sophia	45. Allison	70. Vanessa	95. Claire
21. Anna	46. Mackenzie	71. Angelina	96. Shelby
22. Victoria	47. Paige	72. Riley	97. Melissa
23. Natalie	48. Stephanie	73. Sierra	98. Marissa
24. Chloe	49. Jordan	74. Amber	99. Bailey
25. Sydney	50. Kylie	75. Gabriella	100. Jade

The 100 Most Popular Boys' Names in 2003

1. Jacob	26. Justin	51. Gavin	76. Diego
2. Michael	27. Nathan	52. Jackson	77. Timothy
3. Joshua	28. Jose	53. Kyle	78. Julian
4. Matthew	29. Logan	54. Luis	79. Cody
5. Andrew	30. Gabriel	55. Juan	80. Blake
6. Joseph	31. Kevin	56. Mason	81. Seth
7. Ethan	32. Noah	57. Eric	82. Dominic
8. Daniel	33. Austin	58. Brian	83. Jaden
9. Christopher	34. Caleb	59. Charles	84. Xavier
10. Anthony	35. Robert	60. Adam	85. Hayden
11. William	36. Thomas	61. Sean	86. Richard
12. Ryan	37. Elijah	62. Alex	87. Chase
13. Nicholas	38. Jordan	63. Bryan	88. Sebastian
14. David	39. Aidan	64. Carlos	89. Colin
15. Tyler	40. Cameron	65. Nathaniel	90. Carson
16. Alexander	41. Hunter	66. Ian	91. Jeremiah
17. John	42. Jason	67. Jesus	92. Patrick
18. James	43. Angel	68. Adrian	93. Miguel
19. Dylan	44. Connor	69. Steven	94. Antonio
20. Zachary	45. Evan	70. Cole	95. Victor
21. Brandon	46. Jack	71. Lucas	96. Jesse
22. Jonathan	47. Luke	72. Owen	97. Alejandro
23. Samuel	48. Isaac	73. Aiden	98. Jake
24. Christian	49. Aaron	74. Devin	99. Landon
25. Benjamin	50. Isaiah	75. Jayden	100. Trevor

Most Popular Girls' Names in 2000	Most Popular Boys' Names in 2000	Most Popular Girls' Names in 1990	Most Popular Boys' Names in 1990
Emily	Jacob	Ashley	Michael
Hannah	Michael	Jessica	Christopher
Madison	Matthew	Emily	Matthew
Ashley	Joshua	Sarah	Joshua
Sarah	Christopher	Samantha	Jacob
Alexis	Nicholas	Brittany	Andrew
Samantha	Andrew	Amanda	Daniel
Jessica	Joseph	Elizabeth	Nicholas
Taylor	Daniel	Taylor	Tyler
Elizabeth	Tyler	Megan	Joseph
Lauren	William	Stephanie	David
Alyssa	Ryan	Kayla	Brandon
Kayla	Brandon	Lauren	James
Abigail	John	Jennifer	John
Brianna	Zachary	Rachel	Ryan
Olivia	David	Hannah	Zachary
Emma	Anthony	Nicole	Justin
Megan	James	Amber	Anthony
Grace	Justin	Alexis	William
Victoria	Alexander	Courtney	Robert
Rachel	Jonathan	Victoria	Jonathan
Anna	Christian	Danielle	Kyle
Sydney	Austin	Alyssa	Austin
Destiny	Dylan	Rebecca	Alexander
Morgan	Ethan	Jasmine	Kevin

Most Popular Girls' Names in 1980	Most Popular Boys' Names in 1980	Most Popular Girls' Names in 1970	Most Popular Boys' Names in 1970
Jessica	Michael	Jennifer	Michael
Jennifer	Christopher	Amy	Christopher
Amanda	Matthew	Melissa	Jason
Ashley	Joshua	Michelle	David
Sarah	David	Kimberly	James
Stephanie	Daniel	Lisa	John
Melissa	James	Angela	Robert
Nicole	Robert	Heather	Brian
Elizabeth	John	Stephanie	William
Heather	Joseph	Jessica	Matthew
Tiffany	Jason	Elizabeth	Daniel
Michelle	Justin	Nicole	Joseph
Amber	Andrew	Rebecca	Kevin
Megan	Ryan	Kelly	Eric
Rachel	William	Mary	Jeffrey
Amy	Brian	Christina	Richard
Lauren	Jonathan	Amanda	Scott
Kimberly	Brandon	Sarah	Mark
Christina	Nicholas	Laura	Steven
Brittany	Anthony	Julie	Timothy
Crystal	Eric	Shannon	Thomas
Rebecca	Adam	Christine	Anthony
Laura	Kevin	Tammy	Charles
Emily	Steven	Karen	Jeremy
Danielle	Thomas	Tracy	Joshua

Most Popular Girls' Names in 1960	Most Popular Boys' Names in 1960	Most Popular Girls' Names in 1950	Most Popular Boys' Names in 1950
Lisa	Michael	Mary	Michael
Mary	David	Linda	James
Karen	John	Patricia	Robert
Susan	James	Susan	John
Kimberly	Robert	Deborah	David
Patricia	Mark	Barbara	William
Linda	William	Debra	Richard
Donna	Richard	Karen	Thomas
Michelle	Thomas	Nancy	Mark
Cynthia	Jeffrey	Donna	Charles
Sandra	Steven	Cynthia	Steven
Deborah	Joseph	Sandra	Gary
Pamela	Timothy	Pamela	Joseph
Tammy	Kevin	Sharon	Donald
Laura	Scott	Kathleen	Ronald
Lori	Brian	Carol	Kenneth
Elizabeth	Charles	Diane	Paul
Julie	Daniel	Brenda	Larry
Jennifer	Paul	Cheryl	Daniel
Brenda	Christopher	Elizabeth	Stephen
Angela	Kenneth	Janet	Dennis
Barbara	Anthony	Kathy	Timothy
Debra	Gregory	Margaret	Edward
Sharon	Ronald	Janice	Jeffrey
Teresa	Donald	Carolyn	George

Most Popular Girls' Names in 1940	Most Popular Boys' Names in 1940	Most Popular Girls' Names in 1930	Most Popular Boys' Names in 1930
Mary	James	Mary	Robert
Linda	Robert	Betty	James
Barbara	John	Barbara	John
Patricia	William	Shirley	William
Carol	Richard	Patricia	Richard
Sandra	David	Dorothy	Charles
Nancy	Charles	Joan	Donald
Judith	Thomas	Margaret	George
Sharon	Michael	Nancy	Thomas
Susan	Ronald	Helen	Joseph
Betty	Larry	Carol	David
Carolyn	Donald	Joyce	Edward
Shirley	Joseph	Doris	Ronald
Margaret	Gary	Ruth	Paul
Karen	George	Virginia	Kenneth
Donna	Kenneth	Marilyn	Frank
Judy	Paul	Elizabeth	Raymond
Kathleen	Edward	Jean	Jack
Joyce	Jerry	Frances	Harold
Dorothy	Dennis	Dolores	Billy
Janet	Frank	Beverly	Gerald
Diane	Daniel	Donna	Walter
Elizabeth	Raymond	Alice	Jerry
Janice	Stephen	Lois	Eugene
Joan	Roger	Janet	Henry

Most Popular Girls' Names in 1920	Most Popular Boys' Names in 1920	Most Popular Girls' Names in 1910	Most Popular Boys' Names in 1910
Mary	Robert	Mary	John
Dorothy	John	Helen	William
Helen	James	Dorothy	James
Betty	William	Margaret	Robert
Margaret	Charles	Ruth	Joseph
Ruth	George	Mildred	George
Virginia	Joseph	Anna	Charles
Doris	Richard	Elizabeth	Edward
Mildred	Edward	Frances	Frank
Elizabeth	Donald	Marie	Walter
Frances	Thomas	Evelyn	Thomas
Anna	Frank	Virginia	Henry
Evelyn	Paul	Alice	Harold
Alice	Harold	Florence	Paul
Marie	Walter	Rose	Raymond
Jean	Raymond	Lillian	Arthur
Shirley	Jack	Irene	Richard
Barbara	Henry	Louise	Albert
Irene	Arthur	Edna	Harry
Marjorie	Kenneth	Gladys	Donald
Lois	Albert	Catherine	Ralph
Florence	David	Ethel	Louis
Rose	Harry	Josephine	Clarence
Martha	Ralph	Ruby	Carl
Louise	Eugene	Martha	Fred

Most Popular Girls' Names in 1900	Most Popular Boys' Names in 1900
Mary	John
Helen	William
Margaret	James
Anna	George
Ruth	Joseph
Elizabeth	Charles
Dorothy	Robert
Marie	Frank
Mildred	Edward
Alice	Henry
Florence	Walter
Ethel	Thomas
Lillian	Harry
Rose	Arthur
Gladys	Harold
Frances	Albert
Edna	Paul
Grace	Clarence
Catherine	Fred
Hazel	Carl
Irene	Louis
Gertrude	Raymond
Clara	Ralph
Louise	Roy
Edith	Richard

Popular Names around the World

Family roots, foreign travel, and names in the news—all these are giving people new ideas for baby names. The following lists show the equivalents of Tom, Dick, and Harry (or Ann, Susan, and Elizabeth) from around the world. If you want information from a country not listed, check with its embassy or tourist information office. Incidentally, Mohammed (or Muhammad) is the most commonly given name in the world!

America		Australia		Canada	
Girls	**Boys**	**Girls**	**Boys**	**Girls**	**Boys**
Abelina	Adarius	Alexandra	Adam	Acadia	Alexander
Akayla	Butch	Alison	Alexander	Alice	Andrew
Amberlyn	Caden	Allira	Andrew	Amanda	Brandon
Darilynn	Daevon	Amanda	Benjamin	Ann(e)	Brian
Denisha	Dantrell	Claire	Bradley	Ashley	Christopher
Doneshia	Demarius	Elizabeth	Christopher	Carol(e)	Daniel
Emmylou	Devaughn	Emily	Daniel	Catherine	David
Jaycee	Dionte	Emma	David	Christine	Derek
Jessalyn	Jadrien	Jennifer	Ethan	Danielle	Edward
Johnnessa	Jailen	Jessica	Jack	Elizabeth	George
Karolane	Jamar	Karinya	Jake	Emily	Henry
Krystalynn	Jareth	Kate	James	Jacqueline	James
Kylie	Jayce	Kateena	Jarrah	Jennifer	John
Lakiesha	Lashawn	Katherine	Joshua	Jessica	Joseph
Lashana	Lavon	Kiah	Luke	Laura	Joshua
Latanya	Montel	Lauren	Matthew	Linda	Kyle
Roshawna	Mychal	Michelle	Michael	Lucy	Matthew
Shaniqua	Reno	Nicole	Mitchell	Margaret	Michael
Shantel	Reshawn	Rachel	Nicholas	Mary, Marie	Pierre
Shiquita	Ryker	Rebecca	Riley	Melissa	Robert
Takayla	Tajuan	Samantha	Ryan	Nicole	Ryan
Tenesha	Tevin	Sarah	Samuel	Patricia	Stephen
Trixia	Treshawn	Stephanie	Thomas	Sarah	Thomas
Tyesha	Tyrees	Talia	Timothy	Stephanie	Tyler
Yanet	Ziggy	Tegan	Tirrike	Susan	William

China

Girls	Boys
An	Chen
Bik	Cheung
Bo	Chung
Chun	Cong
Ciana	Dong
Fang	Fai
Gschu	Hung
Huan	Keung
Jai	Kong
Jing	Lei
Kwan	Li
Lai	Mao
Lian	On
Lin	Park
Ling	Po-Sin
Mei	Shilin
Nan	Shing
Ping	Tat
Qing	Tong
Ting	Tung
Xiaoli	Wing
Xiaomei	Xiaogang
Xiaoying	Xiaowei
Xiong Hong	Yang
Yuan	Yu

Czechoslovakia

Girls	Boys
Andela	Alois
Antonie	Antonin
Branka	Bohdan
Dana	Cenek
Denisa	Dominik
Dominika	Emil
Edita	Erik
Eva	Ferdinand
Irena	Filip
Izabela	Havel
Judita	Jan
Kamila	Johan
Katerina	Karel
Kristina	Kolman
Lida	Kornel
Magda	Marek
Marika	Matej
Martina	Michael
Michaela	Milos
Milena	Patrik
Rada	Pavel
Raina	Radovan
Sabina	Stepan
Tatiana	Urban
Tereza	Viktor

Egypt

Girls	Boys
Abeer	Abdu
Aziza	Abdulla
Chavi	Ahmed
Chione	Ali
Efra	Amon
Fatima	Hisham
Halima	Horus
Hind	Hossam
Huda	Kareem
Indihar	Mahmud
Intisar	Mohammed
Maha	Moneim
Monifa	Moses
Nabila	Nassir
Nadine	Omar
Nagwa	Paki
Nakia	Roushdy
Nema	Saled
Ola	Sami
Rakia	Samir
Rasha	Sef
Samira	Tamer
Sanura	Tewfik
Shahira	Yahiya
Sherin	Yahya

England

Girls	Boys
Alexandra	Alexander
Alice	Andrew
Amy	Basil
Anna	Charles
Beatrice	Christopher
Catherine	Daniel
Charlotte	David
Daphne	Edward
Edith	George
Eleonor	Harry
Elizabeth	Henry
Ellen	James
Emily	Jonathan
Emma	Kendall
Isobel	Kendrick
Leola	Mark
Lucy	Martin
Matilda	Maurice
Monica	Nicholas
Olivia	Oliver
Patricia	Richard
Rebecca	Robert
Sarah	Samuel
Sophie	Thomas
Victoria	William

France

Girls	Boys
Angelique	Adrien
Annette	Andre
Aubrey	Antoine
Belle	Bernard
Camille	Christophe
Charlotte	Donatien
Christelle	Eduard
Cosette	Florian
Danielle	Francois
Desiree	Gatien
Estelle	Guillaume
Gabrielle	Jacques
Genevieve	Jean
Juliette	Jerome
Lainey	Joseph
Lourdes	Luc
Margaux	Marc
Maribel	Max
Michelle	Narcisse
Monique	Philippe
Natalie	Russel
Nicolle	Saville
Paris	Sebastian
Raquel	Stephan
Salena	Sylvian

Germany

Girls	Boys
Ada	Adler
Adelaide	Adolf
Amalia	Arnold
Anna	Bern
Annalise	Bogart
Charlee	Bruno
Christa	Claus
Claudia	Clovis
Edda	Diedrich
Elsa	Dieter
Gaby	Emil
Gisela	Emmett
Gretchen	Friedrich
Heidi	Gerhard
Hetta	Helmut
Hilda	Humphrey
Ida	Kurt
Katrina	Leopold
Lona	Lindberg
Margret	Mandel
Milia	Meyer
Monika	Phillipp
Reynalda	Siegfried
Sandra	Stein
Velma	Wagner

Greece		Hawaii		Hungary	
Girls	**Boys**	**Girls**	**Boys**	**Girls**	**Boys**
Aleni	Achilles	Ailani	Aukai	Adrienn	Ambrus
Alexandra	Alexi	Akela	Bane	Alexandra	Andras
Amaryllis	Aristotle	Alamea	Ekewaka	Alida	Aron
Anastasia	Christos	Alana	Elika	Aliz	Attila
Angeline	Constantinos	Ani	Hanale	Amalia	Bandi
Aphrodite	Dimitris	Ikia	Haoa	Anna	Barna
Athena	Elias	Inoa	Havika	Beata	Bela
Callista	Euripedes	Kalia	Hiu	Bianka	Daniel
Daphne	Gaylen	Kalina	Kai	Dora	Demeter
Dimitra	Julius	Kamea	Kane	Edina	Edvard
Ebone	Kimon	Keala	Keawe	Eva	Elek
Ekaterini	Kristo	Keilani	Kele	Felicia	Elias
Emalia	Manolis	Kekona	Kimo	Gabriella	Fabo
Fotini	Mikhail	Kiele	Lani	Ibolya	Filep
Helena	Nicos	Kina	Lei	Ili	Gabi
Hilary	Panayiotis	Lani	Lekek	Ilona	Gazsi
Kaliope	Pericles	Mele	Liban	Izabella	Geza
Katina	Platon	Mohala	Loe	Karola	Imre
Kyriakoula	Stephanos	Nana	Lui	Kata	Jakab
Marina	Thanasi	Noma	Manu	Kornelia	Marcell
Olga	Thanos	Olina	Mauli	Margit	Nikola
Sapphire	Theodor	Peke	Oliwa	Marianna	Orban
Stamata	Vasilis	Pua	Palani	Natalia	Rudi
Stella	Yannis	Suke	Uku	Szilvia	Simon
Yana	Yorgos	Wainani	Wene	Zsa Zsa	Tibor

Ireland

Girls	Boys
Aileen	Aidan
Ashlyn	Barry
Brenna	Blaine
Brianne	Brady
Caitlyn	Clancy
Colleen	Connor
Delainey	Desmond
Erin	Donovan
Gladys	Eagan
Ina	Flynn
Kelly	Garret
Kylie	Grady
Mackenzie	Keegan
Maeve	Keenan
Maura	Kevin
Maureen	Liam
Meagan	Mahon
Nyla	Maloney
Quincy	Nevin
Reagan	Owen
Shaelee	Quinn
Sinead	Reilly
Tara	Ryan
Taryn	Seamus
Una	Sean

Israel

Girls	Boys
Alia	Aaron
Ariel	Abel
Aviva	Azriel
Ayla	Benjamin
Danielle	Boaz
Deborah	Caleb
Dinah	Coby
Eliza	Daniel
Gail	Elijah
Ganya	Emmanuel
Ilana	Ira
Jessica	Isaak
Joan	Isaiah
Jordana	Jacob
Judith	Jeremiah
Laela	Meyer
Levia	Michael
Mariam	Nathaniel
Mikala	Oren
Milena	Reuben
Rachael	Seth
Sabra	Tobin
Talia	Yuri
Tamara	Zachariah
Zilla	Zachary

Italy

Girls	Boys
Adriana	Alessandro
Alessia	Angelo
Anna	Antonio
Aryana	Carlo
Bianca	Dino
Camellia	Drago
Capri	Elmo
Carina	Este
Carlotta	Fabrizio
Chiara	Fortino
Donna	Gino
Elena	Giovanni
Emilia	Giuseppe
Francesca	Guido
Gabriella	Larenzo
Gianna	Luigi
Giulia	Marino
Isabella	Otello
Lucia	Peppe
Mia	Rocco
Mila	Salvatore
Pia	Silvio
Rosa	Tristano
Venecia	Umberto
Zola	Vittorio

Japan		Mexico		Native American	
Girls	**Boys**	**Girls**	**Boys**	**Girls**	**Boys**
Akemi	Akemi	Adriana	Alfonso	Aiyana	Ahanu
Euiki	Akira	Alejandra	Alfredo	Anaba	Anoki
Hiroko	Botan	Alicia	Antonio	Cherokee	Bly
Junko	Danno	Alma	Arturo	Dakota	Chaska
Kadiri	Hiroshi	Ana	Carlos	Dena	Delsin
Kameko	Joben	Ariana	Chavez	Dyana	Elan
Keiko	Joji	Carmen	Enresto	Imala	Elsu
Kimi	Jun	Claudia	Enrique	Izusa	Etu
Kioko	Ken	Cristina	Fernando	Kanda	Hakan
Kumiko	Kenji	Elena	Jaime	Kiona	Huslu
Leiko	Masao	Erika	Javier	Leotie	Inteus
Mai	Miki	Esmeralda	Jesus	Lulu	Istu
Manami	Nobuo	Gabriela	Jorge	Magena	Iye
Mariko	Shigeru	Guadalupe	Jose	Netis	Jolon
Megumi	Sho	Juana	Juan	Nina	Knoton
Michiko	Tadashi	Karla	Julio	Olathe	Lenno
Oki	Takashi	Laura	Luis	Oneida	Masao
Rei	Takeo	Leticia	Marco	Sakuna	Minal
Reiko	Takeshi	Maria	Mario	Sora	Muraco
Sachiko	Toshio	Marta	Miguel	Taima	Neka
Sakuro	Yasuo	Monica	Oscar	Tala	Nodin
Sato	Yoshio	Patricia	Pablo	Utina	Paco
Toshiko	Yuji	Rosa	Pedro	Winona	Son
Yoko	Yujiro	Susana	Raul	Wyanet	Songan
Yoshiko	Yusuke	Valeria	Roman	Wyoming	Wingi

20

Nigeria

Girls	Boys
Abebi	Adebayo
Ada	Adigun
Adanna	Ajani
Akanke	Akins
Alake	Amadi
Amaka	Ayo
Aniweta	Azi
Asabi	Chika
Chi	Chike
Chinwe	Chima
Chinyere	Chinua
Enogi	Ekon
Fayola	Emeka
Femi	Gowon
Ijeoma	Ikenna
Limber	Kayin
Lola	Ndem
Mma	Nnamdi
Nena	Nwa
Ngozi	Okechuku
Nma	Okon
Nnenna	Olu
Nwa	Orji
Oba	Ottah
Oni	Tor

Norway

Girls	Boys
Agnes	Anders
Anne	Andreas
Anne-Lise	Christian
Astrid	Christopher
Berit	Dag
Berta	Erik
Camilla	Gunnar
Gorun	Hans
Grete	Ingolf
Hedda	Ingvar
Hilde	Jan
Inga	Jens
Ingrid	Johannes
Jonette	Jon
Kari	Karl
Karolina	Kasper
Kirsti	Kennet
Marianne	Olaf
Martine	Petter
Merete	Rolf
Signe	Simen
Siri	Stig
Stine	Sverre
Thea	Teodor
Trine	Thomas

Phillippines

Girls	Boys
Aida	Alberto
Alicia	Antonio
Ana	Armando
Aurora	Arturo
Belen	Bayanai
Carmen	Benjamin
Consuela	Carlos
Corazon	Domingo
Elizabeth	Esteban
Elvira	Francisco
Eveline	Gregorio
Fermina	Honorio
Gloria	Jose
Isabel	Juan
Leonor	Juanito
Ligaya	Leopoldo
Malaya	Manuel
Maria	Mariano
Patricia	Pedro
Reyna	Ramon
Roario	Raúl
Socorro	Rizal
Temerlia	Roberto
Teresa	Rolando
Teresita	Rosendo

Poland

Girls	Boys
Agata	Adam
Ania	Andrej
Aniela	Boleslaw
Anka	Danek
Anna	Dawid
Beata	Eugeniusz
Eugenia	Franek
Ewa	Grzegorz
Franciscka	Heniek
Jadwiga	Janos
Joana	Josep
Justina	Karol
Karolina	Krzysctof
Katarzina	Lukasz
Lucia	Marian
Magda	Mateusz
Marinna	Michal
Marta	Milek
Marzena	Natan
Monika	Pawal
Morela	Piotr
Stefa	Rafal
Tawia	Telek
Waleria	Tomasz
Wicktoria	Wincent

Portugal

Girls	Boys
Ana	Americo
Clara	Antonio
Emilia	Carlos
Estela	Donato
Fatima	Edwardo
Fatima	Fernando
Fernanda	Filipe
Francisca	Filipe
Gabriella	Francisco
Gloria	Frederico
Graca	Gaspar
Helena	Germano
Ines	Henrique
Irene	Herberto
Irmelinda	Humberto
Isabel	João
Julia	Joaquin
Luisa	Jorge
Manuela	Luis
Margarida	Manuel
Maria	Mario
Rafaela	Miguel
Rita	Paulo
Sofia	Pedro
Teresa	Ricardo

Russia

Girls	Boys
Anya	Andrei
Anzhela	Adrik
Dasha	Aleksy
Galina	Anatoli
Irina	Arkadij
Kira	Boris
Larisa	Dmitrij
Lelya	Evgenij
Lera	Feodor
Manya	Filya
Marina	Georgi
Mila	Igor
Natalya	Ilya
Natasha	Ivan
Nika	Konstantin
Olga	Leonid
Olya	Misha
Polina	Natan
Sofia	Nikolai
Stepania	Oleg
Tamara	Oleksandr
Tatiana	Pavel
Vera	Sasha
Yelena	Vladimir
Yelizaveta	Yuri

Scotland		Sweden		Vietnam	
Girls	**Boys**	**Girls**	**Boys**	**Girls**	**Boys**
Aileen	Adair	Anna	Adrian	Ai	An
Aili	Ainsley	Anneka	Anders	Am	Antoan
Ainsley	Alastair	Astrid	Arnie	Bian	Binh
Artis	Annan	Birgitte	Axel	Cai	Cadao
Beneen	Arthur	Britta	Bengt	Cam	Chim
Berkley	Brayan	Carina	Bjorn	Cara	Dinh
Blair	Bret	Christina	Bo	Dao	Duc
Davina	Caylan	Dagmar	Burr	Hoa	Gia
Davonna	Connor	Elisabeth	Edvard	Hong	Hai
Elspeth	Craig	Elsa	Erik	Huong	Hung
Isla	Dunham	Erika	Ernst	Kim	Hy
Jeana	Dunn	Eva	Folke	Lan	Lap
Keita	Edan	Gudrun	Frederik	Le	Long
Kelsey	Ennis	Heidi	Greger	Mai	Minh
Kenzie	Ian	Helena	Gunnar	Nghi	Nam
Lesley	Kade	Helga	Gustaf	Nu	Ngai
Maisie	Kendrick	Inga	Halen	Ping	Ngu
Malvina	Kennan	Ingrid	Hans	Tam	Nien
Marjorie	Leith	Karin	Kjell	Thanh	Phuok
Mckenzie	Leslie	Kirsten	Lars	Thao	Tam
Mhairie	Malcom	Margareta	Lukas	Thi	Tan
Paisley	Ronny	Signe	Nils	Thuy	Teo
Rhona	Stratton	Sonja	Oskar	Tuyen	Thai
Roslyn	Tremaine	Ulla	Per	Tuyet	Thian
Scotti	Tyree	Ulrika	Rolle	Xuan	Tu

The Impressions Names Make

Consciously or unconsciously, we all have private pictures of the people who answer to certain names. Jackie could be sophisticated and beautiful, like Jackie Kennedy, or fat and funny, like Jackie Gleason. These pictures come from personal experience as well as from the images we absorb from the mass media and thus may conflict in interesting ways. Charlton strikes many people as a sissified, passive, whiny brat until they think of Charlton Heston. Marilyn may personify voluptuous femininity until you think of your neighbor who hangs out her clothes wearing a ratty bathrobe, with curlers in her hair and a cigarette dangling out of her mouth.

Over the years researchers have been fascinated by this question of the "real" meanings of names and their effects on their bearers. When they are asked to stereotype names by age, trustworthiness, attractiveness, sociability, kindness, aggressiveness, popularity, masculinity/femininity, degree of activity or passivity, etc., people actually do tend to agree on each name's characteristics.

So if people think of Mallory as cute and likeable, does that influence a girl named Mallory to become cute and likeable? Experts agree that names don't guarantee instant success or condemn people to certain failure, but they do affect self-images, influence relationships with others, and help (or hinder) success in work and school.

Robert Rosenthal's classic experiment identified what he named the Pygmalion effect: randomly selected children who'd been labeled "intellectual bloomers" actually did bloom!

Another researcher, S. Gray Garwood, conducted a study on sixth graders in New Orleans. He found that students given names that were popular with teachers scored higher in skills tests, were better adjusted and more consistent in their self-perceptions, were more realistic in their evaluations of themselves, and more frequently expected that they would attain their goals—even though their goals were more ambitious than ones set by their peers.

A research study in San Diego suggested that average essays by Davids, Michaels, Karens, and Lisas got better grades than average essays written by Elmers, Huberts, Adelles, and Berthas. The reason? Teachers expected kids with popular names to do better (the Pygmalion effect again), and thus they assigned higher grades to those kids in a self-fulfilling prophecy.

The Sinrod Marketing Group's International Opinion panel surveyed over 100,000 parents to discover their opinions about names. Results of this poll are presented in *The Baby Name Survey Book* by Bruce Lansky and Barry Sinrod.

Their book contains the names people most often associate with hundreds of adjectives describing personal attributes such as *intelligent, athletic, attractive,* and *nice* (as well as *dumb, klutzy, ugly,* and *nasty*). It also contains personality profiles of over 1,700 common and unusual boys' and girls' names and includes real or fictional famous namesakes who may have influenced people's perception of each name.

What the authors found was that most names have very clear images; some even have multiple images. The following are lists of boys' and girls' names that were found to have either positive or negative multiple images.

Girls

Positive Images	Negative Images
Alana *(bright, mysterious)*	Augusta *(old, stodgy)*
Amy *(educated, calm)*	Bea *(heavy, grandma, old)*
Ava *(beautiful, dreamer)*	Beatrice *(heavy, old)*
Carla *(independent, outgoing)*	Chloris *(unattractive, cold)*
Christy *(friendly, cute)*	Dolores *(overweight, old)*
Courtney *(mischievous, bright)*	Fifi *(airhead, animal name)*
Francesca *(European, exciting)*	Hedda *(ugly, gossip)*
Hope *(calm, gentle)*	Henrietta *(fat, horrible)*
Jody *(athletic, cheerful, cute)*	Hilda *(dowdy, fat, maid)*
Joy *(delightful, friendly)*	Kiki *(dumb, animal name)*
Joyce *(friendly, fun loving)*	Marsha *(average, heavy, loud)*
Kate *(cute, outgoing)*	Matilda *(bossy, big)*
Linda *(beautiful, sweet)*	Maud *(large, opinionated)*
Marlo *(classy, cute)*	Merry *(self-centered, shallow)*
Pam *(sweet, outgoing)*	Milicent *(stuffy, old)*
Randi *(cute, lively)*	Olga *(nasty, fat, strict)*
Roxanne *(feminine, enthusiastic)*	Opal *(weird, old)*
Sandy *(nice, fun loving)*	Thelma *(unattractive, old)*
Stacy *(active, cute)*	Twyla *(dopey, strange)*
Steffi *(cute, free spirited, athletic)*	Wynne *(overweight, silly, whiny)*

Boys

Positive Images	Negative Images
Alexander *(intelligent, leader)*	Ace *(jerk, jock, stupid)*
Allen *(funny, friendly)*	Archibald *(stuffy, fat)*
Bart *(athletic, assertive)*	Boris *(scary, sinister, heavy)*
Ben *(strong, lovable)*	Bruno *(rough, mean, stupid)*
Benjamin *(cute, inventive)*	Butch *(chubby, bully, mean)*
Bradley *(sensitive, fun loving)*	Clem *(klutz, hillbilly)*
Bronson *(strong, tough)*	Clyde *(clumsy, hillbilly)*
Bud *(cheerful, good personality)*	Cyril *(meek, stuffy)*
Christian *(well mannered, honest)*	Damon *(evil, devil)*
Clinton *(rich/wealthy, rugged)*	Dennis *(brat, mischievous)*
Danny *(friendly, cute)*	Ebenezer *(mean, cranky, miserly)*
Dante *(charming, thoughtful, rich)*	Elmo *(awkward, dumb)*
David *(handsome, intelligent)*	Horton *(stuffy, overweight)*
Dmitri *(handsome, sexy)*	Hubert *(fat, old)*
Douglas *(handsome, strong)*	Norman *(fat, nerd)*
Drew *(attractive, independent, trim)*	Percival *(stuffy, snobby)*
Joel *(popular, nice, sensitive)*	Rolf *(hardheaded, rigid)*
John *(intelligent, dependable)*	Vic *(sneaky, old)*
Patrick *(popular, happy)*	Wally *(henpecked, mild mannered)*
Victor *(handsome, sexy)*	Zeke *(dumb, hillbilly, dirty)*

Athletic

Girls	Boys
Bailey	Alex
Billie	Ali
Bobbie	Alonso
Casey	Bart
Chris	Brian
Colleen	Buck
Dena	Chuck
Gabriella	Connor
Jackie	Cooper
Jessie	Daniel
Jill	Derek
Jody	Emmitt
Josie	Hakeem
Katie	Houston
Kelsey	Jake
Lindsay	Jock
Lola	Kareem
Martina	Kevin
Mia	Kirby
Morgan	Lynn
Natalia	Marcus
Nora	Riley
Steffi	Rod
Sue	Terry
Tammy	Trey

Beautiful

Girls
Adrienne
Ariel
Aurora
Bella
Bonita
Carmen
Cassandra
Catherine
Danielle
Ebony
Farrah
Genevieve
Jasmine
Jewel
Kendra
Kiera
Lydia
Marisa
Maya
Sarah
Scarlett
Simone
Tanya
Tessa
Whitney

Blonde

Girls	Boys
Bambie	Aubrey
Barbie	Austin
Bianca	Bjorn
Blanche	Brett
Brigitte	Bud
Bunny	Chance
Candy	Chick
Daisy	Colin
Dolly	Corbin
Heidi	Dalton
Inga	Dane
Jillian	Dennis
Krystal	Dwayne
Lara	Eric
Lorna	Josh
Madonna	Keith
Marcia	Kerry
Marnie	Kipp
Olivia	Kyle
Randi	Lars
Sally	Leif
Shannon	Louis
Sheila	Martin
Tracy	Olaf
Vanna	Sven

Cute

Girls	Boys
Annie	Andrew
Becca	Antoine
Bobbie	Antonio
Cheryl	Barry
Christy	Benjamin
Deanna	Chick
Debbie	Cory
Dee Dee	Danny
Emily	Eric
Jennifer	Francisco
Jody	Franky
Kari	Jon
Lacie	Kipp
Mallory	Linus
Mandy	Louis
Megan	Matthew
Peggy	Mike
Porsha	Nicholas
Randi	Rene
Serena	Robbie
Shannon	Rory
Shirley	Sonny
Stacy	Stevie
Tammy	Timothy
Trudy	Wade

Friendly

Girls	Boys
Bernadette	Allen
Bobbie	Aubrey
Bonnie	Barrett
Carol	Bennie
Christy	Bing
Dorothy	Cal
Elaine	Casper
Gwen	Cole
Joy	Dan
Kathy	Denny
Kenya	Donovan
Kim	Ed
Lila	Fred
Marcie	Gary
Millie	Hakeem
Nancy	Jeff
Nikki	Jerry
Opal	Jim
Patricia	Khalil
Rhoda	Rob
Rose	Russ
Ruby	Sandy
Sandy	Tony
Vivian	Vinny
Wendy	Wally

Funny

Girls	Boys
Dionne	Abbott
Ellen	Ace
Erma	Allen
Fanny	Archie
Gilda	Artie
Gillian	Bennie
Jenny	Bobby
Julie	Carson
Lucille	Chase
Lucy	Diego
Maggie	Dudley
Marge	Eddie
Marsha	Edsel
Maud	Eduardo
Melinda	Fletcher
Mickey	Fraser
Patty	Grady
Paula	Jerome
Rosie	Keenan
Roxanne	Rochester
Sally	Rollie
Stevie	Roscoe
Sunny	Sid
Sydney	Tim
Vivian	Vinny

Handsome

Boys

Adam
Ahmad
Alejandro
Alonzo
Austin
Beau
Blake
Bo
Bryant
Chaz
Christopher
Clint
Damian
David
Demetrius
Denzel
Douglas
Grant
Humphrey
Joe
Jude
Kiefer
Mitchell
Tevin
Vance

Hippie

Girls and Boys

Angel
Autumn
Baby
Breezy
Crystal
Dawn
Happy
Harmony
Honey
Indigo
Kharma
Love
Lucky
Meadow
Misty
Moon
Passion
Rainbow
River
Serenity
Skye
Sparkle
Sprout
Star
Sunshine

Intelligent

Girls	Boys
Abigail	Adlai
Agatha	Alexander
Alexis	Barton
Barbara	Brock
Dana	Clifford
Daria	Colin
Diana	Dalton
Eleanor	David
Grace	Donovan
Helen	Edward
Jade	Esteban
Jillian	Fraser
Kate	Jefferson
Kaylyn	Jerome
Laura	John
Leah	Kelsey
Lillian	Kenneth
Mackenzie	Merlin
Marcella	Ned
Meredith	Nelson
Meryl	Roderick
Michaela	Samuel
Shauna	Sebastian
Shelley	Tim
Vanessa	Virgil

Nerdy	Old-Fashioned		Place Names	
Boys	**Girls**	**Boys**	**Girls**	**Boys**
Arnie	Abigail	Abe	Asia	Afton
Barrett	Adelaide	Amos	Atlanta	Austin
Bernie	Adelle	Arthur	Augusta	Boston
Clarence	Bea	Bertrand	Brittany	Britton
Clifford	Charlotte	Clarence	Brook	Canyon
Creighton	Clementine	Cy	Chelsea	Carson
Dexter	Cora	Cyril	Cheyenne	Cleveland
Egbert	Dinah	Dennis	China	Cuba
Khalil	Edith	Erasmus	Dakota	Dakota
Marvin	Elsie	Erskine	Delta	Dallas
Mortimer	Esther	Ezekiel	Florence	Diego
Myron	Eugenia	Giuseppe	Georgia	Fargo
Newt	Hattie	Grover	India	Finn
Norman	Ida	Herbert	Kenya	Indiana
Sanford	Mamie	Herschel	Madison	Israel
Seymour	Martha	Jerome	Montana	London
Sheldon	Maureen	Kermit	Myrtle	Orlando
Sinclair	Meryl	Lloyd	Olympia	Phoenix
Tracy	Mildred	Sanford	Paris	Rainier
Truman	Nellie	Silas	Persia	Reno
Ulysses	Prudence	Spencer	Russia	Rhodes
Vern	Rosalie	Stanley	Savannah	River
Vladimir	Thelma	Sven	Sierra	Sydney
Waldo	Verna	Vic	Sydney	Texas
Xavier	Wilma	Wilfred	Victoria	Washington

Quiet

Girls	Boys
Bernice	Aaron
Beth	Adrian
Cathleen	Angel
Chloe	Benedict
Diana	Bryce
Donna	Carlo
Faith	Curtis
Fawn	Cy
Fay	Douglas
Grace	Gerald
Jocelyn	Gideon
Leona	Jeremiah
Lisa	Jermaine
Lori	Kiefer
Lydia	Kyle
Moira	Riley
Natalia	Robert
Nina	Robin
Rena	Samson
Sheryl	Spencer
Tessa	Toby
Theresa	Tommy
Ursula	Tucker
Violet	Vaughn
Yoko	Virgil

Rich/Wealthy

Girls	Boys
Alexis	Bartholomew
Amanda	Bradley
Ariel	Brock
Blair	Bryce
Chanel	Burke
Chantal	Cameron
Chastity	Carlos
Chelsea	Chet
Christina	Claybourne
Clara	Clinton
Crystal	Colby
Darlene	Colin
Deandra	Corbin
Jewel	Dane
Larissa	Dante
Madison	Dillon
Marina	Frederick
Meredith	Geoffrey
Moira	Hamilton
Porsha	Harper
Rachel	Montgomery
Taryn	Roosevelt
Tiffany	Sterling
Trisha	Winslow
Zsa Zsa	Winthrop

Sexy

Girls
Alana
Angie
Bambi
Brooke
Caresse
Cari
Carmen
Dani
Desiree
Donna
Honey
Jillian
Kirstie
Kitty
Kyra
Latoya
Leah
Lola
Marilyn
Marlo
Raquel
Sabrina
Sandra
Simone
Zsa Zsa

Southern		Strong/Tough	Sweet
Girls	**Boys**	**Boys**	**Girls**
Ada	Ashley	Amos	Abby
Alma	Beau	Ben	Alyssa
Annabel	Bobby	Brandon	Angela
Belle	Cletus	Brock	Betsy
Carolina	Clint	Bronson	Candy
Charlotte	Dale	Bruce	Cheryl
Clementine	Earl	Bruno	Cindy
Dixie	Jackson	Cain	Dana
Dolly	Jeb	Christopher	Desiree
Dottie	Jed	Clint	Elise
Ellie	Jefferson	Cody	Ellie
Georgeanne	Jesse	Coleman	Esther
Georgia	Jethro	Colin	Heather
Jolene	Jimmy	Delbert	Heidi
LeeAnn	Johnny	Demetrius	Kara
Luella	Lee	Duke	Kristi
Mirabel	Luke	Jed	Laura
Ophelia	Luther	Judd	Linda
Patsy	Moses	Kurt	Marjorie
Polly	Otis	Nick	Melinda
Priscilla	Peyton	Sampson	Melissa
Rosalind	Rhett	Stefan	Olivia
Scarlet	Robert	Thor	Rose
Tara	Roscoe	Vince	Shauna
Winona	Wade	Zeb	Sue

Trendy

Girls	Boys
Alexia	Adrian
Alia	Alec
Britney	Angelo
Chanel	Bradley
Char	Carson
Delia	Connor
Destiny	Davis
Gwyneth	Dominic
Hannah	Ellery
India	Garrett
Isabella	Harley
Jen	Harper
Julianna	Jefferson
Keely	Kellan
Lane	Levi
Macy	Liam
Madeleine	Neil
Madison	Olaf
Morgan	Omar
Nadia	Orlando
Natalia	Parker
Olivia	Pierce
Paris	Remington
Ricki	Simon
Taylor	Warren

Weird

Girls	Boys
Abra	Abner
Aida	Barton
Annelise	Boris
Athalie	Cosmo
Belicia	Earl
Calla	Edward
Devonna	Ferris
Dianthe	Gaylord
Elvira	Ira
Garland	Jules
Giselle	Maynard
Happy	Mervin
Hestia	Neville
Keiko	Newt
Kyrene	Nolan
Mahalia	Rod
Modesty	Roscoe
Novia	Seth
Opal	Siegfried
Poppy	Sylvester
Rani	Thaddeus
Sapphire	Tristan
Tierney	Vernon
Twyla	Victor
Velvet	Ward

Wimpy

Boys
Antoine
Archibald
Barton
Bernard
Bradford
Burke
Cecil
Cyril
Dalton
Darren
Duane
Edwin
Gaylord
Homer
Horton
Napoleon
Percival
Prescott
Roosevelt
Rupert
Ulysses
Wesley
Winslow
Winthrop
Yale

Natural Namesakes

Flowers	Rocks, Gems, Minerals	Nature
Girls	**Girls and Boys**	**Girls and Boys**
Angelica	Beryl	Amber
Calla	Clay	Autumn
Dahlia	Coal	Breezy
Daisy	Coral	Brook
Fern	Crystal	Bunny
Flora	Diamond	Chic
Flower	Esmerelda	Fawn
Holly	Flint	Fielding
Hyacinth	Garnet	Forest
Iris	Gemma	Hailey
Jasmine	Goldie	Honey
Laurel	Jade	Hunter
Lavender	Jasper	Jay
Lilac	Jewel	Kitty
Lily	Mercury	Lark
Marigold	Mica	Misty
Pansy	Opal	Moss
Poppy	Pearl	River
Posy	Rock	Robin
Rose	Ruby	Stormy
Sage	Sandy	Summer
Tulip	Sapphire	Tiger
Verbina	Steele	Windy
Vine	Stone	Wolf
Violet	Topaz	Woody

Gender-Neutral Names

In the past few years, naming trends have been heading in less traditional directions. One of such trends is using gender-neutral names for both boys and girls. We have provided below a list of such popular gender-neutral names. While *all* the names below are given to both boys and girls, we have divided them into three categories: names that are used equally for both genders, names that are used more for girls, and those that are used more for boys.

Used Equally		Used More for Girls		Used More for Boys	
Ali	Kayle	Andrea	Kasey	Aaron	Francis
Ariel	Kerry	Angel	Kelly	Adrian	Jesse
Avery	Kim	Ashley	Kelsey	Alex	Joel
Britt	Kirby	Ashton	Leigh	Bobby	Jordan
Brook	Kristian	Aubrey	Leslie	Brett	Kyle
Carey	Loren	Dana	Lindsay	Charlie	Lee
Casey	Mackenzie	Dominique	Lindsey	Christian	Logan
Dakota	Marion	Elisha	Lynn	Cody	Micah
Daniele	Nicola	Erin	Madison	Colby	Michael
Darcy	Noel	Jade	Robin	Corey	Randall
Devan	Paris	Jaime	Sandy	Dale	Riley
Frankie	Quinn	Jamie	Sasha	Dallas	Ryan
Jackie	Regan	Jessie	Shannon	Daryl	Shawn
Jan	Rene	Jodi	Tracy	Devin	Taylor
Jayme	Shea	Justine	Whitney	Drew	Terry
Jean	Stevie			Dusty	Tyler
Jody	Tory			Evan	
Kacey					

In addition, various spellings of the same name influence how that name is perceived. Below are some examples of how a slightly different spelling determines whether that name is used for girls or boys.

Used for Girls	Used for Boys
Adrienne	Adrien
Bobbie, Bobbi	Bobby
Cameron	Camron
Carie	Cary
Codi	Codey
Cori, Corie, Corrie	Cory, Corry
Frances	Francis
Gabriell	Gabriel
Kori	Korey, Kory
Randi	Randy
Ricki, Rikki	Rickey, Rickie, Ricky
Terri	Terry
Toni	Tony

Famous Namesakes

Famous Artists
Male and Female

Andy (Warhol)
Ansel (Adams)
Claude (Monet)
Edgar (Degas)
Edward (Hopper)
Frida (Kahlo)
Henri (Matisse)
Diego (Rivera)
Georgia (O'Keeffe)
Gustav (Klimt)
Jackson (Pollock)
Jasper (Johns)
Leonardo (da Vinci)
Marc (Chagall)
Mary (Cassatt)
Michelangelo (Buonarroti)
Norman (Rockwell)
Pablo (Picasso)
Paul (Cézanne)
Rembrandt (van Rijn)
Robert (Mapplethorpe)
Roy (Lichtenstein)
Salvador (Dali)
Sandro (Botticelli)
Vincent (van Gogh)

Famous Athletes

Female

Anna (Kournikova)
Annika (Sorenstam)
Diana (Taurasi)
Jackie (Joyner-Kersee)
Jennie (Finch)
Kerri (Strug)
Kristi (Yamaguchi)
Florence (Griffith Joyner)
Laila (Ali)
Lisa (Leslie)
Marion (Jones)
Martina (Hingis)
Mary Lou (Retton)
Mia (Hamm)
Monica (Seles)
Nadia (Comaneci)
Babe (Didrikson Zaharias)
Oksana (Baiul)
Picabo (Street)
Rebecca (Lobo)
Sarah (Hughes)
Serena (Williams)
Sheryl (Swoopes)
Steffi (Graf)
Venus (Williams)

Male

Andre (Agassi)
Andy (Roddick)
Babe (Ruth)
Bernie (Williams)
Dale (Earnhardt)
David (Beckham)
Elvis (Stojko)
Hulk (Hogan)
Kasey (Kahne)
Kobe (Bryant)
Lance (Armstrong)
Mark (Spitz)
Michael (Jordan)
Mike (Tyson)
Muhammad (Ali)
Orenthal James ("O.J." Simpson)
Oscar (De La Hoya)
Red (Grange)
Riddick (Bowe)
Rocky (Balboa)
Scott (Hamilton)
Tiger (Woods)
Tony (Hawk)
Wayne (Gretzky)
Yao (Ming)

Famous Authors

Female	Male
Anne (Tyler)	Ambrose (Bierce)
Barbara (Kingsolver)	Bram (Stoker)
Carolyn (Keene)	Cormac (McCarthy)
Charlotte (Brontë)	Dan (Brown)
Doris (Lessing)	Ernest (Hemingway)
Elizabeth (Barrett Browning)	George (Orwell)
Emily (Dickinson)	Henry David (Thoreau)
Harper (Lee)	Homer
Harriet (Beecher Stowe)	J. D. (Salinger)
Jane (Austen)	Jules (Verne)
Joanne Kathleen (J. K. Rowling)	Leo (Tolstoy)
Judy (Blume)	Lewis (Carroll)
Katherine (Mansfield)	Mario (Puzo)
Louisa (May Alcott)	Nicholas (Sparks)
Lucy Maud (Montgomery)	Oscar (Wilde)
Madeleine (L'Engle)	Ray (Bradbury)
Margaret (Atwood)	Samuel (Clemens)
Marge (Piercy)	Scott (Fitzgerald)
Mary (Shelley)	Stephen (King)
Maya (Angelou)	Tennessee (Williams)
Paula (Danziger)	Tom (Clancy)
Rebecca (Wells)	Truman (Capote)
Sylvia (Plath)	Virgil
Virginia (Woolf)	Walt (Whitman)
Willa (Cather)	William (Faulkner)

Famous Baseball Players

Male

Alex (Rodriguez)
Babe (Ruth)
Barry (Bonds)
Catfish (Hunter)
Cy (Young)
Derek (Jeter)
Dizzy (Dean)
Cal (Ripken, Jr.)
Hank (Aaron)
Ichiro (Suzuki)
Jackie (Robinson)
Ken (Griffey, Jr.)
Kirby (Puckett)
Mark (McGwire)
Mickey (Mantle)
Nolan (Ryan)
Pete (Rose)
Randy (Johnson)
Roger (Clemens)
Rollie (Fingers)
Sammy (Sosa)
Ted (Williams)
Torii (Hunter)
Wade (Boggs)
Willie (Mays)

Famous Basketball Players

Female	Male
Alana (Beard)	Alonzo (Mourning)
Alicia (Thompson)	Anfernee ("Penny" Hardaway)
Chantelle (Anderson)	Bill (Russell)
Coco (Miller)	Carmelo (Anthony)
Dominique (Canty)	Clyde (Drexler)
Ebony (Hoffman)	Dennis (Rodman)
Felicia (Ragland)	Earvin ("Magic" Johnson)
Giuliana (Mendiola)	Isiah (Thomas)
Gwen (Jackson)	Jerry (West)
Jessie (Hicks)	Julius (Erving)
Kaayla (Chones)	Kareem (Abdul-Jabbar)
Katie (Douglas)	Karl (Malone)
Kiesha (Brown)	Kevin (Garnett)
Lisa (Leslie)	Kobe (Bryant)
Lucienne (Berthieu)	Larry (Bird)
Michele (Van Gorp)	Latrell (Sprewell)
Natalie (Williams)	LeBron (James)
Nykesha (Sales)	Michael (Jordan)
Olympia (Scott-Richardson)	Moses (Malone)
Sheryl (Swoopes)	Patrick (Ewing)
Simone (Edwards)	Scottie Pippen
Tai (Dillard)	Shaquille (O'Neal)
Tamicha (Jackson)	Spud (Webb)
Tangela (Smith)	Wilt (Chamberlain)
Tari (Phillips)	Yao (Ming)

Famous Country Western Stars

Female	Male
Alison (Krauss)	Alan (Jackson)
Carolyn Dawn (Johnson)	Billy Ray (Cyrus)
Chely (Wright)	Brad (Paisley)
Crystal (Gayle)	Charley (Pride)
Cyndi (Thomson)	Chet (Atkins)
Dolly (Parton)	Clint (Black)
Faith (Hill)	Darryl (Worley)
Gretchen (Wilson)	Don (Everly)
Jamie (O'Neal)	Garth (Brooks)
Jo Dee (Messina)	Gene (Autry)
Julie (Roberts)	George (Strait)
LeAnn (Rimes)	Hank (Williams)
Loretta (Lynn)	Joe (Nichols)
Martie (Maguire)	Johnny (Cash)
Martina (McBride)	Keith (Urban)
Mary (Chapin Carpenter)	Kenny (Chesney)
Mindy (McCready)	Kix (Brooks)
Natalie (Maines)	Randy (Travis)
Patsy (Cline)	Ronnie (Dunn)
Patty (Loveless)	Tim (McGraw)
Reba (McEntire)	Toby (Keith)
Sara (Evans)	Trace (Adkins)
Shania (Twain)	Vince (Gill)
Tammy (Wynette)	Waylon (Jennings)
Terri (Clark)	Willie (Nelson)

Famous Fictional Characters

Female

Anna (Karenina)
Anne (Shirley)
Antonia (Shimerda)
Bridget (Jones)
Cosette (Valjean)
Daisy (Buchanan)
Dorothea (Brooke)
Edna (Pontellier)
Elizabeth (Bennet)
Emma (Woodhouse)
Hermione (Granger)
Hester (Prynne)
Isabel (Archer)
Jane (Eyre)
Josephine (March)
Juliet (Capulet)
Junie (B. Jones)
Mary (Lennox)
Meg (Murry)
Ophelia
Phoebe (Caulfield)
Pippi (Longstocking)
Scarlett (O'Hara)
Scout (Finch)
Serena (Joy)

Male

Atticus (Finch)
Billy (Coleman)
Boo (Radley)
Cyrus (Trask)
Edmond (Dantés)
Ethan (Frome)
Frodo (Baggins)
Guy (Montag)
Harry (Potter)
Heathcliff
Henry (Fleming)
Holden (Caulfield)
Huck (Finn)
Jake (Barnes)
Jay (Gatsby)
Jean (Valjean)
John (Proctor)
Odysseus
Owen (Meany)
Pip (Philip Pirrip)
Rhett (Butler)
Robinson (Crusoe)
Romer (Montague)
Santiago
Victor (Frankenstein)

Famous Football Players

Male

Barry (Sanders)
Bo (Jackson)
Brett (Favre)
Donovan (McNabb)
Carl (Eller)
Dan (Marino)
Deion (Sanders)
Johnny (Unitas)
Eli (Manning)
Emmitt (Smith)
Frank (Gifford)
Jeremy (Shockey)
Jerry (Rice)
Jim (Kelly)
Joe (Montana)
John (Elway)
Ahman (Green)
Peyton (Manning)
Randy (Moss)
Steve (Young)
Tiki (Barber)
Troy (Aikman)
Vince (Lombardi)
William ("The Refrigerator" Perry)
Woody (Hayes)

Famous Golfers

Female	Male
Amy (Alcott)	Arnold (Palmer)
Annika (Sorenstam)	Chi Chi (Rodriguez)
Babe (Didrikson Zaharias)	Claude (Harmon)
Beth (Daniel)	Craig (Stadler)
Betsy (King)	Eldrick ("Tiger" Woods)
Betty (Jameson)	Ernie (Els)
Carol (Mann)	Gene (Littler)
Dinah (Shore)	Greg (Norman)
Donna (Caponi)	Hale (Irwin)
Dottie (Pepper)	Happy (Gilmore)
Hollis (Stacy)	Harvey (Penick)
JoAnne (Carner)	Jack (Nicklaus)
Judy (Rankin)	Jeff (Maggert)
Juli (Inkster)	Jesper (Parnevik)
Karrie (Webb)	Ken (Venturi)
Kathy (Whitworth)	Nick (Price)
Laura (Davies)	Payne (Stewart)
Louise (Suggs)	Phil (Mickelson)
Marlene (Hagge)	Raymond (Floyd)
Mickey (Wright)	Retief (Goosen)
Nancy (Lopez)	Sam (Snead)
Pat (Bradley)	Sergio (Garcia)
Patty (Berg)	Tommy (Bolt)
Sandra (Haynie)	Vijay (Singh)
Se (Ri Pak)	Walter (Hagen)

Famous Military Figures

Female and Male

Alexander (the Great)
Andrew (Johnson)
Anna (Warner Bailey)
Attila (the Hun)
Charles (de Gaulle)
Douglas (MacArthur)
Dwight (D. Eisenhower)
Genghis (Khan)
George (S. Patton)
Ivan (Stepanovich Konev)
Jennie (Hodgers)
Joan (of Arc)
Julius (Caesar)
Lucy (Brewer)
Moshe (Dayan)
Napoleon (Bonaparte)
Oliver (Cromwell)
Omar (Bradley)
Peter (the Great)
Robert (E. Lee)
Tecumseh
Ulysses (S. Grant)
William (Wallace)
Winfield (Scott)
Winston (Churchill)

Famous Mobsters

Male

Al ("Scarface" Capone)
Bugsy (Siegel)
Carlo (Gambino)
Dominick (Palermo)
Donald ("The Wizard of Odds" Angelini)
Dutch (Schultz)
Ernest ("Rocco" Infelise)
Frank (Nitti)
Hymie (Weiss)
Jack ("Machine Gun" McGurn)
James (DiForti)
Jim (Colosimo)
Jimmy (Hoffa)
John (Gotti)
Joseph ("Oscar" Ferriola)
Louis (Bombacino)
Lucky (Luciano)
Manuel (Noriega)
Michael (Corleone)
Paul (Castellano)
Robert ("Gabeet" Bellavia)
Salvatore (Maranzano)
Sam ("Wings" Carlisi)
Tony (Soprano)
Vito (Corleone)

Famous Movie Stars

Female	Male
Angelina (Jolie)	Benicio (Del Toro)
Anjelica (Huston)	Bing (Crosby)
Audrey (Hepburn)	Bruce (Willis)
Betty (Grable)	Cary (Grant)
Cameron (Diaz)	Chevy (Chase)
Catherine (Zeta-Jones)	Clark (Gable)
Cher	Clint (Eastwood)
Drew (Barrymore)	Dustin (Hoffman)
Elizabeth (Taylor)	Harrison (Ford)
Emma (Thompson)	Jack (Nicholson)
Gwyneth (Paltrow)	John (Wayne)
Halle (Berry)	Leonardo (DiCaprio)
Jodie (Foster)	Martin (Sheen)
Julia (Roberts)	Mel (Gibson)
Katharine (Hepburn)	Mickey (Rooney)
Liv (Tyler)	Orlando (Bloom)
Meg (Ryan)	Patrick (Swayze)
Meryl (Streep)	Robert (De Niro)
Michelle (Pfeiffer)	Robin (Williams)
Nicole (Kidman)	Rock (Hudson)
Penelope (Cruz)	Russell (Crowe)
Salma (Hayek)	Sean (Connery)
Sandra (Bullock)	Spencer (Tracy)
Shirley (Temple)	Sylvester (Stalone)
Sissy (Spacek)	Tom (Cruise)

Famous Mythology Figures

Female	Male
Aphrodite	Achilles
Artemis	Aeolus
Athena	Ajax
Chloe	Apollo
Concordia	Aries
Daphne	Atlas
Diana	Eros
Eros	Hector
Gaia	Helios
Grace	Hercules
Hebe	Hermes
Helen	Hyrem
Hera	Jason
Hestia	Loki
Iris	Mars
Lorelei	Midas
Luna	Neptune
Lyssa	Odysseus
Maia	Orion
Minerva	Pan
Nike	Paris
Penelope	Perseus
Persephone	Pollux
Rhea	Thor
Venus	Zeus

Famous Biblical Figures

Female
Abigail
Bathsheba
Deborah
Delilah
Dinah
Eden
Elizabeth
Esther
Eve
Hagar
Hannah
Jezebel
Joy
Julia
Leah
Maria
Martha
Mary
Miriam
Naomi
Phoebe
Rachel
Rebekah
Ruth
Sarah

Famous New Testament Figues	Famous Old Testament Figures	Famous Opera Composers and Stars
Male	**Male**	**Female and Male**
Agrippa	Abel	Andrea (Bocelli)
Andrew	Abraham	Anne (Sofie von Otter)
Annas	Adam	Camille (Saint-Saëns)
Aquila	Cain	Danielle (Millet)
Gabriel	Caleb	Elisabeth (Schwarzkopf)
Herod	Daniel	Floriana (Cavalli)
James	David	Georges (Bizet)
Jesus	Eli	Giacomo (Puccini)
John	Esau	Gioacchino (Rossini)
Joseph	Ezekiel	Giuseppe (Campora)
Judas	Ezra	Helga (Dernesch)
Jude	Isaac	Jane (Berbié)
Luke	Isaiah	Jeannine (Collard)
Mark	Jacob	José (Carreras)
Matthew	Jeremiah	Kiri (Te Kanawa)
Nicolas	Job	Lucia (Popp)
Paul	Joel	Luciano (Pavarotti)
Peter	Joshua	Mady (Mesplé)
Philip	Moses	Margaret (Marshall)
Simon	Nemiah	Maria (Callas)
Stephen	Noah	Montserrat (Caballe)
Thomas	Samson	Placido (Domingo)
Timothy	Samuel	Renata (Scotto)
Titus	Solomon	Renée (Fleming)
Zechariah		Richard (Wagner)

Famous Pop/Rock Stars

Female	Male
Aaliyah	Alice (Cooper)
Alanis (Morissette)	Axl (Rose)
Alicia (Keys)	B. B. King
Annie (Lennox)	Billy (Joel)
Aretha (Franklin)	Carlos (Santana)
Beyonce (Knowles)	Cat (Stevens)
Britney (Spears)	Don (Henley)
Christina (Aguilera)	Elton (John)
Courtney (Love)	Jack (Johnson)
Dido	Jerry (Garcia)
Fiona (Apple)	Jimi (Hendrix)
Gwen (Stefani)	John (Lennon)
Janet (Jackson)	Justin (Timberlake)
Jennifer (Lopez)	Kurt (Cobain)
Jessica (Simpson)	Marshall ("Eminem" Mathers)
Jewel	Michael (Jackson)
Lauryn (Hill)	Paul (McCartney)
Madonna	Prince
Mariah (Carey)	Ray (Charles)
Melissa (Etheridge)	Ricky (Martin)
Missy (Elliott)	Ringo (Starr)
Natalie (Imbruglia)	Sean ("P. Diddy" Combs)
Norah (Jones)	Steven (Tyler)
Shania (Twain)	Stevie (Wonder)
Whitney (Houston)	Van (Morrison)

Famous Presidents

Male

Abraham (Lincoln)
Andrew (Jackson)
Bill (Clinton)
Calvin (Coolidge)
Chester (Arthur)
Dwight (D. Eisenhower)
Franklin (D. Roosevelt)
George (Washington)
Gerald (Ford)
Grover (Cleveland)
Harry (S. Truman)
Herbert (Hoover)
James (Madison)
Jimmy (Carter)
John (F. Kennedy)
Lyndon (B. Johnson)
Martin (Van Buren)
Millard (Fillmore)
Richard (Nixon)
Ronald (Reagan)
Rutherford (B. Hayes)
Thomas (Jefferson)
Ulysses (S. Grant)
Warren (G. Harding)
Woodrow (Wilson)

Famous Race Car Drivers

Male

A. J. (Foyt)
Al (Unser, Jr.)
Ashton (Lewis)
Bill (Elliott)
Bobby (Labonte)
Cale (Yarborough)
Cole (Trickle)
Dale (Earnhardt)
Darrell (Waltrip)
Jeff (Gordon)
Jimmie (Johnson)
Jimmy (Spencer)
John (Andretti)
Justin (Ashburn)
Kenny (Irwin)
Kevin (Harvick)
Kyle (Petty)
Mario (Andretti)
Matt (Kenseth)
Richard (Petty)
Ricky (Rudd)
Rusty (Wallace)
Sterling (Marlin)
Terry (Labonte)
Tony (Stewart)

Star Kids
What Celebrities Are Naming Their Kids

Aidan Rose
Faith Daniels

Alaia
Stephen Baldwin

Allegra
John Leguizamo and Justine Maurer

Apple
Gwyneth Paltrow and Chris Martin

Aquinnah Kathleen
Tracy Pollan and Michael J. Fox

Arpad Flynn
Elle Macpherson

Atherton
Don and Kelley Johnson

Atticus
Isabella Hoffman

August Anna
Garth Brooks

Aurelius
Elle Macpherson

Bailey (boy)
Tracey Gold and Roby Marshall

Bailey Jean (girl)
Melissa Etheridge

Bechet
Woody Allen and Soon-Yi Previn

Braison Chance
Billy Ray Cyrus

Brawley King
Nick Nolte

Brigidine
Sinead O'Connor

Brooklyn Joseph
Victoria "Posh Spice" Adams and David Beckham

Cannon
Larry King and Shawn Southwick-King

Carys (girl)
Catherine Zeta-Jones and Michael Douglas

Casper
Claudia Schiffer

Castor
James and Francesca Hetfield

Chorde
Snoop Dogg

Coco
Courteney Cox Arquette and David Arquette

Darius
James Rubin and Christiane Amanpour

Declyn Wallace
Cyndi Lauper

Denim (boy)
Toni Braxton

Destry Allyn (girl)
Kate Capshaw and Steven Spielberg

Dexter Dean (girl)
Diane Keaton

Diezel (boy)
Toni Braxton

Dominik (girl)
Andy Garcia

Dree Louise
Mariel Hemingway

Dylan Frances (girl)
Sean and Robin Wright Penn

Elijah
Alison Stewart and Bono

Eliot Pauline
Sting

Emerson Rose
Teri Hatcher

Esme
Samantha Morton and Charlie Creed-Miles

Fifi Trixiebelle
Paula Yates and Bob Geldof

Gaia
Emma Thompson and Greg Wise

Gulliver Flynn
Gary Oldman

Heavenly Hirani Tiger Lily
Paula Yates

Homer
Richard Gere and Carey Lowell

Hopper
Sean Penn

Indio
Deborah Falconer and Robert Downey, Jr.

Ireland Eliesse
Kim Basinger and Alec Baldwin

Jamison (girl)
Billy Baldwin and Chynna Phillips

Jelani (boy)
Wesley Snipes

Jett
Kelly Preston and John Travolta

Karsen (girl)
Ray Liotta and Michelle Grace

Langley Fox (girl)
Mariel Hemingway

Lennon
Patsy Kensit and Liam Gallagher

Letesha
Ice T

Loewy
John Malkovich

Lourdes Maria Ciccone
Madonna

Lyric (girl)
Robby Benson

Maddox
Angelina Jolie

Malu Valentine
David Byrne

Matalin Mary
Mary Matalin and James Carville

McCanna
Gary Sinise

McKenna Lane
Mary Lou Retton

Milo
Camryn Manheim

Mingus
Helena Christensen and Norman Reedus

Najee (boy)
LL Cool J

Nala
Keenan Ivory Wayans

Nayib (boy)
Gloria Estefan

Neve
Conan O'Brien and Liza Powell O'Brien

Ocean
Forest Whitaker

Paris (boy)
Blair Underwood

Paris Michael Katherine
Michael Jackson

Phoenix
Melanie "Scary Spice" Brown and Jimmy Gulzar

Pixie
Paula Yates

Presley Tanita
Tanya Tucker

Rainie
Andie MacDowell

Rio
Sean Young

Ripley (girl)
Oliver Parker and Thandie Newton

Roan
Sharon Stone

Rocco
Madonna and Guy Ritchie

Rory
Bill Gates and Melinda French

Rumer Glenn
Demi Moore and Bruce Willis

Ryan Elizabeth
Rodney and Holly Robinson Peete

Sailor Lee
Christie Brinkley

Salome
Alex Kingston

Saoirse Roisin
Courtney Kennedy and Paul Hill

Satchel Lewis (girl)
Spike Lee

Schuyler Frances (girl)
Tracy Pollan and Michael J. Fox

Scout LaRue (girl)
Demi Moore and Bruce Willis

Seven
Andre 3000 and Erykah Badu

Sindri (boy)
Bjork

Sistine Rose
Jennifer Flavin and Sylvester Stallone

Slade Lucas Moby
David Brenner

Sonnet Noel
Forest Whitaker

Sosie Ruth
Kyra Sedgwick and Kevin Bacon

Speck Wildhorse
John Mellencamp

Spencer (girl)
Debbe Dunning

Tali
Annie Lennox

Tallulah Belle
Demi Moore and Bruce Willis

Taylor Mayne Pearl
Garth Brooks

Trixie
Damon Wayans

Truman Theodore
Rita Wilson and Tom Hanks

Weston
Nicolas Cage

Willow
Will Smith and Jada Pinkett Smith

Zelda
Robin Williams and Marsha Garces Williams

Zephyr
Karla De Vito and Robby Benson

Zion
Lauryn Hill and Rohan Marley

The Name Exchange
Celebrities' Names Before and After

Historical/Political Figures

Professional Name	Original Name
Johnny Appleseed	John Chapman
Sitting Bull	Tatanka Iyotake
Calamity Jane	Martha Jane Burke
Butch Cassidy	Robert LeRoy Parker
Gerald Ford	Leslie Lynch King, Jr.
Mata Hari	Margareth Geertruide Zelle
Gary Hart	Gary Hartpence
Crazy Horse	Tashuna-Uitco
Sundance Kid	Harry Longbaugh
Nancy Reagan	Anne Frances Robbins
Leon Trotsky	Lev Davydovich Bronstein
Woodrow Wilson	Thomas Woodrow Wilson
Malcolm X	Malcolm Little

Sports Figures

Professional Name	Original Name
Kareem Abdul-Jabbar	Ferdinand Lewis Alcindor, Jr.
Muhammad Ali	Cassius Marcellus Clay
Andre the Giant	Andre Roussinoff
Yogi Berra	Lawrence Peter Berra
Hulk Hogan	Terry Bodello
Magic Johnson	Earvin Johnson
Pelé	Edson Arantes do Nascimento
Ahmad Rashad	Bobby Moore
Tom Seaver	George Thomas Seaver
Gene Tunney	James Joseph Tunney
Tiger Woods	Eldrick Woods
Cy Young	Denton True Young

Literary Figures

Professional Name	Original Name
Maya Angelou	Marguerite Annie Johnson
Pearl Buck	Pearl Comfort Sydenstricker
Truman Capote	Truman Steckfus Pearsons
Lewis Carroll	Charles Lutwidge Dodgeson
Michael Crichton	John Michael Crichton
Agatha Christie	Agatha Mary Clarissa Miller
Isak Dinesen	Baroness Karen Blixen
Victoria Holt	Eleanot Burford Hibbert
Judith Krantz	Judith Tarcher
John le Carre	John Moore Carnwell
Toni Morrison	Chloe Anthony Wofford
George Orwell	Eric Arthur Blair
Satchel Paige	Leroy Robert Paige
Anne Rice	Howard Allen O'Brien
Harold Robbins	Francis Kane
J. K. Rowling	Joanne Kathleen Rowling
Mickey Spillane	Frank Morrison
Danielle Steel	Danielle Schuelein-Steel
R. L. Stine	Robert Lawrence Stine
Dr. Suess	Theodore Suess Geisel
J. R. R. Tolkien	John Ronald Reuel Tolkien
Mark Twain	Samuel Clemens
Gore Vidal	Eugene Luther Vidal
Nathaniel West	Nathaniel Wallenstein Weinstein
Tennessee Williams	Thomas Lanier Williams

Entertainment Figures

Professional Name ....Original Name

Eddie Albert ....Edward Albert Heimberger
Alan Alda............................Alphonse D'Abruzzo
Jane Alexander....................Jane Quigley
Jason Alexander ....Jay Scott Greenspan
Tim Allen ....Tim Allen Dick
Woody Allen ....Allen Konigsberg
Don Ameche......................Dominic Felix Amici
Tori Amos ....Myra Ellen Amos
Julie Andrews....................Julia Vernon
Ann-Margret......................Ann-Margret Olsson
Beatrice Arthur ....Bernice Frankel
Ed Asner ....Yitzak Edward Asner
Fred Astaire ....Frederick Austerlitz
Lauren Bacall....................Betty Joan Perske
Anne Bancroft....................Anne Italiano
John Barrymore..................John Blythe
Warren Beatty ....Henry Warren Beaty
Beck ....Beck Hansen
Bonnie Bedelia ....Bonnie Culkin
Pat Benetar ....Patricia Andrejewski
Tony Bennett ....Anthony Dominick Benedetto
Jack Benny ....Joseph Kubelsky
Robbie Benson ....Robert Segal
Ingmar Bergman ....Ernst Ingmar Bergman
Milton Berle ....Milton Berlinger
Irving Berlin ....Israel Baline
Joey Bishop ....Joseph Abraham Gottlieb
Bjork ....Björk Gudmundsdottir
Robert Blake......................Michael James Vijencio Gubitosi
Blondie ....Deborah Harry
Michael Bolton ....Michael Bolotin
Jon Bon Jovi ....John Bonjiovi
Bono ....Paul Hewson
Sonny Bono ....Salvatore Bono
Pat Boone ....Charles Eugene Boone
Victor Borge ....Borge Rosenbaum

Professional Name ....Original Name

Bow Wow ....Shad Moss
David Bowie ....David Hayward-Jones
Max Brand ....Gerald Kenneth Tierney
Brandy................................Brandy Norwood
Beau Bridges ....Lloyd Vernet Bridges III
Charles Bronson ....Charles Buchinsky
Albert Brooks ....Albert Einstein
Garth Brooks......................Troyal Garth Brooks
Mel Brooks ....Melvin Kaminsky
Yul Brynner........................Taidje Kahn, Jr.
George Burns ....Nathan Birnbaum
Ellen Burstyn......................Edna Rae Gillooly
Richard Burton..................Richard Jenkins
Nicolas Cage ....Nicholas Coppola
Michael Caine....................Maurice Joseph Micklewhite
Maria Callas......................Maria Anna Sophia Cecilia
                                         Kalogeropoulos
Dyan Cannon ....Samile Diane Friesen
Kate Capshaw ....Kathleen Sue Nail
Vikki Carr..........................Florencia Bisenta de Casillas Martinez
                                         Cardona
Diahann Carroll ....Carol Diahann Johnson
Johnny Cash ....J. R. Cash
Stockard Channing ....Susan Antonia Williams Stockard
Ray Charles........................Ray Charles Robinson
Charo ....Maria Rosaria Pilar Martinez Molina
                                         Baeza
J. C. Chasez ....Joshua Scott Chasez
Chevy Chase ....Cornelius Crane Chase
Chubby Checker................Ernest Evans
Cher ....Cherilyn Sarkisian LaPierre
Chyna ....Joanie Laurer
Eric Clapton ....Eric Clapp
Patsy Cline ....Virginia Patterson Hensley
Lee J. Cobb ....Leo Jacob
Perry Como ....Pierino Como
Bert Convy ....Bernard Whalen Patrick Convy
Alice Cooper......................Vincent Damon Furnier

Professional Name	Original Name
David Copperfield	David Kotkin
Howard Cosell	Howard William Cohen
Bob Costas	Robert Quinlan Costas
Elvis Costello	Declan Patrick McManus
Joan Crawford	Lucille Le Sueur
Bing Crosby	Harry Lillis Crosby
Tom Cruise	Thomas Cruise Mapother IV
Tony Curtis	Bernard Schwartz
Willem Dafoe	William Dafoe
D'Angelo	Michael D'Angelo Archer
Rodney Dangerfield	Jacob Cohen
Dawn	Joyce Elaine Vincent
Doris Day	Doris Kappelhoff
Sandra Dee	Alexandra Zuck
John Denver	Henry John Deutschendorf, Jr.
Bo Derek	Mary Cathleen Collins
Portia de Rossi	Amanda Rogers
Danny DeVito	Daniel Michaeli
Susan Dey	Susan Smith
Marlene Dietrich	Maria von Losch
Phyllis Diller	Phyllis Driver
Kirk Douglas	Issur Danielovitch Demsky
Mike Douglas	Michael Delaney Dowd, Jr.
Patty Duke	Anna Marie Duke
Faye Dunaway	Dorothy Faye Dunaway
Bob Dylan	Robert Zimmerman
Sheena Easton	Sheena Shirley Orr
Buddy Ebsen	Christian Ebsen, Jr.
Barbara Eden	Barbara Huffman
The Edge	David Evans
Carmen Electra	Tara Leigh Patrick
Jenna Elfman	Jenna Butala
Mama Cass Elliot	Ellen Naomi Cohen
Missy Elliott	Melissa Elliott
Elvira	Cassandra Peterson
Eminem	Marshall Mathers III
Werner Erhard	Jack Rosenberg
Dale Evans	Francis Octavia Smith

Professional Name	Original Name
Chad Everett	Raymond Lee Cramton
Douglas Fairbanks	Julius Ullman
Morgan Fairchild	Patsy Ann McClenny
Mia Farrow	Maria de Lourdes Villiers Farrow
Farrah Fawcett	Mary Farrah Fawcett
Will Ferrell	John William Ferrell
Sally Field	Sally Mahoney
W. C. Fields	William Claude Dukenfield
Dame Margot Fonteyn	Margaret Hookham
Glenn Ford	Gwllyn Samuel Newton Ford
John Forsythe	John Freund
Jodie Foster	Alicia Christian Foster
Michael Fox	Michael Andrew Fox
Jamie Foxx	Eric Bishop
Redd Foxx	John Elroy Sanford
Anthony Franciosa	Anthony Papaleo
Connie Francis	Concetta Franconero
Carlton Fredericks	Harold Casper Frederick Kaplan
Greta Garbo	Greta Gustafson
Andy Garcia	Andres Arturo Garcia-Menendez
Judy Garland	Frances Gumm
James Garner	James Baumgarner
Crystal Gayle	Brenda Gail Webb Gatzimos
Boy George	George Alan O'Dowd
Barry Gibb	Douglas Gibb
Kathie Lee Gifford	Kathie Epstein
Goldberg	Bill Goldberg
Whoopi Goldberg	Caryn Johnson
Cary Grant	Archibald Leach
Lee Grant	Lyova Haskell Rosenthal
Peter Graves	Peter Arness
Macy Gray	Natalie McIntyre
Joel Grey	Joel Katz
Charles Grodin	Charles Grodinsky
Robert Guillaume	Robert Williams
Buddy Hackett	Leonard Hacker
Geri Halliwell	Geraldine Estolle Halliwell
Halston	Roy Halston Frowick

Professional Name	Original Name
Hammer	Stanley Kirk Hacker Burrell
Woody Harrelson	Woodrow Tracy Harrelson
Rex Harrison	Reginald Cary
Laurence Harvey	Lavrushka Skikne
Helen Hayes	Helen Brown
Marg Helgenberger	Mary Margaret Helgenberger
Margaux Hemingway	Margot Hemmingway
Audrey Hepburn	Audrey Hepburn-Ruston
Pee Wee Herman	Paul Rubenfeld
Barbara Hershey	Barbara Herzstine
William Holden	William Beedle
Billie Holiday	Eleanora Fagan
Bob Hope	Leslie Townes Hope
Harry Houdini	Ehrich Weiss
Rock Hudson	Roy Scherer, Jr.
D. L. Hughley	Darryl Lynn Hughley
Engelbert Humperdinck	Arnold Dorsey
Mary Beth Hurt	Mary Supinger
Lauren Hutton	Mary Laurence Hutton
Ice Cube	O'Shea Jackson
Billy Idol	William Broad
Don Imus	John Donald Imus, Jr.
Wolfman Jack	Robert Smith
Wyclef Jean	Nelust Wyclef Jean
Jewel	Jewel Kilcher
Elton John	Reginald Kenneth Dwight
Don Johnson	Donald Wayne
Al Jolson	Asa Yoelson
Tom Jones	Thomas Jones Woodward
Louis Jourdan	Louis Gendre
Donna Karan	Donna Faske
Boris Karloff	William Henry Pratt
Danny Kaye	David Kaminsky
Diane Keaton	Diane Hall
Michael Keaton	Michael Douglas
Alicia Keys	Alicia Augello-Cook
Chaka Khan	Yvette Stevens
Kid Rock	Robert James Ritchie

Professional Name	Original Name
Larry King	Larry Zeiger
Ben Kingsley	Krishna Banji
Nastassia Kinski	Nastassja Naksynznki
Calvin Klein	Richard Klein
Ted Knight	Tadeus Wladyslaw Konopka
Johnny Knoxville	Phillip John Clapp
Kreskin	George Joseph Kresge Jr.
Ashton Kutcher	Christopher Ashton Kutcher
Cheryl Ladd	Cheryl Stoppelmoor
Bert Lahr	Irving Lahrheim
Ann Landers	Esther Pauline Lederer
Michael Landon	Eugene Michael Orowitz
Nathan Lane	Joseph Lane
K. D. Lang	Katherine Dawn Lang
Stan Laurel	Arthur Stanley Jefferson Laurel
Ralph Lauren	Ralph Lifshitz
Piper Laurie	Rosetta Jacobs
Jude Law	David Jude Law
Steve Lawrence	Sidney Leibowitz
Heath Ledger	Heathcliff Andrew Ledger
Bruce Lee	Lee Yuen Kam
Gypsy Rose Lee	Louise Hovick
Peggy Lee	Norma Egstrom
Spike Lee	Shelton Jackson Lee
Jay Leno	James Leno
Téa Leoni	Elizabeth Téa Pantaleoni
Huey Lewis	Hugh Cregg
Jerry Lewis	Joseph Levitch
Shari Lewis	Shari Hurwitz
Jet Li	Li Lian Jie
Liberace	Wladziu Valentino Liberace
Hal Linden	Hal Lipshitz
Meat Loaf	Marvin Lee Aday
Jack Lord	J. J. Ryan
Sophia Loren	Sophia Villani Scicolone
Peter Lorre	Laszlo Loewenstein
Courtney Love	Love Michelle Harrison

Professional Name	Original Name
Myrna Loy	Myrna Williams
Bela Lugosi	Bela Ferenc Blasko
Loretta Lynn	Loretta Webb
Bernie Mac	Bernard Jeffery McCullough
Andie MacDowell	Rosalie Anderson MacDowell
Shirley MacLaine	Shirley Beaty
Elle Macpherson	Eleanor Gow
Madonna	Madonna Louise Veronica Ciccone
Lee Majors	Harvey Lee Yeary II
Karl Malden	Mladen Sekulovich
Camryn Manheim	Debra Manheim
Jayne Mansfield	Vera Jane Palmer
Marilyn Manson	Brian Hugh Warner
Fredric March	Frederick Bickel
Penny Marshall	Carole Penny Marshall
Dean Martin	Dino Crocetti
Ricky Martin	Enrique José Martin Morales
Chico Marx	Leonard Marx
Groucho Marx	Julius Henry Marx
Harpo Marx	Arthur Marx
Zeppo Marx	Herbert Marx
Master P	Percy Miller
Walter Matthau	Walter Matuschanskayasky
Ethel Merman	Ethel Zimmermann
Paul McCartney	James Paul McCartney
A. J. McLean	Alexander James McLean
Steve McQueen	Terence Stephen McQueen
George Michael	Georgios Panayiotou
Joni Mitchell	Roberta Joan Anderson Mitchell
Jay Mohr	Jon Ferguson Mohr
Marilyn Monroe	Norma Jean Baker
Yves Montand	Ivo Livi
Demi Moore	Demetria Gene Guynes
Julianne Moore	Julie Anne Smith
Rita Moreno	Rosita Dolores Alverio
Pat Morita	Noriyuki Morita
Van Morrison	George Ivan Morrison
Zero Mostel	Samuel Joel Mostel

Professional Name	Original Name
Ricky Nelson	Eric Hilliard Nelson
Randy Newman	Randall Stuart Newman
Thandie Newton	Thandiwe Newton
Mike Nichols	Michael Igor Peschkowsky
Stevie Nicks	Stephanie Nicks
Chuck Norris	Carlos Ray Norris
Kim Novak	Marilyn Pauline Novak
Hugh O'Brian	Hugh J. Krampe
Tony Orlando	Michael Anthony Orlando Cassavitis
Suze Orman	Suzie Orman
Ozzy Osbourne	John Michael Osbourne
Marie Osmond	Olive Marie Osmond
Peter O'Toole	Seamus O'Toole
Al Pacino	Alfredo James Pacino
Jack Palance	Walter Jack Palanuik
Jane Pauley	Margaret Jane Pauley
Minnie Pearl	Sarah Ophelia Colley Cannon
Gregory Peck	Eldred Gregory Peck
Bernadette Peters	Bernadette Lazzara
Joaquin Phoenix	Joaquin Raphael Bottom
Christopher Pike	Kevin McFadden
Brad Pitt	William Bradley Pitt
Stephanie Powers	Stefania Federkiewicz
Paula Prentiss	Paula Ragusa
Priscilla Presley	Pricilla Wagner Beaulieu
Prince	Prince Rogers Nelson
William Proxmire	Edward William Proxmire
Tony Randall	Leonard Rosenberg
Robert Redford	Charles Robert Redford
Donna Reed	Donna Belle Mullenger
Della Reese	Delloreese Patricia Early
Judge Reinhold	Edward Ernest Reinhold, Jr.
Lee Remick	Ann Remick
Debbie Reynolds	Mary Frances Reynolds
Busta Rhymes	Trevor Smith
Andy Richter	Paul Andrew Richter
Edward G. Robinson	Emanuel Goldenberg
The Rock	Dwayne Douglas Johnson

Professional Name	Original Name
Ginger Rogers	Virginia McMath
Roy Rogers	Leonard Slye
Mickey Rooney	Joe Yule, Jr.
Diana Ross	Diane Ernestine Ross
Theresa Russell	Theresa Paup
Jeri Ryan	Jeri Lynn Zimmerman
Meg Ryan	Margaret Hyra
Winona Ryder	Winona Laura Horowitz
Buffy Sainte-Marie	Beverly Sainte-Marie
Susan Saint James	Susan Miller
Soupy Sales	Milton Supman
Susan Sarandon	Susan Tomalin
Leo Sayer	Gerald Sayer
John Saxon	Carmen Orrico
Jane Seymour	Joyce Frankenberg
Shaggy	Orville Richard Burrell
Shakira	Shakira Isabel Mebarak Ripoll
Omar Sharif	Michael Shalhouz
Artie Shaw	Arthur Arshowsky
Charlie Sheen	Carlos Irwin Estevez
Martin Sheen	Ramon G. Estevez
Judith Sheindlin	Judy Blum
Brooke Shields	Christa Brooke Shields
Talia Shire	Talia Coppola
Dinah Shore	Frances "Fanny" Rose Shore
Beverly Sills	Belle "Bubbles" Silverman
Neil Simon	Marvin Neil Simon
Sinbad	David Adkins
Sisqo	Mark Andrews
Ione Skye	Ione Skye Leitch
Christian Slater	Christian Hawkins
Snoop Dogg	Calvin Cordozar Broadus
Phoebe Snow	Phoebe Loeb
Leelee Sobieski	Liliane Rudabet Gloria Elsveta Sobieski
Suzanne Somers	Suzanne Mahoney
Elke Sommer	Elke Schletz
Ann Sothern	Harriet Lake

Professional Name	Original Name
Sissy Spacek	Mary Elizabeth Spacek
Robert Stack	Robert Modini
Sylvester Stallone	Michael Sylvester Stallone
Jean Stapleton	Jeanne Murray
Ringo Starr	Richard Starkey
Cat Stevens	(Yusuf Islam) Steven Georgiou
Connie Stevens	Concetta Anne Ingolia
Jon Stewart	Jon Stuart Liebowitz
Sting	Gordon Matthew Sumner
Sly Stone	Sylvester Stone
Meryl Streep	Mary Louise Streep
Barbra Streisand	Barbara Streisand
Donna Summer	LaDonna Gaines
Max von Sydow	Carl Adolph von Sydow
Mr. T	Lawrence Tureaud
Rip Taylor	Charles Elmer, Jr.
Robert Taylor	Spangler Brugh
Danny Thomas	Amos Jacobs
Jonathan Taylor Thomas	Jonathan Weiss
Tiny Tim	Herbert Buckingham Khaury
Lily Tomlin	Mary Jean Tomlin
Rip Torn	Elmore Rual Torn, Jr.
Randy Travis	Randy Traywick
Ted Turner	Robert Edward Turner III
Tina Turner	Anna Mae Bullock
Shania Twain	Eileen Regina Twain
Twiggy	Leslie Hornby
Steven Tyler	Steven Tallarico
Rudolph Valentino	Rudolpho Alphonzo Raffaelo Pierre Filibut Guglielmo di Valentina D'Antonguolla
Rudy Vallee	Hubert Prior Vallée
Abigail Van Buren	Pauline Phillips
Christopher Walken	Ronald Walken
Nancy Walker	Ann Myrtle Swoyer
Mike Wallace	Myron Wallace
Andy Warhol	Andrew Warhola
Muddy Waters	McKinley Morganfield

Professional Name	Original Name
John Wayne	Marion Michael Morrison
Sigourney Weaver	Susan Weaver
Raquel Welch	Raquel Tejada
Tuesday Weld	Susan Kerr Weld
Gene Wilder	Jerome Silberman
Bruce Willis	Walter Bruce Willis
August Wilson	Frederick August Kittel
Flip Wilson	Clerow Wilson
Debra Winger	Mary Debra Winger
Shelley Winters	Shirley Schrift

Professional Name	Original Name
Reese Witherspoon	Laura Jeanne Reese Witherspoon
Stevie Wonder	Steveland Morris Hardaway
Natalie Wood	Natasha Gurdin
Jane Wyman	Sarah Jane Fulks
Tammy Wynette	Wynette Pugh
Wynonna	Christina Claire Ciminella
Ed Wynn	Isaiah Edwin Leopold
Loretta Young	Gretchen Young
Sean Young	Mary Sean Young

Birthstones and Flowers

January
   Birthstone: garnet
   Flower: carnation

February
   Birthstone: amethyst
   Flower: violet

March
   Birthstone: aquamarine
   Flower: jonquil

April
   Birthstone: diamond
   Flower: sweet pea

May
   Birthstone: emerald
   Flower: lily of the valley

June
   Birthstone: pearl
   Flower: rose

July
   Birthstone: ruby
   Flower: larkspur

August
   Birthstone: peridot
   Flower: gladiolus

September
   Birthstone: sapphire
   Flower: aster

October
   Birthstone: opal
   Flower: calendula

November
   Birthstone: topaz
   Flower: chrysanthemum

December
   Birthstone: turquoise
   Flower: narcissus

Baby Name Legal Guide

Shortly after your baby is born, someone on the hospital staff will ask you for information to fill out a birth certificate. If your baby is not born in a hospital, either by choice or accident, you still need to file a birth certificate. If you're on your way but don't make it to the hospital in time, the hospital will still take care of filling in the form and presenting it for your signature after you're admitted. If you plan a home birth, you will have to go to the vital statistics office and file a form there—to be certain, find out what your local laws require.

Basic facts about both parents' names, places and dates of birth, and such details about the baby as its sex, weight, length, exact time of arrival, and date of birth will be needed for a birth certificate. Questions regarding other children (if any), their ages, previous miscarriages or children's deaths, the educational levels of both parents, and so on might be asked at this time for records at your local division of vital statistics. They may not appear on the actual birth certificate, though.

The hospital staffer will type up the form and present it for the mother and doctor to sign before sending it to the vital statistics division to be recorded permanently. Once it's recorded you can request copies (needed for things like passports, some jobs, and some legal transactions).

That's what happens in the usual chain of events. But what about the technicalities and specific legal aspects of naming a child? The first thing to know is that laws that govern baby naming vary greatly throughout the country. If your choice of names is in any way unusual (such as giving your baby a hyphenated surname combining the mother's maiden name with the father's name), be

sure of the law before you name the baby. And sign the official birth certificate only after it has been filled out to your satisfaction.

A few of the most commonly asked questions concerning legalities are considered here but, since state and territory laws are not uniform, even these answers cannot be definite. Your local municipal health department officials can probably lead you to the proper department or official to handle your particular situation. Contact them if you need more detailed answers to your questions.

Q. Are there any restrictions on the choice of first and middle names for a baby?

A. No, with the possible exception that the baby's names should be composed of letters, not numbers. In 1978 a district court judge refused to allow a young Minneapolis social studies teacher to legally change his name to the number 1069, calling such a change "an offense to human dignity" that would "hasten that day in which we all become lost in faceless numbers."

Freedom in choosing given names is not universal. A spokesperson for the French Consulate in Chicago confirmed that an 1813 French law still governs naming practices in France. It decrees that babies must be named after Catholic saints or "persons known in ancient history."

Q. Is a choice allowed in giving the baby its surname?

A. In former generations a baby's surname was not often considered a matter for personal decision. State regulations dictated that if the parents were married, the baby took on the father's surname. If the parents were not married, the baby's surname was that of its mother.

In the past few decades such state regulations have been changing. For example, in Florida, Hawaii, and North Carolina, federal courts have ruled those three states can no longer determine the choice of a baby's surname, leaving that decision to the parent(s).

Such court rulings represent the trend prevalent in most, if not all, states to leave the choice of babies' surnames to parents. However, to be absolutely certain, be sure to check your state's regulations on this matter.

Q. Must the baby's full name be decided upon before the birth certificate can be registered?

A. In most cases no time limit exists in which given names must be recorded. However, depending on the amount of time since the birth, the evidence required to record the name varies, ranging from a letter signed by the parent to a court order.

Q. How can a baby's name be legally changed after its birth is registered?

A. More than 50,000 Americans ask courts to change their names legally every year. Some of these changes are requested by parents for their children when the names originally chosen no longer suit them.

Changes in a minor child's given names are possible in some states without a court order, with time limits ranging from a few days after birth to any time at all. In some states a simple affidavit signed by the parents or a notarized amendment is sufficient to make a name change. Others require various documents to show proof of an established new name, such as a baptismal certificate, an insurance policy, an immunization record, or the

family Bible record. For older children, school records or the school census are usually allowed.

When court procedures are necessary, they involve petitions to a county probate court, a superior court, or a district court, following state laws. Often prior newspaper publication of the intended change is required. The court then issues a "change of name" order or decree. In some states new birth certificates are issued for name changes. In others, certificates are only amended.

Informal name changes can be and often are made simply through the "common law right of choice," which allows individuals to use any names they choose. Such a change is informal, though, and is not legal in official procedures.

Q. What if a mistake is made in the baby's name on the birth certificate?

A. To repeat: the best advice of all is to avoid such an occurrence by being absolutely sure that the completely filled-out certificate is correct in every detail before signing it. If a mistake is made, it is important to handle the matter quickly. Procedures for corrections on certificates vary: sometimes signatures of the parents are sufficient, but in other cases forms must be filled out or documentary evidence supplied.

Q. What are the laws for renaming adopted children?

A. An adoption decree is a court order legally obtained through basically similar procedures in all states and territories. A child's given names are selected by the adoptive parents and the surname is chosen in accordance with whatever state or territory laws exist for surnames of biological children. Then all these names are recorded in the adoption decree. In most places an entirely new birth certificate is drawn up, although the place of birth is not usually changed. Most often, the original birth certificate is sealed with the adoption papers, and the new certificate is filed in place of the original.

Q. How may a child's name be changed by a stepfather, by foster parents, or in the case of legitimization?

A. In the case of a name change by a stepfather or by foster parents, most states require that individuals follow the appropriate procedures for adoption or for legal name change.

Changing a child's surname in the case of legitimization is virtually the same as the adoption procedure in most states and territories. Some require both an affidavit of paternity and a copy of the parents' marriage license, while others do not concern themselves with the marriage of the parents. California has no procedures whatsoever, since illegitimacy is no longer defined in that state.

Fascinating Facts about Names

Birthrights

In some tribal societies children are not considered born until they are named. Frequently the child's name consists of a statement (that is, rather than having a pool of names as Western culture does, parents in these societies name children with a phrase that describes the circumstances of the child's birth, the family's current activities, and so on). Translated, such names might be "We are glad we moved to Memphis," or "A girl at last," or "Too little rain."

Bible Studies

It's been estimated that the majority of people in the Western hemisphere have names from the Bible. Women outnumber men, yet there are 3,037 male names in the Bible and only 181 female names. The New Testament is a more popular source of names than the Old Testament.

Change of Habit

Popes traditionally choose a new name upon their election by the College of Cardinals. The practice began in 844 A.D. when a priest whose real name was Boca de Porco (Pig's Mouth) was elected. He changed his name to Sergious II.

Saint Who?

Saints' names are a common source of names in the U.S. But saints who are popular in other countries contribute very unusual, even unpronounceable, names for children born in the U.S.—like Tamjesdegerd, Borhedbesheba, and Jafkeranaegzia.

Them Bones

Praise-God Barebones had a brother named If-Christ-Had-Not-Died-For-Thee-Thou-Wouldst-Have-Been-Damned, who was called "Damned Barebones" for short.

Hello, God?

Terril William Clark is listed in the phone book under his new name—God. Now he's looking for someone to publish a book he's written. "Let's face it," he reportedly said. "The last book with my name on it was a blockbuster."

The Status Quo

The most commonly given names in English-speaking countries from about 1750 to the present are drawn from a list with only 179 entries (discounting variations in spelling). Essentially the same practice has been followed in naming children since at least the sixteenth century, though the use of middle names has increased over the years.

It's Mainly Relative

A recent study suggests that about two-thirds of the population of the U.S. is named to honor somebody. Of the people who are namesakes, about 60 percent are named after a relative and 40 percent for someone outside the family.

Once Is Enough

Ann Landers wrote about a couple who had six children, all named Eugene Jerome Dupuis, Junior. The children answered to One, Two, Three, Four, Five, and Six, respectively. Can you imagine what the IRS, the

Social Security Administration, and any other institution would do with the Dupuises?

In Sickness and Health
Tonsilitis Jackson has brothers and sisters named Meningitis, Appendicitis, and Peritonitis.

The Old College Try
A couple in Louisiana named their children after colleges: Stanford, Duke, T'Lane, Harvard, Princeton, Auburn, and Cornell. The parents' names? Stanford, Sr., and Loyola.

Peace at All Costs
Harry S. Truman owed his middle name, the initial S, to a compromise his parents worked out. By using only the initial, they were able to please both his grandfathers, whose names were Shippe and Solomon.

Initials Only
A new recruit in the U.S. Army filled out all the forms he was presented with as he always had in school: R. (only) B. (only) Jones. You guessed it—from then on he was, as far as the Army cared about it, Ronly Bonly Jones, and all his records, dogtags, and discharge papers proved the point again and again.

Sticks and Stones May Break My Bones...
The nicknames children make up for each other tend to fall into four patterns: those stemming from the physical appearance of the child, those based on either real or imaginary mental traits (brains or idiocy), those based on social ranking or other relationships, and finally, those based on plays on the child's name. Children who don't conform to the values or looks of their peers are likely to pick up more nicknames than those who do. In these ways nicknames often function as instruments of social control.

The Name's the Game
John Hotvet, of Minnetonka, Minnesota, is—of course—a veterinarian. Sometimes names and occupations get inextricably interwoven. Consider these names and professions:

Dr. Zoltan Ovary, gynecologist

Mr. A. Moron, Commissioner of Education for the Virgin Islands

Reverend Christian Church and Reverend God

Mr. Thomas Crapper of Crapper, Ltd Toilets, in London, who entitled his autobiography "Flushed with Pride"

Assorted physicians named Doctor, Docter, or Doktor

Cardinal Sin, Archbishop of Manila, the Philippines

Mr. Groaner Digger, undertaker in Houston

Mr. I. C. Shivers, iceman

Ms. Justine Tune, chorister in Westminster Choir College, Princeton, New Jersey

Ms. Lavender Sidebottom, masseuse at Elizabeth Arden's in New York City

Mssrs. Lawless and Lynch, attorneys in Jamaica, New York

Major Minor, U.S. Army

Diana Nyad, champion long-distance swimmer

Mssrs. Plummer and Leek, plumbers in Sheringham, Norfolk, England

Mr. Ronald Supena, lawyer

Mrs. Screech, singing teacher in Victoria, British Columbia

Mr. Vroom, motorcycle dealer in Port Elizabeth, South Africa

Mssrs. Wyre and Tapping, detectives in New York City

Ms. A. Forest Burns, professional forester

Dr. McNutt, head of a mental hospital, and Dr. Paul Looney, psychiatrist

Mr. Vice, arrested 820 times and convicted 421 times

Dr. Slaughter, surgeon, Dr. Needles, pediatrician, and Dr. Bonebreak, chiropractor

Time Capsule Names

Celebrities and events often inspire parents in their choices of names for children. Many people are now "dated" by their World War II names, like Pearl (Harbor), Douglas (MacArthur), Dwight (Eisenhower—whose mother named him Dwight David to avoid all nicknames, but whom everyone called Ike!), and Franklin (Roosevelt). Films and film stars contribute their share of names: Scarlett O'Hara and Rhett Butler have countless name-sakes whose parents were swept away by *Gone with the Wind*. Madonna, Elvis, Prince, and virtually all other big stars have their own namesakes as well.

The UN Family

One couple took the time capsule concept to an extreme and named their triplets, born on April 5, 1979, Carter, Begin, and Sadat—to honor U.S. President Jimmy Carter, Israeli Prime Minister Menachem Begin, and Egyptian President Anwar Sadat, the three principle signers of the peace treaty signed in Washington, D.C., on March 1979.

They Add Up

Dick Crouser likes to collect unusual names. Some names tell stories, like Fanny Pistor Bodganoff (although Mr. Crouser admits that he doesn't know what a "bodgan" is); some leave messages, like Hazel Mae Call; some aren't likely to add to their owner's self-esteem, like Seldom Wright and Harley Worthit; some are mere truisms, like Wood Burns; while others announce what you might call philosophies of life, like Daily Goforth and Hazel B. Good.

Truth Stranger than Fiction

Dick Neff, columnist of *Advertising Age*, invited his readers to contribute lists of real names they had encountered that are odd and/or funny, to say the least. Among them were the following: Stanley Zigafoose, Cigar Stubbs, Ladorise Quick, Mad Laughinhouse, Lester Chester Hester, Effie Bong, Dillon C. Quattlebaum, Twila Szwrk, Harry E. Thweatt, Benjamin E. Dymshits, Elmer Ploof, Whipple Filoon, Sweetie Belle Rufus, Peculiar Smith, John Dunwrong, All Dunn, Willie Wunn, H. Whitney Clappsaddle, W. Wesley Muckenfuss, Rudolph J. Ramstack, Sarabelle Scraper Roach, James R. Stufflebeam, Shanda Lear, Arthur Crudder, Mary Crapsey, Memory Lane, Troy Mumpower, Santa Beans, Sividious Stark, Cleveland Biggerstaff, Trinkle Bott, Cleopatra Barksdale, Spring Belch, Fairy Blessing, Royal Fauntleroy Butler, Bozy Ball, Carl W. Gigl, Joy Holy, Peenie Fase, Che Che Creech, J. B. Outhouse, Katz Meow, Stephanie Snatchole, I. O. Silver, Helen Bunpain, Birdie Fawncella Feltis, Elight Starling, Farmer Slusher, Nebraska Minor, Bill Grumbles, Peter Rabbitt, Carbon Petroleum Dubbs, Kick-a-hole-in-the-soup, Wong Bong Fong, Newton Hooton, Sonia Schmeckpeeper, Lewie Wirmelskirchen, Lolita Beanblossom, Liselotte Pook, and Irmgard Quapp.

Popular Names?

In 1979, the Pennsylvania Health Department discovered these two first names among the 159,000 birth certificates issued in the state that year—Pepsi and Cola.

A Boy Named Sue

Researchers have found that boys who had peculiar first names had a higher incidence of mental problems than boys with common ones; no similar correlation was found for girls.

He Who Quacks Last

In a government check of a computer program, researchers turned up a real-life Donald Duck. It seems that programmers used his name to create a bogus G.I.

to check out records—and found out he really existed. The Army Engineer won fame and a visit to the Johnny Carson Show as a result of this discovery.

Too-o-o-o Much
Many people dislike their own names. The most common reasons given for this dislike are that the names "sound too ugly," that they're old-fashioned, too hard to pronounce, too common, too uncommon, too long, sound too foreign, are too easy for people to joke about, and that they sound too effeminate (for men) or too masculine (for women).

What Are Parents Thinking?
It may have seemed like a good joke at the time, but did Mr. Homer Frost consider his children's future when he named them Winter Night, Jack White, Snow, Dew, Hail, and Cold (Frost)? And what was Mr. Wind thinking when he named his four children North, South, East, and West (Wind)?

For the Birds
A. Bird was the assistant manager of Britain's Royal Society for the Protection of Birds. Members of his staff were Barbara Buzzard, John Partridge, Celia Peacock, Helen Peacock, and Dorothy Rook.

Historical Irony
On July 30, 1980, *Good Morning America* announced that Richard Nixon arrested Jimmy Carter in Detroit.

Is Nothing Private Anymore?
Mr. & Mrs. Bra, a couple from South Dakota, named their two daughters Iona and Anita (Bra).

The Power of Disney
Walt Disney's popular movie *Aladdin* was released in 1992. Aladdin's love interest was named Princess Jasmine. In 1995, Jasmine is the #21 name for all girls in the U.S., the #12 name for Hispanic-American girls, and the #2 name for African-American girls.

Last But Not Least
Zachary Zzzzra has been listed in the Guinness Book of World Records as making "the most determined attempt to be the last personal name in a local telephone directory" in San Francisco. That happened before his place was challenged by one Vladimir Zzzzzzabakov. Zzzzra reports that he called Zzzzzzabakov and demanded to know his real name (Zzzzra's name is really his own, he says). Zzzzzzabakov told him it was none of his . . . business. At any rate, true to his reputation for determination, Zzzzra changed his name to regain his former—or latter?—position. When the new phone book appeared, he was relieved to find himself comfortably in the last place again, as Zachary Zzzzzzzzzzra. Unknown to him, the contender, Zzzzzzabakov, had disappeared.

The End
One family that was not terribly successful in limiting its expansion has a series of children called, respectively, Finis, Addenda, Appendix, Supplement, and (last but not least) Errata.

Girls

Aaleyah (Hebrew) a form of Aliya.
*Aalayah, Aalayaha, Aalea, Aaleah,
Aaleaha, Aaleeyah, Aaleyiah, Aaleyyah*

Aaliah (Hebrew) a form of Aliya.
Aaliaya, Aaliayah

Aalisha (Greek) a form of Alisha.
Aaleasha, Aaliesha

Aaliyah (Hebrew) a form of Aliya.
*Aahliyah, Aailiyah, Aailyah, Aalaiya,
Aaleah, Aalia, Aalieyha, Aaliya,
Aaliyaha, Aaliyha, Aalliah, Aalliyah,
Aalyah, Aalyiah*

Abagail (Hebrew) a form of Abigale.
*Abagael, Abagaile, Abagale, Abagayle,
Abageal, Abagil, Abaigael, Abaigeal*

Abbagail (Hebrew) a form of Abigale.
*Abbagale, Abbagayle, Abbegail, Abbegale,
Abbegayle*

Abbey, Abbie, Abby (Hebrew) famil-
iar forms of Abigail.
*Aabbee, Abbe, Abbea, Abbeigh, Abbi,
Abbye, Abeey, Abey, Abi, Abia, Abie, Aby*

Abbygail (Hebrew) a form of Abigale.
*Abbeygale, Abbygale, Abbygayl,
Abbygayle*

Abegail (Hebrew) a form of Abigail.
Abegale, Abegaile, Abegayle

Abelina (American) a combination of
Abbey + Lina.
Abilana, Abilene

Abia (Arabic) great.
Abbia, Abbiah, Abiah, Abya

Abianne (American) a combination of
Abbey + Ann.
Abena, Abeni, Abian, Abinaya

Abida (Arabic) worshiper.
Abedah, Abidah

Abigail (Hebrew) father's joy. Bible:
one of the wives of King David. See
also Gail.
*Abagail, Abbagail, Abbey, Abbiegail,
Abbiegayle, Abbigael, Abbigail, Abbigal,
Abbigale, Abbigayl, Abbigayle, Abbygail,
Abegail, Abgail, Abgale, Abgayle, Abigael,
Abigaile, Abigaill, Abigal, Abigale,
Abigayil, Abigayl, Abigayle, Abigel,
Abigial, Abugail, Abygail, Avigail*

Abinaya (American) a form of
Abiann.
*Abenaa, Abenaya, Abinaa, Abinaiya,
Abinayan*

Abira (Hebrew) my strength.
*Abbira, Abeer, Abeerah, Abeir, Abera,
Aberah, Abhira, Abiir, Abir*

Abra (Hebrew) mother of many
nations.
Abree, Abri, Abria

Abria (Hebrew) a form of Abra.
*Abréa, Abrea, Abreia, Abriah, Abriéa,
Abrya*

Abrial (French) open; secure,
protected.
Abrail, Abreal, Abreale, Abriale, Abrielle

Abriana (Italian) a form of Abra.
*Abbrienna, Abbryana, Abreana,
Abreanna, Abreanne, Abreeana, Abreona,*

**Abreonia, Abriann, Abrianna, Abriannah,
Abrieana, Abrien, Abrienna, Abrienne,
Abrietta, Abrion, Abrionée, Abrionne,
Abriunna, Abryann, Abryanna, Abryona**

Abrielle (French) a form of Abrial.
Aabriella, Abriel, Abriell, Abryell

Abril (French) a form of Abrial.
Abrilla, Abrille

Abygail (Hebrew) a form of Abigail.
Abygael, Abygale, Abygayle

Acacia (Greek) thorny. Mythology: the
acacia tree symbolizes immortality
and resurrection. See also Casey.
*Acasha, Acatia, Accassia, Acey, Acie,
Akacia, Cacia, Casia, Kasia*

Ada (German) a short form of
Adelaide. (English) prosperous; happy.
*Adabelle, Adah, Adan, Adaya, Adda,
Auda*

Adah (Hebrew) ornament.
Ada, Addah

Adair (Greek) a form of Adara.
Adaire

Adalene (Spanish) a form of Adalia.
*Adalane, Adalena, Adalin, Adalina,
Adaline, Adalinn, Adalyn, Adalynn,
Adalynne, Addalyn, Addalynn*

Adalia (German, Spanish) noble.
*Adal, Adala, Adalea, Adaleah, Adalee,
Adalene, Adali, Adalie, Adaly, Addal,
Addala, Addaly*

Adama (Phoenician, Hebrew) a form
of Adam (see Boys' Names).

Adamma (Ibo) child of beauty.

Adana (Spanish) a form of Adama.

Adanna (Nigerian) her father's daughter.
Adanya

Adara (Greek) beauty. (Arabic) virgin.
*Adair, Adaira, Adaora, Adar, Adarah, Adare,
Adaria, Adarra, Adasha, Adauré, Adra*

Adaya (American) a form of Ada.
*Adaija, Adaijah, Adaja, Adajah, Adayja,
Adayjah, Adejah*

Addie (Greek, German) a familiar
form of Adelaide, Adrienne.
*Aday, Adde, Addee, Addey, Addi, Addia,
Addy, Ade, Adee, Adei, Adey, Adeye, Adi,
Adie, Ady, Atti, Attie, Atty*

Addison, Addyson (English) child of
Adam.
Addis, Addisen, Addisson, Adison

Adela (English) a short form of
Adelaide.
Adelae, Adelia, Adelista, Adella

Adelaide (German) noble and serene.
See also Ada, Adela, Adeline, Adelle,
Ailis, Delia, Della, Ela, Elke, Heidi.
*Adelade, Adelaid, Adelaida, Adelei,
Adelheid, Adeliade, Adelka, Aley, Laidey,
Laidy*

Adele (English) a form of Adelle.
Adel, Adelie, Adile

Adelina (English) a form of Adeline.
*Adalina, Adeleana, Adelena, Adellyna,
Adeliana, Adellena, Adileena, Adlena*

Adeline (English) a form of Adelaide.
*Adaline, Adelaine, Adelin, Adelina,
Adelind, Adelita, Adeliya, Adelle, Adelyn,*

*Adelynn, Adelynne, Adilene, Adlin,
Adline, Adlyn, Adlynn, Aline*

Adelle (German, English) a short form
of Adelaide, Adeline.
Adele, Adell

Adena (Hebrew) noble; adorned.
*Adeana, Adeen, Adeena, Aden, Adene,
Adenia, Adenna, Adina*

Adia (Swahili) gift.
Addia, Adéa, Adea, Adiah

Adila (Arabic) equal.
*Adeala, Adeela, Adela, Adelah, Adeola,
Adilah, Adileh, Adilia, Adyla*

Adilene (English) a form of Adeline.
Adilen, Adileni, Adilenne, Adlen, Adlene

Adina (Hebrew) a form of Adena. See
also Dina.
*Adeana, Adiana, Adiena, Adinah, Adine,
Adinna, Adyna*

Adira (Hebrew) strong.
*Ader, Adera, Aderah, Aderra, Adhira,
Adirah, Adirana*

Adison, Adyson (English) forms of
Addison, Addyson.
Adis, Adisa, Adisen, Adisynne, Adysen

Aditi (Hindi) unbound. Religion: the
mother of the Hindu sun gods.
Adithi, Aditti

Adleigh (Hebrew) my ornament.
Adla, Adleni

Adonia (Spanish) beautiful.
*Adonica, Adonis, Adonna, Adonnica,
Adonya*

Adora (Latin) beloved. See also Dora.
Adore, Adoree, Adoria

Adra (Arabic) virgin.
Adara

Adreana, Adreanna (Latin) forms of
Adrienne.
*Adrean, Adreanne, Adreauna, Adreeanna,
Adreen, Adreena, Adreeyana, Adrena,
Adrene, Adrenea, Adréona, Adreonia,
Adreonna*

Adria (English) a short form of
Adriana, Adriene.
Adrea, Adriani, Adrya

Adriana, Adrianna (Italian) forms of
Adrienne.
*Addrianna, Addriyanna, Adreiana,
Adreinna, Adria, Adriannea, Adriannia,
Adrionna*

Adriane, Adrianne (English) forms of
Adrienne.
*Addrian, Adranne, Adria, Adrian,
Adreinne, Adriann, Adriayon, Adrion*

Adrielle (Hebrew) member of God's
flock.
Adriel, Adrielli, Adryelle

Adrien, Adriene (English) forms of
Adrienne.

Adrienna (Italian) a form of Adrienne.
See also Edrianna.
*Adreana, Adrieanna, Adrieaunna,
Adriena, Adrienia, Adriennah, Adrieunna*

Adrienne (Greek) rich. (Latin) dark.
See also Hadriane.
*Addie, Adrien, Adriana, Adriane,
Adrianna, Adrianne, Adrie, Adrieanne,
Adrien, Adrienna, Adriyanna*

Adrina (English) a short form of
Adriana.
Adrinah, Adrinne

Adriyanna (American) a form of
Adrienne.
Adrieyana, Adriyana, Adryan, Adryana,
Adryane, Adryanna, Adryanne

Adya (Hindi) Sunday.
Adia

Aerial, Aeriel (Hebrew) forms of Ariel.
Aeriale, Aeriela, Aerielle, Aeril, Aerile,
Aeryal

Afi (African) born on Friday.
Affi, Afia, Efi, Efia

Afra (Hebrew) young doe. (Arabic)
earth color. See also Aphra.
Affery, Affrey, Affrie, Afraa

Africa (Irish) pleasant. Geography: one
of the seven continents.
Affrica, Afric, Africah, Africaya, Africia,
Africiana, Afrika, Aifric

Afrika (Irish) a form of Africa.
Afrikah

Afrodite, Aphrodite (Greek) Mythology:
the goddess of love and beauty.
Afrodita

Afton (English) from Afton, England.
Aftan, Aftine, Aftinn, Aftyn

Agate (English) a semiprecious stone.
Aggie

Agatha (Greek) good, kind. Literature:
Agatha Christie was a British writer
of more than seventy detective nov-
els. See also Gasha.
Agace, Agaisha, Agasha, Agata, Agatah,

Agathe, Agathi, Agatka, Agetha, Aggie,
Ágota, Ágotha, Agueda, Atka

Agathe (Greek) a form of Agatha.

Aggie (Greek) a short form of Agatha,
Agnes.
Ag, Aggy, Agi

Agnes (Greek) pure. See also Aneesa,
Anessa, Anice, Anisha, Ina, Inez,
Necha, Nessa, Nessie, Neza, Nyusha,
Una, Ynez.
Aganetha, Aggie, Agna, Agne, Agneis,
Agnelia, Agnella, Agnés, Agnesa, Agnesca,
Agnese, Agnesina, Agness, Agnessa,
Agnesse, Agneta, Agneti, Agnetta, Agnies,
Agnieszka, Agniya, Agnola, Agnus,
Aignéis, Aneska, Anka

Ahava (Hebrew) beloved.
Ahivia

Ahliya (Hebrew) a form of Aliya.
Ahlai, Ahlaia, Ahlaya, Ahleah, Ahleeyah,
Ahley, Ahleya, Ahlia, Ahliah, Ahliyah

Aida (Latin) helpful. (English) a form
of Ada.
Aidah, Aidan, Aide, Aidee

Aidan, Aiden (Latin) forms of Aida.

Aiesha (Swahili, Arabic) a form of Aisha.
Aeisha, Aeshia, Aieshia, Aieysha, Aiiesha

Aiko (Japanese) beloved.

Ailani (Hawaiian) chief.
Aelani, Ailana

Aileen (Scottish) light bearer. (Irish) a
form of Helen. See also Eileen.
Ailean, Aileena, Ailen, Ailene, Aili,
Ailina, Ailinn, Aillen

Aili (Scottish) a form of Alice.
(Finnish) a form of Helen.
Aila, Ailee, Ailey, Ailie, Aily

Ailis (Irish) a form of Adelaide.
Ailesh, Ailish, Ailyse, Eilis

Ailsa (Scottish) island dweller. Geography:
Ailsa Craig is an island in Scotland.
Ailsha

Ailya (Hebrew) a form of Aliya.
Ailiyah

Aimee (Latin) a form of Amy. (French)
loved.
Aime, Aimée, Aimey, Aimi, Aimia,
Aimie, Aimy

Ainsley (Scottish) my own meadow.
Ainslee, Ainsleigh, Ainslie, Ainsly, Ansley,
Aynslee, Aynsley, Aynslie

Airiana (English) a form of Ariana,
Arianna.
Airana, Airanna, Aireana, Aireanah,
Aireanna, Aireona, Aireonna, Aireyonna,
Airianna, Airianne, Airiona, Airriana,
Airrion, Airryon, Airyana, Airyanna

Airiél (Hebrew) a form of Ariel.
Aieral, Aierel, Aiiryel, Aire, Aireal,
Aireale, Aireel, Airel, Airele, Airelle, Airi,
Airial, Airiale, Airrel

Aisha (Swahili) life. (Arabic) woman.
See also Asha, Asia, Iesha, Isha,
Keisha, Yiesha.
Aaisha, Aaishah, Aesha, Aeshah,
Aheesha, Aiasha, Aiesha, Aieshah, Aisa,
Aischa, Aish, Aishah, Aisheh, Aishia,
Aishiah, Aiysha, Aiyesha, Ayesha, Aysa,
Ayse, Aytza

Aislinn, Aislynn (Irish) forms of
Ashlyn.
Aishellyn, Aishlinn, Aislee, Aisley, Aislin,
Aisling, Aislyn, Aislynne

Aiyana (Native American) forever
flowering.
Aiyhana, Aiyona, Aiyonia, Ayana

Aiyanna (Hindi) a form of Ayanna.
Aianna, Aiyannah, Aiyonna, Aiyunna

Aja (Hindi) goat.
Ahjah, Aija, Aijah, Ajá, Ajada, Ajah,
Ajara, Ajaran, Ajare, Ajaree, Ajha, Ajia

Ajanae (American) a combination of
the letter A + Janae.
Ajahnae, Ajahne, Ajana, Ajanaé, Ajane,
Ajané, Ajanee, Ajanique, Ajena, Ajenae,
Ajené

Ajia (Hindi) a form of Aja.
Aijia, Ajhia, Aji, Ajjia

Akayla (American) a combination of
the letter A + Kayla.
Akaela, Akaelia, Akaila, Akailah, Akala,
Akaylah, Akaylia

Akeisha (American) a combination of
the letter A + Keisha.
Akaesha, Akaisha, Akasha, Akasia,
Akeecia, Akeesha, Akeishia, Akeshia,
Akisha

Akela (Hawaiian) noble.
Ahkayla, Ahkeelah, Akelah, Akelia,
Akeliah, Akeya, Akeyla, Akeylah

Akeria (American) a form of Akira.
Akera, Akerah, Akeri, Akerra, Akerra

Aki (Japanese) born in autumn.
Akeeye

Akia (American) a combination of the
letter A + Kia.
Akaja, Akeia, Akeya, Akiá, Akiah,
Akiane, Akiaya, Akiea, Akiya, Akiyah,
Akya, Akyan, Akyia, Akyiah

Akiko (Japanese) bright light.

Akilah (Arabic) intelligent.
Aikiela, Aikilah, Akeela, Akeelah,
Akeila, Akeilah, Akeiyla, Akiela,
Akielah, Akila, Akilaih, Akilia, Akilka,
Akillah, Akkila, Akyla, Akylah

Akili (Tanzanian) wisdom.

Akina (Japanese) spring flower.

Akira (American) a combination of
the letter A + Kira.
Akeria, Akiera, Akierra, Akirah, Akire,
Akiria, Akirrah, Akyra

Alaina, Alayna (Irish) forms of Alana.
Aalaina, Alainah, Alaine, Alainna,
Alainnah, Alane, Alaynah, Alayne,
Alaynna, Aleine, Alleyna, Alleynah,
Alleyne

Alair (French) a form of Hilary.
Alaira, Ali, Allaire

Alamea (Hawaiian) ripe; precious.

Alameda (Spanish) poplar tree.

Alana (Irish) attractive; peaceful.
(Hawaiian) offering. See also Lana.
Alaana, Alaina, Alanae, Alanah, Alane,
Alanea, Alani, Alania, Alanis, Alanna,
Alawna, Alayna, Allana, Allanah, Allyn,
Alonna

Alandra, Alandria (Spanish) forms of
Alexandra, Alexandria.
Alandrea, Alantra, Aleandra, Aleandrea

Alani (Hawaiian) orange tree. (Irish) a
form of Alana.
Alaini, Alainie, Alania, Alanie, Alaney,
Alannie

Alanna (Irish) a form of Alana.
Alannah

Alanza (Spanish) noble and eager.

Alaysha, Alaysia (American) forms of
Alicia.
Alaysh, Alayshia

Alba (Latin) from Alba Longa, an
ancient city near Rome, Italy.
Albana, Albani, Albanie, Albany, Albeni,
Albina, Albine, Albinia, Albinka, Elba

Alberta (German, French) noble and
bright. See also Auberte, Bertha,
Elberta.
Albertina, Albertine, Albertyna,
Albertyne, Alverta

Albreanna (American) a combination
of Alberta + Breanna (see Breana).
Albré, Albrea, Albreona, Albreonna,
Albreyon

Alcina (Greek) strong-minded.
Alceena, Alcine, Alcinia, Alseena, Alsinia,
Alsyna, Alzina

Alda (German) old; elder.
Aldina, Aldine

Alden (English) old; wise protector.
Aldan, Aldon, Aldyn

Aldina, Aldine (Hebrew) forms of
Alda.
Aldeana, Aldene, Aldona, Aldyna, Aldyne

Alea, Aleah (Arabic) high, exalted.
(Persian) God's being.
Aileah, Aleea, Aleeah, Aleia, Aleiah,
Allea, Alleah, Alleea, Alleeah

Aleasha, Aleesha (Greek) forms of
Alisha.
Aleashae, Aleashea, Aleashia, Aleassa,
Aleeshia

Alecia (Greek) a form of Alicia.
Aalecia, Ahlasia, Aleacia, Aleacya,
Aleasia, Alecea, Aleceea, Aleceia, Aleciya,
Aleciyah, Alecy, Alecya, Aleeceia, Aleecia,
Aleesia, Aleesiya, Aleicia, Alesha, Alesia,
Allecia, Alleecia

Aleela (Swahili) she cries.
Aleelah, Alila, Alile

Aleena (Dutch) a form of Aleene.
Ahleena, Aleana, Aleeanna

Aleene (Dutch) alone.
Aleen, Aleena, Alene, Alleen

Aleeya (Hebrew) a form of Aliya.
Alee, Aleea, Aleeyah, Aleiya, Aleiyah

Aleeza (Hebrew) a form of Aliza. See
also Leeza.
Aleiza

Alegria (Spanish) cheerful.
Aleggra, Alegra, Allegra, Allegria

Aleisha, Alesha (Greek) forms of
Alecia, Alisha.
Aleasha, Aleashea, Aleasia, Aleesha,
Aleeshah, Aleeshia, Aleeshya, Aleisa,
Alesa, Alesah, Aleisha, Aleshia, Aleshya,
Alesia, Alessia

Alejandra (Spanish) a form of Alexandra.
Aleiandra, Alejanda, Alejandr,

Alejandrea, Alejandria, Alejandrina,
Alejandro

Aleka (Hawaiian) a form of Alice.
Aleeka, Alekah

Aleksandra (Greek) a form of
Alexandra.
Alecsandra, Aleksasha, Aleksandrija,
Aleksandriya

Alena (Russian) a form of Helen.
Alenah, Alene, Alenea, Aleni, Alenia,
Alenka, Alenna, Alennah, Alenya, Alyna

Alesia, Alessia (Greek) forms of Alice,
Alicia, Alisha.
Alessea, Alesya, Allesia

Alessa (Greek) a form of Alice.
Alessi, Allessa

Alessandra (Italian) a form of
Alexandra.
Alesandra, Alesandrea, Alissandra,
Alissondra, Allesand, Allessandra

Aleta (Greek) a form of Alida. See also
Leta.
Aletta, Alletta

Alethea (Greek) truth.
Alathea, Alathia, Aletea, Aletha,
Aletheia, Alethia, Aletia, Alithea, Alithia

Alette (Latin) wing.

Alex (Greek) a short form of
Alexander, Alexandra.
Aleix, Aleks, Alexe, Alexx, Allex, Allexx

Alexa (Greek) a short form of
Alexandra.
Aleixa, Alekia, Aleksa, Aleksha, Aleksi,
Alexah, Alexsa, Alexssa, Alexxa, Allexa,
Alyxa

Alexandra (Greek) defender of
humankind. History: the last czarina of
Russia. See also Lexia, Lexie, Olesia,
Ritsa, Sandra, Sandrine, Sasha, Shura,
Sondra, Xandra, Zandra.
Alandra, Alaxandra, Aleczandra, Alejandra,
Aleksandra, Alessandra, Alex, Alexa,
Alexande, Alexandera, Alexandre, Alexas,
Alexi, Alexina, Alexine, Alexis, Alexsandra,
Alexius, Alexsis, Alexus, Alexxandra,
Alexys, Alexzandra, Alix, Alixandra,
Aljexi, Alla, Alyx, Alyxandra, Lexandra

Alexandrea (Greek) a form of
Alexandria.
Alexandreana, Alexandreia, Alexandriea,
Alexandrieah, Alexanndrea

Alexandria (Greek) a form of
Alexandra. See also Drinka, Xandra,
Zandra.
Alaxandria, Alecsandria, Aleczandria,
Alexanderia, Alexanderine, Alexandrea,
Alexandrena, Alexandrie, Alexandrina,
Alexandrine, Alexanndria, Alexandrya,
Alexendria, Alexendrine, Alexia,
Alixandrea, Alyxandria

Alexandrine (Greek) a form of
Alexandra.
Alexandrina

Alexanne (American) a combination
of Alex + Anne.
Alexan, Alexanna, Alexane, Alexann,
Alexanna, Alexian, Alexiana

Alexas, Alexes (Greek) short forms of
Alexandra.
Alexess

Alexi, Alexie (Greek) short forms of Alexandra.
Aleksey, Aleksi, Alexey, Alexy

Alexia (Greek) a short form of Alexandria. See also Lexia.
Aleksia, Aleska, Alexcia, Alexea, Alexsia, Alexsiya, Allexia, Alyxia

Alexis (Greek) a short form of Alexandra.
Aalexis, Ahlexis, Alaxis, Alecsis, Alecxis, Aleexis, Aleksis, Alexcis, Alexias, Alexiou, Alexiss, Alexiz, Alexxis, Alixis, Allexis, Elexis, Lexis

Alexius, Alexus (Greek) short forms of Alexandra.
Aalexus, Aalexxus, Aelexus, Ahlexus, Alecsus, Alexsus, Alexuss, Alexxus, Alixus, Allexius, Allexus, Elexus, Lexus

Alexsandra (Greek) a form of Alexandra.
Alexsandria, Alexsandro, Alixsandra

Alexsis, Alexxis (Greek) short forms of Alexandra.
Alexxiz

Alexys (Greek) a short form of Alexandra.
Alexsys, Alexyes, Alexyis, Alexyss, Allexys

Alexzandra, Alexzandra (Greek) forms of Alexandra.
Alexzand, Alexzandrea, Alexzandriah, Alexzandrya, Alixzandria

Aleya, Aleyah (Hebrew) forms of Aliya.
Alayah, Aleayah, Aleeya, Aléyah, Aleyia, Aleyiah

Alfie (English) a familiar form of Alfreda.
Alfi, Alfy

Alfreda (English) elf counselor; wise counselor. See also Effie, Elfrida, Freda, Frederica.
Alfie, Alfredda, Alfredia, Alfreeda, Alfreida, Alfrieda

Ali, Aly (Greek) familiar forms of Alice, Alicia, Alisha, Alison.
Allea, Alli, Allie, Ally

Alia, Aliah (Hebrew) forms of Aliya. See also Aaliyah, Alea.
Aelia, Allia, Alya

Alice (Greek) truthful. (German) noble. See also Aili, Aleka, Alie, Alisa, Alison, Alli, Alysa, Alyssa, Alyse, Elke.
Adelice, Alecia, Aleece, Alesia, Alicie, Aliece, Alise, Alix, Alize, Alla, Alleece, Allice, Allis, Allise, Allix

Alicia (English) a form of Alice. See also Elicia, Licia.
Aelicia, Alaysha, Alecea, Alecia, Aleecia, Ali, Alicea, Alicha, Alichia, Aliciah, Alician, Alicja, Alicya, Aliecia, Alisha, Allicea, Allicia, Alycia, Ilysa

Alida (Latin) small and winged. (Spanish) noble. See also Aleta, Lida, Oleda.
Aleda, Aleida, Alidia, Alita, Alleda, Allida, Allidah, Alyda, Alydia, Elida, Elidia

Alie, Allie (Greek) familiar forms of Alice.

Aliesha (Greek) a form of Alisha.
Alieshai, Alieshia, Alliesha

Alika (Hawaiian) truthful. (Swahili) most beautiful.
Aleka, Alica, Alikah, Alike, Alikee, Aliki

Alima (Arabic) sea maiden; musical.

Alina, Alyna (Slavic) bright. (Scottish) fair. (English) short forms of Adeline. See also Alena.
Aliana, Alianna, Alinah, Aline, Alinna, Allyna, Alynna, Alyona

Aline (Scottish) a form of Alina.
Alianne, Allene, Alline, Allyn, Allyne, Alyne, Alynne

Alisa, Alissa (Greek) a form of Alice. See also Elisa, Ilisa.
Aalissah, Aaliysah, Aleessa, Alisah, Alisea, Alisia, Alisza, Alisza, Aliysa, Allissa, Alyssa

Alise, Allise (Greek) forms of Alice.
Alics, Aliese, Alis, Aliss, Alisse, Alisse, Alles, Allesse, Allis, Allisse

Alisha (Greek) truthful. (German) noble. (English) a form of Alicia. See also Elisha, Ilisha, Lisha.
Aalisha, Aleasha, Aleesha, Aleisha, Alesha, Ali, Aliesha, Aliscia, Alisha, Alishay, Alishaye, Alishia, Alishya, Alitsha, Allisha, Allysha, Alysha

Alishia, Alisia, Alissia (English) forms of Alisha.
Alishea, Alisheia, Alishiana, Alyssaya, Alisea, Alissya, Alisyia, Allissia

Alison, Allison (English) forms of Alice. See also Lissie.
Ali, Alicen, Alicyn, Alisan, Alisann, Alisanne, Alisen, Alisenne, Alisin, Alision, Alisonn, Alisson, Alisun, Alles, Allesse, Alleyson, Allie, Allisson, Allisyn, Allix, Allsun

Alita (Spanish) a form of Alida.
Allita

Alivia (Latin) a form of Olivia.
Alivah

Alix (Greek) a short form of Alexandra, Alice.
Alixe, Alixia, Allix, Alyx

Alixandra, Alixandria (Greek) forms of Alexandria.
Alixandriya, Allixandra, Allixandria, Allixandrya

Aliya (Hebrew) ascender.
Aaleyah, Aaliyah, Aeliyah, Ahliya, Ailya, Alea, Aleya, Alia, Alieya, Alieyah, Aliyah, Aliyiah, Aliyyah, Allia, Alliyah, Aly, Alyah

Aliye (Arabic) noble.
Aliyeh

Aliza (Hebrew) joyful. See also Aleeza, Eliza.
Alieza, Aliezah, Alitza, Aliz, Alizah, Alize, Alizee

Alizabeth (Hebrew) a form of Elizabeth.
Alyzabeth

Allana, Allanah (Irish) forms of Alana.
Allanie, Allanna, Allauna

Allegra (Latin) cheerful.
Legra

Allena (Irish) a form of Alana.
Alleen, Alleyna, Alleynah

Alli, Ally (Greek) familiar forms of Alice.
Ali, Alley

Allia, Alliah (Hebrew) forms of Aliya.

Allissa (Greek) a form of Alyssa.
Allisa

Alliyah (Hebrew) a form of Aliya.
Alliya, Alliyha, Alliyia, Alliyyah, Allya, Allyah

Allysa, Allyssa (Greek) a form of Alyssa.
Allissa, Allyisa, Allysa, Allysah, Allyssah

Allysha (English) a form of Alisha.
Alishia, Allysia

Allyson, Alyson (English) forms of Alison.
Allysen, Allyson, Allysonn, Allysson, Allysun, Alyson

Alma (Arabic) learned. (Latin) soul.
Almah

Almeda (Arabic) ambitious.
Allmeda, Allmedah, Allmeta, Allmita, Almea, Almedah, Almeta, Almida, Almita

Almira (Arabic) aristocratic, princess; exalted. (Spanish) from Almeíra, Spain. See also Elmira, Mira.
Allmeera, Allmeria, Allmira, Almeera, Almeeria, Almeira, Almeria, Almire

Aloha (Hawaiian) loving, kindhearted, charitable.
Alohi

Aloisa (German) famous warrior.
Aloisia, Aloysia

Aloma (Latin) a short form of Paloma.

Alondra (Spanish) a form of Alexandra.
Allandra, Alonda

Alonna (Irish) a form of Alana.
Alona, Alonnah, Alonya, Alonyah

Alonza (English) noble and eager.

Alora (American) a combination of the letter A + Lora.
Alorah, Alorha, Alorie, Aloura, Alouria

Alpha (Greek) first-born. Linguistics: the first letter of the Greek alphabet.
Alphia

Alta (Latin) high; tall.
Allta, Altah, Altana, Altanna, Altea, Alto

Althea (Greek) wholesome; healer. History: Althea Gibson was the first African American to win a major tennis title. See also Thea.
Altha, Altheda, Altheya, Althia, Elthea, Eltheya, Elthia

Alva (Latin, Spanish) white; light skinned. See also Elva.
Alvana, Alvanna, Alvannah

Alvina (English) friend to all; noble friend; friend to elves. See also Elva, Vina.
Alveanea, Alveen, Alveena, Alveenia, Alvenea, Alvie, Alvinae, Alvincia, Alvine, Alvinea, Alvinesha, Alvinia, Alvinna, Alvita, Alvona, Alvyna, Alwin, Alwina, Alwyn

Alyah, Alyiah (Hebrew) forms of
Aliya.
Aly, Alya, Aleah, Alyia

Alycia, Alyssia (English) forms of
Alicia.
Allyce, Alycea, Alyciah, Alyse, Lycia

Alysa, Alyse, Alysse (Greek) forms of
Alice.
Allys, Allyse, Allyss, Alys, Alyss

Alysha, Alysia (Greek) forms of
Alisha.
*Allysea, Allyscia, Alysea, Alyshia,
Alyssha, Alyssia*

Alyssa (Greek) rational. Botany:
alyssum is a flowering herb. See also
Alice, Elissa.
*Ahlyssa, Alissa, Allissa, Allyssa, Alyesa,
Alyessa, Alyissa, Alysah, Ilyssa, Lyssa,
Lyssah*

Alysse (Greek) a form of Alice.
Allyce, Allys, Allyse, Allyss, Alys, Alyss

Alyx, Alyxis (Greek) short forms of
Alexandra.

Alyxandra, Alyxandria (Greek) forms
of Alexandria.
Alyxandrea, Alyxzandrya

Am (Vietnamese) lunar; female.

Ama (African) born on Saturday.

Amabel (Latin) lovable. See also Bel,
Mabel.

Amada (Spanish) beloved.
Amadea, Amadi, Amadia, Amadita

Amairani (Greek) a form of Amara.
*Amairaine, Amairane, Amairanie,
Amairany*

Amal (Hebrew) worker. (Arabic)
hopeful.
Amala

Amalia (German) a form of Amelia.
*Ahmalia, Amalea, Amaleah, Amaleta,
Amalija, Amalina, Amalisa, Amalita,
Amaliya, Amalya, Amalyn*

Amalie (German) a form of Amelia.
Amalee, Amali, Amaly

Aman, Amani (Arabic) forms of
Imani.
*Aamani, Ahmani, Amane, Amanee,
Amaney, Amanie, Ammanu*

Amanada (Latin) a form of Amanda.

Amanda (Latin) lovable. See also Manda.
*Amada, Amanada, Amandah,
Amandalee, Amandalyn, Amandi,
Amandie, Amandine, Amandy*

Amandeep (Punjabi) peaceful light.

Amara (Greek) eternally beautiful. See
also Mara.
*Amar, Amaira, Amairani, Amarah,
Amari, Amaria, Amariah*

Amaranta (Spanish) a flower that
never fades.

Amari (Greek) a form of Amara.
Amaree, Amarie, Amarii, Amarri

Amaris (Hebrew) promised by God.
Amarissa, Amarys, Maris

Amaryllis (Greek) fresh; flower.
Amarillis, Amarylis

Amaui (Hawaiian) thrush.

Amaya (Japanese) night rain.

Ambar (French) a form of Amber.

Amber (French) amber.
*Aamber, Ahmber, Ambar, Amberia,
Amberise, Amberly, Ambria, Ambur,
Ambyr, Ambyre, Ammber, Ember*

Amberly (American) a familiar form
of Amber.
*Amberle, Amberlea, Amberlee,
Amberleigh, Amberley, Amberli, Amberlie,
Amberlly, Amberlye*

Amberlyn, Amberlynn (American)
combinations of Amber + Lynn.
*Amberlin, Amberlina, Amberlyne,
Amberlynne*

Ambria (American) a form of Amber.
Ambrea, Ambra, Ambriah

Amelia (German) hard working.
(Latin) a form of Emily. History:
Amelia Earhart, an American aviator,
was the first woman to fly solo across
the Atlantic Ocean. See also Ima,
Melia, Millie, Nuela, Yamelia.
*Aemilia, Aimilia, Amalia, Amalie,
Amaliya, Ameila, Ameilia, Amelie,
Amelina, Ameline, Amelisa, Amelita,
Amella, Amilia, Amilina, Amilisa,
Amilita, Amilyn, Amylia*

Amelie (German) a familiar form of
Amelia.
*Amaley, Amalie, Amelee, Ameleigh,
Ameley, Amélie, Amely, Amilie*

America (Teutonic) industrious.
Americana, Amerika

Ami, Amie (French) forms of Amy.
Aami, Amiee, Amii, Amiiee, Ammee,
Ammie, Ammiee

Amilia, Amilie (Latin, German) forms
of Amelia.
Amilee, Amili, Amillia, Amily, Amilya

Amina (Arabic) trustworthy, faithful.
History: the mother of the prophet
Muhammad.
Aamena, Aamina, Aaminah, Ameena,
Ameenah, Aminah, Aminda, Amindah,
Aminta, Amintah

Amira (Hebrew) speech; utterance.
(Arabic) princess. See also Mira.
Ameera, Ameerah, Amirah

Amissa (Hebrew) truth.
Amissah

Amita (Hebrew) truth.
Amitha

Amity (Latin) friendship.
Amitie

Amlika (Hindi) mother.
Amlikah

Amma (Hindi) god, godlike. Religion:
another name for the Hindu goddess
Shakti.

Amorie (German) industrious leader.

Amparo (Spanish) protected.

Amrit (Sanskrit) nectar.
Amrita

Amy (Latin) beloved. See also Aimee,
Emma, Esmé.
Amata, Ame, Amey, Ami, Amia, Amie,
Amio, Ammy, Amye, Amylyn

An (Chinese) peaceful.

Ana (Hawaiian, Spanish) a form of
Hannah.
Anai, Anaia

Anaba (Native American) she returns
from battle.

Anabel, Anabelle (English) forms of
Annabel.
Anabela, Anabele, Anabell, Anabella

Anahita (Persian) a river and water
goddess.
Anahai, Anahi, Anahit, Anahy

Anais (Hebrew) gracious.
Anaise, Anaïse

Anala (Hindi) fine.

Analisa, Analise (English) combina-
tions of Ana + Lisa.
Analice, Analicia, Analis, Analisha,
Analisia, Analissa

Anamaria (English) a combination of
Ana + Maria.
Anamarie, Anamary

Ananda (Hindi) blissful.

Anastacia (Greek) a form of Anastasia.
Anastace, Anastacie

Anastasia (Greek) resurrection. See
also Nastasia, Stacey, Stacia, Stasya.
Anastacia, Anastase, Anastascia,
Anastasha, Anastashia, Anastasie,
Anastasija, Anastassia, Anastassya,
Anastasya, Anastatia, Anastaysia,
Anastazia, Anastice, Annastasia,
Annastasija, Annastaysia, Annastazia,
Annstás

Anatola (Greek) from the east.

Anci (Hungarian) a form of Hannah.
Annus, Annushka

Andee, Andi, Andie (American) short
forms of Andrea, Fernanda.
Ande, Andea, Andy

Andrea (Greek) strong; courageous.
See also Ondrea.
Aindrea, Andee, Andera, Anderea, Andra,
Andrah, Andraia, Andraya, Andreah,
Andreaka, Andreana, Andreane, Andree,
Andrée, Andreea, Andreia, Andreja, Andreka,
Andrel, Andrell, Andrelle, Andreo, Andressa,
Andrette, Andreya, Andria, Andriana,
Andrieka, Andrietta, Andris, Aundrea

Andreana, Andreanna (Greek) forms
of Andrea.
Ahndrianna, Andreina, Andrena,
Andreyana, Andreyonna, Andrina,
Andriona, Andrionna

Andreane, Andreanne (Greek) forms
of Andrea.
Andrean, Andreeanne, Andree Anne,
Andrene, Andrian, Andrienne

Andria (Greek) a form of Andrea.
Andri, Andriea

Andriana, Andrianna (Greek) forms
of Andrea.

Aneesa, Aneesha (Greek) forms of
Agnes.
Ahnesha, Ahnesia, Ahnesshia, Anee,
Aneesah, Aneese, Aneeshah, Aneesia,
Aneisa, Aneisha, Anessa, Anessia

Aneko (Japanese) older sister.

Anela (Hawaiian) angel.
Anel, Anelle

Anessa (Greek) a form of Agnes.
Anesha, Aneshia, Anesia, Anessia,
Annessa

Anetra (American) a form of Annette.
Anitra

Anezka (Czech) a form of Hannah.

Angel (Greek) a short form of Angela.
Angele, Angéle, Angell, Angelle, Angil, Anjel

Angela (Greek) angel; messenger.
Angala, Anganita, Angel, Angelanell,
Angelanette, Angelee, Angeleigh, Angeles,
Angeli, Angelia, Angelica, Angelina,
Angelique, Angelita, Angella, Angellita,
Angie, Anglea, Anjela, Anjelica

Angelia (Greek) a form of Angela.
Angelea, Angeleah, Angelie

Angelica, Angelika (Greek) forms of
Angela.
Angalic, Angelic, Angelici, Angelicia,
Angelike, Angeliki, Angellica, Angilica

Angelina, Angeline (Russian) forms
of Angela.
Angalena, Angalina, Angeleen, Angelena,
Angelene, Angeliana, Angeleana,
Angellina, Angelyn, Angelyna, Angelyne,
Angelynn, Angelynne, Anhelina, Anjelina

Angelique (French) a form of Angela.
Angeliqua, Angélique, Angilique, Anjelique

Angeni (Native American) spirit.

Angie (Greek) a familiar form of Angela.
Ange, Angee, Angey, Angi, Angy

Ani (Hawaiian) beautiful.
Aany, Aanye

Ania (Polish) a form of Hannah.
Ahnia, Anaya, Aniah

Anica, Anika (Czech) familiar forms
of Anna.
Aanika, Anaka, Aneeky, Aneka, Anekah,
Anicka, Anik, Anikah, Anike, Anikka,
Anikke, Aniko, Anneka, Annik, Annika,
Anouska, Anuska

Anice (English) a form of Agnes.
Anesse, Anis, Anise, Annes, Annice,
Annis, Annus

Anila (Hindi) Religion: an attendant
of the Hindu god Vishnu.
Anilla

Anisa, Anisah (Arabic) friendly.
Annissah

Anissa, Anisha (English) forms of
Agnes, Ann.
Aanisha, Aeniesha, Anis, Anisa, Anissah,
Anise, Annisa, Annisha, Annissa, Anyssa

Anita (Spanish) a form of Ann, Anna.
See also Nita.
Aneeta, Aneetah, Aneethah, Anetha,
Anitha, Anithah, Anitia, Anitra, Anitte

Anjelica (Greek) a form of Angela.
Anjelika

Anka (Polish) a familiar form of
Hannah.
Anke

Ann, Anne (English) gracious.
Anissa, Anita, Annchen, Annette, Annie,
Annik, Annika, Annze, Anouche

Anna (German, Italian, Czech,
Swedish) gracious. Culture: Anna
Pavlova was a famous Russian balle-
rina. See also Anica, Anissa, Nina.
Ahnna, Ana, Anah, Anica, Anita,
Annah, Annina, Annora, Anona, Anya,
Anyu, Aska

Annabel (English) a combination of
Anna + Bel.
Amabel, Anabel, Annabal, Annabelle

Annabelle (English) a form of
Annabel.
Anabelle, Annabell, Annabella

Annalie (Finnish) a form of Hannah.
Analee, Annalea, Annaleah, Annalee,
Annaleigh, Annaleigha, Annali, Anneli,
Annelie

Annalisa, Annalise (English) combi-
nations of Anna + Lisa.
Analisa, Analise, Annaliesa, Annaliese,
Annalissa, Annalisse

Annamarie, Annemarie, Annmarie,
Anne-Marie (English) combinations
of Anne + Marie.
Annamaria, Anna-Maria, Anna-Marie,
Annmaria

Anneka (Swedish) a form of Hannah.
Annaka, Anneke, Annika, Anniki,
Annikki

Annelisa (English) a combination of
Ann + Lisa.
Analiese, Anelisa, Anelise, Anneliese,
Annelise

Annette (French) a form of Ann. See also Anetra, Nettie.
Anet, Aneta, Anetra, Anett, Anetta, Anette, Anneth, Annett, Annetta

Annie (English) a familiar form of Ann.
Anni, Anny

Annik, Annika (Russian) forms of Ann.
Aneka, Anekah, Annick, Annicka, Annike, Annikka, Anninka, Anouk

Annjanette (American) a combination of Ann + Janette (see Janett).
Angen, Angenett, Angenette, Anjane, Anjanetta, Anjani

Anona (English) pineapple.

Anouhea (Hawaiian) cool, soft fragrance.

Ansley (Scottish) forms of Ainsley.
Anslea, Anslee, Ansleigh, Anslie

Anthea (Greek) flower.
Antha, Anthe, Anthia, Thia

Antionette (French) a form of Antonia.
Antionet, Antionett, Anntionett

Antoinette (French) a form of Antonia. See also Netti, Toinette, Toni.
Anta, Antanette, Antoinella, Antoinet, Antonella, Antonetta, Antonette, Antonice, Antonieta, Antonietta, Antonique

Antonia (Greek) flourishing. (Latin) praiseworthy. See also Toni, Tonya, Tosha.
Ansonia, Ansonya, Antania, Antinia, Antionette, Antoinette, Antona, Antoñia,

Antonice, Antonie, Antonina, Antonine, Antoniya, Antonnea, Antonnia, Antonya

Antonice (Latin) a form of Antonia.
Antanise, Antanisha, Antonesha, Antoneshia, Antonise, Antonisha

Anya (Russian) a form of Anna.
Aaniyah, Aniya, Aniyah, Anja

Anyssa (English) a form of Anissa.
Anysa, Anysha

'Aolani (Hawaiian) heavenly cloud.

Aphra (Hebrew) young doe. See also Afra.

April (Latin) opening. See also Avril.
Aprele, Aprelle, Apriell, Aprielle, Aprila, Aprile, Aprilette, Aprili, Aprill, Apryl

Apryl (Latin) a form of April.
Apryle

Aquene (Native American) peaceful.

Ara (Arabic) opinionated.
Ahraya, Aira, Arae, Arah, Araya, Arayah

Arabella (Latin) beautiful altar. See also Belle, Orabella.
Arabela, Arabele, Arabelle

Araceli, Aracely (Latin) heavenly altar.
Aracele, Aracelia, Aracelli, Araseli, Arasely, Arcelia, Arceli

Ardelle (Latin) warm; enthusiastic.
Ardelia, Ardelis, Ardella

Arden (English) valley of the eagle. Literature: in Shakespeare, a romantic place of refuge.
Ardeen, Ardeena, Ardena, Ardene, Ardenia, Ardi, Ardin, Ardina, Ardine

Ardi (Hebrew) a short form of Arden, Ardice, Ardith.
Ardie, Arti, Artie

Ardice (Hebrew) a form of Ardith.
Ardis, Artis, Ardiss, Ardyce, Ardys

Ardith (Hebrew) flowering field.
Ardath, Ardi, Ardice, Ardyth

Areli, Arely (American) forms of Oralee.
Areil, Areile, Arelee, Areli, Arelis, Arelli, Arellia, Arelly

Arella (Hebrew) angel; messenger.
Arela, Arelle, Orella, Orelle

Aretha (Greek) virtuous. See also Oretha.
Areatha, Areetha, Areta, Aretina, Aretta, Arette, Arita, Aritha, Retha, Ritha

Ari, Aria, Arie (Hebrew) short forms of Ariel.
Ariah, Ariea, Aryia

Ariadne (Greek) holy. Mythology: the daughter of King Minos of Crete.

Ariana, Arianna (Greek) holy.
Aeriana, Aerianna, Aerionna, Ahreanna, Ahriana, Ahrianna, Airiana, Arieana, Ariona, Arionna, Aryonna

Ariane (French), Arianne (English) forms of Ariana, Arianna.
Aerian, Aeriann, Aerion, Aerionne, Airiann, Ari, Arianie, Ariann, Ariannie, Arieann, Arien, Ariene, Arienne, Arieon, Arionne, Aryane, Aryann, Aryanne

Arica (Scandinavian) forms of Erica.
Aerica, Aericka, Aeryka, Aricca, Aricka, Arika, Arike, Arikka

Ariel (Hebrew) lion of God.
*Aerial, Aeriale, Aeriel, Aeriela, Aeryal,
Ahriel, Aire, Aireal, Airial, Ari, Aria,
Arial, Ariale, Arieal, Ariela, Arielle,
Arrieal, Arriel, Aryel, Auriel*

Arielle (French) a form of Ariel.
*Aeriell, Ariella, Arriele, Arriell, Arrielle,
Aryelle, Aurielle*

Arin (Hebrew) enlightened. (Arabic)
messenger. See also Erin.
Aaren, Aerin, Aieron, Aieren, Arinn, Aryn

Arista (Greek) best.
Aris, Arissa, Aristana, Aristen

Arla (German) a form of Carla.

Arleigh (English) a form of Harley.
Arlea, Arlee, Arley, Arlie, Arly

Arlene (Irish) pledge. See also Lena,
Lina.
*Airlen, Arlana, Arleen, Arleene, Arlen,
Arlena, Arlenis, Arlette, Arleyne, Arliene,
Arlina, Arlinda, Arline, Arlis*

Arlette (English) a form of Arlene.
Arleta, Arletta, Arletty

Arlynn (American) a combination of
Arlene + Lynn.
Arlyn, Arlyne, Arlynne

Armani (Persian) desire, goal.
Armahni, Arman, Armanee, Armanii

Armine (Latin) noble. (German) sol-
dier. (French) a form of Herman (see
Boys' Names).
Armina

Arnelle (German) eagle.
Arnell, Arnella

Artha (Hindi) wealthy, prosperous.
Arthi, Arti, Artie

Artis (Irish) noble; lofty hill. (Scottish)
bear. (English) rock. (Icelandic) fol-
lower of Thor.
*Arthea, Arthelia, Arthene, Arthette,
Arthurette, Arthurina, Arthurine, Artina,
Artice*

Aryana, Aryanna (Italian) forms of
Ariana.
Aryan, Aryanah, Aryannah

Aryn (Hebrew) a form of Arin.
*Aerryn, Aeryn, Airyn, Aryne, Arynn,
Arynne*

Asa (Japanese) born in the morning.

Asha (Arabic, Swahili) a form of Aisha,
Ashia.

Ashanti (Swahili) from a tribe in West
Africa.
*Achante, Achanti, Asante, Ashanta,
Ashantae, Ashante, Ashanté, Ashantee,
Ashantie, Ashaunta, Ashauntae,
Ashauntee, Ashaunti, Ashonti, Ashuntae,
Ashunti*

Ashely (English) form of Ashley.
*Ashelee, Ashelei, Asheley, Ashelie,
Ashelley, Ashelly*

Ashia (Arabic) life.
Asha, Ashya, Ashyah, Ashyia, Ayshia

Ashlee, Ashli, Ashlie, Ashly (English)
forms of Ashley.
Ashle, Ashlea, Ashleah, Ashleeh, Ashliee

Ashleigh (English) a form of Ashley.
Ahsleigh, Asheleigh, Ashlei, Ashliegh

Ashley (English) ash tree meadow. See
also Lee.
*Ahslee, Aishlee, Ashala, Ashalee, Ashalei,
Ashaley, Ashely, Ashla, Ashlay, Ashleay,
Ashlee, Ashleigh, Ashleye, Ashli, Ashlie,
Ashly, Ashlye*

Ashlin (English) a form of Ashlyn.
Ashlean, Ashliann, Ashlianne, Ashline

Ashlyn, Ashlynn (English) ash tree
pool. (Irish) vision, dream.
*Ashlan, Ashleann, Ashleen, Ashleene,
Ashlen, Ashlene, Ashlin, Ashling,
Ashlyne, Ashlynne*

Ashten, Ashtin (English) forms of
Ashton.
Ashtine

Ashton (English) ash-tree settlement.
Ashten, Ashtyn

Ashtyn (English) a form of Ashton.
Ashtynne

Asia (Greek) resurrection. (English)
eastern sunrise. (Swahili) a form of
Aisha.
*Ahsia, Aisia, Aisian, Asiah, Asian,
Asianae, Asya, Aysia, Aysiah, Aysian,
Ayzia*

Aspen (English) aspen tree.
Aspin, Aspyn

Aster (English) a form of Astra.
Astera, Asteria, Astyr

Astra (Greek) star.
Asta, Astara, Aster, Astraea, Astrea

Astrid (Scandinavian) divine strength.
Astri, Astrida, Astrik, Astrud, Atti, Estrid

Atalanta (Greek) mighty huntress. Mythology: an athletic young woman who refused to marry any man who could not outrun her in a footrace. See also Lani.
Atalaya, Atlanta, Atlante, Atlee

Atara (Hebrew) crown.
Atarah, Ataree

Athena (Greek) wise. Mythology: the goddess of wisdom.
Athenea, Athene, Athina, Atina

Atira (Hebrew) prayer.

Auberte (French) a form of Alberta.
Auberta, Aubertha, Auberthe, Aubine

Aubree, Aubrie (French) forms of Aubrey.
Auberi, Aubre, Aubrei, Aubreigh, Aubri, Aubrielle

Aubrey (German) noble; bearlike. (French) blond ruler; elf ruler.
Aubary, Aubery, Aubray, Aubrea, Aubreah, Aubree, Aubrette, Aubria, Aubrie, Aubry, Aubury, Avery

Aubriana, Aubrianna (English) combinations of Aubrey + Anna.
Aubreyana, Aubreyanna, Aubreyanne, Aubreyena, Aubrianne

Audey (English) a familiar form of Audrey.
Aude, Audi, Audie

Audra (French) a form of Audrey.
Audria, Audriea

Audreanne (English) a combination of Audrey + Anne.
Audrea, Audreen, Audrianne, Audrienne

Audree, Audrie (English) forms of Audrey.
Audre, Audri

Audrey (English) noble strength.
Adrey, Audey, Audra, Audray, Audree, Audrie, Audrin, Audriya, Audry, Audrye

Audriana, Audrianna (English) combinations of Audrey + Anna.
Audreanna, Audrienna, Audrina

Audris (German) fortunate, wealthy.
Audrys

Augusta (Latin) a short form of Augustine. See also Gusta.
Agusta, August, Auguste, Augustia, Augustus, Austina

Augustine (Latin) majestic. Religion: Saint Augustine was the first archbishop of Canterbury. See also Tina.
Agustina, Augusta, Augustina, Augustyna, Augustyne, Austin

'Aulani (Hawaiian) royal messenger.
Lani, Lanie

Aundrea (Greek) a form of Andrea.
Aundreah

Aura (Greek) soft breeze. (Latin) golden. See also Ora.

Aurelia (Latin) golden. See also Oralia.
Auralea, Auralia, Aurea, Aureal, Aurel, Aurele, Aurelea, Aureliana, Aurelie, Auria, Aurie, Aurilia, Aurita

Aurelie (Latin) a form of Aurelia.
Auralee, Auralei, Aurelee, Aurelei, Aurelle

Aurora (Latin) dawn. Mythology: Aurora was the goddess of dawn.
Aurore, Ora, Ori, Orie, Rora

Austin (Latin) a short form of Augustine.
Austen, Austin, Austyn, Austynn

Autumn (Latin) autumn.
Autum

Ava (Greek) a form of Eva.
Avada, Avae, Ave, Aveen

Avalon (Latin) island.
Avallon

Avery (English) a form of Aubrey.
Aivree, Averi, Averie, Avry

Avis (Latin) bird.
Avais, Avi, Avia, Aviana, Avianca, Aviance, Avianna

Aviva (Hebrew) springtime. See also Viva.
Aviv, Avivah, Avivi, Avivice, Avni, Avnit, Avri, Avrit, Avy

Avril (French) a form of April.
Averil, Averyl, Avra, Avri, Avrilia, Avrill, Avrille, Avrillia, Avy

Axelle (Latin) axe. (German) small oak tree; source of life.
Aixa

Aya (Hebrew) bird; fly swiftly.
Aia, Aiah, Aiya, Aiyah

Ayanna (Hindi) innocent.
Ahyana, Aiyanna, Ayan, Ayana, Ayania, Ayannica, Ayna

Ayesha (Persian) a form of Aisha.
Ayasha, Ayeshah, Ayessa, Ayisha, Ayishah, Aysha, Ayshah, Ayshe, Ayshea, Aysia

Ayita (Cherokee) first in the dance.

Ayla (Hebrew) oak tree.
Aylana, Aylee, Ayleen, Aylene, Aylie, Aylin

Aza (Arabic) comfort.
Aiza, Aizha, Aizia, Azia

Aziza (Swahili) precious.
Azize

Baba (African) born on Thursday.
Aba

Babe (Latin) a familiar form of
Barbara. (American) a form of Baby.
Babby

Babette (French, German) a familiar
form of Barbara.
Babita, Barbette

Babs (American) a familiar form of
Barbara.
Bab

Baby (American) baby.
Babby, Babe, Bebe

Bailee, Bailie (English) forms of
Bailey.
*Baelee, Baeli, Bailea, Bailei, Baillee,
Baillie, Bailli*

Baileigh, Baleigh (English) forms of
Bailey.
Baeleigh

Bailey (English) bailiff.
*Baeley, Bailee, Baileigh, Bailley, Bailly,
Baily, Bali, Balley, Baylee, Bayley*

Baka (Hindi) crane.

Bakula (Hindi) flower.

Bambi (Italian) child.
Bambee, Bambie, Bamby

Bandi (Punjabi) prisoner.
Banda, Bandy

Baptista (Latin) baptizer.
Baptiste, Batista, Battista, Bautista

Bara, Barra (Hebrew) chosen.
Bára, Bari

Barb (Latin) a short form of Barbara.
Barba, Barbe

Barbara (Latin) stranger, foreigner. See
also Bebe, Varvara, Wava.
*Babara, Babb, Babbie, Babe, Babette,
Babina, Babs, Barb, Barbara-Ann,
Barbarit, Barbarita, Barbary, Barbeeleen,
Barbera, Barbie, Barbora, Barborah,
Barborka, Barbra, Barbraann, Barbro,
Barùska, Basha, Bebe, Bobbi, Bobbie*

Barbie (American) a familiar form of
Barbara.
Barbee, Barbey, Barbi, Barby, Baubie

Barbra (American) a form of Barbara.
Barbro

Barrett (German) strong as a bear.

Barrie (Irish) spear; markswoman.
Bari, Barri, Berri, Berrie, Berry

Basia (Hebrew) daughter of God.
Basya, Bathia, Batia, Batya, Bitya, Bithia

Bathsheba (Hebrew) daughter of the
oath; seventh daughter. Bible: a wife
of King David. See also Sheba.
*Bathshua, Batsheva, Bersaba, Bethsabee,
Bethsheba*

Batini (Swahili) inner thoughts.

Baylee, Bayleigh, Baylie (English)
forms of Bailey.
*Bayla, Bayle, Baylea, Bayleah, Baylei,
Bayli, Bayliee, Bayliegh*

Bayley (English) a form of Bailey.
Bayly

Bayo (Yoruba) joy is found.

Bea, Bee (American) short forms of
Beatrice.

Beata (Latin) a short form of Beatrice.
Beatta

Beatrice (Latin) blessed; happy;
bringer of joy. See also Trish, Trixie.
*Bea, Beata, Beatrica, Béatrice, Beatricia,
Beatriks, Beatrisa, Beatrise, Beatrissa,
Beatriz, Beattie, Beatty, Bebe, Bee, Trice*

Beatriz (Latin) a form of Beatrice.
Beatris, Beatriss, Beatrix, Beitris

Bebe (Spanish) a form of Barbara,
Beatrice.
BB, Beebee, Bibi

Becca (Hebrew) a short form of
Rebecca.
Beca, Becka, Bekah, Bekka

Becky (American) a familiar form of
Rebecca.
Beckey, Becki, Beckie

Bedelia (Irish) a form of Bridget.
Bedeelia, Biddy, Bidelia

Bel (Hindi) sacred wood of apple
trees. A short form of Amabel,
Belinda, Isabel.

Bela (Czech) white. (Hungarian) bright.
Belah, Biela

Belen (Greek) arrow. (Spanish) Bethlehem.
Belina

Belicia (Spanish) dedicated to God.
Beli, Belia, Belica

Belinda (Spanish) beautiful. Literature: a name coined by English poet Alexander Pope in *The Rape of the Lock*. See also Blinda, Linda.
Bel, Belindra, Belle, Belynda

Bella (Latin) beautiful.
Bellah

Belle (French) beautiful. A short form of Arabella, Belinda, Isabel. See also Billie.
Belita, Bell, Belli, Bellina

Belva (Latin) beautiful view.
Belvia

Bena (Native American) pheasant. See also Bina.
Benea

Benecia (Latin) a short form of Benedicta.
Beneisha, Benicia, Benish, Benisha, Benishia, Bennicia

Benedicta (Latin) blessed.
Bendite, Benecia, Benedetta, Benedicte, Benedikta, Bengta, Benita, Benna, Benni, Bennicia, Benoîte, Binney

Benedicte (Latin) a form of Benedicta.

Benita (Spanish) a form of Benedicta.
Beneta, Benetta, Benitta, Bennita, Neeta

Bennett (Latin) little blessed one.
Bennet, Bennetta

Benni (Latin) a familiar form of Benedicta.
Bennie, Binni, Binnie, Binny

Bente (Latin) blessed.

Berenice (Greek) a form of Bernice.
Berenise, Berenisse, Bereniz, Berenize

Berget (Irish) a form of Bridget.
Bergette, Bergit

Berit (German) glorious.
Beret, Berette, Berta

Berkley (Scottish, English) birch-tree meadow.
Berkeley, Berkly

Berlynn (English) a combination of Bertha + Lynn.
Berla, Berlin, Berlinda, Berline, Berling, Berlyn, Berlyne, Berlynne

Bernadette (French) a form of Bernadine. See also Nadette.
Bera, Beradette, Berna, Bernadet, Bernadete, Bernadett, Bernadetta, Bernarda, Bernardette, Bernedet, Bernedette, Bernessa, Berneta

Bernadine (English, German) brave as a bear.
Bernadene, Bernadette, Bernadin, Bernadina, Bernardina, Bernardine, Berni

Berneta (French) a short form of Bernadette.
Bernatta, Bernetta, Bernette, Bernita

Berni (English) a familiar form of Bernadine, Bernice.
Bernie, Berny

Bernice (Greek) bringer of victory. See also Bunny, Vernice.
Berenice, Berenike, Bernessa, Berni, Bernicia, Bernise, Nixie

Bertha (German) bright; illustrious; brilliant ruler. A short form of Alberta. See also Birdie, Peke.
Barta, Bartha, Berta, Berthe, Bertille, Bertita, Bertrona, Bertus, Birtha

Berti (German, English) a familiar form of Gilberte, Bertina.
Berte, Bertie, Berty

Bertille (French) a form of Bertha.

Bertina (English) bright, shining.
Bertine

Beryl (Greek) sea green jewel.
Beryle

Bess, Bessie (Hebrew) familiar forms of Elizabeth.
Bessi, Bessy

Beth (Hebrew, Aramaic) house of God. A short form of Bethany, Elizabeth.
Betha, Bethe, Bethia

Bethani, Bethanie (Aramaic) forms of Bethany.
Bethanee, Bethania, Bethannie, Bethni, Bethnie

Bethann (English) a combination of Beth + Ann.
Beth-Ann, Bethan, Bethane, Bethanne, Beth-Anne

Bethany (Aramaic) house of figs.
Bible: the site of Lazarus's resurrection.
*Beth, Bethaney, Bethani, Bethanney,
Bethanny, Bethena, Betheny, Bethia,
Bethina, Bethney, Bethny, Betthany*

Betsy (American) a familiar form of
Elizabeth.
Betsey, Betsi, Betsie

Bette (French) a form of Betty.
Beta, Beti, Betka, Bett, Betta

Bettina (American) a combination of
Beth + Tina.
Betina, Betine, Betti, Bettine

Betty (Hebrew) consecrated to God.
(English) a familiar form of
Elizabeth.
*Bette, Bettey, Betti, Bettie, Bettye,
Bettyjean, Betty-Jean, Bettyjo, Betty-Jo,
Bettylou, Betty-Lou, Bety, Boski, Bözsi*

Betula (Hebrew) girl, maiden.

Beulah (Hebrew) married. Bible:
Beulah is a name for Israel.
Beula, Beulla, Beullah

Bev (English) a short form of Beverly.

Bevanne (Welsh) child of Evan.
Bevan, Bevann, Bevany

Beverly (English) beaver field. See also
Buffy.
*Bev, Bevalee, Beverle, Beverlee, Beverley,
Beverlie, Beverlly, Bevlyn, Bevlynn,
Bevlynne, Bevvy, Verly*

Beverlyann (American) a combination
of Beverly + Ann.
Beverliann, Beverlianne, Beverlyanne

Bian (Vietnamese) hidden; secretive.

Bianca (Italian) white. See also Blanca,
Vianca.
*Biancca, Biancha, Biancia, Bianco,
Bianey, Bianica, Bianka, Biannca,
Binney, Bionca, Blanca, Blanche, Byanca*

Bianka (Italian) a form of Bianca.
Beyanka, Biannka

Bibi (Latin) a short form of Bibiana.
(Arabic) lady. (Spanish) a form of Bebe.

Bibiana (Latin) lively.
Bibi

Biddy (Irish) a familiar form of Bedelia.
Biddie

Billi, Billy (English) forms of Billie.
Billye

Billie (English) strong willed.
(German, French) a familiar form of
Belle, Wilhelmina.
*Bilee, Bileigh, Bili, Bilie, Billee, Billi,
Billy, Billye*

Billie-Jean (American) a combination
of Billie + Jean.
Billiejean, Billyjean, Billy-Jean

Billie-Jo (American) a combination of
Billie + Jo.
Billiejo, Billyjo, Billy-Jo

Bina (Hebrew) wise; understanding.
(Swahili) dancer. (Latin) a short form
of Sabina. See also Bena.
Binah, Binney, Binta, Bintah

Binney (English) a familiar form of
Benedicta, Bianca, Bina.
Binnee, Binni, Binnie, Binny

Bionca (Italian) a form of Bianca.
*Beonca, Beyonca, Beyonka, Bioncha,
Bionica, Bionka, Bionnca*

Birdie (English) bird. (German) a
familiar form of Bertha.
*Bird, Birdee, Birdella, Birdena, Birdey,
Birdi, Birdy, Byrd, Byrdey, Byrdie, Byrdy*

Birgitte (Swedish) a form of Bridget.
Birgit, Birgita, Birgitta

Blaine (Irish) thin.
Blane, Blayne

Blair (Scottish) plains dweller.
Blaire

Blaire (Scottish) a form of Blair.
Blare, Blayre

Blaise (French) one who stammers.
*Blaize, Blasha, Blasia, Blaza, Blaze,
Blazena*

Blake (English) dark.
Blaque, Blayke

Blakely (English) dark meadow.
*Blakelea, Blakelee, Blakeleigh, Blakeley,
Blakeli, Blakelyn, Blakelynn, Blakesley,
Blakley, Blakli*

Blanca (Italian) a form of Bianca.
Bellanca, Blancka, Blanka

Blanche (French) a form of Bianca.
Blanch, Blancha, Blinney

Blinda (American) a short form of
Belinda.
Blynda

Bliss (English) blissful, joyful.
Blisse, Blyss, Blysse

Blodwyn (Welsh) flower. See also Wynne.
Blodwen, Blodwynne, Blodyn

Blondelle (French) blond, fair haired.
Blondell, Blondie

Blondie (American) a familiar form of Blondell.
Blondee, Blondey, Blondy

Blossom (English) flower.

Blum (Yiddish) flower.
Bluma

Blythe (English) happy, cheerful.
Blithe, Blyss, Blyth

Bo (Chinese) precious.

Boacha (Hebrew) blessed.

Bobbette (American) a familiar form of Roberta.
Bobbet, Bobbetta

Bobbi, Bobbie (American) familiar forms of Barbara, Roberta.
Baubie, Bobbe, Bobbey, Bobbisue, Bobby, Bobbye, Bobi, Bobie, Bobina, Bobbie-Jean, Bobbie-Lynn, Bobbie-Sue

Bobbi-Ann, Bobbie-Ann (American) combinations of Bobbi + Ann.
Bobbiann, Bobbi-Anne, Bobbianne, Bobbie-Anne, Bobby-Ann, Bobbyann, Bobby-Anne, Bobbyanne

Bobbi-Jo (American) a combination of Bobbi + Jo.
Bobbiejo, Bobbie-Jo, Bobbijo, Bobby-Jo, Bobijo

Bobbi-Lee (American) a combination of Bobbi + Lee.
Bobbie-Lee, Bobbilee, Bobbylee, Bobby-Leigh, Bobile

Bonita (Spanish) pretty.
Bonesha, Bonetta, Bonnetta, Bonnie, Bonny

Bonnie, Bonny (English, Scottish) beautiful, pretty. (Spanish) familiar forms of Bonita.
Boni, Bonie, Bonne, Bonnee, Bonnell, Bonney, Bonni, Bonnin

Bonnie-Bell (American) a combination of Bonnie + Belle.
Bonnebell, Bonnebelle, Bonnibell, Bonnibelle, Bonniebell, Bonniebelle, Bonnybell, Bonnybelle

Bradley (English) broad meadow.
Bradlee, Bradleigh, Bradlie

Brady (Irish) spirited.
Bradee, Bradey, Bradi, Bradie, Braedi, Braidee, Braidi, Braidie, Braidey, Braidy, Braydee

Braeden (English) broad hill.
Bradyn, Bradynn, Braedan, Braedean, Braedyn, Braidan, Braiden, Braidyn, Brayden, Braydn, Braydon

Braelyn (American) a combination of Braeden + Lynn.
Braelee, Braeleigh, Braelin, Braelle, Braelon, Braelynn, Braelynne, Brailee, Brailenn, Brailey, Braili, Brailyn, Braylee, Brayley, Braylin, Braylon, Braylyn, Braylynn

Branda (Hebrew) blessing.

Brandee (Dutch) a form of Brandy.
Brande, Brandea, Brendee

Branden (English) beacon valley.
Brandan, Brandon, Brendan, Brandyn, Brennan

Brandi, Brandie (Dutch) forms of Brandy.
Brandei, Brandice, Brandiee, Brandii, Brandily, Brandin, Brandis, Brandise, Brani, Branndie, Brendi

Brandy (Dutch) an after-dinner drink made from distilled wine.
Brand, Brandace, Brandaise, Brandala, Brandee, Brandeli, Brandell, Brandi, Brandye, Brandylee, Brandy-Lee, Brandy-Leigh, Brann, Brantley, Branyell, Brendy

Brandy-Lynn (American) a combination of Brandy + Lynn.
Brandalyn, Brandalynn, Brandelyn, Brandelynn, Brandelynne, Brandilyn, Brandilynn, Brandilynne, Brandlin, Brandlyn, Brandlynn, Brandlynne, Brandolyn, Brandolynn, Brandolynne, Brandylyn, Brandy-Lyn, Brandylynne, Brandy-Lynne

Braxton (English) Brock's town.
Braxten, Braxtyn

Brea, Bria (Irish) short forms of Breana, Briana.
Breah, Breea, Briah, Brya

Breana, Breanna (Irish) forms of Briana.
Brea, Breanah, Breanda, Bre-Anna, Breannah, Breannea, Breannia, Breasha, Breawna, Breeanna, Breila

Breann, Breanne (Irish) short forms of Briana.
Breane, Bre-Ann, Bre-Anne, Breaunne, Bree, Breean, Breeann, Breeanne, Breelyn, Breeon, Breiann, Breighann, Breyenne, Brieann, Brieon

Breasha (Russian) a familiar form of Breana.

Breauna, Breunna, Briauna (Irish) forms of Briana.
Breaunna, Breeauna, Breuna, Breuna, Briaunna

Breck (Irish) freckled.
Brecken

Bree (English) broth. (Irish) a short form of Breann. See also Brie.
Breay, Brei, Breigh

Breeana, Breeanna (Irish) forms of Briana.
Breeanah, Breeannah

Breena (Irish) fairy palace. A form of Brina.
Breenea, Breene, Breina, Brina

Breiana, Breianna (Irish) forms of Briana.
Breiane, Breiann, Breianne

Brenda (Irish) little raven. (English) sword.
Brendell, Brendelle, Brendette, Brendie, Brendyl, Brenna

Brenda-Lee (American) a combination of Brenda + Lee.
Brendalee, Brendaleigh, Brendali, Brendaly, Brendalys, Brenlee, Brenley

Brenna (Irish) a form of Brenda.
Bren, Brenie, Brenin, Brenn, Brennah, Brennaugh, Brenne

Brennan (English) a form of Brendan (see Boys' Names).
Brennea, Brennen, Brennon, Brennyn

Breona, Breonna (Irish) forms of Briana.
Breeona, Breiona, Breionna, Breonah, Breonia, Breonie, Breonne

Brett (Irish) a short form of Brittany. See also Brita.
Bret, Brette, Brettin, Bretton

Breyana, Breyann, Breyanna (Irish) forms of Briana.
Breyan, Breyane, Breyannah, Breyanne

Breyona, Breyonna (Irish) forms of Briana.
Breyonia

Briana, Brianna (Irish) strong; virtuous, honorable.
Bhrianna, Brana, Brea, Breana, Breann, Breauna, Breeana, Breiana, Breona, Breyana, Breyona, Bria, Briahna, Brianah, Briand, Brianda, Briannah, Brianne, Brianni, Briannon, Brienna, Brina, Briona, Briyana, Bryanna, Bryona

Brianne (Irish) a form of Briana.
Briane, Briann, Brienne, Bryanne

Briar (French) heather.
Brear, Brier, Bryar

Bridey (Irish) a familiar form of Bridget.
Bridi, Bridie, Brydie

Bridget (Irish) strong. See also Bedelia, Bryga, Gitta.
Berget, Birgitte, Bride, Bridey, Bridger, Bridgete, Bridgett, Bridgette, Bridgid, Bridgot, Brietta, Brigada, Briget, Brigid, Brigida, Brigitte, Brita

Bridgett, Bridgette (Irish) forms of Bridget.
Bridgitte, Brigette, Bridggett, Briggitte, Bridgitt, Brigitta

Brie (French) a type of cheese. Geography: a region in France known for its cheese. See also Bree.
Briea, Brielle, Briena, Brieon, Brietta, Briette

Brieana, Brieanna (American) combinations of Brie + Anna.
Brieannah

Brieann, Brieanne (American) combinations of Brie + Ann. See also Briana.
Brie-Ann, Brie-Anne

Brielle (French) a form of Brie.
Briel, Briele, Briell, Briella

Brienna, Brienne (Irish) forms of Briana.
Briene, Brieon, Brieona, Brieonna

Brienne (French) a form of Briana.
Brienn

Brigette (French) a form of Bridget.
Briget, Brigett, Brigetta, Brigettee, Brigget

Brigitte (French) a form of Bridget.
Briggitte, Brigit, Brigita

Brina (Latin) a short form of Sabrina.
(Irish) a familiar form of Briana.
Brin, Brinan, Brinda, Brindi, Brindy,
Briney, Brinia, Brinlee, Brinly, Brinn,
Brinna, Brinnan, Briona, Bryn, Bryna

Briona (Irish) a form of Briana.
Brione, Brionna, Brionne, Briony,
Briunna, Bryony

Brisa (Spanish) beloved. Mythology:
Briseis was the Greek name of
Achilles's beloved.
Breezy, Breza, Brisha, Brishia, Brissa,
Bryssa

Brita (Irish) a form of Bridget.
(English) a short form of Britany.
Bretta, Brieta, Brietta, Brit, Britta

Britaney, Brittaney (English) forms of
Britany, Brittany.
Britanee, Britanny, Britenee, Briteny,
Britianey, British, Britkney, Britley,
Britlyn, Britney, Briton

Britani, Brittani, Brittanie (English)
forms of Britany.
Brit, Britania, Britanica, Britanie,
Britanii, Britanni, Britannia, Britatani,
Britia, Britini, Brittane, Brittanee,
Brittanni, Brittannia, Brittannie,
Brittenie, Brittiani, Brittianni

Britany, Brittany (English) from Britain.
See also Brett.
Brita, Britana, Britaney, Britani, Britanna,
Britlyn, Britney, Britt, Brittainny, Brittainy,
Brittamy, Brittana, Brittaney, Brittani,
Brittania, Brittanica, Brittanny, Brittany-
Ann, Brittanyne, Brittell, Britteny, Brittiany,
Brittini, Brittlin, Brittlynn, Brittnee,
Brittony, Bryttany

Britin, Brittin (English) from Britain.
Britann, Brittan, Brittin, Brittina,
Brittine, Brittini, Brittiny

Britney, Brittney, Brittny (English)
forms of Britany.
Bittney, Bridnee, Bridney, Britnay, Britne,
Britnee, Britnei, Britni, Britny, Britnye,
Brittnay, Brittnaye, Brytnea, Brytni

Britni, Brittni, Brittnie (English)
forms of Britney, Britney.
Britnie

Briton, Brittin (English) forms of
Britin, Brittin.
Britton

Britt, Britta (Latin) short forms of
Britany, Brittany. (Swedish) strong.
Brett, Briet, Brit, Brita, Britte

Britteny (English) a form of Britany,
Brittany.
Britten, Brittenay, Brittenee, Britteney,
Brittenie

Brittini, Brittiny (English) forms of
Britany, Brittany.
Brittinee, Brittiney, Brittinie, Brittiny

Brittnee (English) a form of Britany,
Brittany.
Brittne, Brittnea, Brittnei, Brittneigh

Briyana, Briyanna (Irish) forms of
Briana.

Brodie (Irish) ditch; canal builder.
Brodee, Brodi, Brody

Bronnie (Welsh) a familiar form of
Bronwyn.
Bron, Bronia, Bronney, Bronny, Bronya

Bronwyn (Welsh) white breasted.
Bronnie, Bronwen, Bronwin, Bronwynn,
Bronwynne

Brook, Brooke (English) brook,
stream.
Bhrooke, Brookelle, Brookie, Brooks,
Brooky

Brooklyn, Brooklynn (American)
combinations of Brook + Lynn.
Brookellen, Brookelyn, Brookelyne,
Brookelynn, Brooklen, Brooklin,
Brooklyne, Brooklynne

Bruna (German) a short form of
Brunhilda.
Brona

Brunhilda (German) armored warrior.
Brinhilda, Brinhilde, Bruna, Brunhilde,
Brünnhilde, Brynhild, Brynhilda,
Brynhilde, Hilda

Bryana, Bryanna, Bryanne (Irish)
short forms of Bryana.
Bryann, Bryanni

Bryce (Welsh) alert; ambitious.

Bryga (Polish) a form of Bridget.
Brygid, Brygida, Brygitka

Brylie (American) a combination of
the letter B + Riley.
Brylee, Brylei, Bryley, Bryli

Bryn, Brynn (Latin) from the boundary line. (Welsh) mound.
Brinn, Brynee, Brynne

Bryna (Latin, Irish) a form of Brina.
Brynan, Brynna, Brynnan

Bryona, Bryonna (Irish) forms of Briana.
Bryonia, Bryony

Bryttani, Bryttany (English) forms of Britany.
Brytani, Brytanie, Brytanny, Brytany, Brytnee, Brytnie, Bryton, Bryttanee, Bryttanie, Bryttine, Bryttney, Bryttnie, Brytton

Buffy (American) buffalo; from the plains.
Buffee, Buffey, Buffie, Buffye

Bunny (Greek) a familiar form of Bernice. (English) little rabbit. See also Bonnie.
Bunni, Bunnie

Burgundy (French) Geography: a region of France known for its Burgundy wine.
Burgandi, Burgandie, Burgandy, Burgunde

Cachet (French) prestigious; desirous.
Cachae, Cache, Cachea, Cachee, Cachée

Cadence (Latin) rhythm.
Cadena, Cadenza, Kadena

Cady (English) a form of Kady.
Cade, Cadee, Cadey, Cadi, Cadie, Cadine, Cadye

Caeley, Cailey, Cayley (American) forms of Kaylee, Kelly.
Caela, Caelee, Caeleigh, Caeley, Caeli,

Caelie, Caelly, Caely, Cailee, Caileigh, Caili, Cailie, Cailley, Caillie, Caily, Caylee

Caelin, Caelyn (American) forms of Kaelyn.
Caelan, Caelinn, Caelynn, Cailan, Caylan

Cai (Vietnamese) feminine.
Cae, Cay, Caye

Cailida (Spanish) adoring.
Kailida

Cailin, Cailyn (American) forms of Caitlin.
Caileen, Cailene, Cailine, Cailynn, Cailynne, Calen, Cayleen, Caylen, Caylene, Caylin, Cayline, Caylyn, Caylyne, Caylynne

Caitlan (Irish) a form of Caitlin.
Caitland, Caitlandt

Caitlin (Irish) pure. See also Kaitlin, Katalina, Katelin, Katelyn, Kaytlyn.
Caetlin, Cailin, Caitlan, Caitleen, Caitlen, Caitlene, Caitlenn, Caitline, Caitlinn, Caitlon, Caitlyn, Catlee, Catleen, Catleene, Catlin

Caitlyn, Caitlynn (Irish) forms of Caitlin. See also Kaitlyn.
Caitlyne, Caitlynne, Catelyn, Catlyn, Catlynn, Catlynne

Cala (Arabic) castle, fortress. See also Callie, Kala.
Calah, Calan, Calla, Callah

Calandra (Greek) lark.
Calan, Calandrea, Calandria, Caleida, Calendra, Calendre, Kalandra, Kalandria

Caleigh, Caley (American) forms of Caeley.
Caileigh, Caleah

Cali, Calli (Greek) forms of Calie. See also Kali.
Calee

Calida (Spanish) warm; ardent.
Calina, Calinda, Callida, Callinda, Kalida

Callie (Greek, Arabic) a familiar form of Cala, Callista. See also Kalli.
Cal, Cali, Calie, Callee, Calley, Calli, Cally, Caly

Callista (Greek) most beautiful. See also Kallista.
Calesta, Calista, Callie, Calysta

Calvina (Latin) bald.
Calvine, Calvinetta, Calvinette

Calypso (Greek) concealer. Botany: a pink orchid native to northern regions. Mythology: the sea nymph who held Odysseus captive for seven years.
Caly, Lypsie, Lypsy

Cam (Vietnamese) sweet citrus.
Kam

Camara (American) a form of Cameron.
Camera, Cameri, Cameria, Camira, Camry

Camberly (American) a form of Kimberly.
Camber, Camberlee, Camberleigh

Cambria (Latin) from Wales. See also Kambria.
Camberry, Cambreia, Cambie, Cambrea, Cambree, Cambrie, Cambrina, Cambry, Cambrya, Cami

Camden (Scottish) winding valley.
Camdyn

Camellia (Italian) Botany: a camellia is an evergreen tree or shrub with fragrant roselike flowers.
Camala, Camalia, Camallia, Camela, Camelia, Camelita, Camella, Camellita, Cami, Kamelia, Kamellia

Cameo (Latin) gem or shell on which a portrait is carved.
Cami, Kameo

Cameron (Scottish) crooked nose. See also Kameron, Kamryn.
Camara, Cameran, Cameren, Camira, Camiran, Camiron, Camryn

Cami (French) a short form of Camille. See also Kami.
Camey, Camie, Cammi, Cammie, Cammy, Cammye, Camy

Camila, Camilla (Italian) forms of Camille. See also Kamila, Mila.
Camia, Camilia, Camillia, Camilya, Cammilla, Chamelea, Chamelia, Chamika, Chamila, Chamilia

Camille (French) young ceremonial attendant. See also Millie.
Cam, Cami, Camiel, Camielle, Camil, Camila, Camile, Camill, Cammille, Cammillie, Cammilyn, Cammyl, Cammyll, Camylle, Chamelle, Chamille, Kamille

Camisha (American) a combination of Cami + Aisha.
Cameasha, Cameesha, Cameisha, Camesa, Camesha, Cameshaa, Cameshia, Camiesha, Camyeshia

Camri, Camrie (American) short forms of Camryn. See also Kamri.
Camrea, Camree, Camrey, Camry

Camryn (American) a form of Cameron. See also Kamryn.
Camri, Camrin, Camron, Camrynn

Camylle (French) a form of Camille.
Camyle, Camyll

Candace (Greek) glittering white; glowing. History: the title of the queens of ancient Ethiopia. See also Dacey, Kandace.
Cace, Canace, Canda, Candas, Candece, Candelle, Candi, Candiace, Candice, Candyce

Candi, Candy (American) familiar forms of Candace, Candice, Candida. See also Kandi.
Candee, Candie

Candice, Candis (Greek) forms of Candace.
Candes, Candi, Candias, Candies, Candise, Candiss, Candus

Candida (Latin) bright white.
Candeea, Candi, Candia, Candide, Candita

Candra (Latin) glowing. See also Kandra.
Candrea, Candria

Candyce (Greek) a form of Candace.
Candys, Candyse, Cyndyss

Cantara (Arabic) small crossing.
Cantarah

Cantrelle (French) song.
Cantrella

Capri (Italian) a short form of Caprice. Geography: an island off the west coast of Italy. See also Kapri.
Capria, Caprie, Capry

Caprice (Italian) fanciful.
Cappi, Caprece, Caprecia, Capresha, Capricia, Capriese, Caprina, Capris, Caprise, Caprisha, Capritta

Cara (Latin) dear. (Irish) friend. See also Karah.
Caira, Caragh, Carah, Caralee, Caranda, Carey, Carra

Caralee (Irish) a form of Cara.
Caralea, Caraleigh, Caralia, Caralie, Carely

Caralyn (English) a form of Caroline.
Caralin, Caraline, Caralynn, Caralynna, Caralynne

Caressa (French) a form of Carissa.
Caresa, Carese, Caresse, Carissa, Charessa, Charesse, Karessa

Carey (Welsh) a familiar form of Cara, Caroline, Karen, Katherine. See also Carrie, Kari.
Caree, Cari, Carrey, Cary

Cari, Carie (Welsh) forms of Carey, Kari.

Carina (Italian) dear little one. (Swedish) a form of Karen. (Greek) a familiar form of Cora.
Carena, Carinah, Carine, Carinna

Carine (Italian) a form of Carina.
Carin, Carinn, Carinne

Carisa, Carrisa (Greek) forms of
Carissa.
Carise, Carisha, Carisia, Charisa

Carissa (Greek) beloved. See also
Karissa.
Caressa, Carisa, Carrissa, Charissa

Carita (Latin) charitable.
Caritta, Karita, Karitta

Carla (German) farmer. (English)
strong. (Latin) a form of Carol,
Caroline.
*Carila, Carilla, Carleta, Carlia,
Carliqua, Carliyle, Carlonda, Carlyjo,
Carlyle, Carlysle*

Carlee, Carleigh, Carley (English)
forms of Carly. See also Karlee.
Carle, Carlea, Carleah, Carleh

Carleen, Carlene (English) forms of
Caroline. See also Karlene.
*Carlaen, Carlaena, Carleena, Carlen,
Carlena, Carlenna, Carline, Carlyn,
Carlyne*

Carli, Carlie (English) forms of Carly.
See also Karli.

Carlin (Irish) little champion. (Latin) a
short form of Caroline.
*Carlan, Carlana, Carlandra, Carlina,
Carlinda, Carline, Carling, Carllan,
Carlyn, Carllen, Carrlin*

Carlisa (American) a form of Carlissa.
*Carilis, Carilise, Carilyse, Carleesia,
Carlesia, Carletha, Carlethe, Carlicia,
Carlis, Carlise, Carlisha, Carlisia,
Carlyse*

Carlissa (American) a combination of
Carla + Lissa.
*Carleeza, Carlisa, Carliss, Carlissah,
Carlisse, Carlissia, Carlista*

Carlotta (Italian) a form of Charlotte.
Carletta, Carlita, Carlota

Carly (English) a familiar form of
Caroline, Charlotte. See also Karli.
Carlee, Carli, Carlie, Carlye

Carlyn, Carlynn (Irish) forms of
Carlin.
Carlyna, Carlynne

Carmela, Carmella (Hebrew) garden;
vineyard. Bible: Mount Carmel in
Israel is often thought of as paradise.
See also Karmel.
*Carma, Carmalla, Carmarit, Carmel,
Carmeli, Carmelia, Carmelina,
Carmelit, Carmelle, Carmellia,
Carmellina, Carmesa, Carmesha, Carmi,
Carmie, Carmiel, Carmil, Carmila,
Carmile, Carmilla, Carmille, Carmisha,
Leeta, Lita*

Carmelit (Hebrew) a form of
Carmela.
*Carmaletta, Carmalit, Carmalita,
Carmelita, Carmelitha, Carmelitia,
Carmellit, Carmellita, Carmellitha,
Carmellitia*

Carmen (Latin) song. Religion:
Nuestra Señora del Carmen—Our
Lady of Mount Carmel—is one of
the titles of the Virgin Mary. See also
Karmen.
*Carma, Carmaine, Carman, Carmelina,
Carmencita, Carmene, Carmi, Carmia,
Carmin, Carmina, Carmine, Carmita,
Carmon, Carmynn, Charmaine*

Carol (German) farmer. (French) song
of joy. (English) strong. See also
Charlene, Kalle, Karoll.
*Carel, Cariel, Caro, Carola, Carole,
Carolenia, Carolinda, Caroline, Caroll,
Carrie, Carrol, Carroll, Caryl*

Carolane, Carolann, Carolanne
(American) combinations of Carol +
Ann. Forms of Caroline.
Carolan, Carol Ann, Carole-Anne

Carole (English) a form of Carol.
Carolee, Karole, Karrole

Carolina (Italian) a form of Caroline.
See also Karolina.
*Carilena, Carlena, Carlina, Caroleena,
Caroleina, Carolena, Carrolena*

Caroline (French) little and strong.
See also Carla, Carleen, Carlin,
Karolina.
*Caralin, Caraline, Carileen, Carilene,
Carilin, Cariline, Carling, Carly, Caro,
Carolann, Caroleen, Carolin, Carolina,
Carolyn, Carrie, Carroleen, Carrolene,
Carrolin, Carroline, Cary, Charlene*

Carolyn (English) a form of Caroline.
See also Karolyn.
*Carilyn, Carilynn, Carilynne, Carlyn,
Carlynn, Carlynne, Carolyne, Carolynn,
Carolynne, Carrolyn, Carrolynn,
Carrolynne*

Caron (Welsh) loving, kindhearted,
charitable.
Caronne, Carron, Carrone

Carra (Irish) a form of Cara.
Carrah

Carrie (English) a familiar form of
Carol, Caroline. See also Carey, Kari,
Karri.
*Carree, Carrey, Carri, Carria, Carry,
Cary*

Carson (English) child of Carr.
Carsen, Carsyn

Carter (English) cart driver.

Caryl (Latin) a form of Carol.
Caryle, Caryll, Carylle

Caryn (Danish) a form of Karen.
*Caren, Carren, Carrin, Carryn, Caryna,
Caryne, Carynn*

Carys (Welsh) love.
Caris, Caryse, Ceris, Cerys

Casandra (Greek) a form of
Cassandra.
*Casandera, Casandre, Casandrea,
Casandrey, Casandri, Casandria,
Casanndra, Casaundra, Casaundre,
Casaundri, Casaundria, Casondra,
Casondre, Casondri, Casondria*

Casey (Irish) brave. (Greek) a familiar
form of Acacia. See also Kasey.
*Cacy, Cascy, Casie, Casse, Cassee,
Cassey, Cassye, Casy, Cayce, Cayse,
Caysee, Caysy*

Casidy (Irish) a form of Cassidy.
Casidee, Casidi

Casie (Irish) a form of Casey.
*Caci, Caesi, Caisie, Casci, Cascie, Casi,
Cayci, Caysi, Caysie, Cazzi*

Cass (Greek) a short form of Cassandra.

Cassady (Irish) a form of Cassidy.
*Casadee, Casadi, Casadie, Cassaday,
Cassadee, Cassadey, Cassadi, Cassadie,
Cassadina*

Cassandra (Greek) helper of men.
Mythology: a prophetess of ancient
Greece whose prophesies were not
believed. See also Kassandra, Sandra,
Sandy, Zandra.
*Casandra, Cass, Cassandre, Cassandri,
Cassandry, Cassaundra, Cassie,
Cassondra*

Cassaundra (Greek) a form of
Cassandra.
*Cassaundre, Cassaundri, Cassundra,
Cassundre, Cassundri, Cassundria*

Cassia (Greek) a cinnamon-like spice.
See also Kasia.
Casia, Cass, Casya

Cassidy (Irish) clever. See also Kassidy.
*Casidy, Cassady, Casseday, Cassiddy,
Cassidee, Cassidi, Cassidie, Cassity*

Cassie, Cassey, Cassi (Greek) familiar
forms of Cassandra, Catherine. See
also Kassie.
Cassee, Cassii, Cassy, Casy

Cassiopeia (Greek) clever. Mythology:
the wife of the Ethiopian king
Cepheus; the mother of Andromeda.
Cassio

Cassondra (Greek) a form of Cassandra.
Cassondre, Cassondri, Cassondria

Catalina (Spanish) a form of
Catherine. See also Katalina.
*Cataleen, Catalena, Catalene, Catalin,
Catalyn, Catalyna, Cateline*

Catarina (German) a form of
Catherine.
*Catarena, Catarin, Catarine, Caterin,
Caterina, Caterine*

Catelyn (Irish) a form of Caitlin.
Catelin, Cateline, Catelyne, Catelynn

Catharine (Greek) a form of Catherine.
Catharen, Catharin, Catharina, Catharyn

Catherine (Greek) pure. (English) a
form of Katherine.
*Cat, Catalina, Catarina, Cate, Cathann,
Cathanne, Catharine, Cathenne,
Catheren, Catherene, Catheria, Catherin,
Catherina, Catheryn, Catheryne, Cathi,
Cathleen, Cathrine, Cathryn, Cathy,
Catlaina, Catreeka, Catrelle, Catrice,
Catricia, Catrika, Catrina*

Cathi, Cathy (Greek) familiar forms
of Catherine, Cathleen. See also
Kathy.
Catha, Cathe, Cathee, Cathey, Cathie

Cathleen (Irish) a form of Catherine.
See also Caitlin, Kathleen.
*Caithlyn, Cathaleen, Cathelin, Gathelina,
Cathelyn, Cathi, Cathleana, Cathleene,
Cathlene, Cathleyn, Cathlin, Cathline,
Cathlyn, Cathlyne, Cathlynn, Cathy*

Cathrine (Greek) a form of
Catherine.

Cathryn (Greek) a form of Catherine.
Cathryne, Cathrynn, Catryn

Catrina (Slavic) a form of Catherine,
Katrina.
*Caitriana, Caitriona, Catina, Catreen,
Catreena, Catrene, Catrenia, Catrin,
Catrine, Catrinia, Catriona, Catroina*

Cayla (Hebrew) a form of Kayla.
Caylea, Caylia

Caylee, Caylie (American) forms of Caeley, Cailey, Cayley.
Cayle, Cayleigh, Cayli, Cayly

Ceara (Irish) a form of Ciara.
Ceaira, Ceairah, Ceairra, Cearaa, Cearie, Cearah, Cearra, Cera

Cecelia (Latin) a form of Cecilia. See also Sheila.
Caceli, Cacelia, Cece, Ceceilia, Ceceli, Cecelia, Cecelie, Cecely, Cecelyn, Cecette, Cescelia, Cescelie

Cecilia (Latin) blind. See also Cicely, Cissy, Secilia, Selia, Sissy.
Cacilia, Caecilia, Cecelia, Cecil, Cecila, Cecile, Cecilea, Cecilija, Cecilla, Cecille, Cecillia, Cecily, Cecilya, Ceclia, Cecylia, Cee, Ceil, Ceila, Ceilagh, Ceileh, Ceileigh, Ceilena, Celia, Cesilia, Cicelia

Cecily (Latin) a form of Cecilia.
Cacilie, Cecilee, Ceciley, Cecilie, Cescily, Cicely, Cilley

Ceil (Latin) a short form of Cecilia.
Ceel, Ciel

Ceira, Ceirra (Irish) forms of Ciara.
Ceire

Celena (Greek) a form of Selena.
Celeena, Celene, Celenia, Celine, Cena

Celene (Greek) a form of Celena.
Celeen

Celeste (Latin) celestial, heavenly.
Cele, Celeeste, Celense, Celes, Celesia, Celesley, Celest, Celesta, Celestia, Celestial, Celestin, Celestina, Celestine,

Celestinia, Celestyn, Celestyna, Cellest, Celleste, Selestina

Celia (Latin) a short form of Cecilia.
Ceilia, Celie

Celina (Greek) a form of Celena. See also Selina.
Caleena, Calena, Calina, Celena, Celinda, Celinka, Celinna, Celka, Cellina

Celine (Greek) a form of Celena.
Caline, Celeen, Celene, Céline, Cellinn

Cera (French) a short form of Cerise.
Cerea, Ceri, Ceria, Cerra

Cerella (Latin) springtime.
Cerelisa, Ceres

Cerise (French) cherry; cherry red.
Cera, Cerese, Cerice, Cericia, Cerissa, Cerria, Cerrice, Cerrina, Cerrita, Cerryce, Ceryce, Cherise

Cesilia (Latin) a form of Cecilia.
Cesia, Cesya

Chablis (French) a dry, white wine. Geography: a region in France where wine grapes are grown.
Chabeli, Chabelly, Chabely, Chablee, Chabley, Chabli

Chadee (French) from Chad, a country in north-central Africa. See also Sade.
Chaday, Chadday, Chade, Chadea, Chadi

Chai (Hebrew) life.
Chae, Chaela, Chaeli, Chaella, Chaena, Chaia

Chaka (Sanskrit) a form of Chakra. See also Shaka.
Chakai, Chakia, Chakka, Chakkah

Chakra (Sanskrit) circle of energy.
Chaka, Chakara, Chakaria, Chakena, Chakina, Chakira, Chakrah, Chakria, Chakriya, Chakyra

Chalice (French) goblet.
Chalace, Chalcie, Chalece, Chalicea, Chalie, Chaliese, Chalis, Chalisa, Chalise, Chalisk, Chalissa, Chalisse, Challa, Challaine, Challis, Challisse, Challysse, Chalsey, Chalyce, Chalyn, Chalyse, Chalyssa, Chalysse

Chalina (Spanish) a form of Rose.
Chaline, Chalini

Chalonna (American) a combination of the prefix Cha + Lona.
Chalon, Chalona, Chalonda, Chalonn, Chalonne, Chalonte, Shalon

Chambray (French) a lightweight fabric.
Chambrae, Chambre, Chambree, Chambrée, Chambrey, Chambria, Chambrie

Chan (Cambodian) sweet-smelling tree.

Chana (Hebrew) a form of Hannah.
Chanae, Chanai, Chanay, Chanea, Chanie

Chancey (English) chancellor; church official.
Chance, Chancee, Chancie, Chancy

Chanda (Sanskrit) short tempered. Religion: the demon defeated by the Hindu goddess Chamunda. See also Shanda.
Chandee, Chandey, Chandi, Chandie, Chandin

Chandelle (French) candle.
Chandal, Chandel, Shandal, Shandel

Chandler (Hindi) moon. (Old English) candlemaker.
Chandlar, Chandlier, Chandlor, Chandlyr

Chandra (Sanskrit) moon. Religion: the Hindu god of the moon. See also Shandra.
Chandrae, Chandray, Chandre, Chandrea, Chandrelle, Chandria

Chanel (English) channel. See also Shanel.
Chanal, Chaneel, Chaneil, Chanele, Chanell, Channal, Channel, Chenelle

Chanell, Chanelle (English) forms of Chanel.
Channell, Shanell

Chanise (American) a form of Shanice.
Chanisse, Chenice, Chenise

Channa (Hindi) chickpea.
Channah

Chantal (French) song.
Chandal, Chantaal, Chantael, Chantala, Chantale, Chantall, Chantalle, Chantara, Chantarai, Chantasia, Chante, Chanteau, Chantel, Chantle, Chantoya, Chantrill, Chauntel

Chante (French) a short form of Chantal.
Chanta, Chantae, Chantai, Chantay,

Chantaye, Chanté, Chantéa, Chantee, Chanti, Chantia, Chaunte, Chauntea, Chauntéa, Chauntee

Chantel, Chantell, Chantelle (French) forms of Chantal. See also Shantel.
Chanteese, Chantela, Chantele, Chantella, Chanter, Chantey, Chantez, Chantrel, Chantrell, Chantrelle, Chatell

Chantilly (French) fine lace. See also Shantille.
Chantiel, Chantielle, Chantil, Chantila, Chantilée, Chantill, Chantille

Chantrea (Cambodian) moon; moon-beam.
Chantra, Chantrey, Chantri, Chantria

Chantrice (French) singer. See also Shantrice.
Chantreese, Chantress

Chardae, Charde (Punjabi) charitable. (French) short forms of Chardonnay. See also Shardae.
Charda, Chardai, Charday, Chardea, Chardee, Chardée, Chardese, Chardey, Chardie

Chardonnay (French) a dry white wine.
Char, Chardae, Chardnay, Chardney, Chardon, Chardonae, Chardonai, Chardonay, Chardonaye, Chardonee, Chardonna, Chardonnae, Chardonnai, Chardonnee, Chardonnée, Chardonney, Shardonay, Shardonnay

Charis (Greek) grace; kindness.
Charece, Chareece, Chareeze, Charese, Chari, Charice, Charie, Charish, Charisse

Charissa, Charisse (Greek) forms of Charity.
Charesa, Charese, Charessa, Charesse, Charis, Charisa, Charise, Charisha, Charissee, Charista, Charyssa

Charity (Latin) charity, kindness.
Chariety, Charis, Charissa, Charisse, Charista, Charita, Chariti, Charitie, Sharity

Charla (French, English) a short form of Charlene, Charlotte.
Char, Charlea

Charlaine (English) a form of Charlene.
Charlaina, Charlane, Charlanna, Charlayna, Charlayne

Charlee, Charley (German, English) forms of Charlie.
Charle, Charleigh

Charlene (English) a form of Caroline. See also Carol, Karla, Sharlene.
Charla, Charlaine, Charlean, Charleen, Charleene, Charleesa, Charlena, Charlenae, Charlesena, Charline, Charlyn, Charlyne, Charlynn, Charlynne, Charlzina, Charoline

Charlie (German, English) strong.
Charlee, Charley, Charli, Charyl, Chatty, Sharli, Sharlie

Charlotte (French) a form of Caroline. Literature: Charlotte Brontë was a British novelist and poet best known for her novel *Jane Eyre*. See also Karlotte, Lotte, Sharlotte, Tottie.
Carlotta, Carly, Chara, Charil, Charl, Charla, Charlet, Charlett, Charletta, Charlette, Charlisa, Charlita, Charlott,

Charlotta, Charlottie, Charlotty, Charolet, Charolette, Charolot, Charolotte

Charmaine (French) a form of Carmen. See also Sharmaine.
Charamy, Charma, Charmae, Charmagne, Charmaigne, Charmain, Chamaine, Charmalique, Charman, Charmane, Charmar, Charmara, Charmayane, Charmayne, Charmeen, Charmeine, Charmene, Charmese, Charmian, Charmin, Charmine, Charmion, Charmisa, Charmon, Charmyn, Charmyne, Charmynne

Charnette (American) a combination of Charo + Annette.
Charnetta, Charnita

Charnika (American) a combination of Charo + Nika.
Charneka, Charniqua, Charnique

Charo (Spanish) a familiar form of Rosa.
Charyanna (American) a combination of Charo + Anna.
Charian, Charyian, Cheryn

Chasidy, Chassidy (Latin) forms of Chastity.
Chasa Dee, Chasadie, Chasady, Chasidee, Chasidey, Chasidie, Chassedi, Chassidi, Chasydi

Chasity (Latin) a form of Chastity.
Chasiti, Chasitie, Chasitty, Chassey, Chassie, Chassiti, Chassity, Chassy

Chastity (Latin) pure.
Chasidy, Chasity, Chasta, Chastady, Chastidy, Chastin, Chastitie, Chastney, Chasty

Chauntel (French) a form of Chantal.
Chaunta, Chauntae, Chauntay, Chaunte, Chauntell, Chauntelle, Chawntel, Chawntell, Chawntelle, Chontelle

Chava (Hebrew) life. (Yiddish) bird. Religion: the original name of Eve.
Chabah, Chavae, Chavah, Chavalah, Chavarra, Chavarria, Chave, Chavé, Chavette, Chaviva, Chavvis, Hava, Kaÿa

Chavella (Spanish) a form of Isabel.
Chavel, Chaveli, Chavell, Chavelle, Chevelle, Chavely, Chevie

Chavi (Gypsy) girl.
Chavali

Chavon (Hebrew) a form of Jane.
Chavona, Chavonda, Chavonn, Chavonne, Shavon

Chavonne (Hebrew) a form of Chavon. (American) a combination of the prefix Cha + Yvonne.
Chavondria, Chavonna, Chevon, Chevonn, Chevonna

Chaya (Hebrew) life; living.
Chaike, Chaye, Chayka, Chayla, Chaylah, Chaylea, Chaylee, Chaylene, Chayra

Chelci, Chelcie (English) forms of Chelsea.
Chelce, Chelcee, Chelcey, Chelcy

Chelsea (English) seaport. See also Kelsi, Shelsea.
Chelci, Chelese, Chelesia, Chelsa, Chelsae, Chelsah, Chelse, Chelseah, Chelsee, Chelsey, Chelsia, Chelsie, Chesea, Cheslee, Chessea

Chelsee (English) a form of Chelsea.
Chelsei, Chelseigh

Chelsey, Chelsy (English) forms of Chelsea. See also Kelsey.
Chelcy, Chelsay, Chelssy, Chelssey, Chelsye, Chesley

Chelsie (English) a form of Chelsea.
Chelli, Chellie, Chellise, Chellsie, Chelsi, Chelssie, Cheslie, Chessie

Chenelle (English) a form of Chanel.
Chenel, Chenell

Chenoa (Native American) white dove.
Chenee, Chenika, Chenita, Chenna, Chenoah

Cher (French) beloved, dearest. (English) a short form of Cherilyn.
Chere, Cheri, Cherie, Sher

Cherelle, Cherrelle (French) forms of Cheryl. See also Sherelle.
Charell, Charelle, Cherell, Cherrel, Cherrell

Cherese (Greek) a form of Cherish.
Chereese, Cheresa, Cheresse, Cherice

Cheri, Cherie (French) familiar forms of Cher.
Cheree, Chérie, Cheriee, Cherri, Cherrie

Cherilyn (English) a combination of Cheryl + Lynn.
Cher, Cheralyn, Chereen, Chereena, Cherilynn, Cherlyn, Cherlynn, Cherralyn, Cherrilyn, Cherrylyn, Cherylene, Cherylin, Cheryline, Cheryl-Lyn, Cheryl-Lynn, Cheryl-Lynne, Cherylyn, Cherylynn, Cherylynne, Sherilyn

Cherise (French) a form of Cherish. See also Sharice, Sherice.
Charisa, Charise, Cherece, Chereese, Cheresa, Cherice, Cheriss, Cherissa, Cherisse, Cherrise

Cherish (English) dearly held, precious.
Charish, Charisha, Cheerish, Cherise, Cherishe, Cherrish, Sherish

Cherokee (Native American) a tribal name.
Cherika, Cherkita, Cherrokee, Sherokee

Cherry (Latin) a familiar form of Charity. (French) cherry; cherry red.
Chere, Cheree, Cherey, Cherida, Cherita, Cherrey, Cherrita, Cherry-Ann, Cherry-Anne, Cherrye, Chery, Cherye

Cheryl (French) beloved. See also Sheryl.
Charel, Charil, Charyl, Cherelle, Cherrelle, Cheryl-Ann, Cheryl-Anne, Cheryle, Cherylee, Cheryll, Cherylle, Cheryl-Lee

Chesarey (American) a form of Desiree.
Chesarae, Chessa

Chesna (Slavic) peaceful.
Chesnee, Chesney, Chesnie, Chesny

Chessa (American) a short form of Chesarey.
Chessi, Chessie, Chessy

Cheyanne (Cheyenne) a form of Cheyenne.
Cheyan, Cheyana, Cheyane, Cheyann, Cheyanna, Cheyeana, Cheyeannna, Cheyeannne

Cheyenne (Cheyenne) a tribal name. See also Shaianne, Sheyenne, Shianne, Shyann.
Cheyanne, Cheyeene, Cheyena, Cheyene, Cheyenna, Cheyna, Chi, Chi-Anna, Chie, Chyanne

Cheyla (American) a form of Sheila.
Cheylan, Cheyleigh, Cheylo

Cheyna (American) a short form of Cheyenne.
Chey, Cheye, Cheyne, Cheynee, Cheyney, Cheynna

Chiara (Italian) a form of Clara.
Cheara, Chiarra

Chika (Japanese) near and dear.
Chikaka, Chikako, Chikara, Chikona

Chiku (Swahili) chatterer.

China (Chinese) fine porcelain. Geography: a country in eastern Asia. See also Ciana, Shina.
Chinaetta, Chinah, Chinasa, Chinda, Chinea, Chinesia, Chinita, Chinna, Chinwa, Chyna, Chynna

Chinira (Swahili) God receives.
Chinara, Chinarah, Chinirah

Chinue (Ibo) God's own blessing.

Chiquita (Spanish) little one. See also Shiquita.
Chaqueta, Chaquita, Chica, Chickie, Chicky, Chikata, Chikita, Chiqueta, Chiquila, Chiquite, Chiquitha, Chiquithe, Chiquitia, Chiquitta

Chiyo (Japanese) eternal.
Chiya

Chloe (Greek) blooming, verdant. Mythology: another name for Demeter, the goddess of agriculture.
Chloé, Chlöe, Chloee, Chloie, Cloe, Kloe

Chloris (Greek) pale. Mythology: the only daughter of Niobe to escape the vengeful arrows of Apollo and Artemis. See also Loris.
Cloris, Clorissa

Cho (Korean) beautiful.
Choe

Cholena (Native American) bird.

Chriki (Swahili) blessing.

Chris (Greek) a short form of Christina. See also Kris.
Chrys, Cris

Chrissa (Greek) a short form of Christina. See also Khrissa.
Chrysa, Chryssa, Crissa, Cryssa

Chrissy (English) a familiar form of Christina.
Chrisie, Chrissee, Chrissie, Crissie, Khrissy

Christa (German) a short form of Christina. History: Christa McAuliffe, an American school teacher, was the first civilian on a U. S. space flight. See also Krista.
Chrysta, Crista, Crysta

Christabel (Latin, French) beautiful Christian.
Christabell, Christabella, Christabelle, Christable, Cristabel, Kristabel

Christain (Greek) a form of Christina.
Christana, Christann, Christanna

Christal (Latin) a form of Crystal. (Scottish) a form of Christina.
Christalene, Christalin, Christaline, Christall, Christalle, Christalyn, Christelle, Christle, Chrystal

Christelle (French) a form of Christal.
Christel, Christele, Christell, Chrystel, Chrystelle

Christen, Christin (Greek) forms of Christina. See also Kristen.
Christan, Christyn, Chrystan, Chrysten, Chrystyn, Crestienne

Christena, Christen (Greek) forms of Christina.

Christi, Christie (Greek) short forms of Christina, Christine. See also Kristi.
Christy, Chrysti, Chrystie, Chrysty, Kristi

Christian, Christiana, Christianna (Greek) forms of Christina. See also Kristian, Krystian.
Christiane, Christiann, Christi-Ann, Christianne, Christi-Anne, Christianni, Christiaun, Christiean, Christien, Christiena, Christienne, Christinan, Christy-Ann, Christy-Anne, Crystian, Chrystyann, Chrystyanne, Crystiann, Crystianne

Christin (Greek) a short form of Christina.
Christen, Chrystin

Christina (Greek) Christian; anointed. See also Khristina, Kristina, Stina, Tina.
Chris, Chrissa, Chrissy, Christa, Christain, Christal, Christeena, Christella, Christen, Christena, Christi, Christian,

Christie, Christin, Christinaa, Christine, Christinea, Christinia, Christinna, Christinnah, Christna, Christy, Christyn, Christyna, Christynna, Chrystina, Chrystyna, Cristeena, Cristena, Cristina, Crystina, Chrystena, Cristena

Christine (French, English) a form of Christina. See also Kirsten, Kristen, Kristine.
Chrisa, Christeen, Christen, Christene, Christi, Christie, Christy, Chrystine, Cristeen, Cristene, Cristine, Crystine

Christophe (Greek) Christ-bearer.

Christy (English) a short form of Christina, Christine.
Cristy

Christyn (Greek) a form of Christina.
Christyne

Chrys (English) a form of Chris.
Krys

Chrystal (Latin) a form of Christal.
Chrystale, Chrystalla, Chrystallina, Chrystallynn,

Chu Hua (Chinese) chrysanthemum.

Chumani (Lakota) dewdrops.
Chumany

Chun (Burmese) nature's renewal.

Chyanne, Chyenne (Cheyenne) forms of Cheyenne.
Chyan, Chyana, Chyane, Chyann, Chyanna, Chyeana, Chyenn, Chyenna, Chyennee

Chyna, Chynna (Chinese) forms of China.

Ciana (Chinese) a form of China. (Italian) a form of Jane.
Cian, Ciandra, Ciann, Cianna

Ciara, Ciarra (Irish) black. See also Sierra.
Ceara, Chiairah, Ciaara, Ciaera, Ciaira, Ciarah, Ciaria, Ciarrah, Cieara, Ciearra, Ciearria, Ciera, Cierra, Cioria, Cyarra

Cicely (English) a form of Cecilia. See also Sissy.
Cicelia, Cicelie, Ciciley, Cicilia, Cicilie, Cicily, Cile, Cilka, Cilla, Cilli, Cillie, Cilly

Cidney (French) a form of Sydney.
Cidnee, Cidni, Cidnie

Ciera, Cierra (Irish) forms of Ciara.
Ceira, Cierah, Ciere, Cieria, Cierrah, Cierre, Cierria, Cierro

Cinderella (French, English) little cinder girl. Literature: a fairy tale heroine.
Cindella

Cindy (Greek) moon. (Latin) a familiar form of Cynthia. See also Sindy.
Cindee, Cindi, Cindie, Cyndi

Cinthia, Cinthya (Greek) forms of Cynthia.
Cinthiya, Cintia

Cira (Spanish) a form of Cyrilla.

Cissy (American) a familiar form of Cecelia, Cicely.
Cissey, Cissi, Cissie

Claire (French) a form of Clara.
Clair, Klaire, Klarye

Clairissa (Greek) a form of Clarissa.
Clairisa, Clairisse, Claraissa

Clara (Latin) clear; bright. Music: Clara Shumann was a famous nineteenth-century German composer. See also Chiara, Klara.
Claira, Claire, Clarabelle, Clare, Claresta, Clarice, Clarie, Clarina, Clarinda, Clarine, Clarissa, Clarita

Clarabelle (Latin) bright and beautiful.
Clarabella, Claribel, Claribell

Clare (English) a form of Clara.

Clarie (Latin) a familiar form of Clara.
Clarey, Clari, Clary

Clarice (Italian) a form of Clara.
Claris, Clarise, Clarisse, Claryce, Cleriese, Klarice, Klarise

Clarisa (Greek) a form of Clarissa.
Claresa, Clarise, Clarisia

Clarissa (Greek) brilliant. (Italian) a form of Clara. See also Klarissa.
Clairissa, Clarecia, Claressa, Claresta, Clarisa, Clarissia, Claritza, Clarizza, Clarrisa, Clarrissa, Clerissa

Clarita (Spanish) a form of Clara.
Clairette, Clareta, Claretta, Clarette, Claritza

Claudette (French) a form of Claudia.
Clauddetta

Claudia (Latin) lame. See also Gladys, Klaudia.
Claudeen, Claudel, Claudelle, Claudette, Claudex, Claudiana, Claudiane, Claudie, Claudie-Anne, Claudina, Claudine

Claudie (Latin) a form of Claudia.
Claudee

Clea (Greek) a form of Cleo, Clio.

Clementine (Latin) merciful.
Clemence, Clemencia, Clemencie, Clemency, Clementia, Clementina, Clemenza, Clemette

Cleo (Greek) a short form of Cleopatra.
Chleo, Clea

Cleone (Greek) famous.
Cleonie, Cleonna, Cliona

Cleopatra (Greek) her father's fame. History: a great Egyptian queen.
Cleo

Cleta (Greek) illustrious.

Clio (Greek) proclaimer; glorifier. Mythology: the Muse of history.
Clea

Cloe (Greek) a form of Chloe.
Clo, Cloei, Cloey, Cloie

Clotilda (German) heroine.

Coco (Spanish) coconut. See also Koko.

Codi, Cody (English) cushion. See also Kodi.
Coady, Codee, Codey, Codia, Codie

Colby (English) coal town. Geography: a region in England known for cheese-making. See also Kolby.
Cobi, Cobie, Colbi, Colbie

Colette (Greek, French) a familiar form of Nicole.
Coe, Coetta, Coletta, Collet, Collete, Collett, Colletta, Collette, Kolette, Kollette

Colleen (Irish) girl. See also Kolina.
Coe, Coel, Cole, Coleen, Colene, Coley, Coline, Colleene, Collen, Collene, Collie, Collina, Colline, Colly

Collina (Irish) a form of Colleen.
Colena, Colina, Colinda

Concetta (Italian) pure.
Concettina, Conchetta

Conchita (Spanish) conception.
Chita, Conceptia, Concha, Conciana

Concordia (Latin) harmonious. Mythology: the goddess governing the peace after war.
Con, Cordae, Cordaye

Connie (Latin) a familiar form of Constance.
Con, Connee, Conni, Conny, Konnie, Konny

Connor (Scottish) wise. (Irish) praised; exhalted.
Connar, Conner, Connery, Conor

Constance (Latin) constant; firm. History: Constance Motley was the first African-American woman to be appointed as a U.S. federal judge. See also Konstance, Kosta.
Connie, Constancia, Constancy, Constanta, Constantia, Constantina, Constantine, Constanza, Constynse

Constanza (Spanish) a form of Constance.
Constanz, Constanze

Consuelo (Spanish) consolation. Religion: Nuestra Señora del Consuelo—Our Lady of Consolation—is a name for the Virgin Mary.
Consolata, Consuela, Consuella, Consula, Conzuelo, Konsuela, Konsuelo

Cora (Greek) maiden. Mythology: Kore is another name for Persephone, the goddess of the underworld. See also Kora.
Corah, Coralee, Coretta, Corissa, Corey, Corra

Corabelle (American) a combination of Cora + Belle.
Corabel, Corabella

Coral (Latin) coral. See also Koral.
Coraal, Corral

Coralee (American) a combination of Cora + Lee.
Coralea, Cora-Lee, Coralena, Coralene, Coraley, Coralie, Coraline, Coraly, Coralyn, Corella, Corilee, Koralie

Coralie (American) a form of Coralee.
Corali, Coralia, Coralina, Coralynn, Coralynne

Corazon (Spanish) heart.

Corbin (Latin) raven.
Corbe, Corbi, Corby, Corbyn, Corbynn

Cordasha (American) a combination of Cora + Dasha.

Cordelia (Latin) warm-hearted. (Welsh) sea jewel. See also Delia, Della.
Cordae, Cordelie, Cordett, Cordette,

Cordi, Cordilia, Cordilla, Cordula, Kordelia, Kordula

Cordi (Welsh) a short form of Cordelia.
Cordey, Cordia, Cordie, Cordy

Coretta (Greek) a familiar form of Cora.
Coreta, Corette, Correta, Corretta, Corrette, Koretta, Korretta

Corey, Cory (Irish) from the hollow. (Greek) familiar forms of Cora. See also Kori.
Coree, Cori, Correy, Correye, Corry

Cori, Corie, Corrie (Irish) forms of Corey.

Coriann, Corianne (American) combinations of Cori + Ann, Cori + Anne.
Corian, Coriane, Cori-Ann, Corri, Corrie-Ann, Corrianne, Corrie-Anne

Corina, Corinna (Greek) familiar forms of Corinne. See also Korina.
Coreena, Coriana, Corianna, Corinda, Correna, Corrinna, Coryna

Corinne (Greek) maiden.
Coreen, Coren, Corin, Corina, Corine, Corinee, Corinn, Corinna, Corrina, Coryn, Corynn, Corynne

Corissa (Greek) a familiar form of Cora.
Coresa, Coressa, Corisa, Coryssa, Korissa

Corliss (English) cheerful; goodhearted.
Corlisa, Corlise, Corlissa, Corly, Korliss

Cornelia (Latin) horn colored. See also Kornelia, Nelia, Nellie.
Carna, Carniella, Corneilla, Cornela, Cornelie, Cornella, Cornelle, Cornie, Cornilear, Cornisha, Corny

Corrina, Corrine (Greek) forms of Corinne.
Correen, Corren, Corrin, Corrinn, Corrinna, Corrinne, Corrinne, Corryn

Cortney (English) a form of Courtney.
Cortne, Cortnea, Cortnee, Cortneia, Cortni, Cortnie, Cortny, Cortnye, Corttney

Cosette (French) a familiar form of Nicole.
Cosetta, Cossetta, Cossette, Cozette

Courtenay (English) a form of Courtney.
Courtaney, Courtany, Courteney, Courteny

Courtnee, Courtnie (English) forms of Courtney.
Courtne, Courtnée, Courtnei, Courtneigh, Courtni, Courtnii

Courtney (English) from the court. See also Kortney, Kourtney.
Cortney, Courtena, Courtenay, Courtene, Courtnae, Courtnay, Courtnee, Courtny, Courtonie

Crisbell (American) a combination of Crista + Belle.
Crisbel, Cristabel

Crista, Crysta (Italian) forms of Christa.
Cristah

Cristal (Latin) a form of Crystal.
Cristalie, Cristalina, Cristalle, Cristel, Cristela, Cristelia, Cristella, Cristelle, Cristhie, Cristle

Cristen, Cristin (Irish) forms of Christen, Christin. See also Kristin.
Cristan, Cristyn, Crystan, Crysten, Crystin, Crystyn

Cristina, Cristine (Greek) forms of Christina. See also Kristina.
Cristiona, Cristy

Cristy (English) a familiar form of Cristina. A form of Christy. See also Kristy.
Cristey, Cristi, Cristie, Crysti, Crystie, Crysty

Crystal (Latin) clear, brilliant glass. See also Kristal, Krystal.
Christal, Chrystal, Chrystal-Lynn, Chrystel, Cristal, Crystala, Crystale, Crystalee, Crystalin, Crystall, Crystalle, Crystaly, Crystel, Crystela, Crystelia, Crystelle, Crysthelle, Crystl, Crystle, Crystol, Crystole, Crystyl

Crystalin (Latin) crystal pool.
Crystal-Ann, Cristalanna, Crystal-Anne, Cristalina, Cristallina, Cristalyn, Crystallynn, Crystallynne, Cristilyn, Crystalina, Crystal-Lee, Crystal-Lynn, Crystalyn, Crystalynn

Crystina (Greek) a form of Christina.
Crystin, Crystine, Crystyn, Crystyna, Crystyne

Curran (Irish) heroine.
Cura, Curin, Curina, Curinna

Cybele (Greek) a form of Sybil.
Cybel, Cybil, Cybill, Cybille

Cydney (French) a form of Sydney.
Cydne, Cydnee, Cydnei, Cydni, Cydnie

Cyerra (Irish) a form of Ciara.
Cyera, Cyerria

Cyndi (Greek) a form of Cindy.
Cynda, Cyndal, Cyndale, Cyndall,

Cyndee, Cyndel, Cyndia, Cyndie, Cyndle, Cyndy

Cynthia (Greek) moon. Mythology: another name for Artemis, the moon goddess. See also Hyacinth, Kynthia.
Cindy, Cinthia, Cyneria, Cynethia, Cynithia, Cynthea, Cynthiana, Cynthiann, Cynthie, Cynthria, Cynthy, Cynthya, Cyntia, Cyntreia, Cythia, Synthia

Cyrilla (Greek) noble.
Cerelia, Cerella, Cira, Cirilla, Cyrella, Cyrille

Dacey (Irish) southerner. (Greek) a familiar form of Candace.
Dacee, Dacei, Daci, Dacia, Dacie, Dacy, Daicee, Daici, Daicie, Daicy, Daycee, Daycie, Daycy

Dacia (Irish) a form of Dacey.
Daciah

Dae (English) day. See also Dai.

Daeja (French) a form of Déja.
Daejah, Daejia

Daelynn (American) a combination of Dae + Lynn.
Daeleen, Daelena, Daelin, Daelyn, Daelynne

Daeshandra (American) a combination of Dae + Shandra.
Daeshandria, Daeshaundra,

Daeshaundria, Daeshawndra, Daeshawndria, Daeshondra, Daeshondria

Daeshawna (American) a combination of Dae + Shawna.
Daeshan, Daeshaun, Daeshauna, Daeshavon, Daeshawn, Daeshawntia, Daeshon, Daeshona

Daeshonda (American) a combination of Dae + Shonda.
Daeshanda, Daeshawnda

Dafny (American) a form of Daphne.
Dafany, Daffany, Daffie, Daffy, Dafna, Dafne, Dafney, Dafnie

Dagmar (German) glorious.
Dagmara

Dagny (Scandinavian) day.
Dagna, Dagnanna, Dagne, Dagney, Dagnie

Dahlia (Scandinavian) valley. Botany: a perennial flower. See also Daliah.
Dahliah, Dahlya, Dahlye

Dai (Japanese) great. See also Dae.
Day, Daye

Daija, Daijah (French) forms of Déja.
Daijaah, Daijea, Daijha, Daijhah, Dayja

Daisha (American) a form of Dasha.
Daesha, Daishae, Daishia, Daishya, Daisia

Daisy (English) day's eye. Botany: a white and yellow flower.
Daisee, Daisey, Daisi, Daisia, Daisie, Dasey, Dasi, Dasie, Dasy, Daysi, Deisy

Daja, Dajah (French) forms of Déja.
Dajae, Dajai, Daje, Dajha, Dajia

Dakayla (American) a combination of the prefix Da + Kayla.
Dakala, Dakila

Dakira (American) a combination of the prefix Da + Kira.
Dakara, Dakaria, Dakarra, Dakirah, Dakyra

Dakota (Native American) a tribal name.
Dakkota, Dakoda, Dakotah, Dakotha, Dakotta, Dekoda, Dekota, Dekotah, Dekotha

Dale (English) valley.
Dael, Dahl, Daile, Daleleana, Dalena, Dalina, Dayle

Dalia, Daliah (Hebrew) branch. See also Dahlia.
Daelia, Dailia, Daleah, Daleia, Dalialah, Daliyah

Dalila (Swahili) gentle.
Dalela, Dalida, Dalilah, Dalilia

Dalisha (American) a form of Dallas.
Dalisa, Dalishea, Dalishia, Dalishya, Dalisia, Dalissia

Dallas (Irish) wise.
Dalis, Dalise, Dalisha, Dalisse, Dallace, Dallis, Dallise, Dallus, Dallys, Dalyce, Dalys

Damaris (Greek) gentle girl. See also Maris.
Dama, Damar, Damara, Damarius, Damary, Damarylis, Damarys, Dameress, Dameris, Damiris, Dammaris, Dammeris, Damris, Demaras, Demaris

Damiana (Greek) tamer, soother.
Daimenia, Daimiona, Damia, Damiann, Damianna, Damianne, Damien, Damienne, Damiona, Damon, Demion

Damica (French) friendly.
Damee, Dameeka, Dameka, Damekah, Damicah, Damicia, Damicka, Damie, Damieka, Damika, Damikah, Damyka, Demeeka, Demeka, Demekah, Demica, Demicah

Damita (Spanish) small noblewoman.
Damee, Damesha, Dameshia, Damesia, Dametia, Dametra, Dametrah

Damonica (American) a combination of the prefix Da + Monica.
Damonec, Damoneke, Damonik, Damonika, Damonique, Diamoniqua, Diamonique

Dana (English) from Denmark; bright as day.
Daina, Dainna, Danah, Danaia, Danan, Danarra, Dane, Danean, Danna, Dayna

Danae (Greek) Mythology: the mother of Perseus.
Danaë, Danay, Danayla, Danays, Danai, Danea, Danee, Dannae, Denae, Denee

Danalyn (American) a combination of Dana + Lynn.
Danalee, Donaleen

Daneil (Hebrew) a form of Danielle.
Daneal, Daneala, Daneale, Daneel, Daneela, Daneila

Danella (American) a form of Danielle.
Danayla, Danela, Danelia, Danelle, Danna, Donella, Donnella

Danelle (Hebrew) a form of Danielle.
Danael, Danalle, Danel, Danele, Danell, Danella, Donelle, Donnelle

Danesha, Danisha (American) forms of Danessa.
Daneisha, Daneshia, Daniesha, Danishia

Danessa (American) a combination of Danielle + Vanessa. See also Doneshia.
Danasia, Danesa, Danesha, Danessia, Daniesa, Danisa, Danissa

Danessia (American) a form of Danessa.
Danesia, Danieshia, Danisia, Danissia

Danette (American) a form of Danielle.
Danetra, Danett, Danetta, Donnita

Dani (Hebrew) a familiar form of Danielle.
Danee, Danie, Danne, Dannee, Danni, Dannie, Danny, Dannye, Dany

Dania, Danya (Hebrew) short forms of Danielle.
Daniah, Danja, Dannia, Danyae

Danica, Danika (Slavic) morning star. (Hebrew) forms of Danielle.
Daneca, Daneeka, Daneekah, Danicah, Danicka, Danieka, Danikah, Danikla, Danneeka, Dannica, Dannika, Dannikah, Danyka, Denica, Donica, Donika, Donnaica, Donnica, Donnika

Danice (American) a combination of Danielle + Janice.
Donice

Daniela (Italian) a form of Danielle.
Daniellah, Dannilla, Danijela

Danielan (Spanish) a form of Danielle.

Daniella (English) a form of Dana.
Danka, Danniella, Danyella

Danielle (Hebrew, French) God is my judge.
Daneen, Daneil, Daneille, Danelle, Dani, Danial, Danialle, Danica, Daniel, Daniela, Danielan, Daniele, Danielka, Daniell, Daniella, Danilka, Danille, Danit, Dannielle, Danyel, Donniella

Danille (American) a form of Danielle.
Danila, Danile, Danilla, Dannille

Danit (Hebrew) a form of Danielle.
Danett, Danis, Danisha, Daniss, Danita, Danitra, Danitrea, Danitria, Danitza, Daniz

Danna (Hebrew) a short form of Danella.
Dannah

Dannielle (Hebrew, French) a form of Danielle.
Danniel, Danniele, Danniell

Danyel, Danyell, Danyelle (American) forms of Danielle.
Daniyel, Danyae, Danyail, Danyaile, Danyal, Danyale, Danyea, Danyele, Danyiel, Danyielle, Danyle, Donnyale, Donnyell, Donyale, Donyell

Daphne (Greek) laurel tree.
Dafny, Daphane, Daphany, Dapheney, Daphna, Daphnee, Daphnique, Daphnit, Daphny

Daphnee (Greek) a form of Daphne.
Daphaney, Daphanie, Daphney, Daphni, Daphnie

Dara (Hebrew) compassionate.
Dahra, Daira, Dairah, Darah, Daraka, Daralea, Daralee, Daraleigh, Daralie, Daravie, Darda, Darice, Darisa, Darissa, Darja, Darra, Darrah

Darby (Irish) free. (Scandinavian) deer estate.
Darb, Darbe, Darbee, Darbi, Darbie, Darbra, Darbye

Darcelle (French) a form of Darci.
Darcel, Darcell, Darcella, Darselle

Darci, Darcy (Irish) dark. (French) fortress.
Darcee, Darcelle, Darcey, Darcie, Darsey, Darsi, Darsie

Daria (Greek) wealthy.
Dari, Dariya, Darria, Darya, Daryia

Darian, Darrian (Greek) forms of Daron.
Dariana, Dariane, Dariann, Darianna, Darianne, Dariyan, Dariyanne, Darriana, Darriane, Darriann, Darrianna, Darrianne, Derrian, Driana

Darielle (French) a form of Daryl.
Dariel, Dariela, Dariell, Darriel, Darrielle

Darien, Darrien (Greek) forms of Daron.
Dariene, Darienne, Darriene

Darilynn (American) a form of Darlene.
Daralin, Daralyn, Daralynn, Daralynne, Darilin, Darilyn, Darilynne, Darlin, Darlyn, Darlynn, Darlynne, Darylin, Darylyn, Darylynn, Darylynne

Darion, Darrion (Irish) forms of Daron.
Dariona, Darione, Darionna, Darionne, Darriona, Darrionna

Darla (English) a short form of Darlene.
Darlecia, Darli, Darlice, Darlie, Darlis, Darly, Darlys

Darlene (French) little darling. See also Daryl.
Darilynn, Darla, Darlean, Darlee, Darleen, Darleene, Darlena, Darlenia, Darlenne, Darletha, Darlin, Darline, Darling, Darlyn, Darlynn, Darlynne

Darnee (Irish) a familiar form of Darnelle.

Darnelle (English) hidden place.
Darnee, Darnel, Darnell, Darnella, Darnesha, Darnetta, Darnette, Darnice, Darniece, Darnita, Darnyell

Darnesha, Darnisha (American) forms of Darnelle.
Darneisha, Darneishia, Darneshea, Darneshia, Darnesia, Darniesha, Darnishia, Darnisia, Darrenisha

Daron (Irish) great.
Darian, Darien, Darion, Daronica, Daronice, Darron, Daryn

Darselle (French) a form of Darcelle.
Darsel, Darsell, Darsella

Daru (Hindi) pine tree.

Daryl (English) beloved. (French) a short form of Darlene.
Darelle, Darielle, Daril, Darilynn, Darrel, Darrell, Darrelle, Darreshia, Darryl, Darryll, Daryll, Darylle

Daryn (Greek) gifts. (Irish) great.
Daron, Daryan, Daryne, Darynn, Darynne

Dasha, Dasia (Russian) forms of Dorothy.
Daisha, Dashae, Dashenka, Dashia, Dashiah, Dasiah, Daysha

Dashawna (American) a combination of the prefix Da + Shawna.
Dashawn, Dashawnna, Dashay, Dashell, Dayshana, Dayshawnna, Dayshona, Deshawna

Dashiki (Swahili) loose-fitting shirt worn in Africa.
Dashi, Dashika, Dashka, Desheka, Deshiki

Dashonda (American) a combination of the prefix Da + Shonda.
Dashawnda, Dishante

Davalinda (American) a combination of Davida + Linda.
Davalynda, Davelinda, Davilinda, Davylinda

Davalynda (American) a form of Davalinda.
Davelynda, Davilynda, Davylynda

Davalynn (American) a combination of Davida + Lynn.
Davalin, Davalyn, Davalynne, Davelin, Davelyn, Davelynn, Davelynne, Davilin, Davilyn, Davilynn, Davilynne, Dayleen, Devlyn

Davida (Hebrew) beloved. Bible: David was the second king of Israel. See also Vida.
Daveta, Davetta, Davette, Davika, Davita

Davina (Scottish) a form of Davida. See also Vina.
Dava, Davannah, Davean, Davee, Daveen, Daveena, Davene, Daveon, Davey, Davi, Daviana, Davie, Davin, Davinder, Davine, Davineen, Davinia, Davinna, Davonna, Davria, Devean, Deveen, Devene, Devina

Davisha (American) a combination of the prefix Da + Aisha.
Daveisha, Davesia, Davis, Davisa

Davonna (Scottish, English) a form of Davina, Devonna.
Davion, Daviona, Davionna, Davon, Davona, Davonda, Davone, Davonia, Davonne, Davonnia

Dawn (English) sunrise, dawn.
Dawana, Dawandrea, Dawanna, Dawin, Dawna, Dawne, Dawnee, Dawnetta, Dawnisha, Dawnlynn, Dawnn, Dawnrae

Dawna (English) a form of Dawn.
Dawnna, Dawnya

Dawnyelle (American) a combination of Dawn + Danielle.
Dawnele, Dawnell, Dawnelle, Dawnyel, Dawnyella

Dawnisha (American) a form of Dawn.
Dawnesha, Dawni, Dawniell, Dawnielle, Dawnisia, Dawniss, Dawnita, Dawnnisha, Dawnysha, Dawnysia

Dayana (Latin) a form of Diana.
Dayanara, Dayani, Dayanna, Dayanne, Dayanni, Deyanaira, Dyani, Dyanna, Dyia

Dayle (English) a form of Dale.
Dayla, Daylan, Daylea, Daylee

Dayna (Scandinavian) a form of Dana.
Daynah, Dayne, Daynna, Deyna

Daysha (American) a form of Dasha.
Daysa, Dayshalie, Daysia, Deisha

Daysi, Deysi (English) forms of Daisy.
Daysee, Daysia, Daysie, Daysy, Deysia, Deysy

Dayton, Daytona (English) day town; bright, sunny town.
Daytonia

Deana (Latin) divine. (English) valley.
Deanah, Deane, Deanielle, Deanisha, Deanna, Deeana, Deeann, Deeanna, Deena

Deandra (American) a combination of Dee + Andrea.
Dandrea, Deandre, Deandré, Deandrea, Deandree, Deandreia, Deandria, Deanndra, Deaundra, Deaundria, Deeandra, Deyaneira, Deondra, Diandra, Diandre, Diandrea, Diondria, Dyandra

Deangela (Italian) a combination of the prefix De + Angela.
Deangala, Deangalique, Deangle

Deanna (Latin) a form of Deana, Diana.
Deaana, Deahana, Deandra, Deandre, Déanna, Deannia, Deeanna, Deena

Deanne (Latin) a form of Diane.
Deahanne, Deane, Deann, Déanne, Deeann, Dee-Ann, Deeanne

Debbie (Hebrew) a short form of Deborah.
Debbee, Debbey, Debbi, Debby, Debee, Debi, Debie

Deborah (Hebrew) bee. Bible: a great
Hebrew prophetess.
*Deb, Debbie, Debbora, Debborah,
Deberah, Debor, Debora, Deboran,
Deborha, Deborrah, Debra, Debrena,
Debrina, Debroah, Devora, Dobra*

Debra (American) a form of Deborah.
Debbra, Debbrah, Debrah, Debrea, Debria

Dedra (American) a form of Deirdre.
Deeddra, Deedra, Deedrea, Deedrie

Dedriana (American) a combination
of Dedra + Adriana.
Dedranae

Dee (Welsh) black, dark.
*De, Dea, Deah, Dede, Dedie, Deea,
Deedee, Dee Dee, Didi*

Deena (American) a form of Deana,
Dena, Dinah.

Deidra, Deidre (Irish) forms of
Deirdre.
*Deidrah, Deidrea, Deidrie, Diedra,
Diedre, Dierdra*

Deirdre (Irish) sorrowful; wanderer.
*Dedra, Deerdra, Deerdre, Deidra, Deidre,
Deirdree, Didi, Diedra, Dierdre, Diérdre,
Dierdrie*

Deisy (English) a form of Daisy.
Deisi, Deissy

Deitra (Greek) a short form of
Demetria.
Deetra, Detria

Déja (French) before.
*Daeja, Daija, Deejay, Dejae, Déjah,
Dejai, Dejanae, Dejanelle, Dejon*

Dejanae (French) a form of Déja.
*Dajahnae, Dajona, Dejana, Dejanah,
Dejanae, Dejanai, Dejanay, Dejane,
Dejanea, Dejanee, Dejanna, Dejannaye,
Dejena, Dejonae*

Dejon (French) a form of Déja.
*Daijon, Dajan, Dejone, Dejonee,
Dejonelle, Dejonna*

Deka (Somali) pleasing.
Dekah

Delacy (American) a combination of
the prefix De + Lacy.
Delaceya

Delainey (Irish) a form of Delaney.
*Delaine, Delainee, Delaini, Delainie,
Delainy*

Delana (German) noble protector.
*Dalanna, Dalayna, Daleena, Dalena,
Dalenna, Dalina, Dalinda, Dalinna,
Delaina, Delania, Delanya, Delayna,
Deleena, Delena, Delenya, Delina,
Dellaina*

Delaney (Irish) descendant of the
challenger. (English) a form of
Adeline.
*Dalaney, Dalania, Dalene, Daleney,
Daline, Del, Delainey, Delane, Delanee,
Delanie, Delany, Delayne, Delayney,
Delaynie, Deleani, Déline, Della, Dellaney*

Delanie (Irish) a form of Delaney.
Delani

Delfina (Greek) a form of Delphine.
(Spanish) dolphin.
Delfeena, Delfine

Delia (Greek) visible; from Delos,
Greece. (German, Welsh) a short
form of Adelaide, Cordelia.
Mythology: a festival of Apollo held
in ancient Greece.
*Dehlia, Delea, Deli, Deliah, Deliana,
Delianne, Delinda, Dellia, Dellya, Delya*

Delicia (English) delightful.
*Delecia, Delesha, Delice, Delisa, Delise,
Delisha, Delishia, Delisiah, Delya,
Delys, Delyse, Delysia, Doleesha*

Delilah (Hebrew) brooder. Bible: the
companion of Samson. See also Lila.
Dalialah, Dalila, Daliliah, Delila, Delilia

Della (English) a short form of
Adelaide, Cordelia, Delaney.
Del, Dela, Dell, Delle, Delli, Dellie, Dells

Delores (Spanish) a form of Dolores.
*Delora, Delore, Deloria, Delories, Deloris,
Delorise, Delorita, Delsie*

Delphine (Greek) from Delphi,
Greece. See also Delfina.
*Delpha, Delphe, Delphi, Delphia,
Delphina, Delphinia, Delvina*

Delsie (English) a familiar form of
Delores.
Delsa, Delsey, Delza

Delta (Greek) door. Linguistics: the
fourth letter in the Greek alphabet.
Geography: a triangular land mass at
the mouth of a river.
Delte, Deltora, Deltoria, Deltra

Demetria (Greek) cover of the earth. Mythology: Demeter was the Greek goddess of the harvest.
Deitra, Demeta, Demeteria, Demetra, Demetriana, Demetrianna, Demetrias, Demetrice, Demetriona, Demetris, Demetrish, Demetrius, Demi, Demita, Demitra, Demitria, Dymitra

Demi (French) half. (Greek) a short form of Demetria.
Demia, Demiah, Demii, Demmi, Demmie, Demy

Dena (English, Native American) valley. (Hebrew) a form of Dinah. See also Deana.
Deane, Deena, Deeyn, Denae, Denah, Dene, Denea, Deney, Denna, Deonna

Denae (Hebrew) a form of Dena.
Denaé, Denay, Denee, Deneé

Deni (French) a short form of Denise.
Deney, Denie, Denni, Dennie, Denny, Dinnie, Dinny

Denica, Denika (Slavic) forms of Danica.
Denikah, Denikia

Denise (French) Mythology: follower of Dionysus, the god of wine.
Danice, Danise, Denese, Deni, Denice, Denicy, Deniece, Denisha, Denisse, Denize, Dennise, Dennys, Denyce, Denys, Denyse

Denisha (American) a form of Denise.
Deneesha, Deneichia, Deneisha, Deneishea, Denesha, Deneshia, Deniesha, Denishia

Denisse (French) a form of Denise.
Denesse, Denissa

Deonna (English) a form of Dena.
Deon, Deona, Deonah, Deondra, Deonne

Derika (German) ruler of the people.
Dereka, Derekia, Derica, Dericka, Derrica, Derricka, Derrika

Derry (Irish) redhead.
Deri, Derie

Deryn (Welsh) bird.
Derien, Derienne, Derion, Derin, Deron, Derren, Derrin, Derrine, Derrion, Derriona, Deryne

Desarae (French) a form of Desiree.
Desara, Desarai, Desaraie, Desaray, Desare, Desaré, Desarea, Desaree, Desarie, Dezarae

Deserae, Desirae (French) forms of Desiree.
Desera, Deserai, Deseray, Desere, Deseree, Deseret, Deseri, Deserie, Deserrae, Deserray, Deserré, Dessirae, Dezeray, Dezere, Dezerea, Dezrae, Dezyrae

Deshawna (American) a combination of the prefix De + Shawna.
Dashawna, Deshan, Deshane, Deshaun, Deshawn, Desheania, Deshona, Deshonna

Deshawnda (American) a combination of the prefix De + Shawnda.
Deshanda, Deshandra, Deshaundra, Deshawndra, Deshonda

Desi (French) a short form of Desiree.
Désir, Desira, Dezi, Dezia, Dezzia, Dezzie

Desiree (French) desired, longed for. See also Dessa.
Chesarey, Desarae, Deserae, Desi, Desirae, Desirah, Desirai, Desiray, Desire, Desirea, Desireah, Desirée, Désirée, Desirey, Desiri, Desray, Desree, Dessie, Dessire, Dezarae, Dezirae, Deziree

Dessa (Greek) wanderer. (French) a form of Desiree.

Desta (Ethiopian) happy. (French) a short form of Destiny.
Desti, Destie, Desty

Destany (French) a form of Destiny.
Destanee, Destaney, Destani, Destanie, Destannee, Destannie

Destinee, Destini, Destinie (French) forms of Destiny.
Desteni, Destiana, Destine, Destinée, Destnie

Destiney (French) a form of Destiny.

Destiny (French) fate.
Desnine, Desta, Destany, Destenee, Destenie, Desteny, Destin, Destinee, Destiney, Destini, Destinie, Destonie, Destynee, Dezstany

Destynee, Destyni (French) forms of Destiny.
Desty, Destyn, Destyne, Destyne, Destynie

Deva (Hindi) divine.
Deeva

Devan (Irish) a form of Devin.
*Devana, Devane, Devanee, Devaney,
Devani, Devanie, Devann, Devanna,
Devannae, Devanne, Devany*

Devi (Hindi) goddess. Religion: the
Hindu goddess of power and
destruction.

Devin (Irish) poet.
*Devan, Deven, Devena, Devenje, Deveny,
Devine, Devinn, Devinne, Devyn*

Devon (English) a short form of
Devonna. (Irish) a form of Devin.
*Deaven, Devion, Devione, Devionne,
Devone, Devoni, Devonne*

Devonna (English) from Devonshire.
*Davonna, Devon, Devona, Devonda,
Devondra, Devonia*

Devora (Hebrew) a form of Deborah.
Deva, Devorah, Devra, Devrah

Devyn (Irish) a form of Devin.
Deveyn, Devyne, Devynn, Devynne

Dextra (Latin) adroit, skillful.
Dekstra, Dextria

Dezarae, Dezirae, Deziree (French)
forms of Desiree.
*Dezaraee, Dezarai, Dezaray, Dezare,
Dezaree, Dezarey, Dezerie, Deziray,
Dezirea, Dezirée, Dezorae, Dezra*

Di (Latin) a short form of Diana, Diane.
Dy

Dia (Latin) a short form of Diana,
Diane.

Diamond (Latin) precious gem.
*Diamantina, Diamon, Diamonda,
Diamonde, Diamonia, Diamonique,
Diamonte, Diamontina, Dyamond*

Diana (Latin) divine. Mythology: the
goddess of the hunt, the moon, and
fertility. See also Deanna, Deanne,
Dyan.
*Daiana, Daianna, Dayana, Dayanna,
Di, Dia, Dianah, Dianalyn, Dianarose,
Dianatris, Dianca, Diandra, Diane,
Dianelis, Diania, Dianielle, Dianita,
Dianna, Dianys, Didi*

Diane, Dianne (Latin) short forms of
Diana.
*Deane, Deanne, Deeane, Deeanne, Di,
Dia, Diahann, Dian, Diani, Dianie,
Diann*

Dianna (Latin) a form of Diana.
Diahanna, Diannah

Diantha (Greek) divine flower.
Diandre, Dianthe

Diedra (Irish) a form of Deirdre.
Didra, Diedre

Dillan (Irish) loyal, faithful.
Dillon, Dillyn

Dilys (Welsh) perfect; true.

Dina (Hebrew) a form of Dinah.
Dinna, Dyna

Dinah (Hebrew) vindicated. Bible: a
daughter of Jacob and Leah.
Dina, Dinnah, Dynah

Dinka (Swahili) people.

Dionna (Greek) an alternative form of
Dionne.
*Deona, Deondra, Deonia, Deonna,
Deonyia, Diona, Diondra, Diondrea*

Dionne (Greek) divine queen.
Mythology: Dione was the mother
of Aphrodite, the goddess of love.
*Deonne, Dion, Dione, Dionee, Dionis,
Dionna, Dionte*

Dior (French) golden.
Diora, Diore, Diorra, Diorre

Dita (Spanish) a form of Edith.
Ditka, Ditta

Divinia (Latin) divine.
*Devina, Devinae, Devinia, Devinie,
Devinna, Diveena, Divina, Divine,
Diviniea, Divya*

Dixie (French) tenth. (English) wall;
dike. Geography: a nickname for the
American South.
Dix, Dixee, Dixi, Dixy

Diza (Hebrew) joyful.
Ditza, Ditzah, Dizah

Dodie (Hebrew) beloved. (Greek) a
familiar form of Dorothy.
Doda, Dode, Dodee, Dodi, Dody

Dolly (American) a short form of
Dolores, Dorothy.
*Dol, Doll, Dollee, Dolley, Dolli, Dollie,
Dollina*

Dolores (Spanish) sorrowful. Religion:
Nuestra Señora de los Dolores—Our
Lady of Sorrows—is a name for the
Virgin Mary. See also Lola.
*Delores, Deloria, Dolly, Dolorcitas,
Dolorita, Doloritas*

Dominica, Dominika (Latin) belonging to the Lord. See also Mika.
Domenica, Domenika, Domineca, Domineka, Dominga, Domini, Dominick, Dominicka, Dominique, Dominixe, Domino, Dominyika, Domka, Domnicka, Domonica, Domonice, Domonika

Dominique, Domonique (French) forms of Dominica, Dominika.
Domanique, Domeneque, Domenique, Domineque, Dominiqua, Domino, Dominoque, Dominque, Dominuque, Domique, Domminique, Domoniqua

Domino (English) a short form of Dominica, Dominique.

Dona (English) world leader; proud ruler. (Italian) a form of Donna.
Donae, Donah, Donalda, Donaldina, Donelda, Donellia, Doni

Doña (Italian) a form of Donna.
Donail, Donalea, Donalisa, Donay, Doni, Donia, Donie, Donise, Donitrae

Donata (Latin) gift.
Donatha, Donato, Donatta, Donetta, Donette, Donita, Donnette, Donnita, Donte

Dondi (American) a familiar form of Donna.
Dondra, Dondrea, Dondria

Doneshia, Donisha (American) forms of Danessa.
Donasha, Donashay, Doneisha, Doneishia, Donesha, Donisa, Donisha, Donishia, Donneshia, Donnisha

Donna (Italian) lady.
Doña, Dondi, Donnae, Donnalee,

Donnalen, Donnay, Donne, Donnell, Donni, Donnie, Donnise, Donny, Dontia, Donya

Donniella (American) a form of Danielle.
Donella, Doniele, Doniell, Doniella, Donielle, Donnella, Donnielle, Donnyella, Donyelle

Dora (Greek) gift. A short form of Adora, Eudora, Pandora, Theodora.
Dorah, Doralia, Doralie, Doralisa, Doraly, Doralynn, Doran, Dorchen, Dore, Dorece, Doree, Doreece, Doreen, Dorelia, Dorella, Dorelle, Doresha, Doressa, Doretta, Dori, Dorielle, Dorika, Doriley, Dorilis, Dorinda, Dorion, Dorita, Doro, Dory

Doralynn (English) a combination of Dora + Lynn.
Doralin, Doralyn, Doralynne, Dorlin

Doreen (Irish) moody, sullen. (French) golden. (Greek) a form of Dora.
Doreena, Dorena, Dorene, Dorina, Dorine

Doretta (American) a form of Dora, Dorothy.
Doretha, Dorette, Dorettie

Dori, Dory (American) familiar forms of Dora, Doria, Doris, Dorothy.
Dore, Dorey, Dorie, Dorree, Dorri, Dorrie, Dorry

Doria (Greek) a form of Dorian.
Dori

Dorian (Greek) from Doris, Greece.
Dorean, Doriana, Doriane, Doriann,

Dorianna, Dorianne, Dorin, Dorina, Dorriane

Dorinda (Spanish) a form of Dora.

Doris (Greek) sea. Mythology: wife of Nereus and mother of the Nereids or sea nymphs.
Dori, Dorice, Dorisa, Dorise, Dorris, Dorrise, Dorrys, Dory, Dorys

Dorothea (Greek) a form of Dorothy. See also Thea.
Dorethea, Dorotea, Doroteya, Dorotha, Dorothia, Dorotthea, Dorthea, Dorthia

Dorothy (Greek) gift of God. See also Dasha, Dodie, Lolotea, Theodora.
Dasya, Do, Doa, Doe, Dolly, Doortje, Dorathy, Dordei, Dordi, Doretta, Dori, Dorika, Doritha, Dorka, Dorle, Dorlisa, Doro, Dorolice, Dorosia, Dorota, Dorothea, Dorothee, Dorothi, Dorothie, Dorottya, Dorte, Dortha, Dorthy, Dory, Dosi, Dossie, Dosya, Dottie

Dorrit (Greek) dwelling. (Hebrew) generation.
Dorit, Dorita, Doritt

Dottie, Dotty (Greek) familiar forms of Dorothy.
Dot, Dottee

Drew (Greek) courageous; strong. (Latin) a short form of Drusilla.
Dru, Drue

Drinka (Spanish) a form of Alexandria.
Dreena, Drena, Drina

Drusi (Latin) a short form of Drusilla.
Drucey, Druci, Drucie, Drucy, Drusey, Drusie, Drusy

Drusilla (Latin) descendant of Drusus, the strong one. See also Drew.
Drewsila, Drucella, Drucill, Drucilla, Druscilla, Druscille, Drusi

Dulce (Latin) sweet.
Delcina, Delcine, Douce, Doucie, Dulcea, Dulcey, Dulci, Dulcia, Dulciana, Dulcibel, Dulcibella, Dulcie, Dulcine, Dulcinea, Dulcy, Dulse, Dulsea

Dulcinea (Spanish) sweet. Literature: Don Quixote's love interest.

Duscha (Russian) soul; sweetheart; term of endearment.
Duschah, Dusha, Dushenka

Dusti, Dusty (English) familiar forms of Dustine.
Dustee, Dustie

Dustine (German) valiant fighter. (English) brown rock quarry.
Dusteena, Dusti, Dustin, Dustina, Dustyn

Dyamond, Dymond (Latin) forms of Diamond.
Dyamin, Dyamon, Dyamone, Dymin, Dymon, Dymonde, Dymone, Dymonn

Dyana (Latin) a form of Diana. (Native American) deer.
Dyan, Dyane, Dyani, Dyann, Dyanna, Dyanne

Dylan (Welsh) sea.
Dylaan, Dylaina, Dylana, Dylane, Dylanee, Dylanie, Dylann, Dylanna, Dylen, Dylin, Dyllan, Dylynn

Dyllis (Welsh) sincere.
Dilys, Dylis, Dylys

Dynasty (Latin) powerful ruler.
Dynastee, Dynasti, Dynastie

Dyshawna (American) a combination of the prefix Dy + Shawna.
Dyshanta, Dyshawn, Dyshonda, Dyshonna

Earlene (Irish) pledge. (English) noblewoman.
Earla, Earlean, Earlecia, Earleen, Earlena, Earlina, Earlinda, Earline, Erla, Erlana, Erlene, Erlenne, Erlina, Erlinda, Erline, Erlisha

Eartha (English) earthy.
Ertha

Easter (English) Easter time. History: a name for a child born on Easter.
Eastan, Eastlyn, Easton

Ebone, Ebonee (Greek) forms of Ebony.
Abonee, Ebanee, Eboné, Ebonea, Ebonne, Ebonnee

Eboni, Ebonie (Greek) forms of Ebony.
Ebanie, Ebeni, Ebonni, Ebonnie

Ebony (Greek) a hard, dark wood.
Abony, Eban, Ebanie, Ebany, Ebbony, Ebone, Eboney, Eboni, Ebonie, Ebonique, Ebonisha, Ebonye, Ebonyi

Echo (Greek) repeated sound. Mythology: the nymph who pined for the love of Narcissus until only her voice remained.
Echoe, Ecko, Ekko, Ekkoe

Eda (Irish, English) a short form of Edana, Edith.

Edana (Irish) ardent; flame.
Eda, Edan, Edanna

Edda (German) a form of Hedda.
Etta

Eddy (American) a familiar form of Edwina.
Eady, Eddi, Eddie, Edy

Edeline (English) noble; kind.
Adeline, Edelyne, Ediline, Edilyne

Eden (Babylonian) a plain. (Hebrew) delightful. Bible: the earthly paradise.
Eaden, Ede, Edena, Edene, Edenia, Edin, Edyn

Edie (English) a familiar form of Edith.
Eadie, Edi, Edy, Edye, Eyde, Eydie

Edith (English) rich gift. See also Dita.
Eadith, Eda, Ede, Edetta, Edette, Edie, Edit, Edita, Edite, Editha, Edithe, Editta, Ediva, Edyta, Edyth, Edytha, Edythe

Edna (Hebrew) rejuvenation. Religion: the wife of Enoch, according to the Book of Enoch.
Adna, Adnisha, Ednah, Edneisha, Edneshia, Ednisha, Ednita, Edona

Edrianna (Greek) a form of Adrienne.
Edria, Edriana, Edrina

Edwina (English) prosperous friend. See also Winnie.
Eddy, Edina, Edweena, Edwena, Edwine, Edwyna, Edwynn

Effia (Ghanaian) born on Friday.

Effie (Greek) spoken well of. (English) a short form of Alfreda, Euphemia.
Effi, Effia, Effy, Ephie

Eileen (Irish) a form of Helen. See also Aileen, Ilene.
Eilean, Eileena, Eileene, Eilena, Eilene, Eiley, Eilie, Eilieh, Eilina, Eiline, Eilleen, Eillen, Eilyn, Eleen, Elene

Ekaterina (Russian) a form of Katherine.
Ekaterine, Ekaterini

Ela (Polish) a form of Adelaide.

Elaina (French) a form of Helen.
Elainea, Elainia, Elainna

Elaine (French) a form of Helen. See also Lainey, Laine.
Eilane, Elain, Elaina, Elaini, Elan, Elana, Elane, Elania, Elanie, Elanit, Elauna, Elayna, Ellaine

Elana (Greek) a short form of Eleanor. See also Ilana, Lana.
Elan, Elanee, Elaney, Elani, Elania, Elanie, Elanna, Elanni

Elayna (French) a form of Elaina.
Elayn, Elaynah, Elayne, Elayni

Elberta (English) a form of Alberta.
Elbertha, Elberthina, Elberthine, Elbertina, Elbertine

Eldora (Spanish) golden, gilded.
Eldoree, Eldorey, Eldori, Eldoria, Eldorie, Eldory

Eleanor (Greek) light. History: Anna Eleanor Roosevelt was a U. S. delegate to the United Nations, a writer, and the thirty-second First Lady of the United States. See also Elana, Ella, Ellen, Leanore, Lena, Lenore, Leonore, Leora, Nellie, Nora, Noreen.
Elana, Elanor, Elanore, Eleanora, Eleanore, Elena, Eleni, Elenor, Elenorah, Elenore, Eleonor, Eleonore, Elianore, Elinor, Elinore, Elladine, Ellenor, Ellie, Elliner, Ellinor, Ellinore, Elna, Elnore, Elynor, Elynore

Eleanora (Greek) a form of Eleanor. See also Lena.
Elenora, Eleonora, Elianora, Ellenora, Ellenorah, Elnora, Elynora

Electra (Greek) shining; brilliant. Mythology: the daughter of Agamemnon, leader of the Greeks in the Trojan War.
Elektra

Elena (Greek) a form of Eleanor. (Italian) a form of Helen.
Eleana, Eleen, Eleena, Elen, Elene, Elenitsa, Elenka, Elenna, Elenoa, Elenola, Elina, Ellena, Lena

Eleni (Greek) a familiar form of Eleanor.
Elenie, Eleny

Eleora (Hebrew) the Lord is my light.
Eliora, Elira, Elora

Elexis (Greek) a form of Alexis.
Elexas, Elexes, Elexess, Elexeya, Elexia, Elexiah

Elexus (Greek) a form of Alexius, Alexus.
Elexius, Elexsus, Elexxus, Elexys

Elfrida (German) peaceful. See also Freda.
Elfrea, Elfreda, Elfredda, Elfreeda, Elfreyda, Elfrieda, Elfryda

Elga (Norwegian) pious. (German) a form of Helga.
Elgiva

Elia (Hebrew) a short form of Eliana.
Eliah

Eliana (Hebrew) my God has answered me. See also Iliana.
Elia, Eliane, Elianna, Ellianna, Liana, Liane

Eliane (Hebrew) a form of Eliana.
Elianne, Elliane, Ellianne

Elicia (Hebrew) a form of Elisha. See also Alicia.
Elecia, Elica, Elicea, Elicet, Elichia, Eliscia, Elisia, Elissia, Ellecia, Ellicia

Elida, Elide (Latin) forms of Alida.
Elidee, Elidia, Elidy

Elisa (Spanish, Italian, English) a short form of Elizabeth. See also Alisa, Ilisa.
Elecea, Eleesa, Elesa, Elesia, Elisia, Elisya, Ellisa, Ellisia, Ellissa, Ellissia, Ellissya, Ellisya, Elysa, Elysia, Elyssia, Elyssya, Elysya, Lisa

Elisabeth (Hebrew) a form of Elizabeth.
Elisabet, Elisabeta, Elisabethe, Elisabetta, Elisabette, Elisabith, Elisebet, Elisheba, Elisheva

Elise (French, English) a short form of
Elizabeth, Elysia. See also Ilise, Liese,
Lisette, Lissie.
*Eilis, Eilise, Elese, Élise, Elisee, Elisie,
Elisse, Elizé, Ellice, Ellise, Ellyce, Ellyse,
Ellyze, Elsey, Elsie, Elsy, Elyce, Elyci,
Elyse, Elyze, Lisel, Lisl, Lison*

Elisha (Hebrew) consecrated to God.
(Greek) a form of Alisha. See also
Ilisha, Lisha.
*Eleacia, Eleasha, Eleesha, Eleisha, Elesha,
Eleshia, Eleticia, Elicia, Elishah, Elisheva,
Elishia, Elishua, Eliska, Ellesha, Ellexia,
Ellisha, Elsha, Elysha, Elyshia*

Elissa, Elyssa (Greek, English) forms
of Elizabeth. Short forms of Melissa.
See also Alissa, Alyssa, Lissa.
Elissah, Ellissa, Ellyssa, Ilissa, Ilyssa

Elita (Latin, French) chosen. See also
Lida, Lita.
*Elitia, Elitia, Elitie, Ellita, Ellitia, Ellitie,
Ilida, Ilita, Litia*

Eliza (Hebrew) a short form of
Elizabeth. See also Aliza.
Eliz, Elizaida, Elizalina, Elize, Elizea

Elizabet (Hebrew) a form of Elizabeth.
Elizabete, Elizabette

Elizabeth (Hebrew) consecrated to
God. Bible: the mother of John the
Baptist. See also Bess, Beth, Betsy,
Betty, Elsa, Ilse, Libby, Liese, Liesel,
Lisa, Lisbeth, Lisette, Lissa, Lissie, Liz,
Liza, Lizabeta, Lizabeth, Lizbeth,
Lizina, Lizzy, Veta, Yelisabeta, Zizi.
*Alizabeth, Eliabeth, Elisa, Elisabeth,
Elise, Elissa, Eliza, Elizabee, Elizabet,
Elizaveta, Elizebeth, Elka, Elsabeth,*

*Elsbeth, Elschen, Elspeth, Elysabeth,
Elzbieta, Elzsébet, Helsa, Ilizzabet, Lusa*

Elizaveta (Polish, English) a form of
Elizabeth.
*Elisavet, Elisaveta, Elisavetta, Elisveta,
Elizavet, Elizavetta, Elizveta, Elsveta,
Elzveta*

Elka (Polish) a form of Elizabeth.
Ilka

Elke (German) a form of Adelaide,
Alice.
Elki, Ilki

Ella (English) elfin; beautiful fairy-
woman. (Greek) a short form of
Eleanor.
Ellah, Ellamae, Ellia, Ellie

Elle (Greek) a short form of Eleanor.
(French) she.
El, Ele, Ell

Ellen (English) a form of Eleanor,
Helen.
*Elen, Elenee, Eleny, Elin, Elina, Elinda,
Ellan, Ellena, Ellene, Ellie, Ellin, Ellon,
Ellyn, Ellynn, Ellynne, Elyn*

Ellice (English) a form of Elise.
Ellecia, Ellyce, Elyce

Ellie, Elly (English) short forms of
Eleanor, Ella, Ellen.
Ele, Elie, Ellee, Elleigh, Elli

Elma (Turkish) sweet fruit.

Elmira (Arabic, Spanish) a form of
Almira.
Elmeera, Elmera, Elmeria, Elmyra

Elnora (American) a combination of
Ella + Nora.

Elodie (American) a form of Melody.
(English) a form of Alodie.
Elodee, Elodia, Elody

Eloise (French) a form of Louise.
Elois, Eloisa, Eloisia

Elora (American) a short form of
Elnora.
Ellora, Elloree, Elorie

Elsa (German) noble. (Hebrew) a
short form of Elizabeth. See also Ilse.
Ellsa, Ellse, Else, Elsia, Elsie, Elsje

Elsbeth (German) a form of Elizabeth.
Elsbet, Elzbet, Elzbieta

Elsie (German) a familiar form of Elsa,
Helsa.
Ellsie, Ellsie, Ellsy, Elsi, Elsy

Elspeth (Scottish) a form of Elizabeth.
Elspet, Elspie

Elva (English) elfin. See also Alva,
Alvina.
Elvia, Elvie

Elvina (English) a form of Alvina.
Elvenea, Elvinea, Elvinia, Elvinna

Elvira (Latin) white; blond. (German)
closed up. (Spanish) elfin. Geography:
the town in Spain that hosted a
Catholic synod in 300 A.D.
Elva, Elvera, Elvire, Elwira, Vira

Elyse (Latin) a form of Elysia.
Ellysa, Ellyse, Elyce, Elys, Elysee, Elysse

Elysia (Greek) sweet; blissful.
Mythology: Elysium was the
dwelling place of happy souls.
*Elise, Elishia, Ellicia, Elycia, Elyssa,
Ilysha, Ilysia*

Elyssa (Latin) a form of Elysia.
Ellyssa

Emalee (Latin) a form of Emily.
Emaili, Emalea, Emaleigh, Emali,
Emalia, Emalie

Emani (Arabic) a form of Iman.
Eman, Emane, Emaneé, Emanie, Emann

Emanuelle (Hebrew) a form of
Emmanuelle.
Emanual, Emanuel, Emanuela,
Emanuella

Ember (French) a form of Amber.
Emberlee, Emberly

Emelia, Emelie (Latin) forms of
Emily.
Emellie

Emely (Latin) a form of Emily.
Emelly

Emerald (French) bright green gemstone.
Emelda, Esmeralda

Emery (German) industrious leader.
Emeri, Emerie

Emilee, Emilie (English) forms of
Emily.
Emile, Emilea, Emileigh, Émilie,
Emiliee, Emillee, Emillie, Emmélie,
Emmilee, Emylee

Emilia (Italian) a form of Amelia,
Emily.
Emalia, Emelia, Emila

Emily (Latin) flatterer. (German)
industrious. See also Amelia, Emma,
Millie.
Eimile, Em, Emaily, Emalee, Emeli,

Emelia, Emelie, Emelita, Emely, Emilee,
Emiley, Emili, Emilia, Emilie, Émilie,
Emilis, Emilka, Emillie, Emilly,
Emmaline, Emmaly, Emmélie, Emmey,
Emmi, Emmie, Emmilly, Emmily,
Emmy, Emmye, Emyle

Emilyann (American) a combination
of Emily + Ann.
Emileane, Emileann, Emileanna,
Emileanne, Emiliana, Emiliann,
Emilianna, Emilianne, Emillyane,
Emillyann, Emillyanna, Emillyanne,
Emliana, Emliann, Emlianna, Emlianne

Emma (German) a short form of
Emily. See also Amy.
Em, Ema, Emmah, Emmy

Emmalee (American) a combination
of Emma + Lee. A form of Emily.
Emalea, Emalee, Emilee, Emmalea,
Emmalei, Emmaleigh, Emmaley,
Emmali, Emmalia, Emmalie, Emmaliese,
Emmalyse, Emylee

Emmaline (French) a form of Emily.
Emalina, Emaline, Emelina, Emeline,
Emilienne, Emilina, Emiline, Emmalina,
Emmalene, Emmeline, Emmiline

Emmalynn (American) a combination
of Emma + Lynn.
Emelyn, Emelyne, Emelynne, Emilyn,
Emilynn, Emilynne, Emlyn, Emlynn,
Emlynne, Emmalyn, Emmalynne

Emmanuelle (Hebrew) God is with us.
Emanuelle, Emmanuela, Emmanuella

Emmy (German) a familiar form of
Emma.
Emi, Emie, Emiy, Emmi, Emmie,
Emmye, Emy

Emmylou (American) a combination
of Emmy + Lou.
Emlou, Emmalou, Emmelou, Emmilou,
Emylou

Ena (Irish) a form of Helen.
Enna

Enid (Welsh) life; spirit.

Enrica (Spanish) a form of Henrietta.
See also Rica.
Enrieta, Enrietta, Enrika, Enriqua,
Enriqueta, Enriquetta, Enriquette

Eppie (English) a familiar form of
Euphemia.
Effie, Effy, Eppy

Erica (Scandinavian) ruler of all.
(English) brave ruler. See also Arica,
Rica, Ricki.
Ericca, Ericha, Ericka, Errica

Ericka, Erika (Scandanavian) forms of
Erica.
Erickah, Erikaa, Erikah, Erikka,
Erricka, Errika, Eyka, Erykka, Eyrika

Erin (Irish) peace. History: another
name for Ireland. See also Arin.
Earin, Earrin, Eran, Eren, Erena, Erene,
Ereni, Eri, Erian, Erina, Erine, Erinetta,
Erinn, Errin, Eryn

Erinn (Irish) a form of Erin.
Erinna, Erinne

Erma (Latin) a short form of Ermine,
Hermina. See also Irma.
Ermelinda

Ermine (Latin) a form of Hermina.
Erma, Ermin, Ermina, Erminda,
Erminia, Erminie

Erna (English) a short form of Ernestine.

Ernestine (English) earnest, sincere.
Erna, Ernaline, Ernesia, Ernesta, Ernestina, Ernesztina

Eryn (Irish) a form of Erin.
Eiryn, Eryne, Erynn, Erynne

Eshe (Swahili) life.
Eisha, Esha

Esmé (French) a familiar form of Esmeralda. A form of Amy.
Esma, Esme, Esmëe

Esmeralda (Greek, Spanish) a form of Emerald.
Emelda, Esmé, Esmerelda, Esmerilda, Esmiralda, Ezmerelda, Ezmirilda

Esperanza (Spanish) hope. See also Speranza.
Esparanza, Espe, Esperance, Esperans, Esperansa, Esperanta, Esperanz, Esperenza

Essence (Latin) life; existence.
Essa, Essenc, Essencee, Essences, Essenes, Essense, Essynce

Essie (English) a short form of Estelle, Esther.
Essa, Essey, Essie, Essy

Estee (English) a short form of Estelle, Esther.
Esta, Estée, Esti

Estefani, Estefania, Estefany (Spanish) forms of Stephanie.
Estafania, Estefana, Estefane, Estefanie

Estelle (French) a form of Esther. See also Stella, Trella.
Essie, Estee, Estel, Estela, Estele, Esteley, Estelina, Estelita, Estell, Estella, Estellina, Estellita, Esthella

Estephanie (Spanish) a form of Stephanie.
Estephania, Estephani, Estephany

Esther (Persian) star. Bible: the Jewish captive whom Ahasuerus made his queen. See also Hester.
Essie, Estee, Ester, Esthur, Eszter, Eszti

Estrella (French) star.
Estrela, Estrelinha, Estrell, Estrelle, Estrellita

Ethana (Hebrew) strong; firm.

Ethel (English) noble.
Ethelda, Ethelin, Etheline, Ethelle, Ethelyn, Ethelynn, Ethelynne, Ethyl

Étoile (French) star.

Etta (German) little. (English) a short form of Henrietta.
Etka, Etke, Etti, Ettie, Etty, Itke, Itta

Eudora (Greek) honored gift. See also Dora.

Eugenia (Greek) born to nobility. See also Gina.
Eugenie, Eugenina, Eugina, Evgenia

Eugenie (Greek) a form of Eugenia.
Eugenee, Eugénie

Eulalia (Greek) well spoken. See also Ula.
Eula, Eulalee, Eulalie, Eulalya, Eulia

Eun (Korean) silver.

Eunice (Greek) happy; victorious. Bible: the mother of Saint Timothy.
See also Unice.
Euna, Eunique, Eunise, Euniss

Euphemia (Greek) spoken well of, in good repute. History: a fourth-century Christian martyr.
Effam, Effie, Eppie, Eufemia, Euphan, Euphemie, Euphie

Eurydice (Greek) wide, broad. Mythology: the wife of Orpheus.
Euridice, Euridyce, Eurydyce

Eustacia (Greek) productive. (Latin) stable; calm. See also Stacey.
Eustasia

Eva (Greek) a short form of Evangelina. (Hebrew) a form of Eve. See also Ava, Chava.
Éva, Evah, Evalea, Evalee, Evike

Evaline (French) a form of Evelyn.
Evalin, Evalina, Evalyn, Evalynn, Eveleen, Evelene, Evelina, Eveline

Evangelina (Greek) bearer of good news.
Eva, Evangelene, Evangelia, Evangelica, Evangeline, Evangelique, Evangelyn, Evangelynn

Evania (Irish) young warrior.
Evan, Evana, Evanka, Evann, Evanna, Evanne, Evany, Eveania, Evvanne, Evvunea, Evyan

Eve (Hebrew) life. Bible: the first woman created by God. (French) a short form of Evonne. See also Chava, Hava, Naeva, Vica, Yeva.
Eva, Evie, Evita, Evuska, Evyn, Ewa, Yeva

Evelin (English) a form of Evelyn.
Evelina, Eveline

Evelyn (English) hazelnut.
Avalyn, Aveline, Evaleen, Evalene, Evaline, Evalyn, Evalynn, Evalynne, Eveleen, Evelin, Evelyna, Evelyne, Evelynn, Evelynne, Evline, Ewalina

Everett (German) courageous as a boar.

Evette (French) a form of Yvette. A familiar form of Evonne. See also Ivette.
Evett

Evie (Hungarian) a form of Eve.
Evey, Evi, Evicka, Evike, Evka, Evuska, Evvie, Evvy, Evy, Ewa

Evita (Spanish) a form of Eve.

Evline (English) a form of Evelyn.
Evleen, Evlene, Evlin, Evlina, Evlyn, Evlynn, Evlynne

Evonne (French) a form of Yvonne. See also Ivonne.
Evanne, Eve, Evenie, Evenne, Eveny, Evette, Evin, Evon, Evona, Evone, Evoni, Evonna, Evonnie, Evony, Evyn, Evynn, Eyona, Eyvone

Ezri (Hebrew) helper; strong.
Ezra, Ezria

Fabia (Latin) bean grower.
Fabiana, Fabienne, Fabiola, Fabra, Fabria

Fabiana (Latin) a form of Fabia.
Fabyana

Fabienne (Latin) a form of Fabia.
Fabian, Fabiann, Fabianne, Fabiene, Fabreanne

Fabiola, Faviola (Latin) forms of Fabia.
Fabiole, Fabyola, Faviana, Faviolha

Faith (English) faithful; fidelity. See also Faye, Fidelity.
Fayth, Faythe

Faizah (Arabic) victorious.

Falda (Icelandic) folded wings.
Faida, Fayda

Faline (Latin) catlike.
Faleen, Falena, Falene, Falin, Falina, Fallyn, Fallyne, Faylina, Fayline, Faylyn, Faylynn, Faylynne, Felenia, Felina

Fallon (Irish) grandchild of the ruler.
Falan, Falen, Fallan, Fallen, Fallonne, Falon, Falyn, Falynn, Falynne, Phalon

Fancy (French) betrothed. (English) whimsical; decorative.
Fanchette, Fanchon, Fanci, Fancia, Fancie

Fannie, Fanny (American) familiar forms of Frances.
Fan, Fanette, Fani, Fania, Fannee, Fanney, Fanni, Fannia, Fany, Fanya

Fantasia (Greek) imagination.
Fantasy, Fantasya, Fantaysia, Fantazia, Fiantasi

Farah, Farrah (English) beautiful; pleasant.
Fara, Farra, Fayre

Faren, Farren (English) wanderer.
Faran, Fare, Farin, Faron, Farrahn, Farran, Farrand, Farrin, Farron, Farryn, Farye, Faryn, Feran, Ferin, Feron, Ferran, Ferren, Ferrin, Ferron, Ferryn

Fatima (Arabic) daughter of the Prophet. History: the daughter of Muhammad.
Fatema, Fathma, Fatimah, Fatime, Fatma, Fatmah, Fatme, Fattim

Fawn (French) young deer.
Faun, Fawna, Fawne

Fawna (French) a form of Fawn.
Fauna, Fawnia, Fawnna

Faye (French) fairy; elf. (English) a form of Faith.
Fae, Fay, Fayann, Fayanna, Fayette, Fayina, Fey

Fayola (Nigerian) lucky.
Fayla, Feyla

Felecia (Latin) a form of Felicia.
Flecia

Felica (Spanish) a short form of Felicia.
Falisa, Felisa, Felisca, Felissa, Feliza

Felice (Latin) a short form of Felicia.
Felece, Felicie, Felise, Felize, Felyce, Felysse

Felicia (Latin) fortunate; happy. See also Lecia, Phylicia.
Falecia, Faleshia, Falicia, Fela, Felecia, Felica, Felice, Felicidad, Feliciona, Felicity, Felicya, Felisea, Felisha, Felisia, Felisiana, Felissya, Felita, Felixia, Felizia, Felka, Fellcia, Felycia, Felysia, Felyssia, Fleasia, Fleichia, Fleishia, Flichia

Felicity (English) a form of Felicia.
Falicity, Felicita, Felicitas, Félicité, Feliciti,
Felisita, Felisity

Felisha (Latin) a form of Felicia.
Faleisha, Falesha, Falisha, Falleshia,
Feleasha, Feleisha, Felesha, Felishia,
Fellishia, Felysha, Flisha

Femi (French) woman. (Nigerian) love
me.
Femie, Femmi, Femmie, Femy

Feodora (Greek) gift of God.
Fedora, Fedoria

Fern (English) fern. (German) a short
form of Fernanda.
Ferne, Ferni, Fernlee, Fernleigh, Fernley,
Fernly

Fernanda (German) daring, adventur-
ous. See also Andee, Nan.
Ferdie, Ferdinanda, Ferdinande, Fern,
Fernande, Fernandette, Fernandina,
Nanda

Fiala (Czech) violet

Fidelia (Latin) a form of Fidelity.
Fidela, Fidele, Fidelina

Fidelity (Latin) faithful, true. See also
Faith.
Fidelia, Fidelita

Fifi (French) a familiar form of
Josephine.
Feef, Feefee, Fifine

Filippa (Italian) a form of Philippa.
Felipa, Filipa, Filippina, Filpina

Filomena (Italian) a form of
Philomena.
Fila, Filah, Filemon

Fiona (Irish) fair, white.
Fionna

Fionnula (Irish) white shouldered. See
also Nola, Nuala.
Fenella, Fenula, Finella, Finola, Finula

Flair (English) style; verve.
Flaire, Flare

Flannery (Irish) redhead. Literature:
Flannery O'Connor was a renowned
American writer.
Flan, Flann, Flanna

Flavia (Latin) blond, golden haired.
Flavere, Flaviar, Flavie, Flavien,
Flavienne, Flaviere, Flavio, Flavyere,
Fulvia

Flavie (Latin) a form of Flavia.
Flavi

Fleur (French) flower.
Fleure, Fleuree, Fleurette

Flo (American) a short form of
Florence.

Flora (Latin) flower. A short form of
Florence. See also Lore.
Fiora, Fiore, Fiorenza, Flor, Florann,
Florella, Florelle, Floren, Floria, Floriana,
Florianna, Florica, Florimel

Florence (Latin) blooming; flowery;
prosperous. History: Florence
Nightingale, a British nurse, is con-
sidered the founder of modern nurs-
ing. See also Florida.
Fiorenza, Flo, Flora, Florance, Florencia,
Florency, Florendra, Florentia, Florentina,
Florentyna, Florenza, Floretta, Florette,
Florie, Florina, Florine, Floris, Flossie

Floria (Basque) a form of Flora.
Flori, Florria

Florida (Spanish) a form of Florence.
Floridia, Florinda, Florita

Florie (English) a familiar form of
Florence.
Flore, Flori, Florri, Florrie, Florry, Flory

Floris (English) a form of Florence.
Florisa, Florise

Flossie (English) a familiar form of
Florence.
Floss, Flossi, Flossy

Fola (Yoruba) honorable.

Fonda (Latin) foundation. (Spanish)
inn.
Fondea, Fonta

Fontanna (French) fountain.
Fontaine, Fontana, Fontane, Fontanne,
Fontayne

Fortuna (Latin) fortune; fortunate.
Fortoona, Fortune

Fran (Latin) a short form of Frances.
Frain, Frann

Frances (Latin) free; from France. See
also Paquita.
Fanny, Fran, Franca, France, Francee,
Francena, Francesca, Francess, Francesta,
Franceta, Francetta, Francette, Francine,
Francis, Francisca, Françoise, Frankie,
Frannie, Franny

Francesca (Italian) a form of Frances.
Franceska, Francessca, Francesta,
Franchesca, Franzetta

Franchesca (Italian) a form of
Francesca.
Cheka, Chekka, Chesca, Cheska,
Francheca, Francheka, Franchelle,
Franchesa, Francheska, Franchessca,
Franchesska

Franci (Hungarian) a familiar form of
Francine.
Francey, Francie, Francy

Francine (French) a form of Frances.
Franceen, Franceine, Franceline, Francene,
Francenia, Franci, Francin, Francina,
Francyne

Francis (Latin) a form of Frances.
Francise, Franncia, Francys

Francisca (Italian) a form of Frances.
Franciska, Franciszka, Frantiska,
Franziska

Françoise (French) a form of Frances.
Frankie (American) a familiar form of
Frances.
Francka, Francki, Franka, Frankey,
Franki, Frankia, Franky, Frankye

Frannie, Franny (English) familiar
forms of Frances.
Frani, Frania, Franney, Franni, Frany

Freda, Freida, Frida (German) short
forms of Alfreda, Elfrida, Frederica,
Sigfreda.
Frayda, Fredda, Fredella, Fredia, Fredra,
Freeda, Freeha, Freia, Frida, Frideborg,
Frieda

Freddi, Freddie (English) familiar
forms of Frederica, Winifred.
Fredda, Freddy, Fredi, Fredia, Fredy, Frici

Frederica (German) peaceful ruler.
See also Alfreda, Rica, Ricki.
Farica, Federica, Freda, Fredalena,
Fredaline, Freddi, Freddie, Frederickina,
Frederika, Frederike, Frederina,
Frederine, Frederique, Fredith, Fredora,
Fredreca, Fredrica, Fredricah, Fredricia,
Freida, Fritzi, Fryderica

Frederika (German) a form of
Frederica.
Fredericka, Fredreka, Fredricka, Fredrika,
Fryderyka

Frederike (German) a form of
Frederica.
Fredericke, Friederike

Frederique (French) a form of
Frederica.
Frédérique, Rike

Freja (Scandinavian) a form of Freya.

Freya (Scandinavian) noblewoman.
Mythology: the Norse goddess of love.
Fraya, Freya

Fritzi (German) a familiar form of
Frederica.
Friezi, Fritze, Fritzie, Fritzinn,
Fritzline, Fritzy

Gabriel, Gabriele (French) forms of
Gabrielle.
Gabbriel, Gabbryel, Gabreal, Gabreale,
Gabreil, Gabrial, Gabryel

Gabriela, Gabriella (Italian) forms of
Gabrielle.
Gabriala, Gabrialla, Gabrielia,
Gabriellia, Gabrila, Gabrilla, Gabryella

Gabrielle (French) devoted to God.
Gabbrielle, Gabielle, Gabrealle,
Gabriana, Gabriel, Gabriela, Gabriele,
Gabriell, Gabriella, Gabrille, Gabrina,
Gabriylle, Gabryell, Gabryelle, Gaby,
Gavriella

Gaby (French) a familiar form of
Gabrielle.
Gabbey, Gabbi, Gabbie, Gabby, Gabey,
Gabi, Gabie, Gavi, Gavy

Gada (Hebrew) lucky.
Gadah

Gaea (Greek) planet Earth.
Mythology: the Greek goddess of
Earth.
Gaia, Gaiea, Gaya

Gaetana (Italian) from Gaeta.
Geography: a city in southern Italy.
Gaetan, Gaétane, Gaetanne

Gagandeep (Sikh) sky's light.
Gagandip, Gagnadeep, Gagndeep

Gail (Hebrew) a short form of
Abigail. (English) merry, lively.
Gael, Gaela, Gaelle, Gaila, Gaile, Gale,
Gayla, Gayle

Gala (Norwegian) singer.
Galla

Galen (Greek) healer; calm. (Irish) lit-
tle and lively.
Gaelen, Gaellen, Galyn, Gaylaine,
Gayleen, Gaylen, Gaylene, Gaylyn

Galena (Greek) healer; calm.

Gali (Hebrew) hill; fountain; spring.
Galice, Galie

Galina (Russian) a form of Helen.
Gailya, Galayna, Galenka, Galia,
Galiana, Galiena, Galinka, Galochka,
Galya, Galyna

Ganesa (Hindi) fortunate. Religion:
Ganesha was the Hindu god of wisdom.

Ganya (Hebrew) garden of the Lord.
(Zulu) clever.
Gana, Gani, Gania, Ganice, Ganit

Gardenia (English) Botany: a sweet-smelling flower.
Deeni, Denia, Gardena, Gardinia

Garland (French) wreath of flowers.

Garnet (English) dark red gem.
Garnetta, Garnette

Garyn (English) spear carrier.
Garan, Garen, Garra, Garryn

Gasha (Russian) a familiar form of
Agatha.
Gashka

Gavriella (Hebrew) a form of
Gabrielle.
Gavila, Gavilla, Gavrid, Gavrieela,
Gavriela, Gavrielle, Gavrila, Gavrilla

Gay (French) merry.
Gae, Gai, Gaye

Gayle (English) a form of Gail.
Gayla

Gayna (English) a familiar form of
Guinevere.
Gaynah, Gayner, Gaynor

Geela (Hebrew) joyful.
Gela, Gila

Geena (American) a form of Gena.
Geania, Geeana, Geeanna

Gelya (Russian) angelic.

Gema, Gemma (Latin, Italian) jewel,
precious stone. See also Jemma.
Gem, Gemmey, Gemmie, Gemmy

Gemini (Greek) twin.
Gemelle, Gemima, Gemina, Geminine,
Gemmina

Gen (Japanese) spring. A short form of
names beginning with "Gen."

Gena (French) a form of Gina. A short
form of Geneva, Genevieve, Iphigenia.
Geanna, Geena, Geenah, Gen, Genae,
Genah, Genai, Genea, Geneja, Geni,
Genia, Genie

Geneen (Scottish) a form of Jeanine.
Geanine, Geannine, Gen, Genene,
Genine, Gineen, Ginene

Genell (American) a form of Jenelle.

Genesis (Latin) origin; birth.
Genes, Genese, Genesha, Genesia,
Genesiss, Genessa, Genesse, Genessie,
Genessis, Genicis, Genises, Genysis, Yenesis

Geneva (French) juniper tree. A short
form of Genevieve. Geography: a city
in Switzerland.
Geena, Gen, Gena, Geneieve, Geneiva,
Geneive, Geneve, Ginneva, Janeva, Jeaneva,
Jeneva

Genevieve (German, French) a form
of Guinevere. See also Gwendolyn.
Gen, Gena, Genaveeve, Genaveve,
Genavie, Genavieve, Genavive, Geneva,
Geneveve, Genevie, Geneviéve,
Genevievre, Genevive, Genovieve,
Genvieve, Ginette, Gineveve, Ginevieve,
Ginevive, Guinevieve, Guinivive,
Gwenevieve, Gwenivive, Jennavieve

Genevra (French, Welsh) a form of
Guinevere.
Gen, Genever, Genevera, Ginevra

Genice (American) a form of Janice.
Gen, Genece, Geneice, Genesa, Genesee,
Genessia, Genis, Genise

Genita (American) a form of Janita.
Gen, Genet, Geneta

Genna (English) a form of Jenna.
Gen, Gennae, Gennay, Genni, Gennie,
Genny

Gennifer (American) a form of
Jennifer.
Gen, Genifer, Ginnifer

Genovieve (French) a form of
Genevieve.
Genoveva, Genoveve, Genovive

Georgeanna (English) a combination
of Georgia + Anna.
Georgana, Georganna, Georgeana,
Georgiana, Georgianna, Georgyanna,
Giorgianna

Georgeanne (English) a combination
of Georgia + Anne.
Georgann, Georganne, Georgean,
Georgeann, Georgie, Georgyann,
Georgyanne

Georgene (English) a familiar form of Georgia.
Georgeena, Georgeina, Georgena, Georgenia, Georgiena, Georgienne, Georgina, Georgine

Georgette (French) a form of Georgia.
Georgeta, Georgett, Georgetta, Georjetta

Georgia (Greek) farmer. Art: Georgia O'Keeffe was an American painter known especially for her paintings of flowers. Geography: a southern American state; a country in Eastern Europe. See also Jirina, Jorja.
Georgene, Georgette, Georgie, Giorgia

Georgianna (English) a form of Georgeanna.
Georgiana, Georgiann, Georgianne, Georgie, Georgieann, Georgionna

Georgie (English) a familiar form of Georgeanne, Georgia, Georgianna.
Georgi, Georgy, Giorgi

Georgina (English) a form of Georgia.
Georgena, Georgene, Georgine, Giorgina, Jorgina

Geraldine (German) mighty with a spear. See also Dena, Jeraldine.
Geralda, Geraldina, Geraldyna, Geraldyne, Gerhardine, Geri, Gerianna, Gerianne, Gerrilee, Giralda

Geralyn (American) a combination of Geraldine + Lynn.
Geralisha, Geralynn, Gerilyn, Gerrilyn

Gerardo (English) brave spearwoman.
Gerardine

Gerda (Norwegian) protector. (German) a familiar form of Gertrude.
Gerta

Geri (American) a familiar form of Geraldine. See also Jeri.
Gerri, Gerrie, Gerry

Germaine (French) from Germany. See also Jermaine.
Germain, Germana, Germanee, Germani, Germanie, Germaya, Germine

Gertie (German) a familiar form of Gertrude.
Gert, Gertey, Gerti, Gerty

Gertrude (German) beloved warrior. See also Trudy.
Gerda, Gerta, Gertie, Gertina, Gertraud, Gertrud, Gertruda

Gervaise (French) skilled with a spear.

Gessica (Italian) a form of Jessica.
Gesica, Gesika, Gess, Gesse, Gessy

Geva (Hebrew) hill.
Gevah

Ghada (Arabic) young; tender.
Gada

Ghita (Italian) pearly.
Gita

Gianna (Italian) a short form of Giovanna. See also Jianna, Johana.
Geona, Geonna, Giana, Gianella, Gianetta, Gianina, Gianinna, Gianne, Giannee, Giannella, Giannetta, Gianni, Giannie, Giannina, Gianny, Gianoula

Gigi (French) a familiar form of Gilberte.
Geegee, G. G., Giggi

Gilana (Hebrew) joyful.
Gila, Gilah

Gilberte (German) brilliant; pledge; trustworthy. See also Berti.
Gigi, Gilberta, Gilbertina, Gilbertine, Gill

Gilda (English) covered with gold.
Gilde, Gildi, Gildie, Gildy

Gill (Latin, German) a short form of Gilberte, Gillian.
Gili, Gilli, Gillie, Gilly

Gillian (Latin) a form of Jillian.
Gila, Gilana, Gilenia, Gili, Gilian, Gill, Gilliana, Gilliane, Gilliann, Gillianna, Gillianne, Gillie, Gilly, Gillyan, Gillyane, Gillyann, Gillyanne, Gyllian, Lian

Gin (Japanese) silver. A short form of names beginning with "Gin."

Gina (Italian) a short form of Angelina, Eugenia, Regina, Virginia. See also Jina.
Gena, Gin, Ginah, Ginai, Ginna

Ginette (English) a form of Genevieve.
Gin, Ginata, Ginett, Ginetta, Ginnetta, Ginnette

Ginger (Latin) flower; spice. A familiar form of Virginia.
Gin, Ginja, Ginjer, Ginny

Ginia (Latin) a familiar form of Virginia.
Gin

Ginnifer (English) white; smooth; soft. (Welsh) a form of Jennifer.
Gin, Ginifer

Ginny (English) a familiar form of Ginger, Virginia. See also Jin, Jinny.
Gin, Gini, Ginney, Ginni, Ginnie, Giny, Gionni, Gionny

Giordana (Italian) a form of Jordana.

Giorgianna (English) a form of Georgeanna.
Giorgina

Giovanna (Italian) a form of Jane.
Geovana, Geovanna, Geovonna, Giavanna, Giavonna, Giovana, Giovanne, Giovanni, Giovannica, Giovonna, Givonnie, Jeveny

Gisa (Hebrew) carved stone.
Gazit, Gissa

Gisela (German) a form of Giselle.
Gisella, Gissela, Gissella

Giselle (German) pledge; hostage. See also Jizelle.
Ghisele, Gisel, Gisela, Gisele, Geséle, Giseli, Gisell, Gissell, Gisselle, Gizela, Gysell

Gissel, Gisselle (German) forms of Giselle.
Gissell

Gita (Yiddish) good. (Polish) a short form of Margaret.
Gitka, Gitta, Gituska

Gitana (Spanish) gypsy; wanderer.

Gitta (Irish) a short form of Bridget.
Getta

Giulia (Italian) a form of Julia.
Giulana, Giuliana, Giulianna, Giulliana, Guila, Guiliana, Guilietta

Gizela (Czech) a form of Giselle.
Gizel, Gizele, Gizella, Gizelle, Gizi, Giziki, Gizus

Gladis (Irish) a form of Gladys.
Gladi, Gladiz

Gladys (Latin) small sword. (Irish) princess. (Welsh) a form of Claudia.
Glad, Gladis, Gladness, Gladwys, Glady, Gwladys

Glenda (Welsh) a form of Glenna.
Glanda, Glennda, Glynda

Glenna (Irish) valley, glen. See also Glynnis.
Glenda, Glenetta, Glenina, Glenine, Glenn, Glenne, Glennesha, Glennia, Glennie, Glenora, Gleny, Glyn

Glennesha (American) a form of Glenna.
Glenesha, Glenisha, Glennisha, Glennishia

Gloria (Latin) glory. History: Gloria Steinem, a leading American feminist, founded *Ms.* magazine.
Gloresha, Gloriah, Gloribel, Gloriela, Gloriella, Glorielle, Gloris, Glorisha, Glorvina, Glory

Glorianne (American) a combination of Gloria + Anne.
Gloriana, Gloriane, Gloriann, Glorianna

Glory (Latin) a form of Gloria.

Glynnis (Welsh) a form of Glenna.
Glenice, Glenis, Glenise, Glenyse, Glennis, Glennys, Glenwys, Glenys, Glenyss, Glinnis, Glinys, Glynesha, Glynice, Glynis, Glynisha, Glyniss, Glynitra, Glynys, Glynyss

Golda (English) gold. History: Golda Meir was a Russian-born politician who served as prime minister of Israel.
Goldarina, Golden, Goldie, Goldina

Goldie (English) a familiar form of Golda.
Goldi, Goldy

Goma (Swahili) joyful dance.

Grace (Latin) graceful.
Engracia, Graca, Gracia, Gracie, Graciela, Graciella, Gracinha, Graice, Grata, Gratia, Gray, Grayce, Grecia

Graceanne (English) a combination of Grace + Anne.
Graceann, Graceanna, Gracen, Graciana, Gracianna, Gracin, Gratiana

Gracia (Spanish) a form of Grace.
Gracea, Grecia

Gracie (English) a familiar form of Grace.
Gracee, Gracey, Graci, Gracy, Graecie, Graysie

Grant (English) great; giving.

Grayson (English) bailiff's child.
Graison, Graisyn, Grasien, Grasyn, Graysen

Grazia (Latin) a form of Grace.
Graziella, Grazielle, Graziosa, Grazyna

Grecia (Latin) a form of Grace.

Greer (Scottish) vigilant.
Grear, Grier

Greta (German) a short form of
Gretchen, Margaret.
*Greatal, Greatel, Greeta, Gretal, Grete,
Gretel, Gretha, Grethal, Grethe, Grethel,
Gretta, Grette, Grieta, Gryta, Grytta*

Gretchen (German) a form of
Margaret.
Greta, Gretchin, Gretchyn

Gricelda (German) a form of
Griselda.
Gricelle

Grisel (German) a short form of
Griselda.
*Grisell, Griselle, Grissel, Grissele,
Grissell, Grizel*

Griselda (German) gray woman war-
rior. See also Selda, Zelda.
*Gricelda, Grisel, Griseldis, Griseldys,
Griselys, Grishilda, Grishilde, Grisselda,
Grissely, Grizelda*

Guadalupe (Arabic) river of black
stones. See also Lupe.
*Guadalup, Guadelupe, Guadlupe,
Guadulupe, Gudalupe*

Gudrun (Scandinavian) battler. See
also Runa.
Gudren, Gudrin, Gudrinn, Gudruna

Guillerma (Spanish) a short form of
Guillermina.
Guilla, Guillermina

Guinevere (French, Welsh) white
wave; white phantom. Literature: the

wife of King Arthur. See also Gayna,
Genevieve, Genevra, Jennifer,
Winifred, Wynne.
*Generva, Genn, Ginette, Guenevere,
Guenna, Guinivere, Guinna, Gwen,
Gwenevere, Gwenivere, Gwynnevere*

Gunda (Norwegian) female warrior.
Gundala, Gunta

Gurit (Hebrew) innocent baby.

Gurleen (Sikh) follower of the guru.

Gurpreet (Punjabi) religion.
Gurprit

Gusta (Latin) a short form of Augusta.
*Gus, Gussi, Gussie, Gussy, Gusti,
Gustie, Gusty*

Gwen (Welsh) a short form of
Guinevere, Gwendolyn.
*Gwenesha, Gweness, Gweneta,
Gwenetta, Gwenette, Gweni, Gwenisha,
Gwenita, Gwenn, Gwenna, Gwennie,
Gwenny*

Gwenda (Welsh) a familiar form of
Gwendolyn.
Gwinda, Gwynda, Gwynedd

Gwendolyn (Welsh) white wave; white
browed; new moon. Literature:
Gwendoloena was the wife of
Merlin, the magician. See also
Genevieve, Gwyneth, Wendy.
*Guendolen, Gwen, Gwendalin, Gwenda,
Gwendalee, Gwendaline, Gwendalyn,
Gwendalynn, Gwendela, Gwendelyn,
Gwendelynn, Gwendilyn, Gwendolen,
Gwendolene, Gwendolin, Gwendoline,
Gwendolyne, Gwendolynn,*

*Gwendolynne, Gwendylan, Gwyndolyn,
Gwynndolen*

Gwyn (Welsh) a short form of
Gwyneth.
Gwinn, Gwinne, Gwynn, Gwynne

Gwyneth (Welsh) a form of
Gwendolyn. See also Winnie, Wynne.
*Gweneth, Gwenith, Gwenneth,
Gwennyth, Gwenyth, Gwyn, Gwynneth*

Gypsy (English) wanderer.
Gipsy, Gypsie, Jipsi

H

Habiba (Arabic) beloved.
Habibah, Habibeh

Hachi (Japanese) eight; good luck.
Hachiko, Hachiyo

Hadara (Hebrew) adorned with beauty.
Hadarah

Hadassah (Hebrew) myrtle tree.
*Hadas, Hadasah, Hadassa, Haddasa,
Haddasah*

Hadiya (Swahili) gift.
Hadaya, Hadia, Hadiyah, Hadiyyah

Hadley (English) field of heather.
*Hadlea, Hadlee, Hadleigh, Hadli,
Hadlie, Hadly*

Hadriane (Greek, Latin) a form of
Adrienne.
*Hadriana, Hadrianna, Hadrianne,
Hadriene, Hadrienne*

Haeley (English) a form of Hailey.
Haelee, Haeleigh, Haeli, Haelie,
Haelleigh, Haelli, Haellie, Haely

Hagar (Hebrew) forsaken; stranger.
Bible: Sarah's handmaiden, the
mother of Ishmael.
Haggar

Haidee (Greek) modest.
Hady, Haide, Haidi, Haidy, Haydee,
Haydy

Haiden (English) heather-covered hill.
Haden, Hadyn, Haeden, Haidn, Haidyn

Hailee (English) a form of Hayley.
Haile, Hailei, Haileigh, Haillee

Hailey (English) a form of Hayley.
Haeley, Haiely, Hailea, Hailley, Hailly,
Haily

Haili, Hailie (English) forms of
Hayley.
Haille, Hailli, Haillie

Haldana (Norwegian) half-Danish.

Halee (English) a form of Haley.
Hale, Halea, Haleah, Haleh, Halei

Haleigh (English) a form of Haley.

Haley (Scandinavian) heroine. See also
Hailey, Hayley.
Halee, Haleigh, Hali, Halley, Hallie,
Haly, Halye

Hali, Halie (English) forms of Haley.
Haliegh

Halia (Hawaiian) in loving memory.

Halimah (Arabic) gentle; patient.
Halima, Halime

Halina (Hawaiian) likeness. (Russian) a
form of Helen.
Haleen, Haleena, Halena, Halinka

Halla (African) unexpected gift.
Hala, Hallah, Halle

Halley (English) a form of Haley.
Hally, Hallye

Hallie (Scandinavian) a form of Haley.
Hallee, Hallei, Halleigh, Halli

Halona (Native American) fortunate.
Halonah, Haloona, Haona

Halsey (English) Hall's island.
Halsea, Halsie

Hama (Japanese) shore.

Hana, Hanah (Japanese) flower.
(Arabic) happiness. (Slavic) forms of
Hannah.
Hanae, Hanan, Haneen, Hanicka,
Hanin, Hanita, Hanka

Hanako (Japanese) flower child.

Hania (Hebrew) resting place.
Haniya, Hanja, Hannia, Hanniah,
Hanya

Hanna (Hebrew) a form of Hannah.

Hannah (Hebrew) gracious. Bible: the
mother of Samuel. See also Anci,
Anezka, Ania, Anka, Ann, Anna,
Annalie, Anneka, Chana, Nina, Nusi.
Hana, Hanna, Hanneke, Hannele,
Hanni, Hannon, Honna

Hanni (Hebrew) a familiar form of
Hannah.
Hani, Hanne, Hannie, Hanny

Happy (English) happy.
Happi

Hara (Hindi) tawny. Religion: another
name for the Hindu god Shiva, the
destroyer.

Harlee, Harleigh, Harlie (English)
forms of Harley.
Harlei, Harli

Harley (English) meadow of the hare.
See also Arleigh.
Harlee, Harleey, Harly

Harleyann (English) a combination of
Harley + Ann.
Harlann, Harlanna, Harlanne, Harleen,
Harlene, Harleyanna, Harleyanne,
Harliann, Harlianna, Harlianne,
Harlina, Harline

Harmony (Latin) harmonious.
Harmene, Harmeni, Harmon, Harmonee,
Harmonei, Harmoni, Harmonia,
Harmonie

Harpreet (Punjabi) devoted to God.
Harprit

Harriet (French) ruler of the household. (English) a form of Henrietta.
Literature: Harriet Beecher Stowe
was an American writer noted for
her novel *Uncle Tom's Cabin.*
Harri, Harrie, Harriett, Harrietta,
Harriette, Harriot, Harriott, Hattie

Haru (Japanese) spring.

Hasana (Swahili) she arrived first.
Culture: a name used for the first-
born female twin. See also Huseina.
Hasanna, Hasna, Hassana, Hassna,
Hassona

Hasina (Swahili) good.
Haseena, Hasena, Hassina

Hateya (Moquelumnan) footprints.

Hattie (English) familiar forms of Harriet, Henrietta.
Hatti, Hatty, Hetti, Hettie, Hetty

Hausu (Moquelumnan) like a bear yawning upon awakening.

Hava (Hebrew) a form of Chava. See also Eve.
Havah, Havvah

Haven (English) a form of Heaven.
Havan, Havana, Havanna, Havannah, Havyn

Haviva (Hebrew) beloved.
Havalee, Havelah, Havi, Hayah

Hayden (English) a form of Haiden.
Hayde, Haydin, Haydn, Haydon

Hayfa (Arabic) shapely.

Haylee, Hayleigh, Haylie (English) forms of Hayley.
Hayle, Haylea, Haylei, Hayli, Haylle, Hayllie

Hayley (English) hay meadow. See also Hailey, Haley.
Hailee, Haili, Haylee, Hayly

Hazel (English) hazelnut tree; commanding authority.
Hazal, Hazaline, Haze, Hazeline, Hazell, Hazelle, Hazen, Hazyl

Heather (English) flowering heather.
Heath, Heatherlee, Heatherly

Heaven (English) place of beauty and happiness. Bible: where God and angels are said to dwell.
Haven, Heavan, Heavenly, Heavin, Heavon, Heavyn, Hevean, Heven, Hevin

Hedda (German) battler. See also Edda, Hedy.
Heda, Hedaya, Hedia, Hedvick, Hedvig, Hedvika, Hedwig, Hedwiga, Heida, Hetta

Hedy (Greek) delightful; sweet. (German) a familiar form of Hedda.
Heddey, Heddi, Heddie, Heddy, Hede, Hedi

Heidi, Heidy (German) short forms of Adelaide.
Heida, Heide, Heidee, Heidie, Heydy, Hidee, Hidi, Hidie, Hidy, Hiede, Hiedi, Hydi

Helen (Greek) light. See also Aileen, Aili, Alena, Eileen, Elaina, Elaine, Eleanor, Ellen, Galina, Ila, Ilene, Ilona, Jelena, Leanore, Leena, Lelya, Lenci, Lene, Liolya, Nellie, Nitsa, Olena, Onella, Yalena, Yelena.
Elana, Ena, Halina, Hela, Hele, Helena, Helene, Helle, Hellen, Helli, Hellin, Hellon, Hellyn, Helon

Helena (Greek) a form of Helen. See also Ilena.
Halena, Halina, Helaina, Helana, Helania, Helayna, Heleana, Heleena, Helenia, Helenka, Helenna, Helina, Hellanna, Hellena, Hellenna, Helona, Helonna

Helene (French) a form of Helen.
Helaine, Helanie, Helayne, Heleen, Heleine, Hélène, Helenor, Heline, Hellenor

Helga (German) pious. (Scandinavian) a form of Olga. See also Elga.

Helki (Native American) touched.
Helkey, Helkie, Helky

Helma (German) a short form of Wilhelmina.
Halma, Helme, Helmi, Helmine, Hilma

Heloise (French) a form of Louise.
Héloïse, Hlois

Helsa (Danish) a form of Elizabeth.
Helse, Helsey, Helsi, Helsie, Helsy

Heltu (Moquelumnan) like a bear reaching out.

Henna (English) a familiar form of Henrietta.
Hena, Henaa, Henah, Heni, Henia, Henny, Henya

Henrietta (English) ruler of the household. See also Enrica, Etta, Yetta.
Harriet, Hattie, Hatty, Hendrika, Heneretta, Henka, Henna, Hennrietta, Hennriette, Henretta, Henrica, Henrie, Henrieta, Henriete, Henriette, Henrika, Henrique, Henriquetta, Henryetta, Hetta, Hettie

Hera (Greek) queen; jealous. Mythology: the queen of heaven and the wife of Zeus.

Hermia (Greek) messenger.

Hermina (Latin) noble. (German) soldier. See also Erma, Ermine, Irma.
Herma, Hermenia, Hermia, Herminna

Hermione (Greek) earthy.
Hermalina, Hermia, Hermina, Hermine, Herminia

Hermosa (Spanish) beautiful.

Hertha (English) child of the earth.
Heartha, Hirtha

Hester (Dutch) a form of Esther.
Hessi, Hessie, Hessye, Hesther, Hettie

Hestia (Persian) star. Mythology: the Greek goddess of the hearth and home.
Hestea, Hesti, Hestie, Hesty

Heta (Native American) racer.

Hetta (German) a form of Hedda. (English) a familiar form of Henrietta.

Hettie (German) a familiar form of Henrietta, Hester.
Hetti, Hetty

Hilary, Hillary (Greek) cheerful, merry. See also Alair.
Hilaree, Hilari, Hilaria, Hilarie, Hilery, Hiliary, Hillaree, Hillari, Hillarie, Hilleary, Hilleree, Hilleri, Hillerie, Hillery, Hillianne, Hilliary, Hillory

Hilda (German) a short form of Brunhilda, Hildegarde.
Helle, Hilde, Hildey, Hildie, Hildur, Hildy, Hulda, Hylda

Hildegarde (German) fortress.
Hilda, Hildagard, Hildagarde, Hildegard, Hildred

Hinda (Hebrew) hind; doe.
Hindey, Hindie, Hindy, Hynda

Hisa (Japanese) long lasting.
Hisae, Hisako, Hisay

Hiti (Eskimo) hyena.
Hitty

Hoa (Vietnamese) flower; peace.
Ho, Hoai

Hola (Hopi) seed-filled club.

Holley (English) a form of Holly.
Holleah, Hollee

Holli, Hollie (English) forms of Holly.
Holeigh, Holleigh

Hollis (English) near the holly bushes.
Hollise, Hollyce, Holyce

Holly (English) holly tree.
Holley, Holli, Hollie, Hollye

Hollyann (English) a combination of Holly + Ann.
Holliann, Hollianna, Hollianne, Hollyanne, Hollyn

Hollyn (English) a short form of Hollyann.
Holin, Holeena, Hollina, Hollynn

Honey (English) sweet. (Latin) a familiar form of Honora.
Honalee, Hunney, Hunny

Hong (Vietnamese) pink.

Honora (Latin) honorable. See also Nora, Onora.
Honey, Honner, Honnor, Honnour, Honor, Honorah, Honorata, Honore, Honoree, Honoria, Honorina, Honorine, Honour, Honoure

Hope (English) hope.
Hopey, Hopi, Hopie

Hortense (Latin) gardener. See also Ortensia.
Hortencia, Hortensia

Hoshi (Japanese) star.
Hoshie, Hoshiko, Hoshiyo

Hua (Chinese) flower.

Huata (Moquelumnan) basket carrier.

Hunter (English) hunter.
Hunta, Huntar, Huntter

Huong (Vietnamese) flower.

Huseina (Swahili) a form of Hasana.

Hyacinth (Greek) Botany: a plant with colorful, fragrant flowers. See also Cynthia, Jacinda.
Giacinta, Hyacintha, Hyacinthe, Hyacinthia, Hyacinthie, Hycinth, Hycynth

Hydi, Hydeia (German) forms of Heidi.
Hyde, Hydea, Hydee, Hydia, Hydie, Hydiea

Hye (Korean) graceful.

I

Ian (Hebrew) God is gracious.
Iaian, Iain, Iana, Iann, Ianna, Iannel, Iyana

Ianthe (Greek) violet flower.
Iantha, Ianthia, Ianthina

Icess (Egyptian) a form of Isis.
Ices, Icesis, Icesse, Icey, Icia, Icis, Icy

Ida (German) hard working. (English) prosperous.
Idah, Idaia, Idalia, Idalis, Idaly, Idamae, Idania, Idarina, Idarine, Idaya, Ide, Idelle, Idette, Idys

Idalina (English) a combination of Ida + Lina.
Idaleena, Idaleene, Idalena, Idalene, Idaline

Idalis (English) a form of Ida.
Idalesse, Idalise, Idaliz, Idallas, Idallis, Idelis, Idelys, Idialis

Ideashia (American) a combination of Ida + Iesha.
Idasha, Idaysha, Ideesha, Idesha

Idelle (Welsh) a form of Ida.
Idell, Idella, Idil

Iesha (American) a form of Aisha.
Ieachia, Ieaisha, Ieasha, Ieashe, Ieesha, Ieeshia, Ieisha, Ieishia, Iescha, Ieshah, Ieshea, Iesheia, Ieshia, Iiesha, Iisha

Ignacia (Latin) fiery, ardent.
Ignacie, Ignasha, Ignashia, Ignatia, Ignatzia

Ikia (Hebrew) God is my salvation. (Hawaiian) a form of Isaiah (see Boys' Names).
Ikaisha, Ikea, Ikeea, Ikeia, Ikeisha, Ikeishi, Ikeishia, Ikesha, Ikeshia, Ikeya, Ikeyia, Ikiea, Ikiia

Ila (Hungarian) a form of Helen.

Ilana (Hebrew) tree.
Ilaina, Ilane, Ilani, Ilania, Ilainie, Illana, Illane, Illani, Ilania, Illanie, Ilanit

Ileana (Hebrew) a form of Iliana.
Ilea, Ileah, Ileane, Ileanna, Ileanne, Illeana

Ilena (Greek) a form of Helena.
Ileana, Ileena, Ileina, Ilina, Ilyna

Ilene (Irish) a form of Helen. See also Aileen, Eileen.
Ileen, Ileene, Iline, Ilyne

Iliana (Greek) from Troy.
Ileana, Ili, Ilia, Iliani, Illiana, Illiani, Illianna, Illyana, Illyanna

Ilima (Hawaiian) flower of Oahu.

Ilisa (Scottish, English) a form of Alisa, Elisa.
Ilicia, Ilissa, Iliza, Illisa, Illissa, Illysa, Illyssa, Ilycia, Ilysa, Ilysia, Ilyssa, Ilyza

Ilise (German) a form of Elise.
Ilese, Illytse, Ilyce, Ilyse

Ilisha (Hebrew) a form of Alisha, Elisha. See also Lisha.
Ileshia, Ilishia, Ilysha, Ilyshia

Ilka (Hungarian) a familiar form of Ilona.
Ilke, Milka, Milke

Ilona (Hungarian) a form of Helen.
Ilka, Illona, Illonia, Illonya, Ilonka, Ilyona

Ilse (German) a form of Elizabeth. See also Elsa.
Ilsa, Ilsey, Ilsie, Ilsy

Ima (Japanese) presently. (German) a familiar form of Amelia.

Imala (Native American) strong-minded.

Iman (Arabic) believer.
Aman, Imana, Imane, Imani

Imani (Arabic) a form of Iman.
Amani, Emani, Imahni, Imanie, Imanii, Imonee, Imoni

Imelda (German) warrior.
Imalda, Irmhilde, Melda

Imena (African) dream.
Imee, Imene

Imogene (Latin) image, likeness.
Emogen, Emogene, Imogen, Imogenia, Imojean, Imojeen, Innogen, Innogene

Ina (Irish) a form of Agnes.
Ena, Inanna, Inanne

India (Hindi) from India.
Indea, Indeah, Indee, Indeia, Indeya, Indi, Indiah, Indian, Indiana, Indianna, Indie, Indieya, Indiya, Indy, Indya

Indigo (Latin) dark blue color.
Indiga, Indygo

Indira (Hindi) splendid. History: Indira Nehru Gandhi was an Indian politician and prime minister.
Indiara, Indra, Indre, Indria

Ines, Inez (Spanish) forms of Agnes. See also Ynez.
Inés, Inesa, Inesita, Inésita, Inessa

Inga (Scandinavian) a short form of Ingrid.
Ingaberg, Ingaborg, Inge, Ingeberg, Ingeborg, Ingela

Ingrid (Scandinavian) hero's daughter; beautiful daughter.
Inga, Inger

Inoa (Hawaiian) name.

Ioana (Romanian) a form of Joan.
Ioani, Ioanna

Iola (Greek) dawn; violet colored.
(Welsh) worthy of the Lord.
Iole, Iolee, Iolia

Iolana (Hawaiian) soaring like a hawk.

Iolanthe (English) a form of Yolanda.
See also Jolanda.
Iolanda, Iolande

Iona (Greek) violet flower.
Ione, Ioney, Ioni, Ionia, Iyona, Iyonna

Iphigenia (Greek) sacrifice. Mythology:
the daughter of the Greek leader
Agamemnon. See also Gena.

Irene (Greek) peaceful. Mythology:
the goddess of peace. See also Orina,
Rena, Rene, Yarina.
Irén, Irien, Irina, Jereni

Irina (Russian) a form of Irene.
*Eirena, Erena, Ira, Irana, Iranda, Iranna,
Irena, Irenea, Irenka, Iriana, Irin, Irinia,
Irinka, Irona, Ironka, Irusya, Iryna,
Irynka, Rina*

Iris (Greek) rainbow. Mythology: the
goddess of the rainbow and messenger of the gods.
Irisa, Irisha, Irissa, Irita, Irys, Iryssa

Irma (Latin) a form of Erma.
Irmina, Irminia

Isabeau (French) a form of Isabel.

Isabel (Spanish) consecrated to God.
See also Bel, Belle, Chavella, Ysabel.
Isabal, Isabeau, Isabeli, Isabelita, Isabella,
*Isabelle, Ishbel, Isobel, Issie, Izabel,
Izabele, Izabella*

Isabella (Italian) a form of Isabel.
Isabela, Isabelia, Isabello

Isabelle (French) a form of Isabel.
Isabele, Isabell

Isadora (Latin) gift of Isis.
Isidora

Isela (Scottish) a form of Isla.
Isel

Isha (American) a form of Aisha.
*Ishae, Ishana, Ishanaa, Ishanda, Ishanee,
Ishaney, Ishani, Ishanna, Ishaun,
Ishawna, Ishaya, Ishenda, Ishia, Iysha*

Ishi (Japanese) rock.
Ishiko, Ishiyo, Shiko, Shiyo

Isis (Egyptian) supreme goddess.
Mythology: the goddess of nature
and fertility.
Icess, Issis, Isys

Isla (Scottish) Geography: the River
Isla is in Scotland.
Isela

Isobel (Spanish) a form of Isabel.
Isobell, Isobella, Isobelle

Isoka (Benin) gift from god.
Soka

Isolde (Welsh) fair lady. Literature: a
princess in the Arthurian legends; a
heroine in the medieval romance
Tristan and Isolde. See also Yseult.
Isolda, Isolt, Izolde

Issie (Spanish) a familiar form of
Isabel.
Isa, Issi, Issy, Iza

Ita (Irish) thirsty.

Italia (Italian) from Italy.
Itali, Italie, Italy, Italya

Itamar (Hebrew) palm island.
*Isamar, Isamari, Isamaria, Ithamar,
Ittamar*

Itzel (Spanish) protected.
*Itcel, Itchel, Itesel, Itsel, Itssel, Itza,
Itzallana, Itzayana, Itzell, Ixchel*

Iva (Slavic) a short form of Ivana.
Ivah

Ivana (Slavic) God is gracious. See also
Yvanna.
*Iva, Ivanah, Ivania, Ivanka, Ivanna,
Ivannia, Ivany*

Iverem (Tiv) good fortune; blessing.

Iverna (Latin) from Ireland.
Ivernah

Ivette (French) a form of Yvette. See
also Evette.
Ivet, Ivete, Iveth, Ivetha, Ivett, Ivetta

Ivonne (French) a form of Yvonne.
See also Evonne.
*Ivon, Ivona, Ivone, Ivonna, Iwona,
Iwonka, Iwonna, Iwonne*

Ivory (Latin) made of ivory.
Ivoory, Ivori, Ivorie, Ivorine, Ivree

Ivria (Hebrew) from the land of
Abraham.
Ivriah, Ivrit

Ivy (English) ivy tree.
Ivey, Ivie

Iyabo (Yoruba) mother has returned.

Iyana, Iyanna (Hebrew) forms of Ian.
Iyanah, Iyannah, Iyannia

Izabella (Spanish) a form of Isabel.
Izabela, Izabell, Izabellah, Izabelle, Izobella

Izusa (Native American) white stone.

J

Jabrea, Jabria (American) combinations of the prefix Ja + Brea.
Jabreal, Jabree, Jabreea, Jabreena, Jabrelle, Jabreona, Jabri, Jabriah, Jabriana, Jabrie, Jabriel, Jabrielle, Jabrienna, Jabrina

Jacalyn (American) a form of Jacqueline.
Jacalynn, Jacolyn, Jacolyne, Jacolynn

Jacelyn (American) a form of Jocelyn.
Jaceline, Jacelyne, Jacelynn, Jacilyn, Jacilyne, Jacilynn, Jacylyn, Jacylyne, Jacylynn

Jacey, Jacy (Greek) familiar forms of Jacinda. (American) combinations of the initials J. + C.
Jace, Jac-E, Jacee, Jaci, Jacie, Jacylin, Jaice, Jaicee

Jaci, Jacie (Greek) forms of Jacey.
Jacci, Jacia, Jacie, Jaciel, Jaici, Jaicie

Jacinda, Jacinta (Greek) beautiful, attractive. (Spanish) forms of Hyacinth.
Jacenda, Jacenta, Jacey, Jacinthe, Jacintia, Jacynthe, Jakinda, Jaxine

Jacinthe (Spanish) a form of Jacinda.
Jacinte, Jacinth, Jacintha

Jackalyn (American) a form of Jacqueline.
Jackalene, Jackalin, Jackaline, Jackalynn, Jackalynne, Jackelin, Jackeline, Jackelyn, Jackelynn, Jackelynne, Jackilin, Jackilyn, Jackilynn, Jackilynne, Jackolin, Jackoline, Jackolyn, Jackolynn, Jackolynne

Jackeline, Jackelyn (American) forms of Jacqueline.
Jackelin, Jackelline, Jackellyn, Jockeline

Jacki, Jackie (American) familiar forms of Jacqueline.
Jackee, Jackey, Jackia, Jackielee, Jacky, Jackye

Jacklyn (American) a form of Jacqueline.
Jacklin, Jackline, Jacklyne, Jacklynn, Jacklynne

Jackquel (French) a short form of Jacqueline.
Jackqueline, Jackquetta, Jackquiline, Jackquilyn, Jackquilynn, Jackquilynne

Jaclyn (American) a short form of Jacqueline.
Jacleen, Jaclin, Jacline, Jaclyne, Jaclynn

Jacobi (Hebrew) supplanter, substitute. Bible: Jacob was the son of Isaac, brother of Esau.
Coby, Jacoba, Jacobee, Jacobette, Jacobia, Jacobina, Jacoby, Jacolbi, Jacolbia, Jacolby

Jacqualine (French) a form of Jacqueline.
Jacqualin, Jacqualine, Jacqualyn, Jacqualyne, Jacqualynn

Jacquelin (French) a form of Jacqueline.
Jacquelina

Jacqueline (French) supplanter, substitute; little Jacqui.
Jacalyn, Jackalyn, Jackeline, Jacki, Jacklyn, Jackquel, Jaclyn, Jacqueena, Jacqueine, Jacquel, Jacqueleen, Jacquelene, Jacquelin, Jacquelyn, Jacquelynn, Jacquena, Jacquene, Jacquenetta, Jacquenette, Jacqui, Jacquiline, Jacquine, Jakelin, Jaquelin, Jaqueline, Jaquelyn, Jocqueline

Jacquelyn, Jacquelynn (French) forms of Jacqueline.
Jackquelyn, Jackquelynn, Jacquelyne, Jacquelynne

Jacqui (French) a short form of Jacqueline.
Jacquay, Jacqué, Jacquee, Jacqueta, Jacquete, Jacquetta, Jacquette, Jacquie, Jacquise, Jacquita, Jaquay, Jaqui, Jaquie, Jaquiese, Jaquina, Jaquita

Jacqulin, Jacqulyn (American) forms of Jacqueline.
Jackquilin, Jacqul, Jacqulin, Jacqulyne, Jacqulynn, Jacqulynne, Jacquoline

Jacquiline (French) a form of Jacqueline.
Jacquil, Jacquilin, Jacquilyn, Jacquilyne, Jacquilynn

Jacynthe (Spanish) a form of Jacinda.
Jacynda, Jacynta, Jacynth, Jacyntha

Jada (Spanish) a form of Jade.
Jadah, Jadda, Jadae, Jadzia, Jadziah, Jaeda, Jaedra, Jayda

Jade (Spanish) jade.
Jada, Jadea, Jadeann, Jadee, Jaden, Jadera, Jadi, Jadie, Jadienne, Jady, Jadyn, Jaedra, Jaida, Jaide, Jaiden, Jayde, Jayden

Jadelyn (American) a combination of Jade + Lynn.
Jadalyn, Jadelaine, Jadeline, Jadelyne, Jadelynn, Jadielyn

Jaden (Spanish) a form of Jade.
Jadeen, Jadena, Jadene, Jadeyn, Jadin, Jadine, Jaeden, Jaedine

Jadyn (Spanish) a form of Jade.
Jadynn, Jaedyn, Jaedynn

Jae (Latin) jaybird. (French) a familiar form of Jacqueline.
Jaea, Jaey, Jaya

Jael (Hebrew) mountain goat; climber. See also Yael.
Jaela, Jaelee, Jaeli, Jaelie, Jaelle, Jahla, Jahlea

Jaelyn, Jaelynn (American) combinations of Jae + Lynn.
Jaeleen, Jaelin, Jaelinn, Jaelyn, Jailyn, Jalyn, Jalynn, Jayleen, Jaylyn, Jaylynn, Jaylynne

Jaffa (Hebrew) a form of Yaffa.
Jaffice, Jaffit, Jafit, Jafra

Jaha (Swahili) dignified.
Jahaida, Jahaira, Jaharra, Jahayra, Jahida, Jahira, Jahitza

Jai (Tai) heart. (Latin) a form of Jaye.

Jaida, Jaide (Spanish) forms of Jade.
Jaidah, Jaidan

Jaiden, Jaidyn (Spanish) forms of Jade.
Jaidey, Jaidi, Jaidin, Jaidon

Jailyn (American) a form of Jaelyn.
Jaileen, Jailen, Jailene, Jailin, Jailine

Jaime (French) I love.
Jaima, Jaimee, Jaimey, Jaimie, Jaimini, Jaimme, Jaimy, Jamee

Jaimee (French) a form of Jaime.

Jaimie (French) a form of Jaime.
Jaimi, Jaimmie

Jaira (Spanish) Jehovah teaches.
Jairah, Jairy

Jakeisha (American) a combination of Jakki + Aisha.
Jakeisia, Jakesha, Jakisha

Jakelin (American) a form of Jacqueline.
Jakeline, Jakelyn, Jakelynn, Jakelynne

Jakki (American) a form of Jacki.
Jakala, Jakea, Jakeela, Jakeida, Jakeita, Jakela, Jakelia, Jakell, Jakena, Jaketta, Jakevia, Jaki, Jakia, Jakiah, Jakira, Jakita, Jakiya, Jakiyah, Jakke, Jakkia

Jaleesa (American) a form of Jalisa.
Jaleasa, Jalece, Jalecea, Jaleesah, Jaleese, Jaleesia, Jaleisa, Jaleisha, Jaleisya

Jalena (American) a combination of Jane + Lena.
Jalaina, Jalana, Jalani, Jalanie, Jalayna, Jalean, Jaleen, Jaleena, Jaleene, Jalen, Jalene, Jalina, Jaline, Jallena, Jalyna, Jelayna, Jelena, Jelina, Jelyna

Jalesa, Jalessa (American) forms of Jalisa.
Jalese, Jalesha, Jaleshia, Jalesia

Jalia, Jalea (American) combinations of Jae + Leah.
Jaleah, Jalee, Jaleea, Jaleeya, Jaleia, Jalitza

Jalila (Arabic) great.
Jalile

Jalisa, Jalissa (American) combinations of Jae + Lisa.
Jaleesa, Jalesa, Jalise, Jalisha, Jalisia, Jalysa

Jalyn, Jalynn (American) combinations of Jae + Lynn. See also Jaylyn.
Jaelin, Jaeline, Jaelyn, Jaelyne, Jaelynn, Jaelynne, Jalin, Jaline, Jalyne, Jalynne

Jalysa (American) a form of Jalisa.
Jalyse, Jalyssa, Jalyssia

Jamaica (Spanish) Geography: an island in the Caribbean.
Jameca, Jamecia, Jameica, Jameika, Jameka, Jamica, Jamika, Jamoka, Jemaica, Jemika, Jemyka

Jamani (American) a form of Jami.
Jamana

Jamaria (American) combinations of Jae + Maria.
Jamar, Jamara, Jamarea, Jamaree, Jamari, Jamarie, Jameira, Jamerial, Jamira

Jamecia (Spanish) a form of Jamaica.

Jamee (French) a form of Jaime.

Jameika, Jameka (Spanish) forms of Jamaica.
Jamaika, Jamaka, Jamecka, Jamekia, Jamekka

Jamesha (American) a form of Jami.
Jameisha, Jamese, Jameshia, Jameshyia, Jamesia, Jamesica, Jamesika, Jamesina, Jamessa, Jameta, Jametta, Jamiesha, Jamisha, Jammesha, Jammisha

Jamey (English) a form of Jami, Jamie.

Jami, Jamie (Hebrew, English) supplanter, substitute.
Jama, Jamani, Jamay, Jamesha, Jamey, Jamia, Jamii, Jamis, Jamise, Jammie, Jamy, Jamye, Jayme, Jaymee, Jaymie

Jamia (English) a form of Jami, Jamie.
Jamea, Jamiah, Jamiea, Jamiya, Jamiyah, Jamya, Jamyah

Jamica (Spanish) a form of Jamaica.
Jamika

Jamila (Arabic) beautiful. See also Yamila.
Jahmela, Jahmelia, Jahmil, Jahmilla, Jameela, Jameelah, Jameeliah, Jameila, Jamela, Jamelia, Jameliah, Jamell, Jamella, Jamelle, Jamely, Jamelya, Jamiela, Jamielee, Jamilah, Jamilee, Jamilia, Jamiliah, Jamilla, Jamillah, Jamille, Jamillia, Jamilya, Jamyla, Jemeela, Jemelia, Jemila, Jemilla

Jamilynn (English) a combination of Jami + Lynn.
Jamielin, Jamieline, Jamielyn, Jamielyne, Jamielynn, Jamielynne, Jamilin, Jamiline, Jamilyn, Jamilyne, Jamilynne

Jammie (American) a form of Jami.
Jammi, Jammice, Jammise

Jamonica (American) a combination of Jami + Monica.
Jamoni

Jamylin (American) a form of Jamilynn.
Jamylin, Jamyline, Jamylyn, Jamylyne, Jamylynn, Jamylynne, Jaymylin, Jaymyline, Jaymylyn, Jaymylyne, Jaymylynn, Jaymylynne

Jan (English) a short form of Jane, Janet, Janice.
Jania, Jandy

Jana (Hebrew) gracious, merciful. (Slavic) a form of Jane. See also Yana.
Janalee, Janalisa, Janna, Janne

Janae, Janay (American) forms of Jane.
Janaé, Janaea, Janaeh, Janah, Janai, Janaya, Janaye, Janea, Janee, Janée, Jannae, Jannay, Jenae, Jenay, Jenaya, Jennae, Jennay, Jennaya, Jennaye

Janai (American) a form of Janae.
Janaiah, Janaira, Janaiya

Janalynn (American) a combination of Jana + Lynn.
Janalin, Janaline, Janalyn, Janalyne, Janalynne

Janan (Arabic) heart; soul.
Jananee, Janani, Jananie, Janann, Jananni

Jane (Hebrew) God is gracious. See also Chavon, Jean, Joan, Juanita, Seana, Shana, Shawna, Sheena, Shona, Shunta, Sinead, Zaneta, Zanna, Zhana.
Jaine, Jan, Jana, Janae, Janay, Janelle, Janessa, Janet, Jania, Janice, Janie, Janika, Janine, Janis, Janka, Jannie, Jasia, Jayna, Jayne, Jenica

Janel, Janell (French) forms of Janelle.
Janiel, Jannel, Jannell, Janyll, Jaynel, Jaynell

Janelle (French) a form of Jane.
Janel, Janela, Janele, Janelis, Janell, Janella, Janelli, Janellie, Janelly, Janely, Janelys, Janielle, Janille, Jannelle, Jannellies, Jaynelle

Janesha (American) a form of Janessa.
Janeisha, Janeshia, Janiesha, Janisha, Janishia, Jannesha, Jannisha, Janysha, Jenesha, Jenisha, Jennisha

Janessa (American) a form of Jane.
Janeesa, Janesa, Janesea, Janesha, Janesia, Janeska, Janessi, Janessia, Janiesa, Janissa, Jannesa, Jannessa, Jannisa, Jannissa, Janyssa, Jenesa, Jenessa, Jenissa, Jennisa, Jennissa

Janet (English) a form of Jane. See also Jessie, Yanet.
Jan, Janeta, Janete, Janeth, Janett, Janette, Jannet, Janot, Jante, Janyte

Janeth (English) a form of Janet.
Janetha, Janith, Janneth

Janette, Jannette (French) forms of Janet.
Janett, Janetta, Jannett, Jannetta

Janice (Hebrew) God is gracious. (English) a familiar form of Jane. See also Genice.
Jan, Janece, Janecia, Janeice, Janiece, Janizzette, Jannice, Janniece, Janyce, Jenice, Jhanice, Jynice

Janie (English) a familiar form of Jane.
Janey, Jani, Janiyh, Jannie, Janny, Jany

Janika (Slavic) a form of Jane.
Janaca, Janeca, Janecka, Janeika, Janeka, Janica, Janick, Janicka, Janieka, Janikka, Janikke, Janique, Janka, Jankia, Jannica, Jannick, Jannika, Janyca, Jenica, Jenicka, Jenika, Jeniqua, Jenique, Jennica, Jennika, Jonika

Janine (French) a form of Jane.
Janean, Janeann, Janeanne, Janeen, Janenan, Janene, Janina, Jannen, Jannina, Jannine, Jannyne, Janyne, Jeannine, Jeneen, Jenine

Janis (English) a form of Jane.
Janees, Janese, Janesey, Janess, Janesse, Janise, Jannis, Jannise, Janys, Jenesse, Jenis, Jennise, Jennisse

Janita (American) a form of Juanita. See also Genita.
Janitra, Janitza, Janneta, Jaynita, Jenita, Jennita

Janna (Arabic) harvest of fruit. (Hebrew) a short form of Johana.
Janaya, Janaye, Jannae, Jannah, Jannai

Jannie (English) a familiar form of Jan, Jane.
Janney, Janny

Jaquana (American) a combination of Jacqueline + Anna.
Jaqua, Jaquai, Jaquanda, Jaquania, Jaquanna

Jaquelen (American) a form of Jacqueline.
Jaquala, Jaquera, Jaqulene, Jaquonna

Jaquelin, Jaqueline (French) forms of Jacqueline.
Jaqualin, Jaqualine, Jaquelina, Jaquline, Jaquella

Jaquelyn (French) a form of Jacqueline.
Jaquelyne, Jaquelynn, Jaquelynne

Jardena (Hebrew) a form of Jordan. (French, Spanish) garden.
Jardan, Jardana, Jardane, Jarden, Jardenia, Jardin, Jardine, Jardyn, Jardyne

Jarian (American) a combination of Jane + Marian.

Jarita (Arabic) earthen water jug.
Jara, Jaretta, Jari, Jaria, Jarica, Jarida, Jarietta, Jarika, Jarina, Jaritta, Jaritza, Jarixa, Jarnita, Jarrika, Jarrine

Jas (American) a short form of Jasmine.
Jase, Jass, Jaz, Jazz, Jazze, Jazzi

Jasia (Polish) a form of Jane.
Jaisha, Jasa, Jasea, Jasha, Jashae, Jashala, Jashona, Jashonte, Jasie, Jassie, Jaysa

Jasleen, Jaslyn (Latin) forms of Jocelyn.
Jaslene, Jaslien, Jaslin, Jasline, Jaslynn, Jaslynne

Jasmain (Persian) a short form of Jasmine.
Jasmaine, Jasmane, Jassmain, Jassmaine

Jasmarie (American) a combination of Jasmine + Marie.
Jasmari

Jasmin (Persian) a form of Jasmine.
Jasimin, Jasman, Jasmeen, Jasmen, Jasmon, Jassmin, Jassminn

Jasmine (Persian) jasmine flower. See also Jessamine, Yasmin.
Jas, Jasma, Jasmain, Jasme, Jasmeet, Jasmene, Jasmin, Jasmina, Jasminne, Jasmira, Jasmit, Jasmyn, Jassma, Jassmin, Jassmine, Jassmit, Jassmon, Jassmyn, Jazmin, Jazmyn, Jazzmin

Jasmyn, Jasmyne (Persian) forms of Jasmine.
Jasmynn, Jasmynne, Jassmyn

Jaspreet (Punjabi) virtuous.
Jaspar, Jasparit, Jasparita, Jasper, Jasprit, Jasprita, Jasprite

Jatara (American) a combination of Jane + Tara.
Jataria, Jatarra, Jatori, Jatoria

Javana (Malayan) from Java.
Javanna, Javanne, Javona, Javonna, Jawana, Jawanna, Jawn

Javiera (Spanish) owner of a new house. See also Xaviera.
Javeera, Viera

Javona, Javonna (Malayan) forms of Javana.
Javon, Javonda, Javone, Javoni, Javonne, Javonni, Javonya

Jaya (Hindi) victory.
Jaea, Jaia

Jaycee (American) a combination of the initials J. + C.
Jacee, Jacey, Jaci, Jacie, Jacy, Jayce, Jaycey, Jayci, Jaycie, Jaycy

Jayda (Spanish) a form of Jada.
Jaydah, Jeyda

Jayde (Spanish) a form of Jade.
Jayd

Jaydee (American) a combination of the initials J. + D.
Jadee, Jadey, Jadi, Jadie, Jady, Jaydey, Jaydi, Jaydie, Jaydy

Jayden (Spanish) a form of Jade.
Jaydeen, Jaydene, Jaydin, Jaydn, Jaydon

Jaye (Latin) jaybird.
Jae, Jay

Jayla (American) a short form of Jaylene.
Jaylaa, Jaylah, Jayli, Jaylia, Jayliah, Jaylie

Jaylene (American) forms of Jaylyn.
Jayelene, Jayla, Jaylan, Jayleana, Jaylee, Jayleen, Jayleene, Jaylen, Jaylenne

Jaylin (American) a form of Jaylyn.
Jayline, Jaylinn

Jaylyn, Jaylynn (American) combinations of Jaye + Lynn. See also Jalyn.
Jaylene, Jaylin, Jaylyne, Jaylynne

Jayme, Jaymie (English) forms of Jami.
Jaymi, Jaymia, Jaymine, Jaymini

Jaymee, Jaymi (English) forms of Jami.

Jayna (Hebrew) a form of Jane.
Jaynae, Jaynah, Jaynna

Jayne (Hindi) victorious. (English) a form of Jane.
Jayn, Jaynie, Jaynne

Jaynie (English) a familiar form of Jayne.
Jaynee, Jayni

Jazlyn (American) a combination of Jazmin + Lynn.
Jasleen, Jazaline, Jazalyn, Jazleen, Jazlene, Jazlin, Jazline, Jazlon, Jazlynn, Jazlynne, Jazzalyn, Jazzleen, Jazzlene, Jazzlin, Jazzline, Jazzlyn, Jazzlynn, Jazzlynne

Jazmin, Jazmine (Persian) forms of Jasmine.
Jazmaine, Jazman, Jazmen, Jazminn, Jazmon, Jazzmit

Jazmyn, Jazmyne (Persian) forms of Jasmine.
Jazmynn, Jazmynne, Jazzmyn, Jazzmyne

Jazzmin, Jazzmine (Persian) forms of Jasmine.
Jazzman, Jazzmeen, Jazzmen, Jazzmene, Jazzmenn, Jazzmon

Jean, Jeanne (Scottish) God is gracious. See also Kini.
Jeana, Jeanann, Jeancie, Jeane, Jeaneia, Jeanette, Jeaneva, Jeanice, Jeanie, Jeanine, Jeanmaria, Jeanmarie, Jeanna, Jeanné, Jeannie, Jeannita, Jeannot, Jeantelle

Jeana, Jeanna (Scottish) forms of Jean.
Jeanae, Jeannae, Jeannia

Jeanette, Jeannett (French) forms of Jean.
Jeanet, Jeanete, Jeanett, Jeanetta, Jeanita, Jeannete, Jeannetta, Jeannette, Jeannita, Jenet, Jenett, Jenette, Jennet, Jennett, Jennetta, Jennette, Jennita, Jinetta, Jinette

Jeanie, Jeannie (Scottish) familiar forms of Jean.
Jeannee, Jeanney, Jeani, Jeanny, Jeany

Jeanine, Jenine (Scottish) forms of Jean. See also Geneen.
Jeaneane, Jeaneen, Jeanene, Jeanina, Jeannina, Jeannine, Jennine

Jelena (Russian) a form of Helen. See also Yelena.
Jalaine, Jalane, Jalani, Jalanna, Jalayna, Jalayne, Jaleen, Jaleena, Jaleene, Jalena, Jalene, Jelaina, Jelaine, Jelana, Jelane, Jelani, Jelanni, Jelayna, Jelayne, Jelean, Jeleana, Jeleen, Jeleena, Jelene

Jelisa (American) a combination of Jean + Lisa.
Jalissa, Jelesha, Jelessa, Jelise, Jelissa, Jellese, Jellice, Jelysa, Jelyssa, Jillisa, Jillissa, Julissa

Jem (Hebrew) a short form of Jemima.
Gem, Jemi, Jemia, Jemiah, Jemie, Jemm, Jemmi, Jemmy

Jemima (Hebrew) dove.
Jamim, Jamima, Jem, Jemimah, Jemma

Jemma (Hebrew) a short form of Jemima. (English) a form of Gemma.
Jemmia, Jemmiah, Jemmie, Jemmy

Jena, Jenae (Arabic) forms of Jenna.
Jenah, Jenai, Jenal, Jenay, Jenaya, Jenea

Jendaya (Zimbabwean) thankful.
Daya, Jenda, Jendayah

Jenelle (American) a combination of Jenny + Nell.
Genell, Jeanell, Jeanelle, Jenall, Jenalle, Jenel, Jenela, Jenele, Jenell, Jenella, Jenille, Jennel, Jennell, Jennella, Jennelle, Jennielle, Jennille, Jinelle, Jinnell

Jenessa (American) a form of Jenisa.
Jenesa, Jenese, Jenesia, Jenessia, Jennesa, Jennese, Jennessa, Jinessa

Jenica (Romanian) a form of Jane.
Jeneca, Jenika, Jenikka, Jennica, Jennika

Jenifer, Jeniffer (Welsh) forms of
Jennifer.
Jenefer

Jenilee (American) a combination of
Jennifer + Lee.
*Jenalea, Jenalee, Jenaleigh, Jenaly, Jenelea,
Jenelee, Jeneleigh, Jenely, Jenelly, Jenileigh,
Jenily, Jennalee, Jennely, Jennielee,
Jennilea, Jennilee, Jennilie*

Jenisa (American) a combination of
Jennifer + Nisa.
*Jenessa, Jenisha, Jenissa, Jenisse, Jennisa,
Jennise, Jennisha, Jennissa, Jennisse,
Jennysa, Jennyssa, Jenysa, Jenyse, Jenyssa,
Jenysse*

Jenka (Czech) a form of Jane.

Jenna (Arabic) small bird. (Welsh) a
short form of Jennifer. See also Gen.
*Jena, Jennae, Jennah, Jennai, Jennat,
Jennay, Jennaya, Jennaye, Jhenna*

Jenni, Jennie (Welsh) familiar forms of
Jennifer.
*Jeni, Jenne, Jenné, Jennee, Jenney, Jennia,
Jennier, Jennita, Jennora, Jensine*

Jennifer (Welsh) white wave; white
phantom. A form of Guinevere. See
also Gennifer, Ginnifer, Yenifer.
*Jen, Jenifer, Jeniffer, Jenipher, Jenna,
Jennafer, Jenni, Jenniferanne, Jenniferlee,
Jenniffe, Jenniffer, Jenniffier, Jennifier,
Jennilee, Jenniphe, Jennipher, Jenny,
Jennyfer*

Jennilee (American) a combination of
Jenny + Lee.
*Jennalea, Jennalee, Jennielee, Jennilea,
Jennilie, Jinnalee*

Jennilyn, Jennilynn (American) com-
binations of Jenni + Lynn.
*Jennalin, Jennaline, Jennalyn, Jenalynann,
Jenelyn, Jenilyn, Jennalyne, Jennalynn,
Jennalynne, Jennilin, Jenniline, Jennilyne,
Jennilynne*

Jenny (Welsh) a familiar form of
Jennifer.
Jenney, Jenni, Jennie, Jeny, Jinny

Jennyfer (Welsh) a form of Jennifer.
Jenyfer

Jeraldine (English) a form of
Geraldine.
*Jeraldeen, Jeraldene, Jeraldina, Jeraldyne,
Jeralee, Jeri*

Jereni (Russian) a form of Irene.
Jerena, Jerenae, Jerina

Jeri, Jerri, Jerrie (American) short
forms of Jeraldine. See also Geri.
*Jera, Jerae, JeRae, Jeree, Jeriel, Jerilee,
Jerinda, Jerra, Jerrah, Jerrece, Jerree,
Jerriann, Jerrilee, Jerrine, Jerry, Jerrylee,
Jerryne, Jerzy*

Jerica (American) a combination of
Jeri + Erica.
*Jereca, Jerecka, Jerice, Jericka, Jerika,
Jerrica, Jerrice, Jeryka*

Jerilyn (American) a combination of
Jeri + Lynn.
*Jeralin, Jeraline, Jeralyn, Jeralyne,
Jeralynn, Jeralynne, Jerelin, Jereline,
Jerelyn, Jerelyne, Jerelynn, Jerelynne,
Jerilin, Jeriline, Jerilyne, Jerilynn,
Jerilynne, Jerrilin, Jerriline, Jerrilyn,
Jerrilyne, Jerrilynn, Jerrilynne, Jerrylea*

Jermaine (French) a form of
Germaine.
*Jermain, Jerman, Jermanay, Jermanaye,
Jermane, Jermanee, Jermani, Jermanique,
Jermany, Jermayne, Jermecia, Jermia,
Jermice, Jermicia, Jermika, Jermila*

Jerrica (American) a form of Jerica.
*Jerreka, Jerricah, Jerricca, Jerricha, Jerricka,
Jerrieka, Jerrika*

Jerusha (Hebrew) inheritance.
Jerushah, Yerusha

Jesenia, Jessenia (Arabic) flower.
Jescenia, Jessennia, Jessenya

Jesica, Jesika (Hebrew) forms of
Jessica.
Jesicca, Jesikah, Jesikkah

Jessa (American) a short form of
Jessalyn, Jessamine, Jessica.
Jesa, Jesha, Jessah

Jessalyn (American) a combination of
Jessica + Lynn.
*Jesalin, Jesaline, Jesalyn, Jesalyne,
Jesalynn, Jesalynne, Jesilin, Jesiline,
Jesilyn, Jesilyne, Jesilynn, Jesilynne, Jessa,
Jessalin, Jessaline, Jessalyne, Jessalynn,
Jessalynne, Jesselin, Jesseline, Jesselyn,
Jesselyne, Jesselynn, Jesselynne, Jesslyn*

Jessamine (French) a form of Jasmine.
*Jessa, Jessamin, Jessamon, Jessamy,
Jessamyn, Jessemin, Jessemine, Jessimin,
Jessimine, Jessmin, Jessmine, Jessmon,
Jessmy, Jessmyn*

Jesse, Jessi (Hebrew) forms of Jessie.
Jese, Jesi, Jesie

Jesseca (Hebrew) a form of Jessica.

Jessica (Hebrew) wealthy. Literature: a name perhaps invented by Shakespeare for a character in his play *The Merchant of Venice*. See also Gessica, Yessica.
Jesica, Jesika, Jessa, Jessaca, Jessca, Jesscia, Jesseca, Jessia, Jessicah, Jessicca, Jessicia, Jessicka, Jessie, Jessika, Jessiqua, Jessy, Jessyca, Jessyka, Jezeca, Jezica, Jezika, Jezyca

Jessie, Jessy (Hebrew) short forms of Jessica. (Scottish) forms of Janet.
Jescie, Jesey, Jess, Jesse, Jessé, Jessee, Jessey, Jessi, Jessia, Jessiya, Jessye

Jessika (Hebrew) a form of Jessica.
Jessieka

Jesslyn (American) a short form of Jessalyn.
Jessilyn, Jessilynn, Jesslin, Jesslynn, Jesslynne

Jessyca, Jessyka (Hebrew) forms of Jessica.

Jésusa (Hebrew, Spanish) God is my salvation.

Jetta (English) jet black mineral. (American) a familiar form of Jevette.
Jeta, Jetia, Jetje, Jette, Jettie

Jevette (American) a combination of Jean + Yvette.
Jetta, Jeva, Jeveta, Jevetta

Jewel (French) precious gem.
Jewelann, Jewelia, Jeweliana, Jeweliann, Jewelie, Jewell, Jewelle, Jewellee, Jewellene, Jewellie, Juel, Jule

Jezebel (Hebrew) unexalted; impure. Bible: the wife of King Ahab.
Jesibel, Jessabel, Jessebel, Jez, Jezabel,

Jezabella, Jezabelle, Jezebell, Jezebella, Jezebelle

Jianna (Italian) a form of Giana.
Jiana, Jianina, Jianine, Jianni, Jiannini

Jibon (Hindi) life.

Jill (English) a short form of Jillian.
Jil, Jilli, Jillie, Jilly

Jillaine (Latin) a form of Jillian.
Jilaine, Jilane, Jilayne, Jillana, Jillane, Jillann, Jillanne, Jillayne

Jilleen (Irish) a form of Jillian.
Jileen, Jilene, Jiline, Jillene, Jillenne, Jilline, Jillyn

Jillian (Latin) youthful. See also Gillian.
Jilian, Jiliana, Jiliann, Jilianna, Jilianne, Jilienna, Jilienne, Jill, Jillaine, Jilliana, Jilliane, Jilliann, Jillianne, Jileen, Jillien, Jillienne, Jillion, Jilliyn

Jimi (Hebrew) supplanter, substitute.
Jimae, Jimaria, Jimee, Jimella, Jimena, Jimia, Jimiah, Jimie, Jimiyah, Jimmeka, Jimmet, Jimmi, Jimmia, Jimmie

Jimisha (American) a combination of Jimi + Aisha.
Jimica, Jimicia, Jimmicia, Jimysha

Jin (Japanese) tender. (American) a short form of Ginny, Jinny.

Jina (Swahili) baby with a name. (Italian) a form of Gina.
Jena, Jinae, Jinan, Jinda, Jinna, Jinnae

Jinny (Scottish) a familiar form of Jenny. (American) a familiar form of Virginia. See also Ginny.
Jin, Jinnee, Jinney, Jinni, Jinnie

Jirina (Czech) a form of Georgia.
Jirah, Jireh

Jizelle (American) a form of Giselle.
Jessel, Jezel, Jezell, Jezella, Jezelle, Jisel, Jisela, Jisell, Jisella, Jiselle, Jissel, Jissell, Jissella, Jisselle, Jizel, Jizella, Joselle

Jo (American) a short form of Joanna, Jolene, Josephine.
Joangie, Joetta, Joette, Joey

Joan (Hebrew) God is gracious. History: Joan of Arc was a fifteenth-century heroine and resistance fighter. See also Ioana, Jean, Juanita, Siobahn.
Joane, Joaneil, Joanel, Joanelle, Joanie, Joanmarie, Joann, Joannanette, Joanne, Joannel, Joanny, Jonni

Joana, Joanna (English) a form of Joan. See also Yoanna.
Janka, Jhoana, Jo, Jo-Ana, Joandra, Joanka, Joananna, Jo-Anie, Joanka, Jo-Anna, Joannah, Jo-Annie, Joeana, Joeanna, Johana, Johanna, Johannah

Joanie, Joannie (Hebrew) familiar forms of Joan.
Joanee, Joani, Joanni, Joenie, Johanie, Johnnie, Joni

Joanne (English) a form of Joan.
Joanann, Joananne, Joann, Jo-Ann, Jo-Anne, Joayn, Joeann, Joeanne

Joanny (Hebrew) a familiar form of Joan.
Joany

Joaquina (Hebrew) God will establish.
Joaquine

Jobeth (English) a combination of Jo + Beth.
Joby

Joby (Hebrew) afflicted. (English) a familiar form of Jobeth.
Jobey, Jobi, Jobie, Jobina, Jobita, Jobrina, Jobye, Jobyna

Jocacia (American) a combination of Joy + Acacia.

Jocelin, Joceline (Latin) forms of Jocelyn.
Jocelina, Jocelinn

Jocelyn (Latin) joyous. See also Yocelin, Yoselin.
Jacelyn, Jasleen, Jocelin, Jocelle, Jocelyne, Jocelynn, Joci, Jocia, Jocilyn, Jocilynn, Jocinta, Joclyn, Joclynn, Josalyn, Joscelin, Joselin, Joselyn, Joshlyn, Josilin, Jossalin, Josselyn, Joycelyn

Jocelyne (Latin) a form of Jocelyn.
Joceline, Jocelynne, Joclynne

Jodi, Jodie, Jody (American) familiar forms of Judith.
Jodee, Jodele, Jodell, Jodelle, Jodevea, Jodey, Jodia, Jodiee, Jodilee, Jodi-Lee, Jodilynn, Jodi-Lynn, Joedi, Joedy

Jodiann (American) a combination of Jodi + Ann.
Jodene, Jodi-Ann, Jodianna, Jodi-Anna, Jodianne, Jodi-Anne, Jodine, Jodyann, Jody-Ann, Jodyanna, Jody-Anna, Jodyanne, Jody-Anne, Jodyne

Joelle (Hebrew) God is willing.
Joela, Joele, Joelee, Joeli, Joelia, Joelie, Joell, Joella, Joëlle, Joelli, Joelly, Joely, Joyelle

Joelynn (American) a combination of Joelle + Lynn.
Joeleen, Joelene, Joeline, Joellen, Joellyn, Joelyn, Joelyne

Johana, Johanna, Johannah (German) forms of Joana.
Janna, Joahna, Johanah, Johanka, Johanne, Johnna, Johonna, Jonna, Joyhanna, Joyhannah

Johanie, Johannie (Hebrew) forms of Joanie.
Johani, Johanni, Johanny, Johany

Johnna, Jonna (American) forms of Johana, Joanna.
Jahna, Jahnaya, Jhona, Jhonna, Johna, Johnda, Johnnielynn, Johnnie-Lynn, Johnnquia, Joncie, Jonda, Jondrea, Jontel, Jutta

Johnnie (Hebrew) a form of Joanie.
Johni, Johnie, Johnni, Johnny

Johnnessa (American) a combination of Johnna + Nessa.
Jahnessa, Johneatha, Johnecia, Johnesha, Johnetra, Johnisha, Johnishi, Johnnise, Jonyssa

Joi (Latin) a form of Joy.
Joia, Joie

Jokla (Swahili) beautiful robe.

Jolanda (Greek) a form of Yolanda. See also Iolanthe.
Jola, Jolan, Jolán, Jolande, Jolander, Jolanka, Jolánta, Jolantha, Jolanthe

Joleen, Joline (English) forms of Jolene.
Joleena, Joleene, Jolleen, Jollene

Jolene (Hebrew) God will add, God will increase. (English) a form of Josephine.
Jo, Jolaine, Jolana, Jolane, Jolanna, Jolanne, Jolanta, Jolayne, Jole, Jolean, Joleane, Joleen, Jolena, Joléne, Jolenna, Jolin, Jolina, Jolinda, Joline, Jolinn, Jolinna, Jolleane, Jolleen, Jolline

Jolie (French) pretty.
Jole, Jolea, Jolee, Joleigh, Joley, Joli, Jolibeth, Jollee, Jollie, Jolly, Joly, Jolye

Jolisa (American) a combination of Jo + Lisa.
Joleesa, Joleisha, Joleishia, Jolieasa, Jolise, Jolisha, Jolisia, Jolissa, Jolysa, Jolyssa, Julissa

Jolynn (American) a combination of Jo + Lynn.
Jolyn, Jolyne, Jolynne

Jonatha (Hebrew) gift of God.
Johnasha, Johnasia, Jonesha, Jonisha

Jonelle (American) a combination of Joan + Elle.
Jahnel, Jahnell, Jahnelle, Johnel, Johnell, Johnella, Johnelle, Jonel, Jonell, Jonella, Jonyelle, Jynell, Jynelle

Jonesha, Jonisha (American) forms of Jonatha.
Joneisha, Jonesa, Joneshia, Jonessa, Jonisa, Jonishia, Jonneisha, Jonnesha, Jonnessia

Joni (American) a familiar form of Joan.
Jona, Jonae, Jonai, Jonann, Jonati, Joncey, Jonci, Joncie, Jonice, Jonie, Jonilee, Joni-lee, Jonis, Jony

Jonika (American) a form of Janika.
Johnica, Johnique, Johnquia, Johnnica,
Johnnika, Joneeka, Joneika, Jonica,
Joniqua, Jonique

Jonina (Hebrew) dove. See also
Yonina.
Jona, Jonita, Jonnina

Jonita (Hebrew) a form of Jonina. See
also Yonita.
Johnetta, Johnette, Johnita, Johnittia,
Jonati, Jonetia, Jonetta, Jonette, Jonit,
Jonnita, Jonta, Jontae, Jontaé, Jontaya

Jonni, Jonnie (American) familiar
forms of Joan.
Jonny

Jonquil (Latin, English) Botany: an ornamental plant with fragrant yellow flowers.
Jonquelle, Jonquie, Jonquill, Jonquille

Jontel (American) a form of Johna.
Jontaya, Jontell, Jontelle, Jontia, Jontila,
Jontrice

Jora (Hebrew) autumn rain.
Jorah

Jordan (Hebrew) descending. See also
Jardena.
Jordain, Jordaine, Jordana, Jordane,
Jordann, Jordanna, Jordanne, Jordany,
Jordea, Jordee, Jorden, Jordi, Jordian,
Jordie, Jordin, Jordon, Jordyn, Jori, Jorie,
Jourdan

Jordana, Jordanna (Hebrew) forms of
Jordan. See also Giordana, Yordana.
Jordannah, Jordina, Jordonna, Jourdana,
Jourdanna

Jorden, Jordin, Jordon (Hebrew)
forms of Jordan.
Jordenne, Jordine

Jordyn (Hebrew) a form of Jordan.
Jordyne, Jordynn, Jordynne

Jori, Jorie (Hebrew) familiar forms of
Jordan.
Jorai, Jorea, Joree, Jorée, Jorey, Jorian,
Jorin, Jorina, Jorine, Jorita, Jorre, Jorrey,
Jorri, Jorrian, Jorrie, Jorry, Jory

Joriann (American) a combination of
Jori + Ann.
Jori-Ann, Jorianna, Jori-Anna, Jorianne,
Jori-Anne, Jorriann, Jorrianna, Jorrianne,
Jorryann, Jorryanna, Jorryanne, Joryann,
Joryanna, Joryanne

Jorja (American) a form of Georgia.
Jeorgi, Jeorgia, Jorgana, Jorgi, Jorgia,
Jorgina, Jorjana, Jorji

Josalyn (Latin) a form of Jocelyn.
Josalene, Josalin, Josalind, Josaline,
Josalynn, Joshalyne

Joscelin, Joscelyn (Latin) forms of
Jocelyn.
Josceline, Joscelyne, Joscelynn, Joscelynne,
Joselin, Joseline, Joselyn, Joselyne,
Joselynn, Joselynne, Joshlyn

Josee, Josée (American) familiar
forms of Josephine.
Joesee, Josey, Josi, Josina, Josy, Jozee

Josefina (Spanish) a form of
Josephine.
Josefa, Josefena, Joseffa, Josefine

Joselin, Joseline (Latin) forms of
Jocelyn.
Joselina, Joselinne, Josielina

Joselle (American) a form of Jizelle.
Joesell, Jozelle

Joselyn, Joslyn (Latin) forms of
Jocelyn.
Joselene, Joselyne, Joselynn, Joshely,
Josiline, Josilyn

Josephine (French) God will add, God
will increase. See also Fifi, Pepita,
Yosepha.
Fina, Jo, Joey, Josee, Josée, Josefina, Josepha,
Josephe, Josephene, Josephin, Josephina,
Josephyna, Josephyne, Josette, Josey, Josie,
Jozephine, Jozie, Sefa

Josette (French) a familiar form of
Josephine.
Joesette, Josetta, Joshetta, Jozette

Josey, Josie (Hebrew) familiar forms of
Josephine.
Josi, Josse, Jossee, Jossie, Josy, Josye

Joshann (American) a combination of
Joshlyn + Ann.
Joshana, Joshanna, Joshanne

Joshlyn (Latin) a form of Jocelyn.
(Hebrew) God is my salvation.
Joshalin, Joshalyn, Joshalynn, Joshalynne,
Joshelle, Joshleen, Joshlene, Joshlin,
Joshline, Joshlyne, Joshlynn, Joshlynne

Josiane, Josianne (American) combinations of Josie + Anne.
Josian, Josie-Ann, Josieann

Josilin, Joslin (Latin) forms of Jocelyn.
Josielina, Josiline, Josilyn, Josilyne,
Josilynn, Josilynne, Joslin, Josline, Joslyn,
Joslyne, Joslynn, Joslynne

Jossalin (Latin) a form of Jocelyn.
Jossaline, Jossalyn, Jossalynn, Jossalynne, Josselyn, Josslin, Jossline

Josselyn (Latin) a form of Jocelyn.
Josselen, Josselin, Josseline, Jossellen, Jossellin, Jossellyn, Josselyne, Josselynn, Josselynne, Josslyn, Josslyne, Josslynn, Josslynne

Jourdan (Hebrew) a form of Jordan.
Jourdain, Jourdann, Jourdanne, Jourden, Jourdian, Jourdon, Jourdyn

Jovana (Latin) a form of Jovanna.
Jeovana, Jouvan, Jovan, Jovanah, Jovena, Jovian, Jowan, Jowana

Jovanna (Latin) majestic. (Italian) a form of Giovanna. Mythology: Jove, also known as Jupiter, was the supreme Roman god.
Jeovanna, Jovado, Joval, Jovana, Jovann, Jovannie, Jovena, Jovina, Jovon, Jovonda, Jovonia, Jovonna, Jovonnah, Jovonne, Jowanna

Jovannie (Italian) a familiar form of Jovanna.
Jovanee, Jovani, Jovanie, Jovanne, Jovanni, Jovanny, Jovonnie

Jovita (Latin) jovial.
Joveda, Joveta, Jovetta, Jovida, Jovitta

Joy (Latin) joyous.
Joe, Joi, Joya, Joye, Joyeeta, Joyella, Joyia, Joyous, Joyvina

Joyanne (American) a combination of Joy + Anne.
Joyan, Joyann, Joyanna,

Joyce (Latin) joyous. A short form of Joycelyn.
Joice, Joycey, Joycie, Joyous, Joysel

Joycelyn (American) a form of Jocelyn.
Joycelin, Joyceline, Joycelyne, Joycelynn, Joycelynne

Joylyn (American) a combination of Joy + Lynn.
Joyleen, Joylene, Joylin, Joyline, Joylyne, Joylynn, Joy-Lynn, Joylynne

Jozie (Hebrew) a familiar form of Josephine.
Jozee, Jozée, Jozi, Jozy

Juana (Spanish) a short form of Juanita.
Juanell, Juaney, Juanika, Juanit, Juanna, Juannia

Juandalyn (Spanish) a form of Juanita.
Jualinn, Juandalin, Juandaline, Juandalyne, Juandalynn, Juandalynne

Juanita (Spanish) a form of Jane, Joan. See also Kwanita, Nita, Waneta, Wanika.
Juana, Juandalyn, Juaneice, Juanequa, Juanesha, Juanice, Juanicia, Juaniqua, Juanisha, Juanishia

Juci (Hungarian) a form of Judy.
Jucika

Judith (Hebrew) praised. Mythology: the slayer of Holofernes, according to ancient Jewish legend. See also Yehudit, Yudita.
Giuditta, Ioudith, Jodi, Jodie, Jody, Jude, Judine, Judit, Judita, Judite, Juditha, Judithe, Judy, Judyta, Jutka

Judy (Hebrew) a familiar form of Judith.
Juci, Judi, Judie, Judye

Judyann (American) a combination of Judy + Ann.
Judana, Judiann, Judianna, Judianne, Judyanna, Judyanne

Jula (Polish) a form of Julia.
Julca, Julcia, Juliska, Julka

Julene (Basque) a form of Julia. See also Yulene.
Julena, Julina, Juline, Julinka, Juliska, Julleen, Jullena, Jullene, Julyne

Julia (Latin) youthful. See also Giulia, Jill, Jillian, Sulia, Yulia.
Iulia, Jula, Julea, Juleah, Julene, Juliah, Juliana, Juliann, Julica, Julie, Juliea, Juliet, Julija, Julina, Juline, Julisa, Julissa, Julita, Juliya, Julka, Julyssa

Juliana, Julianna (Czech, Spanish, Hungarian) forms of Julia.
Julieana, Julieanna, Juliena, Julliana, Jullianna, Julyana, Julyanna, Yuliana

Juliann, Julianne (English) forms of Julia.
Julean, Juleann, Julian, Juliane, Julieann, Julie-Ann, Julieanne, Julie-Anne, Julien, Juliene, Julienn, Julienne, Jullian

Julie (English) a form of Julia.
Juel, Jule, Julee, Juli, Julie-Lynn, Julie-Mae, Julle, Jullee, Jullie, Jully, July

Juliet, Juliette (French) forms of Julia.
Julet, Julieta, Juliett, Julietta, Jullet, Julliet, Jullietta

Julisa, Julissa (Latin) forms of Julia.
Julis, Julisha, Julysa, Julyssa

Julita (Spanish) a form of Julia.
Julitta, Julyta

Jumaris (American) a combination of
Julie + Maris.

Jun (Chinese) truthful.

June (Latin) born in the sixth month.
*Juna, Junea, Junel, Junell, Junella,
Junelle, Junette, Juney, Junia, Junie,
Juniet, Junieta, Junietta, Juniette, Junina,
Junita*

Juno (Latin) queen. Mythology: the
supreme Roman goddess.

Justice (Latin) just, righteous.
*Justis, Justise, Justiss, Justisse, Justus,
Justyce, Justys*

Justina (Italian) a form of Justine.
Jestena, Jestina, Justinna, Justyna

Justine (Latin) just, righteous.
*Giustina, Jestine, Juste, Justi, Justice,
Justie, Justina, Justinn, Justy, Justyn,
Justyne, Justynn, Justynne*

Kacey, Kacy (Irish) brave. (American)
forms of Casey. Combinations of the
initials K. + C.
*K. C., Kace, Kacee, Kaci, Kacie, Kaicee,
Kaicey, Kasey, Kasie, Kaycee, Kayci,
Kaycie*

Kachina (Native American) sacred
dancer.
Kachine

Kaci, Kacie (American) forms of
Kacey, Kacy.
Kasci, Kaycie, Kaysie

Kacia (Greek) a short form of Acacia.
Kaycia, Kaysia

Kadedra (American) a combination of
Kady + Dedra.
*Kadeadra, Kadedrah, Kadedria,
Kadeedra, Kadeidra, Kadeidre, Kadeidria*

Kadejah (Arabic) a form of Kadijah.
Kadeija, Kadeijah, Kadejá, Kadejia

Kadelyn (American) a combination of
Kady + Lynn.

Kadesha (American) a combination of
Kady + Aisha.
*Kadeesha, Kadeeshia, Kadeesia,
Kadeesiah, Kadeezia, Kadesa,
Kadesheia, Kadeshia, Kadesia, Kadessa,
Kadezia*

Kadie (English) a form of Kady.
Kadi, Kadia, Kadiah

Kadijah (Arabic) trustworthy.
Kadajah, Kadeeja, Kadeejah, Kadija

Kadisha (American) a form of
Kadesha.
*Kadiesha, Kadieshia, Kadishia, Kadisia,
Kadysha, Kadyshia*

Kady (English) a form of Katy. A
combination of the initials K. + D.
See also Cady.
*K. D., Kade, Kadee, Kadey, Kadie,
Kadya, Kadyn, Kaidi, Kaidy, Kayde,
Kaydee, Kaydey, Kaydi, Kaydie, Kaydy*

Kaedé (Japanese) maple leaf.

Kaela (Hebrew, Arabic) beloved,
sweetheart. A short form of Kalila,
Kelila.
*Kaelah, Kaelea, Kaeleah, Kaelee, Kaeli,
Kayla*

Kaelee, Kaeli (American) forms of
Kaela.
*Kaelei, Kaeleigh, Kaeley, Kaelia, Kaelie,
Kaelii, Kaelly, Kaely, Kaelye*

Kaelin (American) a form of Kaelyn.
*Kaeleen, Kaelene, Kaelina, Kaelinn,
Kalan*

Kaelyn (American) a combination of
Kae + Lynn. See also Caelin, Kaylyn.
*Kaelan, Kaelen, Kaelin, Kaelynn,
Kaelynne*

Kaetlyn (Irish) a form of Kaitlin.
Kaetlin, Kaetlynn

Kagami (Japanese) mirror.

Kahsha (Native American) fur robe.
Kasha, Kashae, Kashia

Kai (Hawaiian) sea. (Hopi, Navaho)
willow tree.
Kae, Kaie

Kaia (Greek) earth. Mythology: Gaea
was the earth goddess.
Kaiah, Kaija

Kaila (Hebrew) laurel; crown.
*Kailah, Kailea, Kaileah, Kailee, Kailey,
Kayla*

Kailee, Kailey (American) familiar
forms of Kaila. Forms of Kaylee.
*Kaile, Kaileh, Kaileigh, Kaili, Kailia,
Kailie, Kailli, Kaillie, Kaily, Kailya*

Kailyn, Kailynn (American) forms of Kaitlin.
Kailan, Kaileen, Kaileena, Kailen, Kailena, Kailene, Kaileyne, Kailin, Kailina, Kailon, Kailynne

Kairos (Greek) last, final, complete. Mythology: the last goddess born to Jupiter.
Kaira, Kairra

Kaishawn (American) a combination of Kai + Shawna.
Kaeshun, Kaisha, Kaishala, Kaishon

Kaitlin (Irish) pure. See also Katelin.
Kaetlyn, Kailyn, Kailynn, Kaitlan, Kaitland, Kaitleen, Kaitlen, Kaitlind, Kaitlinn, Kaitlinne, Kaitlon, Kaytlin

Kaitlyn, Kaitlynn (Irish) forms of Caitlyn.
Kaitelynne, Kaitlynne

Kaiya (Japanese) forgiveness.
Kaiyah, Kaiyia

Kala (Arabic) a short form of Kalila. A form of Cala.
Kalah, Kalla, Kallah

Kalama (Hawaiian) torch.

Kalani (Hawaiian) chieftain; sky.
Kailani, Kalanie, Kaloni

Kalare (Latin, Basque) bright; clear.

Kalea (Hawaiian) bright; clear.
Kahlea, Kahleah, Kailea, Kaileah, Kaleah, Kaleeia, Kaleia, Kalia, Kallea, Kalleah, Kaylea, Kayleah, Khalea, Khaleah

Kalee, Kaleigh, Kaley, Kalie (American) forms of Caley, Kaylee.
Kalei, Kalleigh, Kalley, Kally, Kaly

Kalei (Hawaiian) flower wreath.
Kahlei, Kailei, Kallei, Kaylei, Khalei

Kalena (Hawaiian) pure. See also Kalina.
Kaleen, Kaleena, Kalene, Kalenea, Kalenna

Kalere (Swahili) short woman.
Kaleer

Kali (Hindi) the black one. (Hawaiian) hesitating. Religion: a form of the Hindu goddess Devi. See also Cali.
Kalee, Kaleigh, Kaley, Kalie, Kallee, Kalley, Kalli, Kallie, Kally, Kallye, Kaly

Kalia (Hawaiian) a form of Kalea.
Kaliah, Kaliea, Kalieya

Kalifa (Somali) chaste; holy.

Kalila (Arabic) beloved, sweetheart. See also Kaela.
Kahlila, Kala, Kaleela, Kalilla, Kaylil, Kaylila, Kelila, Khalila, Khalilah, Khalillah, Kylila, Kylilah, Kylillah

Kalina (Slavic) flower. (Hawaiian) a form of Karen. See also Kalena.
Kalin, Kalinna, Kalyna, Kalynah, Kalynna

Kalinda (Hindi) sun.
Kaleenda, Kalindi, Kalynda, Kalyndi

Kalisa (American) a combination of Kate + Lisa.
Kalise, Kalissa, Kalysa, Kalyssa

Kalisha (American) a combination of Kate + Aisha.
Kaleesha, Kaleisha, Kalishia

Kaliska (Moquelumnan) coyote chasing deer.

Kallan (Slavic) stream, river.
Kalahn, Kalan, Kalen, Kallen, Kallon, Kalon

Kalle (Finnish) a form of Carol.
Kaille, Kaylle

Kalli, Kallie (Greek) forms of Callie. Familiar forms of Kalliope, Kallista, Kalliyan.
Kalle, Kallee, Kalley, Kallita, Kally

Kalliope (Greek) a form of Calliope.
Kalli, Kallie, Kallyope

Kallista (Greek) a form of Callista.
Kalesta, Kalista, Kallesta, Kalli, Kallie, Kallysta, Kaysta

Kalliyan (Cambodian) best.
Kalli, Kallie

Kaltha (English) marigold, yellow flower.

Kaluwa (Swahili) forgotten one.
Kalua

Kalyca (Greek) rosebud.
Kalica, Kalika, Kaly

Kalyn, Kalynn (American) forms of Kaylyn.
Kalin, Kallen, Kallin, Kallon, Kallyn, Kalyne, Kalynne

Kama (Sanskrit) loved one. Religion: the Hindu god of love.

Kamala (Hindi) lotus.
Kamalah, Kammala

Kamali (Mahona) spirit guide; protector.
Kamalie

Kamaria (Swahili) moonlight.
Kamar, Kamara, Kamarae, Kamaree, Kamari, Kamariah, Kamarie, Kamariya, Kamariyah, Kamarya

Kamata (Moquelumnan) gambler.

Kambria (Latin) a form of Cambria.
Kambra, Kambrie, Kambriea, Kambry

Kamea (Hawaiian) one and only; precious.
Kameah, Kameo, Kamiya

Kameke (Swahili) blind.

Kameko (Japanese) turtle child. Mythology: the turtle symbolizes longevity.

Kameron (American) a form of Cameron.
Kameran, Kamri

Kami (Japanese) divine aura. (Italian, North African) a short form of Kamila, Kamilah. See also Cami.
Kamie, Kammi, Kammie, Kammy, Kammye, Kamy

Kamila (Slavic) a form of Camila. See also Millie.
Kameela, Kamela, Kamelia, Kamella, Kami, Kamilah, Kamilia, Kamilka, Kamilla, Kamille, Kamma, Kammilla, Kamyla

Kamilah (North African) perfect.
Kameela, Kameelah, Kami, Kamillah, Kammilah

Kamiya (Hawaiian) a form of Kamea.
Kamia, Kamiah, Kamiyah

Kamri (American) a short form of Kameron. See also Camri.
Kamree, Kamrey, Kamrie, Kamry, Kamrye

Kamryn (American) a short form of Kameron. See also Camryn.
Kameryn, Kamren, Kamrin, Kamron, Kamrynn

Kanani (Hawaiian) beautiful.
Kana, Kanae, Kanan

Kanda (Native American) magical power.

Kandace, Kandice (Greek) glittering white; glowing. (American) forms of Candace, Candice.
Kandas, Kandess, Kandi, Kandis, Kandise, Kandiss, Kandus, Kandyce, Kandys, Kandyse

Kandi (American) a familiar form of Kandace, Kandice. See also Candi.
Kandhi, Kandia, Kandie, Kandy, Kendi, Kendie, Kendy, Kenndi, Kenndie, Kenndy

Kandra (American) a form of Kendra. See also Candra.
Kandrea, Kandree, Kandria

Kane (Japanese) two right hands.

Kaneisha, Kanisha (American) forms of Keneisha.
Kaneasha, Kanecia, Kaneesha, Kanesah, Kanesha, Kaneshea, Kaneshia, Kanessa, Kaneysha, Kaniece, Kanishia

Kanene (Swahili) a little important thing.

Kani (Hawaiian) sound.

Kanika (Mwera) black cloth.
Kanica, Kanicka

Kannitha (Cambodian) angel.

Kanoa (Hawaiian) free.

Kanya (Hindi) virgin. (Tai) young lady. Religion: a form of the Hindu goddess Devi.
Kanea, Kania, Kaniya, Kanyia

Kapri (American) a form of Capri.
Kapre, Kapree, Kapria, Kaprice, Kapricia, Kaprisha, Kaprisia

Kapua (Hawaiian) blossom.

Kapuki (Swahili) first-born daughter.

Kara (Greek, Danish) pure.
Kaira, Kairah, Karah, Karalea, Karaleah, Karalee, Karalie, Kari, Karra

Karah (Greek, Danish) a form of Kara. (Irish, Italian) a form of Cara.
Karrah

Karalynn (English) a combination of Kara + Lynn.
Karalin, Karaline, Karalyn, Karalyne, Karalynne

Karelle (American) a form of Carol.
Karel, Kareli, Karell, Karely

Karen (Greek) pure. See also Carey, Carina, Caryn.
Kaaren, Kalina, Karaina, Karan, Karena, Karin, Karina, Karine, Karna, Karon, Karren, Karron, Karyn, Kerron, Koren

Karena (Scandinavian) a form of Karen.
Kareen, Kareena, Kareina, Karenah, Karene, Karreen, Karreena, Karrena, Karrene

Karessa (French) a form of Caressa.

Kari (Greek) pure. (Danish) a form of Caroline, Katherine. See also Carey, Cari, Carrie.
Karee, Karey, Karia, Kariah, Karie, Karrey, Karri, Karrie, Karry, Kary

Kariane, Karianne (American) combinations of Kari + Ann.
Karian, Kariana, Kariann, Karianna

Karida (Arabic) untouched, pure.
Kareeda, Karita

Karilynn (American) a combination of Kari + Lynn.
Kareelin, Kareeline, Kareelinn, Kareelyn, Kareelyne, Kareelynn, Kareelynne, Karilin, Kariline, Karilinn, Karilyn, Karilyne, Karilynne, Karylin, Karyline, Karylinn, Karylyn, Karylyne, Karylynn, Karylynne

Karimah (Arabic) generous.
Kareema, Kareemah, Karima, Karime

Karin (Scandinavian) a form of Karen.
Kaarin, Kareen, Karina, Karine, Karinne, Karrin, Kerrin

Karina (Russian) a form of Karen.
Kaarina, Karinna, Karrina, Karryna, Karyna, Karynna

Karine (Russian) a form of Karen.
Karrine, Karryne, Karyne

Karis (Greek) graceful.
Karess, Karice, Karise, Karisse, Karris, Karys, Karyss

Karissa (Greek) a form of Carissa.
Karese, Karesse, Karisa, Karisha, Karishma, Karisma, Karissimia, Kariza, Karrisa, Karrissa, Karysa, Karyssa, Kerisa

Karla (German) a form of Carla. (Slavic) a short form of Karoline.
Karila, Karilla, Karle, Karlene, Karlicka, Karlinka, Karlisha, Karlisia, Karlitha, Karlla, Karlon, Karlyn

Karlee, Karleigh (American) forms of Karley, Karly. See also Carlee.
Karlea, Karleah, Karlei

Karlene, Karlyn (American) forms of Karla. See also Carleen.
Karleen, Karlen, Karlena, Karlign, Karlin, Karlina, Karlinna, Karlyan, Karlynn, Karlynne

Karley, Karly (Latin) little and strong. (American) forms of Carly.
Karlee, Karley, Karlie, Karlyan, Karlye

Karli, Karlie (American) forms of Karley, Karly. See also Carli.

Karlotte (American) a form of Charlotte.
Karlita, Karletta, Karlette, Karlotta

Karma (Hindi) fate, destiny; action.

Karmel (Hebrew) a form of Carmela.
Karmeita, Karmela, Karmelina, Karmella, Karmelle, Karmiella, Karmielle, Karmyla

Karmen (Latin) song.
Karman, Karmencita, Karmin, Karmina, Karmine, Karmita, Karmon, Karmyn, Karmyne

Karolane (American) a combination of Karoll + Anne.
Karolan, Karolann, Karolanne, Karol-Anne

Karolina, Karoline (Slavic) forms of Caroline. See also Carolina.
Karaleen, Karalena, Karalene, Karalin, Karaline, Karileen, Karilena, Karilene, Karilin, Karilina, Kariline, Karleen, Karlen, Karlena, Karlene, Karling, Karoleena, Karolena, Karolinka, Karroleen, Karrolena, Karrolene, Karrolin, Karroline

Karoll (Slavic) a form of Carol.
Karel, Karilla, Karily, Karol, Karola, Karole, Karoly, Karrol, Karyl, Kerril

Karolyn (American) a form of Carolyn.
Karalyn, Karalyna, Karalynn, Karalynne, Karilyn, Karilyna, Karilynn, Karilynne, Karlyn, Karlynn, Karlynne, Karolyna, Karolynn, Karolynne, Karrolyn, Karrolyna, Karrolynn, Karrolynne

Karri, Karrie (American) forms of Carrie.
Kari, Karie, Karry, Kary

Karsen, Karsyn (English) child of Kar. Forms of Carson.
Karson

Karuna (Hindi) merciful.

Karyn (American) a form of Karen.
Karyne, Karynn, Karynna, Kerrynn, Kerrynne

Kasa (Hopi) fur robe.

Kasandra (Greek) a form of Kassandra.
Kasander, Kasandria, Kasandra, Kasaundra, Kasondra, Kasoundra

Kasey, Kasie (Irish) brave. (American) forms of Casey, Kacey.
Kaisee, Kaisie, Kasci, Kascy, Kasee, Kasi, Kassee, Kassey, Kasy, Kasya, Kaysci, Kaysea, Kaysee, Kaysey, Kaysi, Kaysie, Kaysy

Kashawna (American) a combination of Kate + Shawna.
Kasha, Kashae, Kashana, Kashanna, Kashauna, Kashawn, Kasheana, Kasheanna, Kasheena, Kashena, Kashonda, Kashonna

Kashmir (Sanskrit) Geography: a region located between India and Pakistan.
Cashmere, Kashmear, Kashmere, Kashmia, Kashmira, Kasmir, Kasmira, Kazmir, Kazmira

Kasi (Hindi) from the holy city.

Kasia (Polish) a form of Katherine. See also Cassia.
Kashia, Kasiah, Kasian, Kasienka, Kasja, Kaska, Kassa, Kassia, Kassya, Kasya

Kasinda (Umbundu) our last baby.

Kassandra (Greek) a form of Cassandra.
Kassandr, Kassandre, Kassandré, Kassaundra, Kassi, Kassondra,

Kassondria, Kassundra, Kazandra, Khrisandra, Krisandra, Krissandra

Kassi, Kassie (American) familiar forms of Kassandra, Kassidy. See also Cassie.
Kassey, Kassia, Kassy

Kassidy (Irish) clever. (American) a form of Cassidy.
Kassadee, Kassadi, Kassadie, Kassadina, Kassady, Kasseday, Kassedee, Kassi, Kassiddy, Kassidee, Kassidi, Kassidie, Kassity, Kassydi

Katalina (Irish) a form of Caitlin. See also Catalina.
Kataleen, Kataleena, Katalena, Katalin, Katalyn, Katalynn

Katarina (Czech) a form of Katherine.
Kata, Katareena, Katarena, Katarin, Katarine, Katarinna, Katarinne, Katarrina, Kataryna, Katarzyna, Katinka, Katrika, Katrinka

Kate (Greek) pure. (English) a short form of Katherine.
Kait, Kata, Katee, Kati, Katica, Katie, Katka, Katy, Katya

Katee, Katey (English) familiar forms of Kate, Katherine.

Katelin (Irish) a form of Caitlin. See also Kaitlin.
Kaetlin, Katalin, Katelan, Kateland, Kateleen, Katelen, Katelene, Katelind, Kateline, Katelinn, Katelun, Kaytlin

Katelyn, Katelynn (Irish) forms of Caitlin.
Kaetlyn, Kaetlynn, Kaetlynne, Katelyne, Katelynne, Kaytlyn, Kaytlynn, Kaytlynne

Katerina (Slavic) a form of Katherine.
Katenka, Katerine, Katerini, Katerinka

Katharine (Greek) a form of Katherine.
Katharaine, Katharin, Katharina, Katharyn

Katherine (Greek) pure. See also Carey, Catherine, Ekaterina, Kara, Karen, Kari, Kasia, Katerina, Yekaterina.
Ekaterina, Ekatrinna, Kasienka, Kasin, Kat, Katarina, Katchen, Kate, Katee, Kathann, Kathanne, Katharine, Kathereen, Katheren, Katherene, Katherenne, Katherin, Katherina, Katheryn, Katheryne, Kathi, Kathleen, Kathrine, Kathryn, Kathy, Kathyrine, Katia, Katina, Katlaina, Katoka, Katreeka, Katrina, Kay, Kitty

Kathi, Kathy (English) familiar forms of Katherine, Kathleen. See also Cathi.
Kaethe, Katha, Kathe, Kathee, Kathey, Kathi, Kathie, Katka, Katla, Kató

Kathleen (Irish) a form of Katherine. See also Cathleen.
Katheleen, Kathelene, Kathi, Kathileen, Kathlean, Kathleena, Kathleene, Kathlene, Kathlin, Kathlina, Kathlyn, Kathlyne, Kathlynn, Kathy, Katleen

Kathrine (Greek) a form of Katherine.
Kathreen, Kathreena, Kathrene, Kathrin, Kathrina

Kathryn (English) a form of Katherine.
Kathren, Kathryne, Kathrynn, Kathrynne

Kati (Estonian) a familiar form of
Kate.
Katja, Katya, Katye

Katia, Katya (Russian) forms of
Katherine.
Cattiah, Katiya, Kattia, Kattiah, Katyah

Katie (English) a familiar form of
Kate.
*Katee, Kati, Kātia, Katti, Kattie, Katy,
Kayte, Kaytee, Kaytie*

Katilyn (Irish) a form of Katlyn.
Katilin, Katilynn

Katlin (Irish) a form of Katlyn.
Katlina, Katline

Katlyn (Greek) pure. (Irish) a form of
Katelin.
*Kaatlain, Katilyn, Katland, Katlin,
Katlynd, Katlyne, Katlynn, Katlynne*

Katriel (Hebrew) God is my crown.
Katrelle, Katri, Katrie, Katry, Katryel

Katrina (German) a form of
Katherine. See also Catrina, Trina.
*Katreen, Katreena, Katrene, Katri,
Katrice, Katricia, Katrien, Katrin,
Katrine, Katrinia, Katriona, Katryn,
Katryna, Kattrina, Kattryna, Katus,
Katuska*

Katy (English) a familiar form of Kate.
See also Cady.
Kady, Katey, Katty, Kayte

Kaulana (Hawaiian) famous.
Kaula, Kauna, Kahuna

Kaveri (Hindi) Geography: a sacred
river in India.

Kavindra (Hindi) poet.

Kawena (Hawaiian) glow.
Kawana, Kawona

Kay (Greek) rejoicer. (Teutonic) a fortified place. (Latin) merry. A short
form of Katherine.
Caye, Kae, Kai, Kaye, Kayla

Kaya (Hopi) wise child. (Japanese)
resting place.
Kaja, Kayah, Kayia

Kaycee (American) a combination of
the initials K. + C.
*Kayce, Kaysee, Kaysey, Kaysi, Kaysie,
Kaysii*

Kaydee (American) a combination of
the initials K. + D.
Kayda, Kayde, Kayden, Kaydi, Kaydie

Kayla (Arabic, Hebrew) laurel; crown.
A form of Kaela, Kaila. See also
Cayla.
*Kaylah, Kaylea, Kaylee, Kayleen,
Kaylene, Kaylia, Keila, Keyla*

Kaylah (Arabic, Hebrew) a form of
Kayla.
Kayleah, Kaylia, Keylah

Kaylan, Kaylen (Hebrew) forms of
Kayleen.
*Kaylana, Kayland, Kaylani, Kaylann,
Kaylean, Kayleana, Kayleanna, Kaylenn*

Kaylee (American) a form of Kayla.
See also Caeley, Kalee.
*Kailee, Kayle, Kayleigh, Kayley, Kayli,
Kaylie*

Kayleen, Kaylene (Hebrew) beloved,
sweetheart. Forms of Kayla.
*Kaylan, Kayleena, Kayleene, Kaylen,
Kaylena*

Kayleigh (American) a form of
Kaylee.
Kaylei

Kayley, Kayli, Kaylie (American)
forms of Kaylee.

Kaylin (American) a form of Kaylyn.
Kaylon

Kaylyn, Kaylynn (American) combi-
nations of Kay + Lynn. See also
Kaelyn.
*Kalyn, Kalynn, Kayleen, Kaylene,
Kaylin, Kaylyna, Kaylyne, Kaylynne*

Kaytlin, Kaytlyn (Irish) forms of
Kaitlin.
*Kaytlan, Kaytlann, Kaytlen, Kaytlyne,
Kaytlynn, Kaytlynne*

Keaira (Irish) a form of Keara.
Keair, Keairah, Keairra, Keairre, Keairrea

Keala (Hawaiian) path.

Keana, Keanna (German) bold; sharp.
(Irish) beautiful.
*Keanah, Keanne, Keanu, Keenan,
Keeyana, Keeyanah, Keeyanna,
Keeyona. Keeyonna, Keiana, Keianna,
Keona, Keonna*

Keandra, Keondra (American) forms
of Kenda.
*Keandrah, Keandre, Keandrea, Keandria,
Kedeana, Kedia, Keonda, Keondre,
Keondria*

Keara (Irish) dark; black. Religion: an
Irish saint.
*Keaira, Kearah, Kearia, Kearra, Keera,
Keerra, Keiara, Keiarah, Keiarra, Keira,
Kera*

Kearsten, Keirsten (Greek) forms of
Kirstin.
*Kearstin, Kearston, Kearstyn, Keirstan,
Keirstein, Keirstin, Keirston, Keirstyn,
Keirstynne*

Keeley, Keely (Irish) forms of Kelly.
*Kealee, Kealey, Keali, Kealie, Keallie,
Kealy, Keela, Keelan, Keele, Keelee,
Keeleigh, Keeli, Keelia, Keelie, Keellie,
Keelye, Keighla, Keilee, Keileigh, Keiley,
Keilly, Kiela, Kiele, Kieley, Kielly, Kiely*

Keelyn (Irish) a form of Kellyn.
Kealyn, Keelin, Keilan, Kielyn

Keena (Irish) brave.
Keenya, Kina

Keesha (American) a form of Keisha.
*Keesa, Keeshae, Keeshana, Keeshanne,
Keeshawna, Keeshonna, Keeshya,
Keiosha*

Kei (Japanese) reverent.

Keiana, Keianna (Irish) forms of
Keana. (American) forms of Kiana.
Keiann, Keiannah, Keionna

Keiki (Hawaiian) child.
Keikana, Keikann, Keikanna, Keikanne

Keiko (Japanese) happy child.

Keila (Arabic, Hebrew) a form of
Kayla.
Keilah, Kela, Kelah

Keilani (Hawaiian) glorious chief.
*Kaylani, Keilan, Keilana, Keilany,
Kelana, Kelanah, Kelane, Kelani,
Kelanie*

Keira (Irish) a form of Keara.
*Keiara, Keiarra, Keirra, Keirrah, Kera,
Keyeira*

Keisha (American) a short form of
Keneisha.
*Keasha, Keashia, Keesha, Keishaun,
Keishauna, Keishawn, Kesha, Keysha,
Kiesha, Kisha, Kishanda*

Keita (Scottish) woods; enclosed place.
Keiti

Kekona (Hawaiian) second-born
child.

Kelcey, Kelci, Kelcie (Scottish) forms
of Kelsey.
Kelse, Kelcee, Kelcy

Kelila (Hebrew) crown, laurel. See also
Kaela, Kayla, Kalila.
Kelilah, Kelula

Kelley (Irish) a form of Kelly.

Kelli, Kellie (Irish) familiar forms of
Kelly.
*Keleigh, Keli, Kelia, Keliah, Kelie,
Kellee, Kelleigh, Kellia, Kellisa*

Kelly (Irish) brave warrior. See also
Caeley.
*Keeley, Keely, Kelley, Kelley, Kelli,
Kellie, Kellye*

Kellyanne (Irish) a combination of
Kelly + Anne.
Kelliann, Kellianne, Kellyann

Kellyn (Irish) a combination of Kelly
+ Lyn.
*Keelyn, Kelleen, Kellen, Kellene,
Kellina, Kelline, Kellynn, Kellynne*

Kelsea (Scottish) a form of Kelsey.
*Kelcea, Kelcia, Kelsa, Kelsae, Kelsay,
Kelse*

Kelsey (Scandinavian, Scottish) ship
island. (English) a form of Chelsea.
*Kelcey, Kelda, Kellsee, Kellsei, Kellsey,
Kellsie, Kellsy, Kelsea, Kelsei, Kelsey,
Kelsi, Kelsie, Kelsy, Kelsye*

Kelsi, Kelsie, Kelsy (Scottish) forms of
Chelsea.
Kalsie, Kelci, Kelcie, Kellsi

Kenda (English) water baby. (Dakota)
magical power.
Keandra, Kendra, Kennda

Kendal (English) a form of Kendall.
*Kendahl, Kendale, Kendalie, Kendalin,
Kendalyn, Kendalynn, Kendel, Kendele,
Kendil, Kindal*

Kendall (English) ruler of the valley.
*Kendal, Kendalla, Kendalle, Kendell,
Kendelle, Kendera, Kendia, Kendyl,
Kinda, Kindall, Kindi, Kindle, Kynda,
Kyndal, Kyndall, Kyndel*

Kendra (English) a form of Kenda.
*Kandra, Kendrah, Kendre, Kendrea,
Kendreah, Kendria, Kenndra, Kentra,
Kentrae, Kindra, Kyndra*

Kendyl (English) a form of Kendall.
Kendyle, Kendyll

Keneisha (American) a combination
of the prefix Ken + Aisha.
*Kaneisha, Keisha, Keneesha, Kenesha,
Keneshia, Kenisha, Kenneisha,
Kennesha, Kenneshia, Keosha, Kineisha*

Kenenza (English) a form of Kennice.
Kenza

Kenia (Hebrew) a form of Kenya.
Keniya, Kennia

Kenisha (American) a form of
Keneisha.
*Kenisa, Kenise, Kenishia, Kenissa,
Kennisa, Kennisha, Kennysha*

Kenna (Irish) a short form of Kennice.

Kennedy (Irish) helmeted chief.
History: John F. Kennedy was the
thirty-fifth U. S. president.
*Kenedee, Kenedey, Kenedi, Kenedie,
Kenedy, Kenidee, Kenidi, Kenidie,
Kenidy, Kennadee, Kennadi, Kennadie,
Kennady, Kennedee, Kennedey, Kennedi,
Kennedie, Kennidee, Kennidi, Kennidy,
Kynnedi*

Kennice (English) beautiful.
*Kanice, Keneese, Kenenza, Kenese,
Kennise*

Kenya (Hebrew) animal horn.
Geography: a country in Africa.
*Keenya, Kenia, Kenja, Kenyah,
Kenyana, Kenyatta, Kenyia*

Kenyatta (American) a form of
Kenya.
*Kenyata, Kenyatah, Kenyatte, Kenyattia,
Kenyatta, Kenyette*

Kenzie (Scottish) light skinned. (Irish)
a short form of Mackenzie.
*Kenzea, Kenzee, Kenzey, Kenzi,
Kenzia, Kenzy, Kinzie*

Keona, Keonna (Irish) forms of
Keana.
*Keiona, Keionna, Keoana, Keoni,
Keonia, Keonnah, Keonni, Keonnia*

Keosha (American) a short form of
Keneisha.
Keoshae, Keoshi, Keoshia, Keosia

Kerani (Hindi) sacred bells. See also
Rani.
Kera, Kerah, Keran, Kerana

Keren (Hebrew) animal's horn.
Kerrin, Keryn

Kerensa (Cornish) a form of Karenza.
Karensa, Karenza, Kerenza

Keri, Kerri, Kerrie (Irish) forms of
Kerry.
Keriann, Kerianne, Kerriann, Kerrianne

Kerry (Irish) dark haired. Geography: a
county in Ireland.
*Keary, Keiry, Keree, Kerey, Keri, Kerri,
Kerrie, Kerryann, Kerryanne, Kery,
Kiera, Kierra*

Kerstin (Scandinavian) a form of
Kirsten.
*Kerstan, Kerste, Kerstein, Kersten,
Kerstie, Kerstien, Kerston, Kerstyn,
Kerstynn*

Kesare (Latin) long haired. (Russian) a
form of Caesar (see Boys' Names).

Kesha (American) a form of Keisha.
*Keshah, Keshal, Keshala, Keshan,
Keshana, Keshara, Keshawn, Keshawna,
Keshawnna*

Keshia (American) a form of Keisha.
A short form of Keneisha.
*Kecia, Keishia, Keschia, Keshea, Kesia,
Kesiah, Kessia, Kessiah*

Kesi (Swahili) born during difficult
times.

Kessie (Ashanti) chubby baby.
Kess, Kessa, Kesse, Kessey, Kessi

Kevyn (Irish) beautiful.
*Keva, Kevan, Keven, Kevia, Keviana,
Kevinna, Kevina, Kevion, Kevionna,
Kevon, Kevona, Kevone, Kevonia,
Kevonna, Kevonne, Kevonya, Kevynn*

Keyana, Keyanna (American) forms
of Kiana.
*Keya, Keyanah, Keyanda, Keyandra,
Keyannah*

Keyara (Irish) a form of Kiara.
*Keyarah, Keyari, Keyarra, Keyera,
Keyerah, Keyerra*

Keyona, Keyonna (American) forms
of Kiana.
*Keyonda, Keyondra, Keyonnia,
Keyonnie*

Keysha (American) a form of Keisha.
*Keyosha, Keyoshia, Keyshana,
Keyshanna, Keyshawn, Keyshawna,
Keyshia, Keyshla, Keyshona, Keyshonna*

Keziah (Hebrew) cinnamon-like spice.
Bible: one of the daughters of Job.
*Kazia, Kaziah, Ketzi, Ketzia, Ketziah,
Kezi, Kezia, Kizzy*

Khadijah (Arabic) trustworthy.
History: Muhammed's first wife.
*Khadaja, Khadajah, Khadeeja,
Khadeejah, Khadeja, Khadejah,
Khadejha, Khadija, Khadije, Khadijia,
Khadijiah*

Khalida (Arabic) immortal, everlasting.
*Khali, Khalia, Khaliah, Khalidda,
Khalita*

Khrissa (American) a form of Chrissa. (Czech) a form of Krista.
Khrishia, Khryssa, Krisha, Krisia, Krissa, Krysha, Kryssa

Khristina (Russian, Scandinavian) a form of Kristina, Christina.
Khristeen, Khristen, Khristin, Khristine, Khyristya, Khristyana, Khristyna, Khrystyne

Ki (Korean) arisen.

Kia (African) season's beginning. (American) a short form of Kiana.
Kiah

Kiana (American) a combination of the prefix Ki + Ana.
Keanna, Keiana, Keyana, Keyona, Khiana, Khianah, Khianna, Ki, Kiahna, Kiane, Kiani, Kiania, Kianna, Kiauna, Kiandra, Kiandria, Kiauna, Kiaundra, Kiyana, Kyana

Kianna (American) a form of Kiana.
Kiannah, Kianne, Kianni

Kiara (Irish) little and dark.
Keyara, Kiarra, Kieara, Kiearah, Kiearra, Kyara

Kiaria, Kiarra, Kichi (Japanese) fortunate.

Kiele (Hawaiian) gardenia; fragrant blossom.
Kiela, Kieley, Kieli, Kielli, Kielly

Kiera, Kierra (Irish) forms of Kerry.
Kierana, Kieranna, Kierea

Kiersten, Kierstin (Scandanavian) forms of Kirsten.
Keirstan, Kerstin, Kierstan, Kierston, Kierstyn, Kierstynn

Kiki (Spanish) a familiar form of names ending in "queta."

Kiku (Japanese) chrysanthemum.
Kiko

Kiley (Irish) attractive; from the straits.
Kilea, Kilee, Kileigh, Kili, Kilie, Kylee, Kyli, Kylie

Kim (Vietnamese) needle. (English) a short form of Kimberly.
Kima, Kimette, Kym

Kimana (Shoshone) butterfly.
Kiman, Kimani

Kimber (English) a short form of Kimberly.
Kimbra

Kimberlee, Kimberley (English) forms of Kimberly.
Kimbalee, Kimberlea, Kimberlei, Kimberleigh, Kimbley

Kimberly (English) chief, ruler.
Cymberly, Cymbre, Kim, Kimba, Kimbely, Kimber, Kimbereley, Kimberely, Kimberlee, Kimberli, Kimberlie, Kimberlyn, Kimbery, Kimbria, Kimbrie, Kimbry, Kimmie, Kymberly

Kimberlyn (English) a form of Kimberly.
Kimberlin, Kimberlynn

Kimi (Japanese) righteous.
Kimia, Kimika, Kimiko, Kimiyo, Kimmi, Kimmie, Kimmy

Kimmie (English) a familiar form of Kimberly.
Kimee, Kimme, Kimmee, Kimmi, Kimmy, Kimy

Kina (Hawaiian) from China.

Kineisha (American) a form of Keneisha.
Kineesha, Kinesha, Kineshia, Kinisha, Kinishia

Kineta (Greek) energetic.
Kinetta

Kini (Hawaiian) a form of Jean.
Kina

Kinsey (English) offspring; relative.
Kinsee, Kinsley, Kinza, Kinze, Kinzee, Kinzey, Kinzi, Kinzie, Kinzy

Kinsley (American) a form of Kinsey.
Kinslee, Kinslie, Kinslyn

Kioko (Japanese) happy child.
Kiyo, Kiyoko

Kiona (Native American) brown hills.
Kionah, Kioni, Kionna

Kira (Persian) sun. (Latin) light.
Kirah, Kiri, Kiria, Kiro, Kirra, Kirrah, Kirri

Kiran (Hindi) ray of light.

Kirby (Scandinavian) church village. (English) cottage by the water.
Kirbee, Kirbi

Kirima (Eskimo) hill.

Kirsi (Hindi) amaranth blossoms.
Kirsie

Kirsta (Scandinavian) a form of Kirsten.

Kirsten (Greek) Christian; annointed. (Scandinavian) a form of Christine.
Karsten, Kearsten, Keirstan, Kerstin, Kiersten, Kirsteni, Kirsta, Kirstan, Kirstene, Kirstie, Kirstin, Kirston, Kirsty, Kirstyn, Kjersten, Kursten, Kyersten, Kyrsten, Kyrstin

Kirstin (Scandinavian) a form of Kirsten.
Karstin, Kirsteen, Kirstien, Kirstine

Kirstie, Kirsty (Scandinavian) familiar forms of Kirsten.
Kerstie, Kirsta, Kirste, Kirstee, Kirstey, Kirsti, Kjersti, Kyrsty

Kirstyn (Greek) a form of Kirsten.
Kirstynn

Kisa (Russian) kitten.
Kisha, Kiska, Kissa, Kiza

Kishi (Japanese) long and happy life.

Kissa (Ugandan) born after twins.

Kita (Japanese) north.

Kitra (Hebrew) crowned.

Kitty (Greek) a familiar form of Katherine.
Ketter, Ketti, Ketty, Kit, Kittee, Kitteen, Kittey, Kitti, Kittie

Kiwa (Japanese) borderline.

Kiyana (American) a form of Kiana.
Kiya, Kiyah, Kiyan, Kiyani, Kiyanna, Kiyenna

Kizzy (American) a familiar form of Keziah.
Kezi, Kissie, Kizzi, Kizzie

Klara (Hungarian) a form of Clara.
Klára, Klari, Klarika

Klarise (German) a form of Klarissa.
Klarice, Kláris, Klaryce

Klarissa (German) clear, bright. (Italian) a form of Clarissa.
Klarisa, Klarise, Klarrisa, Klarrissa, Klarrissia, Klarisza, Klarysa, Klaryssa, Kleresa

Klaudia (American) a form of Claudia.
Klaudija

Kloe (American) a form of Chloe.
Khloe, Kloee, Kloey, Klohe, Kloie

Kodi (American) a form of Codi.
Kodee, Kodey, Kodie, Kody, Kodye, Koedi

Koffi (Swahili) born on Friday.
Kaffe, Kaffi, Koffe, Koffie

Koko (Japanese) stork. See also Coco.

Kolby (American) a form of Colby.
Kobie, Koby, Kolbee, Kolbey, Kolbi, Kolbie

Kolina (Swedish) a form of Katherine. See also Colleen.
Koleen, Koleena, Kolena, Kolene, Koli, Kolleen, Kollena, Kollene, Kolyn, Kolyna

Kona (Hawaiian) lady. (Hindi) angular.
Koni, Konia

Konstance (Latin) a form of Constance.
Konstantina, Konstantine, Konstanza, Konstanze

Kora (Greek) a form of Cora.
Korah, Kore, Koren, Koressa, Koretta, Korra

Koral (American) a form of Coral.
Korel, Korele, Korella, Korilla, Korral, Korrel, Korrell, Korrelle

Kori (American) a short form of Korina. See also Corey, Cori.
Koree, Korey, Koria, Korie, Korri, Korrie, Korry, Kory

Korina (Greek) a form of Corina.
Koreena, Korena, Koriana, Korianna, Korine, Korinna, Korreena, Korrina, Korrinna, Koryna, Korynna

Korine (Greek) a form of Korina.
Koreen, Korene, Koriane, Korianne, Korin, Korinn, Korinne, Korrin, Korrine, Korrinne, Korryn, Korrynne, Koryn, Koryne, Korynn

Kornelia (Latin) a form of Cornelia.
Karniela, Karniella, Karnis, Kornelija, Kornelis, Kornelya, Korny

Kortney (English) a form of Courtney.
Kortnay, Kortnee, Kortni, Kortnie, Kortny

Kosma (Greek) order; universe.
Cosma

Kosta (Latin) a short form of Constance.
Kostia, Kostusha, Kostya

Koto (Japanese) harp.

Kourtney (American) a form of Courtney.
Kourtnay, Kourtne, Kourtnee, Kourtnei, Kourtneigh, Kourtni, Kourtny, Kourtynie

Kris (American) a short form of Kristine. A form of Chris.
Khris, Krissy

Krissy (American) a familiar form of Kris.
Krissey, Krissi, Krissie

Krista (Czech) a form of Christina. See also Christa.
Khrissa, Khrista, Khryssa, Khrysta, Krissa, Kryssa, Krysta

Kristal (Latin) a form of Crystal.
Kristale, Kristall, Kristill, Kristl, Kristle, Kristy

Kristan (Greek) a form of Kristen.
Kristana, Kristanna, Kristanne, Kriston, Krystan, Krystane

Kristen (Greek) Christian; anointed. (Scandinavian) a form of Christine.
Christen, Kristan, Kristene, Kristien, Kristin, Kristyn, Krysten

Kristi, Kristie (Scandinavian) short forms of Kristine.
Christi

Kristian, Kristiana (Greek) Christian; anointed. Forms of Christian.
Khristian, Kristian, Kristiane, Kristiann, Kristi-Ann, Kristianna, Kristianne, Kristi-Anne, Kristienne, Kristyan, Kristyana, Kristy-Ann, Kristy-Anne

Kristin (Scandinavian) a form of Kristen. See also Cristen.
Kristiin, Krystin

Kristina (Greek) Christian; annointed. (Scandinavian) a form of Christina. See also Cristina.
Khristina, Kristena, Kristina, Kristeena, Kristena, Kristinka, Krystina

Kristine (Scandinavian) a form of Christine.
Kris, Kristeen, Kristene, Kristi, Kristie, Kristy, Krystine, Krystyne

Kristy (American) a familiar form of Kristine, Krystal. See also Cristy.
Kristi, Kristia, Kristie, Krysia, Krysti

Kristyn (Greek) a form of Kristen.
Kristyne, Kristynn

Krysta (Polish) a form of Krista.
Krystah, Krystka

Krystal (American) clear, brilliant glass.
Kristabel, Kristal, Krystalann, Krystalanne, Krystale, Krystall, Krystalle, Krystel, Krystil, Krystle, Krystol

Krystalee (American) a combination of Krystal + Lee.
Kristalea, Kristaleah, Kristalee, Krystalea, Krystaleah, Krystlea, Krystleah, Krystlee, Krystlelea, Krystleleah, Krystlelee

Krystalynn (American) a combination of Krystal + Lynn.
Kristaline, Kristalyn, Kristalynn, Kristilyn, Kristilynn, Kristlyn, Krystaleen, Krystalene, Krystalin, Krystalina, Krystallyn, Krystalyn, Krystalynne

Krystel (Latin) a form of Krystal.
Kristel, Kristell, Kristelle, Krystelle

Krysten (Greek) a form of Kristen.
Krystene, Krystyn, Krystyne

Krystian, Krystiana (Greek) forms of Christian.
Krystiana, Krystianna, Krystianne, Krysty-Ann, Krystyan, Kristyana, Krystyanna, Krystyanne, Krysty-Anne, Krystyen

Krystin (Czech) a form of Kristin.

Krystina (Greek) a form of Kristina.
Krysteena, Krystena, Krystyna, Krystynka

Krystle (American) a form of Krystal.
Krystl, Krystyl

Kudio (Swahili) born on Monday.

Kuma (Japanese) bear. (Tongan) mouse.

Kumiko (Japanese) girl with braids.
Kumi

Kumuda (Sanskrit) lotus flower.

Kuniko (Japanese) child from the country.

Kunto (Twi) third-born.

Kuri (Japanese) chestnut.

Kusa (Hindi) God's grass.

Kwanita (Zuni) a form of Juanita.

Kwashi (Swahili) born on Sunday.

Kwau (Swahili) born on Thursday.

Kyana (American) a form of Kiana.
Kyanah, Kyani, Kyann, Kyanna,
Kyanne, Kyanni, Kyeana, Kyeanna

Kyara (Irish) a form of Kiara.
Kiyara, Kiyera, Kiyerra, Kyarah, Kyaria,
Kyarie, Kyarra, Kyera, Kyerra

Kyla (Irish) attractive. (Yiddish) crown;
laurel.
Khyla, Kylah, Kylea, Kyleah, Kylia

Kyle (Irish) attractive.
Kial, Kiele, Kylee, Kyleigh, Kylene, Kylie

Kylee (Irish) a familiar form of Kyle.
Kylea, Kyleah, Kylie, Kyliee

Kyleigh (Irish) a form of Kyle.
Kyliegh

Kylene (Irish) a form of Kyle.
Kyleen, Kylen, Kylyn, Kylynn

Kylie (West Australian Aboriginal)
curled stick; boomerang. (Irish) a
familiar form of Kyle.
Keiley, Keilley, Keilly, Keily, Kiley, Kye,
Kylee, Kyley, Kyli, Kyllie

Kymberly (English) a form of
Kimberly.
Kymber, Kymberlee, Kymberleigh,
Kymberley, Kymberli, Kymberlie,
Kymberlyn, Kymberlynn, Kymberlynne

Kyndal, Kyndall (English) forms of
Kendall.
Kyndahl, Kyndalle, Kyndel, Kyndell,
Kyndelle, Kyndle, Kyndol

Kynthia (Greek) a form of Cynthia.
Kyndi

Kyoko (Japanese) mirror.

Kyra (Greek) ladylike. A form of Cyrilla.
Keera, Keira, Kira, Kyrah, Kyrene,
Kyria, Kyriah, Kyriann, Kyrie

Lacey, Lacy (Latin) cheerful. (Greek)
familiar forms of Larissa.
Lacee, Laci, Lacie, Lacye

Lachandra (American) a combination
of the prefix La + Chandra.
Lachanda, Lachandice

Laci, Lacie (Latin) forms of Lacey.
Lacia, Laciann, Lacianne

Lacrecia (Latin) a form of Lucretia.
Lacrasha, Lacreash, Lacreasha, Lacreashia,
Lacreisha, Lacresha, Lacreshia, Lacresia,
Lacretia, Lacricia, Lacriesha, Lacrisah,
Lacrisha, Lacrishia, Lacrissa

Lada (Russian) Mythology: the Slavic
goddess of beauty.

Ladasha (American) a combination of
the prefix La + Dasha.
Ladaesha, Ladaisa, Ladaisha, Ladaishea,
Ladaishia, Ladashiah, Ladaseha,
Ladashia, Ladasia, Ladassa, Ladaysha,
Ladesha, Ladisha, Ladosha

Ladeidra (American) a combination
of the prefix La + Deidra.
Ladedra, Ladiedra

Ladonna (American) a combination
of the prefix La + Donna.
Ladan, Ladana, Ladon, Ladona,
Ladonne, Ladonya

Laela (Arabic, Hebrew) a form of
Leila.
Lael, Laelle

Lahela (Hawaiian) a form of Rachel.

Laila (Arabic) a form of Leila.
Lailah, Laili, Lailie

Laine, Layne (French) short forms of
Elaine.
Lain, Laina, Lainah, Lainee, Lainna,
Layna

Lainey, Layney (French) familiar forms
of Elaine.
Laini, Lainie, Laynee, Layni, Laynie

Lajila (Hindi) shy, coy.

Lajuana (American) a combination of
the prefix La + Juana.
Lajuanna, Lawana, Lawanna, Lawanza,
Lawanze, Laweania

Laka (Hawaiian) attractive; seductive;
tame. Mythology: the goddess of the
hula.

Lakayla (American) a combination of
the prefix La + Kayla.
Lakala, Lakaya, Lakeila, Lakela, Lakella

Lakeisha (American) a combination of
the prefix La + Keisha. See also
Lekasha.
Lakaiesha, Lakaisha, Lakasha, Lakashia,
Lakaysha, Lakaysia, Lakeasha, Lakecia,
Lakeesh, Lakeesha, Lakeeshia, Lakesha,
Lakeshia, Lakeysha, Lakezia, Lakicia,
Lakieshia, Lakisha

Laken, Lakin, Lakyn (American) short
forms of Lakendra.
Lakena, Lakyna, Lakynn

Lakendra (American) a combination
of the prefix La + Kendra.
Lakanda, Lakedra, Laken, Lakenda

Lakenya (American) a combination of
the prefix La + Kenya.
*Lakeena, Lakeenna, Lakeenya, Lakena,
Lakenia, Lakinja, Lakinya, Lakwanya,
Lekenia, Lekenya*

Lakesha, Lakeshia, Lakisha (American)
forms of Lakeisha.
*Lakecia, Lakeesha, Lakesa, Lakese,
Lakeseia, Lakeshya, Lakesi, Lakesia,
Lakeyshia, Lakiesha*

Laketa (American) a combination of the
prefix La + Keita.
*Lakeeta, Lakeetah, Lakeita, Lakeitha,
Lakeithia, Laketha, Laketia, Laketta,
Lakieta, Lakietha, Lakita, Lakitia,
Lakitra, Lakitri, Lakitta*

Lakia (Arabic) found treasure.
Lakiea, Lakkia

Lakota (Dakota) a tribal name.
Lakoda, Lakohta, Lakotah

Lakresha (American) a form of
Lucretia.
*Lacresha, Lacreshia, Lacresia, Lacretia,
Lacrisha, Lakreshia, Lakrisha, Lekresha,
Lekresia*

Lakya (Hindi) born on Thursday.
*Lakeya, Lakeyah, Lakieya, Lakiya,
Lakyia*

Lala (Slavic) tulip.
Lalah, Lalla

Lalasa (Hindi) love.

Laleh (Persian) tulip.
Lalah

Lali (Spanish) a form of Lulani.
Lalia, Lalli, Lally

Lalita (Greek) talkative. (Sanskrit)
charming; candid.

Lallie (English) babbler.
Lalli, Lally

Lamesha (American) a combination
of the prefix La + Mesha.
*Lamees, Lameesha, Lameise, Lameisha,
Lameshia, Lamisha, Lamishia, Lemisha*

Lamia (German) bright land.
Lama, Lamiah

Lamis (Arabic) soft to the touch.
Lamese, Lamise

Lamonica (American) a combination
of the prefix La + Monica.
Lamoni, Lamonika

Lamya (Arabic) dark lipped.
Lama

Lan (Vietnamese) flower.

Lana (Latin) woolly. (Irish) attractive,
peaceful. A short form of Alana,
Elana. (Hawaiian) floating; bouyant.
*Lanae, Lanai, Lanata, Lanay, Laneah,
Laneetra, Lanette, Lanna, Lannah*

Landa (Basque) another name for the
Virgin Mary.

Landon (English) open, grassy
meadow.
*Landan, Landen, Landin, Landyn,
Landynne*

Landra (German, Spanish) counselor.
Landrea

Lane (English) narrow road.
Laina, Laney, Layne

Laneisha (American) a combination
of the prefix La + Keneisha.
*Laneasha, Lanecia, Laneesha, Laneise,
Laneishia, Lanesha, Laneshe, Laneshea,
Laneshia, Lanesia, Lanessa, Lanesse,
Lanisha, Lanishia*

Laney (English) a familiar form of Lane.
Lanie, Lanni, Lanny, Lany

Lani (Hawaiian) sky; heaven. A short
form of Atalanta, 'Aulani, Leilani.
*Lanee, Lanei, Lania, Lanie, Lanita,
Lanney, Lanni, Lannie*

Laporsha (American) a combination
of the prefix La + Porsha.
*Laporcha, Laporche, Laporscha,
Laporsche, Laporschia, Laporshe,
Laporshia, Laportia*

Laqueena (American) a combination
of the prefix La + Queenie.
Laqueen, Laquena, Laquenetta, Laquinna

Laquinta (American) a combination
of the prefix La + Quintana.
*Laquanta, Laqueinta, Laquenda,
Laquenta, Laquinda*

Laquisha (American) a combination
of the prefix La + Queisha.
*Laquasha, Laquaysha, Laqueisha,
Laquesha, Laquiesha*

Laquita (American) a combination of
the prefix La + Queta.
*Laqeita, Laqueta, Laquetta, Laquia,
Laquiata, Laquieta, Laquitta, Lequita*

Lara (Greek) cheerful. (Latin) shining; famous. Mythology: a Roman nymph. A short form of Laraine, Larissa, Laura.
Larae, Larah, Laretta, Larette

Laraine (Latin) a form of Lorraine.
Lara, Laraene, Larain, Larane, Larayn, Larayne, Laraynna, Larein, Lareina, Lareine, Laren, Larenn, Larenya, Lauraine, Laurraine

Larina (Greek) seagull.
Larena, Larine

Larisa (Greek) a form of Larissa.
Lareesa, Lareese, Laresa, Laris, Larise, Larisha, Larrisa, Larysa, Laurisa

Larissa (Greek) cheerful. See also Lacey.
Lara, Laressa, Larisa, Larissah, Larrissa, Larryssa, Laryssa, Laurissa, Laurissah

Lark (English) skylark.

Lashae, Lashay (American) combinations of the prefix La + Shay.
Lasha, Lashai, Lashaia, Lashaya, Lashaye, Lashea

Lashana (American) a combination of the prefix La + Shana.
Lashanay, Lashane, Lashanna, Lashannon, Lashona, Lashonna

Lashanda (American) a combination of the prefix La + Shanda.
Lashandra, Lashanta, Lashante

Lashawna (American) a combination of the prefix La + Shawna.
Lashaun, Lashauna, Lashaune, Lashaunna, Lashaunta, Lashawn, Lashawnd, Lashawnda, Lashawndra, Lashawne, Lashawnia, Leshawn, Leshawna

Lashonda (American) a combination of the prefix La + Shonda.
Lachonda, Lashaunda, Lashaundra, Lashon, Lashond, Lashonde, Lashondia, Lashondra, Lashonta, Lashunda, Lashundra, Lashunta, Lashunte, Leshande, Leshandra, Leshondra, Leshundra

Latanya (American) a combination of the prefix La + Tanya.
Latana, Latandra, Latania, Latanja, Latanna, Latanua, Latonshia

Latara (American) a combination of the prefix La + Tara.

Latasha (American) a combination of the prefix La + Tasha.
Latacha, Latacia, Latai, Lataisha, Latashia, Latasia, Lataysha, Letasha, Letashia, Letasiah

Latavia (American) a combination of the prefix La + Tavia.

Lateefah (Arabic) pleasant. (Hebrew) pat, caress.
Lateefa, Latifa, Latifah, Latipha

Latesha (American) a form of Leticia.
Lataeasha, Lateasha, Lateashia, Latecia, Lateicia, Lateisha, Latesa, Lateshia, Latessa, Lateysha, Latisa, Latissa, Leteisha, Leteshia

Latia (American) a combination of the prefix La + Tia.
Latea, Lateia, Lateka

Latika (Hindi) elegant.
Lateeka, Lateka

Latisha (Latin) joy. (American) a combination of the prefix La + Tisha.
Laetitia, Laetizia, Latashia, Lateasha, Lateashia, Latecia, Lateesha, Lateicia, Lateisha, Latice, Laticia, Latiesha, Latishia, Latishya, Latissha, Latitia, Latysha

Latona (Latin) Mythology: the powerful goddess who bore Apollo and Diana.
Latonna, Latonnah

Latonya (American) a combination of the prefix La + Tonya. (Latin) a form of Latona.
Latoni, Latonia

Latoria (American) a combination of the prefix La + Tori.
Latoira, Latorio, Latorja, Latorray, Latorreia, Latory, Latorya, Latoyra, Latoyria

Latosha (American) a combination of the prefix La + Tosha.
Latoshia, Latoshya, Latosia

Latoya (American) a combination of the prefix La + Toya.
Latoia, Latoiya, LaToya, Latoyia, Latoye, Latoyia, Latoyita, Latoyo

Latrice (American) a combination of the prefix La + Trice.
Latrece, Latreece, Latreese, Latresa, Latrese, Latressa, Letreece, Letrice

Latricia (American) a combination of the prefix La + Tricia.
Latrecia, Latresh, Latresha, Latreshia, Latrica, Latrisha, Latrishia

Laura (Latin) crowned with laurel.
Lara, Laurah, Lauralee, Laurelen, Laurella, Lauren, Lauricia, Laurie, Laurka, Laury, Lauryn, Lavra, Lolly, Lora, Loretta, Lori, Lorinda, Lorna, Loura

Laurel (Latin) laurel tree.
Laural, Laurell, Laurelle, Lorel, Lorelle

Lauren (English) a form of Laura.
Lauran, Laureen, Laurena, Laurene, Laurien, Laurin, Laurine, Lawren, Loren, Lorena

Laurence (Latin) crowned with laurel.
Laurencia, Laurens, Laurent, Laurentana, Laurentina, Lawrencia

Laurianna (English) a combination of Laurie + Anna.
Laurana, Laurann, Laureana, Laureanne, Laureen, Laureena, Laurian, Lauriana, Lauriane, Laurianna, Laurie Ann, Laurie Anne, Laurina

Laurie (English) a familiar form of Laura.
Lari, Larilia, Laure, Lauré, Lauri, Lawrie

Laury (English) a familiar form of Laura.

Lauryn (English) a familiar form of Laura.
Laurynn

Laveda (Latin) cleansed, purified.
Lavare, Lavetta, Lavette

Lavelle (Latin) cleansing.
Lavella

Lavena (Irish, French) joy. (Latin) a form of Lavina.

Laverne (Latin) springtime. (French) grove of alder trees. See also Verna.
Laverine, Lavern, Laverna, La Verne

Lavina (Latin) purified; woman of Rome. See also Vina.
Lavena, Lavenia, Lavinia, Lavinie,

Levenia, Levinia, Livinia, Louvinia, Lovina, Lovinia

Lavonna (American) a combination of the prefix La + Yvonne.
Lavon, Lavonda, Lavonder, Lavondria, Lavone, Lavonia, Lavonica, Lavonn, Lavonne, Lavonnie, Lavonya

Lawan (Tai) pretty.
Lawanne

Lawanda (American) a combination of the prefix La + Wanda.
Lawonda, Lawynda

Layce (American) a form of Lacey.
Laycee, Layci, Laycia, Laycie, Laysa, Laysea, Laysie

Layla (Hebrew, Arabic) a form of Leila.
Laylah, Layli, Laylie

Le (Vietnamese) pearl.

Lea (Hawaiian) Mythology: the goddess of canoe makers. (Hebrew) a form of Leah.

Leah (Hebrew) weary. Bible: the first wife of Jacob. See also Lia.
Lea, Léa, Lee, Leea, Leeah, Leia

Leala (French) faithful, loyal.
Lealia, Lealie, Leial

Lean, Leann, Leanne (English) forms of Leeann, Lian.
Leana, Leane, Leanna

Leandra (Latin) like a lioness.
Leanda, Leandre, Leandrea, Leandria, Leeanda, Leeandra

Leanna, Leeanna (English) forms of Liana.
Leana, Leeana, Leianna

Leanore (Greek) a form of Eleanor. (English) a form of Helen.
Leanora, Lanore

Lecia (Latin) a short form of Felecia.
Leasia, Leecia, Leesha, Leesia, Lesha, Leshia, Lesia

Leda (Greek) lady. Mythology: the queen of Sparta and the mother of Helen of Troy.
Ledah, Lyda, Lydah

Lee (Chinese) plum. (Irish) poetic. (English) meadow. A short form of Ashley, Leah.
Lea, Leigh

Leeann, Leeanne (English) combinations of Lee + Ann. Forms of Lian.
Leane, Leean, Leian, Leiann, Leianne

Leena (Estonian) a form of Helen. (Greek, Latin, Arabic) a form of Lina.

Leeza (Hebrew) a short form of Aleeza. (English) a form of Lisa, Liza.
Leesa

Lei (Hawaiian) a familiar form of Leilani.

Leigh, Leigha (English) forms of Leah.
Leighann, Leighanna, Leighanne

Leiko (Japanese) arrogant.

Leila (Hebrew) dark beauty; night. (Arabic) born at night. See also Laela, Layla, Lila.
Laila, Leela, Leelah, Leilah, Leilia, Lela, Lelah, Leland, Lelia, Leyla

Leilani (Hawaiian) heavenly flower; heavenly child.
Lailanee, Lailani, Lailanie, Lailany, Lailoni, Lani, Lei, Leilany, Leiloni, Leilony, Lelani, Lelania

Lekasha (American) a form of Lakeisha.
Lekeesha, Lekeisha, Lekesha, Lekeshia, Lekesia, Lekicia, Lekisha

Leli (Swiss) a form of Magdalen.
Lelie

Lelia (Greek) fair speech. (Hebrew, Arabic) a form of Leila.
Leliah, Lelika, Lelita, Lellia

Lelya (Russian) a form of Helen.

Lena (Hebrew) dwelling or lodging. (Latin) temptress. (Norwegian) illustrious. (Greek) a short form of Eleanor. Music: Lena Horne, a well-known African American singer and actress.
Lenah, Lene, Lenee, Leni, Lenka, Lenna, Lennah, Lina, Linah

Lenci (Hungarian) a form of Helen.
Lency

Lene (German) a form of Helen.
Leni, Line

Leneisha (American) a combination of the prefix Le + Keneisha.
Lenece, Lenesha, Leniesha, Lenieshia, Leniesia, Leniessia, Lenisa, Lenise, Lenisha, Lennise, Lennisha, Lynesha

Lenia (German) a form of Leona.
Lenayah, Lenda, Lenea, Leneen, Lenna, Lennah, Lennea, Leny

Lenita (Latin) gentle.
Leneta, Lenette, Lennette

Lenore (Greek, Russian) a form of Eleanor.
Lenni, Lenor, Lenora, Lenorah

Leona (German) brave as a lioness. See also Lona.
Lenia, Leoine, Leola, Leolah, Leonae, Leonah, Leondra, Leone, Leonelle, Leonia, Leonice, Leonicia, Leonie, Leonissa, Leonna, Leonne, Liona

Leonie (German) a familiar form of Leona.
Leoni, Léonie, Leony

Leonore (Greek) a form of Eleanor. See also Nora.
Leonor, Leonora, Leonorah, Léonore

Leontine (Latin) like a lioness.
Leona, Leonine, Leontyne, Léontyne

Leora (Hebrew) light. (Greek) a familiar form of Eleanor. See also Liora.
Leorah, Leorit

Leotie (Native American) prairie flower.

Lera (Russian) a short form of Valera.
Lerka

Lesley (Scottish) gray fortress.
Leslea, Leslee, Leslie, Lesly, Lezlee, Lezley

Leslie (Scottish) a form of Lesley.
Leslei, Lesleigh, Lesli, Lesslie, Lezli

Lesly (Scottish) a form of Lesley.
Leslye, Lessly, Lezly

Leta (Latin) glad. (Swahili) bringer. (Greek) a short form of Aleta.
Lita, Lyta

Leticia (Latin) joy. See also Latisha, Tisha.
Laticia, Leisha, Leshia, Let, Leta, Letesa, Letesha, Leteshia, Letha, Lethia, Letice, Letichia, Letisha, Letishia, Letisia, Letissa, Letita, Letitia, Letiticia, Letiza, Letizia, Letty, Letycia, Loutitia

Letty (English) a familiar form of Leticia.
Letta, Letti, Lettie

Levana (Hebrew) moon; white. (Latin) risen. Mythology: the goddess of newborn babies.
Lévana, Levania, Levanna, Levenia, Lewana, Livana

Levani (Fijian) anointed with oil.

Levia (Hebrew) joined, attached.
Leevya, Levi, Levie

Levina (Latin) flash of lightning.
Levene

Levona (Hebrew) spice; incense.
Leavonia, Levonat, Levonna, Levonne, Livona

Lewana (Hebrew) a form of Levana.
Lebhanah, Lewanna

Lexandra (Greek) a short form of Alexandra.
Lisandra

Lexi, Lexie (Greek) familiar forms of Alexandra.
Leksi, Lexey, Lexy

Lexia (Greek) a familiar form of Alexandra.
Leska, Lesya, Lexa, Lexane, Lexina, Lexine

Lexis (Greek) a short form of Alexius, Alexus.
Laexis, Lexius, Lexsis, Lexxis

Lexus (Greek) a short form of Alexis.
Lexuss, Lexxus, Lexyss

Leya (Spanish) loyal. (Tamil) the constellation Leo.
Leyah, Leyla

Lia (Greek) bringer of good news. (Hebrew, Dutch, Italian) dependent. See also Leah.
Liah

Lian (Chinese) graceful willow. (Latin) a short form of Gillian, Lillian.
Lean, Leeann, Liane, Liann, Lianne

Liana, Lianna (Latin) youth. (French) bound, wrapped up; tree covered with vines. (English) meadow. (Hebrew) short forms of Eliana.
Leanna

Liane, Lianne (Hebrew) short forms of Eliane. (English) forms of Lian.
Leeanne

Libby (Hebrew) a familiar form of Elizabeth.
Ibby, Lib, Libbee, Libbey, Libbie

Liberty (Latin) free.
Liberti, Libertie

Licia (Greek) a short form of Alicia.
Licha, Lishia, Lisia, Lycia

Lida (Greek) happy. (Slavic) loved by people. (Latin) a short form of Alida, Elita.
Leeda, Lidah, Lidochka, Lyda

Lide (Latin, Basque) life.

Lidia (Greek) a form of Lydia.
Lidea, Lidi, Lidija, Lidiya, Lidka, Lidya

Lien (Chinese) lotus.
Lienne

Liesabet (German) a short form of Elizabeth.
Liesbeth, Lisbete

Liese (German) a familiar form of Elise, Elizabeth.
Liesa, Lieschen, Lise

Liesel (German) a familiar form of Elizabeth.
Leesel, Leesl, Leezel, Leezl, Liesl, Liezel, Liezl, Lisel

Lila (Arabic) night. (Hindi) free will of God. (Persian) lilac. A short form of Dalila, Delilah, Lillian.
Lilah, Lilia, Lyla, Lylah

Lilac (Sanskrit) lilac; blue purple.

Lilia (Persian) a form of Lila.
Lili

Lilian (Latin) a form of Lillian.
Liliane, Liliann, Lilianne

Liliana (Latin) a form of Lillian.
Lileana, Lilliana, Lilianna, Lilliana, Lillianna

Lilibeth (English) a combination of Lilly + Beth.
Lilibet, Lillibeth, Lillybeth, Lilybet, Lilybeth

Lilith (Arabic) of the night; night demon. Mythology: the first wife of Adam, according to ancient Jewish legends.
Lillis, Lily

Lillian (Latin) lily flower.
Lian, Lil, Lila, Lilas, Lileane, Lilia, Lilian, Liliana, Lilias, Liliha, Lilja, Lilla, Lilli, Lillia, Lilliane, Lilliann, Lillianne, Lillyann, Lis, Liuka

Lillyann (English) a combination of Lilly + Ann. (Latin) a form of Lillian.
Lillyan, Lillyanne, Lily, Lilyan, Lilyana, Lilyann, Lilyanna, Lilyanne

Lily (Latin, Arabic) a familiar form of Lilith, Lillian, Lillyann.
Lil, Líle, Lili, Lilie, Lilijana, Lilika, Lilike, Liliosa, Lilium, Lilka, Lille, Lilli, Lillie, Lilly

Limber (Tiv) joyful.

Lin (Chinese) beautiful jade. (English) a form of Lynn.
Linh, Linn

Lina (Greek) light. (Arabic) tender. (Latin) a form of Lena.

Linda (Spanish) pretty.
Lind, Lindy, Linita, Lynda

Lindsay (English) a form of Lindsey.
Lindsi, Linsay, Lyndsay

Lindsey (English) linden tree island; camp near the stream.
Lind, Lindsea, Lindsee, Lindsi, Linsey, Lyndsey, Lynsey

Lindsi (American) a familiar form of Lindsay, Lindsey.
Lindsie, Lindsy, Lindze, Lindzee, Lindzey, Lindzy

Lindy (Spanish) a familiar form of Linda.
Linde, Lindee, Lindey, Lindi, Lindie

Linette (Welsh) idol. (French) bird.
Lanette, Linet, Linnet, Linnetta, Linnette, Lyannette, Lynette

Ling (Chinese) delicate, dainty.

Linnea (Scandinavian) lime tree. Botany: the national flower of Sweden.
Lin, Linae, Linea, Linnae, Linnaea, Linneah, Lynea, Lynnea

Linsey (English) a form of Lindsey.
Linsea, Linsee, Linsi, Linsie, Linsy, Linzee, Linzey, Linzi, Linzie, Linzy, Linzzi, Lynsey

Liolya (Russian) a form of Helen.

Liora (Hebrew) light. See also Leora.

Lirit (Hebrew) poetic; lyrical, musical.

Liron (Hebrew) my song.
Leron, Lerone, Lirone

Lisa (Hebrew) consecrated to God. (English) a short form of Elizabeth.
Leeza, Liesa, Liisa, Lise, Lisenka, Lisette, Liszka, Litsa, Lysa

Lisbeth (English) a short form of Elizabeth.
Lisbet

Lise (German) a form of Lisa.

Lisette, Lissette (French) forms of Lisa. (English) familiar forms of Elise, Elizabeth.
Liset, Liseta, Lisete, Liseth, Lisett, Lisetta, Lisettina, Lisset, Lissete, Lissett, Lizet, Lizette, Lysette

Lisha (Arabic) darkness before midnight. (Hebrew) a short form of Alisha, Elisha, Ilisha. *Lishe*

Lissa (Greek) honey bee. A short form of Elissa, Elizabeth, Melissa, Millicent.
Lyssa

Lissie (American) a familiar form of Allison, Elise, Elizabeth.
Lissee, Lissey, Lissi, Lissy, Lissye

Lita (Latin) a familiar form of names ending in "lita."
Leta, Litah, Litta

Litonya (Moquelumnan) darting hummingbird.

Liv (Latin) a short form of Livia, Olivia.

Livana (Hebrew) a form of Levana.
Livna, Livnat

Livia (Hebrew) crown. A familiar form of Olivia. (Latin) olive.
Levia, Liv, Livie, Livy, Livya, Livye

Liviya (Hebrew) brave lioness; royal crown.
Leviya, Levya, Livya

Livona (Hebrew) a form of Levona.

Liz (English) a short form of Elizabeth.

Liza (American) a short form of Elizabeth.
Leeza, Lizela, Lizka, Lyza

Lizabeta (Russian) a form of Elizabeth.
Lizabetah, Lizaveta, Lizonka

Lizabeth (English) a short form of Elizabeth.
Lisabet, Lisabeth, Lisabette, Lizabette

Lizbeth (English) a short form of Elizabeth.
Lizbet, Lizbett

Lizet, Lizette (French) forms of Lisette.
Lizet, Lizete, Lizeth, Lizett, Lizzet, Lizzeth, Lizzette

Lizina (Latvian) a familiar form of Elizabeth.

Lizzy (American) a familiar form of Elizabeth.
Lizzie, Lizy

Logan (Irish) meadow.
Logann, Loganne, Logen, Loghan, Logun, Logyn, Logynn

Lois (German) famous warrior.

Lola (Spanish) a familiar form of Carlota, Dolores, Louise.
Lolah, Lolita

Lolita (Spanish) sorrowful. A familiar form of Lola.
Lita, Lulita

Lolly (English) sweet; candy. A familiar form of Laura.

Lolotea (Zuni) a form of Dorothy.

Lomasi (Native American) pretty flower.

Lona (Latin) lioness. (English) solitary. (German) a short form of Leona.
Loni, Lonna

London (English) fortress of the moon. Geography: the capital of the United Kingdom.
Landyn, Londen, Londun, Londyn

Loni (American) a form of Lona.
Lonee, Lonie, Lonni, Lonnie

Lora (Latin) crowned with laurel. (American) a form of Laura.
Lorah, Lorane, Lorann, Lorra, Lorrah, Lorrane

Lore (Basque) flower. (Latin) a short form of Flora.
Lor

Lorelei (German) alluring. Mythology: the siren of the Rhine River who lured sailors to their deaths. See also Lurleen.
Loralee, Loralei, Lorali, Loralie, Loralyn, Loreal, Lorelea, Loreli, Lorilee, Lorilyn

Lorelle (American) a form of Laurel.

Loren (American) a form of Lauren.
Loreen, Lorena, Lorin, Lorne, Lorren, Lorrin, Lorryn, Loryn, Lorynn, Lorynne

Lorena (English) a form of Lauren.
Lorene, Lorenea, Lorenia, Lorenna, Lorina, Lorrina, Lorrine, Lurana

Lorenza (Latin) a form of Laura.
Laurencia, Laurentia, Laurentina

Loretta (English) a familiar form of Laura.
Larretta, Lauretta, Laurette, Loretah, Lorette, Lorita, Lorretta, Lorrette

Lori (Latin) crowned with laurel. (French) a short form of Lorraine. (American) a familiar form of Laura.
Loree, Lorey, Loria, Lorianna, Lorianne, Lorie, Lorree, Lorri, Lorrie, Lory

Lorin (American) a form of Loren.
Lorine

Lorinda (Spanish) a form of Laura.

Loris (Latin) thong. (Dutch) clown. (Greek) a short form of Chloris.
Laurice, Laurys, Lorice

Lorna (Latin) crowned with laurel. Literature: probably coined by Richard Blackmore in his novel *Lorna Doone*.
Lorrna

Lorraine (Latin) sorrowful. (French) from Lorraine, a former province of France. See also Rayna.
Laraine, Lorain, Loraine, Lorayne, Lorein, Loreine, Lori, Lorine, Lorrain, Lorraina, Lorrayne, Lorreine

Lotte (German) a short form of Charlotte.
Lotie, Lotta, Lottchen, Lottey, Lottie, Lotty, Loty

Lotus (Greek) lotus.

Lou (American) a short form of Louise, Luella.
Lu

Louam (Ethiopian) sleep well.

Louisa (English) a familiar form of Louise. Literature: Louisa May Alcott was an American writer and reformer best known for her novel *Little Women*.
Aloisa, Eloisa, Heloisa, Lou, Louisian, Louisane, Louisina, Louiza, Lovisa, Luisa, Luiza, Lujza, Lujzika

Louise (German) famous warrior. See also Alison, Eloise, Heloise, Lois, Lola, Ludovica, Luella, Lulu.
Loise, Lou, Louisa, Louisette, Louisiane, Louisine, Lowise, Loyce, Loyise, Luise

Lourdes (French) from Lourdes, France. Religion: a place where the Virgin Mary was said to have appeared.

Love (English) love, kindness, charity.
Lovely, Lovewell, Lovey, Lovie, Lovy, Luv, Luvvy

Lovisa (German) a form of Louisa.

Luann (Hebrew, German) graceful woman warrior. (Hawaiian) happy; relaxed. (American) a combination of Louise + Ann.
Louann, Louanne, Lu, Lua, Luan, Luane, Luanna, Luanne, Luanni, Luannie

Luanna (German) a form of Luann.
Lewanna, Louanna, Luana, Luwana

Lubov (Russian) love.
Luba, Lubna, Lubochka, Lyuba, Lyubov

Lucerne (Latin) lamp; circle of light. Geography: the Lake of Lucerne is in Switzerland.
Lucerna, Lucero

Lucero (Latin) a form of Lucerne.

Lucetta (English) a familiar form of Lucy.
Lucette

Lucia (Italian, Spanish) a form of Lucy.
Luciana, Lucianna

Lucie (French) a familiar form of Lucy.

Lucille (English) a familiar form of Lucy.
Lucila, Lucile, Lucilla

Lucinda (Latin) a form of Lucy. See also Cindy.

Lucine (Arabic) moon. (Basque) a form of Lucy.
Lucienne, Lucina, Lucyna, Lukene, Lusine, Luzine

Lucita (Spanish) a form of Lucy.
Lusita

Lucretia (Latin) rich; rewarded.
Lacrecia, Lucrece, Lucréce, Lucrecia, Lucreecia, Lucresha, Lucreshia, Lucrezia, Lucrisha, Lucrishia

Lucrezia (Italian) a form of Lucretia. History: Lucrezia Borgia was the Duchess of Ferrara and a patron of learning and the arts.

Lucy (Latin) light; bringer of light.
Luca, Luce, Lucetta, Luci, Lucia, Lucida, Lucie, Lucija, Lucika, Lucille, Lucinda, Lucine, Lucita, Luciya, Lucya, Luzca, Luzi

Ludmilla (Slavic) loved by the people. See also Mila.
Ludie, Ludka, Ludmila, Lyuba, Lyudmila

Ludovica (German) a form of Louise.
Ludovika, Ludwiga

Luella (English) elf. (German) a familiar form of Louise.
Loella, Lou, Louella, Ludella, Luelle, Lula, Lulu

Luisa (Spanish) a form of Louisa.

Lulani (Polynesian) highest point of heaven.

Lulu (Arabic) pearl. (English) soothing, comforting. (Native American) hare. (German) a familiar form of Louise, Luella.
Loulou, Lula, Lulie

Luna (Latin) moon.
Lunetta, Lunette, Lunneta, Lunnete

Lupe (Latin) wolf. (Spanish) a short form of Guadalupe.
Lupi, Lupita, Luppi

Lupita (Latin) a form of Lupe.

Lurleen, Lurlene (Scandinavian) war horn. (German) forms of Lorelei.
Lura, Lurette, Lurline

Lusa (Finnish) a form of Elizabeth.

Lusela (Moquelumnan) like a bear swinging its foot when licking it.

Luvena (Latin, English) little; beloved.
Lovena, Lovina, Luvenia, Luvina

Luyu (Moquelumnan) like a pecking bird.

Luz (Spanish) light. Religion: Nuestra Señora de Luz—Our Lady of the Light—is another name for the Virgin Mary.
Luzi, Luzija

Lycoris (Greek) twilight.

Lyda (Greek) a short form of Lidia, Lydia.

Lydia (Greek) from Lydia, an ancient land in Asia. (Arabic) strife.
Lidia, Lidija, Lidiya, Lyda, Lydie, Lydië

Lyla (French) island. (English) a form of Lyle (see Boys' Names). (Arabic, Hindi, Persian) a form of Lila.
Lila, Lilah

Lynda (Spanish) pretty. (American) a form of Linda.
Lyndah, Lynde, Lyndi, Lynnda

Lyndell (English) a form of Lynelle.
Lyndall, Lyndel, Lyndella

Lyndi (Spanish) a familiar form of Lynda.
Lyndee, Lindie, Lyndy, Lynndie, Lynndy

Lyndsay (American) a form of Lindsay.
Lyndsaye

Lyndsey (English) linden tree island; camp near the stream. (American) a form of Lindsey.
Lyndsea, Lyndsee, Lyndsi, Lyndsie, Lyndsy, Lyndzee, Lyndzey, Lyndzi, Lyndzie, Lynndsie

Lynelle (English) pretty.
Linel, Linell, Linnell, Lyndell, Lynel, Lynell, Lynella, Lynnell

Lynette (Welsh) idol. (English) a form of Linette.
Lynett, Lynetta, Lynnet, Lynnette

Lynn, Lynne (English) waterfall; pool below a waterfall.
Lin, Lina, Linley, Linn, Lyn, Lynlee, Lynley, Lynna, Lynnae, Lynnea

Lynnell (English) a form of Lynelle.
Linnell, Lynnelle

Lynsey (American) a form of Lyndsey.
Lynnsey, Lynnzey, Lynsie, Lynsy, Lynzee, Lynzey, Lynzi, Lynzie, Lynzy

Lyra (Greek) lyre player.
Lyre, Lyric, Lyrica, Lyrie, Lyris

Lysandra (Greek) liberator.
Lisandra, Lysandre, Lytle

Lysanne (American) a combination of Lysandra + Anne.
Lisanne, Lizanne

Mab (Irish) joyous. (Welsh) baby. Literature: queen of the fairies.
Mabry

Mabel (Latin) lovable. A short form of Amabel.
Mabelle, Mable, Mabyn, Maible, Maybel, Maybeline, Maybelle, Maybull

Macawi (Dakota) generous; motherly.

Macayla (American) a form of Michaela.
Macaela, Macaila, Macala, Macalah, Macaylah, Macayle, Macayli, Mackayla

Macey, Macie, Macy (Polish) familiar forms of Macia.
Macee, Maci, Macye

Machaela (Hebrew) a form of Michaela.
Machael, Machaelah, Machaelie, Machaila, Machala, Macheala

Machiko (Japanese) fortunate child.
Machi

Macia (Polish) a form of Miriam.
Macelia, Macey, Machia, Macie, Macy, Masha, Mashia

Mackenna (American) a form of Mackenzie.
Mackena, Makenna, Mckenna

Mackenzie (Irish) child of the wise leader. See also Kenzie.
Macenzie, Mackenna, Mackensi, Mackensie, Mackenze, Mackenzee, Mackenzey, Mackenzi, Mackenzia, Mackenzy, Mackenzye, Mackinsey, Mackynze, Makenzie, McKenzie, Mckinzie, Mekenzie, Mykenzie

Mackinsey (Irish) a form of Mackenzie.
Mackinsie, Mackinze, Mackinzee, Mackinzey, Mackinzi, Mackinzie

Mada (English) a short form of Madaline, Magdalen.
Madda, Mahda

Madaline (English) a form of Madeline.
Mada, Madailéin, Madaleen, Madaleine, Madalene, Madalin, Madaline

Madalyn (Greek) a form of Madeline.
Madalyne, Madalynn, Madalynne

Maddie (English) a familiar form of Madeline.
Maddi, Maddy, Mady, Maidie, Maydey

Maddison (English) a form of Madison.
Maddisan, Maddisen, Maddisson, Maddisyn, Maddyson

Madelaine (French) a form of Madeline.
Madelane, Madelayne

Madeleine (French) a form of Madeline.
Madalaine, Madalayne, Madelaine, Madelein, Madeliene

Madelena (English) a form of Madeline.
Madalaina, Madalena, Madalina, Maddalena, Madelaina, Madeleina, Madelina, Madelyna

Madeline (Greek) high tower. See also Lena, Lina, Maud.
Madaline, Madalyn, Maddie, Madel, Madelaine, Madeleine, Madelena, Madelene, Madelia, Madella, Madelle, Madelon, Madelyn, Madge, Madilyn, Madlen, Madlin, Madline, Madlyn, Madolyn, Maida

Madelyn (Greek) a form of Madeline.
Madelyne, Madelynn, Madelynne, Madilyn, Madlyn, Madolyn

Madge (Greek) a familiar form of Madeline, Margaret.
Madgi, Madgie, Mady

Madilyn (Greek) a form of Madeline.
Madilen, Madiline, Madilyne, Madilynn

Madisen (English) a form of Madison.
Madisan, Madisin, Madissen, Madisun

Madison (English) good; child of Maud.
*Maddison, Madisen, Madisson, Madisyn,
Madyson, Mattison*

Madisyn (English) a form of Madison.
Madissyn, Madisynn, Madisynne

Madolyn (Greek) a form of Madeline.
*Madoline, Madolyne, Madolynn,
Madolynne*

Madonna (Latin) my lady.
Madona

Madrona (Spanish) mother.
Madre, Madrena

Madyson (English) a form of Madison.
Madysen, Madysun

Mae (English) a form of May. History:
Mae Jemison was the first African
American woman in space.
*Maelea, Maeleah, Maelen, Maelle,
Maeona*

Maegan (Irish) a form of Megan.
Maegen, Maeghan, Maegin

Maeko (Japanese) honest child.
Mae, Maemi

Maeve (Irish) joyous. Mythology: a legendary Celtic queen. See also Mavis.
Maevi, Maevy, Maive, Mayve

Magali, Magaly (Hebrew) from the
high tower.
Magalie, Magally

Magan, Magen (Greek) forms of
Megan.
Maggen, Maggin

Magda (Czech, Polish, Russian) a form
of Magdalen.
Mahda, Makda

Magdalen (Greek) high tower. Bible:
Magdala was the home of Saint
Mary Magdalen. See also Madeline,
Malena, Marlene.
*Mada, Magda, Magdala, Magdaleen,
Magdalena, Magdalene, Magdaline,
Magdalyn, Magdalynn, Magdelane,
Magdelene, Magdeline, Magdelyn,
Magdlen, Magdolna, Maggie, Magola,
Maighdlin, Mala, Malaine*

Magdalena (Greek) a form of
Magdalen.
*Magdalina, Magdelana, Magdelena,
Magdelina*

Magena (Native American) coming
moon.

Maggie (Greek) pearl. (English) a
familiar form of Magdalen, Margaret.
*Mag, Magge, Maggee, Maggi, Maggia,
Maggie, Maggiemae, Maggy, Magi,
Magie, Mags*

Maggy, Meggy (English) forms of
Maggie.
Maggey, Magy

Magnolia (Latin) flowering tree. See
also Nollie.
Nola

Mahal (Filipino) love.

Mahala (Arabic) fat, marrow; tender.
(Native American) powerful woman.
*Mahalah, Mahalar, Mahalla, Mahela,
Mahila, Mahlah, Mahlaha, Mehala,
Mehalah*

Mahalia (American) a form of
Mahala.
*Mahaley, Mahaliah, Mahalie, Mahayla,
Mahaylah, Mahaylia, Mahelea,
Maheleah, Mahelia, Mahilia, Mehalia*

Maharene (Ethiopian) forgive us.

Mahesa (Hindi) great lord. Religion: a
name for the Hindu god Shiva.
Maheesa, Mahisa

Mahila (Sanskrit) woman.

Mahina (Hawaiian) moon glow.

Mahira (Hebrew) energetic.
Mahri

Mahogony (Spanish) rich; strong.
*Mahagony, Mahoganey, Mahogani,
Mahoganie, Mahogany, Mahogney,
Mahogny, Mohogany, Mohogony*

Mai (Japanese) brightness.
(Vietnamese) flower. (Navajo) coyote.

Maia (Greek) mother; nurse. (English)
kinswoman; maiden. Mythology: the
loveliest of the Pleiades, the seven
daughters of Atlas, and the mother of
Hermes. See also Maya.
Maiah, Maie, Maiya

Maida (English) maiden. (Greek) a
short form of Madeline.
Maidel, Mayda, Maydena

Maija (Finnish) a form of Mary.
Maiji, Maikki

Maika (Hebrew) a familiar form of
Michaela.
Maikala, Maikka, Maiko

Maira, Maire (Irish) forms of Mary.
Maairah, Mair, Mairi, Mairim, Mairin, Mairona, Mairwen

Maisie (Scottish) familiar forms of Margaret.
Maisa, Maise, Maisey, Maisi, Maisy, Maizie, Maycee, Maysie, Mayzie, Mazey, Mazie, Mazy, Mazzy, Mysie, Myzie

Maita (Spanish) a form of Martha.
Maite, Maitia

Maitlyn (American) a combination of Maita + Lynn.
Maitlan, Maitland, Maitlynn, Mattilyn

Maiya (Greek) a form of Maia.
Maiyah

Maja (Arabic) a short form of Majidah.
Majal, Majalisa, Majalyn, Majalynn

Majidah (Arabic) splendid.
Maja, Majida

Makaela, Makaila (American) forms of Michaela.
Makaelah, Makaelee, Makaella, Makaely, Makail, Makailah, Makailee, Makailla, Makaillah, Makealah, Makell

Makala (Hawaiian) myrtle. (Hebrew) a form of Michaela.
Makalae, Makalah, Makalai, Makalea, Makalee, Makaleh, Makaleigh, Makaley, Makalia, Makalie, Makalya, Makela, Makelah, Makell, Makella

Makana (Hawaiian) gift, present.

Makani (Hawaiian) wind.

Makara (Hindi) Astrology: another name for the zodiac sign Capricorn.

Makayla (American) a form of Michaela.
Macayla, Makaylah, Makaylee, Makayleigh, Makayli, Makaylia, Makaylla, Makell, Makyla, Makylah, Mckayla, Mekayla, Mikayla

Makell (American) a short form of Makaela, Makala, Makayla.
Makele, Makelle, Mckell, Mekel

Makenna (American) a form of Mackenna.
Makena, Makennah, Mikenna

Makenzie (Irish) a form of Mackenzie.
Makense, Makensey, Makensie, Makenze, Makenzee, Makenzey, Makenzi, Makenzy, Makenzye, Makinzey, Makynzey, Mekenzie, Mykenzie

Mala (Greek) a short form of Magdalen.
Malana, Malee, Mali

Malana (Hawaiian) bouyant, light.

Malaya (Filipino) free.
Malayaa, Malayah, Malayna, Malea, Maleah

Malena (Swedish) a familiar form of Magdalen.
Malen, Malenna, Malin, Malina, Maline, Malini, Malinna

Malha (Hebrew) queen.
Maliah, Malkah, Malkia, Malkiah, Malkie, Malkiya, Malkiyah, Miliah

Mali (Tai) jasmine flower. (Tongan) sweet. (Hungarian) a short form of Malika.
Malea, Malee, Maley

Malia (Hawaiian, Zuni) a form of Mary. (Spanish) a form of Maria.
Malea, Maleah, Maleeya, Maleeyah, Maleia, Maliah, Maliasha, Malie, Maliea, Maliya, Maliyah, Malli, Mally

Malika (Hungarian) industrious. (Arabic) queen.
Malak, Maleeka, Maleka, Mali, Maliaka, Malik, Malikah, Malikee, Maliki, Malikia, Malky

Malina (Hebrew) tower. (Native American) soothing. (Russian) raspberry.
Malin, Maline, Malina, Malinna, Mallie

Malinda (Greek) a form of Melinda.
Malinde, Malinna, Malynda

Malini (Hindi) gardener.
Maliny

Malissa (Greek) a form of Melissa.
Malisa, Malisah, Malyssa

Mallalai (Pashto) beautiful.

Malley (American) a familiar form of Mallory.
Mallee, Malli, Mallie, Mally, Maly

Mallorie (French) a form of Mallory.
Malerie, Mallari, Mallerie, Malloreigh, Mallori

Mallory (German) army counselor. (French) unlucky.
Maliri, Mallary, Mallauri, Mallery, Malley, Malloree, Mallorey, Mallorie, Malorie, Malory, Malorym, Malree, Malrie, Mellory

Malorie, Malory (German) forms of Mallory.
Malarie, Maloree, Malori, Melorie, Melory

Malva (English) a form of Melba.
Malvi, Malvy

Malvina (Scottish) a form of Melvina. Literature: a name created by the eighteenth-century romantic poet James Macpherson.
Malvane, Malvi

Mamie (American) a familiar form of Margaret.
Mame, Mamee, Mami, Mammie, Mamy, Mamye

Mamo (Hawaiian) saffron flower; yellow bird.

Mana (Hawaiian) psychic; sensitive.
Manal, Manali, Manna, Mannah

Manar (Arabic) guiding light.
Manayra

Manda (Spanish) woman warrior. (Latin) a short form of Amanda.
Mandy

Mandara (Hindi) calm.

Mandeep (Punjabi) enlightened.

Mandisa (Xhosa) sweet.

Mandy (Latin) lovable. A familiar form of Amanda, Manda, Melinda.
Mandee, Mandi, Mandie

Manette (French) a form of Mary.

Mangena (Hebrew) song, melody.
Mangina

Mani (Chinese) a mantra repeated in Tibetan Buddhist prayer to impart understanding.
Manee

Manka (Polish, Russian) a form of Mary.

Manon (French) a familiar form of Marie.
Mannon

Manpreet (Punjabi) mind full of love.
Manprit

Mansi (Hopi) plucked flower.
Mancey, Manci, Mancie, Mansey, Mansie, Mansy

Manuela (Spanish) a form of Emmanuelle.
Manuala, Manuelita, Manuella, Manuelle

Manya (Russian) a form of Mary.

Mara (Hebrew) melody. (Greek) a short form of Amara. (Slavic) a form of Mary.
Mahra, Marae, Marah, Maralina, Maraline, Marra

Marabel (English) a form of Mirabel.
Marabella, Marabelle

Maranda (Latin) a form of Miranda.

Maraya (Hebrew) a form of Mariah.
Mareya

Marcela (Latin) a form of Marcella.
Marcele, Marcelen, Marcelia, Marcelina, Marceline, Maricela

Marcelen (English) a form of Marcella.
Marcelen, Marcelin, Marcelina, Marceline,

Marcellin, Marcellina, Marcelline, Marcelyn, Marcilen

Marcella (Latin) martial, warlike. Mythology: Mars was the god of war.
Mairsil, Marca, Marce, Marceil, Marcela, Marcelen, Marcell, Marcelle, Marcello, Marcena, Marchella, Marchelle, Marci, Marcia, Marcie, Marciella, Marcile, Marcilla, Marcille, Marella, Marsella, Marselle, Marsiella

Marcena (Latin) a form of Marcella, Marcia.
Maracena, Marceen, Marcene, Marcenia, Marceyne, Marcina

Marci, Marcie (English) familiar forms of Marcella, Marcia.
Marca, Marcee, Marcita, Marcy, Marsi, Marsie

Marcia (Latin) martial, warlike. See also Marquita.
Marcena, Marchia, Marci, Marciale, Marcie, Marcsa, Marsha, Martia

Marciann (American) a combination of Marci + Ann.
Marciane, Marcianna, Marcianne, Marcyane, Marcyanna, Marcyanne

Marcilynn (American) a combination of Marci + Lynn.
Marcilen, Marcilin, Marciline, Marcilyn, Marcilyne, Marcilynne, Marcylen, Marcylin, Marcyline, Marcylyn, Marcylyne, Marcylynn, Marcylynne

Marcy (English) a form of Marci.
Marsey, Marsy

Mardi (French) born on Tuesday. (Aramaic) a familiar form of Martha.

Mare (Irish) a form of Mary.
Mair, Maire

Marelda (German) renowned warrior.
Marella, Marilda

Maren (Latin) sea. (Aramaic) a form of Mary. See also Marina.
Marin, Marine, Marinn, Miren

Maresa, Maressa (Latin) forms of Marisa.
Maresha, Meresa

Maretta (English) a familiar form of Margaret.
Maret, Marette

Margaret (Greek) pearl. History: Margaret Hilda Thatcher served as British prime minister. See also Gita, Greta, Gretchen, Marjorie, Markita, Meg, Megan, Peggy, Reet, Rita.
Madge, Maergrethe, Maggie, Maisie, Mamie, Maretta, Marga, Margalo, Marganit, Margara, Maretha, Margarett, Margarette, Margarida, Margarit, Margarita, Margaro, Margaux, Marge, Margeret, Margeretta, Margerette, Margery, Margetta, Margiad, Margie, Margisia, Margit, Margo, Margot, Margret, Marguerite, Meta

Margarit (Greek) a form of Margaret.
Margalide, Margalit, Margalith, Margarid, Margaritt, Margerit

Margarita (Italian, Spanish) a form of Margaret.
Margareta, Margaretta, Margarida, Margaritis, Margaritta, Margeretta, Margharita, Margherita, Margrieta, Margrita, Marguarita, Marguerita, Margurita

Margaux (French) a form of Margaret.
Margeaux

Marge (English) a short form of Margaret, Marjorie.
Margie

Margery (English) a form of Margaret.
Margerie, Margorie

Margie (English) a familiar form of Marge, Margaret.
Margey, Margi, Margy

Margit (Hungarian) a form of Margaret.
Marget, Margette, Margita

Margo, Margot (French) forms of Margaret.
Mago, Margaro

Margret (German) a form of Margaret.
Margreta, Margrete, Margreth, Margrett, Margretta, Margrette, Margrieta, Margrita

Marguerite (French) a form of Margaret.
Margarete, Margaretha, Margarethe, Margarite, Margerite, Marguaretta, Marguarette, Marguarite, Marguerette, Margurite

Mari (Japanese) ball. (Spanish) a form of Mary.

Maria (Hebrew) bitter; sea of bitterness. (Italian, Spanish) a form of Mary.
Maie, Malia, Marea, Mareah, Mariabella, Mariae, Mariesa, Mariessa, Mariha, Marija, Mariya, Mariyah, Marja, Marya

Mariah (Hebrew) a form of Mary. See also Moriah.
Maraia, Maraya, Mariyah, Marriah, Meriah

Mariam (Hebrew) a form of Miriam.
Mariama, Mariame, Mariem, Meryam

Marian (English) a form of Maryann.
Mariana, Mariane, Mariann, Marianne, Mariene, Marion, Marrian, Marriann

Mariana, Marianna (Spanish) forms of Marian.
Marriana, Marrianna, Maryana, Maryanna

Mariane, Marianne (English) forms of Marian.
Marrianne, Maryanne

Maribel (French) beautiful. (English) a combination of Maria + Bell.
Marabel, Marbelle, Mariabella, Maribella, Maribelle, Maridel, Marybel, Marybella, Marybelle

Marice (Italian) a form of Mary. See also Maris.
Marica, Marise, Marisse

Maricela (Latin) a form of Marcella.
Maricel, Mariceli, Maricelia, Maricella, Maricely

Maridel (English) a form of Maribel.

Marie (French) a form of Mary.
Maree, Marietta, Marrie

Mariel, Marielle (German, Dutch) forms of Mary.
Marial, Marieke, Marielana, Mariele, Marieli, Marielie, Marieline, Mariell, Mariellen, Marielsie, Mariely, Marielys

Mariela, Mariella (German, Dutch) forms of Mary.

Marietta (Italian) a familiar form of Marie.
Maretta, Marette, Mariet, Mariette, Marrietta

Marieve (American) a combination of Mary + Eve.

Marigold (English) Mary's gold. Botany: a plant with yellow or orange flowers.
Marygold

Marika (Dutch, Slavic) a form of Mary.
Marica, Marieke, Marija, Marijke, Marikah, Marike, Marikia, Marikka, Mariska, Mariske, Marrika, Maryk, Maryka, Merica, Merika

Mariko (Japanese) circle.

Marilee (American) a combination of Mary + Lee.
Marili, Marilie, Marily, Marrilee, Marylea, Marylee, Merrilee, Merrili, Merrily

Marilla (Hebrew, German) a form of Mary.
Marella, Marelle

Marilou (American) a form of Marylou.
Marilu, Mariluz

Marilyn (Hebrew) Mary's line of descendants. See also Merilyn.
Maralin, Maralyn, Maralyne, Maralynn, Maralynne, Marelyn, Marilin, Marillyn, Marilyne, Marilynn, Marilynne, Marlyn, Marolyn, Marralynn, Marrilin, Marrilyn, Marrilynn, Marrilynne, Marylin, Marylinn, Marylyn, Marylyne, Marylynn, Marylynne

Marina (Latin) sea. See also Maren.
Mareena, Marena, Marenka, Marinae, Marinah, Marinda, Marindi, Marinka, Marinna, Marrina, Maryna, Merina, Mirena

Marini (Swahili) healthy; pretty.

Marion (French) a form of Mary.
Marrian, Marrion, Maryon, Maryonn

Maris (Latin) sea. (Greek) a short form of Amaris, Damaris. See also Marice.
Maries, Marise, Marris, Marys, Maryse, Meris

Marisa (Latin) sea.
Maresa, Mariesa, Mariessa, Marisela, Marissa, Marita, Mariza, Marrisa, Marrissa, Marysa, Maryse, Maryssa, Merisa

Marisela (Latin) a form of Marisa.
Mariseli, Marisella, Marishelle, Marissela

Marisha (Russian) a familiar form of Mary.
Mareshah, Marishenka, Marishka, Mariska

Marisol (Spanish) sunny sea.
Marise, Marizol, Marysol

Marissa (Latin) a form of Maris, Marisa.
Maressa, Marisa, Marisha, Marissah, Marisse, Marizza, Marrissa, Marrissia, Maryssa, Merissa, Morissa

Marit (Aramaic) lady.
Marita, Marite

Marita (Spanish) a form of Marisa. (Aramaic) a form of Marit.
Marité, Maritha

Maritza (Arabic) blessed.
Maritsa, Marittssa

Mariyan (Arabic) purity.
Mariya, Mariyah, Mariyana, Mariyanna

Marja (Finnish) a form of Mary.
Marjae, Marjatta, Marjie

Marjan (Persian) coral. (Polish) a form of Mary.
Marjaneh, Marjanna

Marjie (Scottish) a familiar form of Marjorie.
Marje, Marjey, Marji, Marjy

Marjolaine (French) marjoram.

Marjorie (Greek) a familiar form of Margaret. (Scottish) a form of Mary.
Majorie, Marge, Margeree, Margerey, Margerie, Margery, Margorie, Margory, Marjarie, Marjary, Marjerie, Marjery, Marjie, Marjorey, Marjori, Marjory

Markayla (American) a combination or Mary + Kayla.
Marka, Markaiah, Markaya, Markayel, Markeela, Markel

Markeisha (English) a combination of Mary + Keisha.
Markasha, Markeisa, Markeisia, Markesha, Markeshia, Markesia, Markiesha, Markisha, Markishia, Marquesha

Markita (Czech) a form of Margaret.
Marka, Markeah, Markeda, Markee, Markeeta, Marketa, Marketta, Marki, Markia, Markie, Markieta, Markita, Markitha, Markketta, Merkate

Marla (English) a short form of
Marlena, Marlene.
Marlah, Marlea, Marleah

Marlana (English) a form of Marlena.
*Marlaena, Marlaina, Marlainna, Marlania,
Marlanna, Marlayna, Marleana*

Marlee (English) a form of Marlene.
Marlea, Marleah, Marleigh

Marlena (German) a form of Marlene.
*Marla, Marlaina, Marlana, Marlanna,
Marleena, Marlina, Marlinda, Marlyna,
Marna*

Marlene (Greek) high tower. (Slavic) a
form of Magdalen.
*Marla, Marlaine, Marlane, Marlayne,
Marlee, Marleen, Marleene, Marlen,
Marlena, Marlenne, Marley, Marlin,
Marline, Marlyne*

Marley (English) a familiar form of
Marlene.
Marlee, Marli, Marlie, Marly

Marlis (English) a combination of
Maria + Lisa.
*Marles, Marlisa, Marlise, Marlys,
Marlyse, Marlyssa*

Marlo (English) a form of Mary.
Marlon, Marlow, Marlowe

Marlyn (Hebrew) a short form of
Marilyn. (Greek, Slavic) a form of
Marlene.
Marlynn, Marlynne

Marmara (Greek) sparkling, shining.
Marmee

Marni (Hebrew) a form of Marnie.
Marnia, Marnique

Marnie (Hebrew) a short form of
Marnina.
*Marna, Marnay, Marne, Marnee,
Marney, Marni, Marnisha, Marnja,
Marny, Marnya, Marnye*

Marnina (Hebrew) rejoice.

Maroula (Greek) a form of Mary.

Marquise (French) noblewoman.
*Markese, Marquees, Marquese, Marquice,
Marquies, Marquiese, Marquis, Marquisa,
Marquisee, Marquisha, Marquisse,
Marquiste*

Marquisha (American) a form of
Marquise.
Marquiesha, Marquisia

Marquita (Spanish) a form of Marcia.
*Marquatte, Marqueda, Marquedia,
Marquee, Marqueita, Marquet, Marqueta,
Marquetta, Marquette, Marquia,
Marquida, Marquietta, Marquitra,
Marquitia, Marquitta*

Marrim (Chinese) tribal name in
Manpur state.

Marsala (Italian) from Marseilles, France.
Marsali, Marseilles

Marsha (English) a form of Marcia.
*Marcha, Marshae, Marshay, Marshel,
Marshele, Marshell, Marshia, Marshiela*

Marta (English) a short form of
Martha, Martina.
*Martá, Martä, Marte, Martia, Marttaha,
Merta*

Martha (Aramaic) lady; sorrowful. Bible:
a friend of Jesus. See also Mardi.
*Maita, Marta, Martaha, Marth,
Marthan, Marthe, Marthy, Marti,
Marticka, Martita, Mattie, Matty,
Martus, Martuska, Masia*

Marti (English) a familiar form of
Martha, Martina.
Martie, Marty

Martina (Latin) martial, warlike. See
also Tina.
*Marta, Martel, Martella, Martelle,
Martene, Marthena, Marthina, Marthine,
Marti, Martine, Martinia, Martino,
Martisha, Martosia, Martoya, Martricia,
Martrina, Martyna, Martyne, Martynne*

Martiza (Arabic) blessed.

Maru (Japanese) round.

Maruca (Spanish) a form of Mary.
Maruja, Maruska

Marvella (French) marvelous.
*Marva, Marvel, Marvela, Marvele,
Marvelle, Marvely, Marvetta, Marvette,
Marvia, Marvina*

Mary (Hebrew) bitter; sea of bitter-
ness. Bible: the mother of Jesus. See
also Maija, Malia, Maren, Mariah,
Marjorie, Maura, Maureen, Miriam,
Mitzi, Moira, Mollie, Muriel.
*Maira, Maire, Manette, Manka, Manon,
Manya, Mara, Mare, Maree, Maren,
Marella, Marelle, Mari, Maria, Maricara,
Marice, Marie, Mariel, Mariela, Marika,
Marilla, Marilyn, Marion, Mariquilla,
Mariquita, Marisha, Marja, Marjan,
Marlo, Maroula, Maruca, Marye, Maryla,
Marynia, Masha, Mavra, Mendi,
Mérane, Meridel, Mhairie, Mirja,
Molara, Morag, Moya*

Marya (Arabic) purity; bright white-
ness.
Maryah

Maryam (Hebrew) a form of Miriam.
Maryama

Maryann, Maryanne (English) combinations of Mary + Ann.
Marian, Marryann, Maryan, Meryem

Marybeth (American) a combination
of Mary + Beth.
Maribeth, Maribette

Maryellen (American) a combination
of Mary + Ellen.
Mariellen

Maryjane (American) a combination
of Mary + Jane.

Maryjo (American) a combination of
Mary + Jo.
Marijo, Maryjoe

Marykate (American) a combination
of Mary + Kate.
Mary-Kate

Marylou (American) a combination of
Mary + Lou.
Marilou, Marylu

Maryssa (Latin) a form of Marissa.
Maryse, Marysia

Masago (Japanese) sands of time.

Masani (Luganda) gap toothed.

Masha (Russian) a form of Mary.
Mashka, Mashenka

Mashika (Swahili) born during the
rainy season.
Masika

Matana (Hebrew) gift.
Matat

Mathena (Hebrew) gift of God.

Mathilde (German) a form of Matilda.
Mathilda

Matilda (German) powerful battler.
See also Maud, Tilda, Tillie.
*Máda, Mahaut, Maitilde, Malkin, Mat,
Matelda, Mathilde, Matilde, Mattie,
Matty, Matusha, Matylda*

Matrika (Hindi) mother. Religion: a
name for the Hindu goddess Shakti
in the form of the letters of the
alphabet.
Matrica

Matsuko (Japanese) pine tree.

Mattea (Hebrew) gift of God.
*Matea, Mathea, Mathia, Matia, Matte,
Matthea, Matthia, Mattia, Matya*

Mattie, Matty (English) familiar forms
of Martha, Matilda.
Matte, Mattey, Matti, Mattye

Matusha (Spanish) a form of Matilda.
Matuja, Matuxa

Maud, Maude (English) short forms
of Madeline, Matilda. See also
Madison.
Maudie, Maudine, Maudlin

Maura (Irish) dark. A form of Mary,
Maureen. See also Moira.
*Maurah, Maure, Maurette, Mauricette,
Maurita*

Maureen (French) dark. (Irish) a form
of Mary.
Maura, Maurene, Maurine, Mo, Moreen,

*Morena, Morene, Morine, Morreen,
Moureen*

Maurelle (French) dark; elfin.
Mauriel, Mauriell, Maurielle

Maurise (French) dark skinned; moor;
marshland.
Maurisa, Maurissa, Maurita, Maurizia

Mausi (Native American) plucked
flower.

Mauve (French) violet colored.

Mavis (French) thrush, songbird. See
also Maeve.
Mavies, Mavin, Mavine, Mavon, Mavra

Maxie (English) a familiar form of
Maxine.
Maxi, Maxy

Maxine (Latin) greatest.
*Max, Maxa, Maxeen, Maxena, Maxene,
Maxie, Maxima, Maxime, Maximiliane,
Maxina, Maxna, Maxyne*

May (Latin) great. (Arabic) discerning.
(English) flower; month of May. See
also Mae, Maia.
*Maj, Mayberry, Maybeth, Mayday,
Maydee, Maydena, Maye, Mayela,
Mayella, Mayetta, Mayrene*

Maya (Hindi) God's creative power.
(Greek) mother; grandmother. (Latin)
great. A form of Maia.
Mayam, Mya

Maybeline (Latin) a familiar form of
Mabel.

Maygan, Maygen (Irish) forms of
Megan.
Mayghan, Maygon

Maylyn (American) a combination of May + Lynn.
Mayelene, Mayleen, Maylen, Maylene, Maylin, Maylon, Maylynn, Maylynne

Mayoree (Tai) beautiful.
Mayra, Mayree, Mayariya

Mayra (Tai) a form of Mayoree.

Maysa (Arabic) walks with a proud stride.

Maysun (Arabic) beautiful.

Mazel (Hebrew) lucky.
Mazal, Mazala, Mazella

Mckayla (American) a form of Makayla.
Mckaela, Mckaila, Mckala, Mckaylah, Mckayle, Mckaylee, Mckayleh, Mckayleigh, Mckayli, Mckaylia, Mckaylie

Mckell (American) a form of Makell.
Mckelle

Mckenna (American) a form of Mackenna.
Mckena, Mckennah, Mckinna, Mckinnah

Mckenzie (Scottish) a form of Mackenzie.
Mckennzie, Mckensee, Mckensey, McKensi, Mckensi, Mckensie, Mckensy, Mckenze, Mckenzee, Mckenzey, Mckenzi, Mckenzy, Mckenzye, Mekensie, Mekenzi, Mekenzie

Mckinley (Irish) daughter of the learned ruler.
Mckinlee, Mckinleigh, Mckinlie, Mckinnley

Mckinzie (American) a form of Mackenzie.
Mckinsey, Mckinze, Mckinzea, Mckinzee, Mckinzi, Mckinzy, Mckynze, Mckynzie

Mead, Meade (Greek) honey wine.

Meagan (Irish) a form of Megan.
Maegan, Meagain, Meagann, Meagen, Meagin, Meagnah, Meagon

Meaghan (Welsh) a form of Megan.
Maeghan, Meaghann, Meaghen, Meahgan

Meara (Irish) mirthful.

Meda (Native American) prophet; priestess.

Medea (Greek) ruling. (Latin) middle. Mythology: a sorceress who helped Jason get the Golden Fleece.
Medeia

Medina (Arabic) History: the site of Muhammed's tomb.
Medinah

Medora (Greek) mother's gift. Literature: a character in Lord Byron's poem *The Corsair.*

Meena (Hindi) blue semiprecious stone; bird. (Greek, German, Dutch) a form of Mena.

Meg (English) a short form of Margaret, Megan.

Megan (Greek) pearl; great. (Irish) a form of Margaret.
Maegan, Magan, Magen, Meagan, Meaghan, Magen, Maygan, Maygen, Meg, Megane, Megann, Megean, Megen, Meggan, Meggen, Meggie, Meghan, Megyn, Meygan

Megane (Irish) a form of Megan.
Magana, Meganna, Meganne

Megara (Greek) first. Mythology: Heracles's first wife.

Meggie (English) a familiar form of Margaret, Megan.
Meggi, Meggy

Meghan (Welsh) a form of Megan.
Meeghan, Meehan, Megha, Meghana, Meghane, Meghann, Meghanne, Meghean, Meghen, Mehgan, Mehgen

Mehadi (Hindi) flower.

Mehira (Hebrew) speedy; energetic.
Mahira

Mehitabel (Hebrew) benefited by trusting God.
Mehetabel, Mehitabelle, Hetty, Hitty

Mehri (Persian) kind; lovable; sunny.

Mei (Hawaiian) great. (Chinese) a short form of Meiying.
Meiko

Meira (Hebrew) light.
Meera

Meit (Burmese) affectionate.

Meiying (Chinese) beautiful flower.
Mei

Meka (Hebrew) a familiar form of Michaela.

Mekayla (American) a form of Michaela.
Mekaela, Mekaila, Mekayela, Mekaylia

Mel (Portuguese, Spanish) sweet as honey.

Mela (Hindi) religious service. (Polish) a form of Melanie.

Melana (Russian) a form of Melanie.
Melanna, Melashka, Melenka, Milana

Melanie (Greek) dark skinned.
Malania, Malanie, Meila, Meilani, Meilin, Melaine, Melainie, Melana, Melane, Melanee, Melaney, Melani, Melania, Mélanie, Melanka, Melanney, Melannie, Melany, Melanya, Melasya, Melayne, Melenia, Mella, Mellanie, Melonie, Melya, Milena, Milya

Melantha (Greek) dark flower.

Melba (Greek) soft; slender. (Latin) mallow flower.
Malva, Melva

Mele (Hawaiian) song; poem.

Melesse (Ethiopian) eternal.
Mellesse

Melia (German) a short form of Amelia.
Melcia, Melea, Meleah, Meleia, Meleisha, Meli, Meliah, Melida, Melika, Mema

Melina (Latin) canary yellow. (Greek) a short form of Melinda.
Melaina, Meleana, Meleena, Melena, Meline, Melinia, Melinna, Melynna

Melinda (Greek) honey. See also Linda, Melina, Mindy.
Maillie, Malinda, Melinde, Melinder, Mellinda, Melynda, Melyne, Milinda, Milynda, Mylenda, Mylinda, Mylynda

Meliora (Latin) better.
Melior, Meliori, Mellear, Melyor, Melyora

Melisa (Greek) a form of Melissa.
Melesa, Mélisa, Melise, Melisha, Melishia, Melisia, Meliza, Melizah, Mellisa, Melosa, Milisa, Mylisa, Mylisia

Melisande (French) a form of Melissa, Millicent.
Lisandra, Malisande, Malissande, Malyssandre, Melesande, Melisandra, Melisandre, Mélisandré, Melisenda, Melissande, Melissandre, Mellisande, Melond, Melysande, Melyssandre

Melissa (Greek) honey bee. See also Elissa, Lissa, Melisande, Millicent.
Malissa, Mallissa, Melessa, Meleta, Melisa, Mélissa, Melisse, Melissia, Mellie, Mellissa, Melly, Melyssa, Milissa, Millie, Milly, Missy, Molissia, Mollissa, Mylissa, Mylissia

Melita (Greek) a form of Melissa. (Spanish) a short form of Carmelita.
Malita, Meleeta, Melitta, Melitza, Melletta, Molita

Melly (American) a familiar form of names beginning with "Mel." See also Millie.
Meli, Melie, Melli, Mellie

Melody (Greek) melody. See also Elodie.
Meladia, Melodee, Melodey, Melodi, Melodia, Melodie, Melodyann, Melodye

Melonie (American) a form of Melanie.
Melloney, Mellonie, Mellony, Melonee, Meloney, Meloni, Melonie, Melonnie, Melony

Melosa (Spanish) sweet; tender.

Melvina (Irish) armored chief. See also Malvina.
Melevine, Melva, Melveen, Melvena, Melvene, Melvonna

Melyne (Greek) a short form of Melinda.
Melyn, Melynn, Melynne

Melyssa (Greek) a form of Melissa.

Mena (German, Dutch) strong. (Greek) a short form of Philomena. History: Menes is believed to be the first king of Egypt.
Menah

Mendi (Basque) a form of Mary.
Menda, Mendy

Meranda (Latin) a form of Miranda.
Merana, Merandah, Merandia, Merannda

Mérane (French) a form of Mary.
Meraine, Merrane

Mercedes (Latin) reward, payment. (Spanish) merciful.
Mercades, Mercadez, Mercadie, Meceades, Merced, Mercede, Mercedees, Mercedeez, Mercedez, Mercedies, Mercedis, Mersade, Mersades

Mercia (English) a form of Marcia. History: an ancient British kingdom.

Mercy (English) compassionate, merciful. See also Merry.
Mercey, Merci, Mercie, Mercille, Mersey

Meredith (Welsh) protector of the sea.
Meredeth, Meredithe, Meredy, Meredyth, Meredythe, Meridath, Merideth, Meridie, Meridith, Merridie, Merridith, Merry

Meri (Finnish) sea. (Irish) a short form of Meriel.

Meriel (Irish) shining sea.
Meri, Merial, Meriol, Meryl

Merilyn (English) a combination of Merry + Lynn. See also Marilyn.
Merelyn, Merlyn, Merralyn, Merrelyn, Merrilyn

Merissa (Latin) a form of Marissa.
Merisa, Merisha

Merle (Latin, French) blackbird.
Merl, Merla, Merlina, Merline, Merola, Murle, Myrle, Myrleen, Myrlene, Myrline

Merry (English) cheerful, happy. A familiar form of Mercy, Meredith.
Merie, Merree, Merri, Merrie, Merrielle, Merrilee, Merrili, Merrilyn, Merris, Merrita

Meryl (German) famous. (Irish) shining sea. A form of Meriel, Muriel.
Meral, Merel, Merrall, Merrell, Merril, Merrile, Merrill, Merryl, Meryle, Meryll

Mesha (Hindi) another name for the zodiac sign Aries.
Meshal

Meta (German) a short form of Margaret.
Metta, Mette, Metti

Mhairie (Scottish) a form of Mary.
Mhaire, Mhairi, Mhari, Mhary

Mia (Italian) mine. A familiar form of Michaela, Michelle.
Mea, Meah, Miah

Micaela (Hebrew) a form of Michaela.
Macaela, Micaella, Micaila, Micala, Miceala

Micah (Hebrew) a short form of Michaela. Bible: one of the Old Testament prophets.
Meecah, Mica, Micha, Mika, Myca, Mycah

Micayla, Michayla (Hebrew) forms of Michaela.
Micayle, Micaylee, Michaylah

Michaela (Hebrew) who is like God?
Machaela, Maika, Makaela, Makaila, Makala, Makayla, Mia, Micaela, Micayla, Michael, Michaelann, Michala, Michayla, Michealia, Michaelina, Michaeline, Michaell, Michaella, Michaelyn, Michaila, Michal, Michala, Micheal, Micheala, Michelia, Michelina, Michelle, Michely, Michelyn, Micheyla, Micheline, Micki, Miguela, Mikaela, Mikala, Misha, Mycala, Mychael, Mychal

Michala (Hebrew) a form of Michaela.
Michalann, Michale, Michalene, Michalin, Mchalina, Michalisha, Michalla, Michalle, Michayla, Michayle, Michela

Michele (Italian) a form of Michaela.
Michaelle, Michal, Michela

Michelle (French) who is like God? See also Shelley.
Machealle, Machele, Machell, Machella, Machelle, Mechelle, Meichelle, Meschell, Meshell, Meshelle, Mia, Michel, Michéle, Michell, Michella, Michellene, Michellyn, Mischel, Mischelle, Mishael, Mishaela, Mishayla, Mishell, Mishelle, Mitchele, Mitchelle

Michi (Japanese) righteous way.
Miche, Michee, Michiko

Micki (American) a familiar form of Michaela.
Mickee, Mickeeya, Mickia, Mickie, Micky, Mickya, Miquia

Midori (Japanese) green.

Mieko (Japanese) prosperous.
Mieke

Mielikki (Finnish) pleasing.

Miette (French) small; sweet.

Migina (Omaha) new moon.

Mignon (French) dainty, petite; graceful.
Mignonette, Minnionette, Minnonette, Minyonette, Minyonne

Miguela (Spanish) a form of Michaela.
Micquel, Miguelina, Miguelita, Miquel, Miquela, Miquella

Mika (Japanese) new moon. (Russian) God's child. (Native American) wise racoon. (Hebrew) a form of Micah. (Latin) a form of Dominica.
Mikah, Mikka

Mikaela (Hebrew) a form of Michaela.
Mekaela, Mekala, Mickael, Mickaela, Mickala, Mickalla, Mickeel, Mickell, Mickelle, Mikael, Mikail, Mikaila, Mikal, Mikalene, Mikalovna, Mikalyn, Mikayla, Mikea, Mikeisha, Mikeita, Mikel, Mikela, Mikele, Mikell, Mikella, Mikesha, Mikeya, Mikhaela, Mikie, Mikiela, Mikkel, Mikyla, Mykaela

Mikala (Hebrew) a form of Michaela.
Mickala, Mikalah, Mikale, Mikalea, Mikalee, Mikaleh

Mikayla (American) a form of Mikaela.
Mekayla, Mickayla, Mikala, Mikayle, Mikyla

Mikhaela (American) a form of Mikaela.
Mikhail, Mikhaila, Mikhala, Mikhalea, Mikhayla, Mikhelle

Miki (Japanese) flower stem.
Mikia, Mikiala, Mikie, Mikita, Mikiyo, Mikki, Mikkie, Mikkiya, Mikko, Miko

Mila (Russian) dear one. (Italian, Slavic) a short form of Camila, Ludmilla.
Milah, Milla

Milada (Czech) my love.
Mila, Milady

Milagros (Spanish) miracle.
Mila, Milagritos, Milagro, Milagrosa, Mirari

Milana (Italian) from Milan, Italy. (Russian) a form of Melana.
Milan, Milane, Milani, Milanka, Milanna, Milanne

Mildred (English) gentle counselor.
Mil, Mila, Mildrene, Mildrid, Millie, Milly

Milena (Greek, Hebrew, Russian) a form of Ludmilla, Magdalen, Melanie.
Mila, Milène, Milenia, Milenny, Milini, Millini

Mileta (German) generous, merciful.

Milia (German) industrious. A short form of Amelia, Emily.
Mila, Milka, Milla, Milya

Miliani (Hawaiian) caress.
Milanni, Miliany

Mililani (Hawaiian) heavenly caress.
Milliani

Milissa (Greek) a form of Melissa.
Milessa, Milisa, Millisa, Millissa

Milka (Czech) a form of Amelia.
Milica, Milika

Millicent (English) industrious. (Greek) a form of Melissa. See also Lissa, Melisande.
Melicent, Meliscent, Mellicent, Mellisent, Melly, Milicent, Milisent, Millie, Milliestone, Millisent, Milly, Milzie, Missy

Millie, Milly (English) familiar forms of Amelia, Camille, Emily, Kamila, Melissa, Mildred, Millicent.
Mili, Milla, Millee, Milley, Millie, Mylie

Mima (Burmese) woman.
Mimma

Mimi (French) a familiar form of Miriam.

Mina (German) love. (Persian) blue sky. (Arabic) harbor. (Japanese) south. A short form of names ending in "mina."
Meena, Mena, Min

Minal (Native American) fruit.

Minda (Hindi) knowledge.

Mindy (Greek) a familiar form of Melinda.
Mindee, Mindi, Mindie, Mindyanne, Mindylee, Myndy

Mine (Japanese) peak; mountain range.
Mineko

Minerva (Latin) wise. Mythology: the goddess of wisdom.
Merva, Minivera, Minnie, Myna

Minette (French) faithful defender
Minnette, Minnita

Minka (Polish) a short form of Wilhelmina.

Minna (German) a short form of Wilhelmina.
Mina, Minka, Minnie, Minta

Minnie (American) a familiar form of Mina, Minerva, Minna, Wilhelmina.
Mini, Minie, Minne, Minni, Minny

Minowa (Native American) singer.
Minowah

Minta (English) Literature: originally coined by playwright Sir John Vanbrugh in his comedy *The Confederacy*.
Minty

Minya (Osage) older sister.

Mio (Japanese) three times as strong.

Mira (Latin) wonderful. (Spanish) look, gaze. A short form of Almira, Amira, Marabel, Mirabel, Miranda.
Mirae, Mirra, Mirah

Mirabel (Latin) beautiful.
Mira, Mirabell, Mirabella, Mirabelle, Mirable

Miracle (Latin) wonder, marvel.

Miranda (Latin) strange; wonderful; admirable. Literature: the heroine of Shakespeare's *The Tempest*. See also Randi.
Maranda, Marenda, Meranda, Mira, Miran, Miranada, Mirandia, Mirinda, Mirindé, Mironda, Mirranda, Muranda, Myranda

Mireille (Hebrew) God spoke. (Latin) wonderful.
Mireil, Mirel, Mirella, Mirelle, Mirelys, Mireya, Mireyda, Mirielle, Mirilla, Myrella, Myrilla

Mireya (Hebrew) a form of Mireille.
Mireea, Miriah, Miryah

Miri (Gypsy) a short form of Miriam.
Miria, Miriah

Miriam (Hebrew) bitter; sea of bitterness. Bible: the original form of Mary. See also Macia, Mimi, Mitzi.
Mairwen, Mariam, Maryam, Miram, Mirham, Miri, Miriain, Miriama, Miriame, Mirian, Mirit, Mirjam, Mirjana, Mirriam, Mirrian, Miryam, Miryan, Myriam

Misha (Russian) a form of Michaela.
Mischa, Mishae

Missy (English) a familiar form of Melissa, Millicent.
Missi, Missie

Misty (English) shrouded by mist.
Missty, Mistee, Mistey, Misti, Mistie, Mistin, Mistina, Mistral, Mistylynn, Mystee, Mysti, Mystie

Mitra (Hindi) Religion: god of daylight. (Persian) angel.
Mita

Mituna (Moquelumnan) like a fish wrapped up in leaves.

Mitzi (German) a form of Mary, Miriam.
Mieze, Mitzee, Mitzie, Mitzy

Miwa (Japanese) wise eyes.
Miwako

Miya (Japanese) temple.
Miyah, Miyana, Miyanna

Miyo (Japanese) beautiful generation.
Miyoko, Miyuko

Miyuki (Japanese) snow.

Moana (Hawaiian) ocean; fragrance.

Mocha (Arabic) chocolate-flavored coffee.
Moka

Modesty (Latin) modest.
Modesta, Modeste, Modestia, Modestie, Modestina, Modestine, Modestus

Moesha (American) a short form of Monisha.
Myesha

Mohala (Hawaiian) flowers in bloom.
Moala

Moira (Irish) great. A form of Mary. See also Maura.
Moirae, Moirah, Moire, Moya, Moyra, Moyrah

Molara (Basque) a form of Mary.

Mollie, Molly (Irish) familiar forms of Mary.
Moli, Molie, Moll, Mollee, Molley, Molli, Mollissa

Mona (Irish) noble. (Greek) a short form of Monica, Ramona, Rimona.
Moina, Monah, Mone, Monea, Monna, Moyna

Monet (French) Art: Claude Monet was a leading French impressionist remembered for his paintings of water lilies.
Monae, Monay, Monee

Monica (Greek) solitary. (Latin) advisor.
Mona, Monca, Monee, Monia, Monic, Monice, Monicia, Monicka, Monika, Monique, Monise, Monn, Monnica, Monnie, Monya

Monifa (Yoruba) I have my luck.

Monika (German) a form of Monica.
Moneka, Monieka, Monike, Monnika

Monique (French) a form of Monica.
Moneeke, Moneik, Moniqua, Moniquea, Moniquie, Munique

Monisha (American) a combination of Monica + Aisha.
Moesha, Moneisha, Monishia

Montana (Spanish) mountain. Geography: a U.S. state.
Montanna

Mora (Spanish) blueberry.
Morae, Morea, Moria, Morita

Morela (Polish) apricot.
Morelia, Morelle

Morena (Irish) a form of Maureen.

Morgan (Welsh) seashore. Literature:
Morgan le Fay was the half-sister of
King Arthur.
Morgana, Morgance, Morgane,
Morganetta, Morganette, Morganica,
Morgann, Morganna, Morganne, Morgen,
Morghan, Morgyn, Morrigan

Morghan (Welsh) a form of Morgan.
Morghen, Morghin, Morghyn

Moriah (Hebrew) God is my teacher.
(French) dark skinned. Bible: the
mountain on which the Temple of
Solomon was built. See also Mariah.
Moria, Moriel, Morit, Morria, Morriah

Morie (Japanese) bay.

Morowa (Akan) queen.

Morrisa (Latin) dark skinned; moor;
marshland.
Morisa, Morissa, Morrissa

Moselle (Hebrew) drawn from the
water. (French) a white wine.
Mozelle

Mosi (Swahili) first-born.

Moswen (Tswana) white.

Mouna (Arabic) wish, desire.
Moona, Moonia, Mounia, Muna, Munia

Mrena (Slavic) white eyes.
Mren

Mumtaz (Arabic) distinguished.

Mura (Japanese) village.

Muriel (Arabic) myrrh. (Irish) shining
sea. A form of Mary. See also Meryl.
Merial, Meriel, Meriol, Merrial, Merriel,
Muire, Murial, Muriell, Murielle

Musetta (French) little bagpipe.
Musette

Muslimah (Arabic) devout believer.

Mya (Burmese) emerald. (Italian) a
form of Mia.
My, Myah, Myia, Myiah

Myesha (American) a form of Moesha.
Myeisha, Myeshia, Myiesha, Myisha

Mykaela, Mykayla (American) forms
of Mikaela.
Mykael, Mykaila, Mykal, Mykala,
Mykaleen, Mykel, Mykela, Mykyla

Myla (English) merciful.

Mylene (Greek) dark.
Mylaine, Mylana, Mylee, Myleen

Myra (Latin) fragrant ointment.
Mayra, Myrena, Myria

Myranda (Latin) a form of Miranda.
Myrandah, Myrandia, Myrannda

Myriam (American) a form of Miriam.
Myriame, Myryam

Myrna (Irish) beloved.
Merna, Mirna, Morna, Muirna

Myrtle (Greek) dark green shrub.
Mertis, Mertle, Mirtle, Myrta, Myrtia,
Myrtias, Myrtice, Myrtie, Myrtilla,
Myrtis

N

Nabila (Arabic) born to nobility.
Nabeela, Nabiha, Nabilah

Nadda (Arabic) generous; dewy.
Nada

Nadette (French) a short form of
Bernadette.

Nadia (French, Slavic) hopeful.
Nadea, Nadenka, Nadezhda, Nadiah,
Nadie, Nadija, Nadijah, Nadine,
Nadiya, Nadiyah, Nadja, Nadjae,
Nadjah, Nadka, Nadusha, Nady, Nadya

Nadine (French, Slavic) a form of
Nadia.
Nadean, Nadeana, Nadeen, Nadena,
Nadene, Nadien, Nadin, Nadina,
Nadyne, Naidene, Naidine

Nadira (Arabic) rare, precious.
Naadirah, Nadirah

Naeva (French) a form of Eve.
Nahvon

Nafuna (Luganda) born feet first.

Nagida (Hebrew) noble; prosperous.
Nagda, Nageeda

Nahid (Persian) Mythology: another
name for Venus, the goddess of love
and beauty.

Nahimana (Dakota) mystic.

Naida (Greek) water nymph.
Naiad, Naiya, Nayad, Nyad

Naila (Arabic) successful.
Nailah

Nairi (Armenian) land of rivers.
History: a name for ancient Armenia.
Naira, Naire, Nayra

Naiya (Greek) a form of Naida.
Naia, Naiyana, Naja, Najah, Naya

Najam (Arabic) star.
Naja, Najma

Najila (Arabic) brilliant eyes.
Naja, Najah, Najia, Najja, Najla

Nakeisha (American) a combination
of the prefix Na + Keisha.
*Nakeesha, Nakesha, Nakeshea,
Nakeshia, Nakeysha, Nakiesha,
Nakisha, Nekeisha*

Nakeita (American) a form of Nikita.
*Nakeeta, Nakeitha, Nakeithra, Nakeitra,
Nakeitress, Nakeitta, Nakeittia, Naketta,
Nakieta, Nakitha, Nakitia, Nakitta,
Nakyta*

Nakia (Arabic) pure.
*Nakea, Nakeia, Nakeya, Nakeyah,
Nakeyia, Nakiah, Nakiaya, Nakiea,
Nakiya, Nakiyah, Nekia*

Nakita (American) a form of Nikita.
Nakkita, Naquita

Nalani (Hawaiian) calm as the heavens.
Nalanie, Nalany

Nami (Japanese) wave.
Namika, Namiko

Nan (German) a short form of
Fernanda. (English) a form of Ann.
Nana, Nanice, Nanine, Nanna, Nanon

Nana (Hawaiian) spring.

Nanci (English) a form of Nancy.
Nancie, Nancsi, Nansi

Nancy (English) gracious. A familiar
form of Nan.
*Nainsi, Nance, Nancee, Nancey, Nanci,
Nancine, Nancye, Nanette, Nanice,
Nanncey, Nanncy, Nanouk, Nansee,
Nansey, Nanuk*

Nanette (French) a form of Nancy.
*Nan, Nanete, Nannette, Nettie, Nineta,
Ninete, Ninetta, Ninette, Nini, Ninita,
Ninnetta, Ninnette, Nynette*

Nani (Greek) charming. (Hawaiian)
beautiful.
Nanni, Nannie, Nanny

Naomi (Hebrew) pleasant, beautiful.
Bible: Ruth's mother-in-law.
*Naoma, Naomia, Naomie, Naomy,
Navit, Neoma, Neomi, Noami, Noemi,
Noma, Nomi, Nyomi*

Naomie (Hebrew) a form of Naomi.
Naome, Naomee, Noemie

Nara (Greek) happy. (English) north.
(Japanese) oak.
Narah

Narcissa (Greek) daffodil. Mythology:
Narcissus was the youth who fell in
love with his own reflection.
*Narcessa, Narcisa, Narcisse, Narcyssa,
Narissa, Narkissa*

Narelle (Australian) woman from the
sea.
Narel

Nari (Japanese) thunder.
Narie, Nariko

Narmada (Hindi) pleasure giver.

Nashawna (American) a combination
of the prefix Na + Shawna.
*Nashan, Nashana, Nashanda, Nashaun,
Nashauna, Nashaunda, Nashauwna,
Nashawn, Nasheena, Nashounda,
Nashuana*

Nashota (Native American) double;
second-born twin.

Nastasia (Greek) a form of Anastasia.
*Nastasha, Nastashia, Nastasja, Nastassa,
Nastassia, Nastassiya, Nastassja,
Nastassya, Nastasya, Nastazia,
Nastisija, Nastka, Nastusya, Nastya*

Nasya (Hebrew) miracle.
Nasia, Nasyah

Nata (Sanskrit) dancer. (Latin) swimmer. (Native American) speaker; creator. (Polish, Russian) a form of
Natalie. See also Nadia.
Natia, Natka, Natya

Natacha (Russian) a form of Natasha.
Natachia, Natacia, Naticha

Natalee, Natali (Latin) forms of
Natalie.
Natale, Nataleh, Nataleigh, Nattlee

Natalia (Russian) a form of Natalie.
See also Talia.
*Nacia, Natala, Natalea, Nataliia,
Natalija, Natalina, Nataliya, Nataliyah,
Natalja, Natalka, Natallea, Natallia,
Natalya, Nathalia, Natka*

Natalie (Latin) born on Christmas day.
See also Nata, Natasha, Noel, Talia.
Nat, Natalee, Natali, Natalia, Nataliee,
Nataline, Natalle, Natallie, Nataly,
Natelie, Nathalie, Nathaly, Natie,
Natilie, Natlie, Nattalie, Nattilie

Nataline (Latin) a form of Natalie.
Natalene, Nataléne, Natalyn

Natalle (French) a form of Natalie.
Natale

Nataly (Latin) a form of Natalie.
Nathaly, Natally, Natallye

Natane (Arapaho) daughter.
Natanne

Natania (Hebrew) gift of God.
Natanya, Natée, Nathania, Nathenia,
Netania, Nethania

Natara (Arabic) sacrifice.
Natori, Natoria

Natasha (Russian) a form of Natalie.
See also Stacey, Tasha.
Nahtasha, Natacha, Natasa, Natascha,
Natashah, Natashea, Natashenka,
Natashia, Natashiea, Natashja, Natashka,
Natasia, Natassia, Natassija, Natassja,
Natasza, Natausha, Natawsha, Natesha,
Nateshia, Nathasha, Nathassa, Natisha,
Natishia, Natosha, Netasha, Notosha

Natesa (Hindi) cosmic dancer.
Religion: another name for the
Hindu god Shiva.
Natisa, Natissa

Nathalie, Nathaly (Latin) forms of
Natalie.
Nathalee, Nathali, Nathalia, Nathalya

Natie (English) a familiar form of
Natalie.
Nati, Natti, Nattie, Natty

Natosha (Russian) a form of Natasha.
Natoshia, Natoshya, Netosha, Notosha

Nava (Hebrew) beautiful; pleasant.
Navah, Naveh, Navit

Nayely (Irish) a form of Neila.
Naeyli, Nayelia, Nayelli, Nayelly, Nayla

Neala (Irish) a form of Neila.
Nayela, Naylea, Naylia, Nealia, Neela,
Neelia, Neila

Necha (Spanish) a form of Agnes.
Necho

Neci (Hungarian) fiery, intense.
Necia, Necie

Neda (Slavic) born on Sunday.
Nedah, Nedi, Nedia, Neida

Nedda (English) prosperous guardian.
Neddi, Neddie, Neddy

Neely (Irish) a familiar form of Neila,
Nelia.
Nealee, Nealie, Nealy, Neelee, Neeley,
Neeli, Neelie, Neili, Neilie

Neema (Swahili) born during prosperous times.

Neena (Spanish) a form of Nina.
Neenah, Nena

Neila (Irish) champion. See also
Neala, Neely.
Nayely, Neilah, Neile, Neilia, Neilla,
Neille

Nekeisha (American) a form of
Nakeisha.
Nechesa, Neikeishia, Nekesha, Nekeshia,
Nekiesha, Nekisha, Nekysha

Nekia (Arabic) a form of Nakia.
Nekeya, Nekiya, Nekiyah, Nekya,
Nekiya

Nelia (Spanish) yellow. (Latin) a famil-
iar form of Cornelia.
Neelia, Neely, Neelya, Nela, Neli,
Nelka, Nila

Nelle (Greek) stone.

Nellie, Nelly (English) familiar forms
of Cornelia, Eleanor, Helen, Prunella.
Nel, Neli, Nell, Nella, Nelley, Nelli,
Nellianne, Nellice, Nellis, Nelma

Nenet (Egyptian) born near the sea.
Mythology: Nunet was the goddess
of the sea.

Neola (Greek) youthful.
Neolla

Neona (Greek) new moon.

Nereida (Greek) a form of Nerine.
Nereyda, Nereyida, Nerida

Nerine (Greek) sea nymph.
Nereida, Nerina, Nerita, Nerline

Nerissa (Greek) sea nymph. See also
Rissa.
Narice, Narissa, Nerice, Nerisa, Nerisse,
Nerrisa, Nerys, Neryssa

Nessa (Scandinavian) promontory.
(Greek) a short form of Agnes. See also
Nessie.
Nesa, Nesha, Neshia, Nesiah, Nessia,
Nesta, Nevsa, Neysa, Neysha, Neyshia

Nessie (Greek) a familiar form of
Agnes, Nessa, Vanessa.
Nese, Neshie, Nesho, Nesi, Ness, Nessi,
Nessy, Nest, Neys

Neta (Hebrew) plant, shrub. See also
Nettie.
Netia, Netta, Nettia

Netis (Native American) trustworthy.

Nettie (French) a familiar form of
Annette, Nanette, Antoinette.
Neti, Netie, Netta, Netti, Netty, Nety

Neva (Spanish) snow. (English) new.
Geography: a river in Russia.
Neiva, Neve, Nevia, Neyva, Nieve,
Niva, Nivea, Nivia

Nevada (Spanish) snow. Geography: a
western U. S. state.
Neiva, Neva

Nevina (Irish) worshipper of the saint.
Neveen, Nevein, Nevena, Neveyan,
Nevin, Nivena

Neylan (Turkish) fulfilled wish.
Neya, Neyla

Neza (Slavic) a form of Agnes.

Nia (Irish) a familiar form of Neila.
Mythology: Nia Ben Aur was a leg-
endary Welsh woman.
Neya, Niah, Niajia, Niya, Nya

Niabi (Osage) fawn.

Nichelle (American) a combination of
Nicole + Michelle. Culture: Nichelle
Nichols was the first African American
woman featured in a television drama
(*Star Trek*).
Nichele, Nichell, Nishelle

Nichole (French) a form of Nicole.
Nichol, Nichola, Nicholas, Nicholle

Nicki (French) a familiar form of
Nicole.
Nicci, Nickey, Nickeya, Nickia, Nickie,
Nickiya, Nicky, Niki

Nickole (French) a form of Nicole.
Nickol

Nicola (Italian) a form of Nicole.
Nacola, Necola, Nichola, Nickola,
Nicolea, Nicolla, Nikkola, Nikola,
Nikolia, Nykola

Nicole (French) a form of Nicholas.
See also Colette, Cosette, Nikita.
Nacole, Necole, Nica, Nichole, Nicia,
Nicki, Nickole, Nicol, Nicola, Nicolette,
Nicoli, Nicolie, Nicoline, Nicolle,
Nikayla, Nikelle, Nikki, Niquole,
Nocole, Nycole

Nicolette (French) a form of Nicole.
Nicholette, Nicoletta, Nicollete, Nicollette,
Nikkolette, Nikoleta, Nikoletta, Nikolette

Nicoline (French) a familiar form of
Nicole.
Nicholine, Nicholyn, Nicoleen, Nicolene,
Nicolina, Nicolyn, Nicolyne, Nicolynn,
Nicolynne, Nikolene, Nikolina, Nikoline

Nicolle (French) a form of Nicole.
Nicholle

Nida (Omaha) Mythology: an elflike
creature.
Nidda

Nidia (Latin) nest.
Nidi, Nidya

Niesha (American) pure.
(Scandinavian) a form of Nissa.
Neisha, Neishia, Neissia, Nesha, Neshia,
Nesia, Nessia, Niessia, Nisha, Nyesha

Nige (Latin) dark night.
Nigea, Nigela, Nija, Nijae, Nijah

Nika (Russian) belonging to God.
Nikka

Nikayla, Nikelle (American) forms of
Nicole.
Nikeille, Nikel, Nikela, Nikelie

Nike (Greek) victorious. Mythology:
the goddess of victory.

Niki (Russian) a short form of Nikita.
(American) a familiar form of
Nicole.
Nikia, Nikiah

Nikita (Russian) victorious people.
Nakeita, Nakita, Niki, Nikitah, Nikitia,
Nikitta, Nikki, Nikkita, Niquita,
Niquitta

Nikki (American) a familiar form of
Nicole, Nikita.
Nicki, Nikia, Nikkea, Nikkey, Nikkia,
Nikkiah, Nikkie, Nikko, Nikky

Nikole (French) a form of Nicole.
Nikkole, Nikkolie, Nikola, Nikole,
Nikolena, Nicolia, Nikolina, Nikolle

Nila (Latin) Geography: the Nile
River is in Africa. (Irish) a form of
Neila.
Nilah, Nilesia, Nyla

Nili (Hebrew) Botany: a pea plant that
yields indigo.

Nima (Hebrew) thread. (Arabic) blessing.
Nema, Niama, Nimali

Nina (Hebrew) a familiar form of Hannah. (Spanish) girl. (Native American) mighty. (Hebrew) a familiar form of Hannah.
Neena, Ninah, Ninacska, Ninja, Ninna, Ninon, Ninosca, Ninoshka

Ninon (French) a form of Nina.

Nirel (Hebrew) light of God.
Nirali, Nirelle

Nirveli (Hindi) water child.

Nisa (Arabic) woman.

Nisha (American) a form of Niesha, Nissa.
Niasha, Nishay

Nishi (Japanese) west.

Nissa (Hebrew) sign, emblem. (Scandinavian) friendly elf; brownie. See also Nyssa.
Nisha, Nisse, Nissie, Nissy

Nita (Hebrew) planter. (Choctaw) bear. (Spanish) a short form of Anita, Juanita.
Nitai, Nitha, Nithai, Nitika

Nitara (Hindi) deeply rooted.

Nitasha (American) a form of Natasha.
Nitasia, Niteisha, Nitisha, Nitishia

Nitsa (Greek) a form of Helen.

Nituna (Native American) daughter.

Nitza (Hebrew) flower bud.
Nitzah, Nitzana, Nitzanit, Niza, Nizah

Nixie (German) water sprite.

Niya (Irish) a form of Nia.
Niyah, Niyana, Niyia, Nyia

Nizana (Hebrew) a form of Nitza.
Nitzana, Nitzania, Zana

Noel (Latin) Christmas. See also Natalie.
Noël, Noela, Noelani, Noele, Noeleen, Noelene, Noelia, Noeline, Noelle, Noelyn, Noelynn, Nohely, Noleen, Novelenn, Novelia, Nowel, Noweleen, Nowell

Noelani (Hawaiian) beautiful one from heaven.
Noela

Noelle (French) Christmas.
Noell, Noella, Noelleen, Noelly, Noellyn

Noemi (Hebrew) a form of Naomi.
Noam, Noemie, Noemy, Nohemi, Nomi

Noemie (Hebrew) a form of Noemi.

Noemy (Hebrew) a form of Noemi.
Noamy

Noga (Hebrew) morning light.

Nohely (Latin) a form of Noel.
Noeli, Noelie, Noely, Nohal, Noheli

Nokomis (Dakota) moon daughter.

Nola (Latin) small bell. (Irish) famous; noble. A short form of Fionnula.
Nuala

Noleta (Latin) unwilling.
Nolita

Nollie (English) a familiar form of Magnolia.
Nolia, Nolle, Nolley, Nolli, Nolly

Noma (Hawaiian) a form of Norma.

Nona (Latin) ninth.
Nonah, Noni, Nonia, Nonie, Nonna, Nonnah, Nonya

Noor (Aramaic) a form of Nura.
Noorie, Nour, Nur

Nora (Greek) light. A familiar form of Eleanor, Honora, Leonore.
Norah, Noreen

Noreen (Irish) a form of Eleanor, Nora. (Latin) a familiar form of Norma.
Noorin, Noreena, Noreene, Noren, Norena, Norene, Norina, Norine, Nureen

Norell (Scandinavian) from the north.
Narell, Narelle, Norela, Norelle, Norely

Nori (Japanese) law, tradition.
Noria, Norico, Noriko, Norita

Norma (Latin) rule, precept.
Noma, Noreen, Normi, Normie

Nova (Latin) new. A short form of Novella, Novia. (Hopi) butterfly chaser. Astronomy: a star that releases bright bursts of energy.

Novella (Latin) newcomer.
Nova, Novela

Novia (Spanish) sweetheart.
Nova, Novka, Nuvia

Nu (Burmese) tender. (Vietnamese) girl.
Nue

Nuala (Irish) a short form of Fionnula.
Nola, Nula

Nuela (Spanish) a form of Amelia.

Nuna (Native American) land.

Nunciata (Latin) messenger.
Nunzia

Nura (Aramaic) light.
Noor, Noora, Noorah, Noura, Nurah

Nuria (Aramaic) the Lord's light.
Nuri, Nuriel, Nurin

Nurita (Hebrew) Botany: a flower with red and yellow blossoms.
Nurit

Nuru (Swahili) daylight.

Nusi (Hungarian) a form of Hannah.

Nuwa (Chinese) mother goddess. Mythology: another name for Nü-gua, the creator of mankind.

Nya (Irish) a form of Nia.
Nyaa, Nyah, Nyia

Nycole (French) a form of Nicole.
Nychelle, Nycolette, Nycolle

Nydia (Latin) nest.
Nyda

Nyesha (American) a form of Niesha.
Nyeisha, Nyeshia

Nyla (Latin, Irish) a form of Nila.
Nylah

Nyoko (Japanese) gem, treasure.

Nyomi (Hebrew) a form of Naomi.
Nyome, Nyomee, Nyomie

Nyree (Maori) sea.
Nyra, Nyrie

Nyssa (Greek) beginning. See also Nissa.
Nisha, Nissi, Nissy, Nyasia, Nysa

Nyusha (Russian) a form of Agnes.
Nyushenka, Nyushka

Oba (Yoruba) chief, ruler.

Obelia (Greek) needle.

Oceana (Greek) ocean. Mythology: Oceanus was the god of the ocean.
Ocean, Oceananna, Oceane, Oceania, Oceanna, Oceanne, Oceaonna, Oceon

Octavia (Latin) eighth. See also Tavia.
Octabia, Octaviah, Octaviais, Octavice, Octavie, Octavienne, Octavio, Octavious, Octavise, Octavya, Octivia, Otavia, Ottavia

Odeda (Hebrew) strong; courageous.

Odele (Greek) melody, song.
Odelet, Odelette, Odell, Odelle

Odelia (Greek) ode; melodic. (Hebrew) I will praise God. (French) wealthy. See also Odetta.
Oda, Odeelia, Odeleya, Odelina, Odelinda, Odelyn, Odila, Odile, Odilia

Odella (English) wood hill.
Odela, Odelle, Odelyn

Odera (Hebrew) plough.

Odessa (Greek) odyssey, long voyage.
Adesha, Adeshia, Adessa, Adessia, Odessia

Odetta (German, French) a form of Odelia.
Oddetta, Odette

Odina (Algonquin) mountain.

Ofelia (Greek) a form of Ophelia.
Ofeelia, Ofilia

Ofira (Hebrew) gold.
Ofarrah, Ophira

Ofra (Hebrew) a form of Aphra.
Ofrat

Ogin (Native American) wild rose.

Ohanna (Hebrew) God's gracious gift.

Okalani (Hawaiian) heaven.
Okilani

Oki (Japanese) middle of the ocean.
Okie

Oksana (Latin) a form of Osanna.
Oksanna

Ola (Greek) a short form of Olesia. (Scandinavian) ancestor.

Olathe (Native American) beautiful.
Olathia

Oleda (Spanish) a form of Alida. See also Leda.
Oleta, Olida, Olita

Olena (Russian) a form of Helen.
Oleena, Olenka, Olenna, Olenya, Olya

Olesia (Greek) a form of Alexandra.
Cesya, Ola, Olecia, Oleesha, Oleishia,
Olesha, Olesya, Olexa, Olice, Olicia,
Olisha, Olishia, Ollicia

Oletha (Scandinavian) nimble.
Oleta, Yaletha

Olethea (Latin) truthful. See also
Alethea.
Oleta

Olga (Scandinavian) holy. See also
Helga, Olivia.
Olenka, Olia, Olja, Ollya, Olva, Olya

Oliana (Polynesian) oleander.

Olina (Hawaiian) filled with happiness.

Olinda (Latin) scented. (Spanish) protector of property. (Greek) a form of
Yolanda.

Olisa (Ibo) God.

Olive (Latin) olive tree.
Oliff, Oliffe, Olivet, Olivette

Olivia (Latin) a form of Olive.
(English) a form of Olga. See also
Liv, Livia.
Alivia, Alyvia, Olevia, Oliva, Olivea,
Oliveia, Olivetta, Olivi, Olivianne,
Olivya, Oliwia, Ollie, Olva, Olyvia

Ollie (English) a familiar form of Olivia.
Olla, Olly, Ollye

Olwen (Welsh) white footprint.
Olwenn, Olwin, Olwyn, Olwyne,
Olwynne

Olympia (Greek) heavenly.
Olimpia, Olympe, Olympie

Olyvia (Latin) a form of Olivia.

Oma (Hebrew) reverent. (German)
grandmother. (Arabic) highest.

Omaira (Arabic) red.
Omar, Omara, Omarah, Omari,
Omaria, Omarra

Omega (Greek) last, final, end.
Linguistics: the last letter in the
Greek alphabet.

Ona (Latin, Irish) a form of Oona,
Una. (English) river.

Onatah (Iroquois) daughter of the
earth and the corn spirit.

Onawa (Native American) wide
awake.
Onaja, Onajah

Ondine (Latin) a form of Undine.
Ondene, Ondina, Ondyne

Ondrea (Czech) a form of Andrea.
Ohndrea, Ohndreea, Ohndreya,
Ohndria, Ondraya, Ondreana, Ondreea,
Ondreya, Ondria, Ondrianna, Ondriea

Oneida (Native American) eagerly
awaited.
Onida, Onyda

Onella (Hungarian) a form of Helen.

Onesha (American) a combination of
Ondrea + Aisha.
Oneshia, Onesia, Onessa, Onessia,
Onethia, Oniesha, Onisha

Oni (Yoruba) born on holy ground.
Onnie

Onora (Latin) a form of Honora.
Onoria, Onorine, Ornora

Oona (Latin, Irish) a form of Una.
Ona, Onna, Onnie, Oonagh, Oonie

Opa (Choctaw) owl. (German) grandfather.

Opal (Hindi) precious stone.
Opale, Opalina, Opaline

Ophelia (Greek) helper. Literature:
Hamlet's love interest in the
Shakespearean play *Hamlet*.
Filia, Ofelia, Ophélie, Ophilia, Phelia

Oprah (Hebrew) a form of Orpah.
Ophra, Ophrah, Opra

Ora (Latin) prayer. (Spanish) gold.
(English) seacoast. (Greek) a form of
Aura.
Orah, Orlice, Orra

Orabella (Latin) a form of Arabella.
Orabel, Orabela, Orabelle

Oralee (Hebrew) the Lord is my light.
See also Yareli.
Areli, Orali, Oralit, Orelie, Orlee, Orli,
Orly

Oralia (French) a form of Aurelia. See
also Oriana.
Oralis, Oriel, Orielda, Orielle, Oriena,
Orlena, Orlene

Orea (Greek) mountains.
Oreal, Oria, Oriah

Orela (Latin) announcement from the
gods; oracle.
Oreal, Orella, Orelle, Oriel, Orielle

Orenda (Iroquois) magical power.

Oretha (Greek) a form of Aretha.
Oreta, Oretta, Orette

Oriana (Latin) dawn, sunrise. (Irish)
golden.
*Orane, Orania, Orelda, Orelle, Ori,
Oria, Orian, Oriane, Orianna, Orieana,
Oryan*

Orina (Russian) a form of Irene.
Orya, Oryna

Orinda (Hebrew) pine tree. (Irish)
light skinned, white.
Orenda

Orino (Japanese) worker's field.
Ori

Oriole (Latin) golden; black-and-
orange bird.
Auriel, Oriel, Oriell, Oriella, Oriola

Orla (Irish) golden woman.
Orlagh, Orlie, Orly

Orlanda (German) famous throughout the land.
Orlandia, Orlantha, Orlenda, Orlinda

Orlenda (Russian) eagle.

Orli (Hebrew) light.
Orlice, Orlie, Orly

Ormanda (Latin) noble. (German)
mariner.
Orma

Ornice (Hebrew) cedar tree. (Irish)
pale; olive colored.
Orna, Ornah, Ornat, Ornette, Ornit

Orpah (Hebrew) runaway. See also
Oprah.
Orpa, Orpha, Orphie

Orquidea (Spanish) orchid.
Orquidia

Orsa (Latin) a short form of Orseline.
See also Ursa.
*Orsaline, Orse, Orsel, Orselina, Orseline,
Orsola*

Ortensia (Italian) a form of Hortense.

Orva (French) golden; worthy.
(English) brave friend.

Osanna (Latin) praise the Lord.
Oksana, Osana

Osen (Japanese) one thousand.

Oseye (Benin) merry.

Osma (English) divine protector.
Ozma

Otilie (Czech) lucky heroine.
Otila, Otilia, Otka, Ottili, Otylia

Ovia (Latin, Danish) egg.

Owena (Welsh) born to nobility;
young warrior.

Oya (Moquelumnan) called forth.

Oz (Hebrew) strength.

Ozara (Hebrew) treasure, wealth.

Paca (Spanish) a short form of
Pancha. See also Paka.

Padget (French) a form of Page.
Padgett, Paget, Pagett

Padma (Hindi) lotus.

Page (French) young assistant.
Padget, Pagen, Pagi, Payge

Paige (English) young child.
Payge

Paisley (Scottish) patterned fabric first
made in Paisley, Scotland.
*Paislay, Paislee, Paisleyann, Paisleyanne,
Paizlei, Paizleigh, Paizley, Pasley, Pazley*

Paiton (English) warrior's town.
*Paiten, Paityn, Paityne, Paiyton, Paten,
Patton*

Paka (Swahili) kitten. See also Paca.

Pakuna (Moquelumnan) deer bound-
ing while running downhill.

Palila (Polynesian) bird.

Pallas (Greek) wise. Mythology: another
name for Athena, the goddess of wisdom.

Palma (Latin) palm tree.
Pallma, Palmira

Palmira (Spanish) a form of Palma.
Pallmirah, Pallmyra, Palmer, Palmyra

Paloma (Spanish) dove. See also
Aloma.
*Palloma, Palometa, Palomita, Paluma,
Peloma*

Pamela (Greek) honey.
*Pam, Pama, Pamala, Pamalla, Pamelia,
Pamelina, Pamella, Pamila, Pamilla,
Pammela, Pammi, Pammie, Pammy,
Pamula*

Pancha (Spanish) free; from France.
Paca, Panchita

Pandita (Hindi) scholar.

Pandora (Greek) all-gifted.
Mythology: a woman who opened a box out of curiosity and released evil into the world. See also Dora.
Pandi, Pandorah, Pandorra, Pandorrah, Pandy, Panndora, Panndorah, Panndorra, Panndorrah

Pansy (Greek) flower; fragrant. (French) thoughtful.
Pansey, Pansie

Panthea (Greek) all the gods.
Pantheia, Pantheya

Panya (Swahili) mouse; tiny baby. (Russian) a familiar form of Stephanie.
Panyia

Panyin (Fante) older twin.

Paola (Italian) a form of Paula.
Paoli, Paolina

Papina (Moquelumnan) vine growing on an oak tree.

Paquita (Spanish) a form of Frances.
Paqua

Pari (Persian) fairy eagle.

Paris (French) Geography: the capital of France. Mythology: the Trojan prince who started the Trojan War by abducting Helen.
Parice, Paries, Parisa, Parise, Parish, Parisha, Pariss, Parissa, Parisse, Parris, Parys, Parysse

Parker (English) park keeper.
Park, Parke

Parris (French) a form of Paris.
Parrise, Parrish, Parrisha, Parrys, Parrysh

Parthenia (Greek) virginal.
Partheenia, Parthenie, Parthinia, Pathina

Parveneh (Persian) butterfly.

Pascale (French) born on Easter or Passover.
Pascalette, Pascaline, Pascalle, Paschale, Paskel

Pasha (Greek) sea.
Palasha, Pascha, Pasche, Pashae, Pashe, Pashel, Pashka, Pasia, Passia

Passion (Latin) passion.
Pashion, Pashonne, Pasion, Passionaé, Passionate, Passionette

Pasua (Swahili) born by cesarean section.

Pat (Latin) a short form of Patricia, Patsy.

Pati (Moquelumnan) fish baskets made of willow branches.

Patia (Gypsy, Spanish) leaf. (Latin, English) a familiar form of Patience, Patricia.

Patience (English) patient.
Paciencia, Patia, Patiance, Patient, Patince, Patishia

Patra (Greek, Latin) a form of Petra.

Patrice (French) a form of Patricia.
Patrease, Patrece, Patreece, Patreese, Patreice, Patriece, Patryce, Pattrice

Patricia (Latin) noblewoman. See also Payton, Peyton, Tricia, Trisha, Trissa.
Pat, Patia, Patresa, Patrica, Patrice,
Patricea, Patriceia, Patrichea, Patriciana, Patricianna, Patricja, Patricka, Patrickia, Patrisha, Patrishia, Patrisia, Patrissa, Patrizia, Patrizzia, Patrycia, Patrycja, Patsy, Patty

Patsy (Latin) a familiar form of Patricia.
Pat, Patsey, Patsi

Patty (English) a familiar form of Patricia.
Patte, Pattee, Patti, Pattie

Paula (Latin) small. See also Pavla, Polly.
Paliki, Paola, Paulane, Paulann, Paule, Paulette, Paulina, Pauline, Paulla, Pavia

Paulette (Latin) a familiar form of Paula.
Paulet, Paulett, Pauletta, Paulita, Paullett, Paulletta, Paullette

Paulina (Slavic) a form of Paula.
Paulena, Paulene, Paulenia, Pauliana, Paulianne, Paullena, Paulyna, Pawlina, Polena, Polina, Polinia

Pauline (French) a form of Paula.
Pauleen, Paulene, Paulien, Paulin, Paulyne, Paulynn, Pouline

Pausha (Hindi) lunar month of Capricorn.

Pavla (Czech, Russian) a form of Paula.
Pavlina, Pavlinka

Paxton (Latin) peaceful town.
Paxtin, Paxtynn

Payge (English) a form of Paige.

Payton (Irish) a form of Patricia.
Paydon, Paytan, Payten, Paytin, Paytn, Paytton

Paz (Spanish) peace.

Pazi (Ponca) yellow bird.

Pazia (Hebrew) golden.
Paz, Paza, Pazice, Pazit

Peace (English) peaceful.

Pearl (Latin) jewel.
Pearle, Pearleen, Pearlena, Pearlene, Pearlette, Pearlina, Pearline, Pearlisha, Pearlyn, Perl, Perla, Perle, Perlette, Perlie, Perline, Perlline

Peggy (Greek) a familiar form of Margaret.
Peg, Pegeen, Pegg, Peggey, Peggi, Peggie, Pegi

Peke (Hawaiian) a form of Bertha.

Pela (Polish) a short form of Penelope.
Pele

Pelagia (Greek) sea.
Pelage, Pelageia, Pelagie, Pelga, Pelgia, Pellagia

Pelipa (Zuni) a form of Philippa.

Pemba (Bambara) the power that controls all life.

Penda (Swahili) loved.

Penelope (Greek) weaver. Mythology: the clever and loyal wife of Odysseus, a Greek hero.
Pela, Pen, Penelopa, Penna, Pennelope, Penny, Pinelopi

Peni (Carrier) mind.

Peninah (Hebrew) pearl.
Penina, Peninit, Peninnah, Penny

Penny (Greek) a familiar form of Penelope, Peninah.
Penee, Peni, Penney, Penni, Pennie

Peony (Greek) flower.
Peonie

Pepita (Spanish) a familiar form of Josephine.
Pepa, Pepi, Peppy, Peta

Pepper (Latin) condiment from the pepper plant.

Perah (Hebrew) flower.

Perdita (Latin) lost. Literature: a character in Shakespeare's play *The Winter's Tale*.
Perdida, Perdy

Perfecta (Spanish) flawless.

Peri (Greek) mountain dweller. (Persian) fairy or elf.
Perita

Perla (Latin) a form of Pearl.
Pearla

Perlie (Latin) a familiar form of Pearl.
Pearley, Pearlie, Pearly, Perley, Perli, Perly, Purley, Purly

Pernella (Greek, French) rock. (Latin) a short form of Petronella.
Parnella, Pernel, Pernell, Pernelle

Perri (Greek, Latin) small rock; traveler. (French) pear tree. (Welsh) child of Harry. (English) a form of Perry.
Perre, Perrey, Perriann, Perrie, Perrin, Perrine, Perry

Persephone (Greek) Mythology: the goddess of the underworld.
Persephanie, Persephany, Persephonie

Persis (Latin) from Persia.
Perssis, Persy

Peta (Blackfoot) golden eagle.

Petra (Greek, Latin) small rock. A short form of Petronella.
Patra, Pet, Peta, Petena, Peterina, Petraann, Petrice, Petrina, Petrine, Petrova, Petrovna, Pier, Pierce, Pietra

Petronella (Greek) small rock. (Latin) of the Roman clan Petronius.
Pernella, Peternella, Petra, Petrona, Petronela, Petronella, Petronelle, Petronia, Petronija, Petronilla, Petronille

Petula (Latin) seeker.
Petulah

Petunia (Native American) flower.

Peyton (Irish) a form of Patricia.
Peyden, Peydon, Peyten, Peytyn

Phaedra (Greek) bright.
Faydra, Phae, Phaidra, Phe, Phedre

Phallon (Irish) a form of Fallon.
Phalaine, Phalen, Phallan, Phallie, Phalon, Phalyn

Phebe (Greek) a form of Phoebe.
Pheba, Pheby

Pheodora (Greek, Russian) a form of Feodora.
Phedora, Phedorah, Pheodorah, Pheydora, Pheydorah

Philana (Greek) lover of mankind.
Phila, Philanna, Philene, Philiane, Philina, Philine

Philantha (Greek) lover of flowers.

Philicia (Latin) a form of Phylicia.
Philecia, Philesha, Philica, Philicha, Philycia

Philippa (Greek) lover of horses. See also Filippa.
Phil, Philipa, Philippe, Phillipina, Phillippine, Phillie, Philly, Pippa, Pippy

Philomena (Greek) love song; loved one. Bible: a first-century saint. See also Filomena, Mena.
Philoméne, Philomina

Phoebe (Greek) shining.
Phaebe, Phebe, Pheobe, Phoebey

Phylicia (Latin) fortunate; happy. (Greek) a form of Felicia.
Philicia, Phylecia, Phylesha, Phylesia, Phylica, Phylisha, Phylisia, Phylissa, Phyllecia, Phyllicia, Phyllisha, Phyllisia, Phyllissa, Phyllyza

Phyllida (Greek) a form of Phyllis.
Fillida, Philida, Phillida, Phillyda

Phyllis (Greek) green bough.
Filise, Fillys, Fyllis, Philis, Phillis, Philliss, Philys, Philyss, Phylis, Phyllida, Phyllis, Phylliss, Phyllys

Pia (Italian) devout.

Piedad (Spanish) devoted; pious.

Pier (French) a form of Petra.
Pierette, Pierrette, Pierra, Pierre

Pierce (English) a form of Petra.

Pilar (Spanish) pillar, column.
Peelar, Pilár, Pillar

Ping (Chinese) duckweed. (Vietnamese) peaceful.

Pinga (Eskimo) Mythology: the goddess of game and the hunt.

Piper (English) pipe player.

Pippa (English) a short form of Phillipa.

Pippi (French) rosy cheeked.
Pippen, Pippie, Pippin, Pippy

Pita (African) fourth daughter.

Placidia (Latin) serene.
Placida

Pleasance (French) pleasant.
Pleasence

Polla (Arabic) poppy.
Pola

Polly (Latin) a familiar form of Paula.
Paili, Pali, Pauli, Paulie, Pauly, Poll, Pollee, Polley, Polli, Pollie

Pollyam (Hindi) goddess of the plague. Religion: the Hindu name invoked to ward off bad spirits.

Pollyanna (English) a combination of Polly + Anna. Literature: an overly optimistic heroine created by Eleanor Porter.

Poloma (Choctaw) bow.

Pomona (Latin) apple. Mythology: the goddess of fruit and fruit trees.

Poni (African) second daughter.

Poppy (Latin) poppy flower.
Popi, Poppey, Poppi, Poppie

Pora, Poria (Hebrew) fruitful.

Porcha (Latin) a form of Portia.
Porchae, Porchai, Porche, Porchia, Porcia

Porscha, Porsche (German) forms of Portia.
Porcsha, Porcshe, Porschah, Porsché, Porschea, Porschia, Pourche

Porsha (Latin) a form of Portia.
Porshai, Porshay, Porshe, Porshea, Porshia

Portia (Latin) offering. Literature: the heroine of Shakespeare's play *The Merchant of Venice*.
Porcha, Porscha, Porsche, Porsha, Portiea

Precious (French) precious; dear.
Pracious, Preciouse, Precisha, Prescious, Preshious, Presious

Presley (English) priest's meadow.
Preslea, Preslee, Preslei, Presli, Preslie, Presly, Preslye, Pressley, Presslie, Pressly

Prima (Latin) first, beginning; first child.
Prema, Primalia, Primetta, Primina, Priminia

Primavera (Italian, Spanish) spring.

Primrose (English) primrose flower.
Primula

Princess (English) daughter of royalty.
Princcess, Princes, Princesa, Princessa, Princetta, Princie, Princilla

Priscilla (Latin) ancient.
*Cilla, Piri, Precila, Precilla, Prescilla,
Presilla, Pressilia, Pricila, Pricilla, Pris,
Prisca, Priscela, Priscella, Priscila,
Priscilia, Priscill, Priscille, Priscillia,
Prisella, Prisila, Prisilla, Prissila, Prissilla,
Prissy, Pryscylla, Prysilla*

Prissy (Latin) a familiar form of Priscilla.
Prisi, Priss, Prissi, Prissie

Priya (Hindi) beloved; sweet natured.
Pria

Procopia (Latin) declared leader.

Promise (Latin) promise, pledge.
Promis, Promiss, Promys, Promyse

Pru (Latin) a short form of Prudence.
Prue

Prudence (Latin) cautious; discreet.
Pru, Prudencia, Prudens, Prudy

Prudy (Latin) a familiar form of
Prudence.
Prudee, Prudi, Prudie

Prunella (Latin) brown; little plum.
See also Nellie.
Prunela

Psyche (Greek) soul. Mythology: a
beautiful mortal loved by Eros, the
Greek god of love.

Pua (Hawaiian) flower.

Pualani (Hawaiian) heavenly flower.
Puni

Purity (English) purity.
Pura, Pureza, Purisima

Pyralis (Greek) fire.
Pyrene

Qadira (Arabic) powerful.
Kadira

Qamra (Arabic) moon.
Kamra

Qitarah (Arabic) fragrant.

Quaashie (Ewe) born on Sunday.

Quadeisha (American) a combination
of Qadira + Aisha.
*Qudaisha, Quadaishia, Quadajah,
Quadasha, Quadasia, Quadayshia,
Quadaza, Quadejah, Quadesha,
Quadeshia, Quadiasha, Quaesha*

Quaneisha (American) a combination
of the prefix Qu + Niesha.
*Quaneasa, Quanece, Quanecia,
Quaneice, Quanesha, Quanisha,
Quansha, Quarnisha, Queisha,
Qwanisha, Qynisha*

Quanesha (American) a form of
Quaneisha.
*Quamesha, Quaneesha, Quaneshia,
Quanesia, Quanessa, Quanessia,
Quannesha, Quanneshia, Quannezia,
Quayneshia, Quinesha*

Quanika (American) a combination of
the prefix Qu + Nika.
*Quanikka, Quanikki, Quaniqua,
Quanique, Quantenique, Quawanica,
Queenika, Queenique*

Quanisha (American) a form of
Quaneisha.
*Quaniesha, Quanishia, Quaynisha,
Queenisha, Quenisha, Quenishia*

Quartilla (Latin) fourth.
Quantilla

Qubilah (Arabic) agreeable.

Queen (English) queen. See also
Quinn.
Queena, Queenie, Quenna

Queenie (English) a form of Queen.
Queenation, Queeneste, Queeny

Queisha (American) a short form of
Quaneisha.
Qeysha, Queshia, Queysha

Quenby (Scandinavian) feminine.

Quenisha (American) a combination
of Queen + Aisha.
*Queneesha, Quenesha, Quennisha,
Quensha, Quinesha, Quinisha*

Quenna (English) a form of Queen.
Quenell, Quenessa

Querida (Spanish) dear; beloved.

Questa (French) searcher.

Queta (Spanish) a short form of
names ending in "queta" or "quetta."
Quenetta, Quetta

Quiana (American) a combination of
the prefix Qu + Anna.
*Quian, Quianah, Quianda, Quiane,
Quiani, Quianita, Quianna, Quianne,
Quionna*

Quinby (Scandinavian) queen's estate.

Quanisha (American) a form of
Quaneisha.
*Quaniesha, Quanishia, Quaynisha,
Queenisha, Quenisha, Quenishia*

Quincy (Irish) fifth.
Quincee, Quincey, Quinci, Quincia,
Quincie

Quinella (Latin) a form of Quintana.

Quinesha, Quinisha (American) forms
of Quenisha.
Quineshia, Quinessa, Quinessia, Quinisa,
Quinishia, Quinnesha, Quinneshia,
Quinnisha, Quneasha, Quonesha,
Quonisha, Quonnisha

Quinetta (Latin) a form of Quintana.
Queenetta, Queenette, Quinette,
Quinita, Quinnette

Quinn (German, English) queen. See
also Queen.
Quin, Quinna, Quinne, Quynn

Quinshawna (American) a combination
of Quinn + Shauna.
Quinshea

Quintana (Latin) fifth. (English)
queen's lawn. See also Quinella,
Quinetta.
Quinntina, Quinta, Quintanna,
Quintara, Quintarah, Quintia, Quintila,
Quintilla, Quintina, Quintona,
Quintonice

Quintessa (Latin) essence. See also
Tess.
Quintaysha, Quintesa, Quintesha,
Quintessia, Quintice, Quinticia,
Quintisha, Quintosha

Quintrell (American) a combination
of Quinn + Trella.
Quintela, Quintella, Quintrelle

Quiterie (Latin, French) tranquil.
Quita

Qwanisha (American) a form of
Quaneisha.
Qwanechia, Qwanesha, Qwanessia,
Qwantasha

Rabecca (Hebrew) a form of
Rebecca.
Rabecka, Rabeca, Rabekah

Rabi (Arabic) breeze.
Rabia, Rabiah

Rachael (Hebrew) a form of Rachel.
Rachaele, Rachaell, Rachail, Rachalle

Racheal (Hebrew) a form of Rachel.

Rachel (Hebrew) female sheep. Bible:
the second wife of Jacob. See also
Lahela, Rae, Rochelle.
Racha, Rachael, Rachal, Racheal,
Rachela, Rachelann, Rachele, Rachelle,
Racquel, Raechel, Rahel, Rahela, Rahil,
Raiche, Raquel, Rashel, Rashelle, Ray,
Raycene, Raychel, Raychelle, Rey, Ruchel

Rachelle (French) a form of Rachel.
See also Shelley.
Rachalle, Rachell, Rachella, Raechell,
Raechelle, Raeshelle, Rashel, Rashele,
Rashell, Rashelle, Raychell, Rayshell,
Ruchelle

Racquel (French) a form of Rachel.
Rackel, Racquell, Racquella, Racquelle

Radella (German) counselor.

Radeyah (Arabic) content, satisfied.
Radeeyah, Radhiya, Radiah, Radiyah

Radinka (Slavic) full of life; happy,
glad.

Radmilla (Slavic) worker for the people.

Rae (English) doe. (Hebrew) a short
form of Rachel.
Raeh, Raeneice, Raeneisha, Raesha, Ray,
Raye, Rayetta, Rayette, Rayma, Rey

Raeann (American) a combination of
Rae + Ann. See also Rayanne.
Raea, Raean, Raeanna, Raeannah,
Raeona, Reanna, Raeanne

Raechel (Hebrew) a form of Rachel.
Raechael, Raechal, Raechele, Raechell,
Raechyl

Raeden (Japanese) Mythology: Raiden
was the god of thunder and
lightning.
Raeda, Raedeen

Raegan (Irish) a form of Reagan.
Raegen, Raegene, Raegine, Raegyn

Raelene (American) a combination of
Rae + Lee.
Rael, Raela, Raelani, Raele, Raeleah,
Raelee, Raeleen, Raeleia, Raeleigh,
Raeleigha, Raelein, Raelene, Raelennia,
Raelesha, Raelin, Raelina, Raelle,
Raelyn, Raelynn

Raelyn, Raelynn (American) forms of
Raelene.
Raelynda, Raelyne, Raelynne

Raena (German) a form of Raina.
Raenah, Raenia, Raenie, Raenna, Raeonna, Raeyauna, Raeyn, Raeyonna

Raeven (English) a form of Raven.
Raevin, Raevion, Raevon, Raevonna, Raevyn, Raevynne, Raewyn, Raewynne, Raivan, Raiven, Raivin, Raivyn

Rafa (Arabic) happy; prosperous.

Rafaela (Hebrew) a form of Raphaela.
Rafaelia, Rafaella

Ragan (Irish) a form of Reagan.
Ragean, Rageane, Rageen, Ragen, Ragene, Rageni, Ragenna, Raggan, Raygan, Raygen, Raygene, Rayghan, Raygin

Ragine (English) a form of Regina.
Raegina, Ragin, Ragina, Raginee

Ragnild (Scandinavian) battle counsel.
Ragna, Ragnell, Ragnhild, Rainell, Renilda, Renilde

Raheem (Punjabi) compassionate God.
Raheema, Rahima

Ráidah (Arabic) leader.

Raina (German) mighty. (English) a short form of Regina. See also Rayna.
Raeinna, Raena, Raheena, Rain, Rainah, Rainai, Raine, Rainea, Rainna, Reanna

Rainbow (English) rainbow.
Rainbeau, Rainbeaux, Rainbo, Raynbow

Raine (Latin) a short form of Regina. A form of Raina, Rane.
Rainee, Rainey, Raini, Rainie, Rainy, Reyne

Raisa (Russian) a form of Rose.
Raisah, Raissa, Raiza, Raysa, Rayza, Razia

Raizel (Yiddish) a form of Rose.
Rayzil, Razil, Reizel, Resel

Raja (Arabic) hopeful.
Raia, Rajaah, Rajae, Rajah, Rajai

Raku (Japanese) pleasure.

Raleigh (Irish) a form of Riley.
Ralea, Raleiah, Raley

Rama (Hebrew) lofty, exalted. (Hindi) godlike. Religion: an incarnation of the Hindu god Vishnu.
Ramah

Raman (Spanish) a form of Ramona.

Ramandeep (Sikh) covered by the light of the Lord's love.

Ramla (Swahili) fortuneteller.
Ramlah

Ramona (Spanish) mighty; wise protector. See also Mona.
Raman, Ramonda, Raymona, Romona, Romonda

Ramsey (English) ram's island.
Ramsha, Ramsi, Ramsie, Ramza

Ran (Japanese) water lily. (Scandinavian) destroyer. Mythology: the Norse sea goddess who destroys.

Rana (Sanskrit) royal. (Arabic) gaze, look.
Rahna, Rahni, Rani

Ranait (Irish) graceful; prosperous.
Rane, Renny

Randall (English) protected.
Randa, Randah, Randal, Randalee, Randel, Randell, Randelle, Randi, Randilee, Randilynn, Randlyn, Randy, Randyl

Randi, Randy (English) familiar forms of Miranda, Randall.
Rande, Randee, Randeen, Randene, Randey, Randie, Randii

Rane (Scandinavian) queen.
Raine

Rani (Sanskrit) queen. (Hebrew) joyful. A short form of Kerani.
Rahni, Ranee, Raney, Rania, Ranie, Ranice, Ranique, Ranni, Rannie

Ranita (Hebrew) song; joyful.
Ranata, Ranice, Ranit, Ranite, Ranitta, Ronita

Raniyah (Arabic) gazing.
Ranya, Ranyah

Rapa (Hawaiian) moonbeam.

Raphaela (Hebrew) healed by God.
Rafaella, Raphaella, Raphaelle

Raphaelle (French) a form of Raphaela.
Rafaelle, Raphael, Raphaele

Raquel (French) a form of Rachel.
Rakel, Rakhil, Rakhila, Raqueal, Raquela, Raquella, Raquelle, Rickelle, Rickquel, Ricquel, Ricquelle, Rikell, Rikelle, Rockell

Rasha (Arabic) young gazelle.
Rahshea, Rahshia, Rashae, Rashai, Rashea, Rashi, Rashia

Rashawna (American) a combination of the prefix Ra + Shawna.
Rashana, Rashanae, Rashanah, Rashanda, Rashane, Rashani, Rashanna, Rashanta, Rashaun, Rashauna, Rashaunda, Rashaundra, Rashaune, Rashawn, Rashawnda, Rashawnna, Rashon, Rashona, Rashonda, Rashunda

Rashel, Rashelle (American) forms of Rachel.
Rashele, Rashell, Rashella

Rashida (Swahili, Turkish) righteous.
Rahshea, Rahsheda, Rahsheita, Rashdah, Rasheda, Rashedah, Rasheeda, Rasheedah, Rasheeta, Rasheida, Rashidah, Rashidi

Rashieka (Arabic) descended from royalty.
Rasheeka, Rasheika, Rasheka, Rashika, Rasika

Rasia (Greek) rose.

Ratana (Tai) crystal.
Ratania, Ratanya, Ratna, Rattan, Rattana

Ratri (Hindi) night. Religion: the goddess of the night.

Raula (French) wolf counselor.
Raoula, Raulla, Raulle

Raven (English) blackbird.
Raeven, Raveen, Raveena, Raveenn, Ravena, Ravene, Ravenn, Ravenna, Ravennah, Ravenne, Raveon, Ravin, Ravon, Ravyn, Rayven, Revena

Ravin (English) forms of Raven.
Ravi, Ravina, Ravine, Ravinne, Ravion

Ravyn (English) a form of Raven.
Ravynn

Rawnie (Gypsy) fine lady.
Rawan, Rawna, Rhawnie

Raya (Hebrew) friend.
Raia, Raiah, Raiya, Ray, Rayah

Rayanne (American) a form of Raeann.
Rayane, Ray-Ann, Rayan, Rayana, Rayann, Rayanna, Rayeanna, Rayona, Rayonna, Reyan, Reyana, Reyann, Reyanna, Reyanne

Raychel, Raychelle (Hebrew) forms of Rachel.
Raychael, Raychele, Raychell, Raychil

Raylene (American) forms of Raylyn.
Ralina, Rayel, Rayele, Rayelle, Rayleana, Raylee, Rayleen, Rayleigh, Raylena, Raylin, Raylinn, Raylona, Raylyn, Raylynn, Raylynne

Raymonde (German) wise protector.
Rayma, Raymae, Raymie

Rayna (Scandinavian) mighty. (Yiddish) pure, clean. (English) king's advisor. (French) a familiar form of Lorraine. See also Raina.
Raynah, Rayne, Raynell, Raynelle, Raynette, Rayona, Rayonna, Reyna

Rayven (English) a form of Raven.
Rayvan, Rayvana, Rayvein, Rayvenne, Rayveona, Rayvin, Rayvon, Rayvonia

Rayya (Arabic) thirsty no longer.

Razi (Aramaic) secretive.
Rayzil, Rayzilee, Raz, Razia, Raziah, Raziela, Razilee, Razili

Raziya (Swahili) agreeable.

Rea (Greek) poppy flower.
Reah

Reagan (Irish) little ruler.
Reagen, Reaghan, Reagine

Reanna (German, English) a form of Raina. (American) a form of Raeann.
Reannah

Reanne (American) a form of Raeann, Reanna.
Reana, Reane, Reann, Reannan, Reanne, Reannen, Reannon, Reeana

Reba (Hebrew) fourth-born child. A short form of Rebecca. See also Reva, Riva.
Rabah, Reeba, Rheba

Rebeca (Hebrew) an alternate form of Rebecca.
Rebbeca, Rebecah

Rebecca (Hebrew) tied, bound. Bible: the wife of Isaac. See also Becca, Becky.
Rabecca, Reba, Rebbecca, Rebeca, Rebeccah, Rebeccea, Rebeccka, Rebecha, Rebecka, Rebeckah, Rebeckia, Rebecky, Rebekah, Rebeque, Rebi, Reveca, Riva, Rivka

Rebekah (Hebrew) a form of Rebecca.
Rebeka, Rebekha, Rebekka, Rebekkah, Rebekke, Revecca, Reveka, Revekka, Rifka

Rebi (Hebrew) a familiar form of Rebecca.
Rebbie, Rebe, Rebie, Reby, Ree, Reebie

Reena (Greek) peaceful. (English) a form of Rina. (Hebrew) a form of Rinah.
Reen, Reenie, Rena, Reyna

Reet (Estonian) a form of Margaret.
Reatha, Reta, Retha

Regan (Irish) a form of Reagan.
Regane, Reghan

Reganne (Irish) a form of Reagan.
Raegan, Ragan, Reagan, Regin

Reggie (English) a familiar form of Regina.
Reggi, Reggy, Regi, Regia, Regie

Regina (Latin) queen. (English) king's advisor. Geography: the capital of Saskatchewan. See also Gina.
Ragine, Raina, Raine, Rega, Regena, Regennia, Reggie, Regiena, Regine, Reginia, Regis, Reina, Rena

Regine (Latin) a form of Regina.
Regin

Rei (Japanese) polite, well behaved.
Reiko

Reilly (Irish) a form of Riley.
Reilee, Reileigh, Reiley, Reili, Reilley, Reily

Reina (Spanish) a short form of Regina. See also Reyna.
Reinah, Reine, Reinette, Reinie, Reinna, Reiny, Reiona, Renia, Rina

Rekha (Hindi) thin line.
Reka, Rekia, Rekiah, Rekiya

Remedios (Spanish) remedy.

Remi (French) from Rheims, France.
Raymi, Remee, Remie, Remy

Remington (English) raven estate.
Remmington

Ren (Japanese) arranger; water lily; lotus.

Rena (Hebrew) song; joy. A familiar form of Irene, Regina, Renata, Sabrina, Serena.
Reena, Rina, Rinna, Rinnah

Renae (French) a form of Renée.
Renay

Renata (French) a form of Renée.
Ranata, Rena, Renada, Renatta, Renita, Rennie, Renyatta, Rinada, Rinata

Rene (Greek) a short form of Irene, Renée.
Reen, Reenie, Reney, Rennie

Renée (French) born again.
Renae, Renata, Renay, Rene, Renea, Reneigh, Renell, Renelle, Renne

Renita (French) a form of Renata.
Reneeta, Renetta, Renitza

Rennie (English) a familiar form of Renata.
Reni, Renie, Renni

Reseda (Spanish) fragrant mignonette blossom.

Reshawna (American) a combination of the prefix Re + Shawna.
Resaunna, Reshana, Reshaunda, Reshawnda, Reshawnna, Reshonda, Reshonn, Reshonta

Resi (German) a familiar form of Theresa.
Resia, Ressa, Resse, Ressie, Reza, Rezka, Rezi

Reta (African) shaken.
Reeta, Retta, Rheta, Rhetta

Reubena (Hebrew) behold a child.
Reubina, Reuvena, Rubena, Rubenia, Rubina, Rubine, Rubyna

Reva (Latin) revived. (Hebrew) rain; one-fourth. A form of Reba, Riva.
Ree, Reeva, Revia, Revida

Reveca, Reveka (Slavic) forms of Rebecca, Rebekah.
Reve, Revecca, Revekka, Rivka

Rexanne (American) queen.
Rexan, Rexana, Rexann, Rexanna

Reyhan (Turkish) sweet-smelling flower.

Reyna (Greek) peaceful. (English) a form of Reina.
Reyana, Reyanna, Reyni, Reynna

Reynalda (German) king's advisor.

Réz (Latin, Hungarian) copper-colored hair.

Reza (Czech) a form of Theresa.
Rezi, Rezka

Rhea (Greek) brook, stream. Mythology: the mother of Zeus.
Rheá, Rhéa, Rhealyn, Rheanna, Rhia, Rhianna

Rheanna, Rhianna (Greek) forms of Rhea.
Rheana, Rheann, Rheanne, Rhiana, Rhiauna

Rhian (Welsh) a short form of Rhiannon.
Rhianne, Rhyan, Rhyann, Rhyanne, Rian, Riane, Riann, Rianne, Riayn

Rhiannon (Welsh) witch; nymph; goddess.
Rheannan, Rheannin, Rheannon, Rheanon, Rhian, Rhianen, Rhianna, Rhiannan, Rhiannen, Rhianon, Rhianwen, Rhinnon, Rhyanna, Riana, Riannon, Rianon

Rhoda (Greek) from Rhodes, Greece.
Rhode, Rhodeia, Rhodie, Rhody, Roda, Rodi, Rodie, Rodina

Rhona (Scottish) powerful, mighty. (English) king's advisor.
Rhonae, Rhonnie

Rhonda (Welsh) grand.
Rhondene, Rhondiesha, Ronda, Ronelle, Ronnette

Ria (Spanish) river.
Riah

Riana, Rianna (Irish) short forms of Briana. (Arabic) forms of Rihana.
Reana, Reanna, Rhianna, Rhyanna, Riana, Rianah

Rica (Spanish) a short form of Erica, Frederica, Ricarda. See also Enrica, Sandrica, Terrica, Ulrica.
Ricca, Rieca, Riecka, Rieka, Rikka, Riqua, Rycca

Ricarda (Spanish) rich and powerful ruler.
Rica, Richanda, Richarda, Richi, Ricki

Richael (Irish) saint.

Richelle (German, French) a form of Ricarda.
Richel, Richela, Richele, Richell, Richella, Richia

Rickelle (American) a form of Raquel.
Rickel, Rickela, Rickell

Ricki, Rikki (American) familiar forms of Erica, Frederica, Ricarda.
Rica, Ricci, Riccy, Rici, Rickee, Rickia, Rickie, Rickilee, Rickina, Rickita, Ricky, Ricquie, Riki, Rikia, Rikita, Rikka, Rikke, Rikkia, Rikkie, Rikky, Riko

Ricquel (American) a form of Raquel.
Rickquell, Ricquelle, Rikell, Rikelle

Rida (Arabic) favored by God.

Rihana (Arabic) sweet basil.
Rhiana, Rhianna, Riana, Rianna

Rika (Swedish) ruler.
Ricka

Rilee (Irish) a form of Riley.
Rielee, Rielle

Riley (Irish) valiant.
Raleigh, Reilly, Rieley, Rielly, Riely, Rilee, Rileigh, Rilie

Rilla (German) small brook.

Rima (Arabic) white antelope.
Reem, Reema, Reemah, Rema, Remah, Rhymia, Rim, Ryma

Rimona (Hebrew) pomegranate. See also Mona.

Rin (Japanese) park. Geography: a Japanese village.
Rini, Rynn

Rina (English) a short form of names ending in "rina." (Hebrew) a form of Rena, Rinah.
Reena, Rena

Rinah (Hebrew) joyful.
Rina

Riona (Irish) saint.

Risa (Latin) laughter.
Reesa, Resa

Risha (Hindi) born during the lunar month of Taurus.
Rishah, Rishay

Rishona (Hebrew) first.
Rishina, Rishon

Rissa (Greek) a short form of Nerissa.
Risa, Rissah, Ryssa, Ryssah

Rita (Sanskrit) brave; honest. (Greek) a short form of Margarita.
Reatha, Reda, Reeta, Reida, Reitha, Rheta, Riet, Ritah, Ritamae, Ritamarie

Ritsa (Greek) a familiar form of Alexandra.
Ritsah, Ritsi, Ritsie, Ritsy

Riva (French) river bank. (Hebrew) a short form of Rebecca. See also Reba, Reva.
Rivalee, Rivi, Rivvy

River (Latin, French) stream, water.
Rivana, Rivanna, Rivers, Riviane

Rivka (Hebrew) a short form of Rebecca.
Rivca, Rivcah, Rivkah

Riza (Greek) a form of Theresa.
Riesa, Rizus, Rizza

Roanna (American) a form of Rosana.
Ranna, Roana, Roanda, Roanne

Robbi, Robbie (English) familiar forms of Roberta.
Robby, Robbye, Robey, Robi, Robia, Roby

Roberta (English) famous brilliance.
Roba, Robbi, Robbie, Robena, Robertena, Robertina

Robin (English) robin. A form of Roberta.
Robann, Robbin, Robeen, Roben, Robena, Robian, Robina, Robine, Robinette, Robinia, Robinn, Robinta, Robyn

Robinette (English) a familiar form of Robin.
Robernetta, Robinet, Robinett, Robinita

Robyn (English) a form of Robin.
Robbyn, Robbynn, Robyne, Robynn, Robynne

Rochelle (French) large stone. (Hebrew) a form of Rachel. See also Shelley.
Reshelle, Roch, Rocheal, Rochealle, Rochel, Rochele, Rochell, Rochella, Rochette, Rockelle, Roshele, Roshell, Roshelle

Rocio (Spanish) dewdrops.
Rocío

Roderica (German) famous ruler.
Rica, Rika, Rodericka, Roderika, Rodreicka, Rodricka, Rodrika

Rodnae (English) island clearing.
Rodna, Rodnetta, Rodnicka

Rodneisha (American) a combination of Rodnae + Aisha.
Rodesha, Rodisha, Rodishah, Rodnecia, Rodnesha, Rodneshia, Rodneycia, Rodneysha, Rodnisha

Rohana (Hindi) sandalwood. (American) a combination of Rose + Hannah.
Rochana, Rohena

Rohini (Hindi) woman.

Rolanda (German) famous throughout the land.
Ralna, Rolande, Rolando, Rolaunda, Roleesha, Rolene, Rolinda, Rollande, Rolonda

Rolene (German) a form of Rolanda.
Rolaine, Rolena, Rolleen, Rollene

Roma (Latin) from Rome.
Romai, Rome, Romeise, Romeka, Romelle, Romesha, Rometta, Romia, Romilda, Romilla, Romina, Romini, Romma, Romonia

Romaine (French) from Rome.
Romana, Romanda, Romanelle, Romania, Romanique, Romany, Romayne, Romona, Romy

Romy (French) a familiar form of Romaine. (English) a familiar form of Rosemary.
Romi, Romie

Rona (Scandinavian) short forms of Ronalda.
Rhona, Roana, Ronalda, Ronna, Ronnae, Ronnay, Ronne, Ronni, Ronsy

Ronaele (Greek) the name Eleanor spelled backwards.
Ronalee, Ronni, Ronnie, Ronny

Ronda (Welsh) a form of Rhonda.
Rondai, Rondesia, Rondi, Rondie, Ronelle, Ronnette, Ronni, Ronnie, Ronny

Rondelle (French) short poem.
Rhondelle, Rondel, Ronndelle

Roneisha (American) a combination of Rhonda + Aisha.
Roneasha, Ronecia, Ronee, Roneeka, Roneesha, Roneice, Ronese, Ronesha, Roneshia, Ronesia, Ronessa, Ronessia, Ronichia, Ronicia, Roniesha, Ronisha, Ronneisha, Ronnesa, Ronnesha, Ronneshia, Ronni, Ronnie, Ronniesha, Ronny

Ronelle (Welsh) a form of Rhonda, Ronda.
Ranell, Ranelle, Ronel, Ronella, Ronielle, Ronnella, Ronnelle

Ronisha (American) a form of Roneisha.
Ronise, Ronnise, Ronnisha, Ronnishia

Ronli (Hebrew) joyful.
Ronia, Ronice, Ronit, Ronlee, Ronlie, Ronni, Ronnie, Ronny

Ronnette (Welsh) a familiar form of Rhonda, Ronda.
Ronetta, Ronette, Ronit, Ronita, Ronnetta, Ronni, Ronnie, Ronny

Ronni, Ronnie, Ronny (American) familiar forms of Veronica and names beginning with "Ron."
Rone, Ronee, Roni, Ronnee, Ronney

Rori, Rory (Irish) famous brilliance; famous ruler.
Rorie

Ros, Roz (English) short forms of Rosalind, Rosalyn.
Rozz, Rozzey, Rozzi, Rozzie, Rozzy

Rosa (Italian, Spanish) a form of Rose. History: Rosa Parks inspired the American Civil Rights movement by refusing to give up her bus seat to a white man in Montgomery, Alabama. See also Charo, Roza.

Rosabel (French) beautiful rose.
Rosabelia, Rosabella, Rosabelle, Rosebelle

Rosalba (Latin) white rose.
Rosalva, Roselba

Rosalie (English) a form of Rosalind.
Rosalea, Rosalee, Rosaleen, Rosaleigh, Rosalene, Rosalia, Rosealee, Rosealie, Roselee, Roselii, Roselia, Roselie, Roseley, Rosely, Rosilee, Rosli, Rozali, Rozália, Rozalie, Rozele

Rosalind (Spanish) fair rose.
Ros, Rosalie, Rosalinda, Rosalinde, Rosalyn, Rosalynd, Rosalynde, Roselind, Roselyn, Rosie, Roz, Rozalind, Rozland

Rosalinda (Spanish) a form of Rosalind.
Rosalina

Rosalyn (Spanish) a form of Rosalind.
Ros, Rosaleen, Rosalin, Rosaline, Rosalyne, Rosalynn, Rosalynne, Rosilyn, Roslin, Roslyn, Roslyne, Roslynn, Roz, Rozalyn, Rozlyn

Rosamond (German) famous guardian.
Rosamund, Rosamunda, Rosemonde, Rozamond

Rosanna, Roseanna (English) combinations of Rose + Anna.
Ranna, Roanna, Rosana, Rosannah, Roseana, Roseannah, Rosehanah, Rosehannah, Rosie, Rossana, Rossanna, Rozana, Rozanna

Rosanne, Roseanne (English) combinations of Rose + Ann.
Roanne, Rosan, Rosann, Roseann, Rose Ann, Rose Anne, Rossann, Rossanne, Rozann, Rozanne

Rosario (Filipino, Spanish) rosary.
Rosarah, Rosaria, Rosarie, Rosary, Rosaura

Rose (Latin) rose. See also Chalina, Raisa, Raizel, Roza.
Rada, Rasia, Rasine, Rois, Róise, Rosa, Rosea, Rosella, Roselle, Roses, Rosetta, Rosie, Rosina, Rosita, Rosse

Roselani (Hawaiian) heavenly rose.

Roselyn (Spanish) a form of Rosalind.
Roseleen, Roselene, Roselin, Roseline, Roselyne, Roselynn, Roselynne

Rosemarie (English) a combination of Rose + Marie.
Rosamaria, Rosamarie, Rosemari, Rosemaria, Rose Marie

Rosemary (English) a combination of Rose + Mary.
Romi, Romy

Rosetta (Italian) a form of Rose.
Roseta, Rosette

Roshan (Sanskrit) shining light.

Roshawna (American) a combination of Rose + Shawna.
Roshan, Roshana, Roshanda, Roshani, Roshann, Roshanna, Roshanta, Roshaun, Roshauna, Roshaunda, Roshawn, Roshawnda, Roshawnna, Roshona, Roshonda, Roshowna, Roshunda

Rosie (English) a familiar form of Rosalind, Rosanna, Rose.
Rosey, Rosi, Rosio, Rosse, Rosy, Rozsi, Rozy

Rosina (English) a familiar form of Rose.
Rosena, Rosenah, Rosene, Rosheen, Rozena, Rozina

Rosita (Spanish) a familiar form of Rose.
Roseeta, Roseta, Rozeta, Rozita, Rozyte

Roslyn (Scottish) a form of Rossalyn.
Roslin, Roslynn, Rosslyn, Rosslynn

Rossalyn (Scottish) cape; promontory.
Roslyn, Rosselyn, Rosylin, Roszaliyn

Rowan (English) tree with red berries. (Welsh) a form of Rowena.
Rowana

Rowena (Welsh) fair-haired. (English) famous friend. Literature: Ivanhoe's love interest in Sir Walter Scott's novel *Ivanhoe*.
Ranna, Ronni, Row, Rowan, Rowe, Roweena, Rowen, Rowina

Roxana, Roxanna (Persian) forms of Roxann.
Rocsana, Roxannah

Roxann, Roxanne (Persian) sunrise.
Literature: Roxanne is the heroine of
Edmond Rostand's play *Cyrano de
Bergerac*.
*Rocxann, Roxan, Roxana, Roxane,
Roxanna, Roxianne, Roxy*

Roxy (Persian) a familiar form of
Roxann.
Roxi, Roxie

Royale (English) royal.
*Royal, Royalene, Royalle, Roylee,
Roylene, Ryal, Ryale*

Royanna (English) queenly, royal.
Roya

Roza (Slavic) a form of Rosa.
*Roz, Rozalia, Roze, Rozel, Rozele,
Rozell, Rozella, Rozelli, Rozia, Rozsa,
Rozsi, Rozyte, Rozza, Rozzie*

Rozene (Native American) rose blossom.
Rozena, Rozina, Rozine, Ruzena

Ruana (Hindi) stringed musical instrument.
Ruan, Ruon

Rubena (Hebrew) a form of
Reubena.
*Rubenia, Rubina, Rubine, Rubinia,
Rubyn, Rubyna*

Rubi (French) a form of Ruby.
Ruba, Rubbie, Rubee, Rubia, Rubie

Ruby (French) precious stone.
*Rubby, Rubetta, Rubette, Rubey, Rubi,
Rubiann, Rubyann, Rubye*

Ruchi (Hindi) one who wishes to
please.

Rudee (German) famous wolf.
*Rudeline, Rudell, Rudella, Rudi, Rudie,
Rudina, Rudy*

Rudra (Hindi) seeds of the rudraksha
plant.

Rue (German) famous. (French) street.
(English) regretful; strong-scented
herbs.
Ru, Ruey

Ruffina (Italian) redhead.
Rufeena, Rufeine, Rufina, Ruphyna

Rui (Japanese) affectionate.

Rukan (Arabic) steady; confident.

Rula (Latin, English) ruler.

Runa (Norwegian) secret; flowing.
Runna

Ruperta (Spanish) a form of Roberta.

Rupinder (Sanskrit) beautiful.

Ruri (Japanese) emerald.
Ruriko

Rusalka (Czech) wood nymph.
(Russian) mermaid.

Russhell (French) redhead; fox
colored.
Rushell, Rushelle, Russellynn, Russhelle

Rusti (English) redhead.
Russet, Rustie, Rusty

Ruth (Hebrew) friendship. Bible: daughter-in-law of Naomi.
*Rutha, Ruthalma, Ruthe, Ruthella,
Ruthetta, Ruthie, Ruthven*

Ruthann (American) a combination of
Ruth + Ann.
*Ruthan, Ruthanna, Ruthannah,
Ruthanne, Ruthina, Ruthine*

Ruthie (Hebrew) a familiar form of
Ruth.
Ruthey, Ruthi, Ruthy

Ruza (Czech) rose.
Ruzena, Ruzenka, Ruzha, Ruzsa

Ryan, Ryann (Irish) little ruler.
*Raiann, Raianne, Rhyann, Riana,
Riane, Ryana, Ryane, Ryanna, Ryanne,
Rye, Ryen, Ryenne*

Ryba (Czech) fish.

Rylee (Irish) valiant.
*Rye, Ryelee, Rylea, Ryleigh, Ryley,
Rylie, Rylina, Rylyn*

Ryleigh, Rylie (Irish) forms of Rylee.
Ryelie, Ryli, Rylleigh, Ryllie

Ryley (Irish) a form of Rylee.
Ryeley, Rylly, Ryly

Ryo (Japanese) dragon.
Ryoko

S

Saarah (Arabic) princess.

Saba (Arabic) morning. (Greek) a
form of Sheba.
Sabaah, Sabah, Sabba, Sabbah

Sabi (Arabic) young girl.

Sabina (Latin) History: the Sabine were a tribe in ancient Italy. See also Bina.
Sabeen, Sabena, Sabienne, Sabin, Sabine, Sabinka, Sabinna, Sabiny, Saby, Sabyne, Savina, Sebina, Sebinah

Sabiya (Arabic) morning; eastern wind.
Saba, Sabaya, Sabiyah

Sable (English) sable; sleek.
Sabel, Sabela, Sabella

Sabra (Hebrew) thorny cactus fruit. (Arabic) resting. History: a name for native-born Israelis, who were said to be hard on the outside and soft and sweet on the inside.
Sabera, Sabira, Sabrah, Sabre, Sabrea, Sabreah, Sabree, Sabreea, Sabri, Sabria, Sabriah, Sabriya, Sebra

Sabreena (English) a form of Sabrina.
Sabreen, Sabrena, Sabrene

Sabrina (Latin) boundary line. (English) princess. (Hebrew) a familiar form of Sabra. See also Bree, Brina, Rena, Zabrina.
Sabre, Sabreena, Sabrinas, Sabrinah, Sabrine, Sabrinia, Sabrinna, Sabryna, Sebree, Sebrina, Subrina

Sabryna (English) a form of Sabrina.
Sabrynna

Sacha (Russian) a form of Sasha.
Sache, Sachia

Sachi (Japanese) blessed; lucky.
Saatchi, Sachie, Sachiko

Sada (Japanese) chaste. (English) a form of Sadie.
Sadá, Sadah, Sadako

Sade (Hebrew) a form of Chadee, Sarah, Shardae, Sharday.
Sáde, Sadé, Sadea, Sadee, Shaday

Sadella (American) a combination of Sade + Ella.
Sadelle, Sydel, Sydell, Sydella, Sydelle

Sadhana (Hindi) devoted.

Sadie (Hebrew) a familiar form of Sarah. See also Sada.
Saddie, Sadee, Sadey, Sadi, Sadiey, Sady, Sadye, Saide, Saidee, Saidey, Saidi, Saidia, Saidie, Saidy, Sayde, Saydee, Seidy

Sadira (Persian) lotus tree. (Arabic) star.
Sadra

Sadiya (Arabic) lucky, fortunate.
Sadi, Sadia, Sadiah, Sadiyah, Sadiyyah, Sadya

Sadzi (Carrier) sunny disposition.

Saffron (English) Botany: a plant with purple or white flowers whose orange stigmas are used as a spice.
Safron

Safiya (Arabic) pure; serene; best friend.
Safa, Safeya, Saffa, Safia, Safiyah

Sagara (Hindi) ocean.

Sage (English) wise. Botany: an herb used as a seasoning.
Sagia, Saige, Salvia

Sahara (Arabic) desert; wilderness.
Sahar, Saharah, Sahari, Saheer, Saher, Sahira, Sahra, Sahrah

Sai (Japanese) talented.
Saiko

Saida (Hebrew) a form of Sarah. (Arabic) happy; fortunate.
Saidah

Saige (English) a form of Sage.

Saira (Hebrew) a form of Sara.
Sairah, Sairi

Sakaë (Japanese) prosperous.

Sakari (Hindi) sweet.
Sakkara

Saki (Japanese) cloak; rice wine.

Sakti (Hindi) energy, power.

Sakuna (Native American) bird.

Sakura (Japanese) cherry blossom; wealthy; prosperous.

Sala (Hindi) sala tree. Religion: the sacred tree under which Buddha died.

Salali (Cherokee) squirrel.

Salama (Arabic) peaceful. See also Zulima.

Salena (French) a form of Salina.
Saleana, Saleen, Saleena, Salene, Salenna, Sallene

Salima (Arabic) safe and sound; healthy.
Saleema, Salema, Salim, Salimah, Salma

Salina (French) solemn, dignified.
Salena, Salin, Salinah, Salinda, Saline

Salliann (English) a combination of Sally + Ann.
Sallian, Sallianne, Sallyann, Sally-Ann, Sallyanne, Sally-Anne

Sally (English) princess. History: Sally Ride, an American astronaut, became the first U. S. woman in space.
Sal, Salaid, Sallee, Salletta, Sallette, Salley, Salli, Sallie

Salome (Hebrew) peaceful. History: Salome Alexandra was a ruler of ancient Judea. Bible: the niece of King Herod.
Saloma, Salomé, Salomey, Salomi

Salvadora (Spanish) savior.

Salvia (Spanish) healthy; saved. (Latin) a form of Sage.
Sallvia, Salviana, Salviane, Salvina, Salvine

Samala (Hebrew) asked of God.
Samale, Sammala

Samanta (Hebrew) a form of Samantha.
Samantah, Smanta

Samantha (Aramaic) listener. (Hebrew) told by God.
Sam, Samana, Samanath, Samanatha, Samanitha, Samanithia, Samanta, Samanth, Samanthe, Samanthi, Samanthia, Samatha, Sami, Sammanth, Sammantha, Semantha, Simantha, Smantha, Symantha

Samara (Latin) elm-tree seed.
Saimara, Samaira, Samar, Samarah, Samari, Samaria, Samariah, Samarie, Samarra, Samarrea, Samary, Samera, Sameria, Samira, Sammar, Sammara, Samora

Samatha (Hebrew) a form of Samantha.
Sammatha

Sameh (Hebrew) listener. (Arabic) forgiving.
Samaiya, Samaya

Sami (Arabic) praised. (Hebrew) a short form of Samantha, Samuela.
Samia, Samiah, Samiha, Samina, Sammey, Sammi, Sammie, Sammijo, Sammy, Sammyjo, Samya, Samye

Samira (Arabic) entertaining.
Samirah, Samire, Samiria, Samirra, Samyra

Samone (Hebrew) a form of Simone.
Samoan, Samoane, Samon, Samona, Samoné, Samonia

Samuela (Hebrew) heard God, asked of God.
Samala, Samelia, Samella, Sami, Samielle, Samille, Sammile, Samuelle

Samuelle (Hebrew) a form of Samuela.
Samuella

Sana (Arabic) mountaintop; splendid; brilliant.
Sanaa, Sanáa, Sanaah, Sane, Sanah

Sancia (Spanish) holy, sacred.
Sanceska, Sancha, Sancharia, Sanchia, Sancie, Santsia, Sanzia

Sandeep (Punjabi) enlightened.
Sandip

Sandi (Greek) a familiar form of Sandra.
Sandee, Sandia, Sandie, Sandiey, Sandine, Sanndie

Sandra (Greek) defender of mankind. A short form of Cassandra. History: Sandra Day O'Connor was the first woman appointed to the U.S. Supreme Court. See also Zandra.
Sahndra, Sandi, Sandira, Sandrea, Sandria, Sandrica, Sandy, Sanndra, Saundra

Sandrea (Greek) a form of Sandra.
Sandreea, Sandreia, Sandrell, Sandria, Sanndria

Sandrica (Greek) a form of Sandra. See also Rica.
Sandricka, Sandrika

Sandrine (Greek) a form of Alexandra.
Sandreana, Sandrene, Sandrenna, Sandrianna, Sandrina

Sandy (Greek) a familiar form of Cassandra, Sandra.
Sandya, Sandye

Sanne (Hebrew, Dutch) lily.
Sanea, Saneh, Sanna, Sanneen

Santana (Spanish) saint.
Santa, Santaniata, Santanna, Santanne, Santena, Santenna, Shantana

Santina (Spanish) little saint.
Santinia

Sanura (Swahili) kitten.
Sanora

Sanuye (Moquelumnan) red clouds at sunset.

Sanya (Sanskrit) born on Saturday.
Saneiya, Sania, Sanyia

Sanyu (Luganda) happiness.

Sapata (Native American) dancing bear.

Sapphira (Hebrew) a form of Sapphire.
Safira, Sapheria, Saphira, Saphyra, Sephira

Sapphire (Greek) blue gemstone.
Saffire, Saphire, Saphyre, Sapphira

Sara (Hebrew) a form of Sarah.
Saira, Sarae, Saralee, Sarra, Sera

Sarah (Hebrew) princess. Bible: the wife of Abraham and mother of Isaac. See also Sadie, Saida, Sally, Saree, Sharai, Shari, Zara, Zarita.
Sahra, Sara, Saraha, Sarahann, Sarahi, Sarai, Sarann, Saray, Sarha, Sariah, Sarina, Sarita, Sarolta, Sarotte, Sarrah, Sasa, Sayra, Sorcha

Sarai, Saray (Hebrew) forms of Sarah.
Saraya

Saralyn (American) a combination of Sarah + Lynn.
Saralena, Saraly, Saralynn

Saree (Arabic) noble. (Hebrew) a familiar form of Sarah.
Sareeka, Sareka, Sari, Sarika, Sarka, Sarri, Sarrie, Sary

Sariah (Hebrew) forms of Sarah.
Saria, Sarie

Sarila (Turkish) waterfall.

Sarina (Hebrew) a familiar form of Sarah.
Sareen, Sareena, Saren, Sarena, Sarene, Sarenna, Sarin, Sarine, Sarinna, Sarinne

Sarita (Hebrew) a familiar form of Sarah.
Saretta, Sarette, Sarit, Saritia, Saritta

Sarolta (Hungarian) a form of Sarah.

Sarotte (French) a form of Sarah.

Sarrah (Hebrew) a form of Sarah.
Sarra

Sasa (Japanese) assistant. (Hungarian) a form of Sarah, Sasha.

Sasha (Russian) defender of mankind. See also Zasha.
Sacha, Sahsha, Sasa, Sascha, Saschae, Sashae, Sashah, Sashai, Sashana, Sashay, Sashea, Sashel, Sashenka, Sashey, Sashi, Sashia, Sashira, Sashsha, Sashya, Sasjara, Sauscha, Sausha, Shasha, Shashi, Shashia

Sass (Irish) Saxon.
Sassie, Sassoon, Sassy

Satara (American) a combination of Sarah + Tara.
Sataria, Satarra, Sateriaa, Saterra, Saterria

Satin (French) smooth, shiny.
Satinder

Satinka (Native American) sacred dancer.

Sato (Japanese) sugar.
Satu

Saundra (English) a form of Sandra, Sondra.
Saundee, Saundi, Saundie, Saundy

Saura (Hindi) sun worshiper.

Savana, Savanna (Spanish) forms of Savannah.
Saveena, Savhana, Savhanna, Savina, Savine, Savona, Savonna

Savanah (Spanish) a form of Savannah.
Savhannah

Savannah (Spanish) treeless plain.
Sahvannah, Savana, Savanah, Savanha, Savanna, Savannha, Savauna, Savonnah, Savonne, Sevan, Sevanah, Sevanh, Sevann, Sevanna, Svannah

Sawa (Japanese) swamp. (Moquelumnan) stone.

Sawyer (English) wood worker.
Sawyar, Sawyor

Sayde, Saydee (Hebrew) forms of Sadie.
Saydi, Saydia, Saydie, Saydy

Sayo (Japanese) born at night.

Sayra (Hebrew) a form of Sarah.
Sayrah, Sayre, Sayri

Scarlett (English) bright red. Literature: Scarlett O'Hara is the heroine of Margaret Mitchell's novel *Gone with the Wind*.
Scarlet, Scarlette, Scarlotte, Skarlette

Schyler (Dutch) sheltering.
Schuyla, Schuyler, Schuylia, Schylar

Scotti (Scottish) from Scotland.
Scota, Scotia, Scottie, Scotty

Seana, Seanna (Irish) forms of Jane.
See also Shauna, Shawna.
Seaana, Sean, Seane, Seann, Seannae,
Seannah, Seannalisa, Seanté, Sianna,
Sina

Sebastiane (Greek) venerable. (Latin)
revered. (French) a form of Sebastian
(see Boys' Names).
Sebastene, Sebastia, Sebastian,
Sebastiana, Sebastien, Sebastienne

Seble (Ethiopian) autumn.

Sebrina (English) a form of Sabrina.
Sebrena, Sebrenna, Sebria, Sebriana

Secilia (Latin) a form of Cecilia.
Saselia, Sasilia, Sesilia, Sileas

Secunda (Latin) second.

Seda (Armenian) forest voices.

Sedna (Eskimo) well-fed. Mythology:
the goddess of sea animals.

Seelia (English) a form of Sheila.

Seema (Greek) sprout. (Afghan) sky;
profile.
Seemah, Sima, Simah

Sefa (Swiss) a familiar form of
Josefina.

Seirra (Irish) a form of Sierra.
Seiara, Seiarra, Seira, Seirria

Seki (Japanese) wonderful.
Seka

Sela (English) a short form of Selena.
Seeley, Selah

Selam (Ethiopian) peaceful.

Selda (German) a short form of
Griselda. (Yiddish) a form of Zelda.
Seldah, Selde, Sellda, Selldah

Selena (Greek) moon. Mythology:
Selene was the goddess of the moon.
See also Celena.
Saleena, Sela, Selana, Seleana, Seleena,
Selen, Selenah, Selene, Séléné, Selenia,
Selenna, Selina, Sena, Syleena, Sylena

Selene (Greek) a form of Selena.
Seleni, Selenie, Seleny

Selia (Latin) a short form of Cecilia.
Seel, Seil, Sela, Silia

Selima (Hebrew) peaceful.
Selema, Selemah, Selimah

Selina (Greek) a form of Celina,
Selena.
Selie, Selin, Selinda, Seline, Selinia,
Selinka, Sellina, Selyna, Selyne, Selynne,
Sylina

Selma (German) devine protector.
(Irish) fair, just. (Scandinavian)
divinely protected. (Arabic) secure.
See also Zelma.
Sellma, Sellmah, Selmah

Sema (Turkish) heaven; divine omen.
Semaj

Sen (Japanese) Mythology: a magical
forest elf that lives for thousands of
years.

Senalda (Spanish) sign.
Sena, Senda, Senna

Seneca (Iroquoian) a tribal name.
Senaka, Seneka, Senequa, Senequae,
Senequai, Seneque

Septima (Latin) seventh.

Sequoia (Cherokee) giant redwood
tree.
Seqoiyia, Seqouyia, Seqoya, Sequoi,
Sequoiah, Sequora, Sequoya, Sequoyah,
Sikoya

Serafina (Hebrew) burning; ardent.
Bible: seraphim are an order of angels.
Sarafina, Serafine, Seraphe, Seraphin,
Seraphina, Seraphine, Seraphita, Serapia,
Serofina

Serena (Latin) peaceful. See also Rena.
Sarina, Saryna, Seraina, Serana, Sereen,
Sereina, Seren, Serenah, Serene, Serenea,
Serenia, Serenna, Serina, Serreana,
Serrena, Serrenna

Serenity (Latin) peaceful.
Serenidy, Serenitee, Serenitey, Sereniti,
Serenitiy, Serinity, Serrennity

Serilda (Greek) armed warrior
woman.

Serina (Latin) a form of Serena.
Sereena, Serin, Serine, Serreena, Serrin,
Serrina, Seryna

Sevilla (Spanish) from Seville.
Seville

Shaba (Spanish) rose.
Shabana, Shabina

Shada (Native American) pelican.
Shadae, Shadea, Shadeana, Shadee,
Shadi, Shadia, Shadiah, Shadie,
Shadiya, Shaida

Shaday (American) a form of Sade.
Shadai, Shadaia, Shadaya, Shadayna, Shadei, Shadeziah, Shaiday

Shadrika (American) a combination of the prefix Sha + Rika.
Shadreeka, Shadreka, Shadrica, Shadricka, Shadrieka

Shae (Irish) a form of Shea.
Shaenel, Shaeya, Shai, Shaia

Shaelee (Irish) a form of Shea.
Shaeleigh, Shaeley, Shaelie, Shaely

Shaelyn (Irish) a form of Shea.
Shael, Shaelaine, Shaelan, Shaelanie, Shaelanna, Shaeleen, Shaelene, Shaelin, Shaeline, Shaelyne, Shaelynn, Shae-Lynn, Shaelynne

Shafira (Swahili) distinguished.
Shaffira

Shahar (Arabic) moonlit.
Shahara

Shahina (Arabic) falcon.
Shaheen, Shaheena, Shahi, Shahin

Shahla (Afghani) beautiful eyes.
Shaila, Shailah, Shalah

Shaianne (Cheyenne) a form of Cheyenne.
Shaeen, Shaeine, Shaian, Shaiana, Shaiandra, Shaiane, Shaiann, Shaianna

Shaila (Latin) a form of Sheila.
Shaela, Shaelea, Shaeyla, Shailah, Shailee, Shailey, Shaili, Shailie, Shailla, Shaily, Shailyn, Shailynn

Shaina (Yiddish) beautiful.
Shaena, Shainah, Shaine, Shainna, Shajna, Shanie, Shayna, Shayndel, Sheina, Sheindel

Shajuana (American) a combination of the prefix Sha + Juanita. See also Shawanna.
Shajuan, Shajuanda, Shajuanita, Shajuanna, Shajuanza

Shaka (Hindi) a form of Shakti. A short form of names beginning with "Shak." See also Chaka.
Shakah, Shakha

Shakarah (American) a combination of the prefix Sha + Kara.
Shacara, Shacari, Shaccara, Shaka, Shakari, Shakkara, Shikara

Shakayla (Arabic) a form of Shakila.
Shakaela, Shakail, Shakaila, Shakala

Shakeena (American) a combination of the prefix Sha + Keena.
Shaka, Shakeina, Shakeyna, Shakina, Shakyna

Shakeita (American) a combination of the prefix Sha + Keita. See also Shaqueita.
Shaka, Shakeeta, Shakeitha, Shakeithia, Shaketa, Shaketha, Shakethia, Shaketia, Shakita, Shakitra, Sheketa, Shekita, Shikita, Shikitha

Shakera (Arabic) a form of Shakira.
Chakeria, Shakeira, Shakeirra, Shakerah, Shakeria, Shakeriah, Shakeriay, Shakerra, Shakerri, Shakerria, Shakerya, Shakeryia, Shakeyra

Shakia (American) a combination of the prefix Sha + Kia.
Shakeeia, Shakeeyah, Shakeia, Shakeya, Shakiya, Shekeia, Shekia, Shekiah, Shikia

Shakila (Arabic) pretty.
Chakila, Shaka, Shakayla, Shakeela, Shakeena, Shakela, Shakelah, Shakilah, Shakyla, Shekila, Shekilla, Shikeela

Shakira (Arabic) thankful.
Shaakira, Shacora, Shaka, Shakeera, Shakeerah, Shakeeria, Shakera, Shakiera, Shakierra, Shakir, Shakirah, Shakirat, Shakirea, Shakirra, Shakora, Shakuria, Shakyra, Shaquira, Shekiera, Shekira, Shikira

Shakti (Hindi) energy, power. Religion: a form of the Hindu goddess Devi.
Sakti, Shaka, Sita

Shakyra (Arabic) a form of Shakira.
Shakyria

Shalana (American) a combination of the prefix Sha + Lana.
Shalaana, Shalain, Shalaina, Shalaine, Shaland, Shalanda, Shalane, Shalann, Shalaun, Shalauna, Shalayna, Shalayne, Shalaynna, Shallan, Shelan, Shelanda

Shaleah (American) a combination of the prefix Sha + Leah.
Shalea, Shalee, Shaleea, Shalia, Shaliah

Shaleisha (American) a combination of the prefix Sha + Aisha.
Shalesha, Shalesia, Shalicia, Shalisha

Shalena (American) a combination of the prefix Sha + Lena.
Shaleana, Shaleen, Shaleena, Shalen, Shálena, Shalene, Shalené, Shalenna, Shalina, Shalinda, Shaline, Shalini, Shalinna, Shelayna, Shelayne, Shelena

Shalisa (American) a combination of the prefix Sha + Lisa.
Shalesa, Shalese, Shalessa, Shalice, Shalicia, Shaliece, Shalise, Shalisha, Shalishea, Shalisia, Shalissa, Shalisse, Shalyce, Shalys, Shalyse

Shalita (American) a combination of the prefix Sha + Lita.
Shaleta, Shaletta, Shalida, Shalitta

Shalona (American) a combination of the prefix Sha + Lona.
Shalon, Shalone, Shálonna, Shalonne

Shalonda (American) a combination of the prefix Sha + Ondine.
Shalonde, Shalondine, Shalondra, Shalondria

Shalyn (American) a combination of the prefix Sha + Lynn.
Shalin, Shalina, Shalinda, Shaline, Shalyna, Shalynda, Shalyne, Shalynn, Shalynne

Shamara (Arabic) ready for battle.
Shamar, Shamarah, Shamare, Shamarea, Shamaree, Shamari, Shamaria, Shamariah, Shamarra, Shamarri, Shammara, Shamora, Shamori, Shamorra, Shamorria, Shamorriah

Shameka (American) a combination of the prefix Sha + Meka.
Shameaka, Shameakah, Shameca, Shamecca, Shamecha, Shamecia, Shameika, Shameke, Shamekia

Shamika (American) a combination of the prefix Sha + Mika.
Shameeca, Shameeka, Shamica, Shamicia, Shamicka, Shamieka, Shamikia

Shamira (Hebrew) precious stone.
Shamir, Shamiran, Shamiria, Shamyra

Shamiya (American) a combination of the prefix Sha + Mia.
Shamea, Shamia, Shamiah, Shamiyah, Shamyia, Shamyiah, Shamyne

Shana (Hebrew) God is gracious. (Irish) a form of Jane.
Shaana, Shan, Shanae, Shanda, Shandi, Shane, Shania, Shanna, Shannah, Shauna, Shawna

Shanae (Irish) a form of Shana.
Shanay, Shanea

Shanda (American) a form of Chanda, Shana.
Shandae, Shandah, Shandra, Shannda

Shandi (English) a familiar form of Shana.
Shandee, Shandeigh, Shandey, Shandice, Shandie

Shandra (American) a form of Shanda. See also Chandra.
Shandrea, Shandreka, Shandri, Shandria, Shandriah, Shandrice, Shandrie, Shandry

Shane (Irish) a form of Shana.
Shanea, Shaneah, Shanee, Shanée, Shanie

Shaneisha (American) a combination of the prefix Sha + Aisha.
Shanesha, Shaneshia, Shanessa, Shanisha, Shanissha

Shaneka (American) a form of Shanika.
Shanecka, Shaneeka, Shaneekah, Shaneequa, Shaneeque, Shaneika, Shaneikah, Shanekia, Shanequa, Shaneyka, Shonneka

Shanel, Shanell, Shanelle (American) forms of Chanel.
Schanel, Schanell, Shanella, Shanelly, Shannel, Shannell, Shannelle, Shenel, Shenela, Shenell, Shenelle, Shenelly, Shinelle, Shonelle, Shynelle

Shaneta (American) a combination of the prefix Sha + Neta.
Seanette, Shaneeta, Shanetha, Shanethis, Shanetta, Shanette, Shineta, Shonetta

Shani (Swahili) a form of Shany.

Shania (American) a form of Shana.
Shanasia, Shanaya, Shaniah, Shaniya, Shanya, Shenia

Shanice (American) a form of Janice. See also Chanise.
Chenise, Shanece, Shaneese, Shaneice, Shanese, Shanicea, Shaniece, Shanise, Shanneice, Shannice, Shanyce, Sheneice

Shanida (American) a combination of the prefix Sha + Ida.
Shaneeda, Shannida

Shanika (American) a combination of the prefix Sha + Nika.
Shaneka, Shanica, Shanicca, Shanicka, Shanieka, Shanike, Shanikia, Shanikka, Shanikqua, Shanikwa, Shaniqua, Shenika, Shineeca, Shonnika

Shaniqua (American) a form of Shanika.
Shaniqa, Shaniquah, Shanique, Shaniquia, Shaniquwa, Shaniqwa, Shenequa, Sheniqua, Shinequa, Shiniqua

Shanise (American) a form of Shanice.
Shanisa, Shanisha, Shanisia, Shanissa, Shanisse, Shineese

Shanita (American) a combination of the prefix Sha + Nita.
Shanitha, Shanitra, Shanitta, Shinita

Shanley (Irish) hero's child.
Shanlee, Shanleigh, Shanlie, Shanly

Shanna (Irish) a form of Shana, Shannon.
Shanea, Shannah, Shannea

Shannen (Irish) a form of Shannon.
Shanen, Shanena, Shanene

Shannon (Irish) small and wise.
Shanan, Shanadoah, Shann, Shanna, Shannan, Shanneen, Shannen, Shannie, Shannin, Shannyn, Shanon

Shanta, Shantae, Shante (French) forms of Chantal.
Shantai, Shantay, Shantaya, Shantaye, Shanté, Shantea, Shantee, Shantée, Shanteia

Shantal (American) a form of Shantel.
Shantall, Shontal

Shantana (American) a form of Santana.
Shantan, Shantanae, Shantanell, Shantanickia, Shantanika, Shantanna

Shantara (American) a combination of the prefix Sha + Tara.
Shantaria, Shantarra, Shantera, Shanteria, Shanterra, Shantira, Shontara, Shuntara

Shanteca (American) a combination of the prefix Sha + Teca.
Shantecca, Shanteka, Shantika, Shantikia

Shantel, Shantell (American) song.
Seantelle, Shanntell, Shanta, Shantal, Shantae, Shantale, Shante, Shanteal, Shanteil, Shantele, Shantella, Shantelle, Shantrell, Shantyl, Shantyle, Shauntel, Shauntell, Shauntelle, Shauntrel, Shauntrell, Shauntrella, Shentel, Shentelle, Shontal, Shontalla, Shontalle, Shontel, Shontelle

Shanteria (American) a form of Shantara.
Shanterica, Shanterria, Shanterrie, Shantieria, Shantirea, Shonteria

Shantesa (American) a combination of the prefix Sha + Tess.
Shantese, Shantice, Shantise, Shantisha, Shontecia, Shontessia

Shantia (American) a combination of the prefix Sha + Tia.
Shanteya, Shanti, Shantida, Shantie, Shaunteya, Shauntia, Shontia

Shantille (American) a form of Chantilly.
Shanteil, Shantil, Shantilli, Shantillie, Shantilly, Shantyl, Shantyle

Shantina (American) a combination of the prefix Sha + Tina.
Shanteena, Shontina

Shantora (American) a combination of the prefix Sha + Tory.
Shantoia, Shantori, Shantoria, Shantory, Shantorya, Shantoya, Shanttoria

Shantrice (American) a combination of the prefix Sha + Trice. See also Chantrice.
Shantrece, Shantrecia, Shantreece, Shantreese, Shantrese, Shantress, Shantrezia, Shantricia, Shantriece, Shantris, Shantrisse, Shontrice

Shany (Swahili) marvelous, wonderful.
Shaney, Shannai, Shannea, Shanni, Shannia, Shannie, Shanny, Shanya

Shappa (Native American) red thunder.

Shaquanda (American) a combination of the prefix Sha + Wanda.
Shaquan, Shaquana, Shaquand, Shaquandey, Shaquandra, Shaquandria, Shaquanera, Shaquani, Shaquania, Shaquanna, Shaquanta, Shaquantae, Shaquantay, Shaquante, Shaquantia, Shaquona, Shaquonda, Shaquondra, Shaquondria

Shaqueita, Shaquita (American) forms of Shakeita.
Shaqueta, Shaquetta, Shaquette, Shaquitta, Shequida, Shequita, Shequittia

Shaquila, Shaquilla (American) forms of Shakila.
Shaquail, Shaquia, Shaquil, Shaquilah, Shaquile, Shaquill, Shaquillah, Shaquille, Shaquillia, Shequela, Shequele, Shequila, Shquiyla

Shaquira (American) a form of Shakira.
Shaquirah, Shaquire, Shaquirra, Shaqura, Shaqurah, Shaquri

Shara (Hebrew) a short form of Sharon.
Shaara, Sharah, Sharal, Sharala, Sharalee, Sharlyn, Sharlynn, Sharra, Sharrah

Sharai (Hebrew) princess. See also Sharon.
Sharae, Sharaé, Sharah, Sharaiah, Sharay, Sharaya, Sharayah

Sharan (Hindi) protector.
Sharaine, Sharanda, Sharanjeet

Shardae, Sharday (Punjabi) charity.
(Yoruba) honored by royalty. (Arabic)
runaway. A form of Chardae.
*Sade, Shadae, Sharda, Shar-Dae, Shardai,
Shar-Day, Sharde, Shardea, Shardee,
Shardée, Shardei, Shardeia, Shardey*

Sharee (English) a form of Shari.
Shareen, Shareena, Sharine

Shari (French) beloved, dearest.
(Hungarian) a form of Sarah. See
also Sharita, Sheree, Sherry.
*Shara, Share, Sharee, Sharia, Shariah,
Sharian, Shariann, Sharianne, Sharie,
Sharra, Sharree, Sharri, Sharrie, Sharry,
Shary*

Sharice (French) a form of Cherice.
*Shareese, Sharesse, Sharese, Sharica,
Sharicka, Shariece, Sharis, Sharise,
Sharish, Shariss, Sharissa, Sharisse,
Sharyse*

Sharik (African) child of God.

Sharissa (American) a form of
Sharice.
*Sharesa, Sharessia, Sharisa, Sharisha,
Shereeza, Shericia, Sherisa, Sherissa*

Sharita (French) a familiar form of
Shari. (American) a form of Charity.
See also Sherita.
Shareeta, Sharrita

Sharla (French) a short form of
Sharlene, Sharlotte.

Sharlene (French) little and strong.
*Scharlane, Scharlene, Shar, Sharla,
Sharlaina, Sharlaine, Sharlane,*

*Sharlanna, Sharlee, Sharleen, Sharleine,
Sharlena, Sharleyne, Sharline, Sharlyn,
Sharlyne, Sharlynn, Sharlynne, Sherlean,
Sherleen, Sherlene, Sherline*

Sharlotte (American) a form of
Charlotte.
Sharlet, Sharlett, Sharlott, Sharlotta

Sharma (American) a short form of
Sharmaine.
Sharmae, Sharme

Sharmaine (American) a form of
Charmaine.
*Sharma, Sharmain, Sharman, Sharmane,
Sharmanta, Sharmayne, Sharmeen,
Sharmene, Sharmese, Sharmin,
Sharmine, Sharmon, Sharmyn*

Sharna (Hebrew) a form of Sharon.
*Sharnae, Sharnay, Sharne, Sharnea,
Sharnease, Sharnee, Sharneese, Sharnell,
Sharnelle, Sharnese, Sharnett, Sharnetta,
Sharnise*

Sharon (Hebrew) desert plain. A form
of Sharai.
*Shaaron, Shara, Sharai, Sharan, Shareen,
Sharen, Shari, Sharin, Sharna,
Sharonda, Sharone, Sharran, Sharren,
Sharrin, Sharron, Sharrona, Sharyn,
Sharyon, Sheren, Sheron, Sherryn*

Sharonda (Hebrew) a form of
Sharon.
Sharronda, Sheronda, Sherrhonda

Sharrona (Hebrew) a form of Sharon.
*Sharona, Sharone, Sharonia, Sharonna,
Sharony, Sharronne, Sheron, Sherona,
Sheronna, Sherron, Sherronna,
Sherronne, Shirona*

Shatara (Hindi) umbrella. (Arabic)
good; industrious. (American) a
combination of Sharon + Tara.
*Shatarea, Shatari, Shataria, Shatarra,
Shataura, Shateira, Shatera, Shaterah,
Shateria, Shaterra, Shaterri, Shaterria,
Shatherian, Shatierra, Shatiria*

Shatoria (American) a combination of
the prefix Sha + Tory.
*Shatora, Shatorea, Shatori, Shatorri,
Shatorria, Shatory, Shatorya, Shatoya*

Shauna (Hebrew) God is gracious.
(Irish) a form of Shana. See also
Seana, Shona.
*Shaun, Shaunah, Shaunda, Shaune,
Shaunee, Shauneen, Shaunelle,
Shaunette, Shauni, Shaunice, Shaunicy,
Shaunie, Shaunika, Shaunisha,
Shaunna, Shaunnea, Shaunta, Shaunua,
Shaunya*

Shaunda (Irish) a form of Shauna. See
also Shanda, Shawnda, Shonda.
*Shaundal, Shaundala, Shaundel,
Shaundela, Shaundell, Shaundelle,
Shaundra, Shaundrea, Shaundree,
Shaundria, Shaundrice*

Shaunta (Irish) a form of Shauna. See
also Shawnta, Shonta.
*Schunta, Shauntae, Shauntay, Shaunte,
Shauntea, Shauntee, Shauntée,
Shaunteena, Shauntei, Shauntia,
Shauntier, Shauntrel, Shauntrell,
Shauntrella*

Shavon (American) a form of
Shavonne.
*Schavon, Schevon, Shavan, Shavana,
Shavaun, Shavona, Shavonda, Shavone,
Shavonia, Shivon*

Shavonne (American) a combination of the prefix Sha + Yvonne. See also Siobhan.
Shavanna, Shavon, Shavondra, Shavonn, Shavonna, Shavonni, Shavonnia, Shavonnie, Shavontae, Shavonte, Shavonté, Shavoun, Shivaun, Shivawn, Shivonne, Shyvon, Shyvonne

Shawanna (American) a combination of the prefix Sha + Wanda. See also Shajuana, Shawna.
Shawan, Shawana, Shawanda, Shawante, Shiwani

Shawna (Hebrew) God is gracious. (Irish) a form of Jane. A form of Shana, Shauna. See also Seana, Shona.
Sawna, Shaw, Shawn, Shawnae, Shawnai, Shawnea, Shawnee, Shawneen, Shawneena, Shawnell, Shawnette, Shawnna, Shawnra, Shawnta, Sheona, Siân, Siana, Sianna

Shawnda (Irish) a form of Shawna. See also Shanda, Shaunda, Shonda.
Shawndal, Shawndala, Shawndan, Shawndel, Shawndra, Shawndrea, Shawndree, Shawndreel, Shawndrell, Shawndria

Shawnee (Irish) a form of Shawna.
Shawne, Shawneea, Shawney, Shawni, Shawnie

Shawnika (American) a combination of Shawna + Nika.
Shawnaka, Shawnequa, Shawneika, Shawnicka

Shawnta (Irish) a form of Shawna. See also Shaunta, Shonta.
Shawntae, Shawntay, Shawnte, Shawnté, Shawntee, Shawntell, Shawntelle, Shawnteria, Shawntia, Shawntil, Shawntile, Shawntill, Shawntille, Shawntina, Shawntish, Shawntrese, Shawntriece

Shay, Shaye (Irish) forms of Shea.
Shaya, Shayah, Shayda, Shayha, Shayia, Shayla, Shey, Sheye

Shayla (Irish) a form of Shay.
Shaylagh, Shaylah, Shaylain, Shaylan, Shaylea, Shayleah, Shaylla, Shaylyn, Sheyla

Shaylee (Irish) a form of Shea.
Shaylei, Shayleigh, Shayley, Shayli, Shaylie, Shayly, Shealy

Shaylyn (Irish) a form of Shea.
Shaylin, Shaylina, Shaylinn, Shaylynn, Shaylynne, Shealyn, Sheylyn

Shayna (Hebrew) beautiful.
Shaynae, Shaynah, Shayne, Shaynee, Shayney, Shayni, Shaynie, Shaynna, Shaynne, Shayny, Sheana, Sheanna

Shea (Irish) fairy palace.
Shae, Shay, Shaylee, Shaylyn, Shealy, Shaelee, Shaelyn, Shealyn, Sheann, Sheannon, Sheanta, Sheaon, Shearra, Sheatara, Sheaunna, Sheavon

Sheba (Hebrew) a short form of Bathsheba. Geography: an ancient country of south Arabia.
Saba, Sabah, Shebah, Sheeba

Sheena (Hebrew) God is gracious. (Irish) a form of Jane.
Sheenagh, Sheenah, Sheenan, Sheeneal, Sheenika, Sheenna, Sheina, Shena, Shiona

Sheila (Latin) blind. (Irish) a form of Cecelia. See also Cheyla, Zelizi.
Seelia, Seila, Selia, Shaila, Sheela, Sheelagh, Sheelah, Sheilagh, Sheilah, Sheileen, Sheiletta, Sheilia, Sheillynn, Sheilya, Shela, Shelagh, Shelah, Shelia, Shiela, Shila, Shilah, Shilea, Shyla

Shelbi, Shelbie (English) forms of Shelby.
Shelbbie, Shellbi, Shellbie

Shelby (English) ledge estate.
Chelby, Schelby, Shel, Shelbe, Shelbee, Shelbey, Shelbi, Shelbie, Shelbye, Shellby

Sheldon (English) farm on the ledge.
Sheldina, Sheldine, Sheldrina, Sheldyn, Shelton

Shelee (English) a form of Shelley.
Shelee, Sheleen, Shelena, Sheley, Sheli, Shelia, Shelina, Shelinda, Shelita

Shelisa (American) a combination of Shelley + Lisa.
Sheleza, Shelica, Shelicia, Shelise, Shelisse, Sheliza

Shelley, Shelly (English) meadow on the ledge. (French) familiar forms of Michelle. See also Rochelle.
Shelee, Shell, Shella, Shellaine, Shellana, Shellany, Shellee, Shellene, Shelli, Shellian, Shelliann, Shellie, Shellina

Shelsea (American) a form of Chelsea.
Shellsea, Shellsey, Shelsey, Shelsie, Shelsy

Shena (Irish) a form of Sheena.
Shenada, Shenae, Shenah, Shenay,
Shenda, Shene, Shenea, Sheneda,
Shenee, Sheneena, Shenica, Shenika,
Shenina, Sheniqua, Shenita, Shenna,
Shennae, Shennah, Shenoa

Shera (Aramaic) light.
Sheera, Sheerah, Sherae, Sherah, Sheralee,
Sheralle, Sheralyn, Sheralynn,
Sheralynne, Sheray, Sheraya

Sheree (French) beloved, dearest.
Scherie, Sheeree, Shere, Shereé, Sherrelle,
Shereen, Shereena

Sherelle (French) a form of Cherelle,
Sheryl.
Sherel, Sherell, Sheriel, Sherrel, Sherrell,
Sherrelle, Shirelle

Sheri, Sherri (French) forms of Sherry.
Sheria, Sheriah, Sherie, Sherrie

Sherian (American) a combination of
Sheri + Ann.
Sherianne, Sherrina

Sherice (French) a form of Cherice.
Scherise, Sherece, Shereece, Sherees,
Shereese, Sherese, Shericia, Sherise,
Sherisse, Sherrish, Sherryse, Sheryce

Sheridan (Irish) wild.
Sherida, Sheridane, Sherideen, Sheriden,
Sheridian, Sheridon, Sherridan, Sherridon

Sherika (Punjabi) relative. (Arabic)
easterner.
Shereka, Sherica, Shericka, Sherrica,
Sherricka, Sherrika

Sherissa (French) a form of Sherry,
Sheryl.
Shereeza, Sheresa, Shericia, Sherrish

Sherita (French) a form of Sherry,
Sheryl. See also Sharita.
Shereta, Sheretta, Sherette, Sherrita

Sherleen (French, English) a form of
Sheryl, Shirley.
Sherileen, Sherlene, Sherlin, Sherlina,
Sherline, Sherlyn, Sherlyne, Sherlynne,
Shirlena, Shirlene, Shirlina, Shirlyn

Sherry (French) beloved, dearest. A
familiar form of Sheryl. See also
Sheree.
Sherey, Sheri, Sherissa, Sherrey, Sherri,
Sherria, Sherriah, Sherrie, Sherye, Sheryy

Sheryl (French) beloved. A familiar
form of Shirley. See also Sherry.
Sharel, Sharil, Sharilyn, Sharyl, Sharyll,
Sheral, Sherell, Sheriel, Sheril, Sherill,
Sherily, Sherilyn, Sherissa, Sherita,
Sherleen, Sherral, Sherrelle, Sherril,
Sherrill, Sherryl, Sherylly

Sherylyn (American) a combination
of Sheryl + Lynn. See also Cherilyn.
Sharolin, Sharolyn, Sharyl-Lynn,
Sheralyn, Sherilyn, Sherilynn,
Sherilynne, Sherralyn, Sherralynn,
Sherrilyn, Sherrilynn, Sherrilynne,
Sherrylyn, Sherryn, Sherylanne

Shevonne (American) a combination
of the prefix She + Yvonne.
Shevaun, Shevon, Shevonda, Shevone

Sheyenne (Cheyenne) a form of
Cheyenne. See also Shyann, Shyanne.
Shayhan, Sheyan, Sheyane, Sheyann,
Sheyanna, Sheyannah, Sheyanne,
Sheyen, Sheyene, Shiante, Shyanne

Shianne (Cheyenne) a form of
Cheyenne.
She, Shian, Shiana, Shianah, Shianda,
Shiane, Shiann, Shianna, Shiannah,
Shiany, Shieana, Shieann, Shieanne,
Shiena, Shiene, Shienna

Shifra (Hebrew) beautiful.
Schifra, Shifrah

Shika (Japanese) gentle deer.
Shi, Shikah, Shikha

Shilo (Hebrew) God's gift. Bible: a
sanctuary for the Israelites where the
Ark of the Covenant was kept.
Shiloh

Shina (Japanese) virtuous, good;
wealthy. (Chinese) a form of China.
Shinae, Shinay, Shine, Shinna

Shino (Japanese) bamboo stalk.

Shiquita (American) a form of
Chiquita.
Shiquata, Shiquitta

Shira (Hebrew) song.
Shirah, Shiray, Shire, Shiree, Shiri, Shirit,
Shyra

Shirlene (English) a form of Shirley.
Shirleen, Shirline, Shirlynn

Shirley (English) bright meadow. See
also Sheryl.
Sherlee, Sherleen, Sherley, Sherli, Sherlie,
Shir, Shirl, Shirlee, Shirlie, Shirly, Shirlly,
Shurlee, Shurley

Shivani (Hindi) life and death.
Shiva, Shivana, Shivanie, Shivanna

Shizu (Japanese) silent.
Shizue, Shizuka, Shizuko, Shizuyo

Shona (Irish) a form of Jane. A form of Shana, Shauna, Shawna.
Shiona, Shonagh, Shonah, Shonalee, Shonda, Shone, Shonee, Shonette, Shoni, Shonie, Shonna, Shonnah, Shonta

Shonda (Irish) a form of Shona. See also Shanda, Shaunda, Shawnda.
Shondalette, Shondalyn, Shondel, Shondelle, Shondi, Shondia, Shondie, Shondra, Shondreka, Shounda

Shonta (Irish) a form of Shona. See also Shaunta, Shawnta.
Shontá, Shontae, Shontai, Shontalea, Shontasia, Shontavia, Shontaviea, Shontay, Shontaya, Shonte, Shonté, Shontedra, Shontee, Shonteral, Shonti, Shontol, Shontoy, Shontrail, Shountáe

Shoshana (Hebrew) a form of Susan.
Shosha, Shoshan, Shoshanah, Shoshane, Shoshanha, Shoshann, Shoshanna, Shoshannah, Shoshauna, Shoshaunah, Shoshawna, Shoshona, Shoshone, Shoshonee, Shoshoney, Shoshoni, Shoushan, Shushana, Sosha, Soshana

Shu (Chinese) kind, gentle.

Shug (American) a short form of Sugar.

Shula (Arabic) flaming, bright.
Shulah

Shulamith (Hebrew) peaceful. See also Sula.
Shulamit, Sulamith

Shunta (Irish) a form of Shonta.
Shuntae, Shunté, Shuntel, Shuntell, Shuntelle, Shuntia

Shura (Russian) a form of Alexandra.
Schura, Shurah, Shuree, Shureen, Shurelle, Shuritta, Shurka, Shurlana

Shyann, Shyanne (Cheyenne) forms of Cheyenne. See also Sheyenne.
Shyan, Shyana, Shyandra, Shyane, Shynee, Shyanna, Shyannah, Shye, Shyene, Shyenna, Shyenne

Shyla (English) a form of Sheila.
Shya, Shyah, Shylah, Shylan, Shylayah, Shylana, Shylane, Shyle, Shyleah, Shylee, Shyley, Shyli, Shylia, Shylie, Shylo, Shyloe, Shyloh, Shylon, Shylyn

Shyra (Hebrew) a form of Shira.
Shyrae, Shyrah, Shyrai, Shyrie, Shyro

Siara (Irish) a form of Sierra.
Siarah, Siarra, Siarrah, Sieara

Sianna (Irish) a form of Seana.
Sian, Siana, Sianae, Sianai, Sianey, Siannah, Sianne, Sianni, Sianny, Siany

Sibeta (Moquelumnan) finding a fish under a rock.

Sibley (English) sibling; friendly. (Greek) a form of Sybil.
Sybley

Sidney (French) a form of Sydney.
Sidne, Sidnee, Sidnei, Sidneya, Sidni, Sidnie, Sidny, Sidnye

Sidonia (Hebrew) enticing.
Sydania, Syndonia

Sidonie (French) from Saint-Denis, France. See also Sydney.
Sedona, Sidaine, Sidanni, Sidelle, Sidoine, Sidona, Sidonae, Sidonia, Sidony

Sidra (Latin) star child.
Sidrah, Sidras

Sienna (American) a form of Ciana.
Seini, Siena

Siera (Irish) a form of Sierra.
Sierah, Sieria

Sierra (Irish) black. (Spanish) saw toothed. Geography: any rugged range of mountains that, when viewed from a distance, has a jagged profile. See also Ciara.
Seara, Searria, Seera, Seirra, Siara, Siearra, Siera, Sierrah, Sierre, Sierrea, Sierriah, Syerra

Sigfreda (German) victorious peace. See also Freda.
Sigfreida, Sigfrida, Sigfrieda, Sigfryda

Sigmunda (German) victorious protector.
Sigmonda

Signe (Latin) sign, signal. (Scandinavian) a short form of Sigourney.
Sig, Signa, Signy, Singna, Singne

Sigourney (English) victorious conquerer.
Signe, Sigournee, Sigourny

Sigrid (Scandinavian) victorious counselor.
Siegrid, Siegrida, Sigritt

Sihu (Native American) flower; bush.

Siko (African) crying baby.

Silvia (Latin) a form of Sylvia.
Silivia, Silva, Silvya

Simcha (Hebrew) joyful.

Simone (Hebrew) she heard. (French) a form of Simon (see Boys' Names).
Samone, Siminie, Simmi, Simmie, Simmona, Simmone, Simoane, Simona, Simonetta, Simonette, Simonia, Simonina, Simonne, Somone, Symone

Simran (Sikh) absorbed in God.
Simren, Simrin, Simrun

Sina (Irish) a form of Seana.
Seena, Sinai, Sinaia, Sinan, Sinay

Sinclaire (French) prayer.
Sinclair

Sindy (American) a form of Cindy.
Sinda, Sindal, Sindee, Sindi, Sindia, Sindie, Sinnedy, Synda, Syndal, Syndee, Syndey, Syndi, Syndia, Syndie, Syndy

Sinead (Irish) a form of Jane.
Seonaid, Sine, Sinéad

Siobhan (Irish) a form of Joan. See also Shavonne.
Shibahn, Shibani, Shibhan, Shioban, Shobana, Shobha, Shobhana, Siobahn, Siobhana, Siobhann, Siobhon, Siovaun, Siovhan

Sirena (Greek) enchanter. Mythology: Sirens were sea nymphs whose singing enchanted sailors and made them crash their ships into nearby rocks.
Sireena, Sirene, Sirine, Syrena, Syrenia, Syrenna, Syrina

Sisika (Native American) songbird.

Sissy (American) a familiar form of Cecelia.
Sisi, Sisie, Sissey, Sissie

Sita (Hindi) a form of Shakti.
Sitah, Sitarah, Sitha, Sithara

Siti (Swahili) respected woman.

Skye (Arabic) water giver. (Dutch) a short form of Skyler. Geography: an island in the Hebrides, Scotland.
Ski, Skie, Skii, Skky, Sky, Skya, Skyy

Skylar (Dutch) a form of Skyler.
Skyela, Skyelar, Skyla, Skylair, Skyylar

Skyler (Dutch) sheltering.
Skila, Skilah, Skye, Skyeler, Skyelur, Skyla, Skylar, Skylee, Skylena, Skyli, Skylia, Skylie, Skylin, Skyllar, Skylor, Skylyn, Skylynn, Skylyr, Skyra

Sloane (Irish) warrior.
Sloan, Sloanne

Socorro (Spanish) helper.

Sofia (Greek) a form of Sophia. See also Zofia, Zsofia.
Sofeea, Sofeeia, Soffi, Sofi, Soficita, Sofie, Sofija, Sofiya, Sofka, Sofya

Solada (Tai) listener.

Solana (Spanish) sunshine.
Solande, Solanna, Soleil, Solena, Soley, Solina, Solinda

Solange (French) dignified.

Soledad (Spanish) solitary.
Sole, Soleda

Solenne (French) solemn, dignified.
Solaine, Solene, Soléne, Solenna, Solina, Soline, Solonez, Souline, Soulle

Soma (Hindi) lunar.

Sommer (English) summer; summoner. (Arabic) black. See also Summer.
Somara, Somer, Sommar, Sommara, Sommers

Sondra (Greek) defender of mankind.
Saundra, Sondre, Sonndra, Sonndre

Sonia (Russian, Slavic) a form of Sonya.
Sonica, Sonida, Sonita, Sonna, Sonni, Sonnia, Sonnie, Sonny

Sonja (Scandinavian) a form of Sonya.
Sonjae, Sonjia

Sonya (Greek) wise. (Russian, Slavic) a form of Sophia.
Sonia, Sonja, Sonnya, Sonyae, Sunya

Sook (Korean) pure.

Sopheary (Cambodian) beautiful girl.

Sophia (Greek) wise. See also Sonya, Zofia.
Sofia, Sophie

Sophie (Greek) a familiar form of Sophia. See also Zocha.
Sophey, Sophi, Sophy

Sophronia (Greek) wise; sensible.
Soffrona, Sofronia

Sora (Native American) chirping songbird.

Soraya (Persian) princess.
Suraya

Sorrel (French) reddish brown. Botany: a plant whose leaves are used as salad greens.

Soso (Native American) tree squirrel dining on pine nuts; chubby-cheeked baby.

Souzan (Persian) burning fire.
Sousan, Souzanne

Spencer (English) dispenser of provisions.
Spenser

Speranza (Italian) a form of Esperanza.
Speranca

Spring (English) springtime.
Spryng

Stacey, Stacy (Greek) resurrection. (Irish) a short form of Anastasia, Eustacia, Natasha.
Stace, Stacee, Staceyan, Staceyann, Staicy, Stasey, Stasya, Stayce, Staycee, Staci, Steacy

Staci, Stacie (Greek) forms of Stacey.
Stacci, Stacia, Stayci

Stacia (English) a short form of Anastasia.
Stasia, Staysha

Starla (English) a form of Starr.
Starrla

Starleen (English) a form of Starr.
Starleena, Starlena, Starlene, Starlin, Starlyn, Starlynn, Starrlen

Starley (English) a familiar form of Starr.
Starle, Starlee, Staly

Starling (English) bird.

Starr (English) star.
Star, Staria, Starisha, Starla, Starleen, Starlet, Starlette, Starley, Starlight, Starre, Starri, Starria, Starrika, Starrsha, Starsha, Starshanna, Startish

Stasya (Greek) a familiar form of Anastasia. (Russian) a form of Stacey.
Stasa, Stasha, Stashia, Stasia, Stasja, Staska

Stefani, Steffani (Greek) forms of Stephanie.
Stafani, Stefanni, Steffane, Steffanee, Stefini, Stefoni

Stefanie (Greek) a form of Stephanie.
Stafanie, Staffany, Stefane, Stefanee, Stefaney, Stefania, Stefanié, Stefanija, Stefannie, Stefcia, Stefenie, Steffanie, Steffi, Stefinie, Stefka

Stefany, Steffany (Greek) forms of Stephanie.
Stefanny, Stefanya, Steffaney

Steffi (Greek) a familiar form of Stefanie, Stephanie.
Stefa, Stefcia, Steffee, Steffie, Steffy, Stefi, Stefka, Stefy, Stepha, Stephi, Stephie, Stephy

Stella (Latin) star. (French) a familiar form of Estelle.
Steile, Stellina

Stepania (Russian) a form of Stephanie.
Stepa, Stepahny, Stepanida, Stepanie, Stepanyda, Stepfanie, Stephana

Stephani (Greek) a form of Stephanie.
Stephania, Stephanni

Stephanie (Greek) crowned. See also Estefani, Estephanie, Panya, Stevie, Zephania.
Stamatios, Stefani, Stefanie, Stefany, Steffie, Stepania, Stephaija, Stephaine, Stephanas, Stephane, Stephanee, Stephani, Stephanida, Stéphanie, Stephanine, Stephann, Stephannie, Stephany, Stephene, Stephenie, Stephianie, Stephney, Stesha, Steshka, Stevanee

Stephany (Greek) a form of Stephanie.
Stephaney, Stephanye

Stephene (Greek) a form of Stephanie.
Stephina, Stephine, Stephyne

Stephenie (Greek) a form of Stephanie.
Stephena, Stephenee, Stepheney, Stepheni, Stephenny, Stepheny, Stephine, Stephinie

Stephney (Greek) a form of Stephanie.
Stephne, Stephni, Stephnie, Stephny

Sterling (English) valuable; silver penny.

Stevie (Greek) a familiar form of Stephanie.
Steva, Stevana, Stevanee, Stevee, Stevena, Stevey, Stevi, Stevy, Stevye

Stina (German) a short form of Christina.
Steena, Stena, Stine, Stinna

Stockard (English) stockyard.

Stormie (English) a form of Stormy.
Stormee, Stormi, Stormii

Stormy (English) impetuous by
nature.
Storm, Storme, Stormey, Stormie, Stormm

Suchin (Tai) beautiful thought.

Sue (Hebrew) a short form of Susan,
Susanna.

Sueann, Sueanna (American) combi-
nations of Sue + Ann, Sue + Anna.
*Suann, Suanna, Suannah, Suanne,
Sueanne*

Suela (Spanish) consolation.
Suelita

Sugar (American) sweet as sugar.
Shug

Sugi (Japanese) cedar tree.

Suke (Hawaiian) a form of Susan.

Sukey (Hawaiian) a familiar form of
Susan.
Suka, Sukee, Suki, Sukie, Suky

Sukhdeep (Sikh) light of peace and
bliss.
Sukhdip

Suki (Japanese) loved one.
(Moquelumnan) eagle-eyed.
Sukie

Sula (Icelandic) large sea bird. (Greek,
Hebrew) a short form of Shulamith,
Ursula. Suletu (Moquelumnan) soar-
ing bird.

Sulia (Latin) a form of Julia.
Suliana

Sulwen (Welsh) bright as the sun.

Sumalee (Tai) beautiful flower.

Sumati (Hindi) unity.

Sumaya (American) a combination of
Sue + Maya.
Sumayah, Sumayya, Sumayyah

Sumi (Japanese) elegant, refined.
Sumiko

Summer (English) summertime. See
also Sommer.
*Sumer, Summar, Summerann,
Summerbreeze, Summerhaze,
Summerine, Summerlee, Summerlin,
Summerlyn, Summerlynn, Summers,
Sumrah, Summyr, Sumyr*

Sun (Korean) obedient.
*Suncance, Sundee, Sundeep, Sundi,
Sundip, Sundrenea, Sunta, Sunya*

Sunee (Tai) good.
Suni

Sun-Hi (Korean) good; joyful.

Suni (Zuni) native; member of our
tribe.
*Sunita, Sunitha, Suniti, Sunne, Sunni,
Sunnie, Sunnilei*

Sunki (Hopi) swift.
Sunkia

Sunny (English) bright, cheerful.
Sunni, Sunnie

Sunshine (English) sunshine.
Sunshyn, Sunshyne

Surata (Pakistani) blessed joy.

Suri (Todas) pointy nose.
Suree, Surena, Surenia

Surya (Sanskrit) Mythology: a sun
god.
Suria, Suriya, Surra

Susammi (French) a combination of
Susan + Aimee.
Suzami, Suzamie, Suzamy

Susan (Hebrew) lily. See also
Shoshana, Sukey, Zsa Zsa, Zusa.
*Sawsan, Siusan, Sosan, Sosana, Sue,
Suesan, Sueva, Suisan, Suke, Susana,
Susann, Susanna, Suse, Susen, Susette,
Susie, Suson, Suzan, Suzanna,
Suzannah, Suzanne, Suzette*

Susana (Hebrew) a form of Susan.
Susanah, Susane

Susanna, Susannah (Hebrew) forms
of Susan. See also Xuxa, Zanna,
Zsuzsanna.
*Sonel, Sosana, Sue, Suesanna, Susana,
Susanah, Susanka, Susette, Susie,
Suzanna*

Suse (Hawaiian) a form of Susan.

Susette (French) a familiar form of
Susan, Susanna.
Susetta

Susie, Suzie (American) familiar
forms of Susan, Susanna.
*Suse, Susey, Susi, Sussi, Sussy, Susy,
Suze, Suzi, Suzy, Suzzie*

Suzanna, Suzannah (Hebrew) forms
of Susan.
Suzana, Suzenna, Suzzanna

Suzanne (English) a form of Susan.
Susanne, Suszanne, Suzane, Suzann, Suzzane, Suzzann, Suzzanne

Suzette (French) a form of Susan.
Suzetta, Suzzette

Suzu (Japanese) little bell.
Suzue, Suzuko

Suzuki (Japanese) bell tree.

Svetlana (Russian) bright light.
Sveta, Svetochka

Syá (Chinese) summer.

Sybella (English) a form of Sybil.
Sebila, Sibbella, Sibeal, Sibel, Sibell, Sibella, Sibelle, Sibilla, Sibylla, Sybel, Sybelle, Sybila, Sybilla

Sybil (Greek) prophet. Mythology: sibyls were oracles who relayed the messages of the gods. See also Cybele, Sibley.
Sib, Sibbel, Sibbie, Sibbill, Sibby, Sibeal, Sibel, Sibyl, Sibylle, Sibylline, Sybella, Sybille, Syble

Sydnee (French) a form of Sydney.
Sydne, Sydnea, Sydnei

Sydney (French) from Saint-Denis, France. See also Sidonie.
Cidney, Cydney, Sidney, Sy, Syd, Sydel, Sydelle, Sydna, Sydnee, Sydni, Sydnie, Sydny, Sydnye, Syndona, Syndonah

Sydni, Sydnie (French) forms of Sydney.

Sying (Chinese) star.

Sylvana (Latin) forest.
Silvaine, Silvana, Silvanna, Silviane,

Sylva, Sylvaine, Sylvanah, Sylvania, Sylvanna, Sylvie, Sylvina, Sylvinnia, Sylvonah, Sylvonia, Sylvonna

Sylvia (Latin) forest. Literature: Sylvia Plath was a well-known American poet. See also Silvia, Xylia.
Sylvette, Sylvie, Sylwia

Sylvianne (American) a combination of Sylvia + Anne.
Sylvian

Sylvie (Latin) a familiar form of Sylvia.
Silvi, Silvie, Silvy, Sylvi

Symone (Hebrew) a form of Simone.
Symmeon, Symmone, Symona, Symoné, Symonne

Symphony (Greek) symphony, harmonious sound.
Symfoni, Symphanie, Symphany, Symphanée, Symphoni, Symphoni

Syreeta (Hindi) good traditions. (Arabic) companion.
Syretta, Syrrita

Tabatha (Greek, Aramaic) a form of Tabitha.
Tabathe, Tabathia, Tabbatha

Tabby (English) a familiar form of Tabitha.
Tabbi

Tabia (Swahili) talented.
Tabea

Tabetha (Greek, Aramaic) a form of Tabitha.

Tabina (Arabic) follower of Muhammad.

Tabitha (Greek, Aramaic) gazelle.
Tabatha, Tabbee, Tabbetha, Tabbey, Tabbi, Tabbie, Tabbitha, Tabby, Tabetha, Tabiatha, Tabita, Tabithia, Tabotha, Tabtha, Tabytha

Tabytha (Greek, Aramaic) a form of Tabitha.
Tabbytha

Tacey (English) a familiar form of Tacita.
Tace, Tacee, Taci, Tacy, Tacye

Taci (Zuni) washtub. (English) a form of Tacey.
Tacia, Taciana, Tacie

Tacita (Latin) silent.
Tacey

Tadita (Omaha) runner.
Tadeta, Tadra

Taelor (English) a form of Taylor.
Taelar, Taeler, Taellor, Taelore, Taelyr

Taesha (Latin) a form of Tisha. (American) a combination of the prefix Ta + Aisha.
Tadasha, Taeshayla, Taeshia, Taheisha, Tahisha, Taiesha, Taisha, Taishae, Teasha, Teashia, Teisha, Tesha

Taffy (Welsh) beloved.
Taffia, Taffine, Taffye, Tafia, Tafisa, Tafoya

Tahira (Arabic) virginal, pure.
Taheera, Taheerah, Tahera, Tahere, Taheria, Taherri, Tahiara, Tahirah, Tahireh

Tahlia (Greek, Hebrew) a form of Talia.
Tahleah, Tahleia

Tailor (English) a form of Taylor.
Tailar, Tailer, Taillor, Tailyr

Taima (Native American) clash of thunder.
Taimi, Taimia, Taimy

Taipa (Moquelumnan) flying quail.
Taite (English) cheerful.
Tate, Tayte, Tayten

Taja (Hindi) crown.
Taiajára, Taija, Tajae, Tajah, Tahai, Tehya, Teja, Tejah, Tejal

Taka (Japanese) honored.

Takala (Hopi) corn tassel.

Takara (Japanese) treasure.
Takarah, Takaria, Takarra, Takra

Takayla (American) a combination of the prefix Ta + Kayla.
Takayler, Takeyli

Takeisha (American) a combination of the prefix Ta + Keisha.
Takecia, Takesha, Takeshia, Takesia, Takisha, Takishea, Takishia, Tekeesha, Tekeisha, Tekeshi, Tekeysia, Tekisha, Tikesha, Tikisha, Tokesia, Tykeisha

Takenya (Hebrew) animal horn. (Moquelumnan) falcon. (American) a combination of the prefix Ta + Kenya.
Takenia, Takenja

Takeria (American) a form of Takira.
Takera, Takeri, Takerian, Takerra, Takerria, Takierria, Takoria

Taki (Japanese) waterfall.
Tiki

Takia (Arabic) worshiper.
Takeia, Takeiyah, Takeya, Takeyah, Takhiya, Takiah, Takija, Takiya, Takiyah, Takkia, Takya, Takyah, Takyia, Taqiyya, Taquaia, Taquaya, Taquiia, Tekeiya, Tekeiyah, Tekeyia, Tekiya, Tekiyah, Tikia, Tykeia, Tykia

Takila (American) a form of Tequila.
Takayla, Takeila, Takela, Takelia, Takella, Takeyla, Takiela, Takilah, Takilla, Takilya, Takyla, Takylia, Tatakyla, Tehilla, Tekeila, Tekela, Tekelia, Tekilaa, Tekilia, Tekilla, Tekilyah, Tekla

Takira (American) a combination of the prefix Ta + Kira.
Takara, Takarra, Takeara, Takeera, Takeira, Takeirah, Takera, Takiara, Takiera, Takierah, Takierra, Takirah, Takiria, Takirra, Takora, Takyra, Takyrra, Taquera, Taquira, Tekeria, Tikara, Tikira, Tykera

Tala (Native American) stalking wolf.

Talasi (Hopi) corn tassel.
Talasea, Talasia

Taleah (American) a form of Talia.
Talaya, Talayah, Talayia, Talea, Taleana, Taleea, Taleéi, Talei, Taleia, Taleiya, Tylea, Tyleah, Tylee

Taleisha (American) a combination of Talia + Aisha.
Taileisha, Taleise, Talesha, Talicia, Taliesha, Talisa, Talisha, Talysha, Telisha, Tilisha, Tyleasha, Tyleisha, Tylicia, Tylisha, Tylishia

Talena (American) a combination of the prefix Ta + Lena.
Talayna, Talihna, Taline, Tallenia, Talná, Tilena, Tilene, Tylena

Talesha (American) a form of Taleisha.
Taleesha, Talesa, Talese, Taleshia, Talesia, Tallese, Tallesia, Tylesha, Tyleshia, Tylesia

Talia (Greek) blooming. (Hebrew) dew from heaven. (Latin, French) birthday. A short form of Natalie. See also Thalia.
Tahlia, Taleah, Taliah, Taliatha, Taliea, Taliyah, Talley, Tallia, Tallya, Talya, Tylia

Talina (American) a combination of Talia + Lina.
Talin, Talinda, Taline, Tallyn, Talyn, Talynn, Tylina, Tyline

Talisa (English) a form of Tallis.
Talisha, Talishia, Talisia, Talissa, Talysa, Talysha, Talysia, Talyssa

Talitha (Arabic) young girl.
Taleetha, Taletha, Talethia, Taliatha, Talita, Talithia, Taliya, Telita, Tiletha

Taliyah (Greek) a form of Talia.
Taleya, Taleyah, Talieya, Talliyah, Talya, Talyah, Talyia

Talley (French) a familiar form of Talia.
Tali, Talle, Tallie, Tally, Taly, Talye

Tallis (French, English) forest.
Talice, Talisa, Talise, Tallys

Tallulah (Choctaw) leaping water.
Tallou, Talula

Tam (Vietnamese) heart.

Tama (Japanese) jewel.
Tamaa, Tamah, Tamaiah, Tamala, Tema

Tamaka (Japanese) bracelet.
Tamaki, Tamako, Timaka

Tamar (Hebrew) a short form of
Tamara. (Russian) History: a twelfth-
century Georgian queen. (Hebrew) a
short form of Tamara.
Tamer, Tamor, Tamour

Tamara (Hebrew) palm tree. See also
Tammy.
*Tamar, Tamará, Tamarae, Tamarah, Tamaria,
Tamarin, Tamarla, Tamarra, Tamarria,
Tamarrian, Tamarsha, Tamary, Tamera,
Tamira, Tamma, Tammara, Tamora, Tamoya,
Tamra, Tamura, Tamyra, Temara, Temarian,
Thama, Thamar, Thamara, Thamarra,
Timara, Tomara, Tymara*

Tamassa (Hebrew) a form of
Thomasina.
*Tamasin, Tamasine, Tamsen, Tamsin,
Tamzen, Tamzin*

Tameka (Aramaic) twin.
*Tameca, Tamecia, Tamecka, Tameeka,
Tamekia, Tamiecka, Tamieka, Temeka,
Timeeka, Timeka, Tomeka, Tomekia,
Trameika, Tymeka, Tymmeeka, Tymmeka*

Tamera (Hebrew) a form of Tamara.
*Tamer, Tamerai, Tameran, Tameria,
Tamerra, Tammera, Thamer, Timera*

Tamesha (American) a combination
of the prefix Ta + Mesha.
*Tameesha, Tameisha, Tameshia,
Tameshkia, Tameshya, Tamisha, Tamishia,
Tamnesha, Temisha, Timesha, Timisha,
Tomesha, Tomiese, Tomise, Tomisha,
Tramesha, Tramisha, Tymesha*

Tamika (Japanese) a form of Tamiko.
*Tamica, Tamieka, Tamikah, Tamikia,
Tamikka, Tammika, Tamyka, Timika,
Timikia, Tomika, Tymika, Tymmicka*

Tamiko (Japanese) child of the people.
*Tami, Tamika, Tamike, Tamiqua, Tamiyo,
Tammiko*

Tamila (American) a combination of
the prefix Ta + Mila.
*Tamala, Tamela, Tamelia, Tamilla, Tamille,
Tamillia, Tamilya*

Tamira (Hebrew) a form of Tamara.
*Tamir, Tamirae, Tamirah, Tamiria, Tamirra,
Tamyra, Tamyria, Tamyrra*

Tammi, Tammie (English) forms of
Tammy.
*Tameia, Tami, Tamia, Tamiah, Tamie,
Tamijo, Tamiya*

Tammy (English) twin. (Hebrew) a famil-
iar form of Tamara.
*Tamilyn, Tamlyn, Tammee, Tammey, Tammi,
Tammie, Tamy, Tamya*

Tamra (Hebrew) a short form of
Tamara.
Tammra, Tamrah

Tamsin (English) a short form of
Thomasina.

Tana (Slavic) a short form of Tanya.
*Taina, Tanae, Tanaeah, Tanah, Tanairi,
Tanairy, Tanalia, Tanara, Tanavia, Tanaya,
Tanaz, Tanna, Tannah*

Tandy (English) team.
*Tanda, Tandalaya, Tandi, Tandie, Tandis,
Tandra, Tandrea, Tandria*

Taneisha, Tanesha (American) com-
binations of the prefix Ta + Nesha.
*Tahniesha, Taineshia, Tanasha, Tanashia,
Tanaysia, Taneasha, Taneesha, Taneshea,
Taneshia, Taneshya, Tanesia, Tanesian,
Tanessa, Tanessia, Taniesha, Tannesha,
Tanneshia, Tanniecia, Tanniesha,
Tantashea*

Taneya (Russian, Slavic) a form of
Tanya.
Tanea, Taneah, Tanee, Taneé, Taneia

Tangia (American) a combination of the
prefix Ta + Angela.
*Tangela, Tangi, Tangie, Tanja, Tanji, Tanjia,
Tanjie*

Tani (Japanese) valley. (Slavic) stand of
glory. A familiar form of Tania.
*Tahnee, Tahni, Tahnie, Tanee, Taney,
Tanie, Tany*

Tania (Russian, Slavic) fairy queen.
*Taneea, Tani, Taniah, Tanija, Tanika,
Tanis, Taniya, Tannia, Tannis, Tanniya,
Tannya, Tarnia*

Taniel (American) a combination of
Tania + Danielle.
Taniele, Tanielle, Teniel, Teniele, Tenielle

Tanika (American) a form of Tania.
*Tanikka, Tanikqua, Taniqua, Tanique,
Tannica, Tianeka, Tianika*

Tanis, Tannis (Slavic) forms of Tania,
Tanya.
*Tanas, Tanese, Taniese, Tanise, Tanisia,
Tanka, Tannese, Tanniece, Tanniese,
Tannis, Tannise, Tannus, Tannyce, Tenice,
Tenise, Tenyse, Tiannis, Tonise, Tranice,
Tranise, Tynice, Tyniece, Tyniese, Tynise*

Tanisha (American) a combination of the prefix Ta + Nisha.
Tahniscia, Tahnisha, Tanasha, Tanashea, Tanicha, Taniesha, Tanish, Tanishah, Tanishia, Tanitia, Tannicia, Tannisha, Tenisha, Tenishka, Tinisha, Tonisha, Tonnisha, Tynisha

Tanissa (American) a combination of the prefix Tania + Nissa.
Tanesa, Tanisa, Tannesa, Tannisa, Tennessa, Tranissa

Tanita (American) a combination of the prefix Ta + Nita.
Taneta, Tanetta, Tanitra, Tanitta, Teneta, Tenetta, Tenita, Tenitta, Tyneta, Tynetta, Tynette, Tynita, Tynitra, Tynitta

Tanith (Phoenician) Mythology: Tanit is the goddess of love.
Tanitha

Tanner (English) leather worker, tanner.
Tannor

Tansy (Greek) immortal. (Latin) tenacious, persistent.
Tancy, Tansee, Tansey, Tanshay, Tanzey

Tanya (Russian, Slavic) fairy queen.
Tahnee, Tahnya, Tana, Tanaya, Taneya, Tania, Tanis, Taniya, Tanka, Tannis, Tannya, Tanoya, Tany, Tanyia, Taunya, Tawnya, Thanya

Tao (Chinese, Vietnamese) peach.

Tara (Aramaic) throw; carry. (Irish) rocky hill. (Arabic) a measurement.
Taira, Tairra, Taraea, Tarah, Taráh, Tarai, Taralee, Tarali, Tarasa, Tarasha, Taraya, Tarha, Tari, Tarra, Taryn, Tayra, Tehra

Taraneh (Persian) melody.

Taree (Japanese) arching branch.
Tarea, Tareya, Tari, Taria

Tari (Irish) a familiar form of Tara.
Taria, Tarika, Tarila, Tarilyn, Tarin, Tarina, Tarita

Tarissa (American) a combination of Tara + Rissa.
Taris, Tarisa, Tarise, Tarisha

Tarra (Irish) a form of Tara.
Tarrah

Taryn (Irish) a form of Tara.
Taran, Tareen, Tareena, Taren, Tarene, Tarin, Tarina, Tarren, Tarrena, Tarrin, Tarrina, Tarron, Tarryn, Taryna

Tasarla (Gypsy) dawn.

Tasha (Greek) born on Christmas day. (Russian) a short form of Natasha. See also Tashi, Tosha.
Tacha, Tachiana, Tahsha, Tasenka, Tashae, Tashana, Tashay, Tashe, Tashee, Tasheka, Tashka, Tasia, Taska, Taysha, Thasha, Tiaisha, Tysha

Tashana (American) a combination of the prefix Ta + Shana.
Tashan, Tashanda, Tashani, Tashanika, Tashanna, Tashiana, Tashianna, Tashina, Tishana, Tishani, Tishanna, Tishanne, Toshanna, Toshanti, Tyshana

Tashara (American) a combination of the prefix Ta + Shara.
Tashar, Tasharah, Tasharia, Tasharna, Tasharra, Tashera, Tasherey, Tasheri, Tasherra, Tashira, Tashirah

Tashawna (American) a combination of the prefix Ta + Shawna.
Tashauna, Tashauni, Tashaunie, Tashaunna, Tashawanna, Tashawn, Tashawnda, Tashawnna, Tashawnnia, Tashonda, Tashondra, Tiashauna, Tishawn, Tishunda, Tishunta, Toshauna, Toshawna, Tyshauna, Tyshawna

Tasheena (American) a combination of the prefix Ta + Sheena.
Tasheana, Tasheeana, Tasheeni, Tashena, Tashenna, Tashennia, Tasheona, Tashina, Tisheena, Tosheena, Tysheana, Tysheena, Tyshyna

Tashelle (American) a combination of the prefix Ta + Shelley.
Tachell, Tashell, Techell, Techelle, Teshell, Teshelle, Tochell, Tochelle, Toshelle, Tychell, Tychelle, Tyshell, Tyshelle

Tashi (Hausa) a bird in flight. (Slavic) a form of Tasha.
Tashia, Tashie, Tashika, Tashima, Tashiya

Tasia (Slavic) a familiar form of Tasha.
Tachia, Tashea, Tasiya, Tassi, Tassia, Tassiana, Tassie, Tasya

Tassos (Greek) a form of Theresa.

Tata (Russian) a familiar form of Tatiana.
Tate, Tatia

Tate (English) a short form of Tatum. A form of Taite, Tata.

Tatiana (Slavic) fairy queen. See also Tanya, Tiana.
Tata, Tatania, Tatanya, Tateana, Tati, Tatia, Tatianna, Tatie, Tatihana, Tatiyana, Tatjana, Tatyana, Tiatiana

Tatianna (Slavic) a form of Tatiana.
Taitiann, Taitianna, Tateanna, Tateonna, Tationna

Tatiyana (Slavic) a form of Tatiana.
Tateyana, Tatiayana, Tatiyanna, Tatiyona, Tatiyonna

Tatum (English) cheerful.
Tate, Tatumn

Tatyana (Slavic) a form of Tatiana.
Tatyanah, Tatyani, Tatyanna, Tatyannah, Tatyona, Tatyonna

Taura (Latin) bull. Astrology: Taurus is a sign of the zodiac.
Taurae, Tauria, Taurina

Tauri (English) a form of Tory.
Taure, Taurie, Taury

Tavia (Latin) a short form of Octavia. See also Tawia.
Taiva, Tauvia, Tava, Tavah, Tavita

Tavie (Scottish) twin.
Tavey, Tavi

Tawanna (American) a combination of the prefix Ta + Wanda.
Taiwana, Taiwanna, Taquana, Taquanna, Tawan, Tawana, Tawanda, Tawanne, Tequana, Tequanna, Tequawna, Tewanna, Tewauna, Tiquana, Tiwanna, Tiwena, Towanda, Towanna, Tywania, Tywanna

Tawia (African) born after twins. (Polish) a form of Tavia.

Tawni (English) a form of Tawny.
Tauni, Taunia, Tawnia, Tawnie, Tawnnie, Tiawni

Tawny (Gypsy) little one. (English) brownish yellow, tan.
Tahnee, Tany, Tauna, Tauné, Taunisha, Tawnee, Tawnesha, Tawney, Tawni, Tawnyell, Tiawna

Tawnya (American) a combination of Tawny + Tonya.
Tawna

Taya, Taye (English) short forms of Taylor.
Tay, Tayah, Tayana, Tayiah, Tayna, Tayra, Taysha, Taysia, Tayva, Tayvonne, Teya, Teyanna, Teyona, Teyuna, Tiaya, Tiya, Tiyah, Tiyana, Tye

Tayla (English) a short form of Taylor.
Taylah, Tayleah, Taylee, Tayleigh, Taylie, Teila

Taylar (English) a form of Taylor.
Talar, Tayla, Taylah, Taylare, Tayllar

Tayler (English) a form of Taylor.
Tayller

Taylor (English) tailor.
Taelor, Tailor, Taiylor, Talor, Talora, Taya, Taye, Tayla, Taylar, Tayler, Tayllor, Tayllore, Tayloir, Taylorann, Taylore, Taylorr, Taylour, Taylur, Teylor

Tazu (Japanese) stork; longevity.
Taz, Tazi, Tazia

Teagan (Welsh) beautiful, attractive.
Taegen, Teage, Teagen, Teaghan, Teaghanne, Teaghen, Teagin, Teague, Teegan, Teeghan, Tegan, Tegwen, Teigan, Tejan, Tiegan, Tigan, Tijan, Tijana

Teaira (Latin) a form of Tiara.
Teairra, Teairre, Teairria, Teara, Tearah, Teareya, Teari, Tearia, Teariea, Tearra, Tearria

Teal (English) river duck; blue green.
Teala, Teale, Tealia, Tealisha

Teanna (American) a combination of the prefix Te + Anna. A form of Tiana.
Tean, Teana, Teanah, Teann, Teannah, Teanne, Teaunna, Teena, Teuana

Teca (Hungarian) a form of Theresa.
Techa, Teka, Tica, Tika

Tecla (Greek) God's fame.
Tekla, Theckla

Teddi (Greek) a familiar form of Theodora.
Tedde, Teddey, Teddie, Teddy, Tedi, Tediah, Tedy

Tedra (Greek) a short form of Theodora.
Teddra, Teddreya, Tedera, Teedra, Teidra

Tegan (Welsh) a form of Teagan.
Tega, Tegen, Teggan, Teghan, Tegin, Tegyn, Teigen

Telisha (American) a form of Taleisha.
Teleesha, Teleisia, Telesa, Telesha, Teleshia, Telesia, Telicia, Telisa, Telishia, Telisia, Telissa, Telisse, Tellisa, Tellisha, Telsa, Telysa

Temira (Hebrew) tall.
Temora, Timora

Tempest (French) stormy.
Tempesta, Tempeste, Tempestt, Tempist, Tempistt, Tempress, Tempteste

Tenesha, Tenisha (American) combinations of the prefix Te + Niesha.
Tenecia, Teneesha, Teneisha, Teneshia, Tenesia, Tenessa, Teneusa, Teniesha, Tenishia

Tennille (American) a combination of the prefix Te + Nellie.
Taniel, Tanille, Teneal, Teneil, Teneille, Teniel, Tenille, Tenneal, Tenneill, Tenneille, Tennia, Tennie, Tennielle, Tennile, Tineal, Tiniel, Tonielle, Tonille

Teodora (Czech) a form of Theodora.
Teadora

Teona, Teonna (Greek) forms of Tiana, Tianna.
Teon, Teoni, Teonia, Teonie, Teonney, Teonnia, Teonnie

Tequila (Spanish) a kind of liquor. See also Takila.
Taquela, Taquella, Taquila, Taquilla, Tequilia, Tequilla, Tiquila, Tiquilia

Tera, Terra (Latin) earth. (Japanese) swift arrow. (American) forms of Tara.
Terah, Terai, Teria, Terrae, Terrah, Terria, Tierra

Teralyn (American) a combination of Terri + Lynn.
Taralyn, Teralyn, Teralynn, Terralin, Terralyn

Teresa (Greek) a form of Theresa. See also Tressa.
Taresa, Taressa, Tarissa, Terasa, Tercza, Tereasa, Tereatha, Terese, Teresea, Teresha, Teresia, Teresina, Teresita, Tereska, Tereson, Teressa, Teretha, Tereza, Terezia, Terezie, Terezilya, Terezinha, Terezka, Terezsa, Terisa, Terisha, Teriza, Terrasa, Terresa,

Terresha, Terresia, Terressa, Terrosina, Tersa, Tersea, Teruska, Terza, Teté, Tyresa, Tyresia

Terese (Greek) a form of Teresa.
Tarese, Taress, Taris, Tarise, Tereece, Tereese, Teress, Terez, Teris, Terrise

Teri (Greek) reaper. A familiar form of Theresa.
Terie

Terrelle (Greek) a form of Theresa.
Tarrell, Teral, Terall, Terel, Terell, Teriel, Terral, Terrall, Terrell, Terrella, Terriel, Terriell, Terrielle, Terrill, Terryelle, Terryl, Terryll, Terrylle, Teryl, Tyrell, Tyrelle

Terrene (Latin) smooth.
Tareena, Tarena, Teran, Teranee, Tereena, Terena, Terencia, Terene, Terenia, Terentia, Terina, Terran, Terren, Terrena, Terrin, Terrina, Terron, Terrosina, Terryn, Terun, Teryn, Teryna, Terynn, Tyreen, Tyrene

Terri (Greek) reaper. A familiar form of Theresa.
Terree, Terria, Terrie

Terriann (American) a combination of Terri + Ann.
Teran, Terian, Teriann, Terianne, Teriyan, Terria, Terrian, Terrianne, Terryann

Terrianna (American) a combination of Terri + Anna.
Teriana, Terianna, Terriana, Terriauna, Terrina, Terriona, Terrionna, Terriyana, Terriyanna, Terryana, Terryauna, Tyrina

Terrica (American) a combination of Terri + Erica. See also Rica.
Tereka, Terica, Tericka, Terika, Terreka, Terricka, Terrika, Tyrica, Tyricka, Tyrika, Tyrikka, Tyronica

Terry (Greek) a short form of Theresa.
Tere, Teree, Terelle, Terene, Teri, Terie, Terrey, Terri, Terrie, Terrye, Tery

Terry-Lynn (American) a combination of Terry + Lynn.
Terelyn, Terelynn, Terri-Lynn, Terrilynn, Terrylynn

Tertia (Latin) third.
Tercia, Tercina, Tercine, Terecena, Tersia, Terza

Tess (Greek) a short form of Quintessa, Theresa.
Tes, Tese

Tessa (Greek) reaper.
Tesa, Tesah, Tesha, Tesia, Tessah, Tessia, Tezia

Tessie (Greek) a familiar form of Theresa.
Tesi, Tessey, Tessi, Tessy, Tezi

Tetsu (Japanese) strong as iron.

Tetty (English) a familiar form of Elizabeth.

Tevy (Cambodian) angel.
Teva

Teylor (English) a form of Taylor.
Teighlor, Teylar

Thaddea (Greek) courageous. (Latin) praiser.
Thada, Thadda

Thalassa (Greek) sea, ocean.

Thalia (Greek) a form of Talia. Mythology: the Muse of comedy.
Thaleia, Thalie, Thalya

Thana (Arabic) happy occasion.
Thaina, Thania, Thanie

Thanh (Vietnamese) bright blue.
(Punjabi) good place.
Thantra, Thanya

Thao (Vietnamese) respectful of parents.

Thea (Greek) goddess. A short form of Althea.
Theo

Thelma (Greek) willful.
Thelmalina

Thema (African) queen.

Theodora (Greek) gift of God. See also Dora, Dorothy, Feodora.
Taedra, Teddi, Tedra, Teodora, Teodory, Teodosia, Theda, Thedorsha, Thedrica, Theo, Theodore, Theodoria, Theodorian, Theodosia, Theodra

Theone (Greek) gift of God.
Theondra, Theoni, Theonie

Theophania (Greek) God's appearance. See also Tiffany.
Theo, Theophanie

Theophila (Greek) loved by God.
Theo

Theresa (Greek) reaper. See also Resi, Reza, Riza, Tassos, Teca, Terrelle, Tracey, Tracy, Zilya.
Teresa, Teri, Terri, Terry, Tersea, Tess, Tessa, Tessie, Theresia, Theresina, Theresita, Theressa, Thereza, Therisa, Therissie, Thersa, Thersea, Tresha, Tressa, Trice

Therese (Greek) a form of Theresa.
Terese, Thérése, Theresia, Theressa, Therra, Therressa, Thersa

Theta (Greek) Linguistics: a letter in the Greek alphabet.

Thetis (Greek) disposed. Mythology: the mother of Achilles.

Thi (Vietnamese) poem.
Thia, Thy, Thya

Thirza (Hebrew) pleasant.
Therza, Thirsa, Thirzah, Thursa, Thurza, Thyrza, Tirshka, Tirza

Thomasina (Hebrew) twin. See also Tamassa.
Tamsin, Thomasa, Thomasia, Thomasin, Thomasine, Thomazine, Thomencia, Thomethia, Thomisha, Thomsina, Toma, Tomasa, Tomasina, Tomasine, Tomina, Tommie, Tommina

Thora (Scandinavian) thunder.
Thordia, Thordis, Thorri, Thyra, Tyra

Thuy (Vietnamese) gentle.

Tia (Greek) princess. (Spanish) aunt.
Téa, Teah, Teeya, Teia, Ti, Tiakeisha, Tialeigh, Tiamarie, Tianda, Tiandria, Tiante, Tiia, Tiye, Tyja

Tiana, Tianna (Greek) princess. (Latin) short forms of Tatiana.
Teana, Teanna, Tiahna, Tianah, Tiane, Tianea, Tianee, Tiani, Tiann, Tiannah, Tianne, Tianni, Tiaon, Tiauna, Tiena, Tiona, Tionna, Tiyana

Tiara (Latin) crowned.
Teair, Teaira, Teara, Téare, Tearia, Tearria, Teearia, Teira, Teirra, Tiaira, Tiare, Tiarea, Tiareah, Tiari, Tiaria, Tiarra, Tiera, Tierra, Tyara

Tiarra (Latin) a form of Tiara.
Tiairra, Tiarrah, Tyarra

Tiauna (Greek) a form of Tiana.
Tiaunah, Tiaunia, Tiaunna

Tiberia (Latin) Geography: the Tiber River in Italy.
Tib, Tibbie, Tibby

Tichina (American) a combination of the prefix Ti + China.
Tichian, Tichin, Tichinia

Tida (Tai) daughter.
Tiera, Tierra (Latin) forms of Tiara.
Tieara, Tiéra, Tierah, Tierre, Tierrea, Tierria

Tierney (Irish) noble.
Tieranae, Tierani, Tieranie, Tieranni, Tierany, Tiernan, Tiernee, Tierny

Tiff (Latin) a short form of Tiffani, Tiffanie, Tiffany.

Tiffani, Tiffanie (Latin) forms of Tiffany.
Tephanie, Tifanee, Tifani, Tifanie, Tiff, Tiffanee, Tiffayne, Tiffeni, Tiffenie, Tiffennie, Tiffiani, Tiffianie, Tiffine, Tiffini, Tiffinie, Tiffni, Tiffy, Tiffynie, Tifni

Tiffany (Latin) trinity. (Greek) a short form of Theophania. See also Tyfany.
Taffanay, Taffany, Tifaney, Tifany, Tiff, Tiffaney, Tiffani, Tiffanie, Tiffanny, Tiffeney, Tiffiany, Tiffiney, Tiffiny, Tiffnay, Tiffney, Tiffny, Tiffy, Tiphanie, Triffany

Tiffy (Latin) a familiar form of Tiffani,
Tiffany.
Tiffey, Tiffi, Tiffie

Tijuana (Spanish) Geography: a border
town in Mexico.
*Tajuana, Tajuanna, Thejuana, Tiajuana,
Tiajuanna, Tiawanna*

Tilda (German) a short form of Matilda.
Tilde, Tildie, Tildy, Tylda, Tyldy

Tillie (German) a familiar form of
Matilda.
Tilia, Tilley, Tilli, Tillia, Tilly, Tillye

Timi (English) a familiar form of
Timothea.
Timia, Timie, Timmi, Timmie

Timothea (English) honoring God.
Thea, Timi

Tina (Spanish, American) a short form
of Augustine, Martina, Christina,
Valentina.
*Teanna, Teena, Teina, Tena, Tenae, Tinai,
Tine, Tinea, Tinia, Tiniah, Tinna, Tinnia,
Tyna, Tynka*

Tinble (English) sound bells make.
Tynble

Tinesha (American) a combination of
the prefix Ti + Niesha.
*Timnesha, Tinecia, Tineisha, Tinesa,
Tineshia, Tinessa, Tinisha, Tinsia*

Tinisha (American) a form of Tenisha.
Tiniesha, Tinieshia, Tinishia, Tinishya

Tiona, Tionna (American) forms of
Tiana.
Teona, Teonna, Tionda, Tiondra, Tiondre,
*Tioné, Tionette, Tioni, Tionia, Tionie,
Tionja, Tionnah, Tionne, Tionya, Tyonna*

Tiphanie (Latin) a form of Tiffany.
Tiphanee, Tiphani, Tiphany

Tiponya (Native American) great
horned owl.
Tipper

Tipper (Irish) water pourer. (Native
American) a short form of Tiponya.

Tira (Hindi) arrow.
Tirah, Tirea, Tirena

Tirtha (Hindi) ford.

Tirza (Hebrew) pleasant.
*Thersa, Thirza, Tierza, Tirsa, Tirzah,
Tirzha, Tyrzah*

Tisa (Swahili) ninth-born.
Tisah, Tysa, Tyssa

Tish (Latin) a short form of Tisha.

Tisha (Latin) joy. A short form of
Leticia.
*Taesha, Tesha, Teisha, Tiesha, Tieshia,
Tish, Tishal, Tishia, Tysha, Tyshia*

Tita (Greek) giant. (Spanish) a short
form of names ending in "tita." A
form of Titus (see Boys' Names).

Titania (Greek) giant. Mythology: the
Titans were a race of giants.
*Tania, Teata, Titanna, Titanya, Titiana,
Tiziana, Tytan, Tytania, Tytiana*

Titiana (Greek) a form of Titania.
*Titianay, Titiania, Titianna, Titiayana,
Titionia, Titiyana, Titiyanna, Tityana*

Tivona (Hebrew) nature lover.

Tiwa (Zuni) onion.

Tiyana (Greek) a form of Tiana.
Tiyan, Tiyani, Tiyania, Tiyanna, Tiyonna

Tobi (Hebrew) God is good.
*Tobe, Tobee, Tobey, Tobie, Tobit, Toby,
Tobye, Tova, Tovah, Tove, Tovi, Tybi, Tybie*

Tocarra (American) a combination of
the prefix To + Cara.
Tocara, Toccara

Toinette (French) a short form of
Antoinette.
*Toinetta, Tola, Tonetta, Tonette, Toni,
Toniette, Twanette*

Toki (Japanese) hopeful.
Toko, Tokoya, Tokyo

Tola (Polish) a form of Toinette.
Tolsia

Tomi (Japanese) rich.
Tomie, Tomiju

Tommie (Hebrew) a short form of
Thomasina.
Tomme, Tommi, Tommia, Tommy

Tomo (Japanese) intelligent.
Tomoko

Tonesha (American) a combination of
the prefix To + Niesha.
*Toneisha, Toneisheia, Tonesha, Tonesia,
Toniece, Tonisha, Tonneshia*

Toni (Greek) flourishing. (Latin) praise-
worthy.
*Tonee, Toney, Tonia, Tonie, Toniee, Tonni,
Tonnie, Tony, Tonye*

Tonia (Latin, Slavic) a form of Toni, Tonya.
Tonea, Toniah, Toniea, Tonja, Tonje, Tonna, Tonni, Tonnia, Tonnie, Tonnja

Tonisha (American) a form of Toneisha.
Toniesha, Tonisa, Tonise, Tonisia, Tonnisha

Tonya (Slavic) fairy queen.
Tonia, Tonnya, Tonyea, Tonyetta, Tonyia

Topaz (Latin) golden yellow gem.

Topsy (English) on top. Literature: a slave in Harriet Beecher Stowe's novel *Uncle Tom's Cabin.*
Toppsy, Topsey, Topsie

Tora (Japanese) tiger.

Tori (Japanese) bird. (English) a form of Tory.
Toria, Toriana, Torie, Torri, Torrie, Torrita

Toria (English) a form of Tori, Tory.
Toriah, Torria

Toriana (English) a form of Tori.
Torian, Toriane, Toriann, Torianna, Torianne, Toriauna, Torin, Torina, Torine, Torinne, Torion, Torionna, Torionne, Toriyanna, Torrina

Torie, Torrie (English) forms of Tori.
Tore, Toree, Torei, Torre, Torree

Torilyn (English) a combination of Tori + Lynn.
Torilynn, Torrilyn, Torrilynn

Torri (English) a form of Tori.

Tory (English) victorious. (Latin) a short form of Victoria.
Tauri, Torey, Tori, Torrey, Torreya, Torry, Torrye, Torya, Torye, Toya

Tosha (Punjabi) armaments. (Polish) a familiar form of Antonia. (Russian) a form of Tasha.
Toshea, Toshia, Toshiea, Toshke, Tosia, Toska

Toshi (Japanese) mirror image.
Toshie, Toshiko, Toshikyo

Toski (Hopi) squashed bug.

Totsi (Hopi) moccasins.

Tottie (English) a familiar form of Charlotte.
Tota, Totti, Totty

Tovah (Hebrew) good.
Tova, Tovia

Toya (Spanish) a form of Tory.
Toia, Toyanika, Toyanna, Toyea, Toylea, Toyleah, Toylenn, Toylin, Toylyn

Tracey (Greek) a familiar form of Theresa. (Latin) warrior.
Trace, Tracee, Tracell, Traci, Tracie, Tracy, Traice, Trasey, Treesy

Traci, Tracie (Latin) forms of Tracey.
Tracia, Tracilee, Tracilyn, Tracilynn, Tracina, Traeci

Tracy (Greek) a familiar form of Theresa. (Latin) warrior.
Treacy

Tralena (Latin) a combination of Tracy + Lena.
Traleen, Tralene, Tralin, Tralinda, Tralyn, Tralynn, Tralynne

Tranesha (American) a combination of the prefix Tra + Niesha.
Traneice, Traneis, Traneise, Traneisha, Tranese, Traneshia, Tranice, Traniece, Traniesha, Tranisha, Tranishia

Trashawn (American) a combination of the prefix Tra + Shawn.
Trashan, Trashana, Trashauna, Trashon, Trayshauna

Trava (Czech) spring grasses.

Treasure (Latin) treasure, wealth; valuable.
Treasa, Treasur, Treasuré, Treasury

Trella (Spanish) a familiar form of Estelle.

Tresha (Greek) a form of Theresa.
Trescha, Trescia, Treshana, Treshia

Tressa (Greek) a short form of Theresa. See also Teresa.
Treaser, Tresa, Tresca, Trese, Treska, Tressia, Tressie, Trez, Treza, Trisa

Trevina (Irish) prudent. (Welsh) homestead.
Treva, Trevanna, Trevena, Trevenia, Treveon, Trevia, Treviana, Trevien, Trevin, Trevona

Trevona (Irish) a form of Trevina.
Trevion, Trevon, Trevonia, Trevonna, Trevonne, Trevonye

Triana (Latin) third. (Greek) a form of Trina.
Tria, Triann, Trianna, Trianne

Trice (Greek) a short form of Theresa.
Treece

Tricia (Latin) a form of Trisha.
Trica, Tricha, Trichelle, Tricina, Trickia

Trilby (English) soft hat.
Tribi, Trilbie, Trillby

Trina (Greek) pure.
Treena, Treina, Trenna, Triana, Trinia, Trinchen, Trind, Trinda, Trine, Trinette, Trini, Trinica, Trinice, Triniece, Trinika, Trinique, Trinisa, Tryna

Trini (Greek) a form of Trina.
Trinia, Trinie

Trinity (Latin) triad. Religion: the Father, the Son, and the Holy Spirit.
Trinita, Trinite, Trinitee, Triniti, Trinnette, Trinty

Trish (Latin) a short form of Beatrice, Trisha.
Trishell, Trishelle

Trisha (Latin) noblewoman. (Hindi) thirsty. See also Tricia.
Treasha, Trish, Trishann, Trishanna, Trishanne, Trishara, Trishia, Trishna, Trissha, Trycia

Trissa (Latin) a familiar form of Patricia.
Trisa, Trisanne, Trisia, Trisina, Trissi, Trissie, Trissy, Tryssa

Trista (Latin) a short form of Tristen.
Trisatal, Tristess, Tristia, Trysta, Trystia

Tristan (Latin) bold.
Trista, Tristane, Tristanni, Tristany, Tristen, Tristian, Tristiana, Tristin, Triston, Trystan, Trystyn

Tristen (Latin) a form of Tristan.
Tristene, Trysten

Tristin (Latin) a form of Tristan.
Tristina, Tristine, Tristinye, Tristn, Trystin

Triston, Trystyn (Latin) forms of Tristan.
Tristony, Trystyn

Trixie (American) a familiar form of Beatrice.
Tris, Trissie, Trissina, Trix, Trixi, Trixy

Troya (Irish) foot soldier.
Troi, Troia, Troiana, Troiya, Troy

Trudel (Dutch) a form of Trudy.

Trudy (German) a familiar form of Gertrude.
Truda, Trude, Trudel, Trudessa, Trudey, Trudi, Trudie

Trycia (Latin) a form of Trisha.

Tryna (Greek) a form of Trina.
Tryane, Tryanna, Trynee

Tryne (Dutch) pure.
Trine

Tsigana (Hungarian) a form of Zigana.
Tsigane, Tzigana, Tzigane

Tu (Chinese) jade.

Tuesday (English) born on the third day of the week.
Tuesdae, Tuesdea, Tuesdee, Tuesdey, Tusdai

Tula (Hindi) born in the lunar month of Capricorn.
Tulah, Tulla, Tullah, Tuula

Tullia (Irish) peaceful, quiet.
Tulia, Tulliah

Tulsi (Hindi) basil, a sacred Hindi herb.
Tulsia

Turquoise (French) blue-green semi-precious stone.
Turkois, Turkoise, Turkoys, Turkoyse

Tusa (Zuni) prairie dog.

Tuyen (Vietnamese) angel.

Tuyet (Vietnamese) snow.

Twyla (English) woven of double thread.
Twila, Twilla

Tyanna (American) a combination of the prefix Ty + Anna.
Tya, Tyana, Tyann, Tyannah, Tyanne, Tyannia

Tyeisha (American) a form of Tyesha.
Tyeesha, Tyeishia, Tyieshia, Tyisha, Tyishea, Tyishia

Tyesha (American) a combination of Ty + Aisha.
Tyasha, Tyashia, Tyasia, Tyasiah, Tyeisha, Tyeshia, Tyeyshia, Tyisha

Tyfany (American) a short form of Tiffany.
Tyfani, Tyfanny, Tyffani, Tyffanni, Tyffany, Tyffini, Typhanie, Typhany

Tykeisha (American) a form of Takeisha.
Tkeesha, Tykeisa, Tykeishia, Tykesha, Tykeshia, Tykeysha, Tykeza, Tykisha

Tykera (American) a form of Takira.
Tykeira, Tykeirah, Tykereiah, Tykeria, Tykeriah, Tykerria, Tykiera, Tykierra, Tykira, Tykiria, Tykirra

Tyler (English) tailor.
Tyller, Tylor

Tyna (Czech) a short form of Kristina.
Tynae, Tynea, Tynia

Tyne (English) river.
Tine, Tyna, Tynelle, Tynessa, Tynetta

Tynesha (American) a combination of Ty + Niesha.
Tynaise, Tynece, Tyneicia, Tynesa, Tynesha, Tyneshia, Tynessia, Tyniesha, Tynisha, Tyseisha

Tynisha (American) a form of Tynesha.
Tyneisha, Tyneisia, Tynisa, Tynise, Tynishi

Tyra (Scandinavian) battler. Mythology: Tyr was the god of war. A form of Thora. (Hindi) a form of Tira.
Tyraa, Tyrah, Tyran, Tyree, Tyria

Tyshanna (American) a combination of Ty + Shawna.
Tyshana, Tyshanae, Tyshane, Tyshaun, Tyshaunda, Tyshawn, Tyshawna, Tyshawnah, Tyshawnda, Tyshawnna, Tysheann, Tysheanna, Tyshonia, Tyshonna, Tyshonya

Tytiana (Greek) a form of Titania.
Tytana, Tytanna, Tyteana, Tyteanna, Tytianna, Tytianni, Tytionna, Tytiyana, Tytiyanna, Tytyana, Tytyauna

U

U (Korean) gentle.

Udele (English) prosperous.
Uda, Udella, Udelle, Yudelle

Ula (Irish) sea jewel. (Scandinavian) wealthy. (Spanish) a short form of Eulalia.
Uli, Ulla

Ulani (Polynesian) cheerful.
Ulana, Ulane

Ulima (Arabic) astute; wise.
Ullima

Ulla (German, Swedish) willful. (Latin) a short form of Ursula. Ulli

Ulrica (German) wolf ruler; ruler of all. See also Rica.
Ulka, Ullrica, Ullricka, Ullrika, Ulrika, Ulrike

Ultima (Latin) last, endmost, farthest.

Ululani (Hawaiian) heavenly inspiration.

Ulva (German) wolf.

Uma (Hindi) mother. Religion: another name for the Hindu goddess Devi.

Umay (Turkish) hopeful.
Umai

Umeko (Japanese) plum-blossom child; patient.
Ume, Umeyo

Una (Latin) one; united. (Hopi) good memory. (Irish) a form of Agnes. See also Oona.
Unna, Uny

Undine (Latin) little wave. Mythology: the undines were water spirits. See also Ondine.
Undeen, Undene

Unice (English) a form of Eunice.

Unika (American) a form of Unique.
Unica, Unicka, Unik, Unikqua, Unikue

Unique (Latin) only one.
Unika, Uniqia, Uniqua, Uniquia

Unity (English) unity.
Uinita, Unita, Unitee

Unn (Norwegian) she who is loved.

Unna (German) woman.

Urania (Greek) heavenly. Mythology: the Muse of astronomy.
Urainia, Uranie, Uraniya, Uranya

Urbana (Latin) city dweller.
Urbanah, Urbanna

Urika (Omaha) useful to everyone.
Ureka

Urit (Hebrew) bright.
Urice

Ursa (Greek) a short form of Ursula. (Latin) a form of Orsa.
Ursey, Ursi, Ursie, Ursy

Ursula (Greek) little bear. See also Sula, Ulla, Vorsila.
Irsaline, Ursa, Ursala, Ursel, Ursela, Ursella, Ursely, Ursilla, Ursillane, Ursola, Ursule, Ursulina, Ursuline, Urszula, Urszuli, Urzula

Usha (Hindi) sunrise.

Ushi (Chinese) ox. Astrology: a sign of the Chinese zodiac.

Uta (German) rich. (Japanese) poem.
Utako

Utina (Native American) woman of my country.
Utahna, Utona, Utonna

Vail (English) valley.
Vale, Vayle

Val (Latin) a short form of Valentina, Valerie.

Vala (German) singled out.
Valla

Valarie (Latin) a form of Valerie.
Valarae, Valaree, Valarey, Valari, Valaria, Vallarie

Valda (German) famous ruler.
Valida, Velda

Valencia (Spanish) strong. Geography: a region in eastern Spain.
Valecia, Valence, Valenica, Valentia, Valenzia

Valene (Latin) a short form of Valentina.
Valaine, Valean, Valeda, Valeen, Valen, Valena, Valeney, Valien, Valina, Valine, Vallan, Vallen

Valentina (Latin) strong. History: Valentina Tereshkova, a Soviet cosmonaut, was the first woman in space. See also Tina, Valene, Valli.
Val, Valantina, Vale, Valenteen, Valentena, Valentijn, Valentin, Valentine, Valiaka, Valtina, Valyn, Valynn

Valera (Russian) a form of Valerie. See also Lera.

Valeria (Latin) a form of Valerie.
Valaria, Valeriana, Valeriane, Veleria

Valerie (Latin) strong.
Vairy, Val, Valarie, Vale, Valera, Valeree, Valeri, Valeria, Valérie, Valery, Valka, Valleree, Valleri, Vallerie, Valli, Vallirie, Valora, Valorie, Valry, Valya, Velerie, Waleria

Valery (Latin) a form of Valerie.
Valerye, Vallary, Vallery

Valeska (Slavic) glorious ruler.
Valesca, Valese, Valeshia, Valeshka, Valezka, Valisha

Valli (Latin) a familiar form of Valentina, Valerie. Botany: a plant native to India.
Vallie, Vally

Valma (Finnish) loyal defender.

Valonia (Latin) shadow valley.
Vallon, Valona

Valora (Latin) a form of Valerie.
Valoria, Valorya, Velora

Valorie (Latin) a form of Valerie.
Vallori, Vallory, Valori, Valory

Vanda (German) a form of Wanda.
Vandana, Vandella, Vandetta, Vandi, Vannda

Vanesa (Greek) a form of Vanessa.
Vanesha, Vaneshah, Vanesia, Vanisa

Vanessa (Greek) butterfly. Literature: a name invented by Jonathan Swift as a nickname for Esther Vanhomrigh. See also Nessie.
Van, Vanassa, Vanesa, Vaneshia, Vanesse, Vanessia, Vanessica, Vanetta, Vaneza, Vaniece, Vaniessa, Vanija, Vanika, Vanissa, Vanita, Vanna, Vannesa, Vannessa, Vanni, Vannie, Vanny, Varnessa, Venessa

Vanetta (English) a form of Vanessa.
Vaneta, Vanita, Vanneta, Vannetta, Vannita, Venetta

Vania, Vanya (Russian) familiar forms of Anna.
Vanija, Vanina, Vaniya, Vanja, Vanka, Vannia

Vanity (English) vain.
Vaniti, Vanitty

Vanna (Cambodian) golden. (Greek) a short form of Vanessa.
Vana, Vanae, Vanelly, Vannah, Vannalee, Vannaleigh, Vannie, Vanny

Vannesa, Vannessa (Greek) forms of Vanessa.
Vannesha, Vanneza

Vanora (Welsh) white wave.
Vannora

Vantrice (American) a combination of the prefix Van + Trice.
Vantrece, Vantricia, Vantrisa, Vantrissa

Varda (Hebrew) rose.
Vadit, Vardia, Vardice, Vardina, Vardis, Vardit

Varvara (Slavic) a form of Barbara.
Vara, Varenka, Varina, Varinka, Varya, Varyusha, Vava, Vavka

Vashti (Persian) lovely. Bible: the wife of Ahasuerus, king of Persia.
Vashtee, Vashtie, Vashty

Veanna (American) a combination of the prefix Ve + Anna.
Veeana, Veena, Veenaya, Veeona

Veda (Sanskrit) sacred lore; knowledge. Religion: the Vedas are the sacred writings of Hinduism.
Vedad, Vedis, Veeda, Veida, Veleda, Vida

Vedette (Italian) sentry; scout. (French) movie star.
Vedetta

Vega (Arabic) falling star.

Velda (German) a form of Valda.

Velika (Slavic) great, wondrous.

Velma (German) a familiar form of Vilhelmina.
Valma, Vellma, Vilma, Vilna

Velvet (English) velvety.

Venecia (Italian) from Venice, Italy.
Vanecia, Vanetia, Veneise, Venesa, Venesha, Venesher, Venesse, Venessia, Venetia, Venette, Venezia, Venice, Venicia, Veniece, Veniesa, Venise, Venisha, Venishia, Venita, Venitia, Venize, Vennesa, Vennice, Vennisa, Vennise, Vonitia, Vonizia

Venessa (Latin) a form of Vanessa.
Veneese, Venesa, Venese, Veneshia, Venesia, Venisa, Venissa, Vennessa

Venus (Latin) love. Mythology: the goddess of love and beauty.
Venis, Venusa, Venusina, Vinny

Vera (Latin) true. (Slavic) faith. A short form of Elvera, Veronica. See also Verena, Wera.
Vara, Veera, Veira, Veradis, Verasha, Vere, Verka, Verla, Viera, Vira

Verbena (Latin) sacred plants.
Verbeena, Verbina

Verda (Latin) young, fresh.
Verdi, Verdie, Viridiana, Viridis

Verdad (Spanish) truthful.

Verena (Latin) truthful. A familiar form of Vera, Verna.
Verene, Verenis, Vereniz, Verina, Verine, Verinka, Veroshka, Verunka, Verusya, Virna

Verenice (Latin) a form of Veronica.
Verenis, Verenise, Vereniz

Verity (Latin) truthful.
Verita, Veritie

Verlene (Latin) a combination of Veronica + Lena.
Verleen, Verlena, Verlin, Verlina, Verlinda, Verline, Verlyn

Verna (Latin) springtime. (French) a familiar form of Laverne. See also Verena, Wera.
Verasha, Verla, Verne, Vernetia, Vernetta, Vernette, Vernia, Vernice, Vernita, Verusya, Viera, Virida, Virna, Virnell

Vernice (Latin) a form of Bernice, Verna.
Vernese, Vernesha, Verneshia, Vernessa, Vernica, Vernicca, Verniece, Vernika, Vernique, Vernis, Vernise, Vernisha, Vernisheia, Vernissia

Veronica (Latin) true image. See also Ronni, Weronika.
Varonica, Vera, Veranique, Verenice, Verhonica, Verinica, Verohnica, Veron, Verona, Verone, Veronic, Véronic, Veronice, Veronika, Veronique, Véronique, Veronne, Veronnica, Veruszhka, Vironica, Vron, Vronica

Veronika (Latin) a form of Veronica.
Varonika, Veronick, Véronick, Veronik, Veronike, Veronka, Veronkia, Veruka

Veronique, Véronique (French) forms of Veronica.
Vespera (Latin) evening star.

Vesta (Latin) keeper of the house. Mythology: the goddess of the home.
Vessy, Vest, Vesteria

Veta (Slavic) a familiar form of Elizabeth.
Veeta, Vita

Vi (Latin, French) a short form of Viola, Violet.
Vye

Vianca (Spanish) a form of Bianca.
Vianeca, Vianica

Vianey (American) a familiar form of Vianna.
Vianney, Viany

Vianna (American) a combination of Vi + Anna.
Viana, Vianey, Viann, Vianne

Vica (Hungarian) a form of Eve.

Vicki, Vickie (Latin) familiar forms of Victoria.
Vic, Vicci, Vicke, Vickee, Vickiana, Vickilyn, Vickki, Vicky, Vika, Viki, Vikie, Vikki, Vikky

Vicky (Latin) a familiar form of Victoria.
Viccy, Vickey, Viky, Vikkey, Vikky

Victoria (Latin) victorious. See also Tory, Wicktoria, Wisia.
Vicki, Vicky, Victoire, Victoriana, Victorianna, Victorie, Victorina, Victorine, Victoriya, Victorria, Victorriah, Victory, Victorya, Viktoria, Vitoria, Vyctoria

Vida (Sanskrit) a form of Veda. (Hebrew) a short form of Davida.
Vidamarie

Vidonia (Portuguese) branch of a vine.
Vedonia, Vidonya

Vienna (Latin) Geography: the capital of Austria.
Veena, Vena, Venna, Vienette, Vienne, Vina

Viktoria (Latin) a form of Victoria.
Viktorie, Viktorija, Viktorina, Viktorine, Viktorka

Vilhelmina (German) a form of Wilhelmina.
Velma, Vilhelmine, Vilma

Villette (French) small town.
Vietta

Vilma (German) a short form of Vilhemina.

Vina (Hindi) Mythology: a musical instrument played by the Hindu goddess of wisdom. (Spanish) vineyard. (Hebrew) a short form of Davina. (English) a short form of Alvina. See also Lavina.
Veena, Vena, Viña, Vinesha, Vinessa, Vinia, Viniece, Vinique, Vinisha, Viñita, Vinna, Vinni, Vinnie, Vinny, Vinora, Vyna

Vincentia (Latin) victor, conqueror.
Vicenta, Vincenta, Vincentena, Vincentina, Vincentine, Vincenza, Vincy, Vinnie

Viñita (Spanish) a form of Vina.
Viñeet, Viñeeta, Viñetta, Viñette, Viñitha, Viñta, Viñti, Viñtia, Vyñetta, Vyñette

Viola (Latin) violet; stringed instrument in the violin family. Literature: the heroine of Shakespeare's play *Twelfth Night*.
Vi, Violaine, Violanta, Violante, Viole, Violeine

Violet (French) Botany: a plant with purplish blue flowers.
Vi, Violeta, Violette, Vyolet, Vyoletta, Vyolette

Violeta (French) a form of Violet.
Violetta

Virgilia (Latin) rod bearer, staff bearer.
Virgillia

Virginia (Latin) pure, virginal. Literature: Virginia Woolf was a well-known British writer. See also Gina, Ginger, Ginny, Jinny.
Verginia, Verginya, Virge, Virgen, Virgenia, Virgenya, Virgie, Virgine, Virginie, Virginië, Virginio, Virginnia, Virgy, Virjeana

Virginie (French) a form of Virginia.

Viridiana (Latin) a form of Viridis.

Viridis (Latin) green.
Virdis, Virida, Viridia, Viridiana

Virtue (Latin) virtuous.

Vita (Latin) life.
Veeta, Veta, Vitaliana, Vitalina, Vitel, Vitella, Vitia, Vitka, Vitke

Vitoria (Spanish) a form of Victoria.
Vittoria

Viv (Latin) a short form of Vivian.

Viva (Latin) a short form of Aviva, Vivian.
Vica, Vivan, Vivva

Viveca (Scandinavian) a form of Vivian.
Viv, Vivecca, Vivecka, Viveka, Vivica, Vivieca, Vyveca

Vivian (Latin) full of life.
Vevay, Vevey, Viv, Viva, Viveca, Vivee, Vivi, Vivia, Viviana, Viviane, Viviann, Vivianne, Vivie, Vivien, Vivienne, Vivina, Vivion, Vivyan, Vivyann, Vivyanne, Vyvyan, Vyvyann, Vyvyanne

Viviana (Latin) a form of Vivian.
Viv, Vivianna, Vivyana, Vyvyana

Vondra (Czech) loving woman.
Vonda, Vondrea

Voneisha (American) a combination of Yvonne + Aisha.
Voneishia, Vonesha, Voneshia

Vonna (French) a form of Yvonne.
Vona

Vonny (French) a familiar form of Yvonne.
Vonney, Vonni, Vonnie

Vontricia (American) a combination of Yvonne + Tricia.
Vontrece, Vontrese, Vontrice, Vontriece

Vorsila (Greek) a form of Ursula.
Vorsilla, Vorsula, Vorsulla, Vorsyla

Wadd (Arabic) beloved.

Waheeda (Arabic) one and only.

Wainani (Hawaiian) beautiful water.

Wakana (Japanese) plant.

Wakanda (Dakota) magical power.
Wakenda

Wakeisha (American) a combination of the prefix Wa + Keisha.
Wakeishia, Wakesha, Wakeshia, Wakesia

Walad (Arabic) newborn.
Waladah, Walidah

Walda (German) powerful; famous.
Waldina, Waldine, Walida, Wallda, Welda

Waleria (Polish) a form of Valerie.
Wala

Walker (English) cloth; walker.
Wallker

Wallis (English) from Wales.
Wallie, Walliss, Wally, Wallys

Wanda (German) wanderer. See also Wendy.
Vanda, Wahnda, Wandah, Wandely, Wandie, Wandis, Wandja, Wandzia, Wannda, Wonda, Wonnda

Wandie (German) a familiar form of Wanda.
Wandi, Wandy

Waneta (Native American) charger. See also Juanita.
Waneeta, Wanita, Wanite, Wanneta, Waunita, Wonita, Wonnita, Wynita

Wanetta (English) pale face.
Wanette, Wannetta, Wannette

Wanika (Hawaiian) a form of Juanita.
Wanicka

Warda (German) guardian.
Wardah, Wardeh, Wardena, Wardenia, Wardia, Wardine

Washi (Japanese) eagle.

Wattan (Japanese) homeland.

Wauna (Moquelumnan) snow geese honking.
Waunakee

Wava (Slavic) a form of Barbara.

Waverly (English) quaking aspen-tree meadow.
Waverley, Waverli, Wavierlee

Waynesha (American) a combination of Waynette + Niesha.
Wayneesha, Wayneisha, Waynie, Waynisha

Waynette (English) wagon maker.
Waynel, Waynelle, Waynetta, Waynlyn

Weeko (Dakota) pretty girl.

Wehilani (Hawaiian) heavenly adornment.

Wenda (Welsh) a form of Wendy.
Wendaine, Wendayne

Wendelle (English) wanderer.
Wendaline, Wendall, Wendalyn, Wendeline, Wendella, Wendelline, Wendelly

Wendi (Welsh) a form of Wendy.
Wendie

Wendy (Welsh) white; light skinned. A familiar form of Gwendolyn, Wanda.
Wenda, Wende, Wendee, Wendey, Wendi, Wendye, Wuendy

Wera (Polish) a form of Vera. See also Verna.
Wiera, Wiercia, Wierka

Weronika (Polish) a form of Veronica.
Weronikra

Wesisa (Musoga) foolish.

Weslee (English) western meadow.
Weslea, Wesleigh, Weslene, Wesley, Wesli, Weslia, Weslie, Weslyn

Whitley (English) white field.
Whitely, Whitlee, Whitleigh, Whitlie, Whittley

Whitney (English) white island.
Whiteney, Whitne, Whitné, Whitnee, Whitneigh, Whitnie, Whitny, Whitnye, Whytne, Whytney, Witney

Whitnie (English) a form of Whitney.
Whitani, Whitnei, Whitni, Whytni, Whytnie

Whittney (English) a form of Whitney.
Whittaney, Whittanie, Whittany, Whitteny, Whittnay, Whittnee, Whittney, Whittni, Whittnie

Whoopi (English) happy; excited.
Whoopie, Whoopy

Wicktoria (Polish) a form of Victoria.
Wicktorja, Wiktoria, Wiktorja

Wilda (German) untamed. (English) willow.
Willda, Wylda

Wileen (English) a short form of Wilhelmina.
Wilene, Willeen, Willene

Wilhelmina (German) a form of Wilhelm (see Boys' Names). See also Billie, Guillerma, Helma, Minka, Minna, Minnie.
Vilhelmina, Wileen, Wilhelmine, Willa, Willamina, Willamine, Willemina, Willette, Williamina, Willie, Willmina, Willmine, Wilma, Wimina

Wilikinia (Hawaiian) a form of Virginia.

Willa (German) a short form of Wilhelmina.
Willabella, Willette, Williabelle

Willette (English) a familiar form of Wilhelmina, Willa.
Wiletta, Wilette, Willetta, Williette

Willie (English) a familiar form of Wilhelmina.
Willi, Willina, Willisha, Willishia, Willy

Willow (English) willow tree.
Willough

Wilma (German) a short form of Wilhelmina.
Williemae, Wilmanie, Wilmayra, Wilmetta, Wilmette, Wilmina, Wilmyne, Wylma

Wilona (English) desired.
Willona, Willone, Wilone

Win (German) a short form of Winifred. See also Edwina.
Wyn

Winda (Swahili) hunter.

Windy (English) windy.
Windee, Windey, Windi, Windie, Wyndee, Wyndy

Winema (Moquelumnan) woman chief.

Winifred (German) peaceful friend. (Welsh) a form of Guinevere. See also Freddi, Una, Winnie.
Win, Winafred, Winefred, Winefride, Winfreda, Winfrieda, Winiefrida, Winifrid, Winifryd, Winnafred, Winnefred, Winniefred, Winnifred, Winnifrid, Wynafred, Wynifred, Wynnifred

Winna (African) friend.
Winnah

Winnie (English) a familiar form of Edwina, Gwyneth, Winnifred, Winona, Wynne. History: Winnie Mandela kept the anti-apartheid movement alive in South Africa while her then-husband, Nelson Mandela, was imprisoned. Literature: the lovable bear in A. A. Milne's children's story *Winnie-the-Pooh*.
Wina, Winne, Winney, Winni, Winny, Wynnie

Winola (German) charming friend.
Wynola

Winona (Lakota) oldest daughter.
Wanona, Wenona, Wenonah, Winnie, Winonah, Wynonna

Winter (English) winter.
Wintr, Wynter

Wira (Polish) a form of Elvira.
Wiria, Wirke

Wisia (Polish) a form of Victoria.
Wicia, Wikta

Wren (English) wren, songbird.

Wyanet (Native American) legendary beauty.
Wyaneta, Wyanita, Wynette

Wynne (Welsh) white, light skinned. A short form of Blodwyn, Guinivere, Gwyneth.
Winnie, Wyn, Wynn

Wynonna (Lakota) a form of Winona.
Wynnona, Wynona

Wynter (English) a form of Winter.
Wynteria

Wyoming (Native American) Geography: a western U. S. state.
Wy, Wye, Wyoh, Wyomia

Xandra (Greek) a form of Zandra. (Spanish) a short form of Alexandra.
Xander, Xandrea, Xandria

Xanthe (Greek) yellow, blond. See also Zanthe.
Xanne, Xantha, Xanthia, Xanthippe

Xanthippe (Greek) a form of Xanthe. History: Socrates's wife.
Xantippie

Xaviera (Basque) owner of the new house. (Arabic) bright. See also Javiera, Zaviera.
Xavia, Xaviére, Xavyera, Xiveria

Xela (Quiché) my mountain home.

Xena (Greek) a form of Xenia.

Xenia (Greek) hospitable. See also Zena, Zina.
Xeenia, Xena, Xenea, Xenya, Xinia

Xiang (Chinese) fragrant.

Xiomara (Teutonic) glorious forest.
Xiomaris, Xiomayra

Xiu Mei (Chinese) beautiful plum.

Xochitl (Aztec) place of many flowers.
Xochil, Xochilt, Xochilth, Xochiti

Xuan (Vietnamese) spring.

Xuxa (Portuguese) a familiar form of Susanna.

Xylia (Greek) a form of Sylvia.
Xylina, Xylona

Yachne (Hebrew) hospitable.

Yadira (Hebrew) friend.
Yadirah, Yadirha, Yadyra

Yael (Hebrew) strength of God. See also Jael.
Yaeli, Yaella, Yeala

Yaffa (Hebrew) beautiful. See also Jaffa.
Yafeal, Yaffit, Yafit

Yahaira (Hebrew) a form of Yakira.
Yahara, Yahayra, Yahira

Yajaira (Hebrew) a form of Yakira.
Yahaira, Yajara, Yajayra, Yajhaira

Yakira (Hebrew) precious; dear.
Yahaira, Yajaira

Yalanda (Greek) a form of Yolanda.
Yalando, Yalonda, Ylana, Ylanda

Yalena (Greek, Russian) a form of Helen. See also Lena, Yelena.

Yaletha (American) a form of Oletha.
Yelitsa

Yamary (American) a combination of the prefix Ya + Mary.
Yamairy, Yamarie, Yamaris, Yamayra

Yamelia (American) a form of Amelia.
Yameily, Yamelya, Yamelys

Yamila (Arabic) a form of Jamila.
Yamela, Yamely, Yamil, Yamile, Yamilet, Yamiley, Yamilla, Yamille

Yaminah (Arabic) right, proper.
Yamina, Yamini, Yemina, Yeminah, Yemini

Yamka (Hopi) blossom.

Yamuna (Hindi) sacred river.

Yana (Slavic) a form of Jana.
Yanae, Yanah, Yanay, Yanaye, Yanesi, Yanet, Yaneth, Yaney, Yani, Yanik, Yanina, Yanis, Yanisha, Yanitza, Yanixia, Yanna, Yannah, Yanni, Yannica, Yannick, Yannina

Yanaba (Navajo) brave.

Yaneli (American) a combination of the prefix Ya + Nellie.
Yanela, Yanelis, Yaneliz, Yanelle, Yanelli, Yanely, Yanelys

Yanet (American) a form of Janet.
Yanete, Yaneth, Yanethe, Yanette, Yannet, Yanneth, Yannette

Yáng (Chinese) sun.

Yareli (American) a form of Oralee.
Yarely, Yaresly

Yarina (Slavic) a form of Irene.
Yaryna

Yaritza (American) a combination of Yana + Ritsa.
Yaritsa, Yaritsa

Yarkona (Hebrew) green.

Yarmilla (Slavic) market trader.

Yashira (Afghan) humble; takes it easy. (Arabic) wealthy.

Yasmeen (Persian) a form of Yasmin.
Yasemeen, Yasemin, Yasmeena, Yasmen, Yasmene, Yasmeni, Yasmenne, Yassmeen, Yassmen

Yasmin, Yasmine (Persian) jasmine flower.
Yashmine, Yasiman, Yasimine, Yasma, Yasmain, Yasmaine, Yasmina, Yasminda, Yasmon, Yasmyn, Yazmin, Yesmean, Yesmeen, Yesmin, Yesmina, Yesmine, Yesmyn

Yasu (Japanese) resting, calm.
Yasuko, Yasuyo

Yazmin (Persian) a form of Yasmin.
Yazmeen, Yazmen, Yazmene, Yazmina,
Yazmine, Yazmyn, Yazmyne, Yazzmien,
Yazzmine, Yazzmine, Yazzmyn

Yecenia (Arabic) a form of Yesenia.

Yehudit (Hebrew) a form of Judith.
Yudit, Yudita, Yuta

Yei (Japanese) flourishing.

Yeira (Hebrew) light.

Yekaterina (Russian) a form of
Katherine.

Yelena (Russian) a form of Helen,
Jelena. See also Lena, Yalena.
Yeleana, Yelen, Yelenna, Yelenne, Yelina,
Ylena, Ylenia, Ylenna

Yelisabeta (Russian) a form of
Elizabeth.
Yelizaveta

Yemena (Arabic) from Yemen.
Yemina

Yen (Chinese) yearning; desirous.
Yeni, Yenih, Yenny

Yenene (Native American) shaman.

Yenifer (Welsh) a form of Jennifer.
Yenefer, Yennifer

Yeo (Korean) mild.
Yee

Yepa (Native American) snow girl.

Yesenia (Arabic) flower.
Yasenya, Yecenia, Yesinia, Yesnia, Yessenia

Yesica (Hebrew) a form of Jessica.
Yesika, Yesiko

Yessenia (Arabic) a form of Yesenia.
Yessena, Yessenya, Yissenia

Yessica (Hebrew) a form of Jessica.
Yessika, Yesyka

Yetta (English) a short form of
Henrietta.
Yette, Yitta, Yitty

Yeva (Ukrainian) a form of Eve.

Yiesha (Arabic, Swahili) a form of
Aisha.
Yiasha

Yín (Chinese) silver.

Ynez (Spanish) a form of Agnes. See
also Inez.
Ynes, Ynesita

Yoanna (Hebrew) a form of Joanna.
Yoana, Yohana, Yohanka, Yohanna,
Yohannah

Yocelin, Yocelyn (Latin) forms of
Jocelyn.
Yoceline, Yocelyne, Yuceli

Yoi (Japanese) born in the evening.

Yoki (Hopi) bluebird.
Yokie

Yoko (Japanese) good girl.
Yo

Yolie (Greek) a familiar form of Yolanda.
Yola, Yoley, Yoli, Yoly

Yolanda (Greek) violet flower. See also
Iolanthe, Jolanda, Olinda.
Yalanda, Yolie, Yolaine, Yolana, Yoland,

Yolande, Yolane, Yolanna, Yolantha,
Yolanthe, Yolette, Yolonda, Yorlanda,
Youlanda, Yulanda, Yulonda

Yoluta (Native American) summer
flower.

Yomara (American) a combination of
Yolanda + Tamara.
Yomaira, Yomarie, Yomira

Yon (Burmese) rabbit. (Korean) lotus
blossom.
Yona, Yonna

Yoné (Japanese) wealth; rice.

Yonina (Hebrew) a form of Jonina.
Yona, Yonah

Yonita (Hebrew) a form of Jonita.
Yonat, Yonati, Yonit

Yoomee (Coos) star.
Yoome

Yordana (Basque) descendant. See also
Jordana.

Yori (Japanese) reliable.
Yoriko, Yoriyo

Yoselin (Latin) a form of Jocelyn.
Yoseline, Yoselyn, Yosselin, Yosseline,
Yosselyn

Yosepha (Hebrew) a form of
Josephine.
Yosefa, Yosifa, Yuseffa

Yoshi (Japanese) good; respectful.
Yoshie, Yoshiko, Yoshiyo

Yovela (Hebrew) joyful heart; rejoicer.

Ysabel (Spanish) a form of Isabel.
Ysabell, Ysabella, Ysabelle, Ysbel, Ysbella, Ysobel

Ysanne (American) a combination of Ysabel + Ann.
Ysande, Ysann, Ysanna

Yseult (German) ice rule. (Irish) fair; light skinned. (Welsh) a form of Isolde.
Yseulte, Ysolt

Yuana (Spanish) a form of Juana.
Yuan, Yuanna

Yudelle (English) a form of Udele.
Yudela, Yudell, Yudella

Yudita (Russian) a form of Judith.
Yudit, Yudith, Yuditt

Yuki (Japanese) snow.
Yukie, Yukiko, Yukiyo

Yulene (Basque) a form of Julia.
Yuleen

Yulia (Russian) a form of Julia.
Yula, Yulenka, Yulinka, Yulka, Yulya

Yuliana (Spanish) a form of Juliana.
Yulenia, Yuliani

Yuri (Japanese) lily.
Yuree, Yuriko, Yuriyo

Yvanna (Slavic) a form of Ivana.
Yvan, Yvana, Yvannia

Yvette (French) a familiar form of Yvonne. See also Evette, Ivette.
Yavette, Yevett, Yevette, Yevetta, Yvet, Yveta, Yvett, Yvetta

Yvonne (French) young archer. (Scandinavian) yew wood; bow wood. See also Evonne, Ivonne, Vonna, Vonny, Yvette.
Yavanda, Yavanna, Yavanne, Yavonda, Yavonna, Yavonne, Yveline, Yvon, Yvone, Yvonna, Yvonnah, Yvonnia, Yvonnie, Yvonny

Z

Zabrina (American) a form of Sabrina.
Zabreena, Zabrinia, Zabrinna, Zabryna

Zacharie (Hebrew) God remembered.
Zacari, Zacceaus, Zacchaea, Zachary, Zachoia, Zackaria, Zackeisha, Zackeria, Zakaria, Zakaya, Zakeshia, Zakiah, Zakiria, Zakiya, Zakiyah, Zechari

Zachary (Hebrew) a form of Zacharie.
Zackery, Zakary

Zada (Arabic) fortunate, prosperous.
Zaida, Zayda, Zayeda

Zafina (Arabic) victorious.

Zafirah (Arabic) successful; victorious.

Zahar (Hebrew) daybreak; dawn.
Zahara, Zaharra, Zahera, Zahira, Zahirah, Zeeherah

Zahavah (Hebrew) golden.
Zachava, Zachavah, Zechava, Zechavah, Zehava, Zehavi, Zehavit, Zeheva, Zehuva

Zahra (Swahili) flower. (Arabic) white.
Zahara, Zahraa, Zahrah, Zahreh, Zahria

Zaira (Hebrew) a form of Zara.
Zaire, Zairea, Zirrea

Zakia (Swahili) smart. (Arabic) chaste.
Zakea, Zakeia, Zakiah, Zakiya

Zakira (Hebrew) a form of Zacharie.
Zaakira, Zakiera, Zakierra, Zakir, Zakirah, Zakiria, Zakiriya, Zykarah, Zykera, Zykeria, Zykerria, Zykira, Zykuria

Zakiya (Arabic) a form of Zakia.
Zakeya, Zakeyia, Zakiyaa, Zakiyah, Zakiyya, Zakiyyah, Zakkiyya, Zakkiyyah, Zakkyyah

Zalika (Swahili) born to royalty.
Zuleika

Zaltana (Native American) high mountain.

Zandra (Greek) a form of Sandra.
Zahndra, Zandrea, Zandria, Zandy, Zanndra, Zondra

Zaneta (Spanish) a form of Jane.
Zanita, Zanitra

Zanna (Spanish) a form of Jane. (English) a short form of Susanna.
Zaina, Zainah, Zainna, Zana, Zanae, Zanah, Zanella, Zanette, Zannah, Zannette, Zannia, Zannie

Zanthe (Greek) a form of Xanthe.
Zanth, Zantha

Zara (Hebrew) a form of Sarah, Zora.
Zaira, Zarah, Zarea, Zaree, Zareea, Zareen, Zareena, Zareh, Zareya, Zari, Zaria, Zariya, Zarria

Zarifa (Arabic) successful.

Zarita (Spanish) a form of Sarah.

Zasha (Russian) a form of Sasha.
Zascha, Zashenka, Zashka, Zasho

Zaviera (Spanish) a form of Xaviera.
Zavera, Zavirah

Zawati (Swahili) gift.

Zayit (Hebrew) olive.

Zaynah (Arabic) beautiful.
Zayn, Zayna

Zea (Latin) grain.

Zelda (Yiddish) gray haired. (German) a short form of Griselda. See also Selda.
Zelde, Zella, Zellda

Zelene (English) sunshine.
Zeleen, Zelena, Zeline

Zelia (Spanish) sunshine.
Zele, Zelene, Zelie, Zélie, Zelina

Zelizi (Basque) a form of Sheila.

Zelma (German) a form of Selma.

Zemirah (Hebrew) song of joy.

Zena (Greek) a form of Xenia. (Ethiopian) news. (Persian) woman. See also Zina.
Zanae, Zanah, Zeena, Zeenat, Zeenet, Zeenia, Zeenya, Zein, Zeina, Zenah, Zenana, Zenea, Zenia, Zenna, Zennah, Zennia, Zenya

Zenaida (Greek) white-winged dove.
Zenaide, Zenaïde, Zenayda, Zenochka

Zenda (Persian) sacred; feminine.

Zenobia (Greek) sign, symbol. History: a queen who ruled the city of Palmyra in ancient Syria.
Zeba, Zeeba, Zenobie, Zenovia

Zephania, Zephanie (Greek) forms of Stephanie.
Zepania, Zephanas, Zephany

Zephyr (Greek) west wind.
Zefiryn, Zephra, Zephria, Zephyer, Zephyrine

Zera (Hebrew) seeds.
Zerah, Zeriah

Zerdali (Turkish) wild apricot.

Zerlina (Latin, Spanish) beautiful dawn. Music: a character in Mozart's opera *Don Giovanni*.
Zerla, Zerlinda

Zerrin (Turkish) golden.
Zerren

Zeta (English) rose. Linguistics: a letter in the Greek alphabet.
Zayit, Zetana, Zetta

Zetta (Portuguese) rose.

Zhana, Zhane (Slavic) forms of Jane.
Zhanae, Zhanay, Zhanaya, Zhané, Zhanea, Zhanee, Zhaney, Zhani, Zhaniah, Zhanna

Zhen (Chinese) chaste.

Zia (Latin) grain. (Arabic) light.
Zea

Zigana (Hungarian) gypsy girl. See also Tsigana.
Zigane

Zihna (Hopi) one who spins tops.

Zilla (Hebrew) shadow.
Zila, Zillah, Zylla

Zilpah (Hebrew) dignified. Bible: Jacob's wife.
Zilpha, Zylpha

Zilya (Russian) a form of Theresa.

Zimra (Hebrew) song of praise.
Zamora, Zemira, Zemora, Zimria

Zina (African) secret spirit. (English) hospitable. (Greek) a form of Zena.
Zinah, Zine

Zinnia (Latin) Botany: a plant with beautiful, rayed, colorful flowers.
Zinia, Zinny, Zinnya, Zinya

Zipporah (Hebrew) bird. Bible: Moses' wife.
Zipora, Ziporah, Zipporia, Ziproh

Zita (Spanish) rose. (Arabic) mistress. A short form of names ending in "sita" or "zita."
Zeeta, Zyta, Zytka

Ziva (Hebrew) bright; radiant.
Zeeva, Ziv, Zivanka, Zivi, Zivit

Zizi (Hungarian) a familiar form of Elizabeth.
Zsi Zsi

Zocha (Polish) a form of Sophie.

Zoe (Greek) life.
Zoé, Zoë, Zoee, Zoelie, Zoeline, Zoelle, Zoey, Zoi, Zoie, Zowe, Zowey, Zowie, Zoya

Zoey (Greek) a form of Zoe.
Zooey

Zofia (Slavic) a form of Sophia. See also Sofia.
Zofka, Zsofia

Zohar (Hebrew) shining, brilliant.
Zoheret

Zohra (Hebrew) blossom.

Zohreh (Persian) happy.
Zahreh, Zohrah

Zola (Italian) piece of earth.
Zoela, Zoila

Zona (Latin) belt, sash.
Zonia

Zondra (Greek) a form of Zandra.
Zohndra

Zora (Slavic) aurora; dawn. See also Zara.
Zorah, Zorana, Zoreen, Zoreena, Zorna, Zorra, Zorrah, Zorya

Zorina (Slavic) golden.
Zorana, Zori, Zorie, Zorine, Zorna, Zory

Zoya (Slavic) a form of Zoe.
Zoia, Zoyara, Zoyechka, Zoyenka, Zoyya

Zsa Zsa (Hungarian) a familiar form of Susan.
Zhazha

Zsofia (Hungarian) a form of Sofia.
Zofia, Zsofi, Zsofika

Zsuzsanna (Hungarian) a form of Susanna.
Zsuska, Zsuzsa, Zsuzsi, Zsuzsika, Zsuzska

Zudora (Sanskrit) laborer.

Zuleika (Arabic) brilliant.
Zeleeka, Zul, Zulay, Zulekha, Zuleyka

Zulima (Arabic) a form of Salama.
Zuleima, Zulema, Zulemah, Zulimah

Zurafa (Arabic) lovely.
Ziraf, Zuruf

Zuri (Basque) white; light skinned. (Swahili) beautiful.
Zuria, Zurie, Zurisha, Zury

Zusa (Czech, Polish) a form of Susan.
Zuzana, Zuzanka, Zuzia, Zuzka, Zuzu

Zuwena (Swahili) good.
Zwena

Zytka (Polish) rose.

Boys

Aakash (Hindi) a form of Akash.

Aaron (Hebrew) enlightened. (Arabic) messenger. Bible: the brother of Moses and the first high priest. See also Ron.
Aahron, Aaran, Aaren, Aareon, Aarin, Aaronn, Aarron, Aaryn, Aeron, Aharon, Ahran, Ahren, Aranne, Arek, Aren, Ari, Arin, Aron, Aronek, Aronne, Aronos, Arran, Arron

Aban (Persian) Mythology: a figure associated with water and the arts.

Abasi (Swahili) stern.

Abbey (Hebrew) a familiar form of Abe.
Abey, Abbie, Abby

Abbott (Hebrew) father; abbot.
Ab, Abba, Abbah, Abbán, Abbé, Abbot, Abott

Abbud (Arabic) devoted.

Abdirahman (Arabic) a form of Abdulrahman.
Abdirehman

Abdul (Arabic) servant.
Abdal, Abdeel, Abdel, Abdoul, Abdual, Abdull, Abul

Abdulaziz (Arabic) servant of the Mighty.
Abdelazim, Abdelaziz, Abdulazaz, Abdulazeez

Abdullah (Arabic) servant of Allah.
Abdalah, Abdalla, Abdallah, Abduala, Abdualla, Abduallah, Abdulah, Abdulahi, Abdulha, Abdulla, Abdullahi

Abdulrahman (Arabic) servant of the Merciful.
Abdelrahim, Abdelrahman, Abdirahman, Abdolrahem, Abdularahman, Abdurrahman, Abdurram

Abe (Hebrew) a short form of Abel, Abraham.

Abel (Hebrew) breath. (Assyrian) meadow. (German) a short form of Abelard. Bible: Adam and Eve's second son.
Abe, Abele, Abell, Able, Adal, Avel

Abelard (German) noble; resolute.
Ab, Abalard, Abel, Abelardo, Abelhard, Abilard, Adalard, Adelard

Abi (Turkish) older brother.

Abiah (Hebrew) God is my father.
Abia, Abiel, Abija, Abijah, Abisha, Abishai, Aviya, Aviyah

Abie (Hebrew) a familiar form of Abraham.

Abiel (Hebrew) a form of Abiah.

Abir (Hebrew) strong.

Abisha (Hebrew) gift of God.
Abijah, Abishai

Abner (Hebrew) father of light. Bible: the commander of Saul's army.
Ab, Avner, Ebner

Abraham (Hebrew) father of many nations. Bible: the first Hebrew patriarch. See also Avram, Bram, Ibrahim.
Abarran, Abe, Aberham, Abey, Abhiram, Abie, Abrahaim, Abrahame, Abrahamo, Abrahan, Abrahán, Abraheem, Abrahem, Abrahim, Abrahm, Abram, Abramo, Abrán, Abrao, Arram, Avram

Abrahan (Spanish) a form of Abraham.
Abrahon

Abram (Hebrew) a short form of Abraham. See also Bram.
Abramo, Abrams, Avram

Absalom (Hebrew) father of peace. Bible: the rebellious third son of King David. See also Avshalom, Axel.
Absalaam, Absalon, Abselon, Absolum

Acar (Turkish) bright.

Ace (Latin) unity.
Acer, Acey, Acie

Achilles (Greek) Mythology: a hero of the Trojan War. Literature: the hero of Homer's epic poem *Iliad*.
Achill, Achille, Achillea, Achillios, Akil, Akili, Akilles

Ackerley (English) meadow of oak trees.
Accerley, Ackerlea, Ackerleigh, Ackersley, Acklea, Ackleigh, Ackley, Acklie

Acton (English) oak-tree settlement.

Adahy (Cherokee) in the woods.

Adair (Scottish) oak-tree ford.
Adaire, Adare

Adam (Phoenician) man; mankind. (Hebrew) earth; man of the red earth. Bible: the first man created by God. See also Adamson, Addison, Damek, Keddy, Macadam.
Ad, Adama, Adamec, Adamo, Adão, Adas, Addam, Addams, Addis, Addy, Adem, Adham, Adhamh, Adné, Adok, Adomas

Adamec (Czech) a form of Adam.
Adamek, Adamik, Adamka, Adamko, Adamok

Adamson (Hebrew) son of Adam.
Adams, Adamsson, Addamson

Adan (Irish) a form of Aidan.
Aden, Adian, Adin

Adar (Syrian) ruler; prince. (Hebrew) noble; exalted.
Addar

Adarius (American) a combination of Adam + Darius.
Adareus, Adarias, Adarrius, Adarro, Adarruis, Adaruis, Adauris

Addison (English) son of Adam.
Addis, Addisen, Addisun, Addyson, Adison, Adisson, Adyson

Addy (Hebrew) a familiar form of Adam, Adlai. (German) a familiar form of Adelard.
Addey, Addi, Addie, Ade, Adi

Ade (Yoruba) royal.

Adelard (German) noble; courageous.
Adal, Adalar, Adalard, Addy, Adel, Adél, Adelar

Aden (Arabic) Geography: a region in southern Yemen. (Irish) a form of Aidan, Aiden.

Adham (Arabic) black.

Adil (Arabic) just; wise.
Adeel, Adeele

Adin (Hebrew) pleasant.

Adir (Hebrew) majestic; noble.
Adeer

Adiv (Hebrew) pleasant; gentle.
Adeev

Adlai (Hebrew) my ornament.
Ad, Addy, Adley

Adler (German) eagle.
Ad, Addler, Adlar

Adli (Turkish) just; wise.

Admon (Hebrew) peony.

Adnan (Arabic) pleasant.
Adnaan

Adney (English) noble's island.
Adny

Adolf (German) noble wolf. History: Adolf Hitler's German army was defeated in World War II. See also Dolf.
Ad, Adolfo, Adolfus, Adolph

Adolfo (Spanish) a form of Adolf.
Adolpho

Adolph (German) a form of Adolf.
Adolphe, Adolpho, Adolphus, Adulphus

Adom (Akan) help from God.

Adon (Hebrew) Lord. (Greek) a short form of Adonis.

Adonis (Greek) highly attractive. Mythology: the attractive youth loved by Aphrodite.
Adon, Adonnis, Adonys

Adri (Indo-Pakistani) rock.
Adrey

Adrian (Greek) rich. (Latin) dark. (Swedish) a short form of Hadrian.
Adarian, Ade, Adorjan, Adrain, Adreian, Adreyan, Adri, Adriaan, Adriane, Adriann, Adrianne, Adriano, Adriean, Adrien, Adrik, Adrion, Adrionn, Adrionne, Adron, Adryan, Adryn, Adryon

Adriano (Italian) a form of Adrian.
Adrianno

Adriel (Hebrew) member of God's flock.
Adrial

Adrien (French) a form of Adrian.
Adriene, Adrienne

Adrik (Russian) a form of Adrian.
Adric

Aeneas (Greek) praised. (Scottish) a form of Angus. Literature: the Trojan hero of Vergil's epic poem *Aeneid*. See also Eneas.

Afram (African) Geography: a river in Ghana, Africa.

Afton (English) from Afton, England.
Affton

Agamemnon (Greek) resolute. Mythology: the king of Mycenae who led the Greeks in the Trojan War.

Agni (Hindi) Religion: the Hindu fire god.

Agu (Ibo) leopard.

Agustin (Latin) a form of Augustine. *Agostino, Agoston, Aguistin, Agustine, Agustis, Agusto, Agustus*

Ahab (Hebrew) father's brother. Literature: the captain of the Pequod in Herman Melville's novel *Moby-Dick*.

Ahanu (Native American) laughter.

Ahdik (Native American) caribou; reindeer.

Ahearn (Scottish) lord of the horses. (English) heron. *Ahearne, Aherin, Ahern, Aherne, Hearn*

Ahir (Turkish) last.

Ahmad (Arabic) most highly praised. See also Muhammad. *Achmad, Achmed, Ahamad, Ahamada, Ahamed, Ahmaad, Ahmaud, Amad, Amahd, Amed*

Ahmed (Swahili) praiseworthy.

Ahsan (Arabic) charitable.

Aidan (Irish) fiery. *Adan, Aden, Aiden, Aydan, Ayden, Aydin*

Aiden, Ayden (Irish) a form of Aidan. *Aden, Aidon, Aidyn, Aydean*

Aiken (English) made of oak. *Aicken, Aikin, Ayken, Aykin*

Aimery (French) a form of Emery. *Aime, Aimerey, Aimeric, Amerey, Aymeric, Aymery*

Aimon (French) house. (Irish) a form of Eamon.

Aindrea (Irish) a form of Andrew. *Aindreas*

Ainsley (Scottish) my own meadow. *Ainsleigh, Ainslie, Ansley, Aynslee, Aynsley, Aynslie*

Aizik (Russian) a form of Isaac.

Ajala (Yoruba) potter.

Ajay (Punjabi) victorious; undefeatable. (American) a combination of the initials A. + J. *Aj, Aja, Ajae, Ajai, Ajaye, Ajaz, Ajé, Ajee, Ajit*

Ajit (Sanskrit) unconquerable. *Ajeet, Ajith*

Akar (Turkish) flowing stream. *Akara*

Akash (Hindi) sky. *Aakash, Akasha, Akshay*

Akbar (Arabic) great.

Akecheta (Sioux) warrior.

Akeem, Akim (Hebrew) short forms of Joachim. *Achim, Ackeem, Ackim, Ahkieme, Akeam, Akee, Akiem, Akima, Arkeem*

Akemi (Japanese) dawn.

Akil (Arabic) intelligent. (Greek) a form of Achilles. *Ahkeel, Akeel, Akeil, Akeyla, Akhil, Akiel, Akila, Akilah, Akile, Akili*

Akins (Yoruba) brave.

Akira (Japanese) intelligent. *Akihito, Akio, Akiyo*

Akiva (Hebrew) a form of Jacob. *Akiba, Kiva*

Akmal (Arabic) perfect.

Aksel (Norwegian) father of peace. *Aksell*

Akshay (American) a form of Akash. *Akshaj, Akshaya*

Akshat (Sanskrit) uninjurable.

Akule (Native American) he looks up.

Al (Irish) a short form of Alan, Albert, Alexander.

Aladdin (Arabic) height of faith. Literature: the hero of a story in the *Arabian Nights*. *Ala, Alaa, Alaaddin, Aladean, Aladin, Aladino*

Alain (French) a form of Alan. *Alaen, Alainn, Alayn, Allain*

Alaire (French) joyful.

Alam (Arabic) universe.

Alan (Irish) handsome; peaceful. *Ailan, Ailin, Al, Alaan, Alain, Alair, Aland, Alande, Alando, Alani, Alann, Alano, Alanson, Alante, Alao, Allan, Allen, Alon, Alun*

Alaric (German) ruler of all. See also Ulrich.
Alarick, Alarico, Alarik, Aleric, Allaric, Allarick, Alric, Alrick, Alrik

Alastair (Scottish) a form of Alexander.
Alaisdair, Alaistair, Alaister, Alasdair, Alasteir, Alaster, Alastor, Aleister, Alester, Alistair, Allaistar, Allastair, Allaster, Allastir, Allysdair, Alystair

Alban (Latin) from Alba, Italy.
Albain, Albany, Albean, Albein, Alby, Auban, Auben

Albern (German) noble; courageous.

Albert (German, French) noble and bright. See also Elbert, Ulbrecht.
Adelbert, Ailbert, Al, Albertik, Alberto, Alberts, Albie, Albrecht, Alby, Alvertos, Aubert

Alberto (Italian) a form of Albert.
Berto

Albie, Alby (German, French) familiar forms of Albert.
Albee, Albi

Albin (Latin) a form of Alvin.
Alben, Albeno, Albinek, Albino, Albins, Albinson, Alby, Auben

Albion (Latin) white cliffs. Geography: a reference to the white cliffs in Dover, England.

Alcandor (Greek) manly; strong.

Alcott (English) old cottage.
Alcot, Alkot, Alkott, Allcot, Allcott, Allkot, Allkott

Aldair (German, English) a form of Alder.
Aldahir, Aldayr

Alden (English) old; wise protector.
Aldan, Aldean, Aldin, Aldous, Elden

Alder (German, English) alder tree.
Aldair

Aldo (Italian) old; elder. (German) a short form of Aldous.

Aldous (German) a form of Alden.
Aldis, Aldo, Aldon, Aldus, Elden

Aldred (English) old; wise counselor.
Alldred, Eldred

Aldrich (English) wise.
Aldric, Aldrick, Aldridge, Aldrige, Aldritch, Alldric, Alldrich, Alldrick, Alldridge, Eldridge

Aldwin (English) old friend.
Aldwyn, Eldwin

Alec, Alek (Greek) short forms of Alexander.
Aleck, Alekko, Elek

Alejándro (Spanish) a form of Alexander.
Alejándra, Aléjo, Alexjándro

Aleksandar, Aleksander (Greek) forms of Alexander.
Aleksandor, Aleksandr, Aleksandras, Aleksandur

Aleksei (Russian) a short form of Alexander.
Aleks, Aleksey, Aleksi, Aleksis, Aleksy, Alexei, Alexey

Alekzander, Alexzander (Greek) forms of Alexander.
Alekxander, Alekxzander, Alexkzandr, Alexzandr, Alexzandyr

Alem (Arabic) wise.

Aleric (German) a form of Alaric.
Alerick, Alleric, Allerick

Aleron (Latin) winged.

Alessandro (Italian) a form of Alexander.
Alessand, Allessandro

Alex (Greek) a short form of Alexander.
Alax, Alix, Allax, Allex, Elek

Alexander (Greek) defender of mankind. History: Alexander the Great was the conqueror of the civilized world. See also Alastair, Alistair, Iskander, Jando, Leks, Lex, Lexus, Macallister, Oleksandr, Olés, Sander, Sándor, Sandro, Sandy, Sasha, Xan, Xander, Zander, Zindel.
Al, Alec, Alecsandar, Alejándro, Alek, Alekos, Aleksandar, Aleksander, Aleksei, Alekzander, Alessandro, Alex, Alexandar, Alexandor, Alexandr, Alexandre, Alexandro, Alexandros, Alexi, Alexis, Alexxander, Alexzander, Alic, Alick, Alisander, Alixander

Alexandre (French) a form of Alexander.

Alexandro (Greek) a form of Alexander.
Alexandras, Alexandros, Alexandru

Alexi (Russian) a form of Aleksei. (Greek) a short form of Alexander.
Alexe, Alexee, Alexey, Alexie, Alexio, Alexy

Alexis (Greek) a short form of Alexander.
Alexei, Alexes, Alexey, Alexios, Alexius, Alexiz, Alexsis, Alexsus, Alexus

Alfie (English) a familiar form of Alfred.
Alfy

Alfonso (Italian, Spanish) a form of Alphonse.
Affonso, Alfons, Alfonse, Alfonsus, Alfonza, Alfonzo, Alfonzus

Alford (English) old river ford.

Alfred (English) elf counselor; wise counselor. See also Fred.
Ailfrid, Ailfryd, Alf, Alfeo, Alfie, Alfredo, Alured

Alfredo (Italian, Spanish) a form of Alfred.
Alfrido

Alger (German) noble spearman. (English) a short form of Algernon. See also Elger.
Algar, Allgar

Algernon (English) bearded, wearing a moustache.
Algenon, Alger, Algie, Algin, Algon

Algie (English) a familiar form of Algernon.
Algee, Algia, Algy

Algis (German) spear.

Ali (Arabic) greatest. (Swahili) exalted.
Aly

Alic (Greek) a short form of Alexander.
Alick, Aliek, Alik, Aliko

Alim (Arabic) scholar. (Arabic) a form of Alem.

Alisander (Greek) a form of Alexander.
Alissander, Alissandre, Alsandair, Alsandare, Alsander

Alistair (English) a form of Alexander.
Alisdair, Alistaire, Alistar, Alister, Allistair, Allistar, Allister, Allistir, Alstair

Alixander (Greek) a form of Alexander.
Alixandre, Alixandru, Alixzander

Allan (Irish) a form of Alan.
Allayne

Allard (English) noble, brave.
Alard, Ellard

Allen (Irish) a form of Alan.
Alen, Alley, Alleyn, Alleyne, Allie, Allin, Allon, Allyn

Almon (Hebrew) widower.

Alois (German) a short form of Aloysius.
Aloys

Aloisio (Spanish) a form of Louis.

Alok (Sanskrit) victorious cry.

Alon (Hebrew) oak.

Alonso, Alonzo (Spanish) forms of Alphonse.
Alano, Alanzo, Alon, Alonza, Elonzo, Lon, Lonnie, Lonso, Lonzo

Aloysius (German) a form of Louis.
Alaois, Alois, Aloisius, Aloisio

Alphonse (German) noble and eager.
Alf, Alfie, Alfonso, Alonzo, Alphons, Alphonsa, Alphonso, Alphonsus, Alphonza, Alphonzus, Fonzie

Alphonso (Italian) a form of Alphonse.
Alphanso, Alphonzo, Fonso

Alpin (Irish) attractive.
Alpine

Alroy (Spanish) king.

Alston (English) noble's settlement.
Allston, Alstun

Altair (Greek) star. (Arabic) flying.

Altman (German) old man.
Altmann, Atman

Alton (English) old town.
Alten

Alva (Hebrew) sublime.
Alvah

Alvan (German) a form of Alvin.
Alvand

Alvar (English) army of elves.
Alvara

Alvaro (Spanish) just; wise.

Alvern (Latin) spring.
Elvern

Alvin (Latin) white; light skinned. (German) friend to all; noble friend; friend of elves. See also Albin, Elvin.
Aloin, Aluin, Aluino, Alvan, Alven, Alvie, Alvino, Alvy, Alvyn, Alwin, Elwin

Alvis (Scandinavian) all-knowing.

Alwin (German) a form of Alvin.
Ailwyn, Alwyn, Alwynn, Aylwin

Amadeo (Italian) a form of Amadeus.

Amadeus (Latin) loves God. Music:
Wolfgang Amadeus Mozart was a
famous eighteenth-century Austrian
composer.
*Amad, Amadeaus, Amadée, Amadeo,
Amadei, Amadio, Amadis, Amado,
Amador, Amadou, Amando, Amedeo,
Amodaos*

Amal (Hebrew) worker. (Arabic)
hopeful.

Amandeep (Punjabi) light of peace.
Amandip, Amanjit, Amanjot, Amanpreet

Amando (French) a form of Amadeus.
Amand, Amandio, Amaniel, Amato

Amani (Arabic) believer. (Yoruba)
strength; builder.
Amanee

Amar (Punjabi) immortal. (Arabic)
builder.
*Amare, Amaree, Amari, Amario, Amaris,
Amarjit, Amaro, Amarpreet, Amarri,
Ammar, Ammer*

Amato (French) loved.
Amatto

Ambar (Sanskrit) sky.
Amber

Ambrose (Greek) immortal.
*Ambie, Ambroise, Ambros, Ambrosi,
Ambrosio, Ambrosius, Ambrus, Amby*

Ameer (Hebrew) a form of Amir.
Ameir, Amer, Amere

Amerigo (Teutonic) industrious.
History: Amerigo Vespucci was the
Italian explorer for whom America is
named.
Americo, Americus

Ames (French) friend.

Amicus (English, Latin) beloved
friend.
Amico

Amiel (Hebrew) God of my people.
Ammiel

Amin (Hebrew, Arabic) trustworthy;
honest. (Hindi) faithful.
Amine

Amir (Hebrew) proclaimed. (Punjabi)
wealthy; king's minister. (Arabic)
prince.
Aamer, Aamir, Ameer, Amire, Amiri

Amish (Sanskrit) honest.

Amit (Punjabi) unfriendly. (Arabic)
highly praised.
Amitan, Amreet

Ammon (Egyptian) hidden.
Mythology: the ancient god associ-
ated with reproduction.
Amman

Amol (Hindi) priceless, valuable.
Amul

Amon (Hebrew) trustworthy; faithful.

Amory (German) a form of Emory.
Amery, Amor

Amos (Hebrew) burdened, troubled.
Bible: an Old Testament prophet.
Amose

Amram (Hebrew) mighty nation.
Amarien, Amran, Amren

Amrit (Sanskrit) nectar. (Punjabi,
Arabic) a form of Amit.

An (Chinese, Vietnamese) peaceful.
Ana

Anand (Hindi) blissful.
Ananda, Anant, Ananth

Anastasius (Greek) resurrection.
*Anas, Anastacio, Anastacios, Anastagio,
Anastas, Anastase, Anastasi, Anastasio,
Anastasios, Anastice, Anastisis, Anaztáz,
Athanasius*

Anatole (Greek) east.
*Anatol, Anatoley, Anatoli, Anatolijus,
Anatolio, Anatoliy, Anatoly, Anitoly*

Anchali (Taos) painter.

Anders (Swedish) a form of Andrew.
Ander

Anderson (Swedish) son of Andrew.
Andersen

Andonios (Greek) a form of Anthony.
Andoni, Andonis, Andonny

Andor (Hungarian) a form of Andrew.

András (Hungarian) a form of
Andrew.
*Andraes, Andri, Andris, Andrius, Andriy,
Aundras, Aundreas*

Andre, André (French) forms of Andrew.
Andra, Andrae, Andrecito, Andree, Andrei, Aundre, Aundré

Andrea (Greek) a form of Andrew.
Andrean, Andreani, Andrian

Andreas (Greek) a form of Andrew.
Andres, Andries

Andrei (Bulgarian, Romanian, Russian) a form of Andrew.
Andreian, Andrej, Andrey, Andreyan, Andrie, Aundrei

Andres (Spanish) a form of Andrew.
Andras, Andrés, Andrez

Andrew (Greek) strong; manly; courageous. Bible: one of the Twelve Apostles. See also Bandi, Drew, Endre, Evangelos, Kendrew, Ondro.
Aindrea, Anders, Andery, Andonis, Andor, András, Andre, André, Andrea, Andreas, Andrei, Andres, Andrews, Andru, Andrue, Andrus, Andy, Anker, Anndra, Antal, Audrew

Andros (Polish) sea. Mythology: the god of the sea.
Andris, Andrius, Andrus

Andy (Greek) a short form of Andrew.
Andino, Andis, Andje

Aneurin (Welsh) honorable; gold. See also Nye.
Aneirin

Anfernee (Greek) a form of Anthony.
Anferney, Anfernie, Anferny, Anfranee, Anfrene, Anfrenee, Anpherne

Angel (Greek) angel. (Latin) messenger. See also Gotzon.
Ange, Angell, Angelo, Angie, Angy

Angelo (Italian) a form of Angel.
Angeleo, Angelito, Angello, Angelos, Anglo

Angus (Scottish) exceptional; outstanding. Mythology: Angus Og was the Celtic god of youth, love, and beauty. See also Ennis, Gus.
Aeneas, Aonghas

Anh (Vietnamese) peace; safety.

Anibal (Phoenician) a form of Hannibal.

Anil (Hindi) wind god.
Aneel, Anel, Aniel, Aniello

Anka (Turkish) phoenix.

Anker (Danish) a form of Andrew.
Ankur

Annan (Scottish) brook. (Swahili) fourth-born son.

Annas (Greek) gift from God.
Anis, Anish, Anna, Annais

Anno (German) a familiar form of Johann.

Anoki (Native American) actor.

Ansel (French) follower of a nobleman.
Ancell, Ansa, Ansell

Anselm (German) divine protector. See also Elmo.
Anse, Anselme, Anselmi, Anselmo

Ansis (Latvian) a form of Janis.

Ansley (Scottish) a form of Ainsley.
Anslea, Anslee, Ansleigh, Anslie, Ansly, Ansy

Anson (German) divine. (English) Anne's son.
Ansun

Antal (Hungarian) a form of Anthony.
Antek, Anti, Antos

Antares (Greek) giant, red star. Astronomy: the brightest star in the constellation Scorpio.
Antar, Antario, Antarious, Antarius, Antarr, Antarus

Antavas (Lithuanian) a form of Anthony.
Antae, Antaeus, Antavious, Antavius, Ante, Anteo

Anthany (Latin, Greek) a form of Anthony.
Antanee, Antanie, Antenee, Anthan, Antheny, Anthine, Anthney

Anthonie (Latin, Greek) a form of Anthony.
Anthone, Anthonee, Anthoni, Anthonia

Anthony (Latin) praiseworthy. (Greek) flourishing. See also Tony.
Anathony, Andonios, Andor, András, Anothony, Antal, Antavas, Anfernee, Anthany, Anthawn, Anthey, Anthian, Anthino, Anthone, Anthoney, Anthonie, Anthonio, Anthonu, Anthonysha, Anthoy, Anthyoine, Anthyonny, Antione, Antjuan, Antoine, Anton, Antonio, Antony, Antwan, Antwon

Antione (French) a form of Anthony.
Antion, Antionio, Antionne, Antiono

Antjuan (Spanish) a form of Anthony.
Antajuan, Anthjuan, Antuan, Antuane

Antoan (Vietnamese) safe, secure.

Antoine (French) a form of Anthony.
Anntoin, Anthoine, Antoiné, Antoinne, Atoine

Anton (Slavic) a form of Anthony.
Anthon, Antone, Antonn, Antonne, Antons, Antos

Antonio (Italian) a form of Anthony. See also Tino, Tonio.
Anthonio, Antinio, Antoinio, Antoino, Antonello, Antoneo, Antonin, Antonín, Antonino, Antonnio, Antonios, Antonius, Antonyia, Antonyio, Antonyo

Antony (Latin) a form of Anthony.
Antin, Antini, Antius, Antoney, Antoni, Antonie, Antonin, Antonios, Antonius, Antonyia, Antonyio, Antonyo, Anty

Antti (Finnish) manly.
Anthey, Anthi, Anti

Antwan (Arabic) a form of Anthony.
Antaw, Antawan, Antawn, Anthawn, Antowan, Antowaun, Antowine, Antowne, Antowyn, Antuwan, Antwain, Antwaina, Antwaine, Antwainn, Antwaion, Antwane, Antwann, Antwanne, Antwarn, Antwaun, Antwen, Antwian, Antwine, Antwuan, Antwun, Antwyné

Antwon (Arabic) a form of Anthony.
Antown, Antuwon, Antwion, Antwione, Antwoan, Antwoin, Antwoine, Antwone, Antwonn, Antwonne, Antwoun,

Antwyon, Antwyone, Antyon, Antyonne, Antywon

Anwar (Arabic) luminous.
Anour, Anouar, Anwi

Apiatan (Kiowa) wooden lance.

Apollo (Greek) manly. Mythology: the god of prophecy, healing, music, poetry, and light. See also Polo.
Apolinar, Apolinario, Apollos, Apolo, Apolonio, Appollo

Aquila (Latin, Spanish) eagle.
Acquilla, Aquil, Aquilas, Aquileo, Aquiles, Aquilino, Aquilla, Aquille, Aquillino

Araldo (Spanish) a form of Harold.
Aralodo, Aralt, Aroldo, Arry

Aram (Syrian) high, exalted.
Ara, Aramia, Arra, Arram

Aramis (French) Literature: one of the title characters in Alexandre Dumas's novel *The Three Musketeers*.
Airamis, Aramith, Aramys

Aran (Tai) forest. (Danish) a form of Aren. (Hebrew, Scottish) a form of Arran.

Archer (English) bowman.
Archie

Archibald (German) bold. See also Arkady.
Arch, Archaimbaud, Archambault, Archibaldo, Archibold, Archie

Archie (German, English) a familiar form of Archer, Archibald.
Archy

Ardal (Irish) a form of Arnold.
Ardale

Ardell (Latin) eager; industrious.
Ardel

Arden (Latin) ardent; fiery.
Ard, Ardan, Ardene, Ardian, Ardie, Ardin, Ardn, Arduino

Ardon (Hebrew) bronzed.

Aren (Danish) eagle; ruler. (Hebrew, Arabic) a form of Aaron.

Aretino (Greek, Italian) victorious.

Argus (Danish) watchful, vigilant.
Agos

Ari (Hebrew) a short form of Ariel. (Greek) a short form of Aristotle.
Aria, Arias, Arie, Arieh, Arih, Arij, Ario, Arri, Ary, Arye

Arian (Greek) a form of Arion.
Ariana, Ariane, Ariann, Arianne, Arrian, Aryan

Aric (German) a form of Richard. (Scandinavian) a form of Eric.
Aaric, Arec, Areck, Arich, Arick, Ariek, Arik, Arrek, Arric, Arrick, Arrik, Aryk

Ariel (Hebrew) lion of God. Bible: another name for Jerusalem. Literature: the name of a sprite in the Shakespearean play *The Tempest*.
Airel, Arel, Areli, Ari, Ariell, Ariya, Ariyel, Arrial, Arriel

Aries (Latin) ram. Astrology: the first sign of the zodiac.
Ares, Arie, Ariez

Arif (Arabic) knowledgeable.
Areef

Arion (Greek) enchanted. (Hebrew) melodious.
Arian, Arien, Ario, Arione, Aryon

Aristides (Greek) son of the best.
Aris, Aristedes, Aristeed, Aristide, Aristides, Aristidis

Aristotle (Greek) best; wise. History: a third-century B.C. philosopher who tutored Alexander the Great.
Ari, Aris, Aristito, Aristo, Aristokles, Aristotelis

Arjun (Hindi) white; milk colored.
Arjen, Arjin, Arju, Arjuna, Arjune

Arkady (Russian) a form of Archibald.
Arcadio, Arkadi, Arkadij, Arkadiy

Arkin (Norwegian) son of the eternal king.
Aricin, Arkeen, Arkyn

Arledge (English) lake with the hares.
Arlidge, Arlledge

Arlen (Irish) pledge.
Arlan, Arland, Arlend, Arlin, Arlinn, Arlyn, Arlynn

Arley (English) a short form of Harley.
Arleigh, Arlie, Arly

Arlo (Spanish) barberry. (English) fortified hill. A form of Harlow. (German) a form of Charles.

Arman (Persian) desire, goal.
Armaan, Armahn, Armaine

Armand (Latin, German) a form of Herman. See also Mandek.
Armad, Arman, Armanda, Armando, Armands, Armanno, Armaude, Armenta, Armond

Armando (Spanish) a form of Armand.
Armondo

Armani (Hungarian) sly. (Hebrew) a form of Armon.
Arman, Armann, Armoni, Armonie, Armonio, Armonni, Armony

Armon (Hebrew) high fortress, stronghold.
Armani, Armen, Armin, Armino, Armonn, Armons

Armstrong (English) strong arm. History: astronaut Neil Armstrong was the commander of Apollo 11 and the first person to walk on the moon.

Arnaud (French) a form of Arnold.
Arnauld, Arnault, Arnoll

Arne (German) a form of Arnold.
Arna, Arnay, Arnel, Arnele, Arnell, Arnelle

Arnette (English) little eagle.
Arnat, Arnet, Arnett, Arnetta, Arnot, Arnott

Arnie (German) a familiar form of Arnold.
Arney, Arni, Arnny, Arny

Arno (German) a short form of Arnold. (Czech) a short form of Ernest.
Arnou, Arnoux

Arnold (German) eagle ruler.
Ardal, Arnald, Arnaldo, Arnaud, Arne, Arnie, Arno, Arnol, Arnoldas, Arnoldo, Arnoll, Arndt, Arnulfo

Arnon (Hebrew) rushing river.
Arnan

Arnulfo (German) a form of Arnold.

Aron, Arron (Hebrew) forms of Aaron. (Danish) forms of Aren.
Arrion

Aroon (Tai) dawn.

Arran (Scottish) island dweller. Geography: an island off the west coast of Scotland. (Hebrew) a form of Aaron.
Arren, Arrin, Arryn, Aryn

Arrigo (Italian) a form of Harry.
Alrigo, Arrighetto

Arrio (Spanish) warlike.
Ario, Arrow, Arryo, Aryo

Arsenio (Greek) masculine; virile. History: Saint Arsenius was a teacher in the Roman Empire.
Arsen, Arsène, Arsenius, Arseny, Arsinio

Arsha (Persian) venerable.

Art (English) a short form of Arthur.

Artemus (Greek) gift of Artemis. Mythology: Artemis was the goddess of the hunt and the moon.
Artemas, Artemio, Artemis, Artimas, Artimis, Artimus

Arthur (Irish) noble; lofty hill. (Scottish) bear. (English) rock. (Icelandic) follower of Thor. See also Turi.
Art, Artair, Artek, Arth, Arther, Arthor, Artie, Artor, Arturo, Artus, Aurthar, Aurther, Aurthur

Artie (English) a familiar form of Arthur.
Arte, Artian, Artis, Arty, Atty

Arturo (Italian) a form of Arthur.
Arthuro, Artur

Arun (Cambodian, Hindi) sun.
Aruns

Arundel (English) eagle valley.

Arve (Norwegian) heir, inheritor.

Arvel (Welsh) wept over.
Arval, Arvell, Arvelle

Arvid (Hebrew) wanderer. (Norwegian) eagle tree. See also Ravid.
Arv, Arvad, Arve, Arvie, Arvind, Arvinder, Arvydas

Arvin (German) friend of the people; friend of the army.
Arv, Arvie, Arvind, Arvinder, Arvon, Arvy

Aryeh (Hebrew) lion.

Asa (Hebrew) physician, healer. (Yoruba) falcon.
Asaa, Ase

Asád (Arabic) lion.
Asaad, Asad, Asid, Assad, Azad

Asadel (Arabic) prosperous.
Asadour, Asadul, Asael

Ascot (English) eastern cottage; style of necktie. Geography: a village near London and the site of the Royal Ascot horseraces.

Asgard (Scandinavian) court of the gods.

Ash (Hebrew) ash tree.
Ashby

Ashanti (Swahili) from a tribe in West Africa.
Ashan, Ashani, Ashante, Ashantee, Ashaunte

Ashby (Scandinavian) ash-tree farm. (Hebrew) a form of Ash.
Ashbey

Asher (Hebrew) happy; blessed.
Ashar, Ashor, Ashur

Ashford (English) ash-tree ford.
Ash, Ashtin

Ashley (English) ash-tree meadow.
Ash, Asheley, Ashelie, Ashely, Ashlan, Ashlee, Ashleigh, Ashlen, Ashlie, Ashlin, Ashling, Ashlinn, Ashlone, Ashly, Ashlyn, Ashlynn, Aslan

Ashon (Swahili) seventh-born son.

Ashton (English) ash-tree settlement.
Ashtan, Ashten, Ashtian, Ashtin, Ashtion, Ashtonn, Ashtun, Ashtyn

Ashur (Swahili) Mythology: the principal Assyrian deity.

Ashwani (Hindi) first. Religion: the first of the twenty-seven galaxies revolving around the moon.
Ashwan

Ashwin (Hindi) star.

Asiel (Hebrew) created by God.

Asker (Turkish) soldier.

Aspen (English) aspen tree.

Aston (English) eastern town.
Asten, Astin

Aswad (Arabic) dark skinned, black.

Ata (Fante) twin.

Atek (Polish) a form of Tanek.

Athan (Greek) immortal.

Atherton (English) town by a spring.

Atid (Tai) sun.

Atif (Arabic) caring.
Ateef, Atef

Atlas (Greek) lifted; carried. Mythology: Atlas was forced by Zeus to carry the heavens on his shoulders as a punishment for his share of the war of the Titans.

Atley (English) meadow.
Atlea, Atlee, Atleigh, Atli, Attley

Attila (Gothic) little father. History: the Hun leader who invaded the Roman Empire.
Atalik, Atila, Atilio, Atilla, Atiya, Attal, Attilio

Atwater (English) at the water's edge.

Atwell (English) at the well.

Atwood (English) at the forest.

Atworth (English) at the farmstead.

Auberon (German) a form of Oberon.
Auberron, Aubrey

Aubrey (German) noble; bearlike. (French) a familiar form of Auberon. See also Avery.
Aubary, Aube, Aubery, Aubie, Aubré, Aubree, Aubreii, Aubrie, Aubry, Aubury

Auburn (Latin) reddish brown.

Auden (English) old friend.

Audie (German) noble; strong. (English) a familiar form of Edward.
Audi, Audiel, Audley, Audy

Audon (French) old; rich.
Audelon

Audrey (English) noble strength.
Audra, Audre, Audrea, Audrius, Audry

Audric (English) wise ruler.
Audrick, Audrik

Audun (Scandinavian) deserted, desolate.

Augie (Latin) a familiar form of August.
Auggie, Augy

August (Latin) a short form of Augustine, Augustus.
Agosto, Augie, Auguste, Augusto

Augustine (Latin) majestic. Religion: Saint Augustine was the first archbishop of Canterbury. See also Austin, Gus, Tino.
August, Agustin, Augustin, Augustinas, Augustino, Austen, Austin, Auston, Austyn

Augustus (Latin) majestic; venerable. History: an honorary title given to the first Roman emperor, Octavius Caesar.
August

Aukai (Hawaiian) seafarer.

Aundre (Greek) a form of Andre.
Aundrae, Aundray, Aundrea, Aundrey, Aundry

Aurek (Polish) golden haired.

Aurelio (Latin) a short form of Aurelius.
Aurel, Aurele, Aureli, Aurellio

Aurelius (Latin) golden. History: Marcus Aurelius was a second-century A.D. philosopher and emperor of Rome.
Arelian, Areliano, Aurèle, Aureliano, Aurelien, Aurélien, Aurelio, Aurey, Auriel, Aury

Aurick (German) protecting ruler.
Auric

Austen, Auston, Austyn (Latin) short forms of Augustine.
Austan, Austun, Austyne

Austin (Latin) a short form of Augustine.
Astin, Austine, Oistin, Ostin

Avel (Greek) breath.

Avent (French) born during Advent.
Aventin, Aventino

Averill (French) born in April.
Ave, Averel, Averell, Averiel, Averil, Averyl, Averyll, Avrel, Avrell, Avrill, Avryll

Avery (English) a form of Aubrey.
Avary, Aveary, Avere, Averee, Averey, Averi, Averie, Avrey, Avry

Avi (Hebrew) God is my father.
Avian, Avidan, Avidor, Aviel, Avion

Aviv (Hebrew) youth; springtime.

Avner (Hebrew) a form of Abner.
Avneet, Avniel

Avram (Hebrew) a form of Abraham, Abram.
Arram, Avraam, Avraham, Avrahom, Avrohom, Avrom, Avrum

Avshalom (Hebrew) father of peace. See also Absalom.
Avsalom

Awan (Native American) somebody.

Axel (Latin) axe. (German) small oak tree; source of life. (Scandinavian) a form of Absalom.
Aksel, Ax, Axe, Axell, Axil, Axill, Axl, Axle, Axyle

Aydin (Turkish) intelligent.

Ayers (English) heir to a fortune.

Ayinde (Yoruba) we gave praise and he came.

Aylmer (English) a form of Elmer.
Aillmer, Ailmer, Allmer, Ayllmer

Aymil (Greek) a form of Emil.

Aymon (French) a form of Raymond.

Ayo (Yoruba) happiness.

Azad (Turkish) free.

Azeem (Arabic) a form of Azim.
Aseem, Asim

Azi (Nigerian) youth.

Azim (Arabic) defender.
Azeem

Aziz (Arabic) strong.

Azizi (Swahili) precious.

Azriel (Hebrew) God is my aid.

Azuriah (Hebrew) aided by God.
Azaria, Azariah, Azuria

Baden (German) bather.
Baeden, Bayden, Baydon

Bahir (Arabic) brilliant, dazzling.

Bahram (Persian) ancient king.

Bailey (French) bailiff, steward.
*Bail, Bailee, Bailie, Bailio, Baillie, Baily,
Bailye, Baley, Bayley*

Bain (Irish) a short form of
Bainbridge.
Baine, Bayne, Baynn

Bainbridge (Irish) fair bridge.
Bain, Baynbridge, Bayne, Baynebridge

Baird (Irish) traveling minstrel, bard;
poet.
Bairde, Bard

Bakari (Swahili) noble promise.
Bacari, Baccari, Bakarie

Baker (English) baker. See also Baxter.
Bakir, Bakory, Bakr

Bal (Sanskrit) child born with lots of
hair.

Balasi (Basque) flat footed.

Balbo (Latin) stammerer.
Bailby, Balbi, Ballbo

Baldemar (German) bold; famous.
Baldemer, Baldomero, Baumar, Baumer

Balder (Scandinavian) bald.
Mythology: the Norse god of light,
summer, purity, and innocence.
Baldier, Baldur, Baudier

Baldric (German) brave ruler.
Baldrick, Baudric

Baldwin (German) bold friend.
*Bald, Baldovino, Balduin, Baldwinn,
Baldwyn, Baldwynn, Balldwin, Baudoin*

Balfour (Scottish) pastureland.
Balfor, Balfore

Balin (Hindi) mighty soldier.
Bali, Baylen, Baylin, Baylon, Valin

Ballard (German) brave; strong.
Balard

Balraj (Hindi) strongest.

Baltazar (Greek) a form of Balthasar.
Baltasar

Balthasar (Greek) God save the king.
Bible: one of the three wise men
who bore gifts for the infant Jesus.
*Badassare, Baldassare, Baltazar,
Balthasaar, Balthazar, Balthazzar,
Baltsaros, Belshazar, Belshazzar,
Boldizsár*

Bancroft (English) bean field.
*Ban, Bancrofft, Bank, Bankroft, Banky,
Binky*

Bandi (Hungarian) a form of Andrew.
Bandit

Bane (Hawaiian) a form of
Bartholomew.

Banner (Scottish, English) flag bearer.
Bannor, Banny

Banning (Irish) small and fair.
Bannie, Banny

Barak (Hebrew) lightning bolt. Bible:
the valiant warrior who helped
Deborah.
Barrak

Baran (Russian) ram.
Baren

Barasa (Kikuyu) meeting place.

Barclay (Scottish, English) birch-tree
meadow.
*Bar, Barcley, Barklay, Barkley, Barklie,
Barrclay, Berkeley*

Bard (Irish) a form of Baird.
Bar, Barde, Bardia, Bardiya, Barr

Bardolf (German) bright wolf.
*Bardo, Bardolph, Bardou, Bardoul,
Bardulf, Bardulph*

Bardrick (Teutonic) axe ruler.
Bardric, Bardrik

Baris (Turkish) peaceful.

Barker (English) lumberjack; advertiser
at a carnival.

Barlow (English) bare hillside.
Barlowe, Barrlow, Barrlowe

Barnabas (Greek, Hebrew, Aramaic, Latin) son of the missionary. Bible: Christian apostle and companion of Paul on his first missionary journey.
Bane, Barna, Barnaba, Barnabus, Barnaby, Barnebas, Barnebus, Barney

Barnaby (English) a form of Barnabas.
Barnabe, Barnabé, Barnabee, Barnabey, Barnabi, Barnabie, Bernabé, Burnaby

Barnard (French) a form of Bernard.
Barn, Barnard, Barnhard, Barnhardo

Barnes (English) bear; son of Barnett.

Barnett (English) nobleman; leader.
Barn, Barnet, Barney, Baronet, Baronett, Barrie, Barron, Barry

Barney (English) a familiar form of Barnabas, Barnett.
Barnie, Barny

Barnum (German) barn; storage place. (English) baron's home.
Barnham

Baron (German, English) nobleman, baron.
Baaron, Barion, Baronie, Barrin, Barrion, Barron, Baryn, Bayron, Berron

Barrett (German) strong as a bear.
Bar, Baret, Barrat, Barret, Barretta, Barrette, Barry, Berrett, Berrit

Barric (English) grain farm.
Barrick, Beric, Berric, Berrick, Berrik

Barrington (English) fenced town. Geography: a town in England.

Barry (Welsh) son of Harry. (Irish) spear, marksman. (French) gate, fence.
Baris, Barri, Barrie, Barris, Bary

Bart (Hebrew) a short form of Bartholomew, Barton.
Barrt, Bartel, Bartie, Barty

Bartholomew (Hebrew) son of Talmaí. Bible: one of the Twelve Apostles. See also Jerney, Parlan, Parthalán.
Balta, Bane, Bart, Bartek, Barth, Barthel, Barthelemy, Barthélemy, Barthélmy, Bartho, Bartholo, Bartholomaus, Bartholome, Bartholomeo, Bartholomeus, Bartholomieu, Bartimous, Bartlet, Barto, Bartolome, Bartolomé, Bartolomeo, Bartolomeð, Bartolommeo, Bartome, Bartz, Bat

Bartlet (English) a form of Bartholomew.
Bartlett, Bartley

Barto (Spanish) a form of Bartholomew.
Bardo, Bardol, Bartol, Bartoli, Bartolo, Bartos

Barton (English) barley town; Bart's town.
Barrton, Bart

Bartram (English) a form of Bertram.
Barthram

Baruch (Hebrew) blessed.
Boruch

Basam (Arabic) smiling.
Basem, Basim, Bassam

Basil (Greek, Latin) royal, kingly. Religion: a saint and founder of monasteries. Botany: an herb often used in cooking. See also Vasilis, Wasili.
Bas, Basal, Base, Baseal, Basel, Basle, Basile, Basilio, Basilios, Basilius, Bassel, Bazek, Bazel, Bazil, Bazyli

Basir (Turkish) intelligent, discerning.
Bashar, Basheer, Bashir, Bashiyr, Bechir, Bhasheer

Bassett (English) little person.
Basett, Basit, Basset, Bassit

Bastien (German) a short form of Sebastian.
Baste, Bastiaan, Bastian, Bastion

Bat (English) a short form of Bartholomew.

Baul (Gypsy) snail.

Bavol (Gypsy) wind; air.

Baxter (English) a form of Baker.
Bax, Baxie, Baxty, Baxy

Bay (Vietnamese) seventh son. (French) chestnut brown color; evergreen tree. (English) howler.

Bayard (English) reddish brown hair.
Baiardo, Bay, Bayardo, Bayerd, Bayrd

Bayley (French) a form of Bailey.
Baylee, Bayleigh, Baylie, Bayly

Beacan (Irish) small.
Beacán, Becan

Beacher (English) beech trees.
Beach, Beachy, Beech, Beecher, Beechy

Beagan (Irish) small.
Beagen, Beagin

Beale (French) a form of Beau.
Beal, Beall, Bealle, Beals

Beaman (English) beekeeper.
Beamann, Beamen, Beeman, Beman

Beamer (English) trumpet player.

Beasley (English) field of peas.

Beattie (Latin) blessed; happy; bringer of joy.
Beatie, Beatty, Beaty

Beau (French) handsome.
Beale, Beaux, Bo

Beaufort (French) beautiful fort.

Beaumont (French) beautiful mountain.

Beauregard (French) handsome; beautiful; well regarded.

Beaver (English) beaver.
Beav, Beavo, Beve, Bevo

Bebe (Spanish) baby.

Beck (English, Scandinavian) brook.
Beckett

Bede (English) prayer. Religion: the patron saint of lectors.

Bela (Czech) white. (Hungarian) bright.
Béla, Belaal, Belal, Belall, Belay, Bellal

Belden (French, English) pretty valley.
Beldin, Beldon, Bellden, Belldon

Belen (Greek) arrow.

Bell (French) handsome. (English) bell ringer.

Bellamy (French) beautiful friend.
Belamy, Bell, Bellamey, Bellamie

Bello (African) helper or promoter of Islam.

Belmiro (Portuguese) good-looking; attractive.

Bem (Tiv) peace.
Behm

Ben (Hebrew) a short form of Benjamin.
Behn, Benio, Benn, Benne, Benno

Ben-ami (Hebrew) son of my people.
Baram, Barami

Benedict (Latin) blessed. See also Venedictos, Venya.
Benci, Bendick, Bendict, Bendino, Bendix, Bendrick, Benedetto, Benedick, Benedicto, Benedictus, Benedikt, Bengt, Benito, Benoit

Benedikt (German, Slavic) a form of Benedict.
Bendek, Bendik, Benedek, Benedik

Bengt (Scandinavian) a form of Benedict.
Beng, Benke, Bent

Beniam (Ethiopian) a form of Benjamin.
Beneyam, Beniamin, Beniamino

Benito (Italian) a form of Benedict. History: Benito Mussolini led Italy during World War II.
Benedo, Benino, Benno, Beno, Betto, Beto

Benjamen (Hebrew) a form of Benjamin.
Benejamen, Benjermen, Benjjmen

Benjamin (Hebrew) son of my right hand. See also Peniamina, Veniamin.
Behnjamin, Bejamin, Bemjiman, Ben, Benejaminas, Bengamin, Beniam, Benja, Benjahmin, Benjaim, Benjam, Benjamaim, Benjaman, Benjamen, Benjamine, Benjaminn, Benjamino, Benjamon, Benjamyn, Benjamynn, Benjemin, Benjermain, Benjermin, Benji, Benjie, Benjiman, Benjy, Benkamin, Bennjamin, Benny, Benyamin, Benyamino, Binyamin, Mincho

Benjiman (Hebrew) a form of Benjamin.
Benjimen, Benjimin, Benjimon, Benjmain

Benjiro (Japanese) enjoys peace.

Bennett (Latin) little blessed one.
Benet, Benett, Bennet, Benette, Bennete, Bennette

Benny (Hebrew) a familiar form of Benjamin.
Bennie

Beno (Hebrew) son. (Mwera) band member.

Benoit (French) a form of Benedict.
Benott

Benoni (Hebrew) son of my sorrow. Bible: Ben-oni was the son of Jacob and Rachel.
Ben-Oni

Benson (Hebrew) son of Ben. A short form of Ben Zion.
Bensan, Bensen, Benssen, Bensson

Bentley (English) moor; coarse grass meadow.
Bent, Bentlea, Bentlee, Bentlie, Lee

Benton (English) Ben's town; town on the moors.
Bent

Benzi (Hebrew) a familiar form of Ben Zion.

Ben Zion (Hebrew) son of Zion.
Benson, Benzi

Beppe (Italian) a form of Joseph.
Beppy

Ber (English) boundary. (Yiddish) bear.

Beredei (Russian) a form of Hubert.
Berdry, Berdy, Beredej, Beredy

Berg (German) mountain.
Berdj, Berge, Bergh, Berje

Bergen (German, Scandinavian) hill dweller.
Bergin, Birgin

Berger (French) shepherd.

Bergren (Scandinavian) mountain stream.
Berg

Berk (Turkish) solid, rugged.

Berkeley (English) a form of Barclay.
Berk, Berkely, Berkie, Berkley, Berklie, Berkly, Berky

Berl (German) a form of Burl.
Berle, Berlie, Berlin, Berlyn

Berlyn (German) boundary line. See also Burl.
Berlin, Burlin

Bern (German) a short form of Bernard.
Berne

Bernal (German) strong as a bear.
Bernald, Bernaldo, Bernel, Bernhald, Bernhold, Bernold

Bernard (German) brave as a bear. See also Bjorn.
Barnard, Bear, Bearnard, Benek, Ber, Berend, Bern, Bernabé, Bernadas, Bernardel, Bernardin, Bernardo, Bernardus, Bernardyn, Bernarr, Bernat, Bernek, Bernal, Bernel, Bernerd, Berngards, Bernhard, Bernhards, Bernhardt, Bernie, Bjorn, Burnard

Bernardo (Spanish) a form of Bernard.
Barnardino, Barnardo, Barnhardo, Benardo, Bernardino, Bernhardo, Berno, Burnardo, Nardo

Bernie (German) a familiar form of Bernard.
Berney, Berni, Berny, Birney, Birnie, Birny, Burney

Berry (English) berry; grape.
Berrie

Bersh (Gypsy) one year.

Bert (German, English) bright, shining. A short form of Berthold, Berton, Bertram, Bertrand, Egbert, Filbert.
Bertie, Bertus, Birt, Burt

Berthold (German) bright; illustrious; brilliant ruler.
Bert, Berthoud, Bertold, Bertolde

Bertie (English) a familiar form of Bert, Egbert.
Berty, Birt, Birtie, Birty

Bertín (Spanish) distinguished friend.
Berti

Berto (Spanish) a short form of Alberto.

Berton (English) bright settlement; fortified town.
Bert

Bertram (German) bright; illustrious. (English) bright raven. See also Bartram.
Beltran, Beltrán, Beltrano, Bert, Berton, Bertrae, Bertraim, Bertraum, Bertron

Bertrand (German) bright shield.
Bert, Bertran, Bertrando, Bertranno

Berwyn (Welsh) white head.
Berwin, Berwynn, Berwynne

Bevan (Welsh) son of Evan.
Beavan, Beaven, Beavin, Bev, Beve, Beven, Bevin, Bevo, Bevon

Beverly (English) beaver meadow.
Beverlea, Beverleigh, Beverley, Beverlie

Bevis (French) from Beauvais, France; bull.
Beauvais, Bevys

Bhagwandas (Hindi) servant of God.

Bickford (English) axe-man's ford.

Bienvenido (Filipino) welcome.

Bijan (Persian) ancient hero.
Bihjan, Bijann, Bijhan, Bijhon, Bijon

Bilal (Arabic) chosen.
Bila, Bilaal, Bilale, Bile, Bilel, Billaal, Billal

Bill (German) a short form of William.
Bil, Billee, Billijo, Billye, Byll, Will

Billy (German) a familiar form of Bill, William.
Bille, Billey, Billie, Billy, Bily, Willie

Binah (Hebrew) understanding; wise.
Bina

Bing (German) kettle-shaped hollow.

Binh (Vietnamese) peaceful.

Binkentios (Greek) a form of Vincent.

Binky (English) a familiar form of Bancroft, Vincent.
Bink, Binkentios, Binkie

Birch (English) white; shining; birch tree.
Birk, Burch

Birger (Norwegian) rescued.

Birkey (English) island with birch trees.
Birk, Birkie, Birky

Birkitt (English) birch-tree coast.
Birk, Birket, Birkit, Burket, Burkett, Burkitt

Birley (English) meadow with the cow barn.
Birlee, Birlie, Birly

Birney (English) island with a brook.
Birne, Birnie, Birny, Burney, Burnie, Burny

Birtle (English) hill with birds.

Bishop (Greek) overseer. (English) bishop.
Bish, Bishup

Bjorn (Scandinavian) a form of Bernard.
Bjarne

Blackburn (Scottish) black brook.

Blade (English) knife, sword.
Bladen, Bladon, Bladyn, Blae, Blaed, Blayde

Bladimir (Russian) a form of Vladimir.
Bladimer

Blaine (Irish) thin, lean. (English) river source.
Blain, Blane, Blayne

Blair (Irish) plain, field. (Welsh) place.
Blaire, Blare, Blayr, Blayre

Blaise, Blaize (French) forms of Blaze.
Ballas, Balyse, Blais, Blaisot, Blas, Blase, Blasi, Blasien, Blasius, Blass, Blaz, Blaze, Blayz, Blayze, Blayzz

Blake (English) attractive; dark.
Blaik, Blaike, Blakely, Blakeman, Blakey, Blayke

Blakely (English) dark meadow.
Blakelee, Blakeleigh, Blakeley, Blakelie, Blakelin, Blakelyn, Blakeny, Blakley, Blakney

Blanco (Spanish) light skinned; white; blond.

Blane (Irish) a form of Blaine.
Blaney, Blanne

Blayne (Irish) a form of Blaine.
Blayn, Blayney

Blaze (Latin) stammerer. (English) flame; trail mark made on a tree.
Balázs, Biaggio, Biagio, Blaise, Blaize, Blazen, Blazer

Bliss (English) blissful; joyful.

Bly (Native American) high.

Blythe (English) carefree; merry, joyful.
Blithe, Blyth

Bo (English) a form of Beau, Beauregard. (German) a form of Bogart.
Boe

Boaz (Hebrew) swift; strong.
Bo, Boas, Booz, Bos, Boz

Bob (English) a short form of Robert.
Bobb, Bobby, Bobek, Rob

Bobby (English) a familiar form of Bob, Robert.
Bobbey, Bobbi, Bobbie, Bobbye, Boby

Bobek (Czech) a form of Bob, Robert.

Boden (Scandinavian) sheltered. (French) messenger, herald.
Bodie, Bodin, Bodine, Bodyne, Boe

Bodie (Scandinavian) a familiar form of Boden.
Boddie, Bode, Bodee, Bodey, Bodhi, Bodi, Boedee, Boedi, Boedy

Bodil (Norwegian) mighty ruler.

Bodua (Akan) animal's tail.

Bogart (German) strong as a bow. (Irish, Welsh) bog, marshland.
Bo, Bogey, Bogie, Bogy

Bohdan (Ukrainian) a form of Donald.
Bogdan, Bogdashka, Bogdon, Bohden, Bohdon

Bonaro (Italian, Spanish) friend.
Bona, Bonar

Bonaventure (Italian) good luck.

Bond (English) tiller of the soil.
Bondie, Bondon, Bonds, Bondy

Boniface (Latin) do-gooder.
Bonifacio, Bonifacius, Bonifacy

Booker (English) bookmaker; book lover; Bible lover.
Bookie, Books, Booky

Boone (Latin, French) good. History: Daniel Boone was an American pioneer.
Bon, Bone, Bonne, Boonie, Boony

Booth (English) hut. (Scandinavian) temporary dwelling.
Boot, Boote, Boothe

Borak (Arabic) lightning. Mythology: the horse that carried Muhammed to seventh heaven.

Borden (French) cottage. (English) valley of the boar; boar's den.
Bord, Bordie, Bordy

Borg (Scandinavian) castle.

Boris (Slavic) battler, warrior. Religion: the patron saint of Moscow, princes, and Russia.
Boriss, Borja, Borris, Borya, Boryenka, Borys

Borka (Russian) fighter.
Borkinka

Boseda (Tiv) born on Saturday.

Bosley (English) grove of trees.

Botan (Japanese) blossom, bud.

Bourey (Cambodian) country.

Bourne (Latin, French) boundary. (English) brook, stream.

Boutros (Arabic) a form of Peter.

Bowen (Welsh) son of Owen.
Bow, Bowe, Bowie

Bowie (Irish) yellow haired. History: James Bowie was an American-born Mexican colonist who died during the defense of the Alamo.
Bow, Bowen

Boyce (French) woods, forest.
Boice, Boise, Boy, Boycey, Boycie

Boyd (Scottish) yellow haired.
Boid, Boyde

Brad (English) a short form of Bradford, Bradley.
Bradd, Brade

Bradburn (English) broad stream.

Braden (English) broad valley.
Bradan, Bradden, Bradeon, Bradin, Bradine, Bradyn, Braeden, Braiden, Brayden, Bredan, Bredon

Bradford (English) broad river crossing.
Brad, Braddford, Ford

Bradlee (English) a form of Bradley.
Bradlea, Bradleigh, Bradlie

Bradley (English) broad meadow.
Brad, Braddly, Bradlay, Bradlee, Bradly, Bradlyn, Bradney

Bradly (English) a form of Bradley.

Bradon (English) broad hill.
Braedon, Braidon, Braydon

Bradshaw (English) broad forest.

Brady (Irish) spirited. (English) broad island.
Bradey, Bradi, Bradie, Bradye, Braidy

Bradyn (English) a form of Braden.
Bradynne, Breidyn

Braeden, Braiden (English) forms of Braden.
Braedan, Braedin, Braedyn, Braidyn

Braedon (English) a form of Bradon.
Breadon

Bragi (Scandinavian) poet. Mythology: the god of poetry, eloquence, and song.
Brage

Braham (Hindi) creator.
Braheem, Braheim, Brahiem, Brahima, Brahm

Brainard (English) bold raven; prince.
Brainerd

Bram (Scottish) bramble, brushwood.
(Hebrew) a short form of Abraham,
Abram.
Brame, Bramm, Bramdon

Bramwell (English) bramble spring.
Brammel, Brammell, Bramwel, Bramwyll

Branch (Latin) paw; claw; tree branch.

Brand (English) firebrand; sword. A
short form of Brandon.
*Brandall, Brande, Brandel, Brandell,
Brander, Brandley, Brandol, Brandt,
Brandy, Brann*

Brandeis (Czech) dweller on a burned
clearing.
Brandis

Branden (English) beacon valley.
*Brandden, Brandene, Brandin, Brandine,
Brandyn, Breandan*

Brandon (English) beacon hill.
*Bran, Brand, Brandan, Branddon,
Brandone, Brandonn, Brandyn,
Branndan, Branndon, Brannon,
Breandon, Brendon*

Brandt (English) a form of Brant.

Brandy (Dutch) brandy. (English) a
familiar form of Brand.
Branddy, Brandey, Brandi, Brandie

Brandyn (English) a form of Branden,
Brandon.
Brandynn

Brannon (Irish) a form of Brandon.
Branen, Brannan, Brannen, Branon

Branson (English) son of Brandon,
Brant. A form of Bronson.
Bransen, Bransin, Brantson

Brant (English) proud.
Brandt, Brannt, Brante, Brantley, Branton

Brantley (English) a form of Brant.
*Brantlie, Brantly, Brentlee, Brentley,
Brently*

Braulio (Italian) a form of Brawley.
Brauli, Brauliuo

Brawley (English) meadow on the
hillside.
Braulio, Brawlee, Brawly

Braxton (English) Brock's town.
*Brax, Braxdon, Braxston, Braxten,
Braxtin, Braxxton*

Brayan (Irish, Scottish) a form of
Brian.
Brayn, Brayon

Brayden (English) a form of Braden.
*Braydan, Braydn, Bradyn, Breydan,
Breyden, Brydan, Bryden*

Braydon (English) a form of Bradon.
Braydoon, Brydon, Breydon

Breck (Irish) freckled.
*Brec, Breckan, Brecken, Breckie, Breckin,
Breckke, Breckyn, Brek, Brexton*

Brede (Scandinavian) iceberg, glacier.

Brencis (Latvian) a form of Lawrence.
Brence

Brendan (Irish) little raven. (English)
sword.
*Breandan, Bren, Brenden, Brendis,
Brendon, Brendyn, Brenn, Brennan,
Brennen, Brenndan, Brenyan, Bryn*

Brenden (Irish) a form of Brendan.
*Bren, Brendene, Brendin, Brendine,
Brennden*

Brendon (English) a form of Brandon.
(Irish, English) a form of Brendan.
Brenndon

Brennan, Brennen (English, Irish)
forms of Brendan.
*Bren, Brenan, Brenen, Brenin, Brenn,
Brenna, Brennann, Brenner, Brennin,
Brennon, Brennor, Brennyn, Brenon*

Brent (English) a short form of
Brenton.
Brendt, Brente, Brentson, Brentt

Brenton (English) steep hill.
*Brent, Brentan, Brenten, Brentin,
Brentten, Brentton, Brentyn*

Bret, Brett (Scottish) from Great
Britain. See also Britton.
*Bhrett, Braten, Braton, Brayton, Bretin,
Bretley, Bretlin, Breton, Brettan, Brette,
Bretten, Bretton, Brit, Britt*

Brewster (English) brewer.
Brew, Brewer, Bruwster

Breyon (Irish, Scottish) a form of
Brian.
Breon, Breyan

Brian (Irish, Scottish) strong; virtuous;
honorable. History: Brian Boru was
an eleventh-century Irish king and
national hero. See also Palaina.
*Brayan, Breyon, Briana, Briann,
Brianna, Brianne, Briano, Briant,
Briante, Briaun, Briayan, Brien, Brience,
Brient, Brin, Briny, Brion, Bryan, Bryen*

Briar (French) heather.
Brier, Brierly, Bryar, Bryer, Bryor

Brice (Welsh) alert; ambitious.
(English) son of Rice.
Bricen, Briceton, Bryce

Brick (English) bridge.
Bricker, Bricklen, Brickman, Brik

Bridger (English) bridge builder.
Bridd, Bridge, Bridgeley, Bridgely

Brigham (English) covered bridge.
(French) troops, brigade.
Brig, Brigg, Briggs, Brighton

Brighton (English) bright town.
Breighton, Bright, Brightin, Bryton

Brion (Irish, Scottish) a form of Brian.
Brieon, Brione, Brionn, Brionne

Brit, Britt (Scottish) forms of Bret,
Brett. See also Britton.
Brit, Brityce

Britton (Scottish) from Great Britain.
See also Bret, Brett, Brit, Britt.
*Britain, Briten, Britian, Britin, Briton,
Brittain, Brittan, Britten, Brittian,
Brittin, Britton*

Brock (English) badger.
*Broc, Brocke, Brockett, Brockie, Brockley,
Brockton, Brocky, Brok, Broque*

Brod (English) a short form of
Broderick.
Brode, Broden

Broderick (Welsh) son of the famous
ruler. (English) broad ridge. See also
Roderick.
*Brod, Broddie, Brodderick, Brodderrick,
Broddy, Broderic, Broderrick, Brodrick*

Brodie (Irish) a form of Brody.
Brodi, Broedi

Brodrick (Welsh, English) a form of
Broderick.
Broddrick, Brodric, Brodryck

Brody (Irish) ditch; canal builder.
Brodee, Broden, Brodey, Brodie, Broedy

Brogan (Irish) a heavy work shoe.
Brogen, Broghan, Broghen

Bromley (English) brushwood
meadow.

Bron (Afrikaans) source.

Bronislaw (Polish) weapon of glory.

Bronson (English) son of Brown.
*Bransen, Bransin, Branson, Bron,
Bronnie, Bronnson, Bronny, Bronsan,
Bronsen, Bronsin, Bronsonn, Bronsson,
Bronsun, Bronsyn, Brunson*

Brook (English) brook, stream.
Brooke, Brooker, Brookin, Brooklyn

Brooks (English) son of Brook.
Brookes, Broox

Brown (English) brown; bear.

Bruce (French) brushwood thicket;
woods.
Brucey, Brucy, Brue, Bruis

Bruno (German, Italian) brown haired;
brown skinned.
Brunon, Bruns

Bryan (Irish) a form of Brian.
Brayan, Bryann, Bryant, Bryen

Bryant (Irish) a form of Bryan.
Bryent

Bryce (Welsh) a form of Brice.
Brycen, Bryceton, Bryson, Bryston

Bryon (German) cottage. (English)
bear.
*Bryeon, Bryn, Bryne, Brynn, Brynne,
Bryone*

Bryson (Welsh) son of Brice.
Brysan, Brysen, Brysun, Brysyn

Bryton (English) a form of Brighton.
*Brayten, Brayton, Breyton, Bryeton,
Brytan, Bryten, Brytin, Brytten, Brytton*

Bubba (German) a boy.
Babba, Babe, Bebba

Buck (German, English) male deer.
Buckie, Buckley, Buckner, Bucko, Bucky

Buckley (English) deer meadow.
Bucklea, Bucklee

Buckminster (English) preacher.

Bud (English) herald, messenger.
Budd, Buddy

Buddy (American) a familiar form of
Bud.
Budde, Buddey, Buddie

Buell (German) hill dweller. (English)
bull.

Buford (English) ford near the castle.
Burford

Burgess (English) town dweller; shop-
keeper.
Burg, Burges, Burgh, Burgiss, Burr

Burian (Ukrainian) lives near weeds.

Burke (German, French) fortress, castle.
Berk, Berke, Birk, Bourke, Burk, Burkley

Burl (English) cup bearer; wine servant; knot in a tree. (German) a short form of Berlyn
Berl, Burley, Burlie, Byrle

Burleigh (English) meadow with knotted tree trunks.
Burlee, Burley, Burlie, Byrleigh, Byrlee

Burne (English) brook.
Beirne, Burn, Burnell, Burnett, Burney, Byrn, Byrne

Burney (English) island with a brook. A familiar form of Rayburn.

Burr (Swedish) youth. (English) prickly plant.

Burris (English) town dweller.

Burt (English) a form of Bert. A short form of Burton.
Burrt, Burtt, Burty

Burton (English) fortified town.
Berton, Burt

Busby (Scottish) village in the thicket; tall military hat made of fur.
Busbee, Buzby, Buzz

Buster (American) hitter, puncher.

Butch (American) a short form of Butcher.

Butcher (English) butcher.
Butch

Buzz (Scottish) a short form of Busby.
Buzzy

Byford (English) by the ford.

Byram (English) cattle yard.

Byrd (English) birdlike.
Bird, Birdie, Byrdie

Byrne (English) a form of Burne.
Byrn, Byrnes

Byron (French) cottage. (English) barn.
Beyren, Beyron, Biren, Biron, Buiron, Byram, Byran, Byrann, Byren, Byrom, Byrone

C

Cable (French, English) rope maker.
Cabell

Cadao (Vietnamese) folksong.

Cadby (English) warrior's settlement.

Caddock (Welsh) eager for war.

Cade (Welsh) a short form of Cadell.
Cady

Cadell (Welsh) battler.
Cade, Cadel, Cedell

Caden (American) a form of Kadin.
Cadan, Caddon, Cadian, Cadien, Cadin, Cadon, Cadyn, Caeden, Caedon, Caid, Caiden, Cayden

Cadmus (Greek) from the east. Mythology: a Phoenician prince who founded Thebes and introduced writing to the Greeks.

Caelan (Scottish) a form of Nicholas.
Cael, Caelon, Caelyn, Cailan, Cailean, Caillan, Cailun, Cailyn, Calan, Calen, Caleon, Caley, Calin, Callan, Callon, Callyn, Calon, Calyn, Caylan, Cayley

Caesar (Latin) long-haired. History: a title for Roman emperors. See also Kaiser, Kesar, Sarito.
Caesarae, Caesear, Caeser, Caezar, Caseare, Ceasar, Cesar, Ceseare, Cezar, Cézar, Czar, Seasar

Cahil (Turkish) young, naive.

Cai (Welsh) a form of Gaius.
Caio, Caius, Caw

Cain (Hebrew) spear; gatherer. Bible: Adam and Eve's oldest son. See also Kabil, Kane, Kayne.
Cainaen, Cainan, Caine, Cainen, Caineth, Cayn, Cayne

Cairn (Welsh) landmark made of a mound of stones.
Cairne, Carn, Carne

Cairo (Arabic) Geography: the capital of Egypt.
Kairo

Cal (Latin) a short form of Calvert, Calvin.

Calder (Welsh, English) brook, stream.

Caldwell (English) cold well.

Cale (Hebrew) a short form of Caleb.

Caleb (Hebrew) dog; faithful. (Arabic) bold, brave. Bible: one of the twelve spies sent by Moses. See also Kaleb, Kayleb.
Caeleb, Calab, Calabe, Cale, Caley, Calib, Calieb, Callob, Calob, Calyb, Cayleb, Caylebb, Caylib, Caylob

Calen, Calin (Scottish) forms of Caelan.
Caelen, Caelin, Caellin, Cailen, Cailin, Caillin, Calean, Callen, Caylin

Caley (Irish) a familiar form of Caleb.
Calee, Caleigh

Calhoun (Irish) narrow woods. (Scottish) warrior.
Colhoun, Colhoune, Colquhoun

Callahan (Irish) descendant of Ceallachen.
Calahan, Callaghan

Callum (Irish) dove.
Callam, Calum, Calym

Calvert (English) calf herder.
Cal, Calbert, Calvirt

Calvin (Latin) bald. See also Kalvin, Vinny.
Cal, Calv, Calvien, Calvon, Calvyn

Cam (Gypsy) beloved. (Scottish) a short form of Cameron. (Latin, French, Scottish) a short form of Campbell.
Camm, Cammie, Cammy, Camy

Camaron (Scottish) a form of Cameron.
Camar, Camari, Camaran, Camaren

Camden (Scottish) winding valley.
Kamden

Cameron (Scottish) crooked nose. See also Kameron.
Cam, Camaron, Cameran, Cameren, Camerin, Cameroun, Camerron, Camerson, Camerun, Cameryn, Camiren, Camiron, Cammeron, Camron

Camille (French) young ceremonial attendant.
Camile

Camilo (Latin) child born to freedom; noble.
Camiel, Camillo, Camillus

Campbell (Latin, French) beautiful field. (Scottish) crooked mouth.
Cam, Camp, Campy

Camron (Scottish) a short form of Cameron.
Camren, Cammrin, Cammron, Camran, Camreon, Camrin, Camryn, Camrynn

Canaan (French) a form of Cannon. History: an ancient region between the Jordan River and the Mediterranean.
Canan, Canen, Caynan

Candide (Latin) pure; sincere.
Candid, Candido, Candonino

Cannon (French) church official; large gun. See also Kannon.
Canaan, Cannan, Cannen, Cannin, Canning, Canon

Canute (Latin) white haired. (Scandinavian) knot. History: a Danish king who became king of England after 1016. See also Knute.
Cnut, Cnute

Cappi (Gypsy) good fortune.

Car (Irish) a short form of Carney.

Carey (Greek) pure. (Welsh) castle; rocky island. See also Karey.
Care, Caree, Cari, Carre, Carree, Carrie, Cary

Carl (German, English) a short form of Carlton. A form of Charles. See also Carroll, Kale, Kalle, Karl, Karlen, Karol.
Carle, Carles, Carless, Carlis, Carll, Carlo, Carlos, Carlson, Carlston, Carlus, Carolos

Carlin (Irish) little champion.
Carlan, Carlen, Carley, Carlie, Carling, Carlino, Carly

Carlisle (English) Carl's island.
Carlyle, Carlysle

Carlito (Spanish) a familiar form of Carlos.
Carlitos

Carlo (Italian) a form of Carl, Charles.
Carolo

Carlos (Spanish) a form of Carl, Charles.
Carlito

Carlton (English) Carl's town.
Carl, Carleton, Carllton, Carlston, Carltonn, Carltton, Charlton

Carmel (Hebrew) vineyard, garden. See also Carmine.
Carmello, Carmelo, Karmel

Carmichael (Scottish) follower of Michael.

Carmine (Latin) song; crimson. (Italian) a form of Carmel.
Carmain, Carmaine, Carman, Carmen, Carmon

Carnelius (Greek, Latin) a form of Cornelius.
Carnealius, Carneilius, Carnellius, Carnilious

Carnell (English) defender of the castle. (French) a form of Cornell.

Carney (Irish) victorious. (Scottish) fighter. See also Kearney.
Car, Carny, Karney

Carr (Scandinavian) marsh. See also Kerr.
Karr

Carrick (Irish) rock.
Carooq, Carricko

Carrington (Welsh) rocky town.

Carroll (Irish) champion. (German) a form of Carl.
Carel, Carell, Cariel, Cariell, Carol, Carole, Carolo, Carols, Carollan, Carolus, Carrol, Cary, Caryl

Carson (English) son of Carr.
Carsen, Carsino, Carrson, Karson

Carsten (Greek) a form of Karsten.
Carston

Carter (English) cart driver.
Cart

Cartwright (English) cart builder.

Carvell (French, English) village on the marsh.
Carvel, Carvelle, Carvellius

Carver (English) wood-carver; sculptor.

Cary (Welsh) a form of Carey. (German, Irish) a form of Carroll.
Carray, Carry

Case (Irish) a short form of Casey. (English) a short form of Casimir.

Casey (Irish) brave.
Case, Casie, Casy, Cayse, Caysey, Kacey, Kasey

Cash (Latin) vain. (Slavic) a short form of Casimir.
Cashe

Casimir (Slavic) peacemaker.
Cachi, Cas, Case, Cash, Cashemere, Cashi, Cashmeire, Cashmere, Casimere, Casimire, Casimiro, Castimer, Kasimir, Kazio

Casper (Persian) treasurer. (German) imperial. See also Gaspar, Jasper, Kasper.
Caspar, Cass

Cass (Irish, Persian) a short form of Casper, Cassidy.

Cassidy (Irish) clever; curly haired. See also Kazio.
Casidy, Cass, Cassady, Cassie, Kassidy

Cassie (Irish) a familiar form of Cassidy.
Casi, Casie, Casio, Cassey, Cassy, Casy

Cassius (Latin, French) box; protective cover.
Cassia, Cassio, Cazzie

Castle (Latin) castle.
Cassle, Castel

Castor (Greek) beaver. Astrology: one of the twins in the constellation Gemini. Mythology: one of the patron saints of mariners.
Caster, Caston

Cater (English) caterer.

Cato (Latin) knowledgeable, wise.
Caton, Catón

Cavan (Irish) handsome. See also Kevin.
Caven, Cavin, Cavan, Cawoun

Cayden (American) a form of Caden.
Cayde, Caydin

Caylan (Scottish) a form of Caelan.
Caylans, Caylen, Caylon

Cazzie (American) a familiar form of Cassius.
Caz, Cazz, Cazzy

Ceasar (Latin) a form of Caesar.
Ceaser

Cecil (Latin) blind.
Cece, Cecile, Cecilio, Cecilius, Cecill, Celio, Siseal

Cedric (English) battle chieftain. See also Kedrick, Rick.
Cad, Caddaric, Ced, Cederic, Cedrec, Cédric, Cedrick, Cedryche, Sedric

Cedrick (English) a form of Cedric.
Ceddrick, Cederick, Cederrick, Cedirick, Cedrik

Ceejay (American) a combination of the initials C. + J.
Cejay, C.J.

Cemal (Arabic) attractive.

Cephas (Latin) small rock. Bible: the term used by Jesus to describe Peter.
Cepheus, Cephus

Cerdic (Welsh) beloved.
Caradoc, Caradog, Ceredig, Ceretic

Cerek (Polish) lordly. (Greek) a form of Cyril.

Cesar (Spanish) a form of Caesar.
Casar, César, Cesare, Cesareo, Cesario, Cesaro, Cessar

Cestmir (Czech) fortress.

Cezar (Slavic) a form of Caesar.
Cézar, Cezary, Cezek, Chezrae, Sezar

Chace (French) a form of Chase.
Chayce

Chad (English) warrior. A short form of Chadwick. Geography: a country in north-central Africa.
Ceadd, Chaad, Chadd, Chaddie, Chaddy, Chade, Chadleigh, Chadler, Chadley, Chadlin, Chadlyn, Chadmen, Chado, Chadron, Chady

Chadrick (German) mighty warrior.
Chaddrick, Chaderic, Chaderick, Chadrack, Chadric

Chadwick (English) warrior's town.
Chad, Chaddwick, Chadvic, Chadwyck

Chago (Spanish) a form of Jacob.
Chango, Chanti

Chaim (Hebrew) life. See also Hyman.
Chai, Chaimek, Haim, Khaim

Chaise (French) a form of Chase.
Chais, Chaisen, Chaison

Chal (Gypsy) boy; son.
Chalie, Chalin

Chalmers (Scottish) son of the lord.
Chalmer, Chalmr, Chamar, Chamarr

Cham (Vietnamese) hard worker.
Chams

Chan (Sanskrit) shining. (English) a form of Chauncey. (Spanish) a form of Juan.
Chann, Chano, Chayo

Chanan (Hebrew) cloud.

Chance (English) a short form of Chancellor, Chauncey.
Chanc, Chancee, Chancey, Chancie, Chancy, Chanse, Chansy, Chants, Chantz, Chanze, Chanz, Chaynce

Chancellor (English) record keeper.
Chance, Chancelar, Chancelen, Chanceleor, Chanceler, Chanceller, Chancelor, Chanselor, Chanslor

Chander (Hindi) moon.
Chand, Chandan, Chandany, Chandara, Chandon

Chandler (English) candle maker.
Chandelar, Chandlan, Chandlar, Chandlier, Chandlor, Chandlyr

Chane (Swahili) dependable.

Chaney (French) oak.
Chayne, Cheaney, Cheney, Cheyn, Cheyne, Cheyney

Chankrisna (Cambodian) sweet smelling tree.

Channing (English) wise. (French) canon; church official.
Chane, Chann

Chanse (English) a form of Chance.
Chans, Chansey

Chante (French) singer.
Chant, Chantha, Chanthar, Chantra, Chantry, Shantae

Chapman (English) merchant.
Chap, Chappie, Chappy

Charles (German) farmer. (English) strong and manly. See also Carl, Searlas, Tearlach, Xarles.
Arlo, Chareles, Charels, Charlese, Carlo, Carlos, Charl, Charle, Charlen, Charlie, Charlot, Charlz, Charlzell, Chaz, Chick, Chip, Chuck

Charlie (German, English) a familiar form of Charles.
Charle, Charlee, Charley, Charli, Charly

Charlton (English) a form of Carlton.
Charlesten, Charleston, Charleton, Charlotin

Charro (Spanish) cowboy.

Chase (French) hunter.
Chace, Chaise, Chasen, Chason, Chass, Chasse, Chastan, Chasten, Chastin, Chastinn, Chaston, Chasyn, Chayse

Chaska (Sioux) first-born son.

Chauncey (English) chancellor; church official.
Chan, Chance, Chancey, Chaunce, Chauncei, Chauncy, Chauncey, Chaunesy, Chaunszi

Chavez (Hispanic) a surname used as a first name.
Chavaz, Chaves, Chaveze, Chavies, Chavis, Chavius, Chevez, Cheveze, Cheviez, Chevious, Chevis, Chivass, Chivez

Chayse (French) a form of Chase.
Chaysea, Chaysen, Chayson, Chaysten

Chayton (Lakota) falcon.

Chaz (English) a familiar form of
Charles.
*Chas, Chasz, Chaze, Chazwick,
Chazy, Chazz, Chez*

Ché (Spanish) a familiar form of José.
History: Ernesto "Che" Guevara was
a revolutionary who fought at Fidel
Castro's side in Cuba.
Chay

Checha (Spanish) a familiar form of
Jacob.

Cheche (Spanish) a familiar form of
Joseph.

Chen (Chinese) great, tremendous.

Chencho (Spanish) a familiar form of
Lawrence.

Chepe (Spanish) a familiar form of
Joseph.
Cepito

Cherokee (Cherokee) people of a different speech.
Cherrakee

Chesmu (Native American) gritty.

Chester (English) a short form of
Rochester.
Ches, Cheslav, Cheston, Chet

Chet (English) a short form of Chester.
Chett, Chette

Cheung (Chinese) good luck.

Chevalier (French) horseman, knight.
Chev, Chevy

Chevy (French) a familiar form of
Chevalier. Geography: Chevy Chase is
a town in Maryland. Culture: a short
form of Chevrolet, an American auto-
mobile company.
*Chev, Chevey, Chevi, Chevie, Chevvy,
Chewy*

Cheyenne (Cheyenne) a tribal name.
*Chayann, Chayanne, Cheyeenne,
Cheyene, Chyenne, Shayan*

Chi (Chinese) younger generation.
(Nigerian) personal guardian angel.

Chick (English) a familiar form of
Charles.
Chic, Chickie, Chicky

Chico (Spanish) boy.

Chik (Gypsy) earth.

Chike (Ibo) God's power.

Chiko (Japanese) arrow; pledge.

Chilo (Spanish) a familiar form of
Francisco.

Chilton (English) farm by the spring.
Chil, Chill, Chillton, Chilt

Chim (Vietnamese) bird.

Chinua (Ibo) God's blessing.
Chino, Chinou

Chioke (Ibo) gift of God.

Chip (English) a familiar form of
Charles.
Chipman, Chipper

Chiram (Hebrew) exalted; noble.

Chris (Greek) a short form of
Christian, Christopher. See also Kris.
Chriss, Christ, Chrys, Cris, Crist

Christain (Greek) a form of Christian.
*Christai, Christan, Christane, Christaun,
Christein*

Christian (Greek) follower of Christ;
anointed. See also Jaan, Kerstan,
Khristian, Kit, Krister, Kristian,
Krystian.
*Chretien, Chris, Christa, Christain,
Christé, Christen, Christensen,
Christiaan, Christiana, Christiane,
Christiann, Christianna, Christianno,
Christiano, Christianos, Christien,
Christin, Christino, Christion, Christon,
Christos, Christyan, Christyon, Chritian,
Chrystian, Cristian, Crystek*

Christien (Greek) a form of Christian.
Christienne, Christinne, Chrystien

Christofer (Greek) a form of
Christopher.
*Christafer, Christafur, Christefor,
Christerfer, Christifer, Christoffer,
Christofher, Christofper, Chrystofer*

Christoff (Russian) a form of
Christopher.
Chrisof, Christif, Christof, Cristofe

Christophe (French) a form of
Christopher.
Christoph

Christopher (Greek) Christ-bearer. Religion: the patron saint of travelers. See also Cristopher, Kester, Kit, Kristopher, Risto, Stoffel, Tobal, Topher.
Chris, Chrisopherson, Christapher, Christepher, Christerpher, Christhoper, Christipher, Christobal, Christofer, Christoff, Christoforo, Christoher, Christopehr, Christoper, Christophe, Christopherr, Christophor, Christophoros, Christophr, Christophre, Christophyer, Christophyr, Christorpher, Christos, Christovao, Christpher, Christphere, Christphor, Christpor, Christrpher, Chrystopher, Cristobal

Christophoros (Greek) a form of Christopher.
Christoforo, Christoforos, Christophor, Christophorus, Christphor, Cristoforo, Cristopher

Christos (Greek) a form of Christopher. See also Khristos.

Chucho (Hebrew) a familiar form of Jesus.

Chuck (American) a familiar form of Charles.
Chuckey, Chuckie, Chucky

Chui (Swahili) leopard.

Chul (Korean) firm.

Chuma (Ibo) having many beads, wealthy. (Swahili) iron.

Chuminga (Spanish) a familiar form of Dominic.
Chumin

Chumo (Spanish) a familiar form of Thomas.

Chun (Chinese) spring.

Chung (Chinese) intelligent.
Chungo, Chuong

Churchill (English) church on the hill. History: Sir Winston Churchill served as British prime minister and won a Nobel Prize for literature.

Cian (Irish) ancient.
Céin, Cianán, Kian

Cicero (Latin) chickpea. History: a famous Roman orator, philosopher, and statesman.
Cicerón

Cid (Spanish) lord. History: title for Rodrigo Díaz de Vivar, an eleventh-century Spanish soldier and national hero.
Cyd

Ciqala (Dakota) little.

Cirrillo (Italian) a form of Cyril.
Cirilio, Cirillo, Cirilo, Ciro

Cisco (Spanish) a short form of Francisco.

Clancy (Irish) redheaded fighter.
Clancey, Claney

Clare (Latin) a short form of Clarence.
Clair, Clarey, Clary

Clarence (Latin) clear; victorious.
Clarance, Clare, Clarrance, Clarrence, Clearence

Clark (French) cleric; scholar.
Clarke, Clerc, Clerk

Claude (Latin, French) lame.
Claud, Claudan, Claudel, Claudell, Claudey, Claudi, Claudian, Claudianus, Claudie, Claudien, Claudin, Claudio, Claudis, Claudius, Claudy

Claudio (Italian) a form of Claude.

Claus (German) a short form of Nicholas. See also Klaus.
Claas, Claes, Clause

Clay (English) clay pit. A short form of Clayborne, Clayton.
Klay

Clayborne (English) brook near the clay pit.
Claibern, Claiborn, Claiborne, Claibrone, Clay, Claybon, Clayborn, Claybourn, Claybourne, Clayburn, Clebourn

Clayton (English) town built on clay.
Clay, Clayten, Cleighton, Cleyton, Clyton, Klayton

Cleary (Irish) learned.

Cleavon (English) cliff.
Clavin, Clavion, Clavon, Clavone, Clayvon, Claywon, Clévon, Clevonn, Clyvon

Clem (Latin) a short form of Clement.
Cleme, Clemmy, Clim

Clement (Latin) merciful. Bible: a coworker of Paul. See also Klement, Menz.
Clem, Clemens, Clément, Clemente, Clementius, Clemmons

Clemente (Italian, Spanish) a form of Clement.
Clemento, Clemenza

Cleon (Greek) famous.
Kleon

Cletus (Greek) illustrious. History: a Roman pope and martyr.
Cleatus, Cledis, Cleotis, Clete, Cletis

Cleveland (English) land of cliffs.
Cleaveland, Cleavland, Cleavon, Cleve, Clevelend, Clevelynn, Clevey, Clevie, Clevon

Cliff (English) a short form of Clifford, Clifton.
Clif, Clift, Clive, Clyff, Clyph, Kliff

Clifford (English) cliff at the river crossing.
Cliff, Cliford, Clyfford, Klifford

Clifton (English) cliff town.
Cliff, Cliffton, Clift, Cliften, Clyfton

Clint (English) a short form of Clinton.
Klint

Clinton (English) hill town.
Clenten, Clint, Clinten, Clintion, Clintton, Clynton, Klinton

Clive (English) a form of Cliff.
Cleve, Clivans, Clivens, Clyve, Klyve

Clovis (German) famous soldier. See also Louis.

Cluny (Irish) meadow.

Clyde (Welsh) warm. (Scottish) Geography: a river in Scotland.
Cly, Clywd, Klyde

Coby (Hebrew) a familiar form of Jacob.
Cob, Cobby, Cobe, Cobey, Cobi, Cobia, Cobie

Cochise (Apache) hardwood. History: a famous Chiricahua Apache leader.

Coco (French) a familiar form of Jacques.
Coko, Koko

Codey (English) a form of Cody.
Coday

Codi, Codie (English) forms of Cody.
Coadi, Codea

Cody (English) cushion. History: William "Buffalo Bill" Cody was an American frontier scout who toured America and Europe with his Wild West show. See also Kody.
Coady, Coddy, Code, Codee, Codell, Codey, Codi, Codiak, Codie, Coedy

Coffie (Ewe) born on Friday.

Cola (Italian) a familiar form of Nicholas, Nicola.
Colas

Colar (French) a form of Nicholas.

Colbert (English) famous seafarer.
Cole, Colt, Colvert, Culbert

Colby (English) dark; dark haired.
Colbey, Colbi, Colbie, Colbin, Colebee, Coleby, Collby, Kolby

Cole (Latin) cabbage farmer. (English) a short form of Coleman.
Colet, Coley, Colie, Kole

Coleman (Latin) cabbage farmer. (English) coal miner.
Cole, Colemann, Colm, Colman, Koleman

Colin (Irish) young cub. (Greek) a short form of Nicholas.
Cailean, Colan, Cole, Colen, Coleon, Colinn, Collin, Colyn, Kolin

Colley (English) black haired; swarthy.
Colee, Collie, Collis

Collier (English) miner.
Colier, Collayer, Collie, Collyer, Colyer

Collin (Scottish) a form of Colin, Collins.
Collan, Collen, Collian, Collon, Collyn

Collins (Greek) son of Colin. (Irish) holly.
Collin, Collis

Colson (Greek, English) son of Nicholas.
Colsen, Coulson

Colt (English) young horse; frisky. A short form of Colter, Colton.
Colte

Colten (English) a form of Colton.

Colter (English) herd of colts.
Colt

Colton (English) coal town.
Colt, Coltan, Colten, Coltin, Coltinn, Coltn, Coltrane, Colttan, Coltton, Coltun, Coltyn, Coltyne, Kolton

Columba (Latin) dove.
Coim, Colum, Columbia, Columbus

Colwyn (Welsh) Geography: a river in Wales.
Colwin, Colwinn

Coman (Arabic) noble. (Irish) bent.
Comán

Conall (Irish) high, mighty.
Conal, Connal, Connel, Connell, Connelly, Connolly

Conan (Irish) praised; exalted. (Scottish) wise.
Conant, Conary, Connen, Connie, Connon, Connor, Conon

Conary (Irish) a form of Conan.
Conaire

Conlan (Irish) hero.
Conlen, Conley, Conlin, Conlyn

Conner (Irish) a form of Connor.
Connar, Connary, Conneer, Connery, Konner

Connie (English, Irish) a familiar form of Conan, Conrad, Constantine, Conway.
Con, Conn, Conney, Conny

Connor (Scottish) wise. (Irish) a form of Conan.
Conner, Connoer, Connory, Connyr, Conor, Konner, Konnor

Conor (Irish) a form of Connor.
Conar, Coner, Conour, Konner

Conrad (German) brave counselor.
Connie, Conrade, Conrado, Corrado, Konrad

Conroy (Irish) wise.
Conry, Roy

Constant (Latin) a short form of Constantine.

Constantine (Latin) firm, constant. History: Constantine the Great was the Roman emperor who adopted the Christian faith. See also Dinos, Konstantin, Stancio.
Connie, Constadine, Constandine, Constandios, Constanstine, Constant, Constantin, Constantino, Constantinos, Constantios, Costa

Conway (Irish) hound of the plain.
Connie, Conwy

Cook (English) cook.
Cooke

Cooper (English) barrel maker. See also Keiffer.
Coop, Couper

Corbett (Latin) raven.
Corbbitt, Corbet, Corbette, Corbit, Corbitt

Corbin (Latin) raven.
Corban, Corben, Corbey, Corbie, Corbon, Corby, Corbyn, Korbin

Corcoran (Irish) ruddy.

Cordaro (Spanish) a form of Cordero.
Coradaro, Cordairo, Cordara, Cordarel, Cordarell, Cordarelle, Cordareo, Cordarin, Cordario, Cordarion, Cordarious, Cordarius, Cordarrel, Cordarrell, Cordarris, Cordarrius, Cordarro, Cordarrol, Cordarus, Cordarryl, Cordaryal, Corddarro, Corrdarl

Cordell (French) rope maker.
Cord, Cordae, Cordale, Corday, Cordeal,

Cordeil, Cordel, Cordele, Cordelle, Cordie, Cordy, Kordell

Cordero (Spanish) little lamb.
Cordaro, Cordeal, Cordeara, Cordearo, Cordeiro, Cordelro, Corder, Cordera, Corderall, Corderias, Corderious, Corderral, Corderro, Corderryn, Corderun, Corderus, Cordiaro, Cordierre, Cordy, Corrderio

Corey (Irish) hollow. See also Korey, Kory.
Core, Coreaa, Coree, Cori, Corian, Corie, Corio, Correy, Corria, Corrie, Corry, Corrye, Cory

Cormac (Irish) raven's son. History: a third-century king of Ireland who was a great lawmaker.
Cormack, Cormick

Cornelius (Greek) cornel tree. (Latin) horn colored. See also Kornel, Kornelius, Nelek.
Carnelius, Conny, Cornealous, Corneili, Corneilius, Corneilus, Corneliaus, Cornelious, Cornelias, Cornelis, Corneliu, Cornell, Cornellious, Cornellis, Cornellius, Cornelous, Corneluis, Cornelus, Corney, Cornie, Cornielius, Corniellus, Corny, Cournelius, Cournelyous, Nelius, Nellie

Cornell (French) a form of Cornelius.
Carnell, Cornall, Corneil, Cornel, Cornelio, Corney, Cornie, Corny, Nellie

Cornwallis (English) from Cornwall.

Corrado (Italian) a form of Conrad.
Carrado

Corrigan (Irish) spearman.
Carrigan, Carrigen, Corrigon, Corrigun, Korrigan

Corrin (Irish) spear carrier.
Corin, Corion

Corry (Latin) a form of Corey.

Cort (German) bold. (Scandinavian) short. (English) a short form of Courtney.
Corte, Cortie, Corty, Kort

Cortez (Spanish) conqueror. History: Hernando Cortés was a Spanish conquistador who conquered Aztec Mexico.
Cartez, Cortes, Cortis, Cortize, Courtes, Courtez, Curtez, Kortez

Corwin (English) heart's companion; heart's delight.
Corwinn, Corwyn, Corwynn, Corwynne

Cory (Latin) a form of Corey. (French) a familiar form of Cornell. (Greek) a short form of Corydon.
Corye

Corydon (Greek) helmet, crest.
Coridon, Corradino, Cory, Coryden, Coryell

Cosgrove (Irish) victor, champion.

Cosmo (Greek) orderly; harmonious; universe.
Cos, Cosimo, Cosme, Cosmé, Cozmo, Kosmo

Costa (Greek) a short form of Constantine.
Costandinos, Costantinos, Costas, Costes

Coty (French) slope, hillside.
Cote, Cotee, Cotey, Coti, Cotie, Cotty, Cotye

Courtland (English) court's land.
Court, Courtlan, Courtlana, Courtlandt, Courtlin, Courtlind, Courtlon, Courtlyn, Kourtland

Courtney (English) court.
Cort, Cortnay, Cortne, Cortney, Court, Courten, Courtenay, Courteney, Courtnay, Courtnee, Curt, Kortney

Cowan (Irish) hillside hollow.
Coe, Coven, Covin, Cowen, Cowey, Cowie

Coy (English) woods.
Coye, Coyie, Coyt

Coyle (Irish) leader in battle.

Coyne (French) modest.
Coyan

Craddock (Welsh) love.
Caradoc, Caradog

Craig (Irish, Scottish) crag; steep rock.
Crag, Craige, Craigen, Craigery, Craigh, Craigon, Creag, Creg, Cregan, Cregg, Creig, Creigh, Criag, Kraig

Crandall (English) crane's valley.
Cran, Crandal, Crandel, Crandell, Crendal

Crawford (English) ford where crows fly.
Craw, Crow, Ford

Creed (Latin) belief.
Creedon

Creighton (English) town near the rocks.
Cray, Crayton, Creighm, Creight, Creighto, Crichton

Crepin (French) a form of Crispin.

Crispin (Latin) curly haired.
Crepin, Cris, Crispian, Crispien, Crispino, Crispo, Krispin

Cristian (Greek) a form of Christian.
Crétien, Cristean, Cristhian, Cristiano, Cristien, Cristino, Cristle, Criston, Cristos, Cristy, Cristyan, Crystek, Crystian

Cristobal (Greek) a form of Christopher.
Cristóbal, Cristoval, Cristovao

Cristoforo (Italian) a form of Christopher.
Cristofor

Cristopher (Greek) a form of Christopher.
Cristaph, Cristhofer, Cristifer, Cristofer, Cristoph, Cristophe, Crystapher, Crystifer

Crofton (Irish) town with cottages.

Cromwell (English) crooked spring, winding spring.

Crosby (Scandinavian) shrine of the cross.
Crosbey, Crosbie, Cross

Crosley (English) meadow of the cross.
Cross

Crowther (English) fiddler.

Cruz (Portuguese, Spanish) cross.
Cruze, Kruz

Crystek (Polish) a form of Christian.

Cullen (Irish) handsome.
Cull, Cullan, Cullie, Cullin

Culley (Irish) woods.
Cullie, Cully

Culver (English) dove.
Colver, Cull, Cullie, Cully

Cunningham (Irish) village of the
milk pail.

Curran (Irish) hero.
*Curan, Curon, Curr, Curren, Currey,
Curri, Currie, Currin, Curry*

Currito (Spanish) a form of Curtis.
Curcio

Curt (Latin) a short form of Courtney,
Curtis. See also Kurt.

Curtis (Latin) enclosure. (French)
courteous. See also Kurtis.
*Curio, Currito, Curt, Curtice, Curtiss,
Curtus*

Cuthbert (English) brilliant.

Cutler (English) knife maker.
Cut, Cuttie, Cutty

Cy (Persian) a short form of Cyrus.

Cyle (Irish) a form of Kyle.

Cyprian (Latin) from the island of
Cyprus.
Ciprian, Cipriano, Ciprien, Cyprien

Cyrano (Greek) from Cyrene, an
ancient city in North Africa.
Literature: *Cyrano de Bergerac* is a play
by Edmond Rostand about a great
guardsman and poet whose large nose
prevented him from pursuing the
woman he loved.

Cyril (Greek) lordly. See also Kiril.
*Cerek, Cerel, Cyrell, Ceril, Ciril, Cirillo,
Cirillo, Cyra, Cyrel, Cyrell, Cyrelle,
Cyrill, Cyrille, Cyrillus, Syrell, Syril*

Cyrus (Persian) sun. Historical: Cyrus
the Great was a king in ancient
Persia. See also Kir.
*Ciro, Cy, Cyress, Cyris, Cyriss, Cyruss,
Syris, Syrus*

Dabi (Basque) a form of David.

Dabir (Arabic) tutor.

Dacey (Latin) from Dacia, an area now
in Romania. (Irish) southerner.
*Dace, Dache, Dacian, Dacias, Dacio,
Dacy, Daicey, Daicy*

Dada (Yoruba) curly haired.
Dadi

Daegel (English) from Daegel,
England.

Daelen (English) a form of Dale.
*Daelan, Daelin, Daelon, Daelyn,
Daelyne*

Daemon (Greek) a form of Damian.
(Greek, Latin) a form of Damon.
*Daemean, Daemeon, Daemien, Daemin,
Daemion, Daemyen*

Daequan (American) a form of
Daquan.
*Daequane, Daequon, Daequone,
Daeqwan*

Daeshawn (American) a combination
of the prefix Da + Shawn.
*Daesean, Daeshaun, Daeshon, Daeshun,
Daisean, Daishaun, Daishawn, Daishon,
Daishoun*

Daevon (American) a form of Davon.
*Daevion, Daevohn, Daevonne, Daevonte,
Daevontey*

Dafydd (Welsh) a form of David.
Dafyd

Dag (Scandinavian) day; bright.
Daeg, Daegan, Dagen, Dagny, Deegan

Dagan (Hebrew) corn; grain.
*Daegan, Daegon, Dagen, Dageon,
Dagon*

Dagwood (English) shining forest.

Dai (Japanese) big.

Daimian (Greek) a form of Damian.
*Daiman, Daimean, Daimen, Daimeon,
Daimeyon, Daimien, Daimin, Daimion,
Daimyan*

Daimon (Greek, Latin) a form of
Damon.
Daimone

Daiquan (American) a form of
Dajuan.
*Daekwaun, Daekwon, Daiqone, Daiqua,
Daiquane, Daiquawn, Daiquon,
Daiqwan, Daiqwon*

Daivon (American) a form of Davon.
Daivain, Daivion, Daivonn, Daivonte,
Daiwan

Dajon (American) a form of Dajuan.
Dajean, Dajiawn, Dajin, Dajion, Dajn,
Dajohn, Dajonae

Dajuan (American) a combination of
the prefix Da + Juan. See also Dejuan.
Daejon, Daejuan, Daiquan, Dajon, Da
Jon, Da-Juan, Dajwan, Dajwoun,
Dakuan, Dakwan, Dawan, Dawaun,
Dawawn, Dawon, Dawoyan, Dijuan,
Diuan, Dujuan, D'Juan, D'juan,
Dwaun

Dakarai (Shona) happy.
Dakairi, Dakar, Dakaraia, Dakari,
Dakarri

Dakoda (Dakota) a form of Dakota.
Dacoda, Dacodah, Dakodah, Dakodas

Dakota (Dakota) friend; partner; tribal
name.
Dac, Dack, Dackota, Dacota, DaCota,
Dak, Dakcota, Dakkota, Dakoata,
Dakoda, Dakotah, Dakotha, Dakotta,
Dekota

Dakotah (Dakota) a form of Dakota.
Dakottah

Daksh (Hindi) efficient.

Dalal (Sanskrit) broker.

Dalbert (English) bright, shining. See
also Delbert.

Dale (English) dale, valley.
Dael, Daelen, Dal, Dalen, Daley,
Dalibor, Dallan, Dallin, Dallyn, Daly,
Dayl, Dayle

Dalen (English) a form of Dale.
Dailin, Dalaan, Dalan, Dalane, Daleon,
Dalian, Dalibor, Dalione, Dallan, Dalon,
Daylan, Daylen, Daylin, Daylon

Daley (Irish) assembly. (English) a familiar form of Dale.
Daily, Daly, Dawley

Dallan (English) a form of Dale.
Dallen, Dallon

Dallas (Scottish) valley of
the water; resting place. Geography: a
town in Scotland; a city in Texas.
Dal, Dalieass, Dall, Dalles, Dallis, Dalys,
Dellis

Dallin, Dallyn (English) pride's people.
Dalin, Dalyn

Dalston (English) Daegel's place.
Dalis, Dallon

Dalton (English) town in the valley.
Dal, Dalaton, Dallton, Dalt, Daltan,
Dalten, Daltin, Daltyn, Daulton, Delton

Dalvin (English) a form of Delvin.
Dalven, Dalvon, Dalvyn

Dalziel (Scottish) small field.

Damar (American) a short form of
Damarcus, Damario.
Damare, Damari, Damarre, Damauri

Damarcus (American) a combination
of the prefix Da + Marcus.
Damacus, Damar, Damarco, Damarcue,
Damarick, Damark,
Damarkco, Damarkis, Damarko,
Damarkus, Damarques, Damarquez,
Damarquis, Damarrco

Damario (Greek) gentle. (American) a
combination of the prefix Da +
Mario.
Damar, Damarea, Damareus, Damaria,
Damarie, Damarino, Damarion,
Damarious, Damaris, Damarius,
Damarrea, Damarrion, Damarrious,
Damarrius, Damaryo, Dameris,
Damerius

Damek (Slavic) a form of Adam.
Damick, Damicke

Dameon (Greek) a form of Damian.
Damein, Dameion, Dameone

Dametrius (Greek) a form of
Demetrius.
Dametri, Dametries, Dametrious,
Damitri, Damitric, Damitrie, Damitrious,
Damitrius

Damian (Greek) tamer; soother.
Daemon, Daimian, Damaiaon,
Damaian, Damaien, Damain, Damaine,
Damaion, Damani, Damanni, Damaun,
Damayon, Dame, Damean, Dameon,
Damián, Damiane, Damiann, Damiano,
Damianos, Damien, Damion, Damiyan,
Damján, Damyan, Daymian, Dema,
Demyan

Damien (Greek) a form of Damian.
Religion: Father Damien ministered
to the leper colony on the Hawaiian
island Molokai.
Daemien, Daimien, Damie, Damienne,
Damyen

Damion (Greek) a form of Damian.
Damieon, Damiion, Damin, Damine,
Damionne, Damiyon, Dammion,
Damyon

Damon (Greek) constant, loyal. (Latin) spirit, demon.
Daemen, Daemon, Daemond, Daimon, Daman, Damen, Damond, Damone, Damoni, Damonn, Damonni, Damonta, Damontae, Damonte, Damontez, Damontis, Damyn, Daymon, Daymond

Dan (Vietnamese) yes. (Hebrew) a short form of Daniel.
Dahn, Danh, Danne

Dana (Scandinavian) from Denmark.
Dain, Daina, Dayna

Dandin (Hindi) holy man.

Dandré (French) a combination of the prefix De + André.
D'André, Dandrae, D'andrea, Dandras, Dandray, Dandre, Dondrea

Dane (English) from Denmark. See also Halden.
Dain, Daine, Danie, Dayne, Dhane

Danek (Polish) a form of Daniel.

Danforth (English) a form of Daniel.

Danial (Hebrew) a form of Daniel.
Danal, Daneal, Danieal, Daniyal, Dannial

Danick, Dannick (Slavic) familiar forms of Daniel.
Danek, Danieko, Danik, Danika, Danyck

Daniel (Hebrew) God is my judge. Bible: a Hebrew prophet. See also Danno, Kanaiela.
Dacso, Dainel, Dan, Daneel, Daneil, Danek, Danel, Danforth, Danial, Danick, Dániel, Daniël, Daniele,

Danielius, Daniell, Daniels, Danielson, Danilo, Daniyel, Dan'l, Dannel, Dannick, Danniel, Dannil, Danno, Danny, Dano, Danukas, Dany, Danyel, Danyell, Daoud, Dasco, Dayne, Deniel, Doneal, Doniel, Donois, Dusan, Nelo

Daniele (Hebrew) a form of Daniel.
Danile, Danniele

Danilo (Slavic) a form of Daniel.
Danielo, Danil, Danila, Danilka, Danylo

Danior (Gypsy) born with teeth.

Danladi (Hausa) born on Sunday.

Danno (Hebrew) a familiar form of Daniel. (Japanese) gathering in the meadow. (Hebrew) a familiar form of Daniel.
Dannon, Dano

Dannon (American) a form of Danno.
Daenan, Daenen, Dainon, Danaan, Danen, Danon

Danny, Dany (Hebrew) familiar forms of Daniel.
Daney, Dani, Dannee, Danney, Danni, Dannie, Dannye

Dano (Czech) a form of Daniel.
Danko, Danno

Dante, Danté (Latin) lasting, enduring.
Danatay, Danaté, Dant, Dantae, Dantay, Dantee, Dauntay, Dauntaye, Daunté, Dauntrae, Deante, Dontae, Donté

Dantrell (American) a combination of Dante + Darell.
Dantrel, Dantrey, Dantril, Dantyrell, Dontrell

Danyel (Hebrew) a form of Daniel.
Danya, Danyal, Danyale, Danyele, Danyell, Danyiel, Danyl, Danyle, Danylets, Danylo, Donyell

Daoud (Arabic) a form of David.
Daudi, Daudy, Dauod, Dawud

Daquan (American) a combination of the prefix Da + Quan.
Daequan, Daqon, Daquain, Daquaine, Da'quan, Daquandre, Daquandrey, Daquane, Daquann, Daquantae, Daquante, Daquarius, Daquaun, Daquawn, Daquin, Daquon, Daquone, Daquwon, Daqwain, Daqwan, Daqwane, Daqwann, Daqwon, Daqwone, Dayquan, Dequain, Dequan, Dequann, Dequaun

Dar (Hebrew) pearl.

Dara (Cambodian) stars.

Daran (Irish) a form of Darren.
Darann, Darawn, Darian, Darran, Dayran, Deran

Darby (Irish) free. (English) deer park.
Dar, Darb, Darbee, Darbey, Darbie, Derby

Darcy (Irish) dark. (French) from Arcy, France.
Dar, Daray, D'Aray, Darce, Darcee, Darcel, Darcey, Darcio, D'Arcy, Darsey, Darsy

Dareh (Persian) wealthy.

Darell (English) a form of Darrell.
Darall, Daralle, Dareal, Darel, Darelle, Darral, Darrall

Daren (Hausa) born at night. (Irish, English) a form of Darren.
Dare, Dayren, Dheren

Darian, Darrian (Irish) forms of Darren.
Daryan

Darick (German) a form of Derek.
Darek, Daric, Darico, Darieck, Dariek, Darik, Daryk

Darien, Darrien (Irish) forms of Darren.

Darin (Irish) a form of Darren.
Daryn, Darynn, Dayrin, Dearin, Dharin

Dario (Spanish) affluent.

Darion Darrion (Irish) forms of Darren.
Daryeon, Daryon

Darius (Greek) wealthy.
Dairus, Dare, Darieus, Darioush, Dariuse, Dariush, Dariuss, Dariusz, Darrius

Darnell (English) hidden place.
Dar, Darn, Darnall, Darneal, Darneil, Darnel, Darnelle, Darnyell, Darnyll

Daron (Irish) a form of Darren.
Daeron, Dairon, Darone, Daronn, Darroun, Dayron, Dearon, Dharon, Diron

Darrell (French) darling, beloved; grove of oak trees.
Dare, Darel, Darell, Darral, Darrel, Darrill, Darrol, Darryl, Derrell

Darren (Irish) great. (English) small; rocky hill.
Daran, Dare, Daren, Darian, Darien,

Darin, Darion, Daron, Darran, Darrian, Darrien, Darrience, Darrin, Darrion, Darron, Darryn, Darun, Daryn, Dearron, Deren, Dereon, Derren, Derron

Darrick (German) a form of Derek.
Darrec, Darrek, Darric, Darrik, Darryk

Darrin (Irish) a form of Darren.

Darrion (Irish) a form of Darren.
Dairean, Dairion, Darian, Darien, Darion, Darrian, Darrien, Darrione, Darriyun, Derrian, Derrion

Darrius (Greek) a form of Darius.
Darreus, Darrias, Darrious, Darris, Darriuss, Darrus, Darryus, Derrious, Derris, Derrius

Darron (Irish) a form of Darren.
Darriun, Darroun

Darryl (French) darling, beloved; grove of oak trees. A form of Darrell.
Dahrll, Darryle, Darryll, Daryl, Daryle, Daryll, Derryl

Darshan (Hindi) god; godlike. Religion: another name for the Hindu god Shiva.
Darshaun, Darshon

Darton (English) deer town.
Dartel, Dartrel

Darwin (English) dear friend. History: Charles Darwin was the British naturalist who established the theory of evolution.
Darvin, Darvon, Darwyn, Derwin, Derwynn, Durwin

Daryl (French) a form of Darryl.
Darel, Daril, Darl, Darly, Daryell, Daryle, Daryll, Darylle, Daroyl

Dasan (Pomo) leader of the bird clan.
Dassan

Dashawn (American) a combination of the prefix Da + Shawn.
Dasean, Dashan, Dashane, Dashante, Dashaun, Dashaunte, Dashean, Dashon, Dashonnie, Dashonte, Dashuan, Dashun, Dashwan, Dayshawn

Dauid (Swahili) a form of David.

Daulton (English) a form of Dalton.

Davante (American) a form of Davonte.
Davanta, Davantay, Davinte

Davaris (American) a combination of Dave + Darius.
Davario, Davarious, Davarius, Davarrius, Davarus

Dave (Hebrew) a short form of David, Davis.

Davey (Hebrew) a familiar form of David.
Davee, Davi, Davie, Davy

David (Hebrew) beloved. Bible: the second king of Israel. See also Dov, Havika, Kawika, Taaveti, Taffy, Tevel.
Dabi, Daevid, Dafydd, Dai, Daivid, Daoud, Dauid, Dav, Dave, Daved, Daveed, Daven, Davey, Davidde, Davide, Davidek, Davido, Davon, Davoud, Davyd, Dawid, Dawit, Dawud, Dayvid, Dodya, Dov

Davin (Scandinavian) brilliant Finn.
Daevin, Davion, Davon, Davyn,
Dawan, Dawin, Dawine, Dayvon,
Deavan, Deaven

Davion (American) a form of Davin.
Davione, Davionne, Daviyon, Davyon,
Deaveon

Davis (Welsh) son of David.
Dave, Davidson, Davies, Davison

Davon (American) a form of Davin.
Daevon, Daivon, Davon, Davone,
Davonn, Davonne, Deavon, Deavone,
Devon

Davonte (American) a combination of
Davon + the suffix Te.
Davante, Davonnte, Davonta, Davontae,
Davontah, Davontai, Davontay,
Davontaye, Davontea, Davontee, Davonti

Dawan (American) a form of Davin.
Dawann, Dawante, Dawaun, Dawayne,
Dawon, Dawone, Dawoon, Dawyne,
Dawyun

Dawit (Ethiopian) a form of David.

Dawson (English) son of David.
Dawsyn

Dax (French, English) water.
Daylon (American) a form of Dillon.
Daylan, Daylen, Daylin, Daylun,
Daylyn

Daymian (Greek) a form of Damian.
Daymayne, Daymen, Daymeon,
Daymiane, Daymien, Daymin,
Dayminn, Daymion, Daymn

Dayne (Scandinavian) a form of Dane.
Dayn

Dayquan (American) a form of
Daquan.
Dayquain, Dayquawane, Dayquin,
Dayqwan

Dayshawn (American) a form of
Dashawn.
Daysean, Daysen, Dayshaun, Dayshon,
Dayson

Dayton (English) day town; bright,
sunny town.
Daeton, Daiton, Daythan, Daython,
Daytona, Daytonn, Deyton

Dayvon (American) a form of Davin.
Dayven, Dayveon, Dayvin, Dayvion,
Dayvonn

De (Chinese) virtuous.

Deacon (Greek) one who serves.
Deke

Dean (French) leader. (English) valley.
See also Dino.
Deane, Deen, Dene, Deyn, Deyne

Deandre (French) a combination of
the prefix De + André.
D'andre, D'andré, D'André, D'andrea,
Deandra, Deandrae, Déandre, Deandré,
De André, Deandrea, De Andrea,
Deandres, Deandrey, Deaundera,
Deaundra, Deaundray, Deaundre, De
Aundre, Deaundrey, Deaundry, Deondre,
Diandre, Dondre

Deangelo (Italian) a combination of
the prefix De + Angelo.
Dang, Dangelo, D'Angelo, Danglo,
Deaengelo, Deangelio, Deangello,
Déangelo, De Angelo, Deangilio,
Deangleo, Deanglo, Deangulo, Diangelo,
Di'angelo

Deante (Latin) a form of Dante.
Deanta, Deantai, Deantay, Deanté, De
Anté, Deanteé, Deaunta, Diantae,
Diante, Diantey

Deanthony (Italian) a combination of
the prefix De + Anthony.
D'anthony, Danton, Dianthony

Dearborn (English) deer brook.
Dearbourn, Dearburne, Deaurburn,
Deerborn

Decarlos (Spanish) a combination of
the prefix De + Carlos.
Dacarlos, Decarlo, Di'carlos

Decha (Tai) strong.

Decimus (Latin) tenth.

Declan (Irish) man of prayer.
Religion: Saint Declan was a fifth-
century Irish bishop.
Deklan

Dedrick (German) ruler of the peo-
ple. See also Derek, Theodoric.
Deadrick, Deddrick, Dederick, Dedrek,
Dedreko, Dedric, Dedrix, Dedrrick,
Deedrick, Diedrich, Diedrick, Dietrich,
Detrick

Deems (English) judge's child.

Deion (Greek) a form of Dion.
Deione, Deionta, Deionte

Dejuan (American) a combination of the prefix De + Juan. See also Dajuan.
Dejan, Dejon, Dejuane, Dejun, Dewan, Dewaun, Dewon, Dijaun, Djuan, D'Juan, Dujuan, Dujuane, D'Won

Dekel (Hebrew, Arabic) palm tree, date tree.

Dekota (Dakota) a form of Dakota.
Decoda, Dekoda, Dekodda, Dekotes

Del (English) a short form of Delbert, Delvin, Delwin.

Delaney (Irish) descendant of the challenger.
Delaine, Delainey, Delainy, Delan, Delane, Delanny, Delany

Delano (French) nut tree. (Irish) dark.
Delanio, Delayno, Dellano

Delbert (English) bright as day. See also Dalbert.
Bert, Del, Dilbert

Delfino (Latin) dolphin.
Delfine

Déli (Chinese) virtuous.

Dell (English) small valley. A short form of Udell.

Delling (Scandinavian) scintillating.

Delmar (Latin) sea.
Dalmar, Dalmer, Delmare, Delmario, Delmarr, Delmer, Delmor, Delmore

Delon (American) a form of Dillon.
Deloin, Delone, Deloni, Delonne

Delroy (French) belonging to the king. See also Elroy, Leroy.
Delray, Delree, Delroi

Delshawn (American) a combination of Del + Shawn.
Delsean, Delshon, Delsin, Delson

Delsin (Native American) he is so.
Delsy

Delton (English) a form of Dalton.
Delten, Deltyn

Delvin (English) proud friend; friend from the valley.
Dalvin, Del, Delavan, Delvian, Delvon, Delvyn, Delwin

Delwin (English) a form of Delvin.
Dalwin, Dalwyn, Del, Dellwin, Dellwyn, Delwyn, Delwynn

Deman (Dutch) man.

Demarco (Italian) a combination of the prefix De + Marco.
Damarco, Demarcco, Demarceo, Demarcio, Demarkco, Demarkeo, Demarko, Demarquo, D'Marco

Demarcus (American) a combination of the prefix De + Marcus.
Damarcius, Damarcus, Demarces, Demarcis, Demarcius, Demarcos, Demarcuse, Demarkes, Demarkis, Demarkos, Demarkus, Demarqus, D'Marcus

Demario (Italian) a combination of the prefix De + Mario.
Demarea, Demaree, Demareo, Demari, Demaria, Demariea, Demarion, Demarreio, Demariez, Demarious,

Demaris, Demariuz, Demarrio, Demerio, Demerrio

Demarius (American) a combination of the prefix De + Marius.

Demarquis (American) a combination of the prefix De + Marquis.
Demarques, Demarquez, Demarqui

Dembe (Luganda) peaceful.
Damba

Demetri, Demitri (Greek) short forms of Demetrius.
Dametri, Damitré, Demeter, Demetre, Demetrea, Demetriel, Demitre, Demitrie, Domotor

Demetris (Greek) a short form of Demetrius.
Demeatric, Demeatrice, Demeatris, Demetres, Demetress, Demetric, Demetrice, Demetrick, Demetrics, Demetricus, Demetrik, Demitrez, Demitries, Demitris

Demetrius (Greek) lover of the earth. Mythology: a follower of Demeter, the goddess of the harvest. See also Dimitri, Mimis, Mitsos.
Dametrius, Demeitrius, Demeterious, Demetreus, Demetri, Demetrias, Demetrio, Demetrios, Demetrious, Demetris, Demetriu, Demetrium, Demetrois, Demetruis, Demetrus, Demitirus, Demitri, Demitrias, Demitriu, Demitrius, Demitrus, Demtrius, Demtrus, Dimitri, Dimitrios, Dimitrius, Dmetrius, Dymek

Demichael (American) a combination of the prefix De + Michael.
Dumichael

Demond (Irish) a short form of Desmond.
Demonde, Demonds, Demone, Dumonde

Demont (French) mountain.
Démont, Demonta, Demontae, Demontay, Demontaz, Demonte, Demontez, Demontre

Demorris (American) a combination of the prefix De + Morris.
Demoris, DeMorris, Demorus

Demos (Greek) people.
Demas, Demosthenes

Demothi (Native American) talks while walking.

Dempsey (Irish) proud.
Demp, Demps, Dempsie, Dempsy

Dempster (English) one who judges.
Demster

Denby (Scandinavian) Geography: a Danish village.
Danby, Den, Denbey, Denney, Dennie, Denny

Denham (English) village in the valley.

Denholm (Scottish) Geography: a town in Scotland.

Denis (Greek) a form of Dennis.
Denise, Deniz

Denley (English) meadow; valley.
Denlie, Denly

Denman (English) man from the valley.

Dennis (Greek) Mythology: a follower of Dionysus, the god of wine. See also Dion, Nicho.
Den, Dénes, Denies, Denis, Deniz,

Dennes, Dennet, Dennez, Denny, Dennys, Denya, Denys, Deon, Dinis

Dennison (English) son of Dennis. See also Dyson, Tennyson.
Den, Denison, Denisson, Dennyson

Denny (Greek) a familiar form of Dennis.
Den, Denney, Dennie, Deny

Denton (English) happy home.
Dent, Denten, Dentin

Denver (English) green valley. Geography: the capital of Colorado.

Denzel (Cornish) a form of Denzil.
Danzel, Danzell, Dennzel, Denzal, Denzale, Denzall, Denzell, Denzelle, Denzle, Denzsel

Denzell (Cornish) Geography: a location in Cornwall, England.
Dennzil, Dennzyl, Denzel, Denzial, Denziel, Denzil, Denzill, Denzyel, Denzyl, Donzell

Deon (Greek) a form of Dennis. See also Dion.
Deion, Deone, Deonn, Deonno

Deondre (French) a form of Deandre.
Deiondray, Deiondre, Deondra, Deondrae, Deondray, Deondré, Deondrea, Deondree, Deondrei, Deondrey, Diondra, Diondrae, Diondre, Diondrey

Deontae (American) a combination of the prefix De + Dontae.
Deonta, Deontai, Deontay, Deontaye, Deonte, Deonté, Deontea, Deonteya, Deonteye, Deontia, Deontre, Dionte

Deonte, Deonté (American) forms of Deontae.
D'Ante, Deante, Deontée, Deontie

Deontre (American) forms of Deontae.
Deontrae, Deontrais, Deontray, Deontrea, Deontrey, Deontrez, Deontreze, Deontrus

Dequan (American) a combination of the prefix De + Quan.
Dequain, Dequane, Dequann, Dequante, Dequantez, Dequantis, Dequaun, Dequavius, Dequawn, Dequian, Dequin, Dequine, Dequinn, Dequion, Dequoin, Dequon, Dequan, Dequon, Deqwone

Dereck, Derick (German) forms of Derek.
Derekk, Dericka, Derico, Deriek, Derique, Deryck, Deryk, Deryke, Detrek

Derek (German) a short form of Theodoric. See also Dedrick, Dirk.
Darek, Darick, Darrick, Derak, Dereck, Derecke, Derele, Deric, Derick, Derik, Derk, Derke, Derrek, Derrick, Deryek

Deric, Derik (German) forms of Derek.
Deriek, Derikk

Dermot (Irish) free from envy. (English) free. (Hebrew) a short form of Jeremiah. See also Kermit.
Der, Dermod, Dermott, Diarmid, Diarmuid

Deron (Hebrew) bird; freedom. (American) a combination of the prefix De + Ron.
Daaron, Daron, Da-Ron, Darone, Darron, Dayron, Dereon, Deronn, Deronne, Derrin, Derrion, Derron,

*Derronn, Derronne, Derryn, Diron,
Duron, Durron, Dyron*

Deror (Hebrew) lover of freedom.
Derori, Derorie

Derrek (German) a form of Derek.
Derrec, Derreck

Derrell (French) a form of Darrell.
*Derel, Derele, Derell, Derelle, Derrel,
Dérrell, Derriel, Derril, Derrill, Deryl,
Deryll*

Derren (Irish, English) a form of
Darren.
*Deren, Derran, Derraun, Derreon,
Derrian, Derrien, Derrin, Derrion,
Derron, Derryn, Deryan, Deryn, Deryon*

Derrick (German) ruler of the people.
A form of Derek.
Derric, Derrik, Derryck, Derryk

Derry (Irish) redhead. Geography: a
city in Northern Ireland.
Darrie, Darry, Derri, Derrie, Derrye, Dery

Derryl (French) a form of Darryl.
Deryl, Deryll

Derward (English) deer keeper.

Derwin (English) a form of Darwin.
Derwyn

Desean (American) a combination of
the prefix De + Sean.
Dasean, D'Sean, Dusean

Deshane (American) a combination
of the prefix De + Shane.
Deshan, Deshayne

Deshaun (American) a combination
of the prefix De + Shaun.
*Deshan, Deshane, Deshann, Deshaon,
Deshaune, D'shaun, D'Shaun, Dushaun*

Deshawn (American) a combination
of the prefix De + Shawn.
*Dashaun, Dashawn, Deshauwn,
Deshawan, Deshawon, Deshon,
D'shawn, D'Shawn, Dushan, Dushawn*

Deshea (American) a combination of
the prefix De + Shea.
Deshay

Déshì (Chinese) virtuous.

Deshon (American) a form of
Deshawn.
*Deshondre, Deshone, Deshonn,
Deshonte, Deshun, Deshunn*

Desiderio (Spanish) desired.

Desmond (Irish) from south Munster.
*Demond, Des, Desi, Desimon, Desman,
Desmand, Desmane, Desmen, Desmine,
Desmon, Desmound, Desmund,
Desmyn, Dezmon, Dezmond*

Destin (French) destiny, fate.
*Destan, Desten, Destine, Deston, Destry,
Destyn*

Destry (American) a form of Destin.
Destrey, Destrie

Detrick (German) a form of Dedrick.
Detrek, Detric, Detrich, Detrik, Detrix

Devan (Irish) a form of Devin.
*Devaan, Devain, Devane, Devann,
Devean, Devun, Diwan*

Devante (American) a combination of
Devan + the suffix Te.
*Devanta, Devantae, Devantay, Devanté,
Devantée, Devantez, Devanty,
Devaughntae, Devaughnte, Devaunte,
Deventae, Deventay, Devente, Divante*

Devaughn (American) a form of
Devin.
Devaugh, Devaun

Devayne (American) a form of
Dewayne.
*Devain, Devaine, Devan, Devane,
Devayn, Devein, Deveion*

Deven (Hindi) for God. (Irish) a form
of Devin.
*Deaven, Deiven, Devein, Devenn,
Devven, Diven*

Deverell (English) riverbank.

Devin (Irish) poet.
*Deavin, Deivin, Dev, Devan, Devaughn,
Deven, Devlyn, Devon, Devvin, Devy,
Devyn, Dyvon*

Devine (Latin) divine. (Irish) ox.
*Davon, Devinn, Devon, Devyn, Devyne,
Dewine*

Devlin (Irish) brave, fierce.
*Dev, Devlan, Devland, Devlen, Devlon,
Devlyn*

Devon (Irish) a form of Devin.
*Deavon, Deivon, Deivone, Deivonne,
Deveon, Deveone, Devion, Devoen,
Devohn, Devonae, Devone, Devoni,
Devonio, Devonn, Devonne,
Devontaine, Devvon, Devvonne, Dewon,
Dewone, Divon, Diwon*

Devonta (American) a combination of Devon + the suffix Ta.
Deveonta, Devonnta, Devonntae, Devontae, Devontai, Devontay, Devontaye

Devonte (American) a combination of Devon + the suffix Te.
Deveonte, Devionte, Devonté, Devontea, Devontee, Devonti, Devontia, Devontre

Devyn (Irish) a form of Devin.
Devyin, Devynn, Devynne

Dewayne (Irish) a form of Dwayne. (American) a combination of the prefix De + Wayne.
Deuwayne, Devayne, Dewain, Dewaine, Dewan, Dewane, Dewaun, Dewaune, Dewayen, Dewean, Dewon, Dewune

Dewei (Chinese) highly virtuous.

Dewey (Welsh) prized.
Dew, Dewi, Dewie

DeWitt (Flemish) blond.
Dewitt, Dwight, Wit

Dexter (Latin) dexterous, adroit. (English) fabric dyer.
Daxter, Decca, Deck, Decka, Dekka, Dex, Dextar, Dextor, Dextrel, Dextron

Dezmon, Dezmond (Irish) forms of Desmond.
Dezman, Dezmand, Dezmen, Dezmin

Diamond (English) brilliant gem; bright guardian.
Diaman, Diamanta, Diamante, Diamend, Diamenn, Diamont, Diamonta, Diamonte, Diamund, Dimond, Dimonta, Dimontae, Dimonte

Dick (German) a short form of Frederick, Richard.
Dic, Dicken, Dickens, Dickie, Dickon, Dicky, Dik

Dickran (Armenian) History: an ancient Armenian king.
Dicran, Dikran

Dickson (English) son of Dick.
Dickenson, Dickerson, Dikerson, Diksan

Didi (Hebrew) a familiar form of Jedidiah, Yedidyah.

Didier (French) desired, longed for.

Diedrich (German) a form of Dedrick, Dietrich.
Didrich, Didrick, Didrik, Diederick

Diego (Spanish) a form of Jacob, James.
Iago, Diaz, Jago

Dietbald (German) a form of Theobald.
Dietbalt, Dietbolt

Dieter (German) army of the people.
Deiter

Dietrich (German) a form of Dedrick.
Deitrich, Deitrick, Deke, Diedrich, Dietrick, Dierck, Dieter, Dieterich, Dieterick, Dietz

Digby (Irish) ditch town; dike town.

Dillan (Irish) a form of Dillon.
Dilan, Dillian, Dilun, Dilyan

Dillon (Irish) loyal, faithful. See also Dylan.
Daylon, Delon, Dil, Dill, Dillan, Dillen,

Dillie, Dillin, Dillion, Dilly, Dillyn, Dilon, Dilyn, Dilynn

Dilwyn (Welsh) shady place.
Dillwyn

Dima (Russian) a familiar form of Vladimir.
Dimka

Dimitri (Russian) a form of Demetrius.
Dimetra, Dimetri, Dimetric, Dimetrie, Dimitr, Dimitric, Dimitrie, Dimitrik, Dimitris, Dimitry, Dimmy, Dmitri, Dymitr, Dymitry

Dimitrios (Greek) a form of Demetrius.
Dhimitrios, Dimitrius, Dimos, Dmitrios

Dimitrius (Greek) a form of Demetrius.
Dimetrius, Dimitricus, Dimitrius, Dimetrus, Dmitrius

Dingbang (Chinese) protector of the country.

Dinh (Vietnamese) calm, peaceful.
Din

Dino (German) little sword. (Italian) a form of Dean.
Deano

Dinos (Greek) a familiar form of Constantine, Konstantin.

Dinsmore (Irish) fortified hill.
Dinnie, Dinny, Dinse

Diogenes (Greek) honest. History: an ancient philosopher who searched with a lantern in daylight for an honest man.
Diogenese

Dion (Greek) a short form of Dennis, Dionysus.
Deion, Deon, Dio, Dione, Dionigi, Dionis, Dionn, Dionne, Diontae, Dionte, Diontray

Dionte (American) a form of Deontae.
Diante, Dionta, Diontae, Diontay, Diontaye, Dionté, Diontea

Dionysus (Greek) celebration. Mythology: the god of wine.
Dion, Dionesios, Dionicio, Dionisio, Dionisios, Dionusios, Dionysios, Dionysius, Dunixi

Diquan (American) a combination of the prefix Di + Quan.
Diqawan, Diqawn, Diquane

Dirk (German) a short form of Derek, Theodoric.
Derk, Dirck, Dirke, Durc, Durk, Dyrk

Dixon (English) son of Dick.
Dickson, Dix

Dmitri (Russian) a form of Dimitri.
Dmetriy, Dmitiri, Dmitri, Dmitrik, Dmitriy

Doane (English) low, rolling hills.
Doan

Dob (English) a familiar form of Robert.
Dobie

Dobry (Polish) good.

Doherty (Irish) harmful.
Docherty, Dougherty, Douherty

Dolan (Irish) dark haired.
Dolin, Dolyn

Dolf, Dolph (German) short forms of Adolf, Adolph, Rudolf, Rudolph.
Dolfe, Dolfi, Dolphe, Dolphus

Dom (Latin) a short form of Dominic.
Dome, Domó

Domenic (Latin) an alternate form of Dominic.
Domanick, Domenick

Domenico (Italian) a form of Dominic.
Domenic, Domicio, Dominico, Menico

Domingo (Spanish) born on Sunday. See also Mingo.
Demingo, Domingos

Dominic (Latin) belonging to the Lord. See also Chuminga.
Deco, Demenico, Dom, Domanic, Domeka, Domenic, Domenico, Domini, Dominie, Dominik, Dominique, Dominitric, Dominy, Domminic, Domnenique, Domokos, Domonic, Nick

Dominick (Latin) a form of Dominic.
Domiku, Domineck, Dominick, Dominicke, Dominiek, Dominik, Dominnick, Dominyck, Domminick, Dommonick, Domnick, Domokos, Domonick, Donek, Dumin

Dominik (Latin) an alternte form of Dominic.
Domenik, Dominiko, Dominyk, Domonik

Dominique (French) a form of Dominic.
Domeniq, Domeniqu, Domenique, Domenque, Dominiqu, Dominque, Dominiqueia, Domnenique, Domnique, Domoniqu, Domonique, Domunique

Domokos (Hungarian) a form of Dominic.
Dedo, Dome, Domek, Domok, Domonkos

Don (Scottish) a short form of Donald. See also Kona.
Donn

Donahue (Irish) dark warrior.
Donohoe, Donohue

Donal (Irish) a form of Donald.

Donald (Scottish) world leader; proud ruler. See also Bohdan, Tauno.
Don, Donal, Dónal, Donaldo, Donall, Donalt, Donát, Donaugh, Donnie

Donatien (French) gift.
Donathan, Donathon

Donato (Italian) gift.
Dodek, Donatello, Donati, Donatien, Donatus

Donavan (Irish) a form of Donovan.
Donaven, Donavin, Donavon, Donavyn

Dondre (French) a form of Deandre.
Dondra, Dondrae, Dondray, Dondré, Dondrea

Dong (Vietnamese) easterner.
Duong

Donkor (Akan) humble.

Donnell (Irish) brave; dark.
Doneal, Donel, Donele, Donell, Donelle, Donnel, Donnele, Donnelly, Doniel, Donielle, Donnel, Donnelle, Donniel, Donyel, Donyell

Donnelly (Irish) a form of Donnell.
Donelly, Donlee, Donley

Donnie, Donny (Irish) familiar forms of Donald.

Donovan (Irish) dark warrior.
Dohnovan, Donavan, Donevan, Donevon, Donivan, Donnivan, Donnovan, Donnoven, Donoven, Donovin, Donovon, Donvan

Dontae, Donté (American) forms of Dante.
Donta, Dontai, Dontao, Dontate, Dontavious, Dontavius, Dontay, Dontaye, Dontea, Dontee, Dontez

Dontrell (American) a form of Dantrell.
Dontral, Dontrall, Dontray, Dontre, Dontreal, Dontrel, Dontrelle, Dontriel, Dontriell

Donzell (Cornish) a form of Denzell.
Donzeil, Donzel, Donzelle, Donzello

Dooley (Irish) dark hero.
Dooly

Dor (Hebrew) generation.

Doran (Greek, Hebrew) gift. (Irish) stranger; exile.
Dore, Dorin, Dorran, Doron, Dorren, Dory

Dorian (Greek) from Doris, Greece. See also Isidore.
Dore, Dorey, Dorie, Dorien, Dorin, Dorion, Dorján, Doron, Dorrian,

Dorrien, Dorrin, Dorrion, Dorron, Dorryen, Dory

Dorrell (Scottish) king's doorkeeper. See also Durell.
Dorrel, Dorrelle

Dotan (Hebrew) law.
Dothan

Doug (Scottish) a short form of Dougal, Douglas.
Dougie, Dougy, Dugey, Dugie, Dugy

Dougal (Scottish) dark stranger. See also Doyle.
Doug, Dougall, Dugal, Dugald, Dugall, Dughall

Douglas (Scottish) dark river, dark stream. See also Koukalaka.
Doug, Douglass, Dougles, Dugaid, Dughlas

Dov (Yiddish) bear. (Hebrew) a familiar form of David.
Dovid, Dovidas, Dowid

Dovev (Hebrew) whisper.

Dow (Irish) dark haired.

Doyle (Irish) a form of Dougal.
Doy, Doyal, Doyel

Drago (Italian) a form of Drake.

Drake (English) dragon; owner of the inn with the dragon trademark.
Drago

Draper (English) fabric maker.
Dray, Draypr

Draven (American) a combination of the letter D + Raven.
Dravian, Dravin, Dravion, Dravon, Dravone, Dravyn, Drayven, Drevon

Dreng (Norwegian) hired hand; brave.

Dreshawn (American) a combination of Drew + Shawn.
Dreshaun, Dreshon, Dreshown

Drevon (American) a form of Draven.
Drevan, Drevaun, Dreven, Drevin, Drevion, Drevone

Drew (Welsh) wise. (English) a short form of Andrew.
Drewe, Dru

Dru (English) a form of Drew.
Druan, Drud, Drue, Drugi, Drui

Drummond (Scottish) druid's mountain.
Drummund, Drumond, Drumund

Drury (French) loving. Geography: Drury Lane is a street in London's theater district.

Dryden (English) dry valley.
Dry

Duane (Irish) a form of Dwayne.
Deune, Duain, Duaine, Duana

Duarte (Portuguese) rich guard. See also Edward.

Duc (Vietnamese) moral.
Duoc, Duy

Dudd (English) a short form of Dudley.
Dud, Dudde, Duddy

Dudley (English) common field.
Dudd, Dudly

Duer (Scottish) heroic.

Duff (Scottish) dark.
Duffey, Duffie, Duffy

Dugan (Irish) dark.
Doogan, Dougan, Douggan, Duggan

Duke (French) leader; duke.
Dukey, Dukie, Duky

Dukker (Gypsy) fortuneteller.

Dulani (Nguni) cutting.

Dumaka (Ibo) helping hand.

Duman (Turkish) misty, smoky.

Duncan (Scottish) brown warrior.
Literature: King Duncan was
Macbeth's victim in Shakespeare's
play *Macbeth*.
Dunc, Dunn

Dunham (Scottish) brown.

Dunixi (Basque) a form of Dionysus.

Dunley (English) hilly meadow.

Dunlop (Scottish) muddy hill.

Dunmore (Scottish) fortress on the
hill.

Dunn (Scottish) a short form of
Duncan.
Dun, Dune, Dunne

Dunstan (English) brownstone
fortress.
Dun, Dunston

Dunton (English) hill town.

Dur (Hebrew) stacked up. (English) a
short form of Durwin.

Durand (Latin) a form of Durant.

Durant (Latin) enduring.
*Duran, Durance, Durand, Durante,
Durontae, Durrant*

Durell (Scottish, English) king's doorkeeper. See also Dorrell.
Durel, Durial, Durreil, Durrell, Durrelle

Durko (Czech) a form of George.

Durriken (Gypsy) fortuneteller.

Durril (Gypsy) gooseberry.
Durrel, Durrell

Durward (English) gatekeeper.
Dur, Ward

Durwin (English) a form of Darwin.

Dushawn (American) a combination
of the prefix Du + Shawn.
*Dusan, Dusean, Dushan, Dushane,
Dushaun, Dushon, Dushun*

Dustin (German) valiant fighter.
(English) brown rock quarry.
*Dust, Dustain, Dustan, Dusten, Dustie,
Dustine, Dustion, Duston, Dusty,
Dustyn, Dustynn*

Dusty (English) a familiar form of
Dustin.
Dustyn (English) a form of Dustin.

Dutch (Dutch) from the Netherlands;
from Germany.

Duval (French) a combination of the
prefix Du + Val.
Duvall, Duveuil

Dwaun (American) a form of Dajuan.
*Dwan, Dwaunn, Dwawn, Dwon,
Dwuann*

Dwayne (Irish) dark. See also
Dewayne.
*Dawayne, Dawyne, Duane, Duwain,
Duwan, Duwane, Duwayn, Duwayne,
Dwain, Dwaine, Dwan, Dwane,
Dwyane, Dywan, Dywane, Dywayne,
Dywone*

Dwight (English) a form of DeWitt.

Dyami (Native American) soaring
eagle.

Dyer (English) fabric dyer.

Dyke (English) dike; ditch.
Dike

Dylan (Welsh) sea. See also Dillon.
*Dylane, Dylann, Dylen, Dylian, Dylin,
Dyllan, Dyllen, Dyllian, Dyllin, Dyllyn,
Dylon, Dylyn*

Dylon (Welsh) a form of Dylan.
Dyllion, Dyllon

Dyre (Norwegian) dear heart.

Dyson (English) a short form of
Dennison.
Dysen, Dysonn

E

Ea (Irish) a form of Hugh.

Eachan (Irish) horseman.

Eagan (Irish) very mighty.
Egan, Egon

Eamon (Irish) a form of Edmond, Edmund.
Aimon, Eammon, Eamonn

Ean (English) a form of Ian.
Eaen, Eann, Eayon, Eion, Eon, Eyan, Eyon

Earl (Irish) pledge. (English) nobleman.
Airle, Earld, Earle, Earlie, Earlson, Early, Eorl, Erl, Erle, Errol

Earnest (English) a form of Ernest.
Earn, Earnesto, Earnie, Eranest

Easton (English) eastern town.
Eason, Easten, Eastin, Eastton

Eaton (English) estate on the river.
Eatton, Eton, Eyton

Eb (Hebrew) a short form of Ebenezer.
Ebb, Ebbie, Ebby

Eben (Hebrew) rock.
Eban, Ebin, Ebon

Ebenezer (Hebrew) foundation stone. Literature: Ebenezer Scrooge is a miserly character in Charles Dickens's *A Christmas Carol*.
Eb, Ebbaneza, Eben, Ebeneezer, Ebeneser, Ebenezar, Eveneser

Eberhard (German) courageous as a boar. See also Everett.
Eber, Ebere, Eberardo, Eberhardt, Evard, Everard, Everardo, Everhardt, Everhart

Ebner (English) a form of Abner.

Ebo (Fante) born on Tuesday.

Ed (English) a short form of Edgar, Edsel, Edward.
Edd

Edan (Scottish) fire.
Edain

Edbert (English) wealthy; bright.
Ediberto

Eddie (English) a familiar form of Edgar, Edsel, Edward.
Eddee, Eddy, Edi, Edie

Eddy (English) a form of Eddie.
Eddye, Edy

Edel (German) noble.
Adel, Edell, Edelmar, Edelweiss

Eden (Hebrew) delightful. Bible: the garden that was first home to Adam and Eve.
Eaden, Eadin, Edan, Edenson, Edin, Edyn, Eiden

Eder (Hebrew) flock.
Ederick, Edir

Edgar (English) successful spearman. See also Garek, Gerik, Medgar.
Ed, Eddie, Edek, Edgard, Edgardo, Edgars

Edgardo (Spanish) a form of Edgar.

Edison (English) son of Edward.
Eddison, Edisen, Edson

Edmond (English) a form of Edmund.
Eamon, Edmon, Edmonde, Edmondo, Edmondson, Esmond

Edmund (English) prosperous protector.
Eadmund, Eamon, Edmand, Edmaund, Edmond, Edmun, Edmundo, Edmunds

Edmundo (Spanish) a form of Edmund.
Edmando, Mundo

Edo (Czech) a form of Edward.

Edoardo (Italian) a form of Edward.

Edorta (Basque) a form of Edward.

Edouard (French) a form of Edward.
Édoard, Édouard

Edric (English) prosperous ruler.
Eddric, Eddrick, Ederick, Edrek, Edrice, Edrick, Edrico

Edsel (English) rich man's house.
Ed, Eddie, Edsell

Edson (English) a short form of Edison.
Eddson, Edsen

Eduardo (Spanish) a form of Edward.
Estuardo, Estvardo

Edur (Basque) snow.

Edward (English) prosperous guardian. See also Audie, Duarte, Ekewaka, Ned, Ted, Teddy.
Ed, Eddie, Edik, Edko, Edo, Edoardo, Edorta, Édouard, Eduard, Eduardo, Edus, Edvard, Edvardo, Edwardo, Edwards, Edwy, Edzio, Ekewaka, Etzio, Ewart

Edwin (English) prosperous friend. See also Ned, Ted.
Eadwinn, Edik, Edlin, Eduino, Edwan, Edwen, Edwon, Edwyn

Efrain (Hebrew) fruitful.
Efran, Efrane, Efrayin, Efren, Efrian, Eifraine

Efrat (Hebrew) honored.

Efrem (Hebrew) a short form of Ephraim.
Efe, Efraim, Efrim, Efrum

Efren (Hebrew) a form of Efrain, Ephraim.

Egan (Irish) ardent, fiery.
Egann, Egen, Egon

Egbert (English) bright sword. See also Bert, Bertie.

Egerton (English) Edgar's town.
Edgarton, Edgartown, Edgerton, Egeton

Egil (Norwegian) awe inspiring.
Eigil

Eginhard (German) power of the sword.
Eginhardt, Einhard, Einhardt, Enno

Egon (German) formidable.

Egor (Russian) a form of George. See also Igor, Yegor.

Ehren (German) honorable.

Eikki (Finnish) ever powerful.

Einar (Scandinavian) individualist.
Ejnar, Inar

Eion (Irish) a form of Ean, Ian.
Eann, Eian, Ein, Eine, Einn

Eitan (Hebrew) a form of Ethan.
Eita, Eithan, Eiton

Ejau (Ateso) we have received.

Ekewaka (Hawaiian) a form of Edward.

Ekon (Nigerian) strong.

Elam (Hebrew) highlands.

Elan (Hebrew) tree. (Native American) friendly.
Elann

Elbert (English) a form of Albert.
Elberto

Elchanan (Hebrew) a form of John.
Elchan, Elchonon, Elhanan, Elhannan

Elden (English) a form of Alden, Aldous.
Eldan, Eldin

Elder (English) dweller near the elder trees.

Eldon (English) holy hill.

Eldred (English) a form of Aldred.
Eldrid

Eldridge (English) a form of Aldrich.
El, Eldred, Eldredge, Eldrege, Eldrid, Eldrige, Elric

Eldwin (English) a form of Aldwin.
Eldwinn, Eldwyn, Eldwynn

Eleazar (Hebrew) God has helped. See also Lazarus.
Elazar, Elazaro, Eleasar, Eléazar, Eliazar, Eliezer

Elek (Hungarian) a form of Alec, Alex.
Elec, Elic, Elik

Elger (German) a form of Alger.
Elgar, Ellgar, Ellger

Elgin (English) noble; white.
Elgan, Elgen

Eli (Hebrew) uplifted. A short form of Elijah, Elisha. Bible: the high priest who trained the prophet Samuel. See also Elliot.
Elie, Elier, Ellie, Eloi, Eloy, Ely

Elia (Zuni) a short form of Elijah.
Eliah, Elio, Eliya, Elya

Elian (English) a form of Elijah. See also Trevelyan.
Elion

Elias (Greek) a form of Elijah.
Elia, Eliasz, Elice, Eliyas, Ellias, Ellice, Ellis, Elyas, Elyes

Eliazar (Hebrew) a form of Eleazar.
Eliasar, Eliazer, Elizar, Elizardo

Elie (Hebrew) a form of Eli.

Eliezer (Hebrew) a form of Eleazar.
Elieser

Elihu (Hebrew) a short form of Eliyahu.
Elih, Eliu, Ellihu

Elijah (Hebrew) a form of Eliyahu. Bible: a Hebrew prophet. See also Eli, Elisha, Elliot, Ilias, Ilya.
El, Elia, Elian, Elias, Elija, Elijha, Elijiah, Elijio, Elijuah, Elijuo, Elisjsha, Eliya, Eliyah, Ellis

Elika (Hawaiian) a form of Eric.

Eliseo (Hebrew) a form of Elisha.
Elisee, Elisée, Elisei, Elisiah, Elisio

Elisha (Hebrew) God is my salvation. Bible: a Hebrew prophet, successor to Elijah. See also Eli, Elijah.
Elijsha, Eliseo, Elish, Elishah, Elisher, Elishia, Elishua, Elysha, Lisha

Eliyahu (Hebrew) the Lord is my God.
Eliyahou, Elihu

Elkan (Hebrew) God is jealous.
Elkana, Elkanah, Elkin, Elkins

Elki (Moquelumnan) hanging over the top.

Ellard (German) sacred; brave.
Allard, Ellerd

Ellery (English) from a surname derived from the name Hilary.
Ellary, Ellerey

Elliot, Elliott (English) forms of Eli, Elijah.
Elio, Eliot, Eliott, Eliud, Eliut, Elliotte, Elyot, Elyott

Ellis (English) a form of Elias.
Elis

Ellison (English) son of Ellis.
Elison, Ellson, Ellyson, Elson

Ellsworth (English) nobleman's estate.
Ellswerth, Elsworth

Elman (German) like an elm tree.
Elmen

Elmer (English) noble; famous.
Aylmer, Elemér, Ellmer, Elmir, Elmo

Elmo (Greek) lovable, friendly. (Italian) guardian. (Latin) a familiar form of Anselm. (English) a form of Elmer.

Elmore (English) moor where the elm trees grow.

Elonzo (Spanish) a form of Alonzo.
Elon, Élon, Elonso

Eloy (Latin) chosen.
Eloi

Elrad (Hebrew) God rules.
Rad, Radd

Elroy (French) a form of Delroy, Leroy.
Elroi

Elsdon (English) nobleman's hill.

Elston (English) noble's town.
Ellston

Elsu (Native American) swooping, soaring falcon.

Elsworth (English) noble's estate.

Elton (English) old town.
Alton, Eldon, Ellton, Elthon, Eltonia

Elvern (Latin) a form of Alvern.
Elver, Elverne

Elvin (English) a form of Alvin.
El, Elvyn, Elwin, Elwyn, Elwynn

Elvio (Spanish) light skinned; blond.

Elvis (Scandinavian) wise.
El, Elviz, Elvys

Elvy (English) elfin warrior.

Elwell (English) old well.

Elwood (English) old forest. See also Wood, Woody.

Ely (Hebrew) a form of Eli. Geography: a region of England with extensive drained fens.
Elya, Elyie

Eman (Czech) a form of Emmanuel.
Emaney, Emani

Emanuel (Hebrew) a form of Emmanuel.
Emaniel, Emannual, Emannuel, Emanual, Emanueal, Emanuele, Emanuell, Emanuell, Emanuelle

Emerson (German, English) son of Emery.
Emmerson, Emreson

Emery (German) industrious leader.
Aimery, Emari, Emarri, Emeri, Emerich, Emerio, Emmerich, Emmerie, Emmery, Emmo, Emory, Emrick, Emry, Inre, Imrich

Emil (Latin) flatterer. (German) industrious. See also Milko, Milo.
Aymil, Emiel, Émile, Emilek, Emiliano, Emilio, Emill, Emils, Emilyan, Emlyn

Émile (French) a form of Emil.
Emiel, Emile, Emille

Emiliano (Italian) a form of Emil.
Emilian, Emilion

Emilien (Latin) friendly; industrious.

Emilio (Italian, Spanish) a form of Emil.
Emielio, Emileo, Emilio, Emilios, Emillio, Emilo

Emlyn (Welsh) waterfall.
Emelen, Emlen, Emlin

Emmanuel (Hebrew) God is with us. See also Immanuel, Maco, Mango, Manuel.
Eman, Emanuel, Emanuell, Emek, Emmahnuel, Emmanel, Emmaneuol, Emmanle, Emmanual, Emmanueal, Emmanuele, Emmanuell, Emmanuelle, Emmanuil, Enmanuel

Emmett (German) industrious; strong. (English) ant. History: Robert Emmett was an Irish patriot.
Em, Emet, Emett, Emitt, Emmet, Emmette, Emmitt, Emmot, Emmott, Emmy

Emmitt (German, English) a form of Emmett.
Emmit

Emory (German) a form of Emery.
Amory, Emmory, Emorye

Emre (Turkish) brother.
Emra, Emrah, Emreson

Emrick (German) a form of Emery.
Emeric, Emerick, Emric, Emrique, Emryk

Enapay (Sioux) brave appearance; he appears.

Endre (Hungarian) a form of Andrew.
Ender

Eneas (Greek) a form of Aeneas.
Eneias, Enné

Engelbert (German) bright as an angel. See also Ingelbert.
Bert, Englebert

Enli (Dene) that dog over there.

Ennis (Greek) mine. (Scottish) a form of Angus.
Eni, Enni

Enoch (Hebrew) dedicated, consecrated. Bible: the father of Methuselah.
Enoc, Enock, Enok

Enos (Hebrew) man.
Enosh

Enric (Romanian) a form of Henry.
Enrica

Enrick (Spanish) a form of Henry.
Enricky

Enrico (Italian) a form of Henry.
Enzio, Enzo, Rico

Enrikos (Greek) a form of Henry.

Enrique (Spanish) a form of Henry. See also Quiqui.
Enrigué, Enriqué, Enriquez, Enrrique

Enver (Turkish) bright; handsome.

Enyeto (Native American) walks like a bear.

Enzi (Swahili) powerful.

Eoin (Welsh) a form of Evan.

Ephraim (Hebrew) fruitful. Bible: the second son of Joseph.
Efraim, Efrayim, Efrem, Efren, Ephraen, Ephrain, Ephram, Ephrem, Ephriam

Erasmus (Greek) lovable.
Érasme, Erasmo, Rasmus

Erastus (Greek) beloved.
Éraste, Erastious, Ras, Rastus

Erbert (German) a short form of Herbert.
Ebert, Erberto

Ercole (Italian) splendid gift.

Erek (Scandinavian) a form of Eric.
Erec

Erhard (German) strong; resolute.
Erhardt, Erhart

Eriberto (Italian) a form of Herbert.
Erberto, Heriberto

Eric (Scandinavian) ruler of all. (English) brave ruler. (German) a short form of Frederick. History: Eric the Red was a Norwegian explorer who founded Greenland's first colony.
Aric, Ehrich, Elika, Erek, Éric, Erica, Ericc, Erich, Erick, Erico, Erik, Erikur, Erric, Eryc, Rick

Erich (Czech, German) a form of Eric.

Erick (English) a form of Eric.
Errick, Eryck

Erickson (English) son of Eric.
Erickzon, Erics, Ericson, Ericsson, Erikson, Erikzzon, Eriqson

Erik (Scandinavian) a form of Eric.
Erek, Erike, Eriks, Erikur, Errick, Errik, Eryk

Erikur (Icelandic) a form of Eric, Erik.

Erin (Irish) peaceful. History: an ancient name for Ireland.
Erine, Erinn, Erino, Eron, Errin, Eryn, Erynn

Erland (English) nobleman's land.
Erlend

Erling (English) nobleman's son.

Ermanno (Italian) a form of Herman.
Erman

Ermano (Spanish) a form of Herman.
Ermin, Ermine, Erminio, Ermon

Ernest (English) earnest, sincere. See also Arno.
Earnest, Ernestino, Ernesto, Ernestus, Ernie, Erno, Ernst

Ernesto (Spanish) a form of Ernest.
Ernester, Neto

Ernie (English) a familiar form of Ernest.
Earnie, Erney, Erny

Erno (Hungarian) a form of Ernest.
Ernö

Ernst (German) a form of Ernest.
Erns

Erol (Turkish) strong, courageous.
Eroll

Eron (Irish) a form of Erin.
Erran, Erren, Errion, Erron

Errando (Basque) bold.

Errol (Latin) wanderer. (English) a form of Earl.
Erol, Erold, Erroll, Erryl

Erroman (Basque) from Rome.

Erskine (Scottish) high cliff. (English) from Ireland.
Ersin, Erskin, Kinny

Ervin, Erwin (English) sea friend. Forms of Irving, Irwin.
Earvin, Erv, Erven, Ervyn, Erwan, Erwinek, Erwinn, Erwyn, Erwynn

Ervine (English) a form of Irving.
Erv, Ervin, Ervince, Erving, Ervins

Esau (Hebrew) rough; hairy. Bible: Jacob's twin brother.
Esaw

Esequiel (Hebrew) a form of Ezekiel.

Eshkol (Hebrew) grape clusters.

Eskil (Norwegian) god vessel.

Esmond (English) rich protector.

Espen (Danish) bear of the gods.

Essien (Ochi) sixth-born son.

Este (Italian) east.
Estes

Estéban (Spanish) a form of Stephen.
Estabon, Esteben, Estefan, Estefano, Estefen, Estephan, Estephen

Estebe (Basque) a form of Stephen.

Estevan (Spanish) a form of Stephen.
Esteven, Estevon, Estiven

Estevao (Spanish) a form of Stephen.
Estevez

Ethan (Hebrew) strong; firm.
Eathan, Eathen, Eathon, Eeathen, Eitan, Etan, Ethaen, Ethe, Ethen, Ethian

Étienne (French) a form of Stephen.
Etian, Etien, Étienn, Ettien

Ettore (Italian) steadfast.
Etor, Etore

Etu (Native American) sunny.

Euclid (Greek) intelligent. History: the founder of Euclidean geometry.

Eugen (German) a form of Eugene.

Eugene (Greek) born to nobility. See also Ewan, Gene, Gino, Iukini, Jenö, Yevgenyi, Zenda.
Eoghan, Eugen, Eugéne, Eugeni, Eugenio, Eugenius, Evgeny, Ezven

Eugenio (Spanish) a form of Eugene.

Eulises (Latin) a form of Ulysses.

Eustace (Greek) productive. (Latin) stable, calm. See also Stacey.
Eustache, Eustachius, Eustachy, Eustashe, Eustasius, Eustatius, Eustazio, Eustis, Eustiss

Evan (Irish) young warrior. (English) a form of John. See also Bevan, Owen.
Eavan, Eoin, Ev, Evaine, Evann, Evans, Even, Evens, Evin, Evon, Evyn, Ewan, Ewen

Evangelos (Greek) a form of Andrew.
Evagelos, Evaggelos, Evangelo

Evelyn (English) hazelnut.
Evelin

Everardo (German) strong as a boar.
Everado

Everett (English) a form of Eberhard.
Ev, Evered, Everet, Everette, Everhett, Everit, Everitt, Everrett, Evert, Evrett

Everley (English) boar meadow.
Everlea, Everlee

Everton (English) boar town.

Evgeny (Russian) a form of Eugene. See also Zhek.
Evgeni, Evgenij, Evgenyi

Evin (Irish) a form of Evan.
Evian, Evinn, Evins

Ewald (German) always powerful. (English) powerful lawman.

Ewan (Scottish) a form of Eugene, Evan. See also Keon.
Euan, Euann, Euen, Ewen, Ewhen

Ewert (English) ewe herder, shepherd.
Ewart

Ewing (English) friend of the law.
Ewin, Ewynn

Exavier (Basque) a form of Xavier.
Exaviar, Exavior, Ezavier

Eyota (Native American) great.

Ezekiel (Hebrew) strength of God.
Bible: a Hebrew prophet. See also
Haskel, Zeke.
*Esequiel, Ezakeil, Ezéchiel, Ezeck,
Ezeckiel, Ezeeckel, Ezekeial, Ezekeil,
Ezekeyial, Ezekial, Ezekielle, Ezell,
Ezequiel, Eziakah, Eziechiele*

Ezequiel (Hebrew) a form of Ezekiel.
Esequiel, Eziequel

Ezer (Hebrew) a form of Ezra.

Ezra (Hebrew) helper; strong. Bible: a
Jewish priest who led the Jews back
to Jerusalem.
*Esdras, Esra, Ezer, Ezera, Ezrah, Ezri,
Ezry*

Ezven (Czech) a form of Eugene.
Esven, Esvin, Ezavin, Ezavine

Faber (German) a form of Fabian.

Fabian (Latin) bean grower.
*Fabain, Fabayan, Fabe, Fabein, Fabek,
Fabeon, Faber, Fabert, Fabi, Fabiano,
Fabien, Fabin, Fabio, Fabion, Fabius,*

*Fabiyan, Fabiyus, Fabyan, Fabyen,
Faybian, Faybien*

Fabiano (Italian) a form of Fabian.
Fabianno, Fabio

Fabio (Latin) a form of Fabian.
(Italian) a short form of Fabiano.
Fabbio

Fabrizio (Italian) craftsman.
Fabrice, Fabricio, Fabrizius

Fabron (French) little blacksmith;
apprentice.
Fabre, Fabroni

Fadey (Ukrainian) a form of
Thaddeus.
*Faday, Faddei, Faddey, Faddy, Fade,
Fadeyka, Fadie, Fady*

Fadi (Arabic) redeemer.
Fadhi

Fadil (Arabic) generous.
Fadeel, Fadel

Fagan (Irish) little fiery one.
Fagin

Fahd (Arabic) lynx.
Fahaad, Fahad

Fai (Chinese) beginning.

Fairfax (English) blond.
Fair, Fax

Faisal (Arabic) decisive.
*Faisel, Faisil, Faisl, Faiyaz, Faiz, Faizal,
Faize, Faizel, Faizi, Fasel, Fasil, Faysal,
Fayzal, Fayzel*

Fakhir (Arabic) excellent.
Fahkry, Fakher

Fakih (Arabic) thinker; reader of the
Koran.

Falco (Latin) falconer.
Falcon, Falk, Falke, Falken

Falito (Italian) a familiar form of
Rafael, Raphael.

Falkner (English) trainer of falcons.
See also Falco.
*Falconer, Falconner, Faulconer, Faulconner,
Faulkner*

Fane (English) joyful, glad.
Fanes, Faniel

Faraji (Swahili) consolation.

Farid (Arabic) unique.

Faris (Arabic) horseman.
*Faraz, Fares, Farhaz, Farice, Fariez,
Farris*

Farley (English) bull meadow; sheep
meadow. See also Lee.
*Fairlay, Fairlee, Fairleigh, Fairley, Fairlie,
Far, Farlay, Farlee, Farleigh, Farlie, Farly,
Farrleigh, Farrley*

Farnell (English) fern-covered hill.
Farnall, Fernald, Fernall, Furnald

Farnham (English) field of ferns.
Farnam, Farnum, Fernham

Farnley (English) fern meadow.
*Farnlea, Farnlee, Farnleigh, Farnly,
Fernlea, Fernlee, Fernleigh, Fernley*

Faroh (Latin) a form of Pharaoh.

Farold (English) mighty traveler.

Farquhar (Scottish) dear.
Fark, Farq, Farquar, Farquarson, Farque, Farquharson, Farquy, Farqy

Farr (English) traveler.
Faer, Farran, Farren, Farrin, Farrington, Farron

Farrell (Irish) heroic; courageous.
Farrel, Farrill, Farryll, Ferrell

Farrow (English) piglet.

Farruco (Spanish) a form of Francis, Francisco.
Frascuelo

Faruq (Arabic) honest.
Farook, Farooq, Faroque, Farouk, Faruqh

Faste (Norwegian) firm.

Fath (Arabic) victor.

Fatin (Arabic) clever.

Faust (Latin) lucky, fortunate. History: the sixteenth-century German necromancer who inspired many legends.
Faustino, Faustis, Fausto, Faustus

Faustino (Italian) a form of Faust.

Fausto (Italian) a form of Faust.

Favian (Latin) understanding.
Favain, Favio, Favyen

Faxon (German) long-haired.

Federico (Italian, Spanish) a form of Frederick.
Federic, Federigo, Federoquito

Feivel (Yiddish) God aids.

Feliks (Russian) a form of Felix.

Felipe (Spanish) a form of Philip.
Feeleep, Felipino, Felo, Filip, Filippo, Filips, Fillip, Flip

Felippo (Italian) a form of Philip.
Felip, Filippo, Lipp, Lippo, Pip, Pippo

Felix (Latin) fortunate; happy. See also Pitin.
Fee, Felic, Félice, Feliciano, Felicio, Felike, Feliks, Felo, Félix, Felizio, Phelix

Felton (English) field town.
Felten, Feltin

Fenton (English) marshland farm.
Fen, Fennie, Fenny, Fintan, Finton

Feodor (Slavic) a form of Theodore.
Dorek, Fedar, Fedinka, Fedor, Fedya, Fyodor

Feoras (Greek) smooth rock.

Ferdinand (German) daring, adventurous. See also Hernando.
Feranado, Ferd, Ferda, Ferdie, Ferdinánd, Ferdy, Ferdynand, Fernando, Nando

Ferenc (Hungarian) a form of Francis.
Feri, Ferke, Ferko

Fergus (Irish) strong; manly.
Fearghas, Fearghus, Feargus, Ferghus, Fergie, Ferguson, Fergusson

Fermin (French, Spanish) firm, strong.
Ferman, Firmin, Furman

Fernando (Spanish) a form of Ferdinand.
Ferando, Ferdinando, Ferdnando, Ferdo, Fernand, Fernandez, Fernendo

Feroz (Persian) fortunate.

Ferran (Arabic) baker.
Feran, Feron, Ferrin, Ferron

Ferrand (French) iron gray hair.
Farand, Farrand, Farrant, Ferrant

Ferrell (Irish) a form of Farrell.
Ferrel, Ferrill, Ferryl

Ferris (Irish) a form of Peter.
Fares, Faris, Fariz, Farris, Farrish, Feris, Ferriss

Fico (Spanish) a familiar form of Frederick.

Fidel (Latin) faithful. History: Fidel Castro was the Cuban revolutionary who overthrew a dictatorship in 1959 and established a communist regime in Cuba.
Fidele, Fidèle, Fidelio, Fidelis, Fidell, Fido

Field (English) a short form of Fielding.
Fields

Fielding (English) field; field worker.
Field

Fife (Scottish) from Fife, Scotland.
Fyfe

Fifi (Fante) born on Friday.

Fil (Polish) a form of Phil.
Filipek

Filbert (English) brilliant. See also Bert.
Filberte, Filberto, Filiberto, Philbert

Filiberto (Spanish) a form of Filbert.

Filip (Greek) a form of Philip.
Filip, Filippo

Fillipp (Russian) a form of Philip.
Filip, Filipe, Filipek, Filips, Fill, Fillip, Filya

Filmore (English) famous.
Fillmore, Filmer, Fyllmer, Fylmer, Philmore

Filya (Russian) a form of Philip.

Fineas (Irish) a form of Phineas.
Finneas

Finian (Irish) light skinned; white.
Finnen, Finnian, Fionan, Fionn, Phinean

Finlay (Irish) blond-haired soldier.
Findlay, Findley, Finlea, Finlee, Finley, Finn, Finnlea, Finnley

Finn (German) from Finland. (Irish) blond haired; light skinned. A short form of Finlay. (Norwegian) from the Lapland.
Fin, Finnie, Finnis, Finny

Finnegan (Irish) light skinned; white.
Finegan

Fiorello (Italian) little flower.
Fiore

Firas (Arabic) persistent.

Firman (French) firm; strong.
Ferman, Firmin

Firth (English) woodland.

Fischel (Yiddish) a form of Phillip.

Fiske (English) fisherman.
Fisk

Fitch (English) weasel, ermine.
Fitche

Fitz (English) son.
Filz

Fitzgerald (English) son of Gerald.

Fitzhugh (English) son of Hugh.
Hugh

Fitzpatrick (English) son of Patrick.

Fitzroy (Irish) son of Roy.

Flaminio (Spanish) Religion: Marcantonio Flaminio coauthored one of the most important texts of the Italian Reformation.

Flann (Irish) redhead.
Flainn, Flannan, Flannery

Flavian (Latin) blond, yellow haired.
Flavel, Flavelle, Flavien, Flavio, Flawiusz

Flavio (Italian) a form of Flavian.
Flabio, Flavious, Flavius

Fleming (English) from Denmark; from Flanders.
Flemming, Flemmyng, Flemyng

Fletcher (English) arrow featherer, arrow maker.
Flecher, Fletch

Flint (English) stream; flint stone.
Flynt

Flip (Spanish) a short form of Felipe. (American) a short form of Philip.

Florencio (Italian) a form of Florent.

Florent (French) flowering.
Florenci, Florencio, Florentin, Florentino, Florentyn, Florentz, Florinio, Florino

Florian (Latin) flowering, blooming.
Florien, Florrian, Flory, Floryan

Floyd (English) a form of Lloyd.

Flurry (English) flourishing, blooming.

Flynn (Irish) son of the red-haired man.
Flin, Flinn, Flyn

Folke (German) a form of Volker.
Folker

Foluke (Yoruba) given to God.

Foma (Bulgarian, Russian) a form of Thomas.
Fomka

Fonso (German, Italian) a short form of Alphonso.
Fonzo

Fontaine (French) fountain.

Fonzie (German) a familiar form of Alphonse.
Fons, Fonsie, Fonsy, Fonz

Forbes (Irish) prosperous.
Forbe

Ford (English) a short form of names ending in "ford."

Fordel (Gypsy) forgiving.

Forest (French) a form of Forrest.
Forestt, Foryst

Forester (English) forest guardian.
Forrester, Forrie, Forry, Forster, Foss, Foster

Forrest (French) forest; woodsman.
Forest, Forester, Forrestar, Forrester, Forrestt, Forrie

Fortino (Italian) fortunate, lucky.

Fortune (French) fortunate, lucky.
Fortun, Fortunato, Fortuné, Fortunio

Foster (Latin) a short form of Forester.

Fowler (English) trapper of wildfowl.

Fran (Latin) a short form of Francis.
Franh

Francesco (Italian) a form of Francis.

Franchot (French) a form of Francis.

Francis (Latin) free; from France.
Religion: Saint Francis of Assisi was
the founder of the Franciscan order.
See also Farruco, Ferenc.
*Fran, France, Frances, Francesco,
Franchot, Francisco, Franciskus, Franco,
François, Frang, Frank, Frannie, Franny,
Frans, Franscis, Fransis, Franta, Frantisek,
Frants, Franus, Frantisek, Franz, Frencis*

Francisco (Portuguese, Spanish) a
form of Francis. See also Chilo,
Cisco, Farruco, Paco, Pancho.
Franco, Fransisco, Fransysco, Frasco, Frisco

Franco (Latin) a short form of Francis.
Franko

François (French) a form of Francis.
Francoise

Frank (English) a short form of Francis,
Franklin. See also Palani, Pancho.
*Franc, Franck, Franek, Frang, Franio,
Franke, Frankie, Franko*

Frankie (English) a familiar form of
Frank.
*Francky, Franke, Frankey, Franki,
Franky, Franqui*

Franklin (English) free landowner.
*Fran, Francklen, Francklin, Francklyn,
Francylen, Frank, Frankin, Franklen,
Franklinn, Franklyn, Franquelin*

Franklyn (English) a form of Franklin.
Franklynn

Frans (Swedish) a form of Francis.
Frants

Frantisek (Czech) a form of Francis.
Franta

Franz (German) a form of Francis.
*Fransz, Frantz, Franzen, Franzie,
Franzin, Franzl, Franzy*

Fraser (French) strawberry. (English)
curly haired.
Fraizer, Frasier, Fraze, Frazer, Frazier

Frayne (French) dweller at the ash
tree. (English) stranger.
Fraine, Frayn, Frean, Freen, Freyne

Fred (German) a short form of Alfred,
Frederick, Manfred.
Fredd, Fredde, Fredo, Fredson

Freddie (German) a familiar form of
Frederick.
Freddi, Freddy, Fredi, Fredy

Freddy, Fredy (German) familiar
forms of Frederick.

Frederic (German) a form of Frederick.
*Frédéric, Frederich, Frederric, Fredric,
Fredrich*

Frederick (German) peaceful ruler.
See also Dick, Eric, Fico, Peleke,
Rick.
*Federico, Fico, Fred, Fredderick, Freddie,
Freddrick, Freddy, Fredek, Frederic,*

Frederico (Spanish) a form of
Frederick.
Fredrico, Frederigo

Frederik (German) a form of
Frederick.
Frédérik, Frederrik, Fredrik

Frederique (French) a form of
Frederick.

Fredo (Spanish) a form of Fred.

Fredrick (German) a form of
Frederick.
Fredric, Fredricka, Fredricks

Freeborn (English) child of freedom.
Free

Freeman (English) free.
*Free, Freedman, Freemin, Freemon,
Friedman, Friedmann*

Fremont (German) free; noble protector.

Frewin (English) free; noble friend.
Frewen

Frey (English) lord. (Scandinavian)
Mythology: the Norse god who dispenses peace and prosperity.

Frick (English) bold.

Fridolf (English) peaceful wolf.
Freydolf, Freydulf, Fridulf

Friedrich (German) a form of
Frederick.
*Friedel, Friedrick, Fridrich, Fridrick,
Friedrike, Friedryk, Fryderyk*

*Fréderick, Frédérick, Frederik, Frederique,
Frederrick, Fredo, Fredrick, Fredwick,
Fredwyck, Fredy, Friedrich, Fritz*

Frisco (Spanish) a short form of Francisco.

Fritz (German) a familiar form of Frederick.
Fritson, Fritts, Fritzchen, Fritzl

Frode (Norwegian) wise.

Fulbright (German) very bright.
Fulbert

Fuller (English) cloth thickener.

Fulton (English) field near town.

Funsoni (Nguni) requested.

Fyfe (Scottish) a form of Fife.
Fyffe

Fynn (Ghanaian) Geography: another name for the Offin River in Ghana.

Fyodor (Russian) a form of Theodore.

Gabby (American) a familiar form of Gabriel.
Gabbi, Gabbie, Gabi, Gabie, Gaby

Gabe (Hebrew) a short form of Gabriel.

Gabino (American) a form of Gabriel.
Gabin, Gabrino

Gábor (Hungarian) God is my strength.
Gabbo, Gabko, Gabo

Gabrial (Hebrew) a form of Gabriel.
Gaberial, Gabrael, Gabraiel, Gabrail, Gabreal, Gabriael, Gabrieal, Gabryalle

Gabriel (Hebrew) devoted to God. Bible: the angel of the Annunciation.
Gab, Gabe, Gabby, Gabino, Gabis, Gábor, Gabreil, Gabrel, Gabrell, Gabrial, Gabriël, Gabriele, Gabriell, Gabrielle, Gabrielli, Gabrile, Gabris, Gabryel, Gabys, Gavril, Gebereal, Ghabriel, Riel

Gabrielli (Italian) a form of Gabriel.
Gabriello

Gadi (Arabic) God is my fortune.
Gad, Gaddy, Gadiel

Gaetan (Italian) from Gaeta, a region in southern Italy.
Gaetano, Gaetono

Gage (French) pledge.
Gager, Gaige, Gaje

Gaige (French) a form of Gage.

Gair (Irish) small.
Gaer, Gearr, Geir

Gaius (Latin) rejoicer. See also Cai.

Galbraith (Irish) Scotsman in Ireland.
Galbrait, Galbreath

Gale (Greek) a short form of Galen.
Gael, Gail, Gaile, Gayle

Galen (Greek) healer; calm. (Irish) little and lively.
Gaelan, Gaelen, Gaelin, Gaelyn, Gailen, Galan, Gale, Galeno, Galin, Galyn, Gaylen

Galeno (Spanish) illuminated child. (Greek, Irish) a form of Galen.

Gallagher (Irish) eager helper.

Galloway (Irish) Scotsman in Ireland.
Gallway, Galway

Galt (Norwegian) high ground.

Galton (English) owner of a rented estate.
Gallton

Galvin (Irish) sparrow.
Gal, Gall, Gallven, Gallvin, Galvan, Galven

Gamal (Arabic) camel. See also Jamal.
Gamall, Gamel, Gamil

Gamble (Scandinavian) old.

Gan (Chinese) daring, adventurous. (Vietnamese) near.

Gannon (Irish) light skinned, white.
Gannan, Gannen, Gannie, Ganny

Ganya (Zulu) clever.

Gar (English) a short form of Gareth, Garnett, Garrett, Garvin.
Garr

Garcia (Spanish) mighty with a spear.

Gardner (English) gardener.
Gard, Gardener, Gardie, Gardiner, Gardy

Garek (Polish) a form of Edgar.

Garen (English) a form of Garry.
Garan, Garen, Garin, Garion, Garon, Garyn, Garyon

Gareth (Welsh) gentle.
Gar, Garith, Garreth, Garrith, Garth, Garyth

Garett (Irish) a form of Garrett.
*Gared, Garet, Garette, Garhett, Garit,
Garitt, Garritt*

Garfield (English) field of spears; battlefield.

Garland (French) wreath of flowers;
prize. (English) land of spears; battleground.
*Garlan, Garlen, Garllan, Garlund,
Garlyn*

Garman (English) spearman.
Garmann, Garrman

Garner (French) army guard, sentry.
Garnier

Garnett (Latin) pomegranate seed;
garnet stone. (English) armed with a
spear.
Gar, Garnet, Garnie, Garrnett

Garnock (Welsh) dweller by the alder
river.

Garrad (English) a form of Garrett.
*Gared, Garrard, Garred, Garrod, Gerred,
Gerrid, Gerrod, Garrode, Jared*

Garret (Irish) a form of Garrett.
*Garrit, Garyt, Gerret, Garrid, Gerrit,
Gerrot*

Garrett (Irish) brave spearman. See
also Jarrett.
*Gar, Gareth, Garett, Garrad, Garret,
Garrette, Gerrett, Gerritt, Gerrott*

Garrick (English) oak spear.
*Gaerick, Garek, Garick, Garik, Garreck,
Garrek, Garric, Garrik, Garryck,
Garryk, Gerreck, Gerrick*

Garren, Garrin (English) forms of
Garry.
*Garran, Garrion, Garron, Garyn,
Gerren, Gerron, Gerryn*

Garrison (French) troops stationed at
a fort; garrison.
Garison, Garisson, Garris

Garroway (English) spear fighter.
Garraway

Garry (English) a form of Gary.
*Garen, Garrey, Garri, Garrie, Garren,
Garrin*

Garson (English) son of Gar.

Garth (Scandinavian) garden,
gardener. (Welsh) a short form of
Gareth.

Garvey (Irish) rough peace.
*Garbhán, Garrvey, Garrvie, Garv,
Garvan, Garvie, Garvy*

Garvin (English) comrade in battle.
*Gar, Garvan, Garven, Garvyn, Garwen,
Garwin, Garwyn, Garwynn*

Garwood (English) evergreen forest.
See also Wood, Woody.
Garrwood

Gary (German) mighty spearman.
(English) a familiar form of Gerald.
See also Kali.
Gare, Garey, Gari, Garry

Gaspar (French) a form of Casper.
*Gáspár, Gaspard, Gaspare, Gaspari,
Gasparo, Gasper, Gazsi*

Gaston (French) from Gascony,
France.
Gascon, Gastaun

Gaute (Norwegian) great.

Gautier (French) a form of Walter.
*Galtero, Gaulterio, Gaultier, Gaultiero,
Gauthier*

Gavin (Welsh) white hawk.
*Gav, Gavan, Gaven, Gavinn, Gavino,
Gavn, Gavohn, Gavon, Gavyn,
Gavynn, Gawain*

Gavriel (Hebrew) man of God.
Gav, Gavi, Gavrel, Gavril, Gavy

Gavril (Russian) a form of Gavriel.
Ganya, Gavrilo, Gavrilushka

Gawain (Welsh) a form of Gavin.
*Gawaine, Gawayn, Gawayne, Gawen,
Gwayne*

Gaylen (Greek) a form of Galen.
Gaylin, Gaylinn, Gaylon, Gaylyn

Gaylord (French) merry lord; jailer.
*Gaillard, Gallard, Gay, Gayelord,
Gayler, Gaylor*

Gaynor (Irish) son of the fair-skinned
man.
Gainer, Gainor, Gay, Gayner, Gaynnor

Geary (English) variable, changeable.
Gearey, Gery

Gedeon (Bulgarian, French) a form of
Gideon.

Geffrey (English) a form of Geoffrey.
See also Jeffrey.
Gefery, Geff, Geffery, Geffrard

Gellert (Hungarian) a form of Gerald.

Gena (Russian) a short form of
Yevgenyi.
Genka, Genya, Gine

Genaro (Latin) consecrated to God.
Genereo, Genero, Gennaro

Gene (Greek) a short form of Eugene.
Genek

Genek (Polish) a form of Gene.

Geno (Italian) a form of John. A short form of Genovese.
Genio, Jeno

Genovese (Italian) from Genoa, Italy.
Geno, Genovis

Gent (English) gentleman.
Gentle, Gentry

Genty (Irish, English) snow.

Geoff (English) a short form of Geoffrey.

Geoffery (English) a form of Geoffrey.
Geofery

Geoffrey (English) a form of Jeffrey. See also Giotto, Godfrey, Gottfried, Jeff.
Geffrey, Geoff, Geoffery, Geoffre, Geoffrie, Geoffroi, Geoffroy, Geoffry, Geofrey, Geofri, Gofery

Geordan (Scottish) a form of Gordon.
Geordann, Geordian, Geordin, Geordon

Geordie (Scottish) a form of George.
Geordi, Geordy

Georg (Scandinavian) a form of George.

George (Greek) farmer. See also Durko, Egor, Iorgos, Jerzy, Jiri, Joji, Jörg, Jorge, Jorgen, Joris, Jorrín, Jur, Jurgis, Keoki, Mahiái, Semer, Yegor, Yorgos, Yoyi, Yrjo, Yuri, Zhora.
Geordie, Georg, Georgas, Georges, Georget, Georgi, Georgii, Georgio,

Georgios, Georgiy, Georgy, Gevork, Gheorghe, Giorgio, Giorgos, Goerge, Goran, Gordios, Gorge, Gorje, Gorya, Grzegorz, Gyorgy

Georges (French) a form of George.
Geórges

Georgio (Italian) a form of George.

Georgios (Greek) a form of George.
Georgious, Georgius

Georgy (Greek) a familiar form of George.
Georgie

Geovanni, Geovanny (Italian) forms of Giovanni.
Geovan, Geovani, Geovanne, Geovannee, Geovannhi, Geovany

Geraint (English) old.

Gerald (German) mighty spearman. See also Fitzgerald, Jarell, Jarrell, Jerald, Jerry, Kharald.
Garald, Garold, Garolds, Gary, Gearalt, Gellert, Gérald, Geralde, Geraldo, Gerale, Geraud, Gerek, Gerick, Gerik, Gerold, Gerrald, Gerrell, Gérrick, Gerrild, Gerrin, Gerrit, Gerrold, Gerry, Geryld, Giraldo, Giraud, Girauld

Geraldo (Italian, Spanish) a form of Gerald.

Gerard (English) brave spearman. See also Jerard, Jerry.
Garrard, Garrat, Garratt, Gearard, Gerad, Gerar, Gérard, Gerardo, Geraro, Géraud, Gerd, Gerek, Gerhard, Gerrard, Gerrit, Gerry, Girard

Gerardo (Spanish) a form of Gerard.
Gherardo

Géraud (French) a form of Gerard.
Gerrad, Gerraud

Gerek (Polish) a form of Gerard.

Geremia (Hebrew) exalted by God. (Italian) a form of Jeremiah.

Geremiah (Italian) a form of Jeremiah.
Geremia, Gerimiah, Geromiah

Gerhard (German) a form of Gerard.
Garhard, Gerhardi, Gerhardt, Gerhart, Gerhort

Gerik (Polish) a form of Edgar.
Geric, Gerick

Germain (French) from Germany. (English) sprout, bud. See also Jermaine.
Germaine, German, Germane, Germano, Germayn, Germayne

Gerome (English) a form of Jerome.

Geronimo (Greek, Italian) a form of Jerome. History: a famous Apache chief.
Geronemo

Gerrit (Dutch) a form of Gerald.

Gerry (English) a familiar form of Gerald, Gerard. See also Jerry.
Geri, Gerre, Gerri, Gerrie, Gerryson

Gershom (Hebrew) exiled. (Yiddish) stranger in exile.
Gersham, Gersho, Gershon, Gerson, Geurson, Gursham, Gurshan

Gerson (English) son of Gar.
Gersan, Gershawn

Gert (German, Danish) fighter.

Gervaise (French) honorable. See also Jervis.
Garvais, Garvaise, Garvey, Gervais, Gervase, Gervasio, Gervaso, Gervayse, Gervis, Gerwazy

Gerwin (Welsh) fair love.

Gethin (Welsh) dusky.
Geth

Ghazi (Arabic) conqueror.

Ghilchrist (Irish) servant of Christ. See also Gil.
Gilchrist, Gilcrist, Gilie, Gill, Gilley, Gilly

Ghislain (French) pledge.

Gi (Korean) brave.

Gia (Vietnamese) family.

Giacinto (Portuguese, Spanish) a form of Jacinto.
Giacintho

Giacomo (Italian) a form of Jacob.
Gaimo, Giacamo, Giaco, Giacobbe, Giacobo, Giacopo

Gian (Italian) a form of Giovanni, John.
Gianetto, Giann, Gianne, Giannes, Gianni, Giannis, Giannos, Ghian

Giancarlo (Italian) a combination of John + Charles.
Giancarlos, Gianncarlo

Gianluca (Italian) a combination of John + Lucas.

Gianni (Italian) a form of Johnny.
Giani, Gionni

Gianpaolo (Italian) a combination of John + Paul.
Gianpaulo

Gib (English) a short form of Gilbert.
Gibb, Gibbie, Gibby

Gibor (Hebrew) powerful.

Gibson (English) son of Gilbert.
Gibbon, Gibbons, Gibbs, Gillson, Gilson

Gideon (Hebrew) tree cutter. Bible: the judge who defeated the Midianites.
Gedeon, Gideone, Gidon, Hedeon

Gidon (Hebrew) a form of Gideon.

Gifford (English) bold giver.
Giff, Giffard, Gifferd, Giffie, Giffy

Gig (English) horse-drawn carriage.

Gil (Greek) shield bearer. (Hebrew) happy. (English) a short form of Ghilchrist, Gilbert.
Gili, Gill, Gilli, Gillie, Gillis, Gilly

Gilad (Arabic) camel hump; from Giladi, Saudi Arabia.
Giladi, Gilead

Gilamu (Basque) a form of William.
Gillen

Gilbert (English) brilliant pledge; trustworthy. See also Gil, Gillett.
Gib, Gilberto, Gilburt, Giselbert, Giselberto, Giselbertus, Guilbert

Gilberto (Spanish) a form of Gilbert.

Gilby (Scandinavian) hostage's estate. (Irish) blond boy.
Gilbey, Gillbey, Gillbie, Gillby

Gilchrist (Irish) a form of Ghilchrist.

Gilen (Basque, German) illustrious pledge.

Giles (French) goatskin shield.
Gide, Gilles, Gyles

Gillean (Irish) Bible: Saint John's servant.
Gillan, Gillen, Gillian

Gillespie (Irish) son of the bishop's servant.
Gillis

Gillett (French) young Gilbert.
Gelett, Gelette, Gillette

Gilmer (English) famous hostage.
Gilmar

Gilmore (Irish) devoted to the Virgin Mary.
Gillmore, Gillmour, Gilmour

Gilon (Hebrew) circle.

Gilroy (Irish) devoted to the king.
Gilderoy, Gildray, Gildroy, Gillroy, Roy

Gino (Greek) a familiar form of Eugene. (Italian) a short form of names ending in "gene," "gino."
Ghino

Giona (Italian) a form of Jonah.

Giordano (Italian) a form of Jordan.
Giordan, Giordana, Giordin, Guordan

Giorgio (Italian) a form of George.

Giorgos (Greek) a form of George.
Georgos, Giorgios

Giosia (Italian) a form of Joshua.

Giotto (Italian) a form of Geoffrey.

Giovani (Italian) a form of Giovanni.
Giavani, Giovan, Giovane, Giovanie, Giovon

Giovanni (Italian) a form of John. See also Jeovanni, Jiovanni.
Geovanni, Geovanny, Gian, Gianni, Giannino, Giovani, Giovann, Giovannie, Giovanno, Giovanny, Giovonathon, Giovonni, Giovonnia, Giovonnie, Givonni

Giovanny (Italian) a form of Giovanni.
Giovany

Gipsy (English) wanderer.
Gipson, Gypsy

Girvin (Irish) small; tough.
Girvan, Girven, Girvon

Gitano (Spanish) gypsy.

Giuliano (Italian) a form of Julius.
Giulano, Giulino, Giulliano

Giulio (Italian) a form of Julius.
Guilano

Giuseppe (Italian) a form of Joseph.
Giuseppi, Giuseppino, Giusseppe, Guiseppe, Guiseppi, Guiseppie, Guisseppe

Giustino (Italian) a form of Justin.
Giusto

Givon (Hebrew) hill; heights.
Givan, Givawn, Givyn

Gladwin (English) cheerful. See also Win.
Glad, Gladdie, Gladdy, Gladwinn, Gladwyn, Gladwynne

Glanville (English) village with oak trees.

Glen (Irish) a form of Glenn.
Glyn

Glendon (Scottish) fortress in the glen.
Glenden, Glendin, Glenn, Glennden, Glennton, Glenton

Glendower (Welsh) from Glyndwr, Wales.

Glenn (Irish) a short form of Glendon.
Gleann, Glen, Glennie, Glennis, Glennon, Glenny, Glynn

Glentworth (English) from Glenton, England.

Glenville (Irish) village in the glen.

Glyn (Welsh) a form of Glen.
Glin, Glynn

Goddard (German) divinely firm.
Godard, Godart, Goddart, Godhardt, Godhart, Gothart, Gotthard, Gotthardt, Gotthart

Godfrey (Irish) God's peace. (German) a form of Jeffrey. See also Geoffrey, Gottfried.
Giotto, Godefroi, Godfree, Godfry, Godofredo, Godoired, Godrey, Goffredo, Gofraidh, Gofredo, Gorry

Godwin (English) friend of God. See also Win.
Godewyn, Godwinn, Godwyn,

Goodwin, Goodwyn, Goodwynn, Goodwynne

Goel (Hebrew) redeemer.

Goldwin (English) golden friend. See also Win.
Golden, Goldewin, Goldewinn, Goldewyn, Goldwyn, Goldwynn

Goliath (Hebrew) exiled. Bible: the giant Philistine whom David slew with a slingshot.
Golliath

Gomda (Kiowa) wind.

Gomer (Hebrew) completed, finished. (English) famous battle.

Gonza (Rutooro) love.

Gonzalo (Spanish) wolf.
Goncalve, Gónsalo, Gonsalve, Gonzales, Gonzelee, Gonzolo

Gordon (English) triangular-shaped hill.
Geordan, Gord, Gordain, Gordan, Gorden, Gordonn, Gordy

Gordy (English) a familiar form of Gordon.
Gordie

Gore (English) triangular-shaped land; wedge-shaped land.

Gorman (Irish) small; blue eyed.

Goro (Japanese) fifth.

Gosheven (Native American) great leaper.

Gottfried (German) a form of Geoffrey, Godfrey.
Gotfrid, Gotfrids, Gottfrid

Gotzon (German) a form of Angel.

Govert (Dutch) heavenly peace.

Gower (Welsh) pure.

Gowon (Tiv) rainmaker.
Gowan

Gozol (Hebrew) soaring bird.
Gozal

Grady (Irish) noble; illustrious.
Gradea, Gradee, Gradey, Gradleigh, Graidey, Graidy

Graeme (Scottish) a form of Graham.
Graem

Graham (English) grand home.
Graeham, Graehame, Graehme, Graeme, Grahamme, Grahm, Grahame, Grahme, Gram, Grame, Gramm, Grayeme, Grayham

Granger (French) farmer.
Grainger, Grange

Grant (English) a short form of Grantland.
Grand, Grantham, Granthem, Grantley

Grantland (English) great plains.
Grant

Granville (French) large village.
Gran, Granvel, Granvil, Granvile, Granvill, Grenville, Greville

Gray (English) gray haired.
Graye, Grey, Greye

Grayden (English) gray haired.
Graden, Graydan, Graydyn, Greyden

Graydon (English) gray hill.
Gradon, Grayton, Greydon

Grayson (English) bailiff's son. See also Sonny.
Graysen, Greyson

Greeley (English) gray meadow.
Greelea, Greeleigh, Greely

Greenwood (English) green forest.
Green, Greener

Greg, Gregg (Latin) short forms of Gregory.
Graig, Greig, Gregson

Greggory (Latin) a form of Gregory.
Greggery

Gregor (Scottish) a form of Gregory.
Gregoor, Grégor, Gregore

Gregorio (Italian, Portuguese) a form of Gregory.
Gregorios

Gregory (Latin) vigilant watchman. See also Jörn, Krikor.
Gergely, Gergo, Greagoir, Greagory, Greer, Greg, Gregary, Greger, Gregery, Greggory, Grégoire, Gregor, Gregorey, Gregori, Grégorie, Gregorio, Gregorius, Gregors, Gregos, Gregrey, Gregroy, Gregry, Greogry, Gries, Grisha, Grzegorz

Gresham (English) village in the pasture.

Greyson (English) a form of Grayson.
Greysen, Greysten, Greyston

Griffin (Latin) hooked nose.
Griff, Griffen, Griffie, Griffon, Griffy, Gryphon

Griffith (Welsh) fierce chief; ruddy.
Grifen, Griff, Griffeth, Griffie, Griffy, Griffyn, Griffynn, Gryphon

Grigori (Bulgarian) a form of Gregory.
Grigoi, Grigor, Grigore, Grigorios, Grigorov, Grigory

Grimshaw (English) dark woods.

Grisha (Russian) a form of Gregory.

Griswold (German, French) gray forest.
Gris, Griz, Grizwald

Grosvener (French) big hunter.

Grover (English) grove.
Grove

Guadalupe (Arabic) river of black stones.
Guadalope

Gualberto (Spanish) a form of Walter.
Gualterio

Gualtiero (Italian) a form of Walter.
Gualterio

Guglielmo (Italian) a form of William.

Guido (Italian) a form of Guy.

Guilford (English) ford with yellow flowers.
Guildford

Guilherme (Portuguese) a form of William.

Guillaume (French) a form of William.
Guillaums, Guilleaume, Guilem, Guyllaume

Guillermo (Spanish) a form of William.
Guillerrmo

Gunnar (Scandinavian) a form of Gunther.
Guner, Gunner

Gunther (Scandinavian) battle army; warrior.
Guenter, Guenther, Gun, Gunnar, Guntar, Gunter, Guntero, Gunthar, Günther

Guotin (Chinese) polite; strong leader.

Gurion (Hebrew) young lion.
Gur, Guri, Guriel

Gurpreet (Sikh) devoted to the guru; devoted to the Prophet.
Gurjeet, Gurmeet, Guruprit

Gurvir (Sikh) guru's warrior.
Gurveer

Gus (Scandinavian) a short form of Angus, Augustine, Gustave.
Guss, Gussie, Gussy, Gusti, Gustry, Gusty

Gustaf (Swedish) a form of Gustave.
Gustaaf, Gustaff

Gustave (Scandinavian) staff of the Goths. History: Gustavus Adolphus was a king of Sweden. See also Kosti, Tabo, Tavo.
Gus, Gustaf, Gustaff, Gustaof, Gustav, Gustáv, Gustava, Gustaves, Gustavo, Gustavs, Gustavus, Gustik, Gustus, Gusztav

Gustavo (Italian, Spanish) a form of Gustave.
Gustabo

Guthrie (German) war hero. (Irish) windy place.
Guthrey, Guthry

Gutierre (Spanish) a form of Walter.

Guy (Hebrew) valley. (German) warrior. (French) guide. See also Guido.
Guyon

Guyapi (Native American) candid.

Gwayne (Welsh) a form of Gawain.
Gwaine, Gwayn

Gwidon (Polish) life.

Gwilym (Welsh) a form of William.
Gwillym

Gwyn (Welsh) fair; blessed.
Gwynn, Gwynne

Gyasi (Akan) marvelous baby.

Gyorgy (Russian) a form of George.
Gyoergy, György, Gyuri, Gyurka

Gyula (Hungarian) youth.
Gyala, Gyuszi

H

Habib (Arabic) beloved.

Hackett (German, French) little wood cutter.
Hacket, Hackit, Hackitt

Hackman (German, French) wood cutter.

Hadar (Hebrew) glory.

Haddad (Arabic) blacksmith.

Hadden (English) heather-covered hill.
Haddan, Haddon, Haden

Haden (English) a form of Hadden.
Hadin, Hadon, Hadyn, Haeden

Hadi (Arabic) guiding to the right.
Hadee, Hady

Hadley (English) heather-covered meadow.
Had, Hadlea, Hadlee, Hadleigh, Hadly, Lee, Leigh

Hadrian (Latin, Swedish) dark.
Adrian, Hadrien

Hadwin (English) friend in a time of war.
Hadwinn, Hadwyn, Hadwynn, Hadwynne

Hagan (German) strong defense.
Haggan

Hagen (Irish) young, youthful.

Hagley (English) enclosed meadow.

Hagos (Ethiopian) happy.

Hahnee (Native American) beggar.

Hai (Vietnamese) sea.

Haidar (Arabic) lion.
Haider

Haiden (English) a form of Hayden.
Haidyn

Haig (English) enclosed with hedges.

Hailey (Irish) a form of Haley.
Haile, Haille, Haily, Halee

Haji (Swahili) born during the pilgrimage to Mecca.

Hakan (Native American) fiery.

Hakeem (Arabic) a form of Hakim.
Hakam, Hakem

Hakim (Arabic) wise. (Ethiopian) doctor.
Hakeem, Hakiem

Hakon (Scandinavian) of Nordic ancestry.
Haaken, Haakin, Haakon, Haeo, Hak, Hakan, Hako

Hal (English) a short form of Halden, Hall, Harold.

Halbert (English) shining hero.
Bert, Halburt

Halden (Scandinavian) half-Danish. See also Dane.
Hal, Haldan, Haldane, Halfdan, Halvdan

Hale (English) a short form of Haley. (Hawaiian) a form of Harry.
Hayle, Heall

Halen (Swedish) hall.
Hale, Hallen, Haylan, Haylen

Haley (Irish) ingenious.
Hailey, Hale, Haleigh, Halley, Hayleigh, Hayley, Hayli

Halford (English) valley ford.

Hali (Greek) sea.

Halian (Zuni) young.

Halil (Turkish) dear friend.
Halill

Halim (Arabic) mild, gentle.
Haleem

Hall (English) manor, hall.
Hal, Halstead, Halsted

Hallam (English) valley.

Hallan (English) dweller at the hall; dweller at the manor.
Halin, Hallene, Hallin

Halley (English) meadow near the hall; holy.
Hallie

Halliwell (English) holy well.
Hallewell, Hellewell, Helliwell

Hallward (English) hall guard.

Halsey (English) Hal's island.

Halstead (English) manor grounds.
Halsted

Halton (English) estate on the hill.

Halvor (Norwegian) rock; protector.
Halvard

Ham (Hebrew) hot. Bible: one of Noah's sons.

Hamal (Arabic) lamb. Astronomy: a bright star in the constellation of Aries.

Hamar (Scandinavian) hammer.

Hamid (Arabic) praised. See also Muhammad.
Haamid, Hamaad, Hamadi, Hamd, Hamdrem, Hamed, Hamedo, Hameed, Hamidi, Hammad, Hammed, Humayd

Hamill (English) scarred.
Hamel, Hamell, Hammill

Hamilton (English) proud estate.
Hamel, Hamelton, Hamil, Hamill, Tony

Hamish (Scottish) a form of Jacob, James.

Hamisi (Swahili) born on Thursday.

Hamlet (German, French) little village; home. Literature: one of Shakespeare's tragic heroes.

Hamlin (German, French) loves his home.
Hamblin, Hamelen, Hamelin, Hamlen, Hamlyn, Lin

Hammet (English, Scandinavian) village.
Hammett, Hamnet, Hamnett

Hammond (English) village.
Hamond

Hampton (English) Geography: a town in England.
Hamp

Hamza (Arabic) powerful.
Hamzah, Hamze, Hamzeh, Hamzia

Hanale (Hawaiian) a form of Henry.
Haneke

Hanan (Hebrew) grace.
Hananel, Hananiah, Johanan

Hanbal (Arabic) pure. History: Ahmad Ibn Hanbal founded an Islamic school of thought.

Handel (German, English) a form of John. Music: George Frideric Handel was a German composer whose works include *Messiah* and *Water Music*.

Hanford (English) high ford.

Hanif (Arabic) true believer.
Haneef, Hanef

Hank (American) a familiar form of Henry.

Hanley (English) high meadow.
Handlea, Handleigh, Handley, Hanlea, Hanlee, Hanleigh, Hanly, Henlea, Henlee, Henleigh, Henley

Hannes (Finnish) a form of John.

Hannibal (Phoenician) grace of God. History: a famous Carthaginian general who fought the Romans.
Anibal

Hanno (German) a short form of Johan.
Hanna, Hannah, Hannon, Hannu, Hanon

Hans (Scandinavian) a form of John.
Hanschen, Hansel, Hants, Hanz

Hansel (Scandinavian) a form of Hans.
Haensel, Hansell, Hansl, Hanzel

Hansen (Scandinavian) son of Hans.
Hanson

Hansh (Hindi) god; godlike.

Hanson (Scandinavian) a form of Hansen.
Hansen, Hanssen, Hansson

Hanus (Czech) a form of John.

Haoa (Hawaiian) a form of Howard.

Hara (Hindi) seizer. Religion: another name for the Hindu god Shiva.

Harald (Scandinavian) a form of Harold.
Haraldo, Haralds, Haralpos

Harb (Arabic) warrior.

Harbin (German, French) little bright warrior.
Harben, Harbyn

Harcourt (French) fortified dwelling.
Court, Harcort

Hardeep (Punjabi) a form of Harpreet.

Harden (English) valley of the hares.
Hardian, Hardin

Harding (English) brave; hardy.
Hardin

Hardwin (English) brave friend.

Hardy (German) bold, daring.
Hardie

Harel (Hebrew) mountain of God.
Harell, Hariel, Harrell

Harford (English) ford of the hares.

Hargrove (English) grove of the hares.
Hargreave, Hargreaves

Hari (Hindi) tawny.
Hariel, Harin

Harith (Arabic) cultivator.

Harjot (Sikh) light of God.
Harjeet, Harjit, Harjodh

Harkin (Irish) dark red.
Harkan, Harken

Harlan (English) hare's land; army land.
Harland, Harlen, Harlenn, Harlin, Harlon, Harlyn, Harlynn

Harland (English) a form of Harlan.
Harlend

Harley (English) hare's meadow; army meadow.
Arley, Harlea, Harlee, Harleigh, Harly

Harlow (English) hare's hill; army hill. See also Arlo.

Harman, Harmon (English) forms of Herman.
Harm, Harmen, Harmond, Harms

Harold (Scandinavian) army ruler. See also Jindra.
Araldo, Garald, Garold, Hal, Harald, Haraldas, Haraldo, Haralds, Harry, Heraldo, Herold, Heronim, Herrick, Herryck

Haroun (Arabic) lofty; exalted.
Haarun, Harin, Haron, Haroon, Harron, Harun

Harper (English) harp player.
Harp, Harpo

Harpreet (Punjabi) loves God, devoted to God.
Hardeep

Harris (English) a short form of Harrison.
Haris, Hariss

Harrison (English) son of Harry.
Harison, Harreson, Harris, Harrisen, Harrisson

Harrod (Hebrew) hero; conqueror.

Harry (English) a familiar form of Harold. See also Arrigo, Hale, Parry.
Harm, Harray, Harrey, Harri, Harrie

Hart (English) a short form of Hartley.

Hartley (English) deer meadow.
Hart, Hartlea, Hartlee, Hartleigh, Hartly

Hartman (German) hard; strong.

Hartwell (English) deer well.
Harwell, Harwill

Hartwig (German) strong advisor.

Hartwood (English) deer forest.
Harwood

Harvey (German) army warrior.
Harv, Hervé, Hervey, Hervie, Hervy

Harvir (Sikh) God's warrior.
Harvier

Hasad (Turkish) reaper, harvester.

Hasan (Arabic) a form of Hassan.
Hasaan, Hasain, Hasaun, Hashaan, Hason

Hasani (Swahili) handsome.
Hasan, Hasanni, Hassani, Heseny, Hassen, Hassian, Husani

Hashim (Arabic) destroyer of evil.
Haashim, Hasham, Hasheem, Hashem

Hasin (Hindi) laughing.
Haseen, Hasen, Hassin, Hazen, Hesen

Haskel (Hebrew) a form of Ezekiel.
Haskell

Haslett (English) hazel-tree land.
Haze, Hazel, Hazlett, Hazlitt

Hassan (Arabic) handsome.
Hasan, Hassen, Hasson

Hassel (German, English) witches' corner.
Hassal, Hassall, Hassell, Hazael, Hazell

Hastin (Hindi) elephant.

Hastings (Latin) spear. (English) house council.
Hastie, Hasty

Hatim (Arabic) judge.
Hateem, Hatem

Hauk (Norwegian) hawk.
Haukeye

Havelock (Norwegian) sea battler.

Haven (Dutch, English) harbor, port; safe place.
Haeven, Havin, Hevin, Hevon, Hovan

Havika (Hawaiian) a form of David.

Hawk (English) hawk.
Hawke, Hawkin, Hawkins

Hawley (English) hedged meadow.
Hawleigh, Hawly

Hawthorne (English) hawthorn tree.

Hayden (English) hedged valley.
Haiden, Haydan, Haydenn, Haydn, Haydon

Hayes (English) hedged valley.
Hayse

Hayward (English) guardian of the hedged area.
Haward, Heyvard, Heyward

Haywood (English) hedged forest.
Heywood, Woody

Hearn (Scottish, English) a short form of Ahearn.
Hearne, Herin, Hern

Heath (English) heath.
Heathe, Heith

Heathcliff (English) cliff near the heath. Literature: the hero of Emily Brontë's novel *Wuthering Heights*.

Heaton (English) high place.

Heber (Hebrew) ally, partner.

Hector (Greek) steadfast. Mythology: the greatest hero of the Trojan War in Homer's epic poem *Iliad*.

Hedley (English) heather-filled meadow.
Headley, Headly, Hedly

Heinrich (German) a form of Henry.
Heindrick, Heiner, Heinreich, Heinrick, Heinrik, Hinrich

Heinz (German) a familiar form of Henry.

Helaku (Native American) sunny day.

Helge (Russian) holy.

Helki (Moquelumnan) touching.

Helmer (German) warrior's wrath.

Helmut (German) courageous.
Helmuth

Heman (Hebrew) faithful.

Henderson (Scottish, English) son of Henry.
Hendrie, Hendries, Hendron, Henryson

Hendrick (Dutch) a form of Henry.
Hendricks, Hendrickson, Hendrik, Hendriks, Hendrikus, Hendrix, Henning

Heniek (Polish) a form of Henry.
Henier

Henley (English) high meadow.

Henning (German) a form of Hendrick, Henry.

Henoch (Yiddish) initiator.
Enoch, Henock, Henok

Henri (French) a form of Henry.
Henrico, Henrri

Henrick (Dutch) a form of Henry.
Heinrick, Henerik, Henrich, Henrik, Henryk

Henrique (Portuguese) a form of Henry.

Henry (German) ruler of the household. See also Arrigo, Enric, Enrick, Enrico, Enrikos, Enrique, Hanale, Honok, Kiki.
Hagan, Hank, Harro, Harry, Heike, Heinrich, Heinz, Hendrick, Henery, Heniek, Henning, Henraoi, Henri, Henrick, Henrim, Henrique, Henrry, Heromin, Hersz

Heraldo (Spanish) a form of Harold.
Herald, Hiraldo

Herb (German) a short form of Herbert.
Herbie, Herby

Herbert (German) glorious soldier.
Bert, Erbert, Eriberto, Harbert, Hebert, Hébert, Heberto, Herb, Heriberto, Hurbert

Hercules (Latin) glorious gift. Mythology: a Greek hero of fabulous strength, renowned for his twelve labors.
Herakles, Herc, Hercule, Herculie

Heriberto (Spanish) a form of Herbert.
Heribert

Herman (Latin) noble. (German) soldier. See also Armand, Ermanno, Ermano, Mandek.
Harmon, Hermaan, Hermann, Hermie, Herminio, Hermino, Hermon, Hermy, Heromin

Hermes (Greek) messenger. Mythology: the divine herald of Greek mythology.

Hernan (German) peacemaker.

Hernando (Spanish) a form of Ferdinand.
Hernandes, Hernandez

Herrick (German) war ruler.
Herrik, Herryck

Herschel (Hebrew) a form of Hershel.
Herchel, Hersch, Herschel, Herschell

Hersh (Hebrew) a short form of Hershel.
Hersch, Hirsch

Hershel (Hebrew) deer.
Herschel, Hersh, Hershal, Hershall, Hershell, Herzl, Hirschel, Hirshel

Hertz (Yiddish) my strife.
Herzel

Hervé (French) a form of Harvey.

Hesperos (Greek) evening star.
Hespero

Hesutu (Moquelumnan) picking up a yellow jacket's nest.

Hew (Welsh) a form of Hugh.
Hewe, Huw

Hewitt (German, French) little smart one.
Hewe, Hewet, Hewett, Hewie, Hewit, Hewlett, Hewlitt, Hugh

Hewson (English) son of Hugh.

Hezekiah (Hebrew) God gives strength.
Hezekyah, Hazikiah, Hezikyah

Hiamovi (Cheyenne) high chief.

Hibah (Arabic) gift.

Hideaki (Japanese) smart, clever.
Hideo

Hieremias (Greek) God will uplift.

Hieronymos (Greek) a form of Jerome. Art: Hieronymus Bosch was a fifteenth-century Dutch painter.
Hierome, Hieronim, Hieronimo, Hieronimos, Hieronymo, Hieronymus

Hieu (Vietnamese) respectful.

Hilario (Spanish) a form of Hilary.

Hilary (Latin) cheerful. See also Ilari.
*Hi, Hilair, Hilaire, Hilarie, Hilario,
Hilarion, Hilarius, Hil, Hill, Hillary,
Hillery, Hilliary, Hillie, Hilly*

Hildebrand (German) battle sword.
Hildebrando, Hildo

Hilel (Arabic) new moon.

Hillel (Hebrew) greatly praised. Religion:
Rabbi Hillel originated the Talmud.

Hilliard (German) brave warrior.
*Hillard, Hiller, Hillier, Hillierd, Hillyard,
Hillyer, Hillyerd*

Hilmar (Swedish) famous noble.

Hilton (English) town on a hill.
Hylton

Hinto (Dakota) blue.

Hinun (Native American) spirit of the
storm.

Hippolyte (Greek) horseman.
*Hipolito, Hippolit, Hippolitos,
Hippolytus, Ippolito*

Hiram (Hebrew) noblest; exalted.
Hi, Hirom, Huram, Hyrum

Hiromasa (Japanese) fair, just.

Hiroshi (Japanese) generous.

Hisoka (Japanese) secretive, reserved.

Hiu (Hawaiian) a form of Hugh.

Ho (Chinese) good.

Hoang (Vietnamese) finished.

Hobart (German) Bart's hill.
Hobard, Hobbie, Hobby, Hobie, Hoebart

Hobert (German) Bert's hill.
Hobey

Hobson (English) son of Robert.
Hobbs, Hobs

Hoc (Vietnamese) studious.

Hod (Hebrew) a short form of
Hodgson.

Hodgson (English) son of Roger.
Hod

Hogan (Irish) youth.
Hogin

Holbrook (English) brook in the hollow.
Brook, Holbrooke

Holden (English) hollow in the valley.
Holdan, Holdin, Holdon, Holdun, Holdyn

Holic (Czech) barber.

Holland (French) Geography: a former province of the Netherlands.

Holleb (Polish) dove.
Hollub, Holub

Hollis (English) grove of holly trees.
Hollie, Holly

Holmes (English) river islands.

Holt (English) forest.
Holten, Holton

Homer (Greek) hostage; pledge; security. Literature: a renowned Greek
epic poet.
*Homar, Homere, Homère, Homero,
Homeros, Homerus*

Hondo (Shona) warrior.

Honesto (Filipino) honest.

Honi (Hebrew) gracious.
Choni

Honok (Polish) a form of Henry.

Honon (Moquelumnan) bear.

Honorato (Spanish) honorable.

Honoré (Latin) honored.
*Honor, Honoratus, Honoray, Honorio,
Honorius*

Honovi (Native American) strong.

Honza (Czech) a form of John.

Hop (Chinese) agreeable.

Horace (Latin) keeper of the hours.
Literature: a famous Roman lyric
poet and satirist.
Horacio, Horaz

Horacio (Latin) a form of Horace.

Horatio (Latin) clan name. See also
Orris.
Horatius, Oratio

Horst (German) dense grove; thicket.
Hurst

Horton (English) garden estate.
Hort, Horten, Orton

Hosa (Arapaho) young crow.

Hosea (Hebrew) salvation. Bible: a
Hebrew prophet.
Hose, Hoseia, Hoshea, Hosheah

Hotah (Lakota) white.

Hototo (Native American) whistler.

Houghton (English) settlement on the headland.

Houston (English) hill town. Geography: a city in Texas.
Housten, Houstin, Hustin, Huston

Howard (English) watchman. See also Haoa.
Howie, Ward

Howe (German) high.
Howey, Howie

Howell (Welsh) remarkable.
Howel

Howi (Moquelumnan) turtledove.

Howie (English) a familiar form of Howard, Howland.
Howey

Howin (Chinese) loyal swallow.

Howland (English) hilly land.
Howie, Howlan, Howlen

Hoyt (Irish) mind; spirit.

Hu (Chinese) tiger.

Hubbard (German) a form of Hubert.

Hubert (German) bright mind; bright spirit. See also Beredei, Uberto.
Bert, Hobart, Hubbard, Hubbert, Huber, Hubertek, Huberto, Hubertson, Hubie, Huey, Hugh, Hugibert, Huibert, Humberto

Huberto (Spanish) a form of Hubert.
Humberto

Hubie (English) a familiar form of Hubert.
Hube, Hubi

Hud (Arabic) Religion: a Muslim prophet.

Hudson (English) son of Hud.

Huey (English) a familiar form of Hugh.
Hughey, Hughie, Hughy, Hui

Hugh (English) a short form of Hubert. See also Ea, Hewitt, Huxley, Maccoy, Ugo.
Fitzhugh, Hew, Hiu, Hue, Huey, Hughes, Hugo, Hugues

Hugo (Latin) a form of Hugh.
Ugo

Hulbert (German) brilliant grace.
Bert, Hulbard, Hulburd, Hulburt, Hull

Humbert (German) brilliant strength. See also Umberto.
Hum, Humberto

Humberto (Portuguese) a form of Humbert.

Humphrey (German) peaceful strength. See also Onofrio, Onufry.
Hum, Humfredo, Humfrey, Humfrid, Humfried, Humfry, Hump, Humph, Humphery, Humphry, Humphrys, Hunfredo

Hung (Vietnamese) brave.

Hunt (English) a short form of names beginning with "Hunt."

Hunter (English) hunter.
Hunt, Huntur

Huntington (English) hunting estate.
Hunt, Huntingdon

Huntley (English) hunter's meadow.
Hunt, Huntlea, Huntlee, Huntleigh, Huntly

Hurley (Irish) sea tide.
Hurlee, Hurleigh

Hurst (English) a form of Horst.
Hearst, Hirst

Husam (Arabic) sword.

Husamettin (Turkish) sharp sword.

Huslu (Native American) hairy bear.

Hussain (Arabic) a form of Hussein.
Hossain, Husain, Husani, Husayn, Hussan, Hussayn

Hussein (Arabic) little; handsome.
Hossein, Houssein, Houssin, Huissien, Huossein, Husein, Husien, Hussain, Hussien

Hussien (Arabic) a form of Hussein.
Husian, Hussin

Hutchinson (English) son of the hutch dweller.
Hutcheson

Hute (Native American) star.

Hutton (English) house on the jutting ledge.
Hut, Hutt, Huttan

Huxley (English) Hugh's meadow.
Hux, Huxlea, Huxlee, Huxleigh, Lee

Huy (Vietnamese) glorious.

Hy (Vietnamese) hopeful. (English) a short form of Hyman.

Hyacinthe (French) hyacinth.

Hyatt (English) high gate.
Hyat

Hyde (English) cache; measure of land equal to 120 acres; animal hide.

Hyder (English) tanner, preparer of animal hides for tanning.

Hyman (English) a form of Chaim.
Haim, Hayim, Hayvim, Hayyim, Hy, Hyam, Hymie

Hyun-Ki (Korean) wise.

Hyun-Shik (Korean) clever.

I

Iago (Spanish, Welsh) a form of Jacob, James. Literature: the villain in Shakespeare's *Othello*.
Jago

Iain (Scottish) a form of Ian.

Iakobos (Greek) a form of Jacob.
Iakov, Iakovos, Iakovs

Ian (Scottish) a form of John. See also Ean, Eion.
Iain, Iane, Iann

Ianos (Czech) a form of John.
Iannis

Ib (Phoenician, Danish) oath of Baal.

Iban (Basque) a form of John.

Ibon (Basque) a form of Ivor.

Ibrahim (Hausa) my father is exalted.
Ibrahaim, Ibraham, Ibraheem, Ibrahem, Ibrahiem, Ibrahiim, Ibrahmim

Ichabod (Hebrew) glory is gone. Literature: Ichabod Crane is the main character of Washington Irving's story "The Legend of Sleepy Hollow."

Idi (Swahili) born during the Idd festival.

Idris (Welsh) eager lord. (Arabic) Religion: a Muslim prophet.
Idrease, Idrees, Idres, Idress, Idreus, Idriece, Idriss, Idrissa, Idriys

Iestyn (Welsh) a form of Justin.

Igashu (Native American) wanderer; seeker.
Igasho

Iggy (Latin) a familiar form of Ignatius.

Ignacio (Italian) a form of Ignatius.
Ignazio

Ignatius (Latin) fiery, ardent. Religion: Saint Ignatius of Loyola founded the Jesuit order. See also Inigo, Neci.
Iggie, Iggy, Ignac, Ignác, Ignace, Ignacio, Ignacius, Ignatios, Ignatious, Ignatz, Ignaz, Ignazio

Igor (Russian) a form of Inger, Ingvar. See also Egor, Yegor.
Igoryok

Ihsan (Turkish) compassionate.

Ike (Hebrew) a familiar form of Isaac. History: the nickname of the thirty-fourth U.S. president Dwight D. Eisenhower.
Ikee, Ikey

Iker (Basque) visitation.

Ilan (Hebrew) tree. (Basque) youth.

Ilari (Basque) a form of Hilary.
Ilario

Ilias (Greek) a form of Elijah.
Illias, Illyas, Ilyas, Ilyes

Illan (Basque, Latin) youth.

Ilom (Ibo) my enemies are many.

Ilya (Russian) a form of Elijah.
Ilia, Ilie, Ilija, Iliya, Ilja, Illia, Illya

Imad (Arabic) supportive; mainstay.

Iman (Hebrew) a short form of Immanuel.
Imani, Imanni

Immanuel (Hebrew) a form of Emmanuel.
Iman, Imanol, Imanuel, Immanual, Immanuele, Immuneal

Imran (Arabic) host.
Imraan

Imre (Hungarian) a form of Emery.
Imri

Imrich (Czech) a form of Emery.
Imrus

Inay (Hindi) god; godlike.

Ince (Hungarian) innocent.

Inder (Hindi) god; godlike.
Inderbir, Inderdeep, Inderjeet, Inderjit, Inderpal, Inderpreet, Inderveer, Indervir, Indra, Indrajit

Indiana (Hindi) from India.
Indi, Indy

Inek (Welsh) a form of Irvin.

Ing (Scandinavian) a short form of Ingmar.
Inge

Ingelbert (German) a form of Engelbert.
Inglebert

Inger (Scandinavian) son's army.
Igor, Ingemar, Ingmar

Ingmar (Scandinavian) famous son.
Ing, Ingamar, Ingamur, Ingemar

Ingram (English) angel.
Inglis, Ingra, Ingraham, Ingrim

Ingvar (Scandinavian) Ing's soldier.
Igor, Ingevar

Inigo (Basque) a form of Ignatius.
Iñaki, Iniego, Iñigo

Iniko (Ibo) born during bad times.

Innis (Irish) island.
Innes, Inness, Inniss

Innocenzio (Italian) innocent.
Innocenty, Inocenci, Inocencio, Inocente, Inosente

Inteus (Native American) proud; unashamed.

Ioakim (Russian) a form of Joachim.
Ioachime, Ioakimo, Iov

Ioan (Greek, Bulgarian, Romanian) a form of John.
Ioane, Ioann, Ioannes, Ioannikios, Ioannis, Ionel

Iokepa (Hawaiian) a form of Joseph.
Keo

Iolo (Welsh) the Lord is worthy.
Iorwerth

Ionakana (Hawaiian) a form of Jonathan.

Iorgos (Greek) a form of George.

Iosif (Greek, Russian) a form of Joseph.

Iosua (Romanian) a form of Joshua.

Ipyana (Nyakyusa) graceful.

Ira (Hebrew) watchful.

Iram (English) bright.

Irumba (Rutooro) born after twins.

Irv (Irish, Welsh, English) a short form of Irvin, Irving.

Irvin (Irish, Welsh, English) a short form of Irving. See also Ervine.
Inek, Irv, Irven, Irvine, Irvinn, Irvon

Irving (Irish) handsome. (Welsh) white river. (English) sea friend. See also Ervin, Ervine.
Irv, Irvin, Irvington, Irwin, Irwing

Irwin (English) a form of Irving. See also Ervin.
Irwinn, Irwyn

Isa (Arabic) a form of Jesus.
Isaah

Isaac (Hebrew) he will laugh. Bible: the son of Abraham and Sarah. See also Itzak, Izak, Yitzchak.
Aizik, Icek, Ike, Ikey, Ikie, Isaak, Isaakios, Isac, Isacc, Isacco, Isack, Isaic, Ishaq, Isiac, Isiacc, Issac, Issca, Itzak, Izak, Izzy

Isaak (Hebrew) a form of Isaac.
Isack, Isak, Isik, Issak

Isaiah (Hebrew) God is my salvation. Bible: a Hebrew prophet.
Isa, Isai, Isaia, Isaias, Isaid, Isaih, Isaish, Ishaq, Isia, Isiah, Isiash, Issia, Issiah, Izaiah, Izaiha, Izaya, Izayah, Izayaih, Izayiah, Izeyah, Izeyha

Isaias (Hebrew) a form of Isaiah.
Isaiahs, Isais, Izayus

Isam (Arabic) safeguard.

Isas (Japanese) meritorious.

Isekemu (Native American) slow-moving creek.

Isham (English) home of the iron one.

Ishan (Hindi) direction.
Ishaan, Ishaun

Ishaq (Arabic) a form of Isaac.
Ishaac, Ishak

Ishmael (Hebrew) God will hear. Literature: the narrator of Herman Melville's novel *Moby-Dick*.
Isamael, Isamail, Ishma, Ishmail, Ishmale, Ishmeal, Ishmeil, Ishmel, Ishmil, Ismael, Ismail

Isidore (Greek) gift of Isis. See also Dorian, Ysidro.
Isador, Isadore, Isadorios, Isidor, Isidro, Issy, Ixidor, Izadore, Izidor, Izidore, Izydor, Izzy

Isidro (Greek) a form of Isidore.
Isidoro, Isidoros

Iskander (Afghan) a form of Alexander.

Ismael (Arabic) a form of Ishmael.

Ismail (Arabic) a form of Ishmael.
Ismeil, Ismiel

Israel (Hebrew) prince of God; wrestled with God. History: the nation of Israel took its name from the name given Jacob after he wrestled with the angel of the Lord. See also Yisrael.
Iser, Isreal, Israhel, Isrell, Isrrael, Isser, Izrael, Izzy, Yisrael

Isreal (Hebrew) a form of Israel.
Isrieal

Issa (Swahili) God is our salvation.

Issac (Hebrew) a form of Isaac.
Issacc, Issaic, Issiac

Issiah (Hebrew) a form of Isaiah.
Issaiah, Issia

Istu (Native American) sugar pine.

István (Hungarian) a form of Stephen.
Isti, Istvan, Pista

Ithel (Welsh) generous lord.

Ittamar (Hebrew) island of palms.
Itamar

Itzak (Hebrew) a form of Isaac, Yitzchak.
Itzik

Iukini (Hawaiian) a form of Eugene.
Kini

Iustin (Bulgarian, Russian) a form of Justin.

Ivan (Russian) a form of John.
Iván, Ivanchik, Ivanichek, Ivann, Ivano, Ivas, Iven, Ivin, Ivon, Ivyn, Vanya

Ivar (Scandinavian) a form of Ivor. See also Yves, Yvon.
Iv, Iva

Ives (English) young archer.
Ive, Iven, Ivey, Yves

Ivo (German) yew wood; bow wood.
Ibon, Ivar, Ives, Ivon, Ivonnie, Ivor, Yvo

Ivor (Scandinavian) a form of Ivo.
Ibon, Ifor, Ivar, Iver, Ivory, Ivry

Iwan (Polish) a form of John.

Iyapo (Yoruba) many trials; many obstacles.

Iye (Native American) smoke.

Izak (Czech) a form of Isaac.
Itzhak, Ixaka, Izaac, Izaak, Izac, Izaic, Izak, Izec, Izeke, Izick, Izik, Izsak, Izsák, Izzak

Izzy (Hebrew) a familiar form of Isaac, Isidore, Israel.
Issy

J

J (American) an initial used as a first name.
J.

Ja (Korean) attractive, magnetic.

Jaali (Swahili) powerful.

Jaan (Estonian) a form of Christian.

Jaap (Dutch) a form of Jim.

Jabari (Swahili) fearless, brave.
Jabaar, Jabahri, Jabar, Jabarae, Jabare, Jabaree, Jabarei, Jabarie, Jabarri, Jabarrie, Jabary, Jabbar, Jabbaree, Jabbari, Jaber, Jabiari, Jabier, Jabori, Jaborie

Jabez (Hebrew) born in pain.
Jabe, Jabes, Jabesh

Jabin (Hebrew) God has created.
Jabain, Jabien, Jabon

Jabir (Arabic) consoler, comforter.
Jabiri, Jabori

Jabril (Arabic) a form of Jibril.
Jabrail, Jabree, Jabreel, Jabrel, Jabrell, Jabrelle, Jabri, Jabrial, Jabrie, Jabriel, Jabrielle, Jabrille

Jabulani (Shona) happy.

Jacan (Hebrew) trouble.
Jachin

Jacari (American) a form of Jacorey.
Jacarey, Jacaris, Jacarius, Jacarre, Jacarri, Jacarrus, Jacarus, Jacary, Jacaure, Jacauri, Jaccar, Jaccari

Jace (American) a combination of the initials J. + C.
JC, J.C., Jacee, Jacek, Jacey, Jacie, Jaice, Jaicee

Jacen (Greek) a form of Jason.
Jaceon

Jacinto (Portuguese, Spanish) hyacinth. See also Giacinto.
Jacindo, Jacint, Jacinta

Jack (American) a familiar form of Jacob, John. See also Keaka.
Jackie, Jacko, Jackub, Jak, Jax, Jock, Jocko

Jackie, Jacky (American) familiar forms of Jack.
Jackey

Jackson (English) son of Jack.
Jacksen, Jacksin, Jacson, Jakson, Jaxon

Jaco (Portuguese) a form of Jacob.

Jacob (Hebrew) supplanter, substitute. Bible: son of Isaac, brother of Esau. See also Akiva, Chago, Checha, Coby, Diego, Giacomo, Hamish, Iago, Iakobos, James, Kiva, Koby, Kuba, Tiago, Yakov, Yasha, Yoakim.
Jaap, Jachob, Jack, Jackob, Jackub, Jaco, Jacobb, Jacobe, Jacobi, Jacobo, Jacoby, Jacolbi, Jacolby, Jacque, Jacques, Jacub, Jaecob, Jago, Jaicob, Jaime, Jake, Jakob, Jalu, Jasha, Jaycob, Jecis, Jeks, Jeska, Jim, Jocek, Jock, Jocob, Jocobb, Jocoby, Jocolby, Jokubas

Jacobi, Jacoby (Hebrew) forms of Jacob.
Jachobi, Jacobbe, Jacobee, Jacobey, Jacobie, Jacobii, Jacobis

Jacobo (Hebrew) a form of Jacob.

Jacobson (English) son of Jacob.
Jacobs, Jacobsen, Jacobsin, Jacobus

Jacorey (American) a combination of Jacob + Corey.
Jacari, Jacori, Jacoria, Jacorie, Jacoris, Jacorius, Jacorrey, Jacorrien, Jacorry, Jacory, Jacouri, Jacourie, Jakari

Jacque (French) a form of Jacob.
Jacquay, Jacqui, Jocque, Jocqui

Jacques (French) a form of Jacob, James. See also Coco.
Jackque, Jackques, Jackquise, Jacot, Jacquan, Jacquees, Jacquese, Jacquess, Jacquet, Jacquett, Jacquez, Jacquis, Jacquise, Jaquez, Jarques, Jarquis

Jacquez, Jaquez (French) forms of Jacques.
Jaques, Jaquese, Jaqueus, Jaqueze, Jaquis, Jaquise, Jaquze, Jocquez

Jacy (Tupi-Guarani) moon.
Jaicy, Jaycee

Jade (Spanish) jade, precious stone.
Jaeid, Jaid, Jaide

Jaden (Hebrew) a form of Jadon.
Jadee, Jadeen, Jadenn, Jadeon, Jadin, Jaeden

Jadon (Hebrew) God has heard.
Jaden, Jadyn, Jaedon, Jaiden, Jaydon

Jadrien (American) a combination of Jay + Adrien.
Jad, Jada, Jadd, Jader, Jadrian

Jadyn (Hebrew) a form of Jadon.
Jadyne, Jaedyn

Jaegar (German) hunter.
Jaager, Jaeger, Jagur

Jae-Hwa (Korean) rich, prosperous.

Jael (Hebrew) mountain goat.
Yael

Jaelen (American) a form of Jalen.
Jaelan, Jaelaun, Jaelin, Jaelon, Jaelyn

Ja'far (Sanskrit) little stream.
Jafar, Jafari, Jaffar, Jaffer, Jafur

Jagger (English) carter.
Jagar, Jager, Jaggar

Jago (English) a form of James.

Jaguar (Spanish) jaguar.
Jagguar

Jahi (Swahili) dignified.

Jahlil (Hindi) a form of Jalil.
Jahlal, Jahlee, Jahleel, Jahliel

Jahmar (American) a form of Jamar.
Jahmare, Jahmari, Jahmarr, Jahmer

Jahvon (Hebrew) a form of Javan.
Jahvan, Jahvine, Jahwaan, Jahwon

Jai (Tai) heart.
Jaie, Jaii

Jaiden (Hebrew) a form of Jadon.
Jaidan, Jaidon, Jaidyn

Jailen (American) a form of Jalen.
Jailan, Jailani, Jaileen, Jailen, Jailon, Jailyn, Jailynn

Jaime (Spanish) a form of Jacob, James.
Jaimee, Jaimey, Jaimie, Jaimito, Jaimy, Jayme, Jaymie

Jairo (Spanish) God enlightens.
Jair, Jairay, Jaire, Jairus, Jarius

Jaison (Greek) a form of Jason.
Jaisan, Jaisen, Jaishon, Jaishun

Jaivon (Hebrew) a form of Javan.
Jaiven, Jaivion, Jaiwon

Jaja (Ibo) honored.

Jajuan (American) a combination of the prefix Ja + Juan.
Ja Juan, Jauan, Jawaun, Jejuan, Jujuan, Juwan

Jakari (American) a form
of Jacorey.
Jakaire, Jakar, Jakaray, Jakarie, Jakarious,
Jakarius, Jakarre, Jakarri, Jakarus

Jake (Hebrew) a short form of Jacob.
Jakie, Jayk, Jayke

Jakeem (Arabic) uplifted.

Jakob (Hebrew) a form of Jacob.
Jaekob, Jaikab, Jaikob, Jakab, Jakeb, Jakeob,
Jakeub, Jakib, Jakiv, Jakobe, Jakobi,
Jakobus, Jakoby, Jakov, Jakovian, Jakub,
Jakubek, Jekebs

Jakome (Basque) a form of James.
Xanti

Jal (Gypsy) wanderer.

Jalan (American) a form of Jalen.
Jalaan, Jalaen, Jalain, Jaland, Jalane,
Jalani, Jalanie, Jalann, Jalaun, Jalean,
Jallan

Jaleel (Hindi) a form of Jalil.
Jaleell, Jaleil, Jalel

Jalen (American) a combination of the
prefix Ja + Len.
Jaelen, Jailen, Jalan, Jaleen, Jalend, Jalene,
Jalin, Jallen, Jalon, Jalyn

Jalil (Hindi) revered.
Jahlil, Jalaal, Jalal

Jalin, Jalyn (American) forms of Jalen.
Jalian, Jaline, Jalynn, Jalynne

Jalon (American) a form of Jalen.
Jalone, Jaloni, Jalun

Jam (American) a short form of Jamal,
Jamar.
Jama

Jamaal (Arabic) a form of Jamal.

Jamaine (Arabic) a form of Germain.

Jamal (Arabic) handsome. See also
Gamal.
Jahmal, Jahmall, Jahmalle, Jahmeal,
Jahmeel, Jahmeil, Jahmel, Jahmelle,
Jahmil, Jahmile, Jaimal, Jam, Jamaal,
Jamael, Jamahl, Jamail, Jamaile, Jamala,
Jamale, Jamall, Jamalle, Jamar, Jamaul,
Jamel, Jamil, Jammal, Jamor, Jamual,
Jarmal, Jaumal, Jemal, Jermal, Jomal,
Jomall

Jamar (American) a form of Jamal.
Jam, Jamaar, Jamaari, Jamahrae, Jamair,
Jamara, Jamaras, Jamaraus, Jamarl, Jamarr,
Jamarre, Jamarrea, Jamarree, Jamarri,
Jamarvis, Jamaur, Jamir, Jamire, Jamiree,
Jammar, Jarmar, Jarmarr, Jaumar, Jemaar,
Jemar, Jimar, Jomar

Jamarcus (American) a combination
of the prefix Ja + Marcus.
Jamarco, Jamarkus, Jemarcus, Jimarcus

Jamari (American) a form of Jamario.
Jamare, Jamarea, Jamaree, Jamareh,
Jamaria, Jamarie, Jamaul

Jamario (American) a combination of
the prefix Ja + Mario.
Jamareo, Jamari, Jamariel, Jamarious,
Jamaris, Jamarius, Jamariya, Jemario,
Jemarus

Jamarquis (American) a combination
of the prefix Ja + Marquis.
Jamarkees, Jamarkeus, Jamarkis,
Jamarqese, Jamarqueis, Jamarques,
Jamarquez, Jamarquios, Jamarqus

Jamel (Arabic) a form of Jamal.
Jameel, Jamele, Jamell, Jamelle, Jammel,
Jamuel, Jamul, Jarmel, Jaumal, Jaumell,
Je-Mell, Jimell

James (Hebrew) supplanter, substitute.
(English) a form of Jacob. Bible:
James the Great and James the Less
were two of the Twelve Apostles. See
also Diego, Hamish, Iago, Kimo,
Santiago, Seamus, Seumas, Yago,
Yasha.
Jacques, Jago, Jaime, Jaimes, Jakome,
Jamesie, Jamesy, Jamez, Jameze, Jamie,
Jamies, Jamse, Jamyes, Jamze, Jas, Jasha,
Jay, Jaymes, Jem, Jemes, Jim

Jameson (English) son of James.
Jamerson, Jamesian, Jamison, Jaymeson

Jamie (English) a familiar form of
James.
Jaime, Jaimey, Jaimie, Jame, Jamee, Jamey,
Jameyel, Jami, Jamia, Jamiah, Jamian,
Jamme, Jammie, Jamiee, Jammy, Jamy,
Jamye, Jayme, Jaymee, Jaymie

Jamil (Arabic) a form of Jamal.
Jamiel, Jamiell, Jamielle, Jamile, Jamill,
Jamille, Jamyl, Jarmil

Jamin (Hebrew) favored.
Jamen, Jamian, Jamien, Jamion, Jamionn,
Jamon, Jamun, Jamyn, Jarmin, Jarmon,
Jaymin

Jamison (English) son of James.
Jamiesen, Jamieson, Jamis, Jamisen,
Jamyson, Jaymison

Jamon (Hebrew) a form of Jamin.
Jamohn, Jamone, Jamoni

Jamond (American) a combination of James + Raymond.
Jamod, Jamont, Jamonta, Jamontae, Jamontay, Jamonte, Jarmond

Jamor (American) a form of Jamal.
Jamoree, Jamori, Jamorie, Jamorius, Jamorrio, Jamorris, Jamory, Jamour

Jamsheed (Persian) from Persia.
Jamshaid, Jamshed

Jan (Dutch, Slavic) a form of John.
Jaan, Jana, Janae, Jann, Janne, Jano, Janson, Jenda, Yan

Janco (Czech) a form of John.
Jancsi, Janke, Janko

Jando (Spanish) a form of Alexander.
Jandino

Janeil (American) a combination of the prefix Ja + Neil.
Janal, Janel, Janell, Janelle, Janiel, Janielle, Janile, Janille, Jarnail, Jarneil, Jarnell

Janek (Polish) a form of John.
Janak, Janik, Janika, Janka, Jankiel, Janko

Janis (Latvian) a form of John.
Ansis, Jancis, Zanis

Janne (Finnish) a form of John.
Jann, Jannes

János (Hungarian) a form of John.
Jancsi, Jani, Jankia, Jano

Janson (Scandinavian) son of Jan.
Janse, Jansen, Jansin, Janssen, Jansun, Jantzen, Janzen, Jensen, Jenson

Jantzen (Scandinavian) a form of Janson.
Janten, Jantsen, Jantson

Janus (Latin) gate, passageway; born in January. Mythology: the Roman god of beginnings and endings.
Jannese, Jannus, Januario, Janusz

Japheth (Hebrew) handsome. (Arabic) abundant. Bible: a son of Noah. See also Yaphet.
Japeth, Japhet

Jaquan (American) a combination of the prefix Ja + Quan.
Jaequan, Jaiqaun, Jaiquan, Jaqaun, Jaqawan, Jaquaan, Jaquain, Ja'quan, Jaquane, Jaquann, Jaquanne, Jaquavius, Jaquawn, Jaquin, Jaquon, Jaqwan

Jaquarius (American) a combination of Jaquan + Darius.
Jaquari, Jaquarious, Jaquaris

Jaquavius (American) a form of Jaquan.
Jaquavas, Jaquaveis, Jaquaveius, Jaquaveon, Jaquaveous, Jaquavias, Jaquavious, Jaquavis, Jaquavus

Jaquon (American) a form of Jaquan.
Jaequon, Jaqoun, Jaquinn, Jaqune, Jaquoin, Jaquone, Jaqwon

Jarad (Hebrew) a form of Jared.
Jaraad, Jaraed

Jarah (Hebrew) sweet as honey.
Jerah

Jardan (Hebrew) a form of Jordan.
Jarden, Jardin, Jardon

Jareb (Hebrew) contending.
Jarib

Jared (Hebrew) a form of Jordan.
Jahred, Jaired, Jarad, Jaredd, Jareid, Jarid, Jarod, Jarred, Jarrett, Jarrod, Jarryd, Jerad, Jered, Jerod, Jerrad, Jerred, Jerrod, Jerryd, Jordan

Jarek (Slavic) born in January.
Janiuszck, Januarius, Januisz, Jarec, Jarrek, Jarric, Jarrick

Jarell (Scandinavian) a form of Gerald.
Jairell, Jarael, Jareil, Jarel, Jarelle, Jariel, Jarrell, Jarryl, Jayryl, Jerel, Jerell, Jerrell, Jharell

Jaren (Hebrew) a form of Jaron.
Jarian, Jarien, Jarin, Jarion

Jareth (American) a combination of Jared + Gareth.
Jarreth, Jereth, Jarreth

Jarett (English) a form of Jarrett.
Jaret, Jarette

Jarl (Scandinavian) earl, nobleman.

Jarlath (Latin) in control.
Jarl, Jarlen

Jarman (German) from Germany.
Jerman

Jarod (Hebrew) a form of Jared.
Jarodd, Jaroid

Jaron (Hebrew) he will sing; he will cry out.
Jaaron, Jairon, Jaren, Jarone, Jarren, Jarron, Jaryn, Jayron, Jayronn, Je Ronn, J'ron

Jaroslav (Czech) glory of spring.
Jarda

Jarred (Hebrew) a form of Jared.
Ja'red, Jarrad, Jarrayd, Jarrid, Jarrod, Jarryd, Jerrid

Jarrell (English) a form of Gerald.
Jarel, Jarell, Jarrel, Jerall, Jerel, Jerell

Jarren (Hebrew) a form of Jaron.
Jarrain, Jarran, Jarrian, Jarrin

Jarrett (English) a form of Garrett, Jared.
Jairett, Jareth, Jarett, Jaretté, Jarhett, Jarratt, Jarret, Jarrette, Jarrot, Jarrott, Jerrett

Jarrod (Hebrew) a form of Jared.
Jarod, Jerod, Jerrod

Jarryd (Hebrew) a form of Jared.
Jarrayd, Jaryd

Jarvis (German) skilled with a spear.
Jaravis, Jarv, Jarvaris, Jarvas, Jarvaska, Jarvey, Jarvez, Jarvie, Jarvios, Jarvious, Jarvius, Jarvorice, Jarvoris, Jarvous, Jarvus, Javaris, Jervey, Jervis

Jaryn (Hebrew) a form of Jaron.
Jarryn, Jarynn, Jaryon

Jas (Polish) a form of John. (English) a familiar form of James.
Jasio

Jasha (Russian) a familiar form of Jacob, James.
Jascha

Jashawn (American) a combination of the prefix Ja + Shawn.
Jasean, Jashan, Jashaun, Jashion, Jashon

Jaskaran (Sikh) sings praises to the Lord.
Jaskaren, Jaskarn, Jaskiran

Jasmin (Persian) jasmine flower.
Jasman, Jasmanie, Jasmine, Jasmon, Jasmond

Jason (Greek) healer. Mythology: the hero who led the Argonauts in search of the Golden Fleece.
Jacen, Jaeson, Jahson, Jaison, Jasan, Jasaun, Jase, Jasen, Jasin, Jasson, Jasten, Jasun, Jasyn, Jathan, Jathon, Jay, Jayson

Jaspal (Punjabi) living a virtuous lifestyle.

Jasper (French) brown, red, or yellow ornamental stone. (English) a form of Casper. See also Kasper.
Jaspar, Jazper, Jespar, Jesper

Jasson (Greek) a form of Jason.
Jassen, Jassin

Jatinra (Hindi) great Brahmin sage.

Javan (Hebrew) Bible: son of Japheth.
Jaewan, Jahvaughan, Jahvon, Jaivon, Javante, Javaon, JaVaughn, Javen, Javian, Javien, Javin, Javine, Javoanta, Javon, Javona, Javone, Javonte, Jayvin, Jayvion, Jayvon, Jevan, Jevon

Javante (American) a form of Javan.
Javantae, Javantai, Javantée, Javanti

Javaris (English) a form of Jarvis.
Javaor, Javar, Javaras, Javare, Javares, Javari, Javarias, Javaries, Javario, Javarius, Javaro, Javaron, Javarous, Javarre, Javarreis, Javarri, Javarrious, Javarris, Javarro, Javarous, Javarte, Javarus, Javorious, Javoris, Javorius, Javouris

Javas (Sanskrit) quick, swift.
Jayvas, Jayvis

Javier (Spanish) owner of a new house. See also Xavier.
Jabier, Javer, Javere, Javiar

Javon (Hebrew) a form of Javan.
Jaavon, Jaevin, Jaevon, Jaewon, Javeon, Javion, Javionne, Javohn, Javona, Javone, Javoney, Javoni, Javonn, Javonne, Javonni, Javonnie, Javonnte, Javoun, Jayvon

Javonte (American) a form of Javan.
Javona, Javontae, Javontai, Javontay, Javontaye, Javonté, Javontee, Javonteh, Javontey

Jawaun (American) a form of Jajuan.
Jawaan, Jawan, Jawann, Jawn, Jawon, Jawuan

Jawhar (Arabic) jewel; essence.

Jaxon (English) a form of Jackson.
Jaxen, Jaxsen, Jaxson, Jaxsun, Jaxun

Jay (French) blue jay. (English) a short form of James, Jason.
Jae, Jai, Jave, Jaye, Jeays, Jeyes

Jayce (American) a combination of the initials J. + C.
JC, J.C., Jayc, Jaycee, Jay Cee, Jaycey, Jecie

Jaycob (Hebrew) a form of Jacob.
Jaycub, Jaykob

Jayde (American) a combination of the initials J. + D.
JD, J.D., Jayd, Jaydee, Jayden

Jayden (American) a form of Jayde.
Jaydan, Jaydin, Jaydn, Jaydon

Jaylee (American) a combination of
Jay + Lee.
Jayla, Jayle, Jaylen

Jaylen (American) a combination of
Jay + Len.
*Jaylaan, Jaylan, Jayland, Jayleen, Jaylend,
Jaylin, Jayln, Jaylon, Jaylun, Jaylund,
Jaylyn*

Jaylin (American) a form of Jaylen.
Jaylian, Jayline

Jaylon (American) a form of Jaylen.
Jayleon

Jaylyn (American) a form of Jaylen.
Jaylynd, Jaylynn, Jaylynne

Jayme (English) a form of Jamie.
Jaymie

Jaymes (English) a form of James.
Jaymis, Jayms, Jaymz

Jayquan (American) a combination of
Jay + Quan.
*Jaykwan, Jaykwon, Jayqon, Jayquawn,
Jayqunn*

Jayson (Greek) a form of Jason.
*Jaycent, Jaysean, Jaysen, Jayshaun,
Jayshawn, Jayshon, Jayshun, Jaysin,
Jaysn, Jayssen, Jaysson, Jaysun*

Jayvon (American) a form of Javon.
*Jayvion, Jayvohn, Jayvone, Jayvonn,
Jayvontay, Jayvonte, Jaywan, Jaywaun,
Jaywin*

Jazz (American) jazz.
*Jaz, Jazze, Jazzlee, Jazzman, Jazzmen,
Jazzmin, Jazzmon, Jazztin, Jazzton,
Jazzy*

Jean (French) a form of John.
*Jéan, Jeane, Jeannah, Jeannie, Jeannot,
Jeano, Jeanot, Jeanty, Jene*

Jeb (Hebrew) a short form of
Jebediah.
Jebb, Jebi, Jeby

Jebediah (Hebrew) a form of
Jedidiah.
Jeb, Jebadia, Jebadiah, Jebadieh, Jebidiah

Jed (Hebrew) a short form of Jedidiah.
(Arabic) hand.
Jedd, Jeddy, Jedi

Jediah (Hebrew) hand of God.
Jedaia, Jedaiah, Jedeiah, Jedi, Yedaya

Jedidiah (Hebrew) friend of God,
beloved of God. See also Didi.
*Jebediah, Jed, Jedadiah, Jeddediah,
Jedediah, Jedediha, Jedidia, Jedidiah,
Jedidiyah, Yedidya*

Jedrek (Polish) strong; manly.
Jedric, Jedrik, Jedrus

Jeff (English) a short form of Jefferson,
Jeffrey. A familiar form of Geoffrey.
Jef, Jefe, Jeffe, Jeffey, Jeffie, Jeffy, Jhef

Jefferson (English) son of Jeff.
History: Thomas Jefferson was the
third U.S. president.
Jeferson, Jeff, Jeffers

Jeffery (English) a form of Jeffrey.
*Jefery, Jeffari, Jeffary, Jeffeory, Jefferay,
Jeffereoy, Jefferey, Jefferie, Jeffory*

Jefford (English) Jeff's ford.

Jeffrey (English) divinely peaceful. See
also Geffrey, Geoffrey, Godfrey.
Jeff, Jefferies, Jeffery, Jeffre, Jeffree, Jeffrie,

*Jeffrey, Jeffrie, Jeffries, Jeffry, Jefre, Jefri,
Jefry, Jeoffroi, Joffre, Joffrey*

Jeffry (English) a form of Jeffrey.

Jehan (French) a form of John.
Jehann

Jehu (Hebrew) God lives. Bible: a military commander and king of Israel.
Yehu

Jelani (Swahili) mighty.
Jel, Jelan, Jelanie, Jelaun

Jem (English) a short form of James,
Jeremiah.
Jemmie, Jemmy

Jemal (Arabic) a form of Jamal.
Jemaal, Jemael, Jemale, Jemel

Jemel (Arabic) a form of Jemal.
*Jemeal, Jemehl, Jemehyl, Jemell, Jemelle,
Jemello, Jemeyle, Jemile, Jemmy*

Jemond (French) worldly.
Jemon, Jémond, Jemonde, Jemone

Jenkin (Flemish) little John.
Jenkins, Jenkyn, Jenkyns, Jennings

Jenö (Hungarian) a form of Eugene.
Jenci, Jency, Jenoe, Jensi, Jensy

Jens (Danish) a form of John.
Jense, Jensen, Jenson, Jenssen, Jensy, Jentz

Jeovanni (Italian) a form of Giovanni.
Jeovahny, Jeovan, Jeovani, Jeovany

Jequan (American) a combination of
the prefix Je + Quan.
Jeqaun, Jequann, Jequon

Jerad, Jerrad (Hebrew) forms of Jared.
Jeread, Jeredd

Jerahmy (Hebrew) a form of Jeremy.
Jerahmeel, Jerahmeil, Jerahmey

Jerald (English) a form of Gerald.
Jeraldo, Jerold, Jerral, Jerrald, Jerrold, Jerry

Jerall (English) a form of Jarrell.
Jerael, Jerai, Jerail, Jeraile, Jeral, Jerale, Jerall, Jerrail, Jerral, Jerrel, Jerrell, Jerrelle

Jeramie, Jeramy (Hebrew) forms of Jeremy.
Jerame, Jeramee, Jeramey, Jerami, Jerammie

Jerard (French) a form of Gerard.
Jarard, Jarrard, Jerardo, Jeraude, Jerrard

Jere (Hebrew) a short form of Jeremiah, Jeremy.
Jeré, Jeree

Jered, Jerred (Hebrew) forms of Jared.
Jereed, Jerid, Jerryd, Jeryd

Jerel, Jerell, Jerrell (English) forms of Jarell.
Jerelle, Jeriel, Jeril, Jerrail, Jerral, Jerrall, Jerrel, Jerrill, Jerrol, Jerroll, Jerryl, Jerryll, Jeryl, Jeryle

Jereme, Jeremey (Hebrew) forms of Jeremy.
Jarame

Jeremiah (Hebrew) God will uplift. Bible: a Hebrew prophet. See also Dermot, Yeremey, Yirmaya.
Geremiah, Jaramia, Jem, Jemeriah, Jemiah, Jeramiah, Jeramiha, Jere, Jereias, Jeremaya, Jeremi, Jeremia, Jeremial, Jeremias, Jeremija, Jeremy, Jerimiah, Jerimiha, Jerimya, Jermiah, Jermija, Jerry

Jeremie, Jérémie (Hebrew) forms of Jeremy.
Jeremi, Jérémie, Jeremii

Jeremy (English) a form of Jeremiah.
Jaremay, Jaremi, Jaremy, Jem, Jemmy, Jerahmy, Jeramie, Jeramy, Jere, Jereamy, Jereme, Jeremee, Jeremey, Jeremie, Jérémie, Jeremry, Jérémy, Jeremye, Jereomy, Jeriemy, Jerime, Jerimy, Jermey, Jeromy, Jerremy

Jeriah (Hebrew) Jehovah has seen.

Jericho (Arabic) city of the moon. Bible: a city conquered by Joshua.
Jeric, Jerick, Jerico, Jerik, Jerric, Jerrick, Jerrico, Jerricoh, Jerryco

Jermaine (French) a form of Germain. (English) sprout, bud.
Jarman, Jeremaine, Jeremane, Jerimane, Jermain, Jerman, Jermane, Jermanie, Jermanne, Jermany, Jermayn, Jermayne, Jermiane, Jermine, Jer-Mon, Jermone, Jermoney, Jhirmaine

Jermal (Arabic) a form of Jamal.
Jermael, Jermail, Jermall, Jermaul, Jermel, Jermell, Jermil, Jermol, Jermyll

Jermey (English) a form of Jeremy.
Jerme, Jermee, Jermere, Jermery, Jermie, Jermy, Jhermie

Jermiah (Hebrew) a form of Jeremiah.
Jermiha, Jermiya

Jerney (Slavic) a form of Bartholomew.

Jerod, Jerrod (Hebrew) forms of Jarrod.
Jerode, Jeroid

Jerolin (Basque, Latin) holy.

Jerome (Latin) holy. See also Geronimo, Hieronymos.
Gerome, Jere, Jeroen, Jerom, Jérome, Jérôme, Jeromo, Jeromy, Jeron, Jerónimo, Jerrome, Jerromy

Jeromy (Latin) a form of Jerome.
Jeromee, Jeromey, Jeromie

Jeron (English) a form of Jerome.
Jéron, Jerone, Jeronimo, Jerrin, Jerrion, Jerron, Jerrone, J'ron

Jerrett (Hebrew) a form of Jarrett.
Jeret, Jerett, Jeritt, Jerret, Jerrette, Jerriot, Jerritt, Jerrot, Jerrott

Jerrick (American) a combination of Jerry + Derrick.
Jaric, Jarrick, Jerick, Jerrik

Jerry (German) mighty spearman. (English) a familiar form of Gerald, Gerard. See also Gerry, Kele.
Jehri, Jere, Jeree, Jeris, Jerison, Jerri, Jerrie, Jery

Jervis (English) a form of Gervaise, Jarvis.

Jerzy (Polish) a form of George.
Jersey, Jerzey, Jurek

Jeshua (Hebrew) a form of Joshua.
Jeshuah

Jess (Hebrew) a short form of Jesse.

Jesse (Hebrew) wealthy. Bible: the father of David. See also Yishai.
Jese, Jesee, Jesi, Jess, Jessé, Jessee, Jessie, Jessy

Jessie (Hebrew) a form of Jesse.
Jesie, Jessi, Jessi

Jessy (Hebrew) a form of Jesse.
Jescey, Jessey, Jessye, Jessyie, Jesy

Jestin (Welsh) a form of Justin.
Jessten, Jesten, Jeston, Jesstin, Jesston

Jesus (Hebrew) a form of Joshua.
Bible: son of Mary and Joseph,
believed by Christians to be the Son
of God. See also Chucho, Isa, Yosu.
Jecho, Jessus, Jesu, Jesús, Josu

Jesús (Hispanic) a form of Jesus.

Jethro (Hebrew) abundant. Bible: the
father-in-law of Moses. See also
Yitro.
Jeth, Jethroe, Jetro, Jett

Jett (English) hard, black mineral.
(Hebrew) a short form of Jethro.
Jet, Jetson, Jetter, Jetty

Jevan (Hebrew) a form of Javan.
Jevaun, Jeven, Jevin

Jevon (Hebrew) a form of Javan.
*Jevion, Jevohn, Jevone, Jevonn, Jevonne,
Jevonnie*

Jevonte (American) a form of Jevon.
Jevonta, Jevontae, Jevontaye, Jevonté

Jibade (Yoruba) born close to royalty.

Jibben (Gypsy) life.
Jibin

Jibril (Arabic) archangel of Allah.
Jabril, Jibreel, Jibriel

Jilt (Dutch) money.

Jim (Hebrew, English) a short form of
James. See also Jaap.
Jimbo, Jimm, Jimmy

Jimbo (American) a familiar form of
Jim.
Jimboo

Jimell (Arabic) a form of Jamel.
*Jimel, Jimelle, Jimill, Jimmell, Jimmelle,
Jimmiel, Jimmil*

Jimiyu (Abaluhya) born in the dry season.

Jimmie (English) a form of Jimmy.
Jimi, Jimie, Jimmee, Jimmi

Jimmy (English) a familiar form of
Jim.
Jimmey, Jimmie, Jimmye, Jimmyjo, Jimy

Jimoh (Swahili) born on Friday.

Jin (Chinese) gold.
Jinn

Jindra (Czech) a form of Harold.

Jing-Quo (Chinese) ruler of the country.

Jiovanni (Italian) a form of Giovanni.
*Jio, Jiovani, Jiovanie, Jiovann, Jiovannie,
Jiovanny, Jiovany, Jiovoni, Jivan*

Jirair (Armenian) strong; hard working.

Jiri (Czech) a form of George.
Jirka

Jiro (Japanese) second son.

Jivin (Hindi) life giver.
Jivanta

Jo (Hebrew, Japanese) a form of Joe.

Joab (Hebrew) God is father. See also
Yoav.
Joabe, Joaby

Joachim (Hebrew) God will establish.
See also Akeem, Ioakim, Yehoyakem.
*Joacheim, Joakim, Joaquim, Joaquín,
Jokin, Jov*

João (Portuguese) a form of John.

Joaquim (Portuguese) a form of
Joachim.

Joaquín (Spanish) a form of Joachim,
Yehoyakem.
*Jehoichin, Joaquin, Jocquin, Jocquinn,
Joquin, Juaquin*

Job (Hebrew) afflicted. Bible: a righteous man whose faith in God sur-
vived the test of many afflictions.
Jobe, Jobert, Jobey, Jobie, Joby

Joben (Japanese) enjoys cleanliness.
Joban, Jobin

Jobo (Spanish) a familiar form of
Joseph.

Joby (Hebrew) a familiar form of Job.
Jobie

Jock (American) a familiar form of
Jacob.
Jocko, Joco, Jocoby, Jocolby

Jocquez (French) a form of Jacquez.
Jocques, Jocquis, Jocquise

Jodan (Hebrew) a combination of Jo
+ Dan.
*Jodahn, Joden, Jodhan, Jodian, Jodin,
Jodon, Jodonnis*

Jody (Hebrew) a familiar form of
Joseph.
Jodey, Jodi, Jodie, Jodiha, Joedy

Joe (Hebrew) a short form of Joseph.
Jo, Joely, Joey

Joel (Hebrew) God is willing. Bible: an Old Testament Hebrew prophet.
Jôel, Joël, Joell, Joelle, Joely, Jole, Yoel

Joeseph (Hebrew) a form of Joseph.
Joesph

Joey (Hebrew) a familiar form of Joe, Joseph.

Johan, Johann (German) forms of John. See also Anno, Hanno, Yoan, Yohan.
Joahan, Joan, Joannes, Johahn, Johanan, Johane, Johannan, Johannes, Johanthan, Johatan, Johathan, Johathon, Johaun, Johon

Johannes (German) a form of Johan, Johann.
Johanes, Johannas, Johannus, Johansen, Johanson, Johonson

John (Hebrew) God is gracious. Bible: the name honoring John the Baptist and John the Evangelist. See also Elchanan, Evan, Geno, Gian, Giovanni, Handel, Hannes, Hans, Hanus, Honza, Ian, Ianos, Iban, Ioan, Ivan, Iwan, Keoni, Kwam, Ohannes, Sean, Ugutz, Yan, Yanka, Yanni, Yochanan, Yohance, Zane.
Jack, Jacsi, Jaenda, Jahn, Jan, Janak, Janco, Janek, Janis, Janne, János, Jansen, Jantje, Jantzen, Jas, Jean, Jehan, Jen, Jenkin, Jenkyn, Jens, Jhan, Jhanick, Jhon, Jian, João, João, Jock, Joen, Johan, Johann, Johne, Johnl, Johnlee, Johnnie, Johnny, Johnson, Jon, Jonam, Jonas, Jone, Jones, Jonny, Jonté, Jovan, Juan, Juhana

Johnathan (Hebrew) a form of Jonathan.
Jhonathan, Johathe, Johnatan, Johnathann, Johnathaon, Johnathen, Johnathyne, Johnatten, Johniathin, Johnothan, Johnthan

Johnathon (Hebrew) a form of Jonathon. See also Yanton.
Johnaton

Johnnie (Hebrew) a familiar form of John.
Johnie, Johnier, Johnni, Johnsie, Jonni, Jonnie

Johnny (Hebrew) a familiar form of John. See also Gianni.
Jantje, Jhonny, Johney, Johnney, Johny, Jonny

Johnson (English) son of John.
Johnston, Jonson

Joji (Japanese) a form of George.

Jojo (Fante) born on Monday.

Jokim (Basque) a form of Joachim.

Jolon (Native American) valley of the dead oaks.
Jolyon

Jomar (American) a form of Jamar.
Jomari, Jomarie, Jomarri

Jomei (Japanese) spreads light.

Jon (Hebrew) a form of John. A short form of Jonathan.
J'on, Joni, Jonn, Jonnie, Jonny, Jony

Jonah (Hebrew) dove. Bible: an Old Testament prophet who was swallowed by a large fish.
Giona, Jona, Yonah, Yunus

Jonas (Hebrew) he accomplishes. (Lithuanian) a form of John.
Jonahs, Jonass, Jonaus, Jonelis, Jonukas, Jonus, Jonutis, Joonas

Jonatan (Hebrew) a form of Jonathan.
Jonatane, Jonate, Jonattan, Jonnattan

Jonathan (Hebrew) gift of God. Bible: the son of King Saul who became a loyal friend of David. See also Ionakana, Yanton, Yonatan.
Janathan, Johnathan, Johnathon, Jon, Jonatan, Jonatha, Jonathen, Jonathin, Jonathon, Jonathun, Jonathyn, Jonethen, Jonnatha, Jonnathan, Jonnathun, Jonothan, Jonthan

Jonathon (Hebrew) a form of Jonathan.
Joanathon, Johnathon, Jonnathon, Jonothon, Jonthon, Jounathon, Yanaton

Jones (Welsh) son of John.
Joenns, Joness, Jonesy

Jonny (Hebrew) a familiar form of John.
Jonhy, Joni, Jonnee, Jony

Jontae (French) a combination of Jon + the suffix Tae.
Johntae, Jontay, Jontea, Jonteau, Jontez

Jontay (American) a form of Jontae.
Johntay, Johnte, Johntez, Jontai, Jonte, Jonté, Jontez

Joop (Dutch) a familiar form of Joseph.
Jopie

Joost (Dutch) just.

Joquin (Spanish) a form of Joaquin.
Joquan, Joquawn, Joqunn, Joquon

Jora (Hebrew) teacher.
Yora, Jorah

Joram (Hebrew) Jehovah is exalted.
Joran, Jorim

Jordan (Hebrew) descending. See also
Giordano, Yarden.
*Jardan, Jared, Jordaan, Jordae, Jordain,
Jordaine, Jordane, Jordani, Jordanio,
Jordann, Jordanny, Jordano, Jordany,
Jordáo, Jordayne, Jorden, Jordian, Jordin,
Jordon, Jordun, Jordy, Jordyn, Jorrdan,
Jory, Jourdan*

Jorden (Hebrew) a form of Jordan.
Jordenn

Jordon (Hebrew) a form of Jordan.
Jeordon, Johordan

Jordy (Hebrew) a familiar form of
Jordan.
Jordi, Jordie

Jordyn (Hebrew) a form of Jordan.

Jorell (American) he saves. Literature: a
name inspired by the fictional character Jor-El, Superman's father.
Jorel, Jor-El, Jorelle, Jorl, Jorrel, Jorrell

Jörg (German) a form of George.
Jeorg, Juergen, Jungen, Jürgen

Jorge (Spanish) a form of George.
Jorrín

Jorgen (Danish) a form of George.
Joergen, Jorgan, Jörgen

Joris (Dutch) a form of George.

Jörn (German) a familiar form of
Gregory.

Jorrín (Spanish) a form of George.
Jorian, Jorje

Jory (Hebrew) a familiar form of
Jordan.
Joar, Joary, Jorey, Jori, Jorie, Jorrie

José (Spanish) a form of Joseph. See
also Ché, Pepe.
*Josean, Josecito, Josee, Joseito, Joselito,
Josey*

Josef (German, Portuguese, Czech,
Scandinavian) a form of Joseph.
Joosef, Joseff, Josif, Jozef, József, Juzef

Joseluis (Spanish) a combination of
Jose + Luis.

Joseph (Hebrew) God will add, God
will increase. Bible: in the Old
Testament, the son of Jacob who
came to rule Egypt; in the New
Testament, the husband of Mary. See
also Beppe, Cheche, Chepe,
Giuseppe, Iokepa, Iosif, Osip, Pepa,
Peppe, Pino, Sepp, Yeska, Yosef,
Yousef, Youssel, Yusif, Yusuf, Zeusef.
*Jazeps, Jo, Jobo, Jody, Joe, Joeseph, Joey,
Jojo, Joop, Joos, Jooseppi, Jopie, José,
Joseba, Josef, Josep, Josephat, Josephe,
Josephie, Josephus, Josheph, Josip, Jóska,
Joza, Joze, Jozef, Jozeph, Jozhe, Jozio,
Jozka, Jozsi, Jozzepi, Jupp, Juziu*

Josh (Hebrew) a short form of Joshua.
Joshe

Josha (Hindi) satisfied.

Joshi (Swahili) galloping.

Joshua (Hebrew) God is my salvation.
Bible: led the Israelites into the
Promised Land. See also Giosia,
Iosua, Jesus, Yehoshua.
*Jeshua, Johsua, Johusa, Josh, Joshau,
Joshaua, Joshauh, Joshawa, Joshawah,
Joshia, Joshu, Joshuaa, Joshuah, Joshuea,
Joshuia, Joshula, Joshus, Joshusa,
Joshuwa, Joshwa, Josue, Jousha, Jozshua,
Jozsua, Jozua, Jushua*

Josiah (Hebrew) fire of the Lord. See
also Yoshiyahu.
Joshiah, Josia, Josiahs, Josian, Josias, Josie

Joss (Chinese) luck; fate.
Josse, Jossy

Josue (Hebrew) a form of Joshua.
Joshue, Jossue, Josu, Josua, Josuha, Jozus

Jotham (Hebrew) may God complete.
Bible: a king of Judah.

Jourdan (Hebrew) a form of Jordan.
*Jourdain, Jourden, Jourdin, Jourdon,
Jourdyn*

Jovan (Latin) Jove-like, majestic.
(Slavic) a form of John. Mythology:
Jove, also known as Jupiter, was the
supreme Roman deity.
*Johvan, Johvon, Jovaan, Jovane, Jovani,
Jovanic, Jovann, Jovanni, Jovannis,
Jovanny, Jovany, Jovaughn, Jovaun, Joven,
Jovenal, Jovenel, Jovi, Jovian, Jovin,
Jovito, Jovoan, Jovon, Jovone, Jovonn,
Jovonne, Jowan, Jowaun, Yovan, Yovani*

Jovani, Jovanni (Latin) forms of Jovan.
Jovanie, Jovannie, Jovoni, Jovonie, Jovonni

Jovanny, Jovany (Latin) forms of Jovan.
Jovony

Jr (Latin) a short form of Junior.
Jr.

Juan (Spanish) a form of John. See also Chan.
Juanch, Juanchito, Juane, Juanito, Juann, Juaun

Juancarlos (Spanish) a combination of Juan + Carlos.

Juaquin (Spanish) a form of Joaquín.
Juaqin, Juaqine, Juquan, Juaquine

Jubal (Hebrew) ram's horn. Bible: a musician and a descendant of Cain.

Judah (Hebrew) praised. Bible: the fourth of Jacob's sons. See also Yehudi.
Juda, Judas, Judd, Jude

Judas (Latin) a form of Judah. Bible: Judas Iscariot was the disciple who betrayed Jesus.
Jude

Judd (Hebrew) a short form of Judah.
Jud, Judson

Jude (Latin) a short form of Judah, Judas. Bible: one of the Twelve Apostles, author of "The Epistle of Jude."

Judson (English) son of Judd.

Juhana (Finnish) a form of John.
Juha, Juho

Juku (Estonian) a form of Richard.
Jukka

Jules (French) a form of Julius.
Joles, Jule

Julian (Greek, Latin) a form of Julius.
Jolyon, Julean, Juliaan, Julianne, Juliano, Julien, Jullian, Julyan

Julien (Latin) a form of Julian.
Juliene, Julienn, Julienne, Jullien, Jullin

Julio (Hispanic) a form of Julius.

Julius (Greek, Latin) youthful, downy bearded. History: Julius Caesar was a great Roman dictator. See also Giuliano.
Jolyon, Julas, Jule, Jules, Julen, Jules, Julian, Julias, Julie, Julio, Juliusz, Jullius, Juluis

Jumaane (Swahili) born on Tuesday.

Jumah (Arabic, Swahili) born on Friday, a holy day in the Islamic religion.
Jimoh, Juma

Jumoke (Yoruba) loved by everyone.

Jun (Chinese) truthful. (Japanese) obedient; pure.
Junnie

Junior (Latin) young.
Jr, Junious, Junius, Junor

Jupp (German) a form of Joseph.

Jur (Czech) a form of George.
Juraz, Jurek, Jurik, Jurko, Juro

Jurgis (Lithuanian) a form of George.
Jurgi, Juri

Juro (Japanese) best wishes; long life.

Jurrien (Dutch) God will uplift.
Jore, Jurian, Jurre

Justen (Latin) a form of Justin.
Jasten

Justice (Latin) a form of Justis.
Justic, Justiz, Justyc, Justyce

Justin (Latin) just, righteous. See also Giustino, Iestyn, Iustin, Tutu, Ustin, Yustyn.
Jastin, Jaston, Jestin, Jobst, Joost, Jost, Jusa, Just, Justain, Justan, Justas, Justek, Justen, Justian, Justinas, Justine, Justinian, Justinius, Justinn, Justino, Justins, Justinus, Justo, Juston, Justton, Justukas, Justun, Justyn

Justis (French) just.
Justice, Justs, Justus, Justyse

Justyn (Latin) a form of Justin.
Justn, Justyne, Justynn

Juvenal (Latin) young. Literature: a Roman satirist.
Juvon, Juvone

Juwan (American) a form of Jajuan.
Juvon, Juvone, Juvaun, Juwaan, Juwain, Juwane, Juwann, Juwaun, Juwon, Juwonn, Juwuan, Juwuane, Juwvan, Jwan, Jwon

K

Kabiito (Rutooro) born while foreigners are visiting.

Kabil (Turkish) a form of Cain.
Kabel

Kabir (Hindi) History: an Indian mystic poet.
Kabar, Kabeer, Kabier

Kabonero (Runyankore) sign.

Kabonesa (Rutooro) difficult birth.

Kacey (Irish) a form of Casey. (American) a combination of the initials K. + C. See also KC.
Kace, Kacee, Kaci, Kacy, Kaesy, Kase, Kasey, Kasie, Kasy, Kaycee

Kadar (Arabic) powerful.
Kader

Kadarius (American) a combination of Kade + Darius.
Kadairious, Kadarious, Kadaris, Kadarrius, Kadarus, Kaddarrius, Kaderious, Kaderius

Kade (Scottish) wetlands. (American) a combination of the initials K. + D.
Kadee, Kady, Kaid, Kaide, Kaydee

Kadeem (Arabic) servant.
Kadim, Khadeem

Kaden (Arabic) a form of Kadin.
Kadeen, Kadein, Kaidan, Kaiden

Kadin (Arabic) friend, companion.
Caden, Kaden, Kadyn, Kaeden, Kayden

Kadir (Arabic) spring greening.
Kadeer

Kado (Japanese) gateway.

Kaeden (Arabic) a form of Kadin.
Kaedin, Kaedon, Kaedyn

Kaelan, Kaelin (Irish) forms of Kellen.
Kael, Kaelen, Kaelon, Kaelyn

Kaeleb (Hebrew) a form of Kaleb.
Kaelib, Kaelob, Kaelyb, Kailab, Kaileb

Kaemon (Japanese) joyful; right-handed.
Kaeman, Kaemen, Kaemin

Kaenan (Irish) a form of Keenan.
Kaenen, Kaenin, Kaenyn

Ka'eo (Hawaiian) victorious.

Kafele (Nguni) worth dying for.

Kaga (Native American) writer.

Kagan (Irish) a form of Keegan.
Kage, Kagen, Kaghen, Kaigan

Kahale (Hawaiian) home.

Kahil (Turkish) young; inexperienced; naive.
Cahil, Kaheel, Kale, Kayle

Kahlil (Arabic) a form of Khalíl.
Kahleal, Kahlee, Kahleel, Kahleil, Kahli, Kahliel, Kahlill, Kalel, Kalil

Kaholo (Hawaiian) runner.

Kahraman (Turkish) hero.

Kai (Welsh) keeper of the keys. (German) a form of Kay. (Hawaiian) sea.
Kae, Kaie, Kaii

Kaikara (Runyoro) Religion: a Banyoro deity.

Kailen (Irish) a form of Kellen.
Kail, Kailan, Kailey, Kailin, Kailon, Kailyn

Kaili (Hawaiian) Religion: a Hawaiian god.
Kailli

Kain (Welsh, Irish) a form of Kane.
Kainan, Kaine, Kainen, Kainin, Kainon

Kainoa (Hawaiian) name.

Kaipo (Hawaiian) sweetheart.

Kairo (Arabic) a form of Cairo.
Kaire, Kairee, Kairi

Kaiser (German) a form of Caesar.
Kaesar, Kaisar, Kaizer

Kaiven (American) a form of Kevin.
Kaivan, Kaiven, Kaivon, Kaiwan

Kaj (Danish) earth.
Kai, Kaje

Kakar (Hindi) grass.

Kala (Hindi) black; phase. (Hawaiian) sun.

Kalama (Hawaiian) torch.
Kalam

Kalan (Irish) a form of Kalen.
Kalane, Kallan

Kalani (Hawaiian) sky; chief.
Kalan

Kale (Arabic) a short form of Kahlil. (Hawaiian) a familiar form of Carl.
Kalee, Kalen, Kaleu, Kaley, Kali, Kalin, Kalle, Kayle

Kaleb (Hebrew) a form of Caleb.
Kaeleb, Kal, Kalab, Kalabe, Kalb, Kale, Kaleob, Kalev, Kalib, Kalieb, Kallb, Kalleb, Kalob, Kaloeb, Kalub, Kalyb, Kilab

Kalen, Kalin (Arabic, Hawaiian) forms of Kale. (Irish) forms of Kellen.
Kalan

Kalevi (Finnish) hero.

Kali (Arabic) a short form of Kalil. (Hawaiian) a form of Gary.

Kalil (Arabic) a form of Khalíl.
Kaleel, Kalell, Kali, Kaliel, Kaliil

Kaliq (Arabic) a form of Khaliq.
Kalic, Kalique

Kalkin (Hindi) tenth. Religion: Kalki is the final incarnation of the Hindu god Vishnu.
Kalki

Kalle (Scandinavian) a form of Carl. (Arabic, Hawaiian) a form of Kale.

Kallen (Irish) a form of Kellen.
Kallan, Kallin, Kallion, Kallon, Kallun, Kalun

Kalon, Kalyn (Irish) forms of Kellen.
Kalone, Kalonn, Kalyen, Kalyne, Kalynn

Kaloosh (Armenian) blessed event.

Kalvin (Latin) a form of Calvin.
Kal, Kalv, Kalvan, Kalven, Kalvon, Kalvyn, Vinny

Kamaka (Hawaiian) face.

Kamakani (Hawaiian) wind.

Kamal (Hindi) lotus. (Arabic) perfect, perfection.
Kamaal, Kamel, Kamil

Kamau (Kikuyu) quiet warrior.

Kamden (Scottish) a form of Camden.
Kamdon

Kameron (Scottish) a form of Cameron.
Kam, Kamaren, Kamaron, Kameran, Kameren, Kamerin, Kamerion, Kamerron, Kamerun, Kameryn, Kamey, Kammeren, Kammeron, Kammy, Kamoryn, Kamran, Kamron

Kami (Hindi) loving.

Kamil (Arabic) a form of Kamal.
Kameel

Kamran, Kamron (Scottish) forms of Kameron.
Kammron, Kamrein, Kamren, Kamrin, Kamrun, Kamryn

Kamuela (Hawaiian) a form of Samuel.

Kamuhanda (Runyankore) born on the way to the hospital.

Kamukama (Runyankore) protected by God.

Kamuzu (Nguni) medicine.

Kamya (Luganda) born after twin brothers.

Kana (Japanese) powerful; capable. (Hawaiian) Mythology: a demigod.

Kanaiela (Hawaiian) a form of Daniel.
Kana, Kaneii

Kane (Welsh) beautiful. (Irish) tribute. (Japanese) golden. (Hawaiian) eastern sky. (English) a form of Keene. See Kahan, Kain, Kaney, Kayne.

Kange (Lakota) raven.
Kang, Kanga

Kaniel (Hebrew) stalk, reed.
Kan, Kani, Kannie, Kanny

Kannan (Hindi) Religion: another name for the Hindu god Krishna.
Kanaan, Kanan, Kanen, Kanin, Kanine, Kannen

Kannon (Polynesian) free. (French) A form of Cannon.
Kanon

Kanoa (Hawaiian) free.

Kantu (Hindi) happy.

Kanu (Swahili) wildcat.

Kaori (Japanese) strong.

Kapila (Hindi) ancient prophet.
Kapil

Kapono (Hawaiian) righteous.
Kapena

Kardal (Arabic) mustard seed.
Karandal, Kardell

Kare (Norwegian) enormous.
Karee

Kareem (Arabic) noble; distinguished.
Karee, Karem, Kareme, Karim, Karriem

Karel (Czech) a form of Carl.
Karell, Karil, Karrell

Karey (Greek) a form of Carey.
Karee, Kari, Karry, Kary

Karif (Arabic) born in autumn.
Kareef

Kariisa (Runyankore) herdsman.

Karim (Arabic) a form of Kareem.

Karl (German) a form of Carl.
Kaarle, Kaarlo, Kale, Kalle, Kalman, Kálmán, Karcsi, Karel, Kari, Karlen, Karlitis, Karlo, Karlos, Karlton, Karlus, Karol, Kjell

Karlen (Latvian, Russian) a form of Carl.
Karlan, Karlens, Karlik, Karlin, Karlis, Karlon

Karmel (Hebrew) a form of Carmel.

Karney (Irish) a form of Carney.

Karol (Czech, Polish) a form of Carl.
Karal, Karolek, Karolis, Karalos, Károly, Karrel, Karrol

Karr (Scandinavian) a form of Carr.

Karson (English) a form of Carson.
Karrson, Karsen

Karsten (Greek) anointed.
Carsten, Karstan, Karston

Karu (Hindi) cousin.
Karun

Karutunda (Runyankore) little.

Karwana (Rutooro) born during wartime.

Kaseem (Arabic) divided.
Kasceem, Kaseam, Kaseym, Kasim, Kasseem, Kassem, Kazeem

Kaseko (Rhodesian) mocked, ridiculed.

Kasem (Tai) happiness.

Kasen (Basque) protected with a helmet.
Kasean, Kasene, Kaseon, Kasin, Kason, Kassen

Kasey (Irish) a form of Casey.
Kaese, Kaesy, Kasay, Kassey

Kashawn (American) a combination of the prefix Ka + Shawn.
Kashain, Kashan, Kashaun, Kashen, Kashon

Kasib (Arabic) fertile.

Kasim (Arabic) a form of Kaseem.
Kassim

Kasimir (Arabic) peace. (Slavic) a form of Casimir.
Kasim, Kazimierz, Kazimir, Kazio, Kazmer, Kazmér, Kázmér

Kasiya (Nguni) separate.

Kasper (Persian) treasurer. (German) a form of Casper.
Jasper, Kaspar, Kaspero

Kass (German) blackbird.
Kaese, Kasch, Kase

Kassidy (Irish) a form of Cassidy.
Kassady, Kassie, Kassy

Kateb (Arabic) writer.

Kato (Runyankore) second of twins.

Katungi (Runyankore) rich.

Kavan (Irish) handsome.
Cavan, Kavanagh, Kavaugn, Kaven, Kavenaugh, Kavin, Kavon, Kayvan

Kaveh (Persian) ancient hero.

Kavi (Hindi) poet.

Kavin, **Kavon** (Irish) forms of Kavan.
Kaveon, Kavion, Kavone, Kayvon, Kaywon

Kawika (Hawaiian) a form of David.

Kay (Greek) rejoicing. (German) fortified place. Literature: one of King Arthur's knights of the Round Table.
Kai, Kaycee, Kaye, Kayson

Kayden (Arabic) a form of Kadin.
Kayde, Kaydee, Kaydin, Kaydn, Kaydon

Kayin (Nigerian) celebrated. (Yoruba) long-hoped-for child.

Kayle (Hebrew) faithful dog. (Arabic) a short form of Kahlil.
Kayl, Kayla, Kaylee

Kayleb (Hebrew) a form of Caleb.
Kaylib, Kaylob, Kaylub

Kaylen (Irish) a form of Kellen.
Kaylan, Kaylin, Kaylon, Kaylyn, Kaylynn

Kayne (Hebrew) a form of Cain.
Kaynan, Kaynen, Kaynon

Kayode (Yoruba) he brought joy.

Kayonga (Runyankore) ash.

Kazio (Polish) a form of Casimir, Kasimir. See also Cassidy.

Kazuo (Japanese) man of peace.

KC (American) a combination of the initials K. + C. See also Kacey.
Kc, K.C., Kcee, Kcey

Keagan (Irish) a form of Keegan.
Keagean, Keagen, Keaghan, Keagyn

Keahi (Hawaiian) flames.

Keaka (Hawaiian) a form of Jack.

Kealoha (Hawaiian) fragrant.
Ke'ala

Keanan (Irish) a form of Keenan.
Keanen, Keanna, Keannan, Keanon

Keandre (American) a combination of the prefix Ke + Andre.
Keandra, Keandray, Keandré, Keandree, Keandrell, Keondre

Keane (German) bold; sharp. (Irish) handsome. (English) a form of Keene.
Kean

Keanu (Irish) a form of Keenan.
Keaneu, Keani, Keanno, Keano, Keanue, Keeno, Keenu, Kianu

Kearn (Irish) a short form of Kearney.
Kearne

Kearney (Irish) a form of Carney.
Kar, Karney, Karny, Kearn, Kearny

Keary (Irish) a form of Kerry.
Kearie

Keaton (English) where hawks fly.
Keatan, Keaten, Keatin, Keatton, Keatyn, Keeton, Keetun

Keaven (Irish) a form of Kevin.
Keavan, Keavon

Keawe (Hawaiian) strand.

Keb (Egyptian) earth. Mythology: an ancient earth god, also known as Geb.

Kedar (Hindi) mountain lord. (Arabic) powerful. Religion: another name for the Hindu god Shiva.
Kadar, Kedaar, Keder

Keddy (Scottish) a form of Adam.
Keddie

Kedem (Hebrew) ancient.

Kedrick (English) a form of Cedric.
Keddrick, Kederick, Kedrek, Kedric, Kiedric, Kiedrick

Keefe (Irish) handsome; loved.

Keegan (Irish) little; fiery.
Kaegan, Kagan, Keagan, Keagen, Keeghan, Keegon, Keegun, Kegan, Keigan

Keelan (Irish) little; slender.
Keelen, Keelin, Keelyn, Keilan, Kelan

Keeley (Irish) handsome.
Kealey, Kealy, Keeli, Keelian, Keelie, Keely

Keenan (Irish) little Keene.
Kaenan, Keanan, Keanu, Keenen, Keennan, Keenon, Kenan, Keynan, Kienan, Kienon

Keene (German) bold; sharp. (English) smart. See also Kane.
Kaene, Keane, Keen, Keenan

Keenen (Irish) a form of Keenan.
Keenin, Kienen

Kees (Dutch) a form of Kornelius.
Keese, Keesee, Keyes

Keevon (Irish) a form of Kevin.
Keevan, Keeven, Keevin, Keewan, Keewin

Kegan (Irish) a form of Keegan.
Kegen, Keghan, Kegon, Kegun

Kehind (Yoruba) second-born twin.
Kehinde

Keiffer (German) a form of Cooper.
Keefer, Keifer, Kiefer

Keigan (Irish) a form of Keegan.
Keighan, Keighen

Keiji (Japanese) cautious ruler.

Keilan (Irish) a form of Keelan.
Keilen, Keilin, Keillene, Keillyn, Keilon, Keilynn

Keir (Irish) a short form of Kieran.

Keitaro (Japanese) blessed.
Keita

Keith (Welsh) forest. (Scottish) battle place. See also Kika.
Keath, Keeth, Keithen

Keithen (Welsh, Scottish) a form of Keith.
Keithan, Keitheon, Keithon

Keivan (Irish) a form of Kevin.
Keiven, Keivn, Keivon, Keivone

Kekapa (Hawaiian) tapa cloth.

Kekipi (Hawaiian) rebel.

Kekoa (Hawaiian) bold, courageous.

Kelby (German) farm by the spring.
Keelby, Kelbee, Kelbey, Kelbi, Kellby

Kele (Hopi) sparrow hawk. (Hawaiian) a form of Jerry.
Kelle

Kelemen (Hungarian) gentle; kind.
Kellman

Kelevi (Finnish) hero.

Keli (Hawaiian) a form of Terry.

Keli'i (Hawaiian) chief.

Kelile (Ethiopian) protected.

Kell (Scandinavian) spring.

Kellan (Irish) a form of Kellen.
Keillan

Kellen (Irish) mighty warrior.
*Kaelan, Kailen, Kalan, Kalen, Kalin,
Kallen, Kalon, Kalyn, Kaylen, Keelan,
Kelden, Kelin, Kellan, Kelle, Kellin,
Kellyn, Kelyn, Kelynn*

Keller (Irish) little companion.

Kelly (Irish) warrior.
Kelle, Kellen, Kelley, Kelli, Kellie, Kely

Kelmen (Basque) merciful.
Kelmin

Kelsey (Scandinavian) island of ships.
*Kelcy, Kelse, Kelsea, Kelsi, Kelsie, Kelso,
Kelsy, Kesley, Kesly*

Kelton (English) keel town; port.
*Kelden, Keldon, Kelson, Kelston, Kelten,
Keltin, Keltonn, Keltyn*

Kelvin (Irish, English) narrow river.
Geography: a river in Scotland.
*Kelvan, Kelven, Kelvon, Kelvyn,
Kelwin, Kelwyn*

Kemal (Turkish) highest honor.

Kemen (Basque) strong.

Kemp (English) fighter; champion.

Kempton (English) military town.

Ken (Japanese) one's own kind.
(Scottish) a short form of Kendall,
Kendrick, Kenneth.
Kena, Kenn, Keno

Kenan (Irish) a form of Keenan.

Kenaz (Hebrew) bright.

Kendal (English) a form of Kendall.
*Kendale, Kendali, Kendel, Kendul,
Kendyl*

Kendall (English) valley of the river
Kent.
*Ken, Kendal, Kendell, Kendrall,
Kendryll, Kendyll, Kyndall*

Kendarius (American) a combination
of Ken + Darius.
*Kendarious, Kendarrious, Kendarrius,
Kenderious, Kenderius, Kenderyious*

Kendell (English) a form of Kendall.
Kendelle, Kendrel, Kendrell

Kendrew (Scottish) a form of Andrew.

Kendrick (Irish) son of Henry.
(Scottish) royal chieftain.
*Ken, Kenderrick, Kendric, Kendrich,
Kenedrick, Kendricks, Kendrik, Kendrix,
Kendryck, Kenndrick, Keondric, Keondrick*

Kenley (English) royal meadow.
Kenlea, Kenlee, Kenleigh, Kenlie, Kenly

Kenn (Scottish) a form of Ken.

Kennan (Scottish) little Ken.
Kenna, Kenan, Kenen, Kennen, Kennon

Kennard (Irish) brave chieftain.
Kenner

Kennedy (Irish) helmeted chief.
History: John F. Kennedy was the
thirty-fifth U.S. president.
Kenedy, Kenidy, Kennady, Kennedey

Kenneth (Irish) handsome. (English)
royal oath.
Ken, Keneth, Kenneith, Kennet,

*Kennethen, Kennett, Kennieth, Kennith,
Kennth, Kenny, Kennyth, Kenya*

Kenny (Scottish) a familiar form of
Kenneth.
Keni, Kenney, Kenni, Kennie, Kinnie

Kenrick (English) bold ruler; royal
ruler.
Kenric, Kenricks, Kenrik

Kent (Welsh) white; bright. (English) a
short form of Kenton. Geography: a
region in England.

Kentaro (Japanese) big boy.

Kenton (English) from Kent, England.
Kent, Kenten, Kentin, Kentonn

Kentrell (English) king's estate.
Kenreal, Kentrel, Kentrelle

Kenward (English) brave; royal
guardian.

Kenya (Hebrew) animal horn.
(Russian) a form of Kenneth.
Geography: a country in east-central
Africa.
Kenyatta

Kenyatta (American) a form of
Kenya.
*Kenyata, Kenyatae, Kenyatee, Kenyatter,
Kenyatti, Kenyotta*

Kenyon (Irish) white haired, blond.
Kenyan, Kenynn, Keonyon

Kenzie (Scottish) wise leader. See also
Mackenzie.
Kensie

Keoki (Hawaiian) a form of George.

Keola (Hawaiian) life.

Keon (Irish) a form of Ewan.
Keeon, Keion, Keionne, Keondre, Keone,
Keonne, Keonte, Keony, Keyon, Kian,
Kion

Keoni (Hawaiian) a form of John.

Keonte (American) a form of Keon.
Keonntay, Keonta, Keontae, Keontay,
Keontaye, Keontez, Keontia, Keontis,
Keontrae, Keontre, Keontrey, Keontrye

Kerbasi (Basque) warrior.

Kerel (Afrikaans) young.
Kerell

Kerem (Turkish) noble; kind.
Kereem

Kerey (Gypsy) homeward bound.
Ker

Kerman (Basque) from Germany.

Kermit (Irish) a form of Dermot.
Kermey, Kermie, Kermitt, Kermy

Kern (Irish) a short form of Kieran.
Kearn, Kerne

Kerr (Scandinavian) a form of Carr.
Karr

Kerrick (English) king's rule.

Kerry (Irish) dark; dark haired.
Keary, Keri, Kerrey, Kerri, Kerrie

Kers (Todas) Botany: an Indian plant.

Kersen (Indonesian) cherry.

Kerstan (Dutch) a form of Christian.

Kerwin (Irish) little; dark. (English)
friend of the marshlands.
Kervin, Kervyn, Kerwinn, Kerwyn,
Kerwynn, Kirwin, Kirwyn

Kesar (Russian) a form of Caesar.
Kesare

Keshawn (American) a combination
of the prefix Ke + Shawn.
Keeshaun, Keeshawn, Keeshon, Kesean,
Keshan, Keshane, Keshaun, Keshayne,
Keshion, Keshon, Keshone, Keshun,
Kishan

Kesin (Hindi) long-haired beggar.

Kesse (Ashanti, Fante) chubby baby.
Kessie

Kester (English) a form of
Christopher.

Kestrel (English) falcon.
Kes

Keung (Chinese) universe.

Kevan (Irish) a form of Kevin.
Kavan, Kewan, Kewane, Kewaun,
Keyvan, Kiwan, Kiwane

Keven (Irish) a form of Kevin.
Keve, Keveen, Kiven

Kevin (Irish) handsome. See also
Cavan.
Kaiven, Keaven, Keevon, Keivan, Kev,
Kevan, Keven, Keverne, Kevian, Kevien,
Kévin, Kevinn, Kevins, Kevis, Kevn,
Kevon, Kevvy, Kevyn, Kyven

Kevon (Irish) a form of Kevin.
Keveon, Kevion, Kevone, Kevonne,
Kevontae, Kevonte, Kevoyn, Kevron,
Kewon, Kewone, Keyvon, Kivon

Kevyn (Irish) a form of Kevin.
Kevyon

Key (English) key; protected.

Keyon (Irish) a form of Keon.
Keyan, Keyen, Keyin, Keyion

Keyshawn (American) a combination
of Key + Shawn.
Keyshan, Keyshaun, Keyshon, Keyshun

Khachig (Armenian) small cross.
Khachik

Khaim (Russian) a form of Chaim.

Khaldun (Arabic) forever.
Khaldoon, Khaldoun

Khalfani (Swahili) born to lead.
Khalfan

Khälid (Arabic) eternal.
Khaled, Khallid, Khalyd

Khalíl (Arabic) friend.
Kahlil, Kaleel, Kalil, Khahlil, Khailil,
Khailyl, Khalee, Khaleel, Khaleil, Khali,
Khalial, Khaliel, Khalihl, Khalill,
Khaliyl

Khaliq (Arabic) creative.
Kaliq, Khalique

Khamisi (Swahili) born on Thursday.
Kham

Khan (Turkish) prince.
Khanh

Kharald (Russian) a form of Gerald.

Khayru (Arabic) benevolent.
Khiri, Khiry, Kiry

Khoury (Arabic) priest.
Khory

Khristian (Greek) a form of Christian, Kristian.
Khris, Khristan, Khristin, Khriston, Khrystian

Khristopher (Greek) a form of Kristopher.
Khristofer, Khristophar, Khrystopher

Khristos (Greek) a form of Christos.
Khris, Khristophe, Kristo, Kristos

Kibo (Uset) worldly; wise.

Kibuuka (Luganda) brave warrior. History: a Ganda warrior deity.

Kidd (English) child; young goat.

Kiefer (German) a form of Keifer.
Kief, Kieffer, Kiefor, Kiffer, Kiiefer

Kiel (Irish) a form of Kyle.
Kiell

Kiele (Hawaiian) gardenia.

Kieran (Irish) little and dark; little Keir.
Keiran, Keiren, Keiron, Kiaron, Kiarron, Kier, Kieren, Kierian, Kierien, Kierin, Kiernan, Kieron, Kierr, Kierre, Kierron, Kyran

Kiernan (Irish) a form of Kieran.
Kern, Kernan, Kiernen

Kiet (Tai) honor.

Kifeda (Luo) only boy among girls.

Kiho (Rutooro) born on a foggy day.

Kijika (Native American) quiet walker.

Kika (Hawaiian) a form of Keith.

Kiki (Spanish) a form of Henry.

Kile (Irish) a form of Kyle.
Kilee, Kilen, Kiley, Kiyl, Kiyle

Killian (Irish) little Kelly.
Kilean, Kilian, Kilien, Killie, Killien, Killiean, Killion, Killy

Kim (English) a short form of Kimball.
Kimie, Kimmy

Kimball (Greek) hollow vessel. (English) warrior chief.
Kim, Kimbal, Kimbel, Kimbell, Kimble

Kimo (Hawaiian) a form of James.

Kimokeo (Hawaiian) a form of Timothy.

Kin (Japanese) golden.

Kincaid (Scottish) battle chief.
Kincade, Kinkaid

Kindin (Basque) fifth.

King (English) king. A short form of names beginning with "King."

Kingsley (English) king's meadow.
King, Kings, Kingslea, Kingslie, Kingsly, Kingzlee, Kinslea, Kinslee, Kinsley, Kinslie, Kinsly

Kingston (English) king's estate.
King, Kinston

Kingswell (English) king's well.
King

Kini (Hawaiian) a short form of Iukini.

Kinnard (Irish) tall slope.

Kinsey (English) victorious royalty.
Kinze, Kinzie

Kinton (Hindi) crowned.

Kion (Irish) a form of Keon.
Kione, Kionie, Kionne

Kioshi (Japanese) quiet.

Kipp (English) pointed hill.
Kip, Kippar, Kipper, Kippie, Kippy

Kir (Bulgarian) a familiar form of Cyrus.

Kiral (Turkish) king; supreme leader.

Kiran (Sanskrit) beam of light.
Kyran

Kirby (Scandinavian) church village. (English) cottage by the water.
Kerbey, Kerbie, Kerby, Kirbey, Kirbie, Kirkby

Kiri (Cambodian) mountain.

Kiril (Slavic) a form of Cyril.
Kirill, Kiryl, Kyrillos

Kiritan (Hindi) wearing a crown.

Kirk (Scandinavian) church.
Kerk

Kirkland (English) church land.
Kirklin, Kirklind, Kirklynd

Kirkley (English) church meadow.

Kirklin (English) a form of Kirkland.
Kirklan, Kirklen, Kirkline, Kirkloun, Kirklun, Kirklyn, Kirklynn

Kirkwell (English) church well; church spring.

Kirkwood (English) church forest.

Kirton (English) church town.

Kishan (American) a form of Keshawn.
Kishaun, Kishawn, Kishen, Kishon, Kyshon, Kyshun

Kistna (Hindi) sacred, holy. Geography: a sacred river in India.

Kistur (Gypsy) skillful rider.

Kit (Greek) a familiar form of Christian, Christopher, Kristopher.
Kitt, Kitts

Kito (Swahili) jewel; precious child.

Kitwana (Swahili) pledged to live.

Kiva (Hebrew) a short form of Akiva, Jacob.
Kiba, Kivi, Kiwa

Kiyoshi (Japanese) quiet; peaceful.

Kizza (Luganda) born after twins.
Kizzy

Kjell (Swedish) a form of Karl.
Kjel

Klaus (German) a short form of Nicholas. A form of Claus.
Klaas, Klaes, Klas, Klause

Klay (English) a form of Clay.

Klayton (English) a form of Clayton.

Kleef (Dutch) cliff.

Klement (Czech) a form of Clement.
Klema, Klemenis, Klemens, Klemet, Klemo, Klim, Klimek, Kliment, Klimka

Kleng (Norwegian) claw.

Knight (English) armored knight.
Knightly

Knoton (Native American) a form of Nodin.

Knowles (English) grassy slope.
Knolls, Nowles

Knox (English) hill.

Knute (Scandinavian) a form of Canute.
Knud, Knut

Koby (Polish) a familiar form of Jacob.
Kobby, Kobe, Kobey, Kobi, Kobia, Kobie

Kodi (English) a form of Kody.
Kode, Kodee, Kodie

Kody (English) a form of Cody.
Kodey, Kodi, Kodye, Koty

Kofi (Twi) born on Friday.

Kohana (Lakota) swift.

Koi (Choctaw) panther. (Hawaiian) a form of Troy.

Kojo (Akan) born on Monday.

Koka (Hawaiian) Scotsman.

Kokayi (Shona) gathered together.

Kolby (English) a form of Colby.
Kelby, Koalby, Koelby, Kohlbe, Kohlby, Kolbe, Kolbey, Kolbi, Kolbie, Kolebe, Koleby, Kollby

Kole (English) a form of Cole.
Kohl, Kohle

Koleman (English) a form of Coleman.
Kolemann, Kolemen

Kolin (English) a form of Colin.
Kolen, Kollen, Kollin, Kollyn, Kolyn

Kolton (English) a form of Colton.
Kolt, Koltan, Kolte, Kolten, Koltin, Koltn, Koltyn

Kolya (Russian) a familiar form of Nikolai, Nikolos.
Kola, Kolenka, Kolia, Kolja

Kona (Hawaiian) a form of Don.
Konala

Konane (Hawaiian) bright moonlight.

Kondo (Swahili) war.

Kong (Chinese) glorious; sky.

Konner (Irish) a form of Conner, Connor.
Konar, Koner

Konnor (Irish) a form of Connor.
Kohner, Kohnor, Konor

Kono (Moquelumnan) squirrel eating a pine nut.

Konrad (German) a form of Conrad.
Khonrad, Koen, Koenraad, Kon, Konn, Konney, Konni, Konnie, Konny, Konrád, Konrade, Konrado, Kord, Kort, Kunz

Konstantin (German, Russian) a form of Constantine. See also Dinos.
Konstancji, Konstadine, Konstadino, Konstandinos, Konstantinas, Konstantine, Konstantinos, Konstantio, Konstanty, Konstantyn, Konstanz, Konstatino, Kostadino, Kostadinos, Kostandino, Kostandinos, Kostantin, Kostantino, Kostas, Kostenka, Kostya, Kotsos

Kontar (Akan) only child.

Korb (German) basket.

Korbin (English) a form of Corbin.
Korban, Korben, Korbyn

Kordell (English) a form of Cordell.
Kordel

Korey (Irish) a form of Corey, Kory.
Kore, Koree, Korei, Korio, Korre, Korria, Korrye

Kornel (Latin) a form of Cornelius, Kornelius.
Kees, Korneil, Kornél, Korneli, Kornelisz, Kornell, Krelis, Soma

Kornelius (Latin) a form of Cornelius. See also Kees, Kornel.
Karnelius, Korneilius, Korneliaus, Kornelious, Kornellius

Korrigan (Irish) a form of Corrigan.
Korigan, Korigan, Korrigon, Korrigun

Kort (German, Dutch) a form of Cort, Kurt.
Kourt

Kortney (English) a form of Courtney.
Kortni, Kourtney

Korudon (Greek) helmeted one.

Kory (Irish) a form of Corey.
Korey, Kori, Korie, Korrey, Korri, Korrie, Korry

Kosey (African) lion.
Kosse

Kosmo (Greek) a form of Cosmo.
Kosmy, Kozmo

Kostas (Greek) a short form of Konstantin.

Kosti (Finnish) a form of Gustave.

Kosumi (Moquelumnan) spear fisher.

Koukalaka (Hawaiian) a form of Douglas.

Kourtland (English) a form of Courtland.
Kortlan, Kortland, Kortlend, Kortlon, Kourtlin

Kovit (Tai) expert.

Kraig (Irish, Scottish) a form of Craig.
Kraggie, Kraggy, Krayg, Kreg, Kreig, Kreigh

Krikor (Armenian) a form of Gregory.

Kris (Greek) a form of Chris. A short form of Kristian, Kristofer, Kristopher.
Kriss, Krys

Krischan (German) a form of Christian.
Krishan, Krishaun, Krishawn, Krishon, Krishun

Krishna (Hindi) delightful, pleasurable. Religion: the eighth and principal avatar of the Hindu god Vishnu.
Kistna, Kistnah, Krisha, Krishnah

Krispin (Latin) a form of Crispin.
Krispian, Krispino, Krispo

Krister (Swedish) a form of Christian.
Krist, Kristar

Kristian (Greek) a form of Christian, Khristian.
Kerstan, Khristos, Kit, Kris, Krischan, Krist, Kristan, Kristar, Kristek, Kristen, Krister, Kristien, Kristin, Kristine, Kristinn, Kristion, Kristjan, Kristo, Kristos, Krists, Krystek, Krystian, Khrystiyan

Kristo (Greek) a short form of Khristos.

Kristofer (Swedish) a form of Kristopher.
Kris, Kristafer, Kristef, Kristifer, Kristoff, Kristoffer, Kristofo, Kristofor, Kristofyr, Kristufer, Kristus, Krystofer

Kristoff (Greek) a short form of Kristofer, Kristopher.
Kristof, Kristóf

Kristophe (French) a form of Kristopher.

Kristopher (Greek) a form of Christopher. See also Topher.
Khristopher, Kit, Kris, Krisstopher, Kristapher, Kristepher, Kristfer, Kristfor, Kristo, Kristofer, Kristoff, Kristoforo, Kristoph, Kristophe, Kristophor, Kristos, Krists, Krisus, Krystopher, Krystupas, Krzysztof

Kruz (Spanish) a form of Cruz.
Kruise, Kruize, Kruse, Kruze

Krystian (Polish) a form of Christian.
Krys, Krystek, Krystien, Krystin

Kuba (Czech) a form of Jacob.
Kubo, Kubus

Kueng (Chinese) universe.

Kugonza (Rutooro) love.

Kuiril (Basque) lord.

Kumar (Sanskrit) prince.

Kunle (Yoruba) home filled with honors.

Kuper (Yiddish) copper.

Kurt (Latin, German, French) a short form of Kurtis. A form of Curt.
Kirt, Kort, Kuno, Kurtt

Kurtis (Latin, French) a form of Curtis.
Kirtis, Kirtus, Kurt, Kurtes, Kurtez, Kurtice, Kurties, Kurtiss, Kurtus, Kurtys

Kuruk (Pawnee) bear.

Kuzih (Carrier) good speaker.

Kwabena (Akan) born on Tuesday.

Kwacha (Nguni) morning.

Kwako (Akan) born on Wednesday.
Kwaka, Kwaku

Kwam (Zuni) a form of John.

Kwame (Akan) born on Saturday.
Kwamen, Kwami, Kwamin

Kwan (Korean) strong.
Kwane

Kwasi (Akan) born on Sunday. (Swahili) wealthy.
Kwasie, Kwazzi, Kwesi

Kwayera (Nguni) dawn.

Kwende (Nguni) let's go.

Kyele (Irish) a form of Kyle.

Kylan (Irish) a form of Kyle.
Kyelen, Kyleen, Kylen, Kylin, Kyline, Kylon, Kylun

Kyle (Irish) narrow piece of land; place where cattle graze. (Yiddish) crowned with laurels.
Cyle, Kiel, Kilan, Kile, Kilen, Kiley, Ky, Kye, Kyel, Kyele, Kylan, Kylee, Kyler, Kyley, Kylie, Kyll, Kylle, Kyrell

Kyler (English) a form of Kyle.
Kylar, Kylor

Kynan (Welsh) chief.

Kyndall (English) a form of Kendall.
Kyndal, Kyndel, Kyndell, Kyndle

Kyne (English) royal.

Kyran (Sanskrit) a form of Kiran.
Kyren, Kyron, Kyrone

Kyros (Greek) master.

Kyven (American) a form of Kevin.
Kyvan, Kyvaun, Kyvon, Kywon, Kywynn

Laban (Hawaiian) white.
Labon, Lebaan, Leban, Liban

Labaron (American) a combination of the prefix La + Baron.
Labaren, Labarren, Labarron, Labearon, Labron

Labib (Arabic) sensible; intelligent.

Labrentsis (Russian) a form of Lawrence.
Labhras, Labhruinn, Labrencis

Lachlan (Scottish) land of lakes.
Lache, Lachlann, Lachunn, Lakelan, Lakeland

Ladarian (American) a combination of the prefix La + Darian.
Ladarien, Ladarin, Ladarion, Ladarren, Ladarrian, Ladarrien, Ladarrin, Ladarrion, Laderion, Laderrian, Laderrion

Ladarius (American) a combination of the prefix La + Darius.
Ladarious, Ladaris, Ladarrius, Ladauris, Laderius, Ladirus

Ladarrius (American) a form of Ladarius.
Ladarrias, Ladarries, Ladarrious, Laderrious, Laderris

Ladd (English) attendant.
Lad, Laddey, Laddie, Laddy

Laderrick (American) a combination of the prefix La + Derrick.
Ladarrick, Ladereck, Laderic, Laderricks

Ladislav (Czech) a form of Walter.
Laco, Lada, Ladislaus

Lado (Fante) second-born son.

Lafayette (French) History: Marquis de Lafayette was a French soldier and politician who aided the American Revolution.
Lafaiete, Lafayett, Lafette, Laffyette

Laine (English) a form of Lane.
Lain

Laird (Scottish) wealthy landowner.

Lais (Arabic) lion.

Lajos (Hungarian) famous; holy.
Lajcsi, Laji, Lali

Lake (English) lake.
Lakan, Lakane, Lakee, Laken, Lakin

Lakota (Dakota) a tribal name.
Lakoda

Lal (Hindi) beloved.

Lamar (German) famous throughout the land. (French) sea, ocean.
Lamair, Lamario, Lamaris, Lamarr, Lamarre, Larmar, Lemar

Lambert (German) bright land.
Bert, Lambard, Lamberto, Lambirt, Lampard, Landbert

Lamond (French) world.
Lammond, Lamon, Lamonde, Lamondo, Lamondre, Lamund, Lemond

Lamont (Scandinavian) lawyer.
Lamaunt, Lamonta, Lamonte, Lamontie, Lamonto, Lamount, Lemont

Lance (German) a short form of Lancelot.
Lancy, Lantz, Lanz, Launce

Lancelot (French) attendant. Literature: the knight who loved King Arthur's wife, Queen Guinevere.
Lance, Lancelott, Launcelet, Launcelot

Landen (English) a form of Landon.
Landenn

Lander (Basque) lion man. (English) landowner.
Landers, Landor

Lando (Portuguese, Spanish) a short form of Orlando, Rolando.

Landon (English) open, grassy meadow.
Landan, Landen, Landin, Landyn

Landry (French, English) ruler.
Landre, Landré, Landrue

Lane (English) narrow road.
Laine, Laney, Lanie, Layne

Lang (Scandinavian) tall man.
Lange

Langdon (English) long hill.
Landon, Langsdon, Langston

Langford (English) long ford.
Lanford, Lankford

Langley (English) long meadow.
Langlea, Langlee, Langleigh, Langly

Langston (English) long, narrow town.
Langsden, Langsdon

Langundo (Native American) peaceful.

Lani (Hawaiian) heaven.

Lanny (American) a familiar form of Lawrence, Laurence.
Lanney, Lannie, Lennie

Lanu (Moquelumnan) running around the pole.

Lanz (Italian) a form of Lance.
Lanzo, Lonzo

Lao (Spanish) a short form of Stanislaus.

Lap (Vietnamese) independent.

Lapidos (Hebrew) torches.
Lapidoth

Laquan (American) a combination of the prefix La + Quan.
Laquain, Laquann, Laquanta, Laquantae, Laquante, Laquawn,
Laquawne, Laquin, Laquinn, Laqun, Laquon, Laquone, Laqwan, Laqwon

Laquintin (American) a combination of the prefix La + Quintin.
Laquentin, Laquenton, Laquintas, Laquinten, Laquintiss, Laquinton

Laramie (French) tears of love. Geography: a town in Wyoming on the Overland Trail.
Larami, Laramy, Laremy

Larenzo (Italian, Spanish) a form of Lorenzo.
Larenz, Larenza, Larinzo, Laurenzo

Larkin (Irish) rough; fierce.
Larklin

Larnell (American) a combination of Larry + Darnell.

Laron (French) thief.
Laran, La'ron, La Ron, Larone, Laronn, Larron, La Ruan

Larrimore (French) armorer.
Larimore, Larmer, Larmor

Larry (Latin) a familiar form of Lawrence.
Larrie, Lary

Lars (Scandinavian) a form of Lawrence.
Laris, Larris, Larse, Larsen, Larson, Larsson, Larz, Lasse, Laurans, Laurits, Lavrans, Lorens

LaSalle (French) hall.
Lasal, Lasalle, Lascell, Lascelles

Lash (Gypsy) a form of Louis.
Lashi, Lasho

Lashawn (American) a combination of the prefix La + Shawn.
Lasaun, Lasean, Lashajaun, Lashan, Lashane, Lashaun, Lashon, Lashun

Lashon (American) a form of Lashawn.
Lashone, Lashonne

Lasse (Finnish) a form of Nicholas.

László (Hungarian) famous ruler.
Laci, Lacko, Laslo, Lazlo

Lateef (Arabic) gentle; pleasant.
Latif, Letif

Latham (Scandinavian) barn. (English) district.
Laith, Lathe, Lay

Lathan (American) a combination of the prefix La + Nathan.
Lathaniel, Lathen, Lathyn, Leathan

Lathrop (English) barn, farmstead.
Lathe, Lathrope, Lay

Latimer (English) interpreter.
Lat, Latimor, Lattie, Latty, Latymer

Latravis (American) a combination of the prefix La + Travis.
Latavious, Latavius, Latraveus, Latraviaus, Latravious, Latravius, Latrayvious, Latrayvous, Latrivis

Latrell (American) a combination of the prefix La + Kentrell.
Latreal, Latreil, Latrel, Latrelle, Letreal, Letrel, Letrell, Letrelle

Laudalino (Portuguese) praised.
Lino

Laughlin (Irish) servant of Saint Secundinus.
Lanty, Lauchlin, Leachlainn

Laurence (Latin) crowned with laurel. A form of Lawrence. See also Rance, Raulas, Raulo, Renzo.
Lanny, Lauran, Laurance, Laureano, Lauren, Laurencho, Laurencio, Laurens, Laurent, Laurentij, Laurentios, Laurentiu, Laurentius, Laurentz, Laurentzi, Laurie, Laurin, Lauris, Laurits, Lauritz, Laurnet, Lauro, Laurus, Lavrenti, Lurance

Laurencio (Spanish) a form of Laurence.

Laurens (Dutch) a form of Laurence.
Laurenz

Laurent (French) a form of Laurence.
Laurente

Laurie (English) a familiar form of Laurence.
Lauri, Laury, Lorry

Lauris (Swedish) a form of Laurence.

Lauro (Filipino) a form of Laurence.

LaValle (French) valley.
Lavail, Laval, Lavalei, Lavalle, Lavell

Lavan (Hebrew) white.
Lavane, Lavaughan, Laven, Lavon, Levan

Lavaughan (American) a form of Lavan.
Lavaughn, Levaughan, Levaughn

Lave (Italian) lava. (English) lord.

Lavell (French) a form of LaValle.
Lavel, Lavele, Lavelle, Levele, Levell, Levelle

Lavi (Hebrew) lion.

Lavon (American) a form of Lavan.
Lavion, Lavone, Lavonn, Lavonne, Lavont, Lavonte

Lavrenti (Russian) a form of Lawrence.
Larenti, Lavrentij, Lavrusha, Lavrik, Lavro

Lawerence (Latin) a form of Lawrence.
Lawerance

Lawford (English) ford on the hill.
Ford, Law

Lawler (Irish) soft-spoken.
Lawlor, Lollar, Loller

Lawrence (Latin) crowned with laurel. See also Brencis, Chencho.
Labrentsis, Laiurenty, Lanny, Lanty, Larance, Laren, Larian, Larien, Laris, Larka, Larrance, Larrence, Larry, Lars, Larya, Laurence, Lavrenti, Law, Lawerence, Lawrance, Lawren, Lawrey, Lawrie, Lawron, Lawry, Lencho, Lon, Lóránt, Loreca, Loren, Loretto, Lorenzo, Lorne, Lourenco, Lowrance

Lawson (English) son of Lawrence.
Lawsen, Layson

Lawton (English) town on the hill.
Laughton, Law

Layne (English) a form of Lane.
Layn, Laynee

Layton (English) a form of Leighton.
Laydon, Layten, Layth, Laythan,
Laython

Lazaro (Italian) a form of Lazarus.
Lazarillo, Lazarito, Lazzaro

Lazarus (Greek) a form of Eleazar.
Bible: Lazarus was raised from the
dead by Jesus.
Lazar, Lázár, Lazare, Lazarius, Lazaro,
Lazaros, Lazorus

Leander (Greek) lion-man; brave as a
lion.
Ander, Leandro

Leandro (Spanish) a form of Leander.
Leandra, Léandre, Leandrew, Leandros

Leben (Yiddish) life.
Laben, Lebon

Lebna (Ethiopian) spirit; heart.

Ledarius (American) a combination of
the prefix Le + Darius.
Ledarrious, Ledarrius, Lederious, Lederris

Lee (English) a short form of Farley,
Leonard, and names containing "lee."
Leigh

Leggett (French) one who is sent; delegate.
Legate, Legette, Leggitt, Liggett

Lei (Chinese) thunder. (Hawaiian) a
form of Ray.

Leib (Yiddish) roaring lion.
Leibel

Leif (Scandinavian) beloved.
Laif, Leife, Lief

Leigh (English) a form of Lee.

Leighton (English) meadow farm.
Lay, Layton, Leigh, Leyton

Leith (Scottish) broad river.

Lek (Tai) small.

Lekeke (Hawaiian) powerful ruler.

Leks (Estonian) a familiar form of
Alexander.
Leksik, Lekso

Lel (Gypsy) taker.

Leland (English) meadowland; pro-
tected land.
Lealand, Lee, Leeland, Leigh, Leighland,
Lelan, Lelann, Lelend, Lelund, Leyland

Lemar (French) a form of Lamar.
Lemario, Lemarr

Lemuel (Hebrew) devoted to God.
Lem, Lemmie, Lemmy

Len (Hopi) flute. (German) a short
form of Leonard.

Lenard (German) a form of Leonard.
Lennard

Lencho (Spanish) a form of Lawrence.
Lenci, Lenzy

Lennart (Swedish) a form of Leonard.
Lennerd

Lenno (Native American) man.

Lennon (Irish) small cloak; cape.
Lenon

Lennor (Gypsy) spring; summer.

Lennox (Scottish) with many elms.
Lennix, Lenox

Lenny (German) a familiar form of
Leonard.
Leni, Lennie, Leny

Leo (Latin) lion. (German) a short
form of Leon, Leopold.
Lavi, Leão, Lee, Leib, Leibel, Leos,
Leosko, Léo, Léocadie, Leos, Leosoko, Lev,
Lio, Lion, Liutas, Lyon, Nardek

Leobardo (Italian) a form of Leonard.

Leon (Greek, German) a short form of
Leonard, Napoleon.
Leo, Léon, Leonas, Léonce, Leoncio,
Leondris, Leone, Leonek, Leonetti, Leoni,
Leonid, Leonidas, Leonirez, Leonizio,
Leonon, Leons, Leontes, Leontios,
Leontrae, Liutas

Leonard (German) brave as a lion.
Leanard, Lee, Len, Lena, Lenard,
Lennart, Lenny, Leno, Leobardo, Leon,
Léonard, Leonardis, Leonardo, Leonart,
Leonerd, Leonhard, Leonidas, Leonnard,
Leontes, Lernard, Lienard, Linek, Lnard,
Lon, Londard, Lonnard, Lonya, Lynnard

Leonardo (Italian) a form of Leonard.
Leonaldo, Lionardo

Leonel (English) little lion. See also
Lionel.
Leonell

Leonhard (German) a form of
Leonard.
Leonhards

Leonid (Russian) a form of Leonard.
Leonide, Lyonechka, Lyonya

Leonidas (Greek) a form of Leonard.
Leonida, Leonides

Leopold (German) brave people.
Leo, Leopoldo, Leorad, Lipót, Lopolda,
Luepold, Luitpold, Poldi

Leopoldo (Italian) a form of Leopold.

Leor (Hebrew) my light.
Leory, Lior

Lequinton (American) a combination
of the prefix Le + Quinton.
Lequentin, Lequenton, Lequinn

Leron (French) round, circle.
(American) a combination of the
prefix Le + Ron.
Leeron, Le Ron, Lerone, Liron, Lyron

Leroy (French) king. See also Delroy,
Elroy.
Lee, Leeroy, LeeRoy, Leigh, Lerai, Leroi,
LeRoi, LeRoy, Roy

Les (Scottish, English) a short form of
Leslie, Lester.
Lessie

Lesharo (Pawnee) chief.

Leshawn (American) a combination of
the prefix Le + Shawn.
Lashan, Lesean, Leshaun, Leshon,
Leshun

Leslie (Scottish) gray fortress.
Lee, Leigh, Les, Leslea, Leslee, Lesley,
Lesli, Lesly, Lezlie, Lezly

Lester (Latin) chosen camp. (English)
from Leicester, England.
Leicester, Les

Lev (Hebrew) heart. (Russian) a form
of Leo. A short form of Leverett,
Levi.
Leb, Leva, Levka, Levko, Levushka

Leverett (French) young hare.
Lev, Leveret, Leverit, Leveritt

Levi (Hebrew) joined in harmony.
Bible: the third son of Jacob; Levites
are the priestly tribe of the Israelites.
Leavi, Leevi, Leevie, Lev, Levey, Levie,
Levin, Levitis, Levy, Lewi, Leyvi

Levin (Hebrew) a form of Levi.
Levine, Levion

Levon (American) a form of Lavon.
Leevon, Levone, Levonn, Levonne,
Levonte, Lyvonne

Lew (English) a short form of Lewis.

Lewin (English) beloved friend.

Lewis (Welsh) a form of Llewellyn.
(English) a form of Louis.
Lew, Lewes, Lewie, Lewy

Lex (English) a short form of
Alexander.
Lexi, Lexie, Lexin

Lexus (Greek) a short form of
Alexander.
Lexis, Lexius, Lexxus

Leyati (Moquelumnan) shape of an
abalone shell.

Lí (Chinese) strong.

Liam (Irish) a form of William.
Liem, Lliam, Lyam

Liang (Chinese) good, excellent.

Liban (Hawaiian) a form of Laban.
Libaan, Lieban

Liberio (Portuguese) liberation.
Liberaratore, Liborio

Lidio (Greek, Portuguese) ancient.

Ligongo (Yao) who is this?

Likeke (Hawaiian) a form of Richard.

Liko (Chinese) protected by Buddha.
(Hawaiian) bud.
Like

Lin (Burmese) bright. (English) a short
form of Lyndon.
Linh, Linn, Linny, Lyn, Lynn

Linc (English) a short form of Lincoln.
Link

Lincoln (English) settlement by the
pool. History: Abraham Lincoln was
the sixteenth U.S. president.
Linc, Lincon, Lyncoln

Lindberg (German) mountain where
linden grow.
Lindbergh, Lindburg, Lindy

Lindell (English) valley of the linden.
Lendall, Lendel, Lendell, Lindall, Lindel,
Lyndale, Lyndall, Lyndel, Lyndell

Linden (English) a form of Lyndon.

Lindley (English) linden field.
Lindlea, Lindlee, Lindleigh, Lindly

Lindon (English) a form of Lyndon.
Lin, Lindan

Lindsay (English) a form of Lindsey.
Linsay

Lindsey (English) linden-tree island.
Lind, Lindsay, Lindsee, Lindsie, Lindsy,
Lindzy, Linsey, Linzie, Linzy, Lyndsay,
Lyndsey, Lyndsie, Lynzie

Linford (English) linden ford.
Lynford

Linfred (German) peaceful, calm.

Linley (English) flax meadow.
Linlea, Linlee, Linleigh, Linly

Linton (English) flax town.
Lintonn, Lynton, Lyntonn

Linu (Hindi) lily.

Linus (Greek) flaxen haired.
Linas, Linux

Linwood (English) flax wood.

Lio (Hawaiian) a form of Leo.

Lionel (French) lion cub. See also
Leonel.
*Lional, Lionell, Lionello, Lynel, Lynell,
Lyonel*

Liron (Hebrew) my song.
Lyron

Lise (Moquelumnan) salmon's head
coming out of the water.

Lisimba (Yao) lion.
Simba

Lister (English) dyer.

Litton (English) town on the hill.
Liton

Liu (African) voice.

Liuz (Polish) light.
Lius

Livingston (English) Leif's town.
Livingstone

Liwanu (Moquelumnan) growling
bear.

Llewellyn (Welsh) lionlike.
*Lewis, Llewelin, Llewellen, Llewelleyn,
Llewellin, Llewlyn, Llywellyn,
Llywellynn, Llywelyn*

Lloyd (Welsh) gray haired; holy. See
also Floyd.
Loy, Loyd, Loyde, Loydie

Lobo (Spanish) wolf.

Lochlain (Irish, Scottish) land of lakes.
*Laughlin, Lochlan, Lochlann, Lochlin,
Locklynn*

Locke (English) forest.
Lock, Lockwood

Loe (Hawaiian) a form of Roy.

Logan (Irish) meadow.
*Llogan, Loagan, Loagen, Loagon,
Logann, Logen, Loggan, Loghan, Logon,
Logn, Logun, Logunn, Logyn*

Lok (Chinese) happy.

Lokela (Hawaiian) a form of Roger.

Lokni (Moquelumnan) raining
through the roof.

Lomán (Irish) bare. (Slavic) sensitive.

Lombard (Latin) long bearded.
Bard, Barr

Lon (Irish) fierce. (Spanish) a short
form of Alonso, Alonzo, Leonard,
Lonnie.
Lonn

Lonan (Zuni) cloud.

Lonato (Native American) flint stone.

London (English) fortress of the
moon. Geography: the capital of the
United Kingdom.
Londen, Londyn, Lunden, Lundon

Long (Chinese) dragon. (Vietnamese)
hair.

Lonnie (German, Spanish) a familiar
form of Alonso, Alonzo.
*Lon, Loni, Lonie, Lonnell, Lonney,
Lonni, Lonniel, Lonny*

Lono (Hawaiian) Mythology: the god
of learning and intellect.

Lonzo (German, Spanish) a short form
of Alonso, Alonzo.
Lonso

Lootah (Lakota) red.

Lopaka (Hawaiian) a form of Robert.

Loránd (Hungarian) a form of
Roland.

Lóránt (Hungarian) a form of
Lawrence.
Lorant

Lorcan (Irish) little; fierce.

Lord (English) noble title.

Loren (Latin) a short form of
Lawrence.
Lorin, Lorren, Lorrin, Loryn

Lorenzo (Italian, Spanish) a form of
Lawrence.
*Larenzo, Lerenzo, Lewrenzo, Lorenc,
Lorence, Lorenco, Lorencz, Lorens,
Lorenso, Lorentz, Lorenz, Lorenza,
Loretto, Lorinc, Lörinc, Lorinzo, Loritz,
Lorrenzo, Lorrie, Lorry, Lourenza,
Lourenzo, Lowrenzo, Renzo, Zo*

Loretto (Italian) a form of Lawrence.
Loreto

Lorimer (Latin) harness maker.
Lorrie, Lorrimer, Lorry

Loring (German) son of the famous warrior.
Lorrie, Lorring, Lorry

Loris (Dutch) clown.

Loritz (Latin, Danish) laurel.
Lauritz

Lorne (Latin) a short form of Lawrence.
Lorn, Lornie

Lorry (English) a form of Laurie.
Lori, Lorri, Lory

Lot (Hebrew) hidden, covered. Bible: Lot fled from Sodom, but his wife glanced back upon its destruction and was transformed into a pillar of salt.
Lott

Lothar (German) a form of Luther.
Lotaire, Lotarrio, Lothair, Lothaire, Lothario, Lotharrio

Lou (German) a short form of Louis.

Loudon (German) low valley.
Loudan, Louden, Loudin, Lowden

Louie (German) a familiar form of Louis.

Louis (German) famous warrior. See also Aloisio, Aloysius, Clovis, Luigi.
Lash, Lashi, Lasho, Lewis, Lou, Loudovicus, Louie, Louies, Louise, Lucho, Lude, Ludek, Ludirk, Ludis, Ludko,

Ludwig, Lughaidh, Lui, Luigi, Luis, Luiz, Luki, Lutek

Lourdes (French) from Lourdes, France. Religion: a place where the Virgin Mary was said to have appeared.

Louvain (English) Lou's vanity. Geography: a city in Belgium.
Louvin

Lovell (English) a form of Lowell.
Louvell, Lovel, Lovelle, Lovey

Lowell (French) young wolf. (English) beloved.
Lovell, Lowe, Lowel

Loyal (English) faithful, loyal.
Loy, Loyall, Loye, Lyall, Lyell

Lubomir (Polish) lover of peace.

Luboslaw (Polish) lover of glory.
Lubs, Lubz

Luc (French) a form of Luke.
Luce

Luca (Italian) a form of Lucius.
Lucca, Luka

Lucas (German, Irish, Danish, Dutch) a form of Lucius.
Lucais, Lucassie, Lucaus, Luccas, Luccus, Luckas, Lucus

Lucian (Latin) a form of Lucius.
Liuz, Lucan, Lucanus, Luciano, Lucianus, Lucias, Lucjan, Lukianos, Lukyan

Luciano (Italian) a form of Lucian.
Luca, Lucca, Lucino, Lucio

Lucien (French) a form of Lucius.

Lucio (Italian) a form of Lucius.

Lucius (Latin) light; bringer of light.
Loukas, Luc, Luca, Lucais, Lucanus, Lucas, Luce, Lucian, Lucien, Lucio, Lucious, Lucis, Luke, Lusio

Lucky (American) fortunate.
Luckee, Luckie, Luckson, Lucson

Ludlow (English) prince's hill.

Ludovic (German) a form of Ludwig.
Ludovick, Ludovico

Ludwig (German) a form of Louis. Music: Ludwig van Beethoven was a famous nineteenth-century German composer.
Ludovic, Ludvig, Ludvik, Ludwik, Lutz

Lui (Hawaiian) a form of Louis.

Luigi (Italian) a form of Louis.
Lui, Luiggi, Luigino, Luigy

Luis, Luiz (Spanish) forms of Louis.
Luise

Lukas, Lukus (Greek, Czech, Swedish) forms of Luke.
Loukas, Lukais, Lukash, Lukasha, Lukass, Lukasz, Lukaus, Lukkas

Luke (Latin) a form of Lucius. Bible: companion of Saint Paul and author of the third Gospel of the New Testament.
Luc, Luchok, Luck, Lucky, Luk, Luka, Lúkács, Lukas, Luken, Lukes, Lukus, Lukyan, Lusio

Lukela (Hawaiian) a form of Russel.

Luken (Basque) bringer of light.
Lucan, Lucane, Lucano, Luk

Luki (Basque) famous warrior.

Lukman (Arabic) prophet.
Luqman

Lulani (Hawaiian) highest point in heaven.

Lumo (Ewe) born facedown.

Lundy (Scottish) grove by the island.

Lunn (Irish) warlike.
Lon, Lonn

Lunt (Swedish) grove.

Lusila (Hindi) leader.

Lusio (Zuni) a form of Lucius.

Lutalo (Luganda) warrior.

Lutfi (Arabic) kind, friendly.

Luther (German) famous warrior. History: Martin Luther was one of the central figures of the Reformation.
Lothar, Lutero, Luthor

Lutherum (Gypsy) slumber.

Luyu (Moquelumnan) head shaker.

Lyall, Lyell (Scottish) loyal.

Lyle (French) island.
Lisle, Ly, Lysle

Lyman (English) meadow.
Leaman, Leeman, Lymon

Lynch (Irish) mariner.
Linch

Lyndal (English) valley of lime trees.
Lyndale, Lyndall, Lyndel, Lyndell

Lyndon (English) linden hill. History: Lyndon B. Johnson was the thirty-sixth U.S. president.
Lin, Linden, Lindon, Lyden, Lydon, Lyn, Lyndan, Lynden, Lynn

Lynn (English) waterfall; brook.
Lyn, Lynell, Lynette, Lynnard, Lynoll

Lyron (Hebrew) a form of Leron, Liron.

Lysander (Greek) liberator.
Lyzander, Sander

M

Maalik (Punjabi) a form of Malik.
Maalek, Maaliek

Mac (Scottish) son.
Macs

Macadam (Scottish) son of Adam.
MacAdam, McAdam

Macallister (Irish) son of Alistair.
Macalaster, Macalister, MacAlister, McAlister, McAllister

Macario (Spanish) a form of Makarios.

Macarthur (Irish) son of Arthur.
MacArthur, McArthur

Macaulay (Scottish) son of righteousness.
Macaulee, Macauley, Macaully, Macauly, Maccauley, Mackauly, Macualay, McCauley

Macbride (Scottish) son of a follower of Saint Brigid.
Macbryde, Mcbride, McBride

Maccoy (Irish) son of Hugh, Coy.
MacCoy, Mccoy, McCoy

Maccrea (Irish) son of grace.
MacCrae, MacCray, MacCrea, Macrae, Macray, Makray, Mccrea, McCrea

Macdonald (Scottish) son of Donald.
MacDonald, Mcdonald, McDonald, Mcdonna, Mcdonnell, McDonnell

Macdougal (Scottish) son of Dougal.
MacDougal, Mcdougal, McDougal, McDougall, Dougal

Mace (French) club. (English) a short form of Macy, Mason.
Macean, Maceo, Macer, Macey, Macie, Macy

Macgregor (Scottish) son of Gregor.
Macgreggor

Machas (Polish) a form of Michael.

Mack (Scottish) a short form of names beginning with "Mac" and "Mc."
Macke, Mackey, Mackie, Macklin, Macks, Macky

Mackenzie (Irish) son of Kenzie.
Mackensy, Mackenxo, Mackenze, Mackenzey, Mackenzi, MacKenzie, Mackenzly, Mackenzy, Mackienzie, Mackinsey, Mackinzie, Makenzie, McKenzie, Mickenzie

Mackinnley (Irish) son of the learned ruler.
Mackinley, MacKinnley, Mackinnly, Mckinley

Macklain (Irish) a form of Maclean.
Macklaine, Macklane

Maclean (Irish) son of Leander.
Machlin, Macklain, MacLain, MacLean,
Maclin, Maclyn, Makleen, McLaine,
McLean

Macmahon (Irish) son of Mahon.
MacMahon, McMahon

Macmurray (Irish) son of Murray.
McMurray

Macnair (Scottish) son of the heir.
Macknair

Maco (Hungarian) a form of
Emmanuel.

Macon (German, English) maker.

Macy (French) Matthew's estate.
Mace, Macey

Maddock (Welsh) generous.
Madoc, Madock, Madog

Maddox (Welsh, English) benefactor's
son.
Maddux, Madox

Madhar (Hindi) full of intoxication;
relating to spring.

Madison (English) son of Maude;
good son.
Maddie, Maddison, Maddy, Madisen,
Madisson, Madisyn, Madsen, Son,
Sonny

Madongo (Luganda) uncircumcised.

Madu (Ibo) people.

Magar (Armenian) groom's attendant.
Magarious

Magee (Irish) son of Hugh.
MacGee, MacGhee, McGee

Magen (Hebrew) protector.

Magnar (Norwegian) strong; warrior.
Magne

Magnus (Latin) great.
Maghnus, Magnes, Manius, Mayer

Magomu (Luganda) younger of twins.

Maguire (Irish) son of the beige one.
MacGuire, McGuire, McGwire

Mahammed (Arabic) a form of
Muhammad.
Mahamad, Mahamed

Mahdi (Arabic) guided to the right
path.
Mahde, Mahdee, Mahdy

Mahesa (Hindi) great lord. Religion:
another name for the Hindu god
Shiva.

Mahi'ai (Hawaiian) a form of George.

Mahir (Arabic, Hebrew) excellent;
industrious.
Maher

Mahkah (Lakota) earth.

Mahmoud (Arabic) a form of
Muhammad.
Mahamoud, Mahmmoud, Mahmuod

Mahmúd (Arabic) a form of
Muhammad.
Mahmed, Mahmood, Mahmut

Mahomet (Arabic) a form of
Muhammad.
Mehemet, Mehmet

Mahon (Irish) bear.

Mahpee (Lakota) sky.

Maimun (Arabic) lucky.
Maimon

Mairtin (Irish) a form of Martin.
Martain, Martainn

Maitias (Irish) a form of Mathias.
Maithias

Maitiú (Irish) a form of Matthew.

Maitland (English) meadowland.

Majid (Arabic) great, glorious.
Majd, Majde, Majdi, Majdy, Majed,
Majeed

Major (Latin) greater; military rank.
Majar, Maje, Majer, Mayer, Mayor

Makaio (Hawaiian) a form of
Matthew.

Makalani (Mwera) writer.

Makani (Hawaiian) wind.

Makarios (Greek) happy; blessed.
Macario, Macarios, Maccario, Maccarios

Makenzie (Irish) a form of Mackenzie.
Makensie, Makenzy

Makin (Arabic) strong.
Makeen

Makis (Greek) a form of Michael.

Makoto (Japanese) sincere.

Maks (Hungarian) a form of Max.
Makszi

Maksim (Russian) a form of Maximilian.
Maksimka, Maksym, Maxim

Maksym (Polish) a form of Maximilian.
Makimus, Maksim, Maksymilian

Makyah (Hopi) eagle hunter.

Mal (Irish) a short form of names beginning with "Mal."

Malachi (Hebrew) angel of God. Bible: the last canonical Hebrew prophet.
Maeleachlainn, Mal, Malachai, Malachia, Malachie, Malachy, Malakai, Malake, Malaki, Malchija, Malechy, Málik

Malachy (Irish) a form of Malachi.

Malajitm (Sanskrit) garland of victory.

Malcolm (Scottish) follower of Saint Columba who Christianized North Scotland. (Arabic) dove.
Mal, Malcalm, Malcohm, Malcolum, Malcom, Malkolm

Malcom (Scottish) a form of Malcolm.
Malcome, Malcum, Malkom, Malkum

Malden (English) meeting place in a pasture.
Mal, Maldon

Malek (Arabic) a form of Málik.
Maleak, Maleek, Maleik, Maleka, Maleke, Mallek

Maleko (Hawaiian) a form of Mark.

Málik (Punjabi) lord, master. (Arabic) a form of Malachi.

Maalik, Mailik, Malak, Malic, Malick, Malicke, Maliek, Maliik, Malik, Malike, Malikh, Maliq, Malique, Mallik, Malyk, Malyq

Malin (English) strong, little warrior.
Mal, Mallin, Mallon

Mallory (German) army counselor. (French) wild duck.
Lory, Mal, Mallery, Mallori, Mallorie, Malory

Maloney (Irish) church going.
Malone, Malony

Malvern (Welsh) bare hill.
Malverne

Malvin (Irish, English) a form of Melvin.
Mal, Malvinn, Malvyn, Malvynn

Mamo (Hawaiian) yellow flower; yellow bird.

Manchu (Chinese) pure.

Manco (Peruvian) supreme leader. History: a sixteenth-century Incan king.

Mandala (Yao) flowers.
Manda, Mandela

Mandeep (Punjabi) mind full of light.
Mandieep

Mandel (German) almond.
Mandell

Mandek (Polish) a form of Armand, Herman.
Mandie

Mander (Gypsy) from me.

Manford (English) small ford.

Manfred (English) man of peace. See also Fred.
Manfret, Manfrid, Manfried, Maniferd, Mannfred, Mannfryd

Manger (French) stable.

Mango (Spanish) a familiar form of Emmanuel, Manuel.

Manheim (German) servant's home.

Manipi (Native American) living marvel.

Manius (Scottish) a form of Magnus.
Manus, Manyus

Manley (English) hero's meadow.
Manlea, Manleigh, Manly

Mann (German) man.
Manin

Manning (English) son of the hero.

Mannix (Irish) monk.
Mainchin

Manny (German, Spanish) a familiar form of Manuel.
Mani, Manni, Mannie, Many

Mano (Hawaiian) shark. (Spanish) a short form of Manuel.
Manno, Manolo

Manoj (Sanskrit) cupid.

Mansa (Swahili) king. History: a fourteenth-century king of Mali.

Mansel (English) manse; house occupied by a clergyman.
Mansell

Mansfield (English) field by the river; hero's field.

Man-Shik (Korean) deeply rooted.

Mansür (Arabic) divinely aided.
Mansoor, Mansour

Manton (English) man's town; hero's town.
Mannton, Manten

Manu (Hindi) lawmaker. History: the reputed writer of the Hindi compendium of sacred laws and customs. (Hawaiian) bird. (Ghanaian) second-born son.

Manuel (Hebrew) a short form of Emmanuel.
Maco, Mango, Mannuel, Manny, Mano, Manolón, Manual, Manuale, Manue, Manuelli, Manuelo, Manuil, Manyuil, Minel

Manville (French) worker's village. (English) hero's village.
Mandeville, Manvel, Manvil

Man-Young (Korean) ten thousand years of prosperity.

Manzo (Japanese) third son.

Maona (Winnebago) creator, earth maker.

Mapira (Yao) millet.

Marc (French) a form of Mark.

Marcel (French) a form of Marcellus.
Marcell, Marsale, Marsel

Marcelino (Italian) a form of Marcellus.
Marceleno, Marcelin, Marcellin, Marcellino

Marcelo, Marcello (Italian) forms of Marcellus.
Marchello, Marsello, Marselo

Marcellus (Latin) a familiar form of Marcus.
Marceau, Marcel, Marceles, Marcelias, Marcelino, Marcelis, Marcelius, Marcellas, Marcelleous, Marcellis, Marcellous, Marcelluas, Marcelo, Marcelus, Marcely, Marciano, Marcilka, Marcsseau, Marquel, Marsalis

March (English) dweller by a boundary.

Marciano (Italian) a form of Martin.
Marci, Marcio

Marcilka (Hungarian) a form of Marcellus.
Marci, Marcilki

Marcin (Polish) a form of Martin.

Marco (Italian) a form of Marcus. History: Marco Polo was a thirteenth-century Venetian traveler who explored Asia.
Marcko, Marko

Marcos (Spanish) a form of Marcus.
Marckos, Marcous, Markos, Markose

Marcus (Latin) martial, warlike.
Marc, Marcas, Marcellus, Marcio, Marckus, Marco, Marcos, Marcous, Marcuss, Marcuus, Marcux, Marek, Mark, Markov, Markus

Marek (Slavic) a form of Marcus.

Maren (Basque) sea.

Mareo (Japanese) uncommon.

Marian (Polish) a form of Mark.

Mariano (Italian) a form of Mark.

Marid (Arabic) rebellious.

Marin (French) sailor.
Marine, Mariner, Marino, Marius, Marriner

Marino (Italian) a form of Marin.
Marinos, Marinus, Mario, Mariono

Mario (Italian) a form of Marino.
Marios, Marrio

Marion (French) bitter; sea of bitterness.
Mareon, Mariano

Marius (Latin) a form of Marin.
Marious

Mark (Latin) a form of Marcus. Bible: author of the second Gospel in the New Testament. See also Maleko.
Marc, Marek, Marian, Mariano, Marke, Markee, Markel, Markell, Markey, Marko, Markos, Márkus, Markusha, Marque, Martial, Marx

Markanthony (Italian) a combination of Mark + Anthony.

Marke (Polish) a form of Mark.

Markel, Markell (Latin) forms of Mark.
Markelle, Markelo

Markes (Portuguese) a form of Marques.
Markess, Markest

Markese (French) a form of Marquis.
Markease, Markeece, Markees, Markeese, Markei, Markeice, Markeis, Markeise, Markes, Markez, Markeze, Markice

Markham (English) homestead on the boundary.

Markis (French) a form of Marquis.
Markies, Markiese, Markise, Markiss, Markist

Marko (Latin) a form of Marco, Mark.
Markco

Markus (Latin) a form of Marcus.
Markas, Markcus, Markcuss, Markys, Marqus

Marland (English) lake land.

Marley (English) lake meadow.
Marlea, Marleigh, Marly, Marrley

Marlin (English) deep-sea fish.
Marlen, Marlion, Marlyn

Marlon (French) a form of Merlin.

Marlow (English) hill by the lake.
Mar, Marlo, Marlowe

Marmion (French) small.
Marmyon

Marnin (Hebrew) singer; bringer of joy.

Maro (Japanese) myself.

Marquan (American) a combination of Mark + Quan.
Marquane, Marquante

Marquel (American) a form of Marcellus.
Marqueal, Marquelis, Marquell, Marquelle, Marquellis, Marquiel, Marquil, Marquiles, Marquill, Marquille, Marquillus, Marqwel, Marqwell

Marques (Portuguese) nobleman.
Markes, Markqes, Markques, Markquese, Marqese, Marqesse, Marqez, Marqeze, Marquees, Marquese, Marquess, Marquesse, Marquest, Markqueus, Marquez, Marqus

Marquez (Portuguese) a form of Marques.
Marqueze, Marquiez

Marquice (American) a form of Marquis.
Marquaice, Marquece

Marquis, Marquise (French) nobleman.
Marcquis, Marcuis, Markis, Markquis, Markquise, Markuis, Marqise, Marquee, Marqui, Marquice, Marquie, Marquies, Marquiss, Marquist, Marquiz, Marquize

Marquon (American) a combination of Mark + Quon.
Marquin, Marquinn, Marqwan, Marqwon, Marqwyn

Marr (Spanish) divine. (Arabic) forbidden.

Mars (Latin) bold warrior. Mythology: the Roman god of war.

Marsalis (Italian) a form of Marcellus.
Marsalius, Marsallis, Marsellis, Marsellius, Marsellus

Marsden (English) marsh valley.
Marsdon

Marsh (English) swamp land. (French) a short form of Marshall.

Marshal (French) a form of Marshall.
Marschal, Marshel

Marshall (French) caretaker of the horses; military title.
Marsh, Marshal, Marshell

Marshawn (American) a combination of Mark + Shawn.
Marshaine, Marshaun, Marshauwn, Marshean, Marshon, Marshun

Marston (English) town by the marsh.

Martell (English) hammerer.
Martel, Martele, Martellis

Marten (Dutch) a form of Martin.
Maarten, Martein

Martez (Spanish) a form of Martin.
Martaz, Martaze, Martes, Martese, Marteze, Martice, Martiece, Marties, Martiese, Martiez, Martis, Martise, Martize

Marti (Spanish) a form of Martin.
Martee, Martie

Martial (French) a form of Mark.

Martin (Latin, French) a form of Martinus. History: Martin Luther King, Jr. led the Civil Rights movement and won the Nobel Peace Prize. See also Tynek.
Maartin, Mairtin, Marciano, Marcin, Marinos, Marius, Mart, Martan, Marten, Martez, Marti, Martijn, Martinas, Martine, Martinez, Martinho, Martiniano, Martinien, Martinka, Martino, Martins, Marto, Marton, Márton, Marts, Marty, Martyn, Mattin, Mertin, Morten, Moss

Martinez (Spanish) a form of Martin.
Martines

Martinho (Portuguese) a form of
Martin.

Martino (Italian) a form of Martin.
Martinos

Martins (Latvian) a form of Martin.

Martinus (Latin) martial, warlike.
Martin

Marty (Latin) a familiar form of
Martin.
Martey, Marti, Martie

Marut (Hindi) Religion: the Hindu
god of the wind.

Marv (English) a short form of
Marvin.
Marve, Marvi, Marvis

Marvin (English) lover of the sea.
*Marv, Marvein, Marven, Marvion,
Marvn, Marvon, Marvyn, Marwin,
Marwynn, Mervin*

Marwan (Arabic) history personage.

Marwood (English) forest pond.

Masaccio (Italian) twin.
Masaki

Masahiro (Japanese) broad-minded.

Masamba (Yao) leaves.

Masao (Japanese) righteous.

Masato (Japanese) just.

Mashama (Shona) surprising.

Maska (Native American) powerful.
(Russian) mask.

Maslin (French) little Thomas.
Maslen, Masling

Mason (French) stone worker.
*Mace, Maison, Masson, Masun, Masyn,
Sonny*

Masou (Native American) fire god.

Massey (English) twin.
Massi

Massimo (Italian) greatest.
Massimiliano

Masud (Arabic, Swahili) fortunate.
Masood, Masoud, Mhasood

Matai (Basque, Bulgarian) a form of
Matthew.
Máté, Matei

Matalino (Filipino) bright.

Mateo (Spanish) a form of Matthew.
Matías, Matteo

Mateusz (Polish) a form of Matthew.
Matejs, Mateus

Mathe (German) a short form of
Matthew.

Mather (English) powerful army.

Matheu (German) a form of Matthew.
Matheau, Matheus, Mathu

Mathew (Hebrew) a form of Matthew.

Mathias, Matthias (German, Swedish)
forms of Matthew.
*Maitias, Mathi, Mathia, Mathis, Matías,
Matthia, Matthieus, Mattia, Mattias,
Matus*

Mathieu, Matthieu (French) forms of
Matthew.
*Mathie, Mathieux, Mathiew, Matthiew,
Mattieu, Mattieux*

Matías (Spanish) a form of Mathias.
Mattias

Mato (Native American) brave.

Matope (Rhodesian) our last child.

Matoskah (Lakota) white bear.

Mats (Swedish) a familiar form of
Matthew.
Matts, Matz

Matson (Hebrew) son of Matt.
Matison, Matsen, Mattison, Mattson

Matt (Hebrew) a short form of
Matthew.
Mat

Matteen (Afghan) disciplined; polite.

Matteus (Scandinavian) a form of
Matthew.

Matthew (Hebrew) gift of God. Bible:
author of the first Gospel of the
New Testament.
*Mads, Makaio, Maitiú, Mata, Matai,
Matek, Mateo, Mateusz, Matfei, Mathe,
Matheson, Matheu, Mathew, Mathian,
Mathias, Mathieson, Mathieu, Matro,
Mats, Matt, Matteus, Matthaeus,
Matthaios, Matthaus, Matthäus,
Mattheus, Matthews, Mattmias, Matty,
Matvey, Matyas, Mayhew*

Matty (Hebrew) a familiar form of
Matthew.
Mattie

Matus (Czech) a form of Mathias.

Matvey (Russian) a form of Matthew.
*Matviy, Matviyko, Matyash, Motka,
Motya*

Matyas (Polish) a form of Matthew.
Mátyás

Mauli (Hawaiian) a form of Maurice.

Maurice (Latin) dark skinned; moor; marshland. See also Seymour.
Mauli, Maur, Maurance, Maureo, Mauricio, Maurids, Mauriece, Maurikas, Maurin, Maurino, Maurise, Mauritz, Maurius, Maurizio, Mauro, Maurrel, Maurtel, Maury, Maurycy, Meurig, Moore, Morice, Moritz, Morrel, Morrice, Morrie, Morrill, Morris

Mauricio (Spanish) a form of Maurice.
Mauriccio, Mauriceo, Maurico, Maurisio

Mauritz (German) a form of Maurice.

Maurizio (Italian) a form of Maurice.

Mauro (Latin) a short form of Maurice.
Maur, Maurio

Maury (Latin) a familiar form of Maurice.
Maurey, Maurie, Morrie

Maverick (American) independent.
Maverik, Maveryke, Mavric, Mavrick

Mawuli (Ewe) there is a God.

Max (Latin) a short form of Maximilian, Maxwell.
Mac, Mack, Maks, Maxe, Maxx, Maxy, Miksa

Maxfield (English) Mack's field.

Maxi (Czech, Hungarian, Spanish) a familiar form of Maximilian, Máximo.
Makszi, Maxey, Maxie, Maxis, Maxy

Maxim (Russian) a form of Maxime.

Maxime (French) most excellent.
Maxim, Maxyme

Maximilian (Latin) greatest.
Mac, Mack, Maixim, Maksim, Maksym, Max, Maxamillion, Maxemilian, Maxemilion, Maxi, Maximalian, Maximili, Maximilia, Maximiliano, Maximilianus, Maximilien, Maximillian, Máximo, Maximos, Maxmilian, Maxmillion, Maxon, Maxymilian, Maxymillian, Mayhew, Miksa

Maximiliano (Italian) a form of Maximilian.
Massimiliano, Maximiano, Maximino

Maximillian (Latin) a form of Maximilian.
Maximillan, Maximillano, Maximillien, Maximillion, Maxmillian, Maxximillian, Maxximillion

Máximo (Spanish) a form of Maximilian.
Massimo, Maxi, Maximiano, Maximiliano, Maximino, Máximo

Maximos (Greek) a form of Maximilian.

Maxwell (English) great spring.
Max, Maxwel, Maxwill, Maxxwell, Maxy

Maxy (English) a familiar form of Max, Maxwell.
Maxi

Mayer (Hebrew) a form of Meir. (Latin) a form of Magnus, Major.
Mahyar, Mayeer, Mayor, Mayur

Mayes (English) field.
Mayo, Mays

Mayhew (English) a form of Matthew.

Maynard (English) powerful; brave. See also Meinhard.
May, Mayne, Maynhard, Maynor, Ménard

Mayo (Irish) yew-tree plain. (English) a form of Mayes. Geography: a county in Ireland.

Mayon (Indian) person of black complexion. Religion: another name for the Indian god Mal.

Mayonga (Luganda) lake sailor.

Mazi (Ibo) sir.
Mazzi

Mazin (Arabic) proper.
Mazen, Mazinn, Mazzin

Mbita (Swahili) born on a cold night.

Mbwana (Swahili) master.

McGeorge (Scottish) son of George.
MacGeorge

Mckade (Scottish) son of Kade.
Mccade

Mckay (Scottish) son of Kay.
Mackay, MacKay, Mckae, Mckai, McKay

McKenzie (Irish) a form of Mackenzie.
Mccenzie, Mckennzie, Mckensey, Mckensie, Mckenson, Mckensson, Mckenzi, Mckenzy, Mckinzie

Mckinley (Irish) a form of Mackinnley.
Mckinely, Mckinnely, Mckinnlee,
Mckinnley, McKinnley

Mead (English) meadow.
Meade, Meed

Medgar (German) a form of Edgar.

Medwin (German) faithful friend.

Mehetabel (Hebrew) who God benefits.

Mehrdad (Persian) gift of the sun.

Mehtar (Sanskrit) prince.
Mehta

Meinhard (German) strong, firm. See also Maynard.
Meinhardt, Meinke, Meino, Mendar

Meinrad (German) strong counsel.

Meir (Hebrew) one who brightens, shines; enlightener. History: Golda Meir was the prime minister of Israel.
Mayer, Meyer, Muki, Myer

Meka (Hawaiian) eyes.

Mel (English, Irish) a familiar form of Melvin.

Melbourne (English) mill stream.
Melborn, Melburn, Melby, Milborn,
Milbourn, Milbourne, Milburn, Millburn,
Millburne

Melchior (Hebrew) king.
Meilseoir, Melchor, Melker, Melkior

Meldon (English) mill hill.
Melden

Melrone (Irish) servant of Saint Ruadhan.

Melvern (Native American) great chief.

Melville (French) mill town. Literature: Herman Melville was a well-known nineteenth-century American writer.
Milville

Melvin (Irish) armored chief. (English) mill friend; council friend. See also Vinny.
Malvin, Mel, Melvino, Melvon, Melvyn,
Melwin, Melwyn, Melwynn

Menachem (Hebrew) comforter.
Menahem, Nachman

Menassah (Hebrew) cause to forget.
Menashe, Menashi, Menashia,
Menashiah, Menashya, Manasseh

Mendel (English) repairman.
Mendeley, Mendell, Mendie, Mendy

Mengesha (Ethiopian) kingdom.

Menico (Spanish) a short form of Domenico.

Mensah (Ewe) third son.

Menz (German) a short form of Clement.

Mercer (English) storekeeper.
Merce

Mered (Hebrew) revolter.

Meredith (Welsh) guardian from the sea.
Meredyth, Merideth, Meridith, Merry

Merion (Welsh) from Merion, Wales.
Merrion

Merle (French) a short form of Merlin, Merrill.
Meryl

Merlin (English) falcon. Literature: the magician who served as counselor in King Arthur's court.
Marlon, Merle, Merlen, Merlinn, Merlyn,
Merlynn

Merrick (English) ruler of the sea.
Merek, Meric, Merick, Merik, Merric,
Merrik, Meryk, Meyrick, Myrucj

Merrill (Irish) bright sea. (French) famous.
Meril, Merill, Merle, Merrel, Merrell,
Merril, Meryl

Merritt (Latin, Irish) valuable; deserving.
Merit, Meritt, Merrett

Merton (English) sea town.
Murton

Merv (Irish) a short form of Mervin.

Merville (French) sea village.

Mervin (Irish) a form of Marvin.
Merv, Mervyn, Mervynn, Merwin,
Merwinn, Merwyn, Murvin, Murvyn,
Myrvyn, Myrvynn, Myrwyn

Meshach (Hebrew) artist. Bible: one of Daniel's three friends who emerged unharmed from the fiery furnace of Babylon.

Mesut (Turkish) happy.

Metikla (Moquelumnan) reaching a hand underwater to catch a fish.

Mette (Greek, Danish) pearl.
Almeta, Mete

Meurig (Welsh) a form of Maurice.

Meyer (German) farmer.
Mayer, Meier, Myer

Mhina (Swahili) delightful.

Micah (Hebrew) a form of Michael. Bible: a Hebrew prophet.
Mic, Micaiah, Michiah, Mika, Mikah, Myca, Mycah

Micha (Hebrew) a short form of Michael.
Mica, Micha, Michah

Michael (Hebrew) who is like God? See also Micah, Miguel, Mika, Miles.
Machael, Machas, Mahail, Maichail, Maikal, Makael, Makal, Makel, Makell, Makis, Meikel, Mekal, Mekhail, Mhichael, Micael, Micah, Micahel, Mical, Micha, Michaele, Michaell, Michail, Michak, Michal, Michale, Michalek, Michalel, Michau, Micheal, Micheil, Michel, Michele, Michelet, Michiel, Micho, Michoel, Mick, Mickael, Mickey, Mihail, Mihalje, Mihkel, Mika, Mikael, Mikáele, Mikal, Mike, Mikeal, Mikel, Mikelis, Mikell, Mikhail, Mikkel, Mikko, Miksa, Milko, Miquel, Misael, Misi, Miska, Mitchell, Mychael, Mychajlo, Mychal, Mykal, Mykhas

Michail (Russian) a form of Michael.
Mihas, Mikail, Mikale, Misha

Michal (Polish) a form of Michael.
Michak, Michalek, Michall

Micheal (Irish) a form of Michael.

Michel (French) a form of Michael.
Michaud, Miche, Michee, Michell, Michelle, Michon

Michelangelo (Italian) a combination of Michael + Angelo. Art: Michelangelo Buonarroti was one of the greatest Renaissance painters.
Michelange, Miguelangelo

Michele (Italian) a form of Michael.

Michio (Japanese) man with the strength of three thousand.

Mick (English) a short form of Michael, Mickey.
Mickerson

Mickael (English) a form of Michael.
Mickaele, Mickal, Mickale, Mickeal, Mickel, Mickell, Mickelle, Mickle

Mickenzie (Irish) a form of Mackenzie.
Mickenze, Mickenzy, Mikenzie

Mickey (Irish) a familiar form of Michael.
Mick, Micki, Mickie, Micky, Miki, Mique

Micu (Hungarian) a form of Nick.

Miguel (Portuguese, Spanish) a form of Michael.
Migeel, Migel, Miguelly, Migui

Miguelangel (Spanish) a combination of Miguel + Angel.

Mihail (Greek, Bulgarian, Romanian) a form of Michael.
Mihailo, Mihal, Mihalis, Mikail

Mika (Ponca) raccoon. (Hebrew) a form of Micah. (Russian) a familiar form of Michael.
Miika, Mikah

Mikael (Swedish) a form of Michael.
Mikaeel, Mikaele

Mikáele (Hawaiian) a form of Michael.
Mikele

Mikal (Hebrew) a form of Michael.
Mekal, Mikahl, Mikale

Mikasi (Omaha) coyote.

Mike (Hebrew) a short form of Michael.
Mikey, Myk

Mikeal (Irish) a form of Michael.

Mikel (Basque) a form of Michael.
Mekel, Mikele, Mekell, Mikell, Mikelle

Mikelis (Latvian) a form of Michael.
Mikus, Milkins

Mikhail (Greek, Russian) a form of Michael.
Mekhail, Mihály, Mikhael, Mikhale, Mikhalis, Mikhalka, Mikhall, Mikhel, Mikhial, Mikhos

Miki (Japanese) tree.
Mikio

Mikkel (Norwegian) a form of Michael.
Mikkael, Mikle

Mikko (Finnish) a form of Michael.
Mikk, Mikka, Mikkohl, Mikkol, Miko, Mikol

Mikolaj (Polish) a form of Nicholas.
Mikolai

Mikolas (Greek) a form of Nicholas.
Miklós, Milek

Miksa (Hungarian) a form of Max.
Miks

Milan (Italian) northerner. Geography: a city in northern Italy.
Milaan, Milano, Milen, Millan, Millen, Mylan, Mylen, Mylon, Mylynn

Milap (Native American) giving.

Milborough (English) middle borough.
Milbrough

Milek (Polish) a familiar form of Nicholas.

Miles (Greek) millstone. (Latin) soldier. (German) merciful. (English) a short form of Michael.
Milas, Milles, Milo, Milson, Myles

Milford (English) mill by the ford.

Mililani (Hawaiian) heavenly caress.

Milko (Czech) a form of Michael. (German) a familiar form of Emil.
Milkins

Millard (Latin) caretaker of the mill.
Mill, Millar, Miller, Millward, Milward, Myller

Miller (English) miller; grain grinder.
Mellar, Millard, Millen

Mills (English) mills.

Milo (German) a form of Miles. A familiar form of Emil.
Millo, Mylo

Milos (Greek, Slavic) pleasant.

Miloslav (Czech) lover of glory.
Milda

Milt (English) a short form of Milton.

Milton (English) mill town.
Milt, Miltie, Milty, Mylton

Mimis (Greek) a familiar form of Demetrius.

Min (Burmese) king.
Mina

Mincho (Spanish) a form of Benjamin.

Minel (Spanish) a form of Manuel.

Miner (English) miner.

Mingan (Native American) gray wolf.

Mingo (Spanish) a short form of Domingo.

Minh (Vietnamese) bright.
Minhao, Minhduc, Minhkhan, Minhtong, Minhy

Minkah (Akan) just, fair.

Minor (Latin) junior; younger.
Mynor

Minoru (Japanese) fruitful.

Mique (Spanish) a form of Mickey.
Mequel, Mequelin, Miquel

Miron (Polish) peace.

Miroslav (Czech) peace; glory.
Mirek, Miroslaw, Miroslawy

Mirwais (Afghan) noble ruler.

Misael (Hebrew) a form of Michael.
Mischael, Mishael, Missael

Misha (Russian) a short form of Michail.
Misa, Mischa, Mishael, Mishal, Mishe, Mishenka, Mishka

Miska (Hungarian) a form of Michael.
Misi, Misik, Misko, Miso

Mister (English) mister.
Mistur

Misu (Moquelumnan) rippling water.

Mitch (English) a short form of Mitchell.

Mitchel (English) a form of Mitchell.
Mitchael, Mitchal, Mitcheal, Mitchele, Mitchil, Mytchel

Mitchell (English) a form of Michael.
Mitch, Mitchall, Mitchel, Mitchelle, Mitchem, Mytch, Mytchell

Mitsos (Greek) a familiar form of Demetrius.

Modesto (Latin) modest.

Moe (English) a short form of Moses.
Mo

Mogens (Dutch) powerful.
Mohamad (Arabic) a form of Muhammad.
Mohamid

Mohamed (Arabic) a form of Muhammad.
Mohamd, Mohameed

Mohamet (Arabic) a form of Muhammad.
Mahomet, Mehemet, Mehmet

Mohammad (Arabic) a form of Muhammad.
Mahammad, Mohammadi, Mohammd, Mohammid, Mohanad, Mohmad

Mohammed (Arabic) a form of Muhammad.
Mahammed, Mahomet, Mohamad, Mohaned, Mouhamed, Muhammad

Mohamud (Arabic) a form of Muhammad.
Mohammud, Mohamoud

Mohan (Hindi) delightful.

Moises (Portuguese, Spanish) a form of Moses.
Moices, Moise, Moisés, Moisey, Moisis

Moishe (Yiddish) a form of Moses.
Moshe

Mojag (Native American) crying baby.

Molimo (Moquelumnan) bear going under shady trees.

Momuso (Moquelumnan) yellow jackets crowded in their nests for the winter.

Mona (Moquelumnan) gathering jimsonweed seed.

Monahan (Irish) monk.
Monaghan, Monoghan

Mongo (Yoruba) famous.

Monroe (Irish) Geography: the mouth of the Roe River.
Monro, Munro, Munroe

Montague (French) pointed mountain.
Montagne, Montagu, Monte

Montana (Spanish) mountain. Geography: a U.S. state.
Montaine, Montanna

Montaro (Japanese) big boy.
Montario, Monterio, Montero

Monte (Spanish) a short form of Montgomery.
Montae, Montaé, Montay, Montea, Montee, Monti, Montoya, Monty

Montel (American) a form of Montreal.
Montele, Montell, Montelle

Montez (Spanish) dweller in the mountains.
Monteiz, Monteze, Montezz, Montisze

Montgomery (English) rich man's mountain.
Monte, Montgomerie, Monty

Montre (French) show.
Montra, Montrae, Montray, Montraz, Montres, Montrey, Montrez, Montreze

Montreal (French) royal mountain. Geography: a city in Quebec.
Montel, Monterial, Monterrell, Montrail, Montrale, Montrall, Montreall, Montrell, Montrial

Montrell (French) a form of Montreal.
Montral, Montrel, Montrele, Montrelle

Montsho (Tswana) black.

Monty (English) a familiar form of Montgomery.

Moore (French) dark; moor; marshland.
Moor, Mooro, More

Mordecai (Hebrew) martial, warlike. Mythology: Marduk was the Babylonian god of war. Bible: wise counselor to Queen Esther.
Mord, Mordachai, Mordechai, Mordie, Mordy, Mort

Mordred (Latin) painful. Literature: the bastard son of King Arthur.
Modred

Morel (French) an edible mushroom.
Morrel

Moreland (English) moor; marshland.
Moorland, Morland

Morell (French) dark; from Morocco.
Moor, Moore, Morelle, Morelli, Morill, Morrell, Morrill, Murrel, Murrell

Morey (Greek) a familiar form of Moris. (Latin) a form of Morrie.
Morrey, Morry

Morgan (Scottish) sea warrior.
Morgen, Morghan, Morgin, Morgon, Morgun, Morgunn, Morgwn, Morgyn, Morrgan

Morio (Japanese) forest.

Moris (Greek) son of the dark one. (English) a form of Morris.
Morey, Morisz, Moriz

Moritz (German) a form of Maurice, Morris.
Morisz

Morley (English) meadow by the moor.
Moorley, Moorly, Morlee, Morleigh, Morlon, Morly, Morlyn, Morrley

Morrie (Latin) a familiar form of Maurice, Morse.
Maury, Morey, Mori, Morie, Morry, Mory, Morye

Morris (Latin) dark skinned; moor; marshland. (English) a form of Maurice.
Moris, Moriss, Moritz, Morrese, Morrise, Morriss, Morry, Moss

Morse (English) son of Maurice.
Morresse, Morrie, Morrison, Morrisson

Mort (French, English) a short form of Morten, Mortimer, Morton.
Morte, Mortey, Mortie, Mortty, Morty

Morten (Norwegian) a form of Martin.
Mort

Mortimer (French) still water.
Mort, Mortymer

Morton (English) town near the moor.
Mort

Morven (Scottish) mariner.
Morvien, Morvin

Mose (Hebrew) a short form of Moses.

Moses (Hebrew) drawn out of the water. (Egyptian) son, child. Bible: the Hebrew lawgiver who brought the Ten Commandments down from Mount Sinai.
Moe, Moise, Moïse, Moisei, Moises, Moishe, Mose, Mosese, Moshe, Mosiah, Mosie, Moss, Mosses, Mosya, Mosze, Moszek, Mousa, Moyses, Moze

Moshe (Hebrew, Polish) a form of Moses.
Mosheh

Mosi (Swahili) first-born.

Moss (Irish) a short form of Maurice, Morris. (English) a short form of Moses.

Moswen (African) light in color.

Motega (Native American) new arrow.

Mouhamed (Arabic) a form of Muhammad.
Mouhamad, Mouhamadou, Mouhammed, Mouhamoin

Mousa (Arabic) a form of Moses.
Moussa

Moze (Lithuanian) a form of Moses.
Mozes, Mózes

Mpasa (Nguni) mat.

Mposi (Nyakyusa) blacksmith.

Mpoza (Luganda) tax collector.

Msrah (Akan) sixth-born.

Mtima (Nguni) heart.

Muata (Moquelumnan) yellow jackets in their nest.

Mugamba (Runyoro) talks too much.

Mugisa (Rutooro) lucky.
Mugisha, Mukisa

Muhammad (Arabic) praised. History: the founder of the Islamic religion. See also Ahmad, Hamid, Yasin.
Mahmoud, Mahmúd, Mohamad, Mohamed, Mohamet, Mohamud, Mohammed, Mouhamed, Muhamad, Muhamed, Muhamet, Muhammadali, Muhammed

Muhannad (Arabic) sword.
Muhanad

Muhsin (Arabic) beneficent; charitable.

Muhtadi (Arabic) rightly guided.

Muir (Scottish) moor; marshland.

Mujahid (Arabic) fighter in the way of Allah.

Mukasa (Luganda) God's chief administrator.

Mukhtar (Arabic) chosen.
Mukhtaar

Mukul (Sanskrit) bud, blossom; soul.

Mulogo (Musoga) wizard.

Mundan (Rhodesian) garden.

Mundo (Spanish) a short form of Edmundo.

Mundy (Irish) from Reamonn.

Mungo (Scottish) amiable.

Mun-Hee (Korean) literate; shiny.

Munir (Arabic) brilliant; shining.

Munny (Cambodian) wise.

Muraco (Native American) white moon.

Murali (Hindi) flute. Religion: the instrument the Hindu god Krishna is usually depicted as playing.

Murat (Turkish) wish come true.

Murdock (Scottish) wealthy sailor.
Murdo, Murdoch, Murtagh

Murphy (Irish) sea warrior.
Murfey, Murfy

Murray (Scottish) sailor.
Macmurray, Moray, Murrey, Murry

Murtagh (Irish) a form of Murdock.
Murtaugh

Musa (Swahili) child.

Musád (Arabic) untied camel.

Musoke (Rukonjo) born while a rainbow was in the sky.

Mustafa (Arabic) chosen; royal.
Mostafa, Mostaffa, Moustafa, Mustafaa, Mustafah, Mustafe, Mustaffa, Mustafo, Mustapha, Mustoffa, Mustofo

Mustapha (Arabic) a form of Mustafa.
Mostapha, Moustapha

Muti (Arabic) obedient.

Mwaka (Luganda) born on New Year's Eve.

Mwamba (Nyakyusa) strong.

Mwanje (Luganda) leopard.

Mwinyi (Swahili) king.

Mwita (Swahili) summoner.

Mychajlo (Latvian) a form of Michael.
Mykhaltso, Mykhas

Mychal (American) a form of Michael.
Mychall, Mychalo, Mycheal

Myer (English) a form of Meir.
Myers, Myur

Mykal, Mykel (American) forms of Michael.
Mykael, Mikele, Mykell

Myles (Latin) soldier. (German) a form of Miles.
Myels, Mylez, Mylles, Mylz

Mynor (Latin) a form of Minor.

Myo (Burmese) city.

Myron (Greek) fragrant ointment.
Mehran, Mehrayan, My, Myran, Myrone, Ron

Myung-Dae (Korean) right; great.

Mzuzi (Swahili) inventive

N

Naaman (Hebrew) pleasant.

Nabiha (Arabic) intelligent.

Nabil (Arabic) noble.
Nabeel, Nabiel

Nachman (Hebrew) a short form of Menachem.
Nachum, Nahum

Nada (Arabic) generous.

Nadav (Hebrew) generous; noble.
Nadiv

Nadidah (Arabic) equal to anyone else.

Nadim (Arabic) friend.
Nadeem

Nadir (Afghan, Arabic) dear, rare.
Nader

Nadisu (Hindi) beautiful river.

Naeem (Arabic) benevolent.
Naem, Naim, Naiym, Nieem

Naftali (Hebrew) wreath.
Naftalie

Nagid (Hebrew) ruler; prince.

Nahele (Hawaiian) forest.

Nahma (Native American) sturgeon.

Nailah (Arabic) successful.

Nairn (Scottish) river with alder trees.
Nairne

Najee (Arabic) a form of Naji.
Najae, Najée, Najei, Najiee

Naji (Arabic) safe.
Najee, Najih

Najíb (Arabic) born to nobility.
Najib, Nejeeb

Najji (Muganda) second child.

Nakia (Arabic) pure.
Nakai, Nakee, Nakeia, Naki, Nakiah, Nakii

Nakos (Arapaho) sage, wise.

Naldo (Spanish) a familiar form of Reginald.

Nalren (Dene) thawed out.

Nam (Vietnamese) scrape off.

Namaka (Hawaiian) eyes.

Namid (Ojibwa) star dancer.

Namir (Hebrew) leopard.
Namer

Nandin (Hindi) Religion: a servant of the Hindu god Shiva.
Nandan

Nando (German) a familiar form of Ferdinand.
Nandor

Nangila (Abaluhya) born while parents traveled.

Nangwaya (Mwera) don't mess with me.

Nansen (Swedish) son of Nancy.

Nantai (Navajo) chief.

Nantan (Apache) spokesman.

Naoko (Japanese) straight, honest.

Napayshni (Lakota) he does not flee; courageous.

Napier (Spanish) new city.
Neper

Napoleon (Greek) lion of the woodland. (Italian) from Naples, Italy. History: Napoleon Bonaparte was a famous nineteenth-century French emperor.
Leon, Nap, Napolean, Napoléon, Napoleone, Nappie, Nappy

Naquan (American) a combination of the prefix Na + Quan.
Naqawn, Naquain, Naquen, Naquon

Narain (Hindi) protector. Religion: another name for the Hindu god Vishnu.
Narayan

Narcisse (French) a form of Narcissus.
Narcis, Narciso, Narkis, Narkissos

Narcissus (Greek) daffodil. Mythology: the youth who fell in love with his own reflection.
Narcisse

Nard (Persian) chess player.

Nardo (German) strong, hardy. (Spanish) a short form of Bernardo.

Narve (Dutch) healthy, strong.

Nashashuk (Fox, Sauk) loud thunder.

Nashoba (Choctaw) wolf.

Nasim (Persian) breeze; fresh air.
Naseem, Nassim

Nasser (Arabic) victorious.
Naseer, Naser, Nasier, Nasir, Nasr, Nassir, Nassor

Nat (English) a short form of Nathan, Nathaniel.
Natt, Natty

Natal (Spanish) a form of Noël.
Natale, Natalie, Natalino, Natalio, Nataly

Natan (Hebrew, Hungarian, Polish, Russian, Spanish) God has given.
Naten

Natanael (Hebrew) a form of Nathaniel.
Natanel, Nataniel

Nate (Hebrew) a short form of Nathan, Nathaniel.

Natesh (Hindi) destroyer. Religion: another name for the Hindu god Shiva.

Nathan (Hebrew) a short form of Nathaniel. Bible: a prophet during the reigns of David and Solomon.
Naethan, Nat, Nate, Nathann, Nathean, Nathen, Nathian, Nathin, Nathon, Nathyn, Natthan, Naythan, Nethan

Nathanael (Hebrew) gift of God. Bible: one of the Twelve Apostles. Also known as Bartholomew.
Nathanae, Nathanal, Nathaneal, Nathaneil, Nathanel, Nathaneol

Nathanial (Hebrew) a form of Nathaniel.
Nathanyal, Nathanual

Nathanie (Hebrew) a familiar form of Nathaniel.
Nathania, Nathanni

Nathaniel (Hebrew) gift of God. Bible: one of the Twelve Apostles.
Nat, Natanael, Nate, Nathan, Nathanael, Nathanial, Nathanie, Nathanielle, Nathanil, Nathanile, Nathanuel, Nathanyel, Nathanyl, Natheal, Nathel, Nathinel, Nethaniel, Thaniel

Nathen (Hebrew) a form of Nathan.

Nav (Gypsy) name.

Navarro (Spanish) plains.
Navarre

Navdeep (Sikh) new light.
Navdip

Navin (Hindi) new, novel.
Naveen, Naven

Nawat (Native American) left-handed.

Nawkaw (Winnebago) wood.

Nayati (Native American) wrestler.

Nayland (English) island dweller.

Nazareth (Hebrew) born in Nazareth, Israel.
Nazaire, Nazaret, Nazarie, Nazario, Nazerene, Nazerine

Nazih (Arabic) pure, chaste.
Nazeeh, Nazeem, Nazeer, Nazieh, Nazim, Nazir, Nazz

Ndale (Nguni) trick.

Neal (Irish) a form of Neil.
Neale, Neall, Nealle, Nealon, Nealy

Neci (Latin) a familiar form of Ignatius.

Nectarios (Greek) saint. Religion: a saint in the Greek Orthodox Church.

Ned (English) a familiar form of Edward, Edwin.
Neddie, Neddym, Nedrick

Nehemiah (Hebrew) compassion of Jehovah. Bible: a Jewish leader.
Nahemiah, Nechemya, Nehemias, Nehemie, Nehemyah, Nehimiah, Nehmia, Nehmiah, Nemo, Neyamia

Nehru (Hindi) canal.

Neil (Irish) champion.
Neal, Neel, Neihl, Neile, Neill, Neille, Nels, Niall, Niele, Niels, Nigel, Nil, Niles, Nilo, Nils, Nyle

Neka (Native American) wild goose.

Nelek (Polish) a form of Cornelius.

Nellie (English) a familiar form of Cornelius, Cornell, Nelson.
Nell, Nelly

Nelius (Latin) a short form of Cornelius.

Nelo (Spanish) a form of Daniel.
Nello, Nilo

Nels (Scandinavian) a form of Neil, Nelson.
Nelse, Nelson, Nils

Nelson (English) son of Neil.
Nealson, Neilsen, Neilson, Nellie, Nels, Nelsen, Nilson, Nilsson

Nemesio (Spanish) just.
Nemi

Nemo (Greek) glen, glade. (Hebrew) a short form of Nehemiah.

Nen (Egyptian) ancient waters.

Neptune (Latin) sea ruler. Mythology: the Roman god of the sea.

Nero (Latin, Spanish) stern. History: a cruel Roman emperor.
Neron, Nerone, Nerron

Nesbit (English) nose-shaped bend in a river.
Naisbit, Naisbitt, Nesbitt, Nisbet, Nisbett

Nestor (Greek) traveler; wise.
Nester

Nethaniel (Hebrew) a form of Nathaniel.
Netanel, Netania, Netaniah, Netaniel, Netanya, Nethanel, Nethanial, Nethaniel, Nethanyal, Nethanyel

Neto (Spanish) a short form of Ernesto.

Nevada (Spanish) covered in snow. Geography: a U.S. state.
Navada, Nevade

Nevan (Irish) holy.
Nevean

Neville (French) new town.
Nev, Nevil, Nevile, Nevill, Nevyle

Nevin (Irish) worshiper of the saint. (English) middle; herb.
Nefen, Nev, Nevan, Neven, Nevins, Nevyn, Niven

Newbold (English) new tree.

Newell (English) new hall.
Newall, Newel, Newyle

Newland (English) new land.
Newlan

Newlin (Welsh) new lake.
Newlyn

Newman (English) newcomer.
Neiman, Neimann, Neimon, Neuman,
Numan, Numen

Newton (English) new town.
Newt

Ngai (Vietnamese) herb.

Nghia (Vietnamese) forever.

Ngozi (Ibo) blessing.

Ngu (Vietnamese) sleep.

Nguyen (Vietnamese) a form of Ngu.

Nhean (Cambodian) self-knowledge.

Niall (Irish) a form of Neil. History:
Niall of the Nine Hostages was a
famous Irish king.
Nial, Nialle

Nibal (Arabic) arrows.
Nibel

Nibaw (Native American) standing
tall.

Nicabar (Gypsy) stealthy.

Nicho (Spanish) a form of Dennis.

Nicholas (Greek) victorious people.
Religion: Nicholas of Myra is a
patron saint of children. See also
Caelan, Claus, Cola, Colar, Cole,
Colin, Colson, Klaus, Lasse, Mikolaj,
Mikolas, Milek.
Niccolas, Nichalas, Nichelas, Nichele,
Nichlas, Nichlos, Nichola, Nicholaas,
Nicholaes, Nicholase, Nicholaus, Nichole,
Nicholias, Nicholl, Nichollas, Nicholos,
Nichols, Nicholus, Nick, Nickalus,
Nicklaus, Nickolas, Nicky, Niclas,
Niclasse, Nico, Nicola, Nicolai, Nicolas,

Nicoles, Nicolis, Nicoll, Nicolo, Nikhil,
Niki, Nikili, Nikita, Nikko, Niklas,
Niko, Nikolai, Nikolas, Nikolaus,
Nikolos, Nils, Nioclás, Niocol, Nycholas

Nicholaus (Greek) a form of Nicholas.
Nichalaus, Nichalous, Nichaolas,
Nichlaus, Nichloas, Nichlous, Nicholaos,
Nicholous

Nichols, Nicholson (English) son of
Nicholas.
Nicholes, Nicholis, Nicolls, Nickelson,
Nickoles

Nick (English) a short form of
Dominic, Nicholas. See also Micu.
Nic, Nik

Nickalus (Greek) a form of Nicholas.
Nickalas, Nickalis, Nickalos, Nickelas,
Nickelus

Nicklaus, Nicklas (Greek) forms of
Nicholas.
Nickalaus, Nickalous, Nickelous,
Nicklauss, Nicklos, Nicklous, Nicklus,
Nickolau, Nickolaus, Nicolaus, Niklaus,
Nikolaus

Nickolas (Greek) a form of Nicholas.
Nickolaos, Nickolis, Nickolos, Nickolus,
Nickolys, Nickoulas

Nicky (Greek) a familiar form of
Nicholas.
Nickey, Nicki, Nickie, Niki, Nikki

Nico (Greek) a short form of Nicholas.
Nicco

Nicodemus (Greek) conqueror of the
people.
Nicodem, Nicodemius, Nikodem,
Nikodema, Nikodemious, Nikodim

Nicola (Italian) a form of Nicholas.
See also Cola.
Nicolá, Nikolah

Nicolai (Norwegian, Russian) a form
of Nicholas.
Nicholai, Nickolai, Nicolaj, Nicolau,
Nicolay, Nicoly, Nikalai

Nicolas (Italian) a form of Nicholas.
Nico, Nicolaas, Nicolás, Nicolaus, Nicoles,
Nicolis, Nicolus

Nicolo (Italian) a form of Nicholas.
Niccolo, Niccolò, Nicol, Nicolao, Nicollo

Niels (Danish) a form of Neil.
Niel, Nielsen, Nielson, Niles, Nils

Nien (Vietnamese) year.

Nigan (Native American) ahead.
Nigen

Nigel (Latin) dark night.
Niegel, Nigal, Nigale, Nigele, Nigell,
Nigiel, Nigil, Nigle, Nijel, Nye, Nygel,
Nyigel, Nyjil

Nika (Yoruba) ferocious.

Nike (Greek) victorious.
Nikka

Niki (Hungarian) a familiar form of
Nicholas.
Nikia, Nikiah, Nikki, Nikkie, Nykei,
Nykey

Nikita (Russian) a form of Nicholas.
Nakita, Nakitas, Nikula

Nikiti (Native American) round and
smooth like an abalone shell.

Nikko, Niko (Hungarian) forms of Nicholas.
Nikoe, Nyko

Niklas (Latvian, Swedish) a form of Nicholas.
Niklaas, Niklaus

Nikola (Greek) a short form of Nicholas.
Nikolao, Nikolay, Nykola

Nikolai (Estonian, Russian) a form of Nicholas.
Kolya, Nikolais, Nikolaj, Nikolajs, Nikolay, Nikoli, Nikolia, Nikula, Nikulas

Nikolas (Greek) a form of Nicholas.
Nicanor, Nikalas, Nikalis, Nikalus, Nikholas, Nikolaas, Nikolaos, Nikolis, Nikolos, Nikos, Nilos, Nykolas, Nykolus

Nikolaus (Greek) a form of Nicholas.
Nikalous, Nikolaos

Nikolos (Greek) a form of Nicholas. See also Kolya.
Niklos, Nikolaos, Nikolò, Nikolous, Nikolus, Nikos, Nilos

Nil (Russian) a form of Neil.
Nilya

Nila (Hindi) blue.

Niles (English) son of Neil.
Nilesh, Nyles

Nilo (Finnish) a form of Neil.

Nils (Swedish) a short form of Nicholas.

Nimrod (Hebrew) rebel. Bible: a great-grandson of Noah.

Niño (Spanish) young child.

Niran (Tai) eternal.

Nishan (Armenian) cross, sign, mark.
Nishon

Nissan (Hebrew) sign, omen; miracle.
Nisan, Nissim, Nissin, Nisson

Nitis (Native American) friend.
Netis

Nixon (English) son of Nick.
Nixan, Nixson

Nizam (Arabic) leader.

Nkunda (Runyankore) loves those who hate him.

N'namdi (Ibo) his father's name lives on.

Noach (Hebrew) a form of Noah.

Noah (Hebrew) peaceful, restful. Bible: the patriarch who built the ark to survive the Flood.
Noach, Noak, Noe, Noé, Noi

Noam (Hebrew) sweet; friend.

Noble (Latin) born to nobility.
Nobe, Nobie, Noby

Nodin (Native American) wind.
Knoton, Noton

Noe (Czech, French) a form of Noah.

Noé (Hebrew, Spanish) quiet, peaceful. See also Noah.

Noël (French) day of Christ's birth. See also Natal.
Noel, Noël, Noell, Nole, Noli, Nowel, Nowell

Nohea (Hawaiian) handsome.
Noha, Nohe

Nokonyu (Native American) katydid's nose.
Noko, Nokoni

Nolan (Irish) famous; noble.
Noland, Nolande, Nolane, Nolen, Nolin, Nollan, Nolyn

Nollie (Latin, Scandinavian) a familiar form of Oliver.
Noll, Nolly

Norbert (Scandinavian) brilliant hero.
Bert, Norberto, Norbie, Norby

Norberto (Spanish) a form of Norbert.

Norman (French) Norseman. History: a name for the Scandinavians who settled in northern France in the tenth century, and who later conquered England in 1066.
Norm, Normand, Normen, Normie, Normy

Norris (French) northerner. (English) Norman's horse.
Norice, Norie, Noris, Norreys, Norrie, Norry, Norrys

Northcliff (English) northern cliff.
Northcliffe, Northclyff, Northclyffe

Northrop (English) north farm.
North, Northup

Norton (English) northern town.

Norville (French, English) northern town.
Norval, Norvel, Norvell, Norvil, Norvill, Norvylle

Norvin (English) northern friend.
Norvyn, Norwin, Norwinn, Norwyn,
Norwynn

Norward (English) protector of the
north.
Norwerd

Norwood (English) northern woods.

Notaku (Moquelumnan) growing
bear.

Nowles (English) a short form of
Knowles.

Nsoah (Akan) seventh-born.

Numa (Arabic) pleasant.

Numair (Arabic) panther.

Nuncio (Italian) messenger.
Nunzi, Nunzio

Nuri (Hebrew, Arabic) my fire.
Nery, Noori, Nur, Nuris, Nurism, Nury

Nuriel (Hebrew, Arabic) fire of the
Lord.
Nuria, Nuriah, Nuriya

Nuru (Swahili) born in daylight.

Nusair (Arabic) bird of prey.

Nwa (Nigerian) son.

Nwake (Nigerian) born on market
day.

Nye (English) a familiar form of
Aneurin, Nigel.

Nyle (English) island. (Irish) a form of
Neil.
Nyal, Nyll

O

Oakes (English) oak trees.
Oak, Oakie, Oaks, Ochs

Oakley (English) oak-tree field.
Oak, Oakes, Oakie, Oaklee, Oakleigh,
Oakly, Oaks

Oalo (Spanish) a form of Paul.

Oba (Yoruba) king.

Obadele (Yoruba) king arrives at the
house.

Obadiah (Hebrew) servant of God.
Obadias, Obed, Obediah, Obie,
Ovadiach, Ovadiah, Ovadya

Obed (English) a short form of
Obadiah.

Oberon (German) noble; bearlike.
Literature: the king of the fairies in
the Shakespearean play *A Midsummer*
Night's Dream.
See also Auberon, Aubrey.
Oberen, Oberron, Oeberon

Obert (German) wealthy; bright.

Obie (English) a familiar form of
Obadiah.
Obbie, Obe, Obey, Obi, Oby

Ocan (Luo) hard times.

Octavio (Latin) eighth. See also Tavey,
Tavian.
Octave, Octavia, Octavian, Octaviano,
Octavien, Octavious, Octavius, Octavo,
Octavous, Octavus, Ottavio

Octavious, Octavius (Latin) forms of
Octavio.
Octavaius, Octaveous, Octaveus, Octavias,
Octaviaus, Octavis, Octavous, Octavus

Odakota (Lakota) friendly.
Oda

Odd (Norwegian) point.
Oddvar

Ode (Benin) born along the road.
(Irish, English) a short form of Odell.
Odey, Odie, Ody

Oded (Hebrew) encouraging.

Odell (Greek) ode, melody. (Irish)
otter. (English) forested hill.
Dell, Odall, Ode

Odin (Scandinavian) ruler. Mythology:
the Norse god of wisdom and war.
Oden

Odion (Benin) first of twins.

Odo (Norwegian) a form of Otto.

Odolf (German) prosperous wolf.
Odolff

Odom (Ghanaian) oak tree.

Odon (Hungarian) wealthy protector.
Odi

Odran (Irish) pale green.
Odhrán, Oran, Oren, Orin, Orran,
Orren, Orrin

Odysseus (Greek) wrathful. Literature:
the hero of Homer's epic poem
Odyssey.

Ofer (Hebrew) young deer.

Og (Aramaic) king. Bible: the king of Basham.

Ogaleesha (Lakota) red shirt.

Ogbay (Ethiopian) don't take him from me.

Ogbonna (Ibo) image of his father.
Ogbonnia

Ogden (English) oak valley. Literature: Ogden Nash was a twentieth-century American writer of light verse.
Ogdan, Ogdon

Ogima (Chippewa) chief.

Ogun (Nigerian) Mythology: the god of war.
Ogunkeye, Ogunsanwo, Ogunsheye

Ohanko (Native American) restless.

Ohannes (Turkish) a form of John.

Ohanzee (Lakota) comforting shadow.

Ohin (African) chief.
Ohan

Ohitekah (Lakota) brave.

Oistin (Irish) a form of Austin.
Osten, Ostyn, Ostynn

OJ (American) a combination of the initials O. + J.
O.J., Ojay

Ojo (Yoruba) difficult delivery.

Okapi (Swahili) an African animal related to the giraffe but having a short neck.

Oke (Hawaiian) a form of Oscar.

Okechuku (Ibo) God's gift.

Okeke (Ibo) born on market day.
Okorie

Okie (American) from Oklahoma.
Okee, Okey

Oko (Ghanaian) older twin. (Yoruba) god of war.

Okorie (Ibo) a form of Okeke.

Okpara (Ibo) first son.

Okuth (Luo) born in a rain shower.

Ola (Yoruba) wealthy, rich.

Olaf (Scandinavian) ancestor. History: a patron saint and king of Norway.
Olaff, Olafur, Olav, Ole, Olef, Olof, Oluf

Olajuwon (Yoruba) wealth and honor are God's gifts.
Olajawon, Olajawun, Olajowuan, Olajuan, Olajuanne, Olajuawon, Olajuwa, Olajuwan, Olaujawon, Oljuwoun

Olamina (Yoruba) this is my wealth.

Olatunji (Yoruba) honor reawakens.

Olav (Scandinavian) a form of Olaf.
Ola, Olave, Olavus, Ole, Olen, Olin, Olle, Olov, Olyn

Ole (Scandinavian) a familiar form of Olaf, Olav.
Olay, Oleh, Olle

Oleg (Latvian, Russian) holy.
Olezka

Oleksandr (Russian) a form of Alexander.
Olek, Olesandr, Olesko

Olés (Polish) a familiar form of Alexander.

Olin (English) holly.
Olen, Olney, Olyn

Olindo (Italian) from Olinthos, Greece.

Oliver (Latin) olive tree. (Scandinavian) kind; affectionate.
Nollie, Oilibhéar, Oliverio, Oliverios, Olivero, Olivier, Oliviero, Oliwa, Ollie, Olliver, Ollivor, Olvan

Olivier (French) a form of Oliver.

Oliwa (Hawaiian) a form of Oliver.

Ollie (English) a familiar form of Oliver.
Olie, Olle, Olley, Olly

Olo (Spanish) a short form of Orlando, Rolando.

Olubayo (Yoruba) highest joy.

Olufemi (Yoruba) wealth and honor favors me.

Olujimi (Yoruba) God gave me this.

Olushola (Yoruba) God has blessed me.

Omar (Arabic) highest; follower of the Prophet. (Hebrew) reverent.
Omair, Omari, Omarr, Omer, Umar

Omari (Swahili) a form of Omar.
Omare, Omaree, Omarey

Omer (Arabic) a form of Omar.
Omeer, Omero

Omolara (Benin) child born at the right time.

On (Burmese) coconut. (Chinese) peace.

Onan (Turkish) prosperous.

Onaona (Hawaiian) pleasant fragrance.

Ondro (Czech) a form of Andrew.
Ondra, Ondre, Ondrea, Ondrey

O'neil (Irish) son of Neil.
Oneal, O'neal, Oneil, O'neill, Onel, Oniel, Onil

Onkar (Hindi) God in his entirety.

Onofrio (German) a form of Humphrey.
Oinfre, Onfre, Onfrio, Onofre, Onofredo

Onslow (English) enthusiast's hill.
Ounslow

Onufry (Polish) a form of Humphrey.

Onur (Turkish) honor.

Ophir (Hebrew) faithful. Bible: an Old Testament people and country.

Opio (Ateso) first of twin boys.

Oral (Latin) verbal; speaker.

Oran (Irish) green.
Odhran, Odran, Ora, Orane, Orran

Oratio (Latin) a form of Horatio.
Orazio

Orbán (Hungarian) born in the city.

Ordell (Latin) beginning.
Orde

Oren (Hebrew) pine tree. (Irish) light skinned, white.
Oran, Orin, Oris, Orono, Orren, Orrin

Orestes (Greek) mountain man. Mythology: the son of the Greek leader Agamemnon.
Aresty, Oreste

Ori (Hebrew) my light.
Oree, Orie, Orri, Ory

Orien (Latin) visitor from the east.
Orian, Orie, Orin, Oris, Oron, Orono, Orrin, Oryan

Orion (Greek) son of fire. Mythology: a giant hunter who was killed by Artemis. See also Zorion.

Orji (Ibo) mighty tree.

Orlando (German) famous throughout the land. (Spanish) a form of Roland.
Lando, Olando, Olo, Orlan, Orland, Orlanda, Orlandas, Orlandes, Orlandis, Orlandos, Orlandus, Orlo, Orlondo, Orlondon

Orleans (Latin) golden.
Orlean, Orlin

Orman (German) mariner, seaman. (Scandinavian) serpent, worm.
Ormand

Ormond (English) bear mountain; spear protector.
Ormande, Ormon, Ormonde

Oro (Spanish) golden.

Orono (Latin) a form of Oren.
Oron

Orrick (English) old oak tree.
Orric

Orrin (English) river.
Orin, Oryn, Orynn

Orris (Latin) a form of Horatio.
Oris, Orriss

Orry (Latin) from the Orient.
Oarrie, Orrey, Orrie

Orsino (Italian) a form of Orson.

Orson (Latin) bearlike.
Orscino, Orsen, Orsin, Orsini, Orsino, Son, Sonny, Urson

Orton (English) shore town.

Ortzi (Basque) sky.

Orunjan (Yoruba) born under the midday sun.

Orval (English) a form of Orville.
Orvel

Orville (French) golden village. History: Orville Wright and his brother Wilbur were the first men to fly an airplane.
Orv, Orval, Orvell, Orvie, Orvil

Orvin (English) spear friend.
Orwin, Owynn

Osahar (Benin) God hears.

Osayaba (Benin) God forgives.

Osaze (Benin) whom God likes.

Osbert (English) divine; bright.

Osborn (Scandinavian) divine bear. (English) warrior of God.
Osbern, Osbon, Osborne, Osbourn, Osbourne, Osburn, Osburne, Oz, Ozzie

Oscar (Scandinavian) divine spearman.
Oke, Oskar, Osker, Oszkar

Osei (Fante) noble.
Osee

Osgood (English) divinely good.

O'Shea (Irish) son of Shea.
Oshae, Oshai, Oshane, O'Shane, Oshaun, Oshay, Oshaye, Oshe, Oshea, Osheon

Osip (Russian, Ukrainian) a form of Joseph, Yosef. See also Osya.

Oskar (Scandinavian) a form of Oscar.
Osker, Ozker

Osman (Turkish) ruler. (English) servant of God.
Osmanek, Osmen, Osmin, Otthmor, Ottmar

Osmar (English) divine; wonderful.

Osmond (English) divine protector.
Osmand, Osmonde, Osmont, Osmund, Osmunde, Osmundo

Osric (English) divine ruler.
Osrick

Ostin (Latin) a form of Austin.
Ostan, Osten, Ostyn

Osvaldo (Spanish) a form of Oswald.
Osbaldo, Osbalto, Osvald, Osvalda

Oswald (English) God's power; God's crest. See also Waldo.
Osvaldo, Oswaldo, Oswall, Oswell, Oswold, Oz, Ozzie

Oswaldo (Spanish) a form of Oswald.

Oswin (English) divine friend.
Osvin, Oswinn, Oswyn, Oswynn

Osya (Russian) a familiar form of Osip.

Ota (Czech) prosperous.
Otik

Otadan (Native American) plentiful.

Otaktay (Lakota) kills many; strikes many.

Otek (Polish) a form of Otto.

Otello (Italian) a form of Othello.

Otem (Luo) born away from home.

Othello (Spanish) a form of Otto. Literature: the title character in the Shakespearean tragedy *Othello*.
Otello

Othman (German) wealthy.
Ottoman

Otis (Greek) keen of hearing. (German) son of Otto.
Oates, Odis, Otes, Otess, Otez, Otise, Ottis, Otys

Ottah (Nigerian) thin baby.

Ottar (Norwegian) point warrior; fright warrior.

Ottmar (Turkish) a form of Osman.
Otomars, Ottomar

Otto (German) rich.
Odo, Otek, Otello, Otfried, Othello, Otho, Othon, Otik, Otilio, Otman, Oto, Otón, Otton, Ottone

Ottokar (German) happy warrior.
Otokars, Ottocar

Otu (Native American) collecting seashells in a basket.

Ouray (Ute) arrow. Astrology: born under the sign of Sagittarius.

Oved (Hebrew) worshiper, follower.

Owen (Irish) born to nobility; young warrior. (Welsh) a form of Evan.
Owain, Owens, Owin, Uaine

Owney (Irish) elderly.
Oney

Oxford (English) place where oxen cross the river.
Ford

Oya (Moquelumnan) speaking of the jacksnipe.

Oystein (Norwegian) rock of happiness.
Ostein, Osten, Ostin, Øystein

Oz (Hebrew) a short form of Osborn, Oswald.

Ozturk (Turkish) pure; genuine Turk.

Ozzie (English) a familiar form of Osborn, Oswald.
Ossie, Ossy, Ozee, Ozi, Ozzi, Ozzy

P

Paavo (Finnish) a form of Paul.
Paaveli

Pablo (Spanish) a form of Paul.
Pable, Paublo

Pace (English) a form of Pascal.
Payce

Pacifico (Filipino) peaceful.

Paco (Italian) pack. (Spanish) a familiar form of Francisco. (Native American) bald eagle. See also Quico.
Pacorro, Panchito, Pancho, Paquito

Paddy (Irish) a familiar form of Padraic, Patrick.
Paddey, Paddi, Paddie

Paden (English) a form of Patton.

Padget (English) a form of Page.
Padgett, Paget, Pagett

Padraic (Irish) a form of Patrick.
Paddrick, Paddy, Padhraig, Padrai, Pádraig, Padraigh, Padreic, Padriac, Padric, Padron, Padruig

Page (French) youthful assistant.
Padget, Paggio, Paige, Payge

Paige (English) a form of Page.

Pakelika (Hawaiian) a form of Patrick.

Paki (African) witness.

Pal (Swedish) a form of Paul.

Pál (Hungarian) a form of Paul.
Pali, Palika

Palaina (Hawaiian) a form of Brian.

Palani (Hawaiian) a form of Frank.

Palash (Hindi) flowery tree.

Palben (Basque) blond.

Palladin (Native American) fighter.
Pallaton, Palleten

Palmer (English) palm-bearing pilgrim.
Pallmer, Palmar

Palti (Hebrew) God liberates.
Palti-el

Panas (Russian) immortal.

Panayiotis (Greek) a form of Peter.
Panagiotis, Panajotis, Panayioti, Panayoti, Panayotis

Pancho (Spanish) a familiar form of Francisco, Frank.
Panchito

Panos (Greek) a form of Peter.
Petros

Paolo (Italian) a form of Paul.

Paquito (Spanish) a familiar form of Paco.

Paramesh (Hindi) greatest. Religion: another name for the Hindu god Shiva.

Pardeep (Sikh) mystic light.
Pardip

Paris (Greek) lover. Geography: the capital of France. Mythology: the prince of Troy who started the Trojan War by abducting Helen.
Paras, Paree, Pares, Parese, Parie, Parris, Parys

Park (Chinese) cypress tree. (English) a short form of Parker.
Parke, Parkes, Parkey, Parks

Parker (English) park keeper.
Park

Parkin (English) little Peter.
Perkin

Parlan (Scottish) a form of Bartholomew. See also Parthalán.

Parnell (French) little Peter. History: Charles Stewart Parnell was a famous Irish politician.
Nell, Parle, Parnel, Parrnell, Pernell

Parr (English) cattle enclosure, barn.

Parrish (English) church district.
Parish, Parrie, Parrisch, Parrysh

Parry (Welsh) son of Harry.
Parrey, Parrie, Pary

Parth (Irish) a short form of Parthalán.
Partha, Parthey

Parthalán (Irish) plowman. See also Bartholomew.
Parlan, Parth

Parthenios (Greek) virgin. Religion: a Greek Orthodox saint.

Pascal (French) born on Easter or Passover.
Pace, Pascale, Pascalle, Paschal, Paschalis, Pascoe, Pascou, Pascual, Pasquale

Pascual (Spanish) a form of Pascal.
Pascul

Pasha (Russian) a form of Paul.
Pashenka, Pashka

Pasquale (Italian) a form of Pascal.
Pascuale, Pasqual, Pasquali, Pasquel

Pastor (Latin) spiritual leader.

Pat (Native American) fish. (English) a short form of Patrick.
Pattie, Patty

Patakusu (Moquelumnan) ant biting a person.

Patamon (Native American) raging.

Patek (Polish) a form of Patrick.
Patick

Patric (Latin) a form of Patrick.

Patrice (French) a form of Patrick.

Patricio (Spanish) a form of Patrick.
Patricius, Patrizio

Patrick (Latin) nobleman. Religion: the patron saint of Ireland. See also Fitzpatrick, Ticho.
Paddy, Padraic, Pakelika, Pat, Patek, Patric, Patrice, Patricio, Patrickk, Patrik, Patrique, Patrizius, Patryk, Pats, Patsy, Pattrick

Patrin (Gypsy) leaf trail.

Patryk (Latin) a form of Patrick.
Patryck

Patterson (Irish) son of Pat.
Patteson

Pattin (Gypsy) leaf.

Patton (English) warrior's town.
Paden, Paten, Patin, Paton, Patten, Pattin, Patty, Payton, Peyton

Patwin (Native American) man.

Patxi (Basque, Teutonic) free.

Paul (Latin) small. Bible: Saul, later renamed Paul, was the first to bring the teachings of Christ to the Gentiles.
Oalo, Paavo, Pablo, Pal, Pál, Pall, Paolo, Pasha, Pasko, Pauli, Paulia, Paulin, Paulino, Paulis, Paulo, Pauls, Paulus, Pavel, Pavlos, Pawel, Pol, Poul

Pauli (Latin) a familiar form of Paul.
Pauley, Paulie, Pauly

Paulin (German, Polish) a form of Paul.

Paulino (Spanish) a form of Paul.

Paulo (Portuguese, Swedish, Hawaiian) a form of Paul.

Pavel (Russian) a form of Paul.
Paavel, Pasha, Pavils, Pavlik, Pavlo, Pavlusha, Pavlushenka, Pawl

Pavit (Hindi) pious, pure.

Pawel (Polish) a form of Paul.
Pawelek, Pawl

Pax (Latin) peaceful.
Paz

Paxton (Latin) peaceful town.
Packston, Pax, Paxon, Paxten, Paxtun

Payat (Native American) he is on his way.
Pay, Payatt

Payden (English) a form of Payton.
Paydon

Payne (Latin) from the country.
Paine, Paynn

Paytah (Lakota) fire.
Pay, Payta

Payton (English) a form of Patton.
Paiton, Pate, Payden, Peaton, Peighton, Peyton

Paz (Spanish) a form of Pax.

Pearce (English) a form of Pierce.
Pears, Pearse

Pearson (English) son of Peter. See also Pierson.
Pearsson, Pehrson, Peirson, Peterson

Peder (Scandinavian) a form of Peter.
Peadar, Pedey

Pedro (Spanish) a form of Peter.
Pedrin, Pedrín, Petronio

Peers (English) a form of Peter.
Peerus, Piers

Peeter (Estonian) a form of Peter.
Peet

Peirce (English) a form of Peter.
Peirs

Pekelo (Hawaiian) a form of Peter.
Pekka

Peleke (Hawaiian) a form of Frederick.

Pelham (English) tannery town.

Pelí (Latin, Basque) happy.

Pell (English) parchment.
Pall

Pello (Greek, Basque) stone.
Peru, Piarres

Pelton (English) town by a pool.

Pembroke (Welsh) headland. (French) wine dealer. (English) broken fence.
Pembrook

Peniamina (Hawaiian) a form of Benjamin.
Peni

Penley (English) enclosed meadow.

Penn (Latin) pen, quill. (English) enclosure. (German) a short form of Penrod.
Pen, Penna, Penney, Pennie, Penny

Penrod (German) famous commander.
Penn, Pennrod, Rod

Pepa (Czech) a familiar form of Joseph.
Pepek, Pepik

Pepe (Spanish) a familiar form of José.
Pepillo, Pepito, Pequin, Pipo

Pepin (German) determined; petitioner. History: Pepin the Short was an eighth-century king of the Franks.
Pepi, Peppie, Peppy

Peppe (Italian) a familiar form of Joseph.
Peppi, Peppo, Pino

Per (Swedish) a form of Peter.

Perben (Greek, Danish) stone.

Percival (French) pierce the valley. Literature: a knight of the Round Table who first appears in Chrétien de Troyes's poem about the quest for the Holy Grail.
Parsafal, Parsefal, Parsifal, Parzival, Perc,

Perce, Perceval, Percevall, Percivall, Percy, Peredur, Purcell

Percy (French) a familiar form of Percival.
Pearcey, Pearcy, Percey, Percie, Piercey, Piercy

Peregrine (Latin) traveler; pilgrim; falcon.
Peregrin, Peregryne, Perine, Perry

Pericles (Greek) just leader. History: an Athenian statesman.

Perico (Spanish) a form of Peter.
Pequin, Perequin

Perine (Latin) a short form of Peregrine.
Perino, Perion, Perrin, Perryn

Perkin (English) little Peter.
Perka, Perkins, Perkyn, Perrin

Pernell (French) a form of Parnell.
Perren, Perrnall

Perry (English) a familiar form of Peregrine, Peter.
Parry, Perrie, Perrye

Perth (Scottish) thorn-bush thicket. Geography: a burgh in Scotland; a city in Australia.

Pervis (Latin) passage.
Pervez

Pesach (Hebrew) spared. Religion: another name for Passover.
Pessach

Petar (Greek) a form of Peter.

Pete (English) a short form of Peter.
Peat, Peet, Petey, Peti, Petie, Piet, Pit

Peter (Greek, Latin) small rock. Bible: Simon, renamed Peter, was the leader of the Twelve Apostles. See also Boutros, Ferris, Takis.
Panayiotos, Panos, Peadair, Peder, Pedro, Peers, Peeter, Peirce, Pekelo, Per, Perico, Perion, Perkin, Perry, Petar, Pete, Péter, Peterke, Peterus, Petr, Petras, Petros, Petru, Petruno, Petter, Peyo, Piaras, Pierce, Piero, Pierre, Pieter, Pietrek, Pietro, Piotr, Piter, Piti, Pjeter, Pyotr

Peterson (English) son of Peter.
Peteris, Petersen

Petiri (Shona) where we are.
Petri

Petr (Bulgarian) a form of Peter.

Petras (Lithuanian) a form of Peter.
Petra, Petrelis

Petros (Greek) a form of Peter.
Petro

Petru (Romanian) a form of Peter.
Petrukas, Petrus, Petruso

Petter (Norwegian) a form of Peter.

Peverell (French) piper.
Peverall, Peverel, Peveril

Peyo (Spanish) a form of Peter.

Peyton (English) a form of Patton, Payton.
Peyt, Peyten, Peython, Peytonn

Pharaoh (Latin) ruler. History: a title for the ancient kings of Egypt.
Faroh, Pharo, Pharoah, Pharoh

Phelan (Irish) wolf.

Phelipe (Spanish) a form of Philip.

Phelix (Latin) a form of Felix.

Phelps (English) son of Phillip.

Phil (Greek) a short form of Philip, Phillip.
Fil, Phill

Philander (Greek) lover of mankind.

Philbert (English) a form of Filbert.
Philibert, Phillbert

Philemon (Greek) kiss.
Phila, Philamina, Phileman, Philémon, Philmon

Philip (Greek) lover of horses. Bible: one of the Twelve Apostles. See also Felipe, Felippo, Filip, Fillipp, Filya, Fischel, Flip.
Phelps, Phelipe, Phil, Philipp, Philippe, Philippo, Phillip, Phillipos, Phillp, Philly, Philp, Phylip, Piers, Pilib, Pilipo, Pippo

Philipp (German) a form of Philip.
Phillipp

Philippe (French) a form of Philip.
Philipe, Phillepe, Phillipe, Phillippe, Phillippee, Phyllipe

Phillip (Greek) a form of Philip.
Phil, Phillipos, Phillipp, Phillips, Philly, Phyllip

Phillipos (Greek) a form of Phillip.

Philly (American) a familiar form of Philip, Phillip.
Phillie

Philo (Greek) love.

Phinean (Irish) a form of Finian.
Phinian

Phineas (English) a form of Pinchas.
Fineas, Phinehas, Phinny

Phirun (Cambodian) rain.

Phoenix (Latin) phoenix, a legendary bird.
Phenix, Pheonix, Phynix

Phuok (Vietnamese) good.
Phuoc

Pias (Gypsy) fun.

Pickford (English) ford at the peak.

Pickworth (English) wood cutter's estate.

Pierce (English) a form of Peter.
Pearce, Peerce, Peers, Peirce, Piercy, Piers

Piero (Italian) a form of Peter.
Pero, Pierro

Pierre (French) a form of Peter.
Peirre, Piere, Pierrot

Pierre-Luc (French) a combination of Pierre + Luc.
Piere Luc

Piers (English) a form of Philip.

Pierson (English) son of Peter. See also Pearson.
Pierrson, Piersen, Piersson, Piersun

Pieter (Dutch) a form of Peter.
Pietr

Pietro (Italian) a form of Peter.

Pilar (Spanish) pillar.

Pili (Swahili) second born.

Pilipo (Hawaiian) a form of Philip.

Pillan (Native American) supreme essence.
Pilan

Pin (Vietnamese) faithful boy.

Pinchas (Hebrew) oracle. (Egyptian) dark skinned.
Phineas, Pincas, Pinchos, Pincus, Pinkas, Pinkus, Pinky

Pinky (American) a familiar form of Pinchas.
Pink

Pino (Italian) a form of Joseph.

Piñon (Tupi-Guarani) Mythology: the hunter who became the constellation Orion.

Pio (Latin) pious.

Piotr (Bulgarian) a form of Peter.
Piotrek

Pippin (German) father.

Piran (Irish) prayer. Religion: the patron saint of miners.
Peran, Pieran

Pirro (Greek, Spanish) flaming hair.

Pista (Hungarian) a familiar form of István.
Pisti

Piti (Spanish) a form of Peter.

Pitin (Spanish) a form of Felix.
Pito

Pitney (English) island of the strong-willed man.
Pittney

Pitt (English) pit, ditch.

Placido (Spanish) serene.
Placide, Placidus, Placyd, Placydo

Plato (Greek) broad shouldered. History: a famous Greek philosopher.
Platon

Platt (French) flatland.
Platte

Pol (Swedish) a form of Paul.
Pól, Pola, Poul

Poldi (German) a familiar form of Leopold.
Poldo

Pollard (German) close-cropped head.
Poll, Pollerd, Pollyrd

Pollock (English) a form of Pollux. Art: American artist Jackson Pollock was a leader of abstract expressionism.
Pollack, Polloch

Pollux (Greek) crown. Astronomy: one of the stars in the constellation Gemini.
Pollock

Polo (Tibetan) brave wanderer. (Greek) a short form of Apollo. Culture: a game played on horseback. History: Marco Polo was a thirteenth-century Venetian explorer who traveled throughout Asia.

Pomeroy (French) apple orchard.
Pommeray, Pommeroy

Ponce (Spanish) fifth. History: Juan Ponce de León of Spain searched for the Fountain of Youth in Florida.

Pony (Scottish) small horse.
Poni

Porfirio (Greek, Spanish) purple stone.
Porphirios, Prophyrios

Porter (Latin) gatekeeper.
Port, Portie, Porty

Poshita (Sanskrit) cherished.

Po Sin (Chinese) grandfather elephant.

Poul (Danish) a form of Paul.
Poulos, Poulus

Pov (Gypsy) earth.

Powa (Native American) wealthy.

Powell (English) alert.
Powel

Pramad (Hindi) rejoicing.

Pravat (Tai) history.

Prem (Hindi) love.

Prentice (English) apprentice.
Prent, Prentis, Prentiss, Printes, Printiss

Prescott (English) priest's cottage. See also Scott.
Prescot, Prestcot, Prestcott

Presley (English) priest's meadow. Music: Elvis Presley was an influential American rock 'n' roll singer.
Presleigh, Presly, Presslee, Pressley, Prestley, Priestley, Priestly

Preston (English) priest's estate.
Prestan, Presten, Prestin, Prestyn

Prewitt (French) brave little one.
Preuet, Prewet, Prewett, Prewit, Pruit, Pruitt

Price (Welsh) son of the ardent one.
Brice, Bryce, Pryce

Pricha (Tai) clever.

Primo (Italian) first; premier quality.
Preemo, Premo

Prince (Latin) chief; prince.
Prence, Prinz, Prinze

Princeton (English) princely town.
Prenston, Princeston, Princton

Proctor (Latin) official, administrator.
Prockter, Procter

Prokopios (Greek) declared leader.

Prosper (Latin) fortunate.
Prospero, Próspero

Pryor (Latin) head of the monastery; prior.
Prior, Pry

Pumeet (Sanskrit) pure.

Purdy (Hindi) recluse.

Purvis (French, English) providing food.
Pervis, Purves, Purviss

Putnam (English) dweller by the pond.
Putnem

Pyotr (Russian) a form of Peter.
Petenka, Petinka, Petrusha, Petya, Pyatr

Q

Qabil (Arabic) able.

Qadim (Arabic) ancient.

Qadir (Arabic) powerful.
Qaadir, Qadeer, Quaadir, Quadeer, Quadir

Qamar (Arabic) moon.
Quamar, Quamir

Qasim (Arabic) divider.
Quasim

Qimat (Hindi) valuable.

Quaashie (Ewe) born on Sunday.

Quadarius (American) a combination of Quan + Darius.
Quadara, Quadarious, Quadaris, Quandarious, Quandarius, Quandarrius, Qudarius, Qudaruis

Quade (Latin) fourth.
Quadell, Quaden, Quadon, Quadre, Quadrie, Quadrine, Quadrion, Quaid, Quayd, Quayde, Qwade

Quamaine (American) a combination of Quan + Jermaine.
Quamain, Quaman, Quamane, Quamayne, Quarmaine

Quan (Comanche) a short form of Quanah.

Quanah (Comanche) fragrant.
Quan

Quandre (American) a combination of Quan + Andre.
Quandrae, Quandré

Quant (Greek) how much?
Quanta, Quantae, Quantai, Quantas, Quantay, Quante, Quantea, Quantey, Quantez, Quantu

Quantavius (American) a combination of Quan + Octavius.
Quantavian, Quantavin, Quantavion, Quantavious, Quantavis, Quantavous, Quatavious, Quatavius

Quashawn (American) a combination of Quan + Shawn.
Quasean, Quashaan, Quashan, Quashaun, Quashaunn, Quashon, Quashone, Quashun, Queshan, Queshon, Qweshawn, Qyshawn

Qudamah (Arabic) courage.

Quenby (Scandinavian) a form of Quimby.

Quennell (French) small oak.
Quenell, Quennel

Quenten (Latin) a form of Quentin.
Quienten

Quentin (Latin) fifth. (English) queen's town.
Qeuntin, Quantin, Quent, Quentan, Quenten, Quentine, Quenton, Quentyn, Quentynn, Quientin, Quinten, Quintin, Quinton, Qwentin

Quenton (Latin) a form of Quentin.
Quienton

Quico (Spanish) a familiar form of many names.
Paco

Quigley (Irish) maternal side.
Quigly

Quillan (Irish) cub.
Quill, Quillen, Quillin, Quillon

Quimby (Scandinavian) woman's estate.
Quenby, Quinby

Quincy (French) fifth son's estate.
Quenci, Quency, Quince, Quincee, Quincey, Quinci, Quinn, Quinncy, Quinnsy, Quinsey, Quinzy

Quindarius (American) a combination of Quinn + Darius.
Quindarious, Quindarrius, Quinderious, Quinderus, Quindrius

Quinlan (Irish) strong; well shaped.
Quindlen, Quinlen, Quinlin, Quinn, Quinnlan, Quinnlin

Quinn (Irish) a short form of Quincy, Quinlan, Quinton.
Quin

Quintavius (American) a combination of Quinn + Octavius.
Quintavious, Quintavis, Quintavus, Quintayvious

Quinten (Latin) a form of Quentin.
Quinnten

Quintin (Latin) a form of Quentin.
Quinntin, Quintine, Quintyn

Quinton (Latin) a form of Quentin.
Quinn, Quinneton, Quinnton, Quint,
Quintan, Quintann, Quintin, Quintion,
Quintus, Quitin, Quito, Quiton,
Qunton, Qwinton

Quiqui (Spanish) a familiar form of
Enrique.
Quinto, Quiquin

Quitin (Latin) a short form of Quinton.
Quiten, Quito, Quiton

Quito (Spanish) a short form of
Quinton.

Quon (Chinese) bright.

Raanan (Hebrew) fresh; luxuriant.

Rabi (Arabic) breeze.
Rabbi, Rabee, Rabeeh, Rabiah, Rabie,
Rabih

Race (English) race.
Racel, Rayce

Racham (Hebrew) compassionate.
Rachaman, Rachamim, Rachim, Rachman,
Rachmiel, Rachum, Raham, Rahamim

Rad (English) advisor. (Slavic) happy.
Raad, Radd, Raddie, Raddy, Rade,
Radee, Radell, Radey, Radi

Radbert (English) brilliant advisor.

Radburn (English) red brook; brook
with reeds.
Radborn, Radborne, Radbourn,
Radbourne, Radburne

Radcliff (English) red cliff; cliff with
reeds.
Radcliffe, Radclyffe

Radford (English) red ford; ford with
reeds.

Radley (English) red meadow;
meadow of reeds.
Radlea, Radlee, Radleigh, Radly

Radman (Slavic) joyful.
Radmen, Radusha

Radnor (English) red shore; shore
with reeds.

Radomil (Slavic) happy peace.

Radoslaw (Polish) happy glory.
Radik, Rado, Radzmir, Slawek

Raekwon (American) a form of
Raquan.
Raekwan, Raikwan, Rakwane, Rakwon

Raequan (American) a form of
Raquan.
Raequon, Raeqwon, Raiquan, Raiquen,
Raiqoun

Raeshawn (American) a form of
Rashawn.
Raesean, Raeshaun, Raeshon, Raeshun

Rafael (Spanish) a form of Raphael.
See also Falito.
Rafaelle, Rafaello, Rafaelo, Rafal, Rafeal,
Rafeé, Rafel, Rafello, Raffael, Raffaelo,
Raffeal, Raffel, Raffiel, Rafiel

Rafaele (Italian) a form of Raphael.
Raffaele

Rafal (Polish) a form of Raphael.

Rafe (English) a short form of
Rafferty, Ralph.
Raff

Rafer (Irish) a short form of Rafferty.
Raffer

Rafferty (Irish) rich, prosperous.
Rafe, Rafer, Raferty, Raffarty, Raffer

Rafi (Arabic) exalted. (Hebrew) a
familiar form of Raphael.
Raffe, Raffee, Raffi, Raffy, Rafi

Rafiq (Arabic) friend.
Raafiq, Rafeeq, Rafic, Rafique

Raghib (Arabic) desirous.
Raquib

Raghnall (Irish) wise power.

Ragnar (Norwegian) powerful army.
Ragnor, Rainer, Rainier, Ranieri, Rayner,
Raynor, Reinhold

Rago (Hausa) ram.

Raheem (Punjabi) compassionate
God.
Rakeem

Rahim (Arabic) merciful.
Raaheim, Rahaeim, Raheam, Raheim,
Rahiem, Rahiim, Rahime, Rahium,
Rakim

Rahman (Arabic) compassionate.
Rahmatt, Rahmet

Rahul (Arabic) traveler.

Raíd (Arabic) leader.

Raiden (Japanese) Mythology: the
thunder god.
Raidan, Rayden

Raimondo (Italian) a form of
Raymond.
Raymondo, Reimundo

Raimund (German) a form of
Raymond.
Rajmund

Raimundo (Portuguese, Spanish) a
form of Raymond.
*Mundo, Raimon, Raimond, Raimonds,
Raymundo*

Raine (English) lord; wise.
Rain, Raines, Rayne

Rainer (German) counselor.
*Rainar, Rainey, Rainier, Rainor, Raynier,
Reinier*

Rainey (German) a familiar form of
Rainer.
*Raine, Rainee, Rainie, Rainney, Rainy,
Reiny*

Raini (Tupi-Guarani) Religion: the
god who created the world.

Raishawn (American) a form of
Rashawn.
Raishon, Raishun

Rajabu (Swahili) born in the seventh
month of the Islamic calendar.

Rajah (Hindi) prince; chief.
*Raj, Raja, Rajaah, Rajae, Rajahe,
Rajan, Raje, Rajeh, Raji*

Rajak (Hindi) cleansing.

Rajan (Hindi) a form of Rajah.
Rajaahn, Rajain, Rajen, Rajin

Rakeem (Punjabi) a form of Raheem.
Rakeeme, Rakeim, Rakem

Rakim (Arabic) a form of Rahim.
Rakiim

Rakin (Arabic) respectable.
Rakeen

Raktim (Hindi) bright red.

Raleigh (English) a form of Rawleigh.
Ralegh

Ralph (English) wolf counselor.
*Radolphus, Rafe, Ralf, Ralpheal,
Ralphel, Ralphie, Ralston, Raoul, Raul,
Rolf*

Ralphie (English) a familiar form of
Ralph.
Ralphy

Ralston (English) Ralph's settlement.

Ram (Hindi) god; godlike. Religion:
another name for the Hindu god
Rama. (English) male sheep. A short
form of Ramsey.
Rami, Ramie, Ramy

Ramadan (Arabic) ninth month of the
Arabic year in the Islamic calendar.
Rama

Ramanan (Hindi) god; godlike.
*Raman, Ramandeep, Ramanjit,
Ramanjot*

Rami (Hindi, English) a form of Ram.
(Spanish) a short form of Ramiro.
Rame, Ramee, Ramey, Ramih

Ramiro (Portuguese, Spanish) supreme
judge.
*Ramario, Rameer, Rameir, Ramere,
Rameriz, Ramero, Rami, Ramires,
Ramirez, Ramos*

Ramón (Spanish) a form of Raymond.
Ramon, Remon, Remone, Romone

Ramone (Dutch) a form of
Raymond.
*Raemon, Raemonn, Ramond, Ramonte,
Remone*

Ramsden (English) valley of rams.

Ramsey (English) ram's island.
*Ram, Ramsay, Ramsee, Ramsie, Ramsy,
Ramzee, Ramzey, Ramzi, Ramzy*

Rance (English) a short form of
Laurence. (American) a familiar form
of Laurence.
*Rancel, Rancell, Rances, Rancey, Rancie,
Rancy, Ransel, Ransell*

Rand (English) shield; warrior.
Randy

Randal (English) a form of Randall.
*Randahl, Randale, Randel, Randl,
Randle*

Randall (English) a form of
Randolph.
Randal, Randell, Randy, Randyll

Randolph (English) shield wolf.
*Randall, Randol, Randolf, Randolfo,
Randolpho, Randy, Ranolph*

Randy (English) a familiar form of
Rand, Randall, Randolph.
*Randdy, Randee, Randey, Randi,
Randie, Ranndy*

Ranger (French) forest keeper.
Rainger, Range

Rangle (American) cowboy.
Rangler, Wrangle

Rangsey (Cambodian) seven kinds of colors.

Rani (Hebrew) my song; my joy.
Ranen, Ranie, Ranon, Roni

Ranieri (Italian) a form of Ragnar.
Raneir, Ranier, Rannier

Ranjan (Hindi) delighted; gladdened.

Rankin (English) small shield.
Randkin

Ransford (English) raven's ford.

Ransley (English) raven's field.

Ransom (Latin) redeemer. (English) son of the shield.
Rance, Ransome, Ranson

Raoul (French) a form of Ralph, Rudolph.
Raol, Raul, Raúl, Reuel

Raphael (Hebrew) God has healed. Bible: one of the archangels. Art: a prominent painter of the Renaissance. See also Falito, Rafi.
Rafael, Rafaele, Rafal, Rafel, Raphaél, Raphale, Raphaello, Rapheal, Raphel, Raphello, Raphiel, Ray, Rephael

Rapheal (Hebrew) a form of Raphael.
Rafel, Raphiel

Rapier (French) blade-sharp.

Raquan (American) a combination of the prefix Ra + Quan.
Raaquan, Rackwon, Racquan, Raekwon, Raequan, Rahquan, Raquané, Raquon, Raquwan, Raquwn, Raquwon, Raqwan, Raqwann

Rashaad (Arabic) a form of Rashad.

Rashaan (American) a form of Rashawn.
Rasaan, Rashan, Rashann

Rashad (Arabic) wise counselor.
Raashad, Rachad, Rachard, Raeshad, Raishard, Rashaad, Rashadd, Rashade, Rashaud, Rasheed, Rashid, Rashod, Reshad, Rhashad, Rishad, Roshad

Rashard (American) a form of Richard.
Rasharrd

Rashaud (Arabic) a form of Rashad.
Rachaud, Rashaude

Rashaun (American) a form of Rashawn.

Rashawn (American) a combination of the prefix Ra + Shawn.
Raashawn, Raashen, Raeshawn, Rahshawn, Raishawn, Rasaun, Rasawn, Rashaan, Rashaun, Rashaw, Rashon, Rashun, Raushan, Raushawn, Rhashan, Rhashaun, Rhashawn

Rashean (American) a combination of the prefix Ra + Sean.
Rahsaan, Rahsean, Rahseen, Rasean, Rashane, Rasheen, Rashien, Rashiena

Rasheed (Arabic) a form of Rashad.
Rashead, Rashed, Rasheid, Rhasheed

Rashid (Arabic) a form of Rashad.
Rasheyd, Rashida, Rashidah, Rashied, Rashieda, Raushaid

Rashida (Swahili) righteous.

Rashidi (Swahili) wise counselor.

Rashod (Arabic) a form of Rashad.
Rashoda, Rashodd, Rashoud, Rayshod, Rhashod

Rashon (American) a form of Rashawn.
Rashion, Rashone, Rashonn, Rashuan, Rashun, Rashunn

Rasmus (Greek, Danish) a short form of Erasmus.

Raul (French) a form of Ralph.

Raulas (Lithuanian) a form of Laurence.

Raulo (Lithuanian) a form of Laurence.
Raulas

Raven (English) a short form of Ravenel.
Ravan, Ravean, Raveen, Ravin, Ravine, Ravon, Ravyn, Reven, Rhaven

Ravenel (English) raven.
Raven, Ravenell, Revenel

Ravi (Hindi) sun.
Ravee, Ravijot

Ravid (Hebrew) a form of Arvid.

Raviv (Hebrew) rain, dew.

Ravon (English) a form of Raven.
Raveon, Ravion, Ravone, Ravonn, Ravonne, Rayvon, Revon

Rawdon (English) rough hill.

Rawleigh (English) deer meadow.
Raleigh, Rawle, Rawley, Rawling, Rawly, Rawylyn

Rawlins (French) a form of Roland.
Rawlings, Rawlinson, Rawson

Ray (French) kingly, royal. (English) a short form of Rayburn, Raymond. See also Lei.
Rae, Raye

Rayan (Irish) a form of Ryan.
Rayaun

Rayburn (English) deer brook.
Burney, Raeborn, Raeborne, Raebourn, Ray, Raybourn, Raybourne, Rayburne

Rayce (English) a form of Race.

Rayden (Japanese) a form of Raiden.
Raidin, Raydun, Rayedon

Rayhan (Arabic) favored by God.
Rayhaan

Rayi (Hebrew) my friend, my companion.

Raymon (English) a form of Raymond.
Rayman, Raymann, Raymen, Raymone, Raymun, Reamonn

Raymond (English) mighty; wise protector. See also Aymon.
Radmond, Raemond, Raimondo, Raimund, Raimundo, Ramón, Ramond, Ramonde, Ramone, Ray, Raymand, Rayment, Raymon, Raymont, Raymund, Raymunde, Raymundo, Redmond, Reymond, Reymundo

Raymundo (Spanish) a form of Raymond.
Raemondo, Raimondo, Raimundo, Raymondo

Raynaldo (Spanish) a form of Reynold.
Raynal, Raynald, Raynold

Raynard (French) a form of Renard, Reynard.
Raynarde

Rayne (English) a form of Raine.
Raynee, Rayno

Raynor (Scandinavian) a form of Ragnar.
Rainer, Rainor, Ranier, Ranieri, Raynar, Rayner

Rayshawn (American) a combination of Ray + Shawn.
Raysean, Rayshaan, Rayshan, Rayshaun, Raysheen, Rayshon, Rayshone, Rayshonn, Rayshun, Rayshunn

Rayshod (American) a form of Rashad.
Raychard, Rayshad, Rayshard, Rayshaud

Rayvon (American) a form of Ravon.
Rayvan, Rayvaun, Rayven, Rayvone, Reyven, Reyvon

Razi (Aramaic) my secret.
Raz, Raziel, Raziq

Read (English) a form of Reed, Reid.
Raed, Raede, Raeed, Reaad, Reade

Reading (English) son of the red wanderer.
Redding, Reeding, Reiding

Reagan (Irish) little king. History: Ronald Wilson Reagan was the fortieth U.S. president.
Raegan, Reagen, Reaghan, Reegan, Reegen, Regan, Reigan, Reighan, Reign, Rheagan

Rebel (American) rebel.
Reb

Red (American) red, redhead.
Redd

Reda (Arabic) satisfied.
Ridha

Redford (English) red river crossing.
Ford, Radford, Reaford, Red, Redd

Redley (English) red meadow; meadow with reeds.
Radley, Redlea, Redleigh, Redly

Redmond (German) protecting counselor. (English) a form of Raymond.
Radmond, Radmund, Reddin, Redmund

Redpath (English) red path.

Reece (Welsh) enthusiastic; stream.
Reace, Rece, Reese, Reice, Reyes, Rhys, Rice, Ryese

Reed (English) a form of Reid.
Raeed, Read, Reyde, Rheed

Reese (Welsh) a form of Reece.
Rease, Rees, Reis, Reise, Reiss, Rhys, Riese, Riess

Reeve (English) steward.
Reave, Reaves, Reeves

Reg (English) a short form of Reginald.

Regan (Irish) a form of Reagan.
Regen

Reggie (English) a familiar form of Reginald.
Regi, Regie

Reginal (English) a form of Reginald.
Reginale, Reginel

Reginald (English) king's advisor. A form of Reynold. See also Naldo.
Reg, Reggie, Regginald, Reggis, Reginal, Reginaldo, Reginalt, Reginauld, Reginault, Reginold, Reginuld, Regnauld, Ronald

Regis (Latin) regal.

Rehema (Swahili) second-born.

Rei (Japanese) rule, law.

Reid (English) redhead.
Read, Reed, Reide, Reyd, Ried

Reidar (Norwegian) nest warrior.

Reilly (Irish) a form of Riley.
Reiley, Reilley, Reily, Rielly

Reinaldo (Spanish) a form of Reynold.

Reinhart (German) a form of Reynard.
Rainart, Rainhard, Rainhardt, Rainhart, Reinart, Reinhard, Reinhardt, Renke

Reinhold (Swedish) a form of Ragnar.
Reinold

Reku (Finnish) a form of Richard.

Remi, Rémi (French) forms of Remy.
Remie, Remmie

Remington (English) raven estate.
Rem, Reminton, Tony

Remus (Latin) speedy, quick. Mythology: Remus and his twin brother, Romulus, founded Rome.

Remy (French) from Rheims, France.
Ramey, Remee, Remi, Rémi, Remmy

Renaldo (Spanish) a form of Reynold.
Raynaldo, Reynaldo, Rinaldo

Renard (French) a form of Reynard.
Ranard, Raynard, Reinard, Rennard

Renardo (Italian) a form of Reynard.

Renato (Italian) reborn.

Renaud (French) a form of Reynard, Reynold.
Renauld, Renauldo, Renault, Renould

Rendor (Hungarian) policeman.

René (French) reborn.
Renat, Renato, Renatus, Renault, Renay, Renee, Renny

Renfred (English) lasting peace.

Renfrew (Welsh) raven woods.

Renjiro (Japanese) virtuous.

Renny (Irish) small but strong. (French) a familiar form of René.
Ren, Renn, Renne, Rennie

Reno (American) gambler. Geography: a city in Nevada known for gambling.
Renos, Rino

Renshaw (English) raven woods.
Renishaw

Renton (English) settlement of the roe deer.

Renzo (Latin) a familiar form of Laurence. (Italian) a short form of Lorenzo.
Renz, Renzy, Renzzo

Reshad (American) a form of Rashad.
Reshade, Reshard, Resharrd, Reshaud, Reshawd, Reshead, Reshod

Reshawn (American) a combination of the prefix Re + Shawn.
Reshaun, Reshaw, Reshon, Reshun

Reshean (American) a combination of the prefix Re + Sean.
Resean, Reshae, Reshane, Reshay, Reshayne, Reshea, Resheen, Reshey

Reuben (Hebrew) behold a son.
Reuban, Reubin, Reuven, Rheuben, Rhuben, Rube, Ruben, Rubey, Rubin, Ruby, Rueben

Reuven (Hebrew) a form of Reuben.
Reuvin, Rouvin, Ruvim

Rex (Latin) king.
Rexx

Rexford (English) king's ford.

Rexton (English) king's town.

Rey (Spanish) a short form of Reynaldo, Reynard, Reynold.

Reyes (English) a form of Reece.
Reyce

Reyhan (Arabic) favored by God.
Reyham

Reymond (English) a form of Raymond.
Reymon. Reymound, Reymund

Reymundo (Spanish) a form of Raymond.
Reimond, Reimonde, Reimundo, Reymon

Reynaldo (Spanish) a form of Reynold.
Renaldo, Rey, Reynauldo

Reynard (French) wise; bold, courageous.
Raynard, Reinhard, Reinhardt, Reinhart, Renard, Renardo, Renaud, Rennard, Rey, Reynardo, Reynaud

Reynold (English) king's advisor. See also Reginald.
Rainault, Rainhold, Ranald, Raynald, Raynaldo, Reinald, Reinaldo, Reinaldos, Reinhart, Reinhold, Reinold, Reinwald, Renald, Renaldi, Renaldo, Renaud, Renauld, Rennold, Renold, Rey, Reynald, Reynaldo, Reynaldos, Reynol, Reynolds, Rinaldo, Ronald

Réz (Hungarian) copper; redhead.
Rezsö

Rhett (Welsh) a form of Rhys. Literature: Rhett Butler was the hero of Margaret Mitchell's novel *Gone with the Wind*.
Rhet

Rhodes (Greek) where roses grow. Geography: an island of southeast Greece.
Rhoads, Rhodas, Rodas

Rhyan (Irish) a form of Rian.
Rhian

Rhys (Welsh) a form of Reece, Reese.
Rhett, Rhyce, Rhyse, Rice

Rian (Irish) little king.
Rhyan

Ric (Italian, Spanish) a short form of Rico.
Ricca, Ricci, Ricco

Ricardo (Portuguese, Spanish) a form of Richard.
Racardo, Recard, Ricaldo, Ricard, Ricardoe, Ricardos, Riccardo, Riccarrdo, Ricciardo, Richardo

Rice (English) rich, noble. (Welsh) a form of Reece.
Ryce

Rich (English) a short form of Richard.
Ritch

Richard (English) a form of Richart. See also Aric, Dick, Juku, Likeke.
Rashard, Reku, Ricardo, Rich, Richar, Richards, Richardson, Richart, Richaud, Richer, Richerd, Richie, Richird, Richshard, Rick, Rickard, Rickert, Rickey, Ricky, Rico, Rihardos, Rihards, Rikard, Riocard, Riócard, Risa, Risardas, Rishard, Ristéard, Ritchard, Rostik, Rye, Rysio, Ryszard

Richart (German) rich and powerful ruler.

Richie (English) a familiar form of Richard.
Richey, Richi, Richy, Rishi, Ritchie

Richman (English) powerful.

Richmond (German) powerful protector.
Richmon, Richmound

Rick (German, English) a short form of Cedric, Frederick, Richard.
Ric, Ricke, Rickey, Ricks, Ricky, Rik, Riki, Rykk

Rickard (Swedish) a form of Richard.

Ricker (English) powerful army.

Rickey (English) a familiar form of Richard, Rick, Riqui.

Rickie (English) a form of Ricky.
Rickee, Ricki

Rickward (English) mighty guardian.
Rickwerd, Rickwood

Ricky (English) a familiar form of Richard, Rick.
Ricci, Rickie, Riczi, Riki, Rikki, Rikky, Riqui

Rico (Spanish) a familiar form of Richard. (Italian) a short form of Enrico.
Ric, Ricco

Rida (Arabic) favor.

Riddock (Irish) smooth field.
Riddick

Rider (English) horseman.
Ridder, Ryder

Ridge (English) ridge of a cliff.
Ridgy, Rig, Rigg

Ridgeley (English) meadow near the ridge.
Ridgeleigh, Ridglea, Ridglee, Ridgleigh, Ridgley

Ridgeway (English) path along the ridge.

Ridley (English) meadow of reeds.
Rhidley, Riddley, Ridlea, Ridleigh, Ridly

Riel (Spanish) a short form of Gabriel.

Rigby (English) ruler' valley

Rigel (Arabic) foot. Astronomy: one of the stars in the constellation Orion

Rigg (English) ridge.
Rigo

Rigoberto (German) splendid; wealthy.
Rigobert

Rikard (Scandinavian) a form of Richard.
Rikárd

Riki (Estonian) a form of Rick.
Rikkey, Rikki, Riks, Riky

Riley (Irish) valiant.
Reilly, Rhiley, Rhylee, Rhyley, Rieley, Rielly, Riely, Rilee, Rilley, Rily, Rilye, Rylee, Ryley

Rinaldo (Italian) a form of Reynold.
Rinald, Rinaldi

Ring (English) ring.
Ringo

Ringo (Japanese) apple. (English) a familiar form of Ring.

Rio (Spanish) river. Geography: Rio de Janeiro is a city in Brazil.

Riordan (Irish) bard, royal poet.
Rearden, Reardin, Reardon

Rip (Dutch) ripe; full grown. (English) a short form of Ripley.
Ripp

Ripley (English) meadow near the river.
Rip, Ripleigh, Ripply

Riqui (Spanish) a form of Rickey.

Rishad (American) a form of Rashad.
Rishaad

Rishawn (American) a combination of the prefix Ri + Shawn.
Rishan, Rishaun, Rishon, Rishone

Rishi (Hindi) sage.

Risley (English) meadow with shrubs.
Rislea, Rislee, Risleigh, Risly, Wrisley

Risto (Finnish) a short form of Christopher.

Riston (English) settlement near the shrubs.
Wriston

Ritchard (English) a form of Richard.
Ritcherd, Ritchyrd, Ritshard, Ritsherd

Ritchie (English) a form of Richie.
Ritchy

Rithisak (Cambodian) powerful.

Ritter (German) knight; chivalrous.
Rittner

River (English) river; riverbank.
Rivers, Riviera, Rivor

Riyad (Arabic) gardens.
Riad, Riyaad, Riyadh, Riyaz, Riyod

Roald (Norwegian) famous ruler.

Roan (English) a short form of Rowan.
Rhoan

Roar (Norwegian) praised warrior.
Roary

Roarke (Irish) famous ruler.
Roark, Rorke, Rourke, Ruark

Rob (English) a short form of Robert.
Robb, Robe

Robbie (English) a familiar form of Robert.
Robie, Robbi

Robby (English) a familiar form of Robert.
Rhobbie, Robbey, Robhy, Roby

Robert (English) famous brilliance. See also Bobek, Dob, Lopaka.
Bob, Bobby, Rab, Rabbie, Raby, Riobard, Riobart, Rob, Robars, Robart, Robbie, Robby, Rober, Roberd, Robers, Roberte, Roberto, Roberts, Robin, Robinson, Roibeárd, Rosertas, Rubert, Ruberto, Rudbert, Rupert

Roberto (Italian, Portuguese, Spanish) a form of Robert.

Roberts, Robertson (English) son of Robert.
Roberson, Robertson, Robeson, Robinson, Robson

Robin (English) a short form of Robert.
Robben, Robbin, Robbins, Robbyn, Roben, Robinet, Robinn, Robins, Robyn, Roibín

Robinson (English) a form of Roberts.
Robbinson, Robens, Robenson, Robson, Robynson

Robyn (English) a form of Robin.

Rocco (Italian) rock.
Rocca, Rocio, Rocko, Rocky, Roko, Roque

Rochester (English) rocky fortress.
Chester, Chet

Rock (English) a short form of Rockwell.
Roch, Rocky

Rockford (English) rocky ford.

Rockland (English) rocky land.

Rockledge (English) rocky ledge.

Rockley (English) rocky field.
Rockle

Rockwell (English) rocky spring. Art: Norman Rockwell was a well-known twentieth-century American illustrator.
Rock

Rocky (American) a familiar form of Rocco, Rock.
Rockey, Rockie

Rod (English) a short form of Penrod, Roderick, Rodney.
Rodd

Rodas (Greek, Spanish) a form of Rhodes.

Roddy (English) a familiar form of Roderick.
Roddie, Rody

Roden (English) red valley. Art: Auguste Rodin was an innovative French sculptor.
Rodin

Roderich (German) a form of Roderick.

Roderick (German) famous ruler. See also Broderick.
Rhoderick, Rod, Rodderick, Roddy, Roderic, Roderich, Roderigo, Roderik, Roderrick, Roderyck, Rodgrick, Rodrick, Rodricki, Rodrigo, Rodrigue, Rodrugue, Roodney, Rory, Rurik, Ruy

Rodger (German) a form of Roger.
Rodge, Rodgy

Rodman (German) famous man, hero.
Rodmond

Rodney (English) island clearing.
Rhodney, Rod, Rodnee, Rodnei, Rodni, Rodnie, Rodnne, Rodny

Rodolfo (Spanish) a form of Rudolph.
Rodolpho, Rodulfo

Rodrick (German) a form of Roderick.
Roddrick, Rodric, Rodrich, Rodrik, Rodrique, Rodryck, Rodryk

Rodrigo (Italian, Spanish) a form of Roderick.

Rodriguez (Spanish) son of Rodrigo.
Roddrigues, Rodrigues, Rodriquez

Rodrik (German) famous ruler.

Rodriquez (Spanish) a form of Rodriguez.
Rodrigquez, Rodriques, Rodriquiez

Roe (English) roe deer.
Row, Rowe

Rogan (Irish) redhead.
Rogein, Rogen

Rogelio (Spanish) famous warrior.
Rojelio

Roger (German) famous spearman. See also Lokela.
Rodger, Rog, Rogelio, Rogerick, Rogerio, Rogers, Rogiero, Rojelio, Rüdiger, Ruggerio, Rutger

Rogerio (Portuguese, Spanish) a form of Roger.
Rogerios

Rohan (Hindi) sandalwood.

Rohin (Hindi) upward path.

Rohit (Hindi) big and beautiful fish.

Roi (French) a form of Roy.

Roja (Spanish) red.
Rojay

Roland (German) famous throughout the land.
Loránd, Orlando, Rawlins, Rolan, Rolanda, Rolando, Rolek, Rolland, Rolle, Rollie, Rollin, Rollo, Rowe, Rowland, Ruland

Rolando (Portuguese, Spanish) a form of Roland.
Lando, Olo, Roldan, Roldán, Rolondo

Rolf (German) a form of Ralph. A short form of Rudolph.
Rolfe, Rolle, Rolph, Rolphe

Rolle (Swedish) a familiar form of Roland, Rolf.

Rollie (English) a familiar form of Roland.
Roley, Rolle, Rolli, Rolly

Rollin (English) a form of Roland.
Rolin, Rollins

Rollo (English) a familiar form of Roland.
Rolla, Rolo

Rolon (Spanish) famous wolf.

Romain (French) a form of Roman.
Romaine, Romane, Romanne

Roman (Latin) from Rome, Italy.
Roma, Romain, Romann, Romanos, Romman, Romochka, Romy

Romanos (Greek) a form of Roman.
Romano

Romario (Italian) a form of Romeo.
Romar, Romarius, Romaro, Romarrio

Romel (Latin) a short form of Romulus.
Romele, Romell, Romello, Rommel

Romello (Italian) of Romel.
Romelo, Rommello

Romeo (Italian) pilgrim to Rome; Roman. Literature: the title character of the Shakespearean play *Romeo and Juliet*.
Romario, Roméo, Romero

Romero (Latin) a form of Romeo.
Romario, Romeiro, Romer, Romere, Romerio, Romeris, Romeryo

Romney (Welsh) winding river.
Romoney

Romulus (Latin) citizen of Rome. Mythology: Romulus and his twin brother, Remus, founded Rome.
Romel, Romolo, Romono, Romulo

Romy (Italian) a familiar form of Roman.
Rommie, Rommy

Ron (Hebrew) a short form of Aaron, Ronald.
Ronn

Ronald (Scottish) a form of Reginald.
Ranald, Ron, Ronal, Ronaldo, Ronnald, Ronney, Ronnie, Ronnold, Ronoldo

Ronaldo (Portuguese) a form of Ronald.

Rónán (Irish) seal.
Renan, Ronan, Ronat

Rondel (French) short poem.
Rondal, Rondale, Rondall, Rondeal, Rondell, Rondey, Rondie, Rondrell, Rondy, Ronel

Ronel (American) a form of Rondel.
Ronell, Ronelle, Ronnel, Ronnell, Ronyell

Roni (Hebrew) my song; my joy.
Rani, Roneet, Roney, Ronit, Ronli, Rony

Ronnie (Scottish) a familiar form of Ronald.
Roni, Ronie, Ronnie, Ronny

Ronny (Scottish) a form of Ronnie.
Ronney

Ronson (Scottish) son of Ronald.
Ronaldson

Ronté (American) a combination of Ron + the suffix Te.
Rontae, Rontay, Ronte, Rontez

Rooney (Irish) redhead.

Roosevelt (Dutch) rose field. History: Theodore and Franklin D. Roosevelt were the twenty-sixth and thirty-second U.S. presidents, respectively.
Roosvelt, Rosevelt

Roper (English) rope maker.

Rory (German) a familiar form of Roderick. (Irish) red king.
Rorey, Rori, Rorrie, Rorry

Rosalio (Spanish) rose.
Rosalino

Rosario (Portuguese) rosary.

Roscoe (Scandinavian) deer forest.
Rosco

Roshad (American) a form of Rashad.
Roshard

Roshean (American) a combination of the prefix Ro + Sean.
Roshain, Roshan, Roshane, Roshaun, Roshawn, Roshay, Rosheen, Roshene

Rosito (Filipino) rose.

Ross (Latin) rose. (Scottish) peninsula. (French) red.
Rosse, Rossell, Rossi, Rossie, Rossy

Rosswell (English) springtime of roses.
Rosvel

Rostislav (Czech) growing glory.
Rosta, Rostya

Roswald (English) field of roses.
Ross, Roswell

Roth (German) redhead.

Rothwell (Scandinavian) red spring.

Rover (English) traveler.

Rowan (English) tree with red berries.
Roan, Rowe, Rowen, Rowney, Rowyn

Rowell (English) roe-deer well.

Rowland (English) rough land.
(German) a form of Roland.
Rowlando, Rowlands, Rowlandson

Rowley (English) rough meadow.
Rowlea, Rowlee, Rowleigh, Rowly

Rowson (English) son of the redhead.

Roxbury (English) rook's town or
fortress.
Roxburghe

Roy (French) king. A short form of
Royal, Royce. See also Conroy,
Delroy, Fitzroy, Leroy, Loe.
Rey, Roi, Roye, Ruy

Royal (French) kingly, royal.
Roy, Royale, Royall, Royell

Royce (English) son of Roy.
Roice, Roy, Royz

Royden (English) rye hill.
Royd, Roydan

Ruben (Hebrew) a form of Reuben.
*Ruban, Rube, Rubean, Rubens, Rubin,
Ruby*

Rubert (Czech) a form of Robert.

Ruby (Hebrew) a familiar form of
Reuben, Ruben.

Rudd (English) a short form of
Rudyard.

Ruda (Czech) a form of Rudolph.
Rude, Rudek

Rudi (Spanish) a familiar form of
Rudolph.
Ruedi

Rudo (Shona) love.

Rudolf (German) a form of Rudolph.
Rodolf, Rodolfo, Rudolfo

Rudolph (German) famous wolf. See
also Dolf.
*Raoul, Rezsó, Rodolfo, Rodolph,
Rodolphe, Rolf, Ruda, Rudek, Rudi,
Rudolf, Rudolpho, Rudolphus, Rudy*

Rudolpho (Italian) a form of
Rudolph.

Rudy (English) a familiar form of
Rudolph.
*Roody, Ruddy, Ruddie, Rudey, Rudi,
Rudie*

Rudyard (English) red enclosure.
Rudd

Rueben (Hebrew) a form of Reuben.
Rueban, Ruebin

Ruff (French) redhead.

Rufin (Polish) redhead.
Rufino

Ruford (English) red ford; ford with
reeds.
Rufford

Rufus (Latin) redhead.
*Rayfus, Rufe, Ruffis, Ruffus, Rufino,
Rufo, Rufous*

Rugby (English) rook fortress. History:
a famous British school after which
the sport of Rugby was named.

Ruggerio (Italian) a form of Roger.
Rogero, Ruggero, Ruggiero

Ruhakana (Rukiga) argumentative.

Ruland (German) a form of Roland.
Rulan, Rulon, Rulondo

Rumford (English) wide river crossing.

Runako (Shona) handsome.

Rune (German, Swedish) secret.

Runrot (Tai) prosperous.

Rupert (German) a form of Robert.
Ruperth, Ruperto, Ruprecht

Ruperto (Italian) a form of Rupert.

Ruprecht (German) a form of
Rupert.

Rush (French) redhead. (English) a
short form of Russell.
Rushi

Rushford (English) ford with rushes.

Rusk (Spanish) twisted bread.

Ruskin (French) redhead.
Rush, Russ

Russ (French) a short form of Russell.

Russel (French) a form of Russell.

Russell (French) redhead; fox colored. See also Lukela.
Roussell, Rush, Russ, Russel, Russelle, Rusty

Rusty (French) a familiar form of Russell.
Ruste, Rusten, Rustie, Rustin, Ruston, Rustyn

Rutger (Scandinavian) a form of Roger.
Ruttger

Rutherford (English) cattle ford.
Rutherfurd

Rutland (Scandinavian) red land.

Rutledge (English) red ledge.

Rutley (English) red meadow.

Ruy (Spanish) a short form of Roderick.
Rui

Ryan (Irish) little king.
Rayan, Rhyan, Rhyne, Ryane, Ryann, Ryen, Ryian, Ryiann, Ryin, Ryne, Ryon, Ryuan, Ryun, Ryyan

Rycroft (English) rye field.
Ryecroft

Ryder (English) a form of Rider.
Rydder, Rye

Rye (English) a short form of Ryder. A grain used in cereal and whiskey. (Gypsy) gentleman.
Ry.

Ryen (Irish) a form of Ryan.
Ryein, Ryien

Ryerson (English) son of Rider, Ryder.

Ryese (English) a form of Reece.
Reyse, Ryez, Ryse

Ryker (American) a surname used as a first name.
Riker, Ryk

Rylan (English) land where rye is grown.
Ryland, Rylean, Rylen, Rylin, Rylon, Rylyn, Rylynn

Ryland (English) a form of Rylan.
Ryeland, Rylund

Ryle (English) rye hill.
Ryal, Ryel

Rylee (Irish) a form of Riley.
Ryeleigh, Ryleigh, Rylie, Rillie

Ryley (Irish) a form of Riley.
Ryely

Ryman (English) rye seller.

Ryne (Irish) a form of Ryan.
Rynn

Ryon (Irish) a form of Ryan.

Sabastian (Greek) a form of Sebastian.
Sabastain, Sabastiano, Sabastien, Sabastin, Sabastion, Sabaston, Sabbastiun, Sabestian

Saber (French) sword.
Sabir, Sabre

Sabin (Basque) ancient tribe of central Italy.
Saban, Saben, Sabian, Sabien, Sabino

Sabiti (Rutooro) born on Sunday.

Sabola (Nguni) pepper.

Saburo (Japanese) third-born son.

Sacha (Russian) a form of Sasha.
Sascha

Sachar (Russian) a form of Zachary.

Saddam (Arabic) powerful ruler.

Sadiki (Swahili) faithful.
Saadiq, Sadeek, Sadek, Sadik, Sadiq, Sadique

Sadler (English) saddle maker.
Saddler

Safari (Swahili) born while traveling.
Safa, Safarian

Safford (English) willow river crossing.

Sage (English) wise. Botany: an herb.
Sagen, Sager, Saige, Saje

Sahale (Native American) falcon.
Sael, Sahal, Sahel, Sahil

Sahen (Hindi) above.
Sahan

Sahil (Native American) a form of Sahale.
Saheel, Sahel

Sahir (Hindi) friend.

Sa'id (Arabic) happy.
Sa'ad, Saaid, Saed, Sa'eed, Saeed,
Sahid, Saide, Sa'ied, Saied, Saiyed,
Saiyeed, Sajid, Sajjid, Sayed, Sayeed,
Sayid, Seyed, Shahid

Sajag (Hindi) watchful.

Saka (Swahili) hunter.

Sakeri (Danish) a form of Zachary.
Sakarai, Sakari

Sakima (Native American) king.

Sakuruta (Pawnee) coming sun.

Sal (Italian) a short form of Salvatore.

Salam (Arabic) lamb.
Salaam

Salamon (Spanish) a form of
Solomon.
Saloman, Salomón

Salaun (French) a form of Solomon.

Sálih (Arabic) right, good.
Saleeh, Saleh, Salehe

Salim (Swahili) peaceful.

Salím (Arabic) peaceful, safe.
Saleem, Salem, Saliym, Salman

Salmalin (Hindi) taloned.

Salman (Czech) a form of Salím,
Solomon.
Salmaan, Salmaine, Salmon

Salomon (French) a form of
Solomon.
Salomone

Salton (English) manor town; willow
town.

Salvador (Spanish) savior.
Salvadore

Salvatore (Italian) savior. See also
Xavier.
Sal, Salbatore, Sallie, Sally, Salvator,
Salvattore, Salvidor, Sauveur

Sam (Hebrew) a short form of
Samuel.
Samm, Sammy, Sem, Shem, Shmuel

Sambo (American) a familiar form of
Samuel.
Sambou

Sameer (Arabic) a form of Samír.

Sami, Samy (Hebrew) forms of
Sammy.
Sameeh, Sameh, Samie, Samih, Sammi

Samír (Arabic) entertaining companion.
Sameer

Samman (Arabic) grocer.
Saman, Sammon

Sammy (Hebrew) a familiar form of
Samuel.
Saamy, Samey, Sami, Sammee, Sammey,
Sammie, Samy

Samo (Czech) a form of Samuel.
Samho, Samko

Samson (Hebrew) like the sun. Bible:
a judge and powerful warrior
betrayed by Delilah
Sampson, Sansao, Sansom, Sansón,
Shem, Shimshon

Samual (Hebrew) a form of Samuel.
Samuael, Samuail

Samuel (Hebrew) heard God; asked of
God. Bible: a famous Old Testament
prophet and judge. See also Kamuela,
Zamiel, Zanvil.
Sam, Samael, Samaru, Samauel,
Samaul, Sambo, Sameul, Samiel,
Sammail, Sammel, Sammuel, Sammy,
Samo, Samouel, Samu, Samual,
Samuele, Samuelis, Samuell, Samuello,
Samuil, Samuka, Samule, Samuru,
Samvel, Sanko, Saumel, Schmuel, Shem,
Shmuel, Simão, Simuel, Somhairle,
Zamuel

Samuele (Italian) a form of Samuel.
Samulle

Samuru (Japanese) a form of Samuel.

Sanat (Hindi) ancient.

Sanborn (English) sandy brook.
Sanborne, Sanbourn, Sanbourne,
Sanburn, Sanburne, Sandborn,
Sandbourne

Sanchez (Latin) a form of Sancho.
Sanchaz, Sancheze

Sancho (Latin) sanctified; sincere.
Literature: Sancho Panza was Don
Quixote's squire.
Sanchez, Sauncho

Sandeep (Punjabi) enlightened.
Sandip

Sander (English) a short form of
Alexander, Lysander.
Sandor, Sándor, Saunder

Sanders (English) son of Sander.
Sanderson, Saunders, Saunderson

Sándor (Hungarian) a short form of
Alexander.
Sanyi

Sandro (Greek, Italian) a short form
of Alexander.
*Sandero, Sandor, Sandre, Saundro,
Shandro*

Sandy (English) a familiar form of
Alexander.
Sande, Sandey, Sandi, Sandie

Sanford (English) sandy river crossing.
Sandford

Sani (Hindi) the planet Saturn.
(Navajo) old.

Sanjay (American) a combination of
Sanford + Jay.
Sanjaya, Sanje, Sanjey, Sanjo

Sanjiv (Hindi) long lived.
Sanjeev

Sankar (Hindi) a form of Shankara,
another name for the Hindu god
Shiva.

Sansón (Spanish) a form of Samson.
Sanson, Sansone, Sansun

Santana (Spanish) History: Antonio
López de Santa Anna was a Mexican
general and political leader.
Santanna

Santiago (Spanish) a form of James.

Santino (Spanish) a form of Santonio.
Santion

Santo (Italian, Spanish) holy.
Santos

Santon (English) sandy town.

Santonio (Spanish) Geography: a short
form of San Antonio, a city in Texas.
Santino, Santon, Santoni

Santos (Spanish) saint.
Santo

Santosh (Hindi) satisfied.

Sanyu (Luganda) happy.

Saqr (Arabic) falcon.

Saquan (American) a combination of
the prefix Sa + Quan.
*Saquané, Saquin, Saquon, Saqwan,
Saqwone*

Sarad (Hindi) born in the autumn.

Sargent (French) army officer.
*Sargant, Sarge, Sarjant, Sergeant,
Sergent, Serjeant*

Sarito (Spanish) a form of Caesar.
Sarit

Sariyah (Arabic) clouds at night.

Sarngin (Hindi) archer; protector.

Sarojin (Hindi) like a lotus.
Sarojun

Sasha (Russian) a short form of
Alexander.
*Sacha, Sash, Sashenka, Sashka, Sashok,
Sausha*

Sasson (Hebrew) joyful.
Sason

Satchel (French) small bag.
Satch

Satordi (French) Saturn.
Satori

Saul (Hebrew) asked for, borrowed.
Bible: in the Old Testament, a king of
Israel and the father of Jonathan; in
the New Testament, Saint Paul's orig-
inal name was Saul.
Saül, Shaul, Sol, Solly

Saverio (Italian) a form of Xavier.

Saville (French) willow town.
*Savelle, Savil, Savile, Savill, Savylle,
Seville, Siville*

Savon (Spanish) a treeless plain.
*Savan, Savaughn, Saveion, Saveon,
Savhon, Saviahn, Savian, Savino,
Savion, Savo, Savone, Sayvon, Sayvone*

Saw (Burmese) early.

Sawyer (English) wood worker.
Sawyere

Sax (English) a short form of Saxon.
Saxe

Saxon (English) swordsman. History:
the Roman name for the Teutonic
raiders who ravaged the Roman
British coasts.
Sax, Saxen, Saxsin, Saxxon

Sayer (Welsh) carpenter.
Say, Saye, Sayers, Sayr, Sayre, Sayres

Sayyid (Arabic) master.
Sayed, Sayid, Sayyad, Sayyed

Scanlon (Irish) little trapper.
Scanlan, Scanlen

Schafer (German) shepherd.
Schaefer, Schaffer, Schiffer, Shaffar, Shäffer

Schmidt (German) blacksmith.
Schmid, Schmit, Schmitt, Schmydt

Schneider (German) tailor.
Schnieder, Snider, Snyder

Schön (German) handsome.
Schoen, Schönn, Shon

Schuyler (Dutch) sheltering.
Schuylar, Schyler, Scoy, Scy, Skuyler, Sky, Skylar, Skyler, Skylor

Schyler (Dutch) a form of Schuyler.
Schylar, Schylre, Schylur

Scorpio (Latin) dangerous, deadly. Astronomy: a southern constellation near Libra and Sagittarius. Astrology: the eighth sign of the zodiac.
Scorpeo

Scott (English) from Scotland. A familiar form of Prescott.
Scot, Scottie, Scotto, Scotty

Scottie (English) a familiar form of Scott.
Scotie, Scotti

Scotty (English) a familiar form of Scott.
Scottey

Scoville (French) Scott's town.

Scully (Irish) town crier.

Seabert (English) shining sea.
Seabright, Sebert, Seibert

Seabrook (English) brook near the sea.

Seamus (Irish) a form of James.
Seamas, Seumas, Shamus

Sean (Hebrew) God is gracious. (Irish) a form of John.
Seaghan, Séan, Seán, Seanán, Seane, Seann, Shaan, Shaine, Shane, Shaun, Shawn, Shayne, Shon, Siôn

Searlas (Irish, French) a form of Charles.
Séarlas, Searles, Searlus

Searle (English) armor.

Seasar (Latin) a form of Caesar.
Seasare, Seazar, Sesar, Sesear, Sezar

Seaton (English) town near the sea.
Seeton, Seton

Sebastian (Greek) venerable. (Latin) revered.
Bastian, Sabastian, Sabastien, Sebashtian, Sebastain, Sebastiane, Sebastiano, Sebastien, Sébastien, Sebastin, Sebastine, Sebastion, Sebbie, Sebestyén, Sebo, Sepasetiano

Sebastien, Sébastien (French) forms of Sebastian.
Sebasten, Sebastyen

Sebastion (Greek) a form of Sebastian.

Sedgely (English) sword meadow.
Sedgeley, Sedgly

Sedric (Irish) a form of Cedric.
Seddrick, Sederick, Sedrick, Sedrik, Sedriq

Seeley (English) blessed.
Sealey, Seely, Selig

Sef (Egyptian) yesterday. Mythology: one of the two lions that make up the Akeru, guardian of the gates of morning and night.

Sefton (English) village of rushes.

Sefu (Swahili) sword.

Seger (English) sea spear; sea warrior.
Seager, Seeger, Segar

Segun (Yoruba) conqueror.

Segundo (Spanish) second.

Seibert (English) bright sea.
Seabert, Sebert

Seif (Arabic) religion's sword.

Seifert (German) a form of Siegfried.

Sein (Basque) innocent.

Sekaye (Shona) laughter.

Selby (English) village by the mansion.
Selbey, Shelby

Seldon (English) willow tree valley.
Selden, Sellden

Selig (German) a form of Seeley.
Seligman, Seligmann, Zelig

Selwyn (English) friend from the palace.
Selvin, Selwin, Selwinn, Selwynn, Selwynne, Wyn

Semanda (Luganda) cow clan.

Semer (Ethiopian) a form of George.
Semere, Semier

Semon (Greek) a form of Simon.
Semion

Sempala (Luganda) born in prosperous times.

Sen (Japanese) wood fairy.
Senh

Sener (Turkish) bringer of joy.

Senior (French) lord.

Sennett (French) elderly.
Sennet

Senon (Spanish) living.

Senwe (African) dry as a grain stalk.

Sepp (German) a form of Joseph.
Seppi

Septimus (Latin) seventh.

Serafino (Portuguese) a form of Seraphim.

Seraphim (Hebrew) fiery, burning. Bible: the highest order of angels, known for their zeal and love.
Saraf, Saraph, Serafim, Serafin, Serafino, Seraphimus, Seraphin

Sereno (Latin) calm, tranquil.

Serge (Latin) attendant.
Seargeoh, Serg, Sergei, Sergio, Sergios, Sergius, Sergiusz, Serguel, Sirgio, Sirgios

Sergei (Russian) a form of Serge.
Sergey, Sergeyuk, Serghey, Sergi, Sergie, Sergo, Sergunya, Serhiy, Serhiyko, Serjiro, Serzh

Sergio (Italian) a form of Serge.
Serginio, Serigo, Serjio

Servando (Spanish) to serve.
Servan, Servio

Seth (Hebrew) appointed. Bible: the third son of Adam.
Set, Sethan, Sethe, Shet

Setimba (Luganda) river dweller. Geography: a river in Uganda.

Seumas (Scottish) a form of James.
Seaumus

Severiano (Italian) a form of Séverin.

Séverin (French) severe.
Seve, Sevé, Severan, Severian, Severiano, Severo, Sevien, Sevrin, Sevryn

Severn (English) boundary.
Sevearn, Sevren, Sevrnn

Sevilen (Turkish) beloved.

Seward (English) sea guardian.
Sewerd, Siward

Sewati (Moquelumnan) curved bear claws.

Sexton (English) church official; sexton.

Sextus (Latin) sixth.
Sixtus

Seymour (French) prayer. Religion: name honoring Saint Maur. See also Maurice.
Seamor, Seamore, Seamour, See

Shabouh (Armenian) king, noble. History: a fourth-century Persian king.

Shad (Punjabi) happy-go-lucky.
Shadd

Shadi (Arabic) singer.
Shadde, Shaddi, Shaddy, Shade, Shadee, Shadeed, Shadey, Shadie, Shady, Shydee, Shydi

Shadrach (Babylonian) god; godlike. Bible: one of three companions who emerged unharmed from the fiery furnace of Babylon.
Shad, Shadrack, Shadrick, Sheddrach, Shedrach, Shedrick

Shadwell (English) shed by a well.

Shah (Persian) king. History: a title for rulers of Iran.

Shaheem (American) a combination of Shah + Raheem.
Shaheim, Shahiem, Shahm

Shahid (Arabic) a form of Sa'id.
Shahed, Shaheed

Shai (Hebrew) a short form of Yeshaya.
Shaie

Shaiming (Chinese) life; sunshine.

Shaine (Irish) a form of Sean.
Shain

Shaka (Zulu) founder, first. History: Shaka Zulu was the founder of the Zulu empire.

Shakeel (Arabic) a form of Shaquille.
Shakeil, Shakel, Shakell, Shakiel, Shakil, Shakille, Shakyle

Shakir (Arabic) thankful.
Shaakir, Shakeer, Shakeir, Shakur

Shakur (Arabic) a form of Shakir.
Shakuur

Shalom (Hebrew) peace.
Shalum, Shlomo, Sholem, Sholom

Shalya (Hindi) throne.

Shaman (Sanskrit) holy man, mystic, medicine man.
Shamaine, Shamaun, Shamin, Shamine, Shammon, Shamon, Shamone

Shamar (Hebrew) a form of Shamir.
Shamaar, Shamare, Shamari

Shamir (Hebrew) precious stone.
Shahmeer, Shahmir, Shamar, Shameer,
Shamyr

Shamus (American) slang for detective.
Shamas, Shames, Shamos, Shemus

Shan (Irish) a form of Shane.
Shann, Shanne

Shanahan (Irish) wise, clever.

Shandy (English) rambunctious
Shandey, Shandie

Shane (Irish) a form of Sean.
Shan, Shayn, Shayne

Shangobunni (Yoruba) gift from
Shango.

Shanley (Irish) small; ancient.
Shaneley, Shannley

Shannon (Irish) small and wise.
Shanan, Shannan, Shannen, Shannin,
Shannone, Shanon

Shantae (French) a form of Chante.
Shant, Shanta, Shantai, Shante,
Shantell, Shantelle, Shanti, Shantia,
Shantie, Shanton, Shanty

Shap (English) a form of Shep.

Shaquan (American) a combination
of the prefix Sha + Quan.
Shaqaun, Shaquand, Shaquane,
Shaquann, Shaquaunn, Shaquawn,
Shaquen, Shaquian, Shaquin, Shaqwan

Shaquell (American) a form of
Shaquille.
Shaqueal, Shaqueil, Shaquel, Shaquelle,
Shaquiel, Shaquiell, Shaquielle

Shaquille (Arabic) handsome.
Shakeel, Shaquell, Shaquil, Shaquile,
Shaquill, Shaqul

Shaquon (American) a combination
of the prefix Sha + Quon.
Shaikwon, Shaqon, Shaquoin, Shaquoné

Sharad (Pakistani) autumn.
Sharod

Sharíf (Arabic) honest; noble.
Shareef, Sharef, Shareff, Shareif, Sharief,
Sharife, Shariff, Shariyf, Sharrif, Sharyif

Sharod (Pakistani) a form of Sharad.
Sharrod

Sharron (Hebrew) flat area, plain.
Sharon, Sharone, Sharonn, Sharonne

Shattuck (English) little shad fish.

Shaun (Irish) a form of Sean.
Shaughan, Shaughn, Shaugn, Shauna,
Shaunahan, Shaune, Shaunn, Shaunne

Shavar (Hebrew) comet.
Shavit

Shavon (American) a combination of
the prefix Sha + Yvon.
Shauvan, Shauvon, Shavan, Shavaughn,
Shaven, Shavin, Shavone, Shawan,
Shawon, Shawun

Shaw (English) grove.

Shawn (Irish) a form of Sean.
Shawen, Shawne, Shawnee, Shawnn,
Shawon

Shawnta (American) a combination of
Shawn + the suffix Ta.
Shawntae, Shawntel, Shawnti

Shay (Irish) a form of Shea.
Shae, Shai, Shaya, Shaye, Shey

Shayan (Cheyenne) a form of
Cheyenne.
Shayaan, Shayann, Shayon

Shayne (Hebrew) a form of Sean.
Shayn, Shaynne, Shean

Shea (Irish) courteous.
Shay

Shedrick (Babylonian) a form of
Shadrach.
Shadriq, Shederick, Shedric, Shedrique

Sheehan (Irish) little; peaceful.
Shean

Sheffield (English) crooked field.
Field, Shef, Sheff, Sheffie, Sheffy

Shel (English) a short form of Shelby,
Sheldon, Shelton.

Shelby (English) ledge estate.
Shel, Shelbe, Shelbey, Shelbie, Shell,
Shellby, Shelley, Shelly

Sheldon (English) farm on the ledge.
Shel, Sheldan, Shelden, Sheldin,
Sheldyn, Shell, Shelley, Shelly, Shelton

Shelley (English) a familiar form of
Shelby, Sheldon, Shelton. Literature:
Percy Bysshe Shelley was a
nineteenth-century British poet.
Shell, Shelly

Shelton (English) town on a ledge.
Shel, Shelley, Shelten

Shem (Hebrew) name; reputation.
(English) a short form of Samuel.
Bible: Noah's oldest son.

Shen (Egyptian) sacred amulet (Chinese) meditation.

Shep (English) a short form of Shepherd.
Shap, Ship, Shipp

Shepherd (English) shepherd.
Shep, Shepard, Shephard, Shepp, Sheppard, Shepperd

Shepley (English) sheep meadow.
Sheplea, Sheplee, Shepply, Shipley

Sherborn (English) clear brook.
Sherborne, Sherbourn, Sherburn, Sherburne

Sheridan (Irish) wild.
Dan, Sheredan, Sheriden, Sheridon, Sherridan

Sherill (English) shire on a hill.
Sheril, Sherril, Sherrill

Sherlock (English) light haired. Literature: Sherlock Holmes is a famous British detective character, created by Sir Arthur Conan Doyle.
Sherlocke, Shurlock, Shurlocke

Sherman (English) sheep shearer; resident of a shire.
Scherman, Schermann, Sherm, Shermain, Shermaine, Shermann, Shermie, Shermon, Shermy

Sherrod (English) clearer of the land.
Sherod, Sherrad, Sherrard, Sherrodd

Sherwin (English) swift runner, one who cuts the wind.
Sherveen, Shervin, Sherwan, Sherwind, Sherwinn, Sherwyn, Sherwynd, Sherwynne, Win

Sherwood (English) bright forest.
Sherwoode, Shurwood, Woody

Shihab (Arabic) blaze.

Shìlín (Chinese) intellectual.
Shilan

Shiloh (Hebrew) God's gift.
Shi, Shile, Shiley, Shilo, Shiloe, Shy, Shyle, Shylo, Shyloh

Shimon (Hebrew) a form of Simon.
Shymon

Shimshon (Hebrew) a form of Samson.
Shimson

Shing (Chinese) victory.
Shingae, Shingo

Shipton (English) sheep village; ship village.

Shiquan (American) a combination of the prefix Shi + Quan.
Shiquane, Shiquann, Shiquawn, Shiquoin, Shiqwan

Shiro (Japanese) fourth-born son.

Shiva (Hindi) life and death. Religion: the most common name for the Hindu god of destruction and reproduction.
Shiv, Shivan, Siva

Shlomo (Hebrew) a form of Solomon.
Shelmu, Shelomo, Shelomoh, Shlomi, Shlomot

Shmuel (Hebrew) a form of Samuel.
Shem, Shemuel, Shmelke, Shmiel, Shmulka

Shneur (Yiddish) senior.
Shneiur

Shon (German) a form of Schön. (American) a form of Sean.
Shoan, Shoen, Shondae, Shondale, Shondel, Shone, Shonn, Shonntay, Shontae, Shontarious, Shouan, Shoun

Shunnar (Arabic) pheasant.

Si (Hebrew) a short form of Silas, Simon.
Sy

Sid (French) a short form of Sidney.
Cyd, Siddie, Siddy, Sidey, Syd

Siddel (English) wide valley.
Siddell

Siddhartha (Hindi) History: Siddhartha Gautama was the original name of Buddha, the founder of Buddhism.
Sida, Siddartha, Siddhaarth, Siddhart, Siddharth, Sidh, Sidharth, Sidhartha, Sidhdharth

Sidney (French) from Saint-Denis, France.
Cydney, Sid, Sidnee, Sidny, Sidon, Sidonio, Sydney, Sydny

Sidonio (Spanish) a form of Sidney.

Sidwell (English) wide stream.

Siegfried (German) victorious peace. See also Zigfrid, Ziggy.
Seifert, Seifried, Siegfred, Siffre, Sig, Sigfrid, Sigfried, Sigfroi, Sigfryd, Siggy, Sigifredo, Sigvard, Singefrid, Sygfried, Szygfrid

Sierra (Irish) black. (Spanish) saw-toothed.
Siera

Sig (German) a short form of Siegfried, Sigmund.

Sigifredo (German) a form of Siegfried.
Sigefriedo, Sigfrido, Siguefredo

Siggy (German) a familiar form of Siegfried, Sigmund.

Sigmund (German) victorious protector. See also Ziggy, Zsigmond, Zygmunt.
Siegmund, Sig, Siggy, Sigismond, Sigismondo, Sigismund, Sigismundo, Sigismundus, Sigmond, Sigsmond, Szygmond

Sigurd (German, Scandinavian) victorious guardian.
Sigord, Sjure, Syver

Sigwald (German) victorious leader.

Silas (Latin) a short form of Silvan.
Si, Sias, Sylas

Silvan (Latin) forest dweller.
Silas, Silvain, Silvano, Silvaon, Silvie, Silvio, Sylvain, Sylvan, Sylvanus, Sylvio

Silvano (Italian) a form of Silvan.
Silvanos, Silvanus, Silvino

Silvester (Latin) a form of Sylvester.
Silvestr, Silvestre, Silvestro, Silvy

Silvestro (Italian) a form of Sylvester.

Silvio (Italian) a form of Silvan.

Simão (Portuguese) a form of Samuel.

Simba (Swahili) lion. (Yao) a short form of Lisimba.
Sim

Simcha (Hebrew) joyful.
Simmy

Simeon (French) a form of Simon.
Simione, Simone

Simms (Hebrew) son of Simon.
Simm, Sims

Simmy (Hebrew) a familiar form of Simcha, Simon.
Simmey, Simmi, Simmie, Symmy

Simon (Hebrew) he heard. Bible: one of the Twelve Disciples. See also Symington, Ximenes.
Saimon, Samien, Semon, Shimon, Si, Sim, Simao, Simen, Simeon, Simion, Simm, Simmon, Simmonds, Simmons, Simms, Simmy, Simonas, Simone, Simson, Simyon, Síomón, Symon, Szymon

Simpson (Hebrew) son of Simon.
Simonson, Simson

Sinclair (French) prayer. Religion: name honoring Saint Clair.
Sinclare, Synclair

Singh (Hindi) lion.
Sing

Sinjon (English) saint, holy man. Religion: name honoring Saint John.
Sinjin, Sinjun, Sjohn, Syngen, Synjen, Synjon

Sipatu (Moquelumnan) pulled out.

Sipho (Zulu) present.

Siraj (Arabic) lamp, light.

Siseal (Irish) a form of Cecil.

Sisi (Fante) born on Sunday.

Siva (Hindi) a form of Shiva.
Siv

Sivan (Hebrew) ninth month of the Jewish year.

Siwatu (Swahili) born during a time of conflict.
Siwazuri

Siwili (Native American) long fox's tail.

Skah (Lakota) white.
Skai

Skee (Scandinavian) projectile.
Ski, Skie

Skeeter (English) swift.
Skeat, Skeet, Skeets

Skelly (Irish) storyteller.
Shell, Skelley, Skellie

Skelton (Dutch) shell town.

Skerry (Scandinavian) stony island.

Skip (Scandinavian) a short form of Skipper.

Skipper (Scandinavian) shipmaster.
Skip, Skipp, Skippie, Skipton

Skiriki (Pawnee) coyote.

Skule (Norwegian) hidden.

Skye (Dutch) a short form of Skylar, Skyler, Skylor.
Sky

Skylar (Dutch) a form of Schuyler.
Skilar, Skkylar, Skye, Skyelar, Skylaar, Skylare, Skylarr, Skylayr

Skyler (Dutch) a form of Schuyler.
Skieler, Skiler, Skye, Skyeler, Skylee, Skyller

Skylor (Dutch) a form of Schuyler.
Skye, Skyelor, Skyloer, Skylore, Skylour, Skylur, Skylyr

Slade (English) child of the valley.
Slaide, Slayde

Slane (Czech) salty.
Slan

Slater (English) roof slater.
Slader, Slate, Slayter

Slava (Russian) a short form of Stanislav, Vladislav, Vyacheslav.
Slavik, Slavoshka

Slawek (Polish) a short form of Radoslaw.

Slevin (Irish) mountaineer.
Slaven, Slavin, Slawin

Sloan (Irish) warrior.
Sloane, Slone

Smedley (English) flat meadow.
Smedleigh, Smedly

Smith (English) blacksmith.
Schmidt, Smid, Smidt, Smitt, Smitty, Smyth, Smythe

Snowden (English) snowy hill.
Snowdon

Socrates (Greek) wise, learned. History: a famous ancient Greek philosopher.
Socratis, Sokrates, Sokratis

Sofian (Arabic) devoted.

Sohrab (Persian) ancient hero.

Soja (Yoruba) soldier.

Sol (Hebrew) a short form of Saul, Solomon.
Soll, Sollie, Solly

Solly (Hebrew) a familiar form of Saul, Solomon.
Sollie, Zollie, Zolly

Solomon (Hebrew) peaceful. Bible: a king of Israel famous for his wisdom. See also Zalman.
Salamen, Salamon, Salamun, Salaun, Salman, Salomo, Salomon, Selim, Shelomah, Shlomo, Sol, Solamh, Solaman, Solly, Solmon, Soloman, Solomonas, Sulaiman

Solon (Greek) wise. History: a noted ancient Athenian lawmaker.

Somerset (English) place of the summer settlers. Literature: William Somerset Maugham was a well-known British writer.
Sommerset, Sumerset, Summerset

Somerville (English) summer village.
Somerton, Summerton, Summerville

Son (Vietnamese) mountain. (Native American) star. (English) son, boy. A short form of Madison, Orson.
Sonny

Songan (Native American) strong.
Song

Sonny (English) a familiar form of Grayson, Madison, Orson, Son.
Soni, Sonnie, Sony

Sono (Akan) elephant.

Sören (Danish) thunder; war.
Sorren

Sorrel (French) reddish brown.
Sorel, Sorell, Sorrell

Soroush (Persian) happy.

Soterios (Greek) savior.
Soteris, Sotero

Southwell (English) south well.

Sovann (Cambodian) gold.

Sowande (Yoruba) wise healer sought me out.

Spalding (English) divided field.
Spaulding

Spangler (German) tinsmith.
Spengler

Spark (English) happy.
Sparke, Sparkie, Sparky

Spear (English) spear carrier.
Speare, Spears, Speer, Speers, Spiers

Speedy (English) quick; successful.
Speed

Spence (English) a short form of Spencer.
Spense

Spencer (English) dispenser of provisions.
Spence, Spencre, Spenser

Spenser (English) a form of Spencer. Literature: Edmund Spenser was the British poet who wrote *The Faerie Queene.*
Spanser, Spense

Spike (English) ear of grain; long nail.
Spyke

Spiro (Greek) round basket; breath.
Spiridion, Spiridon, Spiros, Spyridon, Spyros

Spoor (English) spur maker.
Spoors

Sproule (English) energetic.
Sprowle

Spurgeon (English) shrub.

Spyros (Greek) a form of Spiro.

Squire (English) knight's assistant; large landholder.

Stacey, Stacy (English) familiar forms of Eustace.
Stace, Stacee

Stafford (English) riverbank landing.
Staffard, Stafforde, Staford

Stamford (English) a form of Stanford.

Stamos (Greek) a form of Stephen.
Stamatis, Stamatos

Stan (Latin, English) a short form of Stanley.

Stanbury (English) stone fortification.
Stanberry, Stanbery, Stanburghe, Stansbury

Stancio (Spanish) a form of Constantine.
Stancy

Stancliff (English) stony cliff.
Stanclife, Stancliffe

Standish (English) stony parkland. History: Miles Standish was a leader in colonial America.

Stane (Slavic) a short form of Stanislaus.

Stanfield (English) stony field.
Stansfield

Stanford (English) rocky ford.
Sandy, Stamford, Stan, Standford, Stanfield

Stanislaus (Latin) stand of glory. See also Lao, Tano.
Slavik, Stana, Standa, Stane, Stanislao, Stanislas, Stanislau, Stanislav, Stanislus, Stannes, Stano, Stasik, Stasio

Stanislav (Slavic) a form of Stanislaus. See also Slava.
Stanislaw

Stanley (English) stony meadow.
Stan, Stanely, Stanlea, Stanlee, Stanleigh, Stanly

Stanmore (English) stony lake.

Stannard (English) hard as stone.

Stanton (English) stony farm.
Stan, Stanten, Staunton

Stanway (English) stony road.

Stanwick (English) stony village.
Stanwicke, Stanwyck

Stanwood (English) stony woods.

Starbuck (English) challenger of fate. Literature: a character in Herman Melville's novel *Moby-Dick.*

Stark (German) strong, vigorous.
Starke, Stärke, Starkie

Starling (English) bird.
Sterling

Starr (English) star.
Star, Staret, Starlight, Starlon, Starwin

Stasik (Russian) a familiar form of Stanislaus.
Stas, Stash, Stashka, Stashko, Stasiek

Stasio (Polish) a form of Stanislaus.
Stas, Stasiek, Stasiu, Staska, Stasko

Stavros (Greek) a form of Stephen.

Steadman (English) owner of a farmstead.
Steadmann, Stedman, Stedmen, Steed

Steel (English) like steel.
Steele

Steen (German, Danish) stone.
Steenn, Stein

Steeve (Greek) a short form of Steeven.

Steeven (Greek) a form of Steven.
Steaven, Steavin, Steavon, Steevan, Steeve, Steevn

Stefan (German, Polish, Swedish) a form of Stephen.
Steafan, Steafeán, Stefaan, Stefane, Stefanson, Stefaun, Stefawn, Steffan

Stefano (Italian) a form of Stephen.
Stefanos, Steffano

Stefanos (Greek) a form of Stephen.
Stefans, Stefos, Stephano, Stephanos

Stefen (Norwegian) a form of
Stephen.
Steffen, Steffin, Stefin

Steffan (Swedish) a form of Stefan.
Staffan

Stefon (Polish) a form of Stephon.
*Staffon, Steffon, Steffone, Stefone,
Stefonne*

Stein (German) a form of Steen.
Steine, Steiner

Steinar (Norwegian) rock warrior.

Stepan (Russian) a form of Stephen.
Stepa, Stepane, Stepanya, Stepka, Stipan

Steph (English) a short form of
Stephen.

Stephan (Greek) a form of Stephen.
*Stepfan, Stephanas, Stephano, Stephanos,
Stephanus, Stephaun*

Stéphane (French) a form of Stephen.
Stefane, Stepháne, Stephanne

Stephen (Greek) crowned. See also
Estéban, Estebe, Estevan, Estevao, Éti-
enne, István, Szczepan, Tapani, Teb,
Teppo, Tiennot.
*Stamos, Stavros, Stefan, Stefano, Stefanos,
Stefen, Stenya, Stepan, Stepanos, Steph,
Stephan, Stephanas, Stéphane, Stephens,
Stephenson, Stephfan, Stephin, Stephon,
Stepven, Steve, Steven, Stevie*

Stephon (Greek) a form of Stephen.
*Stefon, Stepfon, Stepfone, Stephfon,
Stephion, Stephone, Stephonne*

Sterling (English) valuable; silver
penny. A form of Starling.
Sterlen, Sterlin, Stirling

Stern (German) star.

Sterne (English) austere.
Stearn, Stearne, Stearns

Stetson (Danish) stepson.
Steston, Steton, Stetsen, Stetzon

Stevan (Greek) a form of Steven.
Stevano, Stevanoe, Stevaughn, Stevean

Steve (Greek) a short form of
Stephen, Steven.
Steave, Stevie, Stevy

Steven (Greek) a form of Stephen.
*Steeven, Steiven, Stevan, Steve, Stevens,
Stevie, Stevin, Stevon, Stiven*

Stevens (English) son of Steven.
Stevenson, Stevinson

Stevie (English) a familiar form of
Stephen, Steven.
Stevey, Stevy

Stevin, Stevon (Greek) forms of
Steven.
Stevieon, Stevion, Stevyn

Stewart (English) a form of Stuart.
Steward, Stu

Stian (Norwegian) quick on his feet.

Stig (Swedish) mount.

Stiggur (Gypsy) gate.

Stillman (English) quiet.
Stillmann, Stillmon

Sting (English) spike of grain.

Stockman (English) tree-stump
remover.

Stockton (English) tree-stump town.

Stockwell (English) tree-stump well.

Stoddard (English) horse keeper.

Stoffel (German) a short form of
Christopher.

Stoker (English) furnace tender.
Stoke, Stokes, Stroker

Stone (English) stone.
*Stoen, Stoner, Stoney, Stonie, Stonie,
Stoniy, Stony*

Storm (English) tempest, storm.
*Storme, Stormey, Stormi, Stormmie,
Stormy*

Storr (Norwegian) great.
Story

Stover (English) stove tender.

Stowe (English) hidden; packed away.

Strahan (Irish) minstrel.
Strachan

Stratford (English) bridge over the
river. Literature: Stratford-upon-Avon
was Shakespeare's birthplace.
Stradford

Stratton (Scottish) river valley town.
Straten, Straton

Strephon (Greek) one who turns.

Strom (Greek) bed, mattress. (German) stream.

Strong (English) powerful.

Stroud (English) thicket.

Struthers (Irish) brook.

Stu (English) a short form of Stewart, Stuart.
Stew

Stuart (English) caretaker, steward. History: a Scottish and English royal family.
Stewart, Stu, Stuarrt

Studs (English) rounded nail heads; shirt ornaments; male horses used for breeding. History: Louis "Studs" Terkel is a famous American journalist.
Stud, Studd

Styles (English) stairs put over a wall to help cross it.
Stiles, Style, Stylz

Subhi (Arabic) early morning.

Suck Chin (Korean) unshakable rock.

Sudi (Swahili) lucky.
Su'ud

Sued (Arabic) master, chief.
Suede

Suffield (English) southern field.

Sugden (English) valley of sows.

Suhail (Arabic) gentle.
Sohail, Sohayl, Souhail, Suhael, Sujal

Suhuba (Swahili) friend.

Sukru (Turkish) grateful.

Sulaiman (Arabic) a form of Solomon.
Sulaman, Sulay, Sulaymaan, Sulayman, Suleiman, Suleman, Suleyman, Sulieman, Sulman, Sulomon, Sulyman

Sullivan (Irish) black eyed.
Sullavan, Sullevan, Sully

Sully (Irish) a familiar form of Sullivan. (French) stain, tarnish. (English) south.
Sulleigh, Sulley

Sultan (Swahili) ruler.
Sultaan

Sum (Tai) appropriate.

Summit (English) peak, top.
Sumeet, Sumit, Summet, Summitt

Sumner (English) church officer; summoner.
Summer

Sundeep (Punjabi) light; enlightened.
Sundip

Sunny (English) sunny, sunshine.
Sun, Sunni

Sunreep (Hindi) pure.
Sunrip

Sutcliff (English) southern cliff.
Sutcliffe

Sutherland (Scandinavian) southern land.
Southerland, Sutherlan

Sutton (English) southern town.

Sven (Scandinavian) youth.
Svein, Svend, Svenn, Swen, Swenson

Swaggart (English) one who sways and staggers.
Swaggert

Swain (English) herdsman; knight's attendant.
Swaine, Swane, Swanson, Swayne

Swaley (English) winding stream.
Swail, Swailey, Swale, Swales

Sweeney (Irish) small hero.
Sweeny

Swinbourne (English) stream used by swine.
Swinborn, Swinborne, Swinburn, Swinburne, Swinbyrn, Swynborn

Swindel (English) valley of the swine.
Swindell

Swinfen (English) swine's mud.

Swinford (English) swine's crossing.
Swynford

Swinton (English) swine town.

Sy (Latin) a short form of Sylas, Symon.
Si

Sydney (French) a form of Sidney.
Syd, Sydne, Sydnee, Syndey

Syed (Arabic) happy.
Syeed, Syid

Sying (Chinese) star.

Sylas (Latin) a form of Silas.
Sy, Syles, Sylus

Sylvain (French) a form of Silvan, Sylvester.
Sylvan, Sylvian

Sylvester (Latin) forest dweller.
Silvester, Silvestro, Sly, Syl, Sylvain, Sylverster, Sylvestre

Symington (English) Simon's town, Simon's estate.

Symon (Greek) a form of Simon.
Sy, Syman, Symeon, Symion, Symms, Symon, Symone

Szczepan (Polish) a form of Stephen.

Szygfrid (Hungarian) a form of Siegfried.
Szigfrid

Szymon (Polish) a form of Simon.

Taaveti (Finnish) a form of David.
Taavi, Taavo

Tab (German) shining, brilliant. (English) drummer.
Tabb, Tabbie, Tabby

Tabari (Arabic) he remembers.
Tabahri, Tabares, Tabarious, Tabarius, Tabarus, Tabur

Tabib (Turkish) physician.
Tabeeb

Tabo (Spanish) a short form of Gustave.

Tabor (Persian) drummer. (Hungarian) encampment.
Tabber, Taber, Taboras, Taibor, Tayber, Taybor, Taver

Tad (Welsh) father. (Greek, Latin) a short form of Thaddeus.
Tadd, Taddy, Tade, Tadek, Tadey

Tadan (Native American) plentiful.
Taden

Tadarius (American) a combination of the prefix Ta + Darius.
Tadar, Tadarious, Tadaris, Tadarrius

Taddeo (Italian) a form of Thaddeus.
Tadeo

Taddeus (Greek, Latin) a form of Thaddeus.
Taddeous, Taddeusz, Taddius, Tadeas, Tades, Tadeusz, Tadio, Tadious

Tadi (Omaha) wind.

Tadzi (Carrier) loon.

Tadzio (Polish, Spanish) a form of Thaddeus.
Taddeusz

Taffy (Welsh) a form of David. (English) a familiar form of Taft.

Taft (English) river.
Taffy, Tafton

Tage (Danish) day.
Tag

Taggart (Irish) son of the priest.
Tagart, Taggert

Tahír (Arabic) innocent, pure.
Taheer

Tai (Vietnamese) weather; prosperous; talented.

Taima (Native American) born during a storm.

Taishawn (American) a combination of Tai + Shawn.
Taisen, Taishaun, Taishon

Tait (Scandinavian) a form of Tate.
Taite, Taitt

Taiwan (Chinese) island; island dweller. Geography: a country off the coast of China.
Taewon, Tahwan, Taivon, Taiwain, Tawain, Tawan, Tawann, Tawaun, Tawon, Taywan, Tywan

Taiwo (Yoruba) first-born of twins.

Taj (Urdu) crown.
Taje, Tajee, Tajeh, Tajh, Taji

Tajo (Spanish) day.
Taio

Tajuan (American) a combination of the prefix Ta + Juan.
Taijuan, Taijun, Taijuon, Tájuan, Tajwan, Taquan, Tyjuan

Takeo (Japanese) strong as bamboo.
Takeyo

Takis (Greek) a familiar form of Peter.
Takias, Takius

Takoda (Lakota) friend to everyone.

Tal (Hebrew) dew; rain.
Tali, Talia, Talley, Talor, Talya

Talbert (German) bright valley.

Talbot (French) boot maker.
Talbott, Tallbot, Tallbott, Tallie, Tally

Talcott (English) cottage near the lake.

Tale (Tswana) green.

Talen (English) a form of Talon.
Talin, Tallen

Talib (Arabic) seeker.

Taliesin (Welsh) radiant brow.
Tallas, Tallis

Taliki (Hausa) fellow.

Talli (Delaware) legendary hero.

Talmadge (English) lake between two towns.
Talmage

Talmai (Aramaic) mound; furrow.
Telem

Talman (Aramaic) injured; oppressed.
Talmon

Talon (French, English) claw, nail.
Taelon, Taelyn, Talen, Tallin, Tallon, Talyn

Talor (English) a form of Tal, Taylor.
Taelor, Taelur

Tam (Vietnamese) number eight. (Hebrew) honest. (English) a short form of Thomas.
Tama, Tamas, Tamás, Tameas, Tamlane, Tammany, Tammas, Tammen, Tammy

Taman (Slavic) dark, black.
Tama, Tamann, Tamin, Tamon, Tamone

Tamar (Hebrew) date; palm tree.
Tamarié, Tamario, Tamarr, Timur

Tambo (Swahili) vigorous.

Tamir (Arabic) tall as a palm tree.
Tameer

Tammy (English) a familiar form of Thomas.
Tammie

Tamson (Scandinavian) son of Thomas.
Tamsen

Tan (Burmese) million. (Vietnamese) new.
Than

Tanek (Greek) immortal. See also Atek.

Taneli (Finnish) God is my judge.
Taneil, Tanell, Tanella

Taner (English) a form of Tanner.
Tanar

Tanguy (French) warrior.

Tani (Japanese) valley.

Tanmay (Sanskrit) engrossed.

Tanner (English) leather worker; tanner.
Tan, Taner, Tanery, Tann, Tannar, Tannir, Tannor, Tanny

Tannin (English) tan colored; dark.
Tanin, Tannen, Tannon, Tanyen, Tanyon

Tanny (English) a familiar form of Tanner.
Tana, Tannee, Tanney, Tannie, Tany

Tano (Spanish) camp glory. (Ghanaian) Geography: a river in Ghana. (Russian) a short form of Stanislaus.
Tanno

Tanton (English) town by the still river.

Tapan (Sanskrit) sun; summer.

Tapani (Finnish) a form of Stephen.
Tapamn, Teppo

Täpko (Kiowa) antelope.

Taquan (American) a combination of the prefix Ta + Quan.
Taquann, Taquawn, Taquon, Taqwan

Tarak (Sanskrit) star; protector.

Taran (Sanskrit) heaven.
Tarran

Tarek (Arabic) a form of Táriq.
Tareek, Tareke

Tarell (German) a form of Terrell.
Tarelle, Tarrel, Tarrell, Taryl

Taren (American) a form of Taron.
Tarren, Tarrin

Tarif (Arabic) uncommon.
Tareef

Tarik (Arabic) a form of Táriq.
Taric, Tarick, Tariek, Tarikh, Tarrick, Tarrik, Taryk

Táriq (Arabic) conqueror. History: Tariq bin Ziyad was the Muslim general who conquered Spain.
Tareck, Tarek, Tarik, Tarique, Tarreq, Tereik

Tarleton (English) Thor's settlement.
Tarlton

Taro (Japanese) first-born male.

Taron (American) a combination of Tad + Ron.
Taeron, Tahron, Taren, Tarone, Tarrion, Tarron, Taryn

Tarrant (Welsh) thunder.
Terrant

Tarun (Sanskrit) young, youth.
Taran

Tarver (English) tower; hill; leader.
Terver

Taryn (American) a form of Taron.
Tarryn, Taryon

Tas (Gypsy) bird's nest.

Tashawn (American) a combination of
the prefix Ta + Shawn.
*Tashaan, Tashan, Tashaun, Tashon,
Tashun*

Tass (Hungarian) ancient mythology
name.

Tasunke (Dakota) horse.

Tate (Scandinavian, English) cheerful.
(Native American) long-winded
talker.
Tait, Tayte

Tatius (Latin) king, ruler. History: a
Sabine king.
Tatianus, Tazio, Titus

Tatum (English) cheerful.

Tau (Tswana) lion.

Tauno (Finnish) a form of Donald.

Taurean (Latin) strong; forceful.
Astrology: born under the sign of
Taurus.
*Tauraun, Taurein, Taurin, Taurion,
Taurone, Taurus*

Taurus (Latin) Astrology: the second
sign of the zodiac.
Taurice, Tauris

Tavares (Aramaic) a form of Tavor.
Tarvarres, Tavarres, Taveress

Tavaris (Aramaic) a form of Tavor.
*Tarvaris, Tavar, Tavaras, Tavari, Tavarian,
Tavarious, Tavarius, Tavarous, Tavarri,
Tavarris, Tavars, Tavarse, Tavarus, Tevaris,
Tevarius, Tevarus*

Tavey (Latin) a familiar form of
Octavio.

Tavi (Aramaic) good.

Tavian (Latin) a form of Octavio.
*Taveon, Taviann, Tavien, Tavieon, Tavin,
Tavio, Tavion, Tavionne, Tavon, Tayvon*

Tavish (Scottish) a form of Thomas.
Tav, Tavi, Tavis

Tavo (Slavic) a short form of Gustave.

Tavon (American) a form of Tavian.
Tavonn, Tavonne, Tavonni

Tavor (Aramaic) misfortune.
*Tarvoris, Tavares, Tavaris, Tavores,
Tavorious, Tavoris, Tavorise, Tavorres,
Tavorris, Tavuris*

Tawno (Gypsy) little one.
Tawn

Tayib (Hindi) good; delicate.

Tayler (English) a form of Taylor.
Tailer, Taylar, Tayller, Teyler

Taylor (English) tailor.
*Tailor, Talor, Tayler, Tayllor, Taylour, Taylr,
Teylor*

Tayshawn (American) a combination
of Taylor + Shawn.
Taysean, Tayshan, Tayshun, Tayson

Tayvon (American) a form of Tavian.
*Tayvan, Tayvaughn, Tayven, Tayveon,
Tayvin, Tayvohn, Tayvon*

Tavaris (Aramaic) a form of Tavor.

Taz (Arabic) shallow ornamental cup.
Tazz

Tazio (Italian) a form of Tatius.

Teagan (Irish) a form of Teague.
Teagen, Teagun, Teegan

Teague (Irish) bard, poet.
Teag, Teagan, Teage, Teak, Tegan, Teige

Tearence (Latin) a form of Terrence.
Tearance, Tearnce, Tearrance

Tearlach (Scottish) a form of Charles.

Tearle (English) stern, severe.

Teasdale (English) river dweller.
Geography: a river in England.

Teb (Spanish) a short form of Stephen.

Ted (English) a short form of Edward,
Edwin, Theodore.
Tedd, Tedek, Tedik, Tedson

Teddy (English) a familiar form of
Edward, Theodore.
Teddey, Teddie, Tedy

Tedmund (English) protector of the
land.
Tedman, Tedmond

Tedorik (Polish) a form of Theodore.
Teodoor, Teodor, Teodorek

Tedrick (American) a combination of
Ted + Rick.
Teddrick, Tederick, Tedric

Teetonka (Lakota) big lodge.

Tefere (Ethiopian) seed.

Tegan (Irish) a form of Teague.
Teghan, Teigan, Tiegan

Tej (Sanskrit) light; lustrous.

Tejas (Sanskrit) sharp.

Tekle (Ethiopian) plant.

Telek (Polish) a form of Telford.

Telem (Hebrew) mound; furrow.
Talmai, Tel

Telford (French) iron cutter.
Telek, Telfer, Telfor, Telfour

Teller (English) storyteller.
Tell, Telly

Telly (Greek) a familiar form of Teller, Theodore.

Telmo (English) tiller, cultivator.

Telutci (Moquelumnan) bear making dust as it runs.

Telvin (American) a combination of the prefix Te + Melvin.
Tellvin, Telvan

Tem (Gypsy) country.

Teman (Hebrew) on the right side; southward.

Tembo (Swahili) elephant.

Tempest (French) storm.

Temple (Latin) sanctuary.

Templeton (English) town near the temple.
Temp, Templeten

Tennant (English) tenant, renter.
Tenant, Tennent

Tennessee (Cherokee) mighty warrior. Geography: a southern U.S. state.
Tennessee, Tennesy, Tennysee

Tennyson (English) a form of Dennison. Literature: Alfred, Lord Tennyson was a nineteenth-century British poet.
Tenney, Tenneyson, Tennie, Tennis, Tennison, Tenny, Tenson

Teo (Vietnamese) a form of Tom.

Teobaldo (Italian, Spanish) a form of Theobald.

Teodoro (Italian, Spanish) a form of Theodore.
Teodore, Teodorico

Teppo (French) a familiar form of Stephen.

Tequan (American) a combination of the prefix Te + Quan.
Tequinn, Tequon

Terance (Latin) a form of Terrence.
Terriance

Terell (German) a form of Terrell.
Tarell, Tereall, Terel, Terelle, Tyrel

Teremun (Tiv) father's acceptance.
Terence (Latin) a form of Terrence.
Teren, Teryn

Terencio (Spanish) a form of Terrence.

Terran (Latin) a short form of Terrance.
Teran, Teren, Terran, Terren

Terrance (Latin) a form of Terrence.
Tarrance, Terran

Terrell (German) thunder ruler.
Terell, Terrail, Terral, Terrale, Terrall, Terreal, Terrel, Terrelle, Terrill, Terryal, Terryel, Tirel, Tirrel, Tirrell, Turrell, Tyrel, Tyrell

Terrence (Latin) smooth.
Tarrance, Tearence, Terance, Terence, Terencio, Terrance, Terren, Terrin, Terry, Torrence, Tyreese

Terrick (American) a combination of the prefix Te + Derrick.
Teric, Terick, Terik, Teriq, Terric, Terrik, Tirek, Tirik

Terrill (German) a form of Terrell.
Teriel, Teriell, Terril, Terryl, Terryll, Teryll, Teryl, Tyrill

Terrin (Latin) a short form of Terrence.
Terin, Terrien, Terryn, Teryn, Tiren

Terris (Latin) son of Terry.

Terron (American) a form of Tyrone.
Tereon, Terion, Terione, Teron, Terone, Terrion, Terrione, Terriyon, Terrone, Terronn, Terryon, Tiron

Terry (English) a familiar form of Terrence. See also Keli.
Tarry, Terrey, Terri, Terrie, Tery

Tertius (Latin) third.

Teshawn (American) a combination of the prefix Te + Shawn.
Tesean, Teshaun, Teshon

Teva (Hebrew) nature.

Tevan (American) a form of Tevin.
Tevaughan, Tevaughn, Teven, Tevvan

Tevel (Yiddish) a form of David.

Tevin (American) a combination of the prefix Te + Kevin.
Teavin, Teivon, Tevan, Tevien, Tevinn, Tevon, Tevvin, Tevyn

Tevis (Scottish) a form of Thomas.
Tevish

Tevon (American) a form of Tevin.
Tevion, Tevohn, Tevone, Tevonne, Tevoun, Teyvon

Tewdor (German) a form of Theodore.

Tex (American) from Texas.
Tejas

Thabit (Arabic) firm, strong.

Thad (Greek, Latin) a short form of Thaddeus.
Thadd, Thade, Thadee, Thady

Thaddeus (Greek) courageous. (Latin) praiser. Bible: one of the Twelve Apostles. See also Fadey.
Tad, Taddeo, Taddeus, Thaddis, Thadeaus, Tadzio, Thad, Thaddaeus, Thaddaus, Thaddeau, Thaddeaus, Thaddeo, Thaddeous, Thaddiaus, Thaddius, Thadeaou, Thadeous, Thadeus, Thadieus, Thadious, Thadius, Thadus

Thady (Irish) praise.
Thaddy

Thai (Vietnamese) many, multiple.

Thaman (Hindi) god; godlike.

Than (Burma) million.
Tan, Thanh

Thane (English) attendant warrior.
Thain, Thaine, Thayne

Thang (Vietnamese) victorious.

Thanh (Vietnamese) finished.

Thaniel (Hebrew) a short form of Nathaniel.

Thanos (Greek) nobleman; bear-man.
Athanasios, Thanasis

Thatcher (English) roof thatcher, repairer of roofs.
Thacher, Thatch, Thaxter

Thaw (English) melting ice.

Thayer (French) nation's army.
Thay

Thel (English) upper story.

Thenga (Yao) bring him.

Theo (English) a short form of Theodore.

Theobald (German) people's prince. See also Dietbald.
Teobaldo, Thebault, Theðbault, Thibault, Tibalt, Tibold, Tiebold, Tiebout, Toiboid, Tybald, Tybalt, Tybault

Theodore (Greek) gift of God. See also Feodor, Fyodor.
Téadóir, Teador, Ted, Teddy, Tedor, Tedorek, Tedorik, Telly, Teodomiro, Teodoro, Teodus, Teos, Tewdor, Theo, Theodor, Theódor, Theodors, Theodorus, Theodosios, Theodrekr, Tivadar, Todor, Tolek, Tudor

Theodoric (German) ruler of the people. See also Dedrick, Derek, Dirk.
Teodorico, Thedric, Thedrick, Thierry, Till

Theophilus (Greek) loved by God.
Teofil, Théophile, Theophlous, Theopolis

Theron (Greek) hunter.
Theran, Theren, Thereon, Therin, Therion, Therrin, Therron, Theryn, Theryon

Thian (Vietnamese) smooth.
Thien

Thibault (French) a form of Theobald.
Thibaud, Thibaut

Thierry (French) a form of Theodoric.
Theirry, Theory

Thom (English) a short form of Thomas.
Thomy

Thoma (German) a form of Thomas.

Thomas (Greek, Aramaic) twin. Bible: one of the Twelve Apostles. See also Chuma, Foma, Maslin.
Tam, Tammy, Tavish, Tevis, Thom, Thoma, Thomason, Thomaz, Thomeson, Thomison, Thommas, Thompson, Thomson, Tom, Toma, Tomas, Tomás, Tomasso, Tomcy, Tomey, Tomey, Tomi, Tommy, Toomas

Thompson (English) son of Thomas.
Thomason, Thomison, Thomsen, Thomson

Thor (Scandinavian) thunder. Mythology: the Norse god of thunder.
Thorin, Tor, Tyrus

Thorald (Scandinavian) Thor's follower.
Terrell, Terrill, Thorold, Torald

Thorbert (Scandinavian) Thor's brightness.
Torbert

Thorbjorn (Scandinavian) Thor's bear.
Thorburn, Thurborn, Thurburn

Thorgood (English) Thor is good.

Thorleif (Scandinavian) Thor's beloved.
Thorlief

Thorley (English) Thor's meadow.
Thorlea, Thorlee, Thorleigh, Thorly, Torley

Thorndike (English) thorny embankment.
Thorn, Thorndyck, Thorndyke, Thorne

Thorne (English) a short form of names beginning with "Thorn."
Thorn, Thornie, Thorny

Thornley (English) thorny meadow.
Thorley, Thorne, Thornlea, Thornleigh, Thornly

Thornton (English) thorny town.
Thorne

Thorpe (English) village.
Thorp

Thorwald (Scandinavian) Thor's forest.
Thorvald

Thuc (Vietnamese) aware.

Thurlow (English) Thor's hill.
Thurlo

Thurmond (English) defended by Thor.
Thormond, Thurmund

Thurston (Scandinavian) Thor's stone.
Thorstan, Thorstein, Thorsten, Thurstain, Thurstan, Thursten, Torsten, Torston

Tiago (Spanish) a form of Jacob.

Tiberio (Italian) from the Tiber River region.
Tiberias, Tiberious, Tiberiu, Tiberius, Tibius, Tyberious, Tyberius, Tyberrius

Tibor (Hungarian) holy place.
Tiburcio

Tichawanna (Shona) we shall see.

Ticho (Spanish) a short form of Patrick.

Tieler (English) a form of Tyler.
Tielar, Tielor, Tielyr

Tiennot (French) a form of Stephen.
Tien

Tiernan (Irish) lord.

Tierney (Irish) lordly.
Tiarnach, Tiernan

Tige (English) a short form of Tiger.
Ti, Tig, Tighe, Ty, Tyg, Tyge, Tygh, Tyghe

Tiger (American) tiger; powerful and energetic.
Tige, Tigger, Tyger

Tiimu (Moquelumnan) caterpillar coming out of the ground.

Tilden (English) tilled valley.
Tildon

Tiktu (Moquelumnan) bird digging up potatoes.

Tilford (English) prosperous ford.

Till (German) a short form of Theodoric.
Thilo, Til, Tillman, Tilman, Tillmann, Tilson

Tilton (English) prosperous town.

Tim (Greek) a short form of Timothy.
Timmie, Timmy

Timin (Arabic) born near the sea.

Timmothy (Greek) a form of Timothy.
Timmathy, Timmithy, Timmoty, Timmthy

Timmy (Greek) a familiar form of Timothy.
Timmie

Timo (Finnish) a form of Timothy.
Timio

Timofey (Russian) a form of Timothy.
Timofei, Timofej, Timofeo

Timon (Greek) honorable.

Timoteo (Portuguese, Spanish) a form of Timothy.

Timothy (Greek) honoring God. See also Kimokeo.
Tadhg, Taidgh, Tiege, Tim, Tima, Timithy, Timka, Timkin, Timmothy, Timmy, Timo, Timofey, Timok, Timon, Timontheo, Timonthy, Timót, Timote, Timotei, Timoteo, Timoteus, Timothé, Timothée, Timotheo, Timotheos, Timotheus, Timothey, Timothie, Timthie, Tiomóid, Tisha, Tomothy, Tymon, Tymothy

Timur (Hebrew) a form of Tamar. (Russian) conqueror.
Timour

Tin (Vietnamese) thinker.

Tino (Spanish) venerable, majestic. (Italian) small. A familiar form of Antonio. (Greek) a short form of Augustine.
Tion

Tinsley (English) fortified field.

Tiquan (American) a combination of the prefix Ti + Quan.
Tiquawn, Tiquine, Tiquon, Tiquwan, Tiqwan

Tisha (Russian) a form of Timothy.
Tishka

Tishawn (American) a combination of the prefix Ti + Shawn.
Tishaan, Tishaun, Tishean, Tishon, Tishun

Tito (Italian) a form of Titus.
Titas, Titis, Titos

Titus (Greek) giant. (Latin) hero. A form of Tatius. History: a Roman emperor.
Tite, Titek, Tito, Tytus

Tivon (Hebrew) nature lover.

TJ (American) a combination of the initials T. + J.
Teejay, Tj, T.J., T Jae, Tjayda

Tobal (Spanish) a short form of Christopher.
Tabalito

Tobar (Gypsy) road.

Tobi (Yoruba) great.

Tobias (Hebrew) God is good.
Tobia, Tobiah, Tobiás, Tobiath, Tobin, Tobit, Toby, Tobyas, Tuvya

Tobin (Hebrew) a form of Tobias.
Toben, Tobian, Tobyn, Tovin

Toby (Hebrew) a familiar form of Tobias.
Tobbie, Tobby, Tobe, Tobee, Tobey, Tobie

Todd (English) fox.
Tod, Toddie, Toddy

Todor (Basque, Russian) a form of Theodore.
Teodor, Todar, Todas, Todos

Toft (English) small farm.

Tohon (Native American) cougar.

Tokala (Dakota) fox.

Toland (English) owner of taxed land.
Tolan

Tolbert (English) bright tax collector.

Toller (English) tax collector.

Tom (English) a short form of Tomas, Thomas.
Teo, Thom, Tommey, Tommie, Tommy

Toma (Romanian) a form of Thomas.
Tomah

Tomas (German) a form of Thomas.
Tom, Tomaisin, Tomaz, Tomcio, Tome, Tomek, Tomelis, Tomico, Tomik, Tomislaw, Tommas, Tomo, Tomson

Tomás (Irish, Spanish) a form of Thomas.
Tomas, Tómas, Tomasz

Tomasso (Italian) a form of Thomas.
Tomaso, Tommaso

Tombe (Kakwa) northerners.

Tomey (Irish) a familiar form of Thomas.
Tome, Tomi, Tomie, Tomy

Tomi (Japanese) rich. (Hungarian) a form of Thomas.

Tomlin (English) little Tom.
Tomkin, Tomlinson

Tommie (Hebrew) a form of Tommy.
Tommi

Tommy (Hebrew) a familiar form of Thomas.
Tommie, Tomy

Tonda (Czech) a form of Tony.
Tonek

Tong (Vietnamese) fragrant.

Toni (Greek, German, Slavic) a form of Tony.
Tonee, Tonie, Tonio, Tonis, Tonnie

Tonio (Portuguese) a form of Tony. (Italian) a short form of Antonio.
Tono, Tonyo

Tony (Greek) flourishing. (Latin) praiseworthy. (English) a short form of Anthony. A familiar form of Remington.
Tonda, Tonek, Toney, Toni, Tonik, Tonio, Tonny

Tooantuh (Cherokee) spring frog.

Toomas (Estonian) a form of Thomas.
Toomis, Tuomas, Tuomo

Topher (Greek) a short form of Christopher, Kristopher.
Tofer, Tophor

Topo (Spanish) gopher.

Topper (English) hill.

Tor (Norwegian) thunder. (Tiv) royalty, king.
Thor

Torian (Irish) a form of Torin.
Toran, Torean, Toriano, Toriaun, Torien, Torrian, Torrien, Torryan

Torin (Irish) chief.
Thorfin, Thorstein, Torian, Torion, Torrin, Toryn

Torkel (Swedish) Thor's cauldron.

Tormey (Irish) thunder spirit.
Tormé, Tormee

Tormod (Scottish) north.

Torn (Irish) a short form of Torrence.
Toran

Torquil (Danish) Thor's kettle.
Torkel

Torr (English) tower.
Tory

Torrance (Irish) a form of Torrence.
Torance

Torren (Irish) a short form of Torrence.
Torehn, Toren

Torrence (Irish) knolls. (Latin) a form of Terrence.
Tawrence, Toreence, Torence, Torenze, Torey, Torin, Torn, Torr, Torrance, Torren, Torreon, Torrin, Torry, Tory, Torynce, Tuarence, Turance

Torrey (English) a form of Tory.
Toreey, Torie, Torre, Torri, Torrie, Torry

Toru (Japanese) sea.

Tory (English) familiar form of Torr, Torrence.
Torey, Tori, Torrey

Toshi-Shita (Japanese) junior.

Tovi (Hebrew) good.
Tov

Townley (English) town meadow.
Townlea, Townlee, Townleigh, Townlie, Townly

Townsend (English) town's end.
Town, Townes, Towney, Townie, Townsen, Townshend, Towny

Trace (Irish) a form of Tracy.
Trayce

Tracey (Irish) a form of Tracy.
Traci

Tracy (Greek) harvester. (Latin) courageous. (Irish) battler.
Trace, Tracey, Tracie, Treacy

Trader (English) well-trodden path; skilled worker.

Trae (English) a form of Trey.
Trai, Traie, Tre, Trea

Trahern (Welsh) strong as iron.
Traherne, Tray

Tramaine (Scottish) a form of Tremaine, Tremayne.
Tramain, Traman, Tramane, Tramayne, Traymain, Traymon

Traquan (American) a combination of Travis + Quan.
Traequan, Traqon, Traquon, Traqwan, Traqwaun, Trayquan, Trayquane, Trayqwon

Trashawn (American) a combination of Travis + Shawn.
Trasen, Trashaun, Trasean, Trashon, Trashone, Trashun, Trayshaun, Trayshawn

Traugott (German) God's truth.

Travaris (French) a form of Travers.
Travares, Travaress, Travarious, Travarius, Travarous, Travarus, Travauris, Traveress, Traverez, Traverus, Travoris, Travorus

Travell (English) traveler.
Travail, Travale, Travel, Travelis, Travelle, Trevel, Trevell, Trevelle

Traven (American) a form of Trevon.
Travin, Travine, Trayven

Travers (French) crossroads.
Travaris, Traver, Travis

Travion (American) a form of Trevon.
Traveon, Travian, Travien, Travione, Travioun

Travis (English) a form of Travers.
Travais, Travees, Traves, Traveus, Travious, Traviss, Travius, Travous, Travus, Travys, Trayvis, Trevais, Trevis

Travon (American) a form of Trevon.
Traevon, Traivon, Travone, Travonn, Travonne

Tray (English) a form of Trey.
Traye

Trayton (English) town full of trees.
Trayten

Trayvon (American) a combination of
Tray + Von.
*Trayveon, Trayvin, Trayvion, Trayvond,
Trayvone, Trayvonne, Trayvyon*

Treavon (American) a form of Trevon.
Treavan, Treavin, Treavion

Tredway (English) well-worn road.
Treadway

Tremaine, Tremayne (Scottish) house
of stone.
*Tramaine, Tremain, Tremane, Treymaine,
Trimaine*

Trent (Latin) torrent, rapid stream.
(French) thirty. Geography: a city in
northern Italy.
Trente, Trentino, Trento, Trentonio

Trenton (Latin) town by the rapid
stream. Geography: the capital of
New Jersey.
*Trendon, Trendun, Trenten, Trentin,
Trentton, Trentyn, Triinten, Trintin, Trinton*

Trequan (American) a combination of
Trey + Quan.
*Trequanne, Trequaun, Trequian, Trequon,
Treqwon, Treyquane*

Treshawn (American) a combination
of Trey + Shawn.
*Treshaun, Treshon, Treshun, Treysean,
Treyshawn, Treyshon*

Treston (Welsh) a form of Tristan.
Trestan, Trestin, Trestton, Trestyn

Trev (Irish, Welsh) a short form of
Trevor.

Trevaughn (American) a combination
of Trey + Vaughn.
*Trevaughan, Trevaugn, Trevaun, Trevaune,
Trevaunn, Treyvaughn*

Trevelyan (English) Elian's homestead.

Trevin (American) a form of Trevon.
*Trevian, Trevien, Trevine, Trevinne, Trevyn,
Treyvin*

Trevion (American) a form of Trevon.
*Trevione, Trevionne, Trevyon, Treyveon,
Treyvion*

Trevis (English) a form of Travis.
Treves, Trevez, Treveze, Trevius

Trevon (American) a combination of
Trey + Von.
*Traven, Travion, Travon, Tre, Treavon,
Trévan, Treveyon, Trevin, Trevion,
Trevohn, Trevoine, Trévon, Trevone,
Trevonn, Trevonne, Treyvon*

Trevor (Irish) prudent. (Welsh) home-
stead.
*Travor, Treavor, Trebor, Trefor, Trev, Trevar,
Trevares, Trevarious, Trevaris, Trevarius,
Trevaros, Trevarus, Trever, Trevore, Trevores,
Trevoris, Trevorus, Trevour, Trevyr, Treyvor*

Trey (English) three; third.
Trae, Trai, Tray, Treye, Tri, Trie

Treyvon (American) a form of Trevon.
*Treyvan, Treyven, Treyvenn, Treyvone,
Treyvonn, Treyvun*

Trigg (Scandinavian) trusty.

Trini (Latin) a short form of Trinity.

Trinity (Latin) holy trinity.
Trenedy, Trini, Trinidy

Trip, Tripp (English) traveler.

Tristan (Welsh) bold. Literature: a
knight in the Arthurian legends who
fell in love with his uncle's wife.
*Treston, Tris, Trisan, Tristain, Tristano,
Tristen, Tristian, Tristin, Triston, Tristyn,
Trystan*

Tristano (Italian) a form of Tristan.

Tristen (Welsh) a form of Tristan.
Trisden, Trissten

Tristin (Welsh) a form of Tristan.
Tristian, Tristinn

Triston (Welsh) a form of Tristan.

Tristram (Welsh) sorrowful. Literature:
the title character in Laurence
Sterne's eighteenth-century novel
Tristram Shandy.
Tristam

Tristyn (Welsh) a form of Tristan.
Tristynne

Trot (English) trickling stream.

Trowbridge (English) bridge by the
tree.

Troy (Irish) foot soldier. (French) curly
haired. (English) water. See also Koi.
Troi, Troye, Troyton

True (English) faithful, loyal.
Tru

Truesdale (English) faithful one's
homestead.

Truitt (English) little and honest.
Truett

Truman (English) honest. History: Harry S. Truman was the thirty-third U.S. president.
Trueman, Trumain, Trumaine, Trumann

Trumble (English) strong; bold.
Trumball, Trumbell, Trumbull

Trustin (English) trustworthy.
Trustan, Trusten, Truston

Trygve (Norwegian) brave victor.

Trystan (Welsh) a form of Tristan.
Tryistan, Trysten, Trystian, Trystin, Trystn, Tryston, Trystyn

Tsalani (Nguni) good-bye.

Tse (Ewe) younger of twins.

Tu (Vietnamese) tree.

Tuaco (Ghanaian) eleventh-born.

Tuan (Vietnamese) goes smoothly.

Tucker (English) fuller, tucker of cloth.
Tuck, Tuckie, Tucky, Tuckyr

Tudor (Welsh) a form of Theodore. History: an English ruling dynasty.
Todor

Tug (Scandinavian) draw, pull.
Tugg

Tuketu (Moquelumnan) bear making dust as it runs.

Tukuli (Moquelumnan) caterpillar crawling down a tree.

Tulio (Italian, Spanish) lively.
Tullio

Tullis (Latin) title, rank.
Tullius, Tullos, Tully

Tully (Irish) at peace with God. (Latin) a familiar form of Tullis.
Tull, Tulley, Tullie, Tullio

Tumaini (Mwera) hope.

Tumu (Moquelumnan) deer thinking about eating wild onions.

Tung (Vietnamese) stately, dignified. (Chinese) everyone.

Tungar (Sanskrit) high; lofty.

Tupi (Moquelumnan) pulled up.

Tupper (English) ram raiser.

Turi (Spanish) a short form of Arthur.
Ture

Turk (English) from Turkey.

Turner (Latin) lathe worker; wood worker.

Turpin (Scandinavian) Finn named after Thor.

Tut (Arabic) strong and courageous. History: a short form of Tutankhamen, an Egyptian king.
Tutt

Tutu (Spanish) a familiar form of Justin.

Tuvya (Hebrew) a form of Tobias.
Tevya, Tuvia, Tuviah

Tuwile (Mwera) death is inevitable.

Tuyen (Vietnamese) angel.

Twain (English) divided in two. Literature: Mark Twain (whose real name was Samuel Langhorne Clemens) was one of the most prominent nineteenth-century American writers.
Tawine, Twaine, Twan, Twane, Tway, Twayn, Twayne

Twia (Fante) born after twins.

Twitchell (English) narrow passage.
Twytchell

Twyford (English) double river crossing.

Txomin (Basque) like the Lord.

Ty (English) a short form of Tyler, Tyrone, Tyrus.
Tye

Tyee (Native American) chief.

Tyger (English) a form of Tiger.
Tige, Tyg, Tygar

Tylar (English) a form of Tyler.
Tyelar, Tylarr

Tyler (English) tile maker.
Tieler, Tiler, Ty, Tyel, Tyeler, Tyelor, Tyhler, Tylar, Tyle, Tylee, Tylere, Tyller, Tylor, Tylyr

Tylor (English) a form of Tyler.
Tylour

Tymon (Polish) a form of Timothy. (Greek) a form of Timon.
Tymain, Tymaine, Tymane, Tymeik, Tymek, Tymen

Tymothy (English) a form of Timothy.
Tymithy, Tymmothy, Tymoteusz, Tymothee, Timothi

Tynan (Irish) dark.
Ty

Tynek (Czech) a form of Martin.
Tynko

Tyquan (American) a combination of Ty + Quan.
Tykwan, Tykwane, Tykwon, Tyquaan, Tyquane, Tyquann, Tyquine, Tyquinn, Tyquon, Tyquone, Tyquwon, Tyqwan

Tyran (American) a form of Tyrone.
Tyraine, Tyrane

Tyree (Scottish) island dweller. Geography: Tiree is an island off the west coast of Scotland.
Tyra, Tyrae, Tyrai, Tyray, Tyre, Tyrea, Tyrée

Tyreese (American) a form of Terrence.
Tyreas, Tyrease, Tyrece, Tyreece, Tyreice, Tyres, Tyrese, Tyresse, Tyrez, Tyreze, Tyrice, Tyriece, Tyriese

Tyrel, Tyrell (American) forms of Terrell.
Tyrelle, Tyrrel, Tyrrell

Tyrick (American) a combination of Ty + Rick.
Tyreck, Tyreek, Tyreik, Tyrek, Tyreke, Tyric, Tyriek, Tyrik, Tyriq, Tyrique

Tyrin (American) a form of Tyrone.
Tyrinn, Tyrion, Tyrrin, Tyryn

Tyron (American) a form of Tyrone.
Tyrohn, Tyronn, Tyronna, Tyronne

Tyrone (Greek) sovereign. (Irish) land of Owen.
Tayron, Tayrone, Teirone, Terron, Ty, Tyerone, Tyhrone, Tyran, Tyrin, Tyron, Tyroney, Tyronne, Tyroon, Tyroun

Tyrus (English) a form of Thor.
Ty, Tyruss, Tyryss

Tyshawn (American) a combination of Ty + Shawn.
Tyshan, Tyshaun, Tyshauwn, Tyshian, Tyshinn, Tyshion, Tyshon, Tyshone, Tyshonne, Tyshun, Tyshunn, Tyshyn

Tyson (French) son of Ty.
Tison, Tiszon, Tyce, Tycen, Tyesn, Tyeson, Tysen, Tysie, Tysin, Tysne, Tysone

Tytus (Polish) a form of Titus.
Tyus

Tyvon (American) a combination of Ty + Von.
Tyvan, Tyvin, Tyvinn, Tyvone, Tyvonne

Tywan (Chinese) a form of Taiwan.
Tywain, Tywaine, Tywane, Tywann, Tywaun, Tywen, Tywon, Tywone, Tywonne

Tzadok (Hebrew) righteous.
Tzadik, Zadok

Tzion (Hebrew) sign from God.
Zion

Tzuriel (Hebrew) God is my rock.
Tzuriya

Tzvi (Hebrew) deer.
Tzevi, Zevi

U

Uaine (Irish) a form of Owen.

Ubadah (Arabic) serves God.

Ubaid (Arabic) faithful.

Uberto (Italian) a form of Hubert.

Uche (Ibo) thought.

Uday (Sanskrit) to rise.

Udell (English) yew-tree valley.
Dell, Eudel, Udale, Udall, Yudell

Udit (Sanskrit) grown; shining.

Udo (Japanese) ginseng plant. (German) a short form of Udolf.

Udolf (English) prosperous wolf.
Udo, Udolfo, Udolph

Ugo (Italian) a form of Hugh, Hugo.

Ugutz (Basque) a form of John.

Uilliam (Irish) a form of William.
Uileog, Uilleam, Ulick

Uinseann (Irish) a form of Vincent.

Uistean (Irish) intelligent.
Uisdean

Uja (Sanskrit) growing.

Uku (Hawaiian) flea, insect; skilled ukulele player.

Ulan (African) first-born twin.

Ulbrecht (German) a form of Albert.

Ulf (German) wolf.

Ulfred (German) peaceful wolf.

Ulger (German) warring wolf.

Ulises (Latin) a form of Ulysses.
Ulishes, Ulisse, Ulisses

Ullock (German) sporting wolf.

Ulmer (English) famous wolf.
Ullmar, Ulmar

Ulmo (German) from Ulm, Germany.

Ulric (German) a form of Ulrich.
Ullric

Ulrich (German) wolf ruler; ruler of all. See also Alaric.
Uli, Ull, Ulric, Ulrick, Ulrik, Ulrike, Ulu, Ulz, Uwe

Ultman (Hindi) god; godlike.

Ulyses (Latin) a form of Ulysses.
Ulysee, Ulysees

Ulysses (Latin) wrathful. A form of Odysseus.
Eulises, Ulick, Ulises, Ulyes, Ulysse, Ulyssees, Ulysses, Ulyssius

Umang (Sanskrit) enthusiastic.
Umanga

Umar (Arabic) a form of Omar.
Umair, Umarr, Umayr, Umer

Umberto (Italian) a form of Humbert.
Uberto

Umi (Yao) life.

Umit (Turkish) hope.

Unai (Basque) shepherd.
Una

Uner (Turkish) famous.

Unika (Lomwe) brighten.

Unique (Latin) only, unique.
Uneek, Unek, Unikque, Uniqué, Unyque

Unwin (English) nonfriend.
Unwinn, Unwyn

Upshaw (English) upper wooded area.

Upton (English) upper town.

Upwood (English) upper forest.

Urban (Latin) city dweller; courteous.
Urbain, Urbaine, Urbane, Urbano, Urbanus, Urvan, Urvane

Urbane (English) a form of Urban.

Urbano (Italian) a form of Urban.

Uri (Hebrew) a short form of Uriah.
Urie

Uriah (Hebrew) my light. Bible: a soldier and the husband of Bathsheba. See also Yuri.
Uri, Uria, Urias, Urijah

Urian (Greek) heaven.
Urihaan

Uriel (Hebrew) God is my light.
Urie

Urson (French) a form of Orson.
Ursan, Ursus

Urtzi (Basque) sky.

Usamah (Arabic) like a lion.
Usama

Useni (Yao) tell me.
Usene, Usenet

Usi (Yao) smoke.

Ustin (Russian) a form of Justin.

Utatci (Moquelumnan) bear scratching itself.

Uthman (Arabic) companion of the Prophet.
Usman, Uthmaan

Uttam (Sanskrit) best.

Uwe (German) a familiar form of Ulrich.

Uzi (Hebrew) my strength.
Uzzia

Uziel (Hebrew) God is my strength; mighty force.
Uzie, Uzziah, Uzziel

Uzoma (Nigerian) born during a journey.

Uzumati (Moquelumnan) grizzly bear.

V

Vachel (French) small cow.
Vache, Vachell

Vaclav (Czech) wreath of glory.
Vasek

Vadin (Hindi) speaker.
Vaden

Vail (English) valley.
Vaile, Vaill, Vale, Valle

Val (Latin) a short form of Valentin.

Valborg (Swedish) mighty mountain.

Valdemar (Swedish) famous ruler.

Valentin (Latin) strong; healthy.
Val, Valencio, Valenté, Valentijn, Valentine, Valentino, Valenton, Valentyn, Velentino

Valentino (Italian) a form of Valentin.

Valerian (Latin) strong; healthy.
Valeriano, Valerii, Valerio, Valeryn

Valerii (Russian) a form of Valerian.
Valera, Valerie, Valerij, Valerik, Valeriy, Valery

Valfrid (Swedish) strong peace.

Valin (Hindi) a form of Balin. Mythology: a tyrannical monkey king.

Vallis (French) from Wales.
Valis

Valter (Lithuanian, Swedish) a form of Walter.
Valters, Valther, Valtr, Vanda

Van (Dutch) a short form of Vandyke.
Vander, Vane, Vann, Vanno

Vance (English) thresher.

Vanda (Lithuanian) a form of Walter.
Vander

Vandyke (Dutch) dyke.
Van

Vanya (Russian) a familiar form of Ivan.
Vanechka, Vanek, Vanja, Vanka, Vanusha, Wanya

Vardon (French) green knoll.
Vardaan, Varden, Verdan, Verdon, Verdun

Varian (Latin) variable.

Varick (German) protecting ruler.
Varak, Varek, Warrick

Vartan (Armenian) rose producer; rose giver.

Varun (Hindi) rain god.
Varron

Vasant (Sanskrit) spring.
Vasanth

Vashawn (American) a combination of the prefix Va + Shawn.
Vashae, Vashan, Vashann, Vashaun, Vashawnn, Vashon, Vashun, Vishon

Vasilis (Greek) a form of Basil.
Vas, Vasaya, Vaselios, Vashon, Vasil, Vasile, Vasileior, Vasileios, Vasilios, Vasilius, Vasilos, Vasilus, Vasily, Vassilios, Vasylko, Vasyltso, Vazul

Vasily (Russian) a form of Vasilis.
Vasilek, Vasili, Vasilii, Vasilije, Vasilik, Vasiliy, Vassili, Vassilij, Vasya, Vasyenka

Vasin (Hindi) ruler, lord.

Vasu (Sanskrit) wealth.

Vasyl (German, Slavic) a form of William.
Vasos, Vassily, Vassos, Vasya, Vasyuta, Va Vaska, Wassily

Vaughn (Welsh) small.
Vaughan, Vaughen, Vaun, Vaune, Von, Voughn

Veasna (Cambodian) lucky.

Ved (Sanskrit) sacred knowledge.

Vedie (Latin) sight.

Veer (Sanskrit) brave.

Vegard (Norwegian) sanctuary; protection.

Velvel (Yiddish) wolf.

Vencel (Hungarian) a short form of Wenceslaus.
Venci, Vencie

Venedictos (Greek) a form of Benedict.
Venedict, Venediktos, Venka, Venya

Veniamin (Bulgarian) a form of Benjamin.
Venyamin, Verniamin

Venkat (Hindi) god; godlike. Religion: another name for the Hindu god Vishnu.

Venya (Russian) a familiar form of Benedict.
Venedict, Venka

Vere (Latin, French) true.

Vered (Hebrew) rose.

Vergil (Latin) a form of Virgil. Literature: a Roman poet best known for his epic poem *Aenid*.
Verge

Vern (Latin) a short form of Vernon.
Verna, Vernal, Verne, Verneal, Vernel, Vernell, Vernelle, Vernial, Vernine, Vernis, Vernol

Vernados (German) courage of the bear.

Verner (German) defending army.
Varner

Verney (French) alder grove.
Vernie

Vernon (Latin) springlike; youthful.
Vern, Varnan, Vernen, Verney, Vernin

Verrill (German) masculine. (French) loyal.
Verill, Verrall, Verrell, Verroll, Veryl

Vian (English) full of life.

Vic (Latin) a short form of Victor.
Vick, Vicken, Vickenson

Vicente (Spanish) a form of Vincent.
Vicent, Visente

Vicenzo (Italian) a form of Vincent.

Victoir (French) a form of Victor.

Victor (Latin) victor, conqueror.
*Vic, Victa, Victer, Victoir, Victoriano,
Victorien, Victorin, Victorio, Viktor, Vitin,
Vittorio, Vitya, Wikoli, Wiktor, Witek*

Victorio (Spanish) a form of Victor.
Victorino

Vidal (Spanish) a form of Vitas.
Vida, Vidale, Vidall, Videll

Vidar (Norwegian) tree warrior.

Vidor (Hungarian) cheerful.

Vidur (Hindi) wise.

Viho (Cheyenne) chief.

Vijay (Hindi) victorious.

Vikas (Hindi) growing.
Vikash, Vikesh

Vikram (Hindi) valorous.
Vikrum

Vikrant (Hindi) powerful.
Vikran

Viktor (German, Hungarian, Russian)
a form of Victor.
Viktoras, Viktors

Vilhelm (German) a form of William.
Vilhelms, Vilho, Vilis, Viljo, Villem

Vili (Hungarian) a short form of
William.
Villy, Vilmos

Viliam (Czech) a form of William.
*Vila, Vilek, Vilém, Viliami, Viliamu,
Vilko, Vilous*

Viljo (Finnish) a form of William.

Ville (Swedish) a short form of
William.

Vimal (Hindi) pure.

Vin (Latin) a short form of Vincent.
Vinn

Vinay (Hindi) polite.

Vince (English) a short form of Vincent.
Vence, Vint

Vincent (Latin) victor, conqueror. See
also Binkentios, Binky.
*Uinseann, Vencent, Vicente, Vicenzo,
Vikent, Vikenti, Vikesha, Vin, Vince,
Vincence, Vincens, Vincente, Vincentius,
Vincents, Vincenty, Vincenzo, Vinci,
Vincien, Vincient, Vinciente, Vincint,
Vinny, Vinsent, Vinsint, Wincent*

Vincente (Spanish) a form of Vincent.
Vencente

Vincenzo (Italian) a form of Vincent.
*Vincenz, Vincenza, Vincenzio,
Vinchenzo, Vinzenz*

Vinci (Hungarian, Italian) a familiar
form of Vincent.
Vinci, Vinco, Vincze

Vinny (English) a familiar form of
Calvin, Melvin, Vincent.
Vinnee, Vinney, Vinni, Vinnie

Vinod (Hindi) happy, joyful.
Vinodh, Vinood

Vinson (English) son of Vincent.
Vinnis

Vipul (Hindi) plentiful.

Viraj (Hindi) resplendent.

Virat (Hindi) very big.

Virgil (Latin) rod bearer, staff bearer.
Vergil, Virge, Virgial, Virgie, Virgilio

Virgilio (Spanish) a form of Virgil.
Virjilio

Virote (Tai) strong, powerful.

Vishal (Hindi) huge; great.
Vishaal

Vishnu (Hindi) protector.

Vitas (Latin) alive, vital.
Vidal, Vitus

Vito (Latin) a short form of Vittorio.
*Veit, Vidal, Vital, Vitale, Vitalis, Vitas,
Vitin, Vitis, Vitus, Vitya, Vytas*

Vittorio (Italian) a form of Victor.
Vito, Vitor, Vitorio, Vittore, Vittorios

Vitya (Russian) a form of Victor.
Vitenka, Vitka

Vivek (Hindi) wisdom.
Vivekinan

Vladimir (Russian) famous prince. See
also Dima, Waldemar, Walter.
*Bladimir, Vimka, Vlad, Vladamir, Vladik,
Vladimar, Vladimeer, Vladimer, Vladimere,
Vladimire, Vladimyr, Vladjimir, Vladka,
Vladko, Vladlen, Vladmir, Volodimir,
Volodya, Volya, Vova, Wladimir*

Vladislav (Slavic) glorious ruler. See also Slava.
Vladik, Vladya, Vlas, Vlasislava, Vyacheslav, Wladislav

Vlas (Russian) a short form of Vladislav.

Volker (German) people's guard.
Folke

Volney (German) national spirit.

Von (German) a short form of many German names.

Vova (Russian) a form of Walter.
Vovka

Vuai (Swahili) savior.

Vyacheslav (Russian) a form of Vladislav. See also Slava.

Waban (Ojibwa) white.
Wabon

Wade (English) ford; river crossing.
Wad, Wadesworth, Wadi, Wadie, Waed, Waid, Waide, Wayde, Waydell, Whaid

Wadley (English) ford meadow.
Wadleigh, Wadly

Wadsworth (English) village near the ford.
Waddsworth

Wagner (German) wagoner, wagon maker. Music: Richard Wagner was a famous nineteenth-century German composer.
Waggoner

Wahid (Arabic) single; exclusively unequaled.
Waheed

Wahkan (Lakota) sacred.

Wahkoowah (Lakota) charging.

Wain (English) a short form of Wainwright. A form of Wayne.

Wainwright (English) wagon maker.
Wain, Wainright, Wayne, Wayneright, Waynewright, Waynright, Wright

Waite (English) watchman.
Waitman, Waiton, Waits, Wayte

Wakefield (English) wet field.
Field, Wake

Wakely (English) wet meadow.

Wakeman (English) watchman.
Wake

Wakiza (Native American) determined warrior.

Walcott (English) cottage by the wall.
Wallcot, Wallcott, Wolcott

Waldemar (German) powerful; famous. See also Vladimir.
Valdemar, Waldermar, Waldo

Walden (English) wooded valley. Literature: Henry David Thoreau made Walden Pond famous with his book *Walden*.
Waldi, Waldo, Waldon, Welti

Waldo (German) a familiar form of Oswald, Waldemar, Walden.
Wald, Waldy

Waldron (English) ruler.

Waleed (Arabic) newborn.
Waled, Walid

Walerian (Polish) strong; brave.

Wales (English) from Wales.
Wael, Wail, Wali, Walie, Waly

Walford (English) Welshman's ford.

Walfred (German) peaceful ruler.
Walfredo, Walfried

Wali (Arabic) all-governing.

Walker (English) cloth walker; cloth cleaner.
Wallie, Wally

Wallace (English) from Wales.
Wallach, Wallas, Wallie, Wallis, Wally, Walsh, Welsh

Wallach (German) a form of Wallace.
Wallache

Waller (German) powerful. (English) wall maker.

Wally (English) a familiar form of Walter.
Walli, Wallie

Walmond (German) mighty ruler.

Walsh (English) a form of Wallace.
Welch, Welsh

Walt (English) a short form of Walter, Walton.
Waltey, Waltli, Walty

Walter (German) army ruler, general. (English) woodsman. See also Gautier, Gualberto, Gualtiero, Gutierre, Ladislav, Vladimir. *Valter, Vanda, Vova, Walder, Wally, Walt, Waltli, Walther, Waltr, Wat, Waterio, Watkins, Watson, Wualter*

Walther (German) a form of Walter.

Walton (English) walled town. *Walt*

Waltr (Czech) a form of Walter.

Walworth (English) fenced-in farm.

Walwyn (English) Welsh friend. *Walwin, Walwinn, Walwynn, Walwynne, Welwyn*

Wamblee (Lakota) eagle.

Wang (Chinese) hope; wish.

Wanikiya (Lakota) savior.

Wanya (Russian) a form of Vanya. *Wanyai*

Wapi (Native American) lucky.

Warburton (English) fortified town.

Ward (English) watchman, guardian. *Warde, Warden, Worden*

Wardell (English) watchman's hill.

Wardley (English) watchman's meadow. *Wardlea, Wardleigh*

Ware (English) wary, cautious.

Warfield (English) field near the weir or fish trap.

Warford (English) ford near the weir or fish trap.

Warley (English) meadow near the weir or fish trap.

Warner (German) armed defender. (French) park keeper. *Werner*

Warren (German) general; warden; rabbit hutch. *Ware, Waring, Warrenson, Warrin, Warriner, Worrin*

Warton (English) town near the weir or fish trap.

Warwick (English) buildings near the weir or fish trap. *Warick, Warrick*

Washburn (English) overflowing river.

Washington (English) town near water. History: George Washington was the first U.S. president. *Wash*

Wasili (Russian) a form of Basil. *Wasyl*

Wasim (Arabic) graceful; good-looking. *Waseem, Wasseem, Wassim*

Watende (Nyakyusa) there will be revenge.

Waterio (Spanish) a form of Walter. *Gualtiero*

Watford (English) wattle ford; dam made of twigs and sticks.

Watkins (English) son of Walter. *Watkin*

Watson (English) son of Walter. *Wathson, Whatson*

Waverly (English) quaking aspen-tree meadow. *Waverlee, Waverley*

Wayland (English) a form of Waylon. *Weiland, Weyland*

Waylon (English) land by the road. *Wallen, Walon, Way, Waylan, Wayland, Waylen, Waylin, Weylin*

Wayman (English) road man; traveler. *Waymon*

Wayne (English) wagon maker. A short form of Wainwright. *Wain, Wanye, Wayn, Waynell, Waynne, Wene, Whayne*

Wazir (Arabic) minister.

Webb (English) weaver. *Web, Weeb*

Weber (German) weaver. *Webber, Webner*

Webley (English) weaver's meadow. *Webbley, Webbly, Webly*

Webster (English) weaver.

Weddel (English) valley near the ford.

Wei-Quo (Chinese) ruler of the country. *Wei*

Welborne (English) spring-fed stream. *Welborn, Welbourne, Welburn, Wellborn, Wellborne, Wellbourn, Wellburn*

Welby (German) farm near the well. *Welbey, Welbie, Wellbey, Wellby*

Weldon (English) hill near the well.
Weldan

Welfel (Yiddish) a form of William.
Welvel

Welford (English) ford near the well.

Wells (English) springs.
Welles

Welsh (English) a form of Wallace, Walsh.
Welch

Welton (English) town near the well.

Wemilat (Native American) all give to him.

Wemilo (Native American) all speak to him.

Wen (Gypsy) born in winter.

Wenceslaus (Slavic) wreath of honor.
Vencel, Wenceslao, Wenceslas, Wenzel, Wenzell, Wiencyslaw

Wendell (German) wanderer. (English) good dale, good valley.
Wandale, Wendall, Wendel, Wendle, Wendy

Wene (Hawaiian) a form of Wayne.

Wenford (English) white ford.
Wynford

Wentworth (English) pale man's settlement.

Wenutu (Native American) clear sky.

Werner (English) a form of Warner.
Wernhar, Wernher

Wes (English) a short form of Wesley.
Wess

Wesh (Gypsy) woods.

Wesley (English) western meadow.
Wes, Weseley, Wesle, Weslee, Wesleyan, Weslie, Wesly, Wessley, Westleigh, Westley, Wezley

West (English) west.

Westbrook (English) western brook.
Brook, West, Westbrooke

Westby (English) western farmstead.

Westcott (English) western cottage.
Wescot, Wescott, Westcot

Westley (English) a form of Wesley.
Westlee, Westly

Weston (English) western town.
West, Westen, Westin

Wetherby (English) wether-sheep farm.
Weatherbey, Weatherbie, Weatherby, Wetherbey, Wetherbie

Wetherell (English) wether-sheep corner.

Wetherly (English) wether-sheep meadow.

Weylin (English) a form of Waylon.
Weylan, Weylyn

Whalley (English) woods near a hill.
Whaley

Wharton (English) town on the bank of a lake.
Warton

Wheatley (English) wheat field.
Whatley, Wheatlea, Wheatleigh, Wheatly

Wheaton (English) wheat town.

Wheeler (English) wheel maker; wagon driver.

Whistler (English) whistler, piper.

Whit (English) a short form of Whitman, Whitney.
Whitt, Whyt, Whyte, Wit, Witt

Whitby (English) white house.

Whitcomb (English) white valley.
Whitcombe, Whitcumb

Whitelaw (English) small hill.
Whitlaw

Whitey (English) white skinned; white haired.

Whitfield (English) white field.

Whitford (English) white ford.

Whitley (English) white meadow.
Whitlea, Whitlee, Whitleigh

Whitman (English) white-haired man.
Whit

Whitmore (English) white moor.
Whitmoor, Whittemore, Witmore, Wittemore

Whitney (English) white island; white water.
Whit, Whittney, Widney, Widny

Whittaker (English) white field.
Whitacker, Whitaker, Whitmaker

Wicasa (Dakota) man.

Wicent (Polish) a form of Vincent.
Wicek, Wicus

Wichado (Native American) willing.

Wickham (English) village enclosure.
Wick

Wickley (English) village meadow.
Wilcley

Wid (English) wide.

Wies (German) renowned warrior.

Wikoli (Hawaiian) a form of Victor.

Wiktor (Polish) a form of Victor.

Wilanu (Moquelumnan) pouring water on flour.

Wilbert (German) brilliant; resolute.
Wilberto, Wilburt

Wilbur (English) wall fortification; bright willows.
Wilber, Wilburn, Wilburt, Willbur, Wilver

Wilder (English) wilderness, wild.
Wylder

Wildon (English) wooded hill.
Wilden, Willdon

Wile (Hawaiian) a form of Willie.

Wiley (English) willow meadow; Will's meadow.
Whiley, Wildy, Willey, Wylie

Wilford (English) willow-tree ford.
Wilferd

Wilfred (German) determined peace-maker.
Wilferd, Wilfredo, Wilfrid, Wilfride,

Wilfried, Wilfryd, Will, Willfred, Willfried, Willie, Willy

Wilfredo (Spanish) a form of Wilfred.
Fredo, Wifredo, Wilfrido, Willfredo

Wilhelm (German) determined guardian.
Wilhelmus, Willem

Wiliama (Hawaiian) a form of William.
Pila, Wile

Wilkie (English) a familiar form of Wilkins.
Wikie, Wilke

Wilkins (English) William's kin.
Wilkens, Wilkes, Wilkie, Wilkin, Wilks, Willkes, Willkins

Wilkinson (English) son of little William.
Wilkenson, Willkinson

Will (English) a short form of William.
Wil, Wilm, Wim

Willard (German) determined and brave.
Williard

Willem (German) a form of William.
Willim

William (English) a form of Wilhelm. See also Gilamu, Guglielmo, Guilherme, Guillaume, Guillermo, Gwilym, Liam, Uilliam, Wilhelm.
Bill, Billy, Vasyl, Vilhelm, Vili, Viliam, Viljo, Ville, Villiam, Welfel, Wilek, Wiliam, Wiliama, Wiliame, Wiliame, Will, Willaim, Willam, Willeam, Willem, Williams, Willie,

Willil, Willis, Willium, Williw, Willyam, Wim

Williams (German) son of William.
Wilams, Willaims, Williamson, Wuliams

Willie (German) a familiar form of William.
Wile, Wille, Willi, Willia, Willy

Willis (German) son of Willie.
Willice, Wills, Willus, Wyllis

Willoughby (English) willow farm.
Willoughbey, Willoughbie

Wills (English) son of Will.

Willy (German) a form of Willie.
Willey, Wily

Wilmer (German) determined and famous.
Willimar, Willmer, Wilm, Wilmar, Wylmar, Wylmer

Wilmot (Teutonic) resolute spirit.
Willmont, Willmot, Wilm, Wilmont

Wilny (Native American) eagle singing while flying.

Wilson (English) son of Will.
Wilkinson, Willson, Wilsen, Wolson

Wilt (English) a short form of Wilton.

Wilton (English) farm by the spring.
Will, Wilt

Wilu (Moquelumnan) chicken hawk squawking.

Win (Cambodian) bright. (English) a short form of Winston and names ending in "win."
Winn, Winnie, Winny

Wincent (Polish) a form of Vincent.
Wicek, Wicenty, Wicus, Wince, Wincenty

Winchell (English) bend in the road;
bend in the land.

Windsor (English) riverbank with a
winch. History: the surname of the
British royal family.
Wincer, Winsor, Wyndsor

Winfield (English) friendly field.
*Field, Winfred, Winfrey, Winifield,
Winnfield, Wynfield, Wynnfield*

Winfried (German) friend of peace.

Wing (Chinese) glory.
Wing-Chiu, Wing-Kit

Wingate (English) winding gate.

Wingi (Native American) willing.

Winslow (English) friend's hill.

Winston (English) friendly town; vic-
tory town.
*Win, Winsten, Winstin, Winstonn,
Winton, Wynstan, Wynston*

Winter (English) born in winter.
Winterford, Wynter

Winthrop (English) victory at the
crossroads.

Winton (English) a form of Winston.
Wynten, Wynton

Winward (English) friend's guardian;
friend's forest.

Wit (Polish) life. (English) a form of
Whit. (Flemish) a short form of
DeWitt.
Witt, Wittie, Witty

Witek (Polish) a form of Victor.

Witha (Arabic) handsome.

Witter (English) wise warrior.

Witton (English) wise man's estate.

Wladislav (Polish) a form of Vladislav.
Wladislaw

Wolcott (English) cottage in the
woods.

Wolf (German, English) a short form
of Wolfe, Wolfgang.
Wolff, Wolfie, Wolfy

Wolfe (English) wolf.
Wolf, Woolf

Wolfgang (German) wolf quarrel.
Music: Wolfgang Amadeus Mozart
was a famous eighteenth-century
Austrian composer.
Wolf, Wolfegang, Wolfgans

Wood (English) a short form of
Elwood, Garwood, Woodrow.
Woody

Woodfield (English) forest meadow.

Woodford (English) ford through the
forest.

Woodrow (English) passage in the
woods. History: Thomas Woodrow
Wilson was the twenty-eighth U.S.
president.
Wood, Woodman, Woodroe, Woody

Woodruff (English) forest ranger.

Woodson (English) son of Wood.
Woods, Woodsen

Woodward (English) forest warden.
Woodard

Woodville (English) town at the edge
of the woods.

Woody (American) a familiar form of
Elwood, Garwood, Woodrow.
Wooddy, Woodie

Woolsey (English) victorious wolf.

Worcester (English) forest army camp.

Wordsworth (English) wolf-guardian's
farm. Literature: William Wordsworth
was a famous British poet.
Worth

Worie (Ibo) born on market day.

Worth (English) a short form of
Wordsworth.
Worthey, Worthington, Worthy

Worton (English) farm town.

Wouter (German) powerful warrior.

Wrangle (American) a form of
Rangle.
Wrangler

Wray (Scandinavian) corner property.
(English) crooked.
Wreh

Wren (Welsh) chief, ruler. (English)
wren.

Wright (English) a short form of
Wainwright.

Wrisley (English) a form of Risley.
Wrisee, Wrislie, Wrisly

Wriston (English) a form of Riston.
Wryston

Wuliton (Native American) will do well.

Wunand (Native American) God is good.

Wuyi (Moquelumnan) turkey vulture flying.

Wyatt (French) little warrior.
Wiatt, Wyat, Wyatte, Wye, Wyeth, Wyett, Wyitt, Wytt

Wybert (English) battle bright.

Wyborn (Scandinavian) war bear.

Wyck (Scandinavian) village.

Wycliff (English) white cliff; village near the cliff.
Wyckliffe, Wycliffe

Wylie (English) charming.
Wiley, Wye, Wyley, Wyllie, Wyly

Wyman (English) fighter, warrior.

Wymer (English) famous in battle.

Wyn (Welsh) light skinned; white. (English) friend. A short form of Selwyn.
Win, Wyne, Wynn, Wynne

Wyndham (Scottish) village near the winding road.
Windham, Wynndham

Wynono (Native American) first-born son.

Wythe (English) willow tree.

Xabat (Basque) savior.

Xaiver (Basque) a form of Xavier.
Xajavier, Xzaiver

Xan (Greek) a short form of Alexander.
Xane

Xander (Greek) a short form of Alexander.
Xande, Xzander

Xanthus (Latin) golden haired.
Xanthos

Xarles (Basque) a form of Charles.

Xavier (Arabic) bright. (Basque) owner of the new house. See also Exavier, Javier, Salvatore, Saverio.
Xabier, Xaiver, Xavaeir, Xaver, Xavian, Xaviar, Xavior, Xavon, Xavyer, Xever, Xizavier, Xxavier, Xzavier, Zavier

Xenophon (Greek) strange voice.
Xeno, Zennie

Xenos (Greek) stranger; guest.
Zenos

Xerxes (Persian) ruler. History: a king of Persia.
Zerk

Ximenes (Spanish) a form of Simon.
Ximenez, Ximon, Ximun, Xymenes

Xylon (Greek) forest.

Xzavier (Basque) a form of Xavier.
Xzavaier, Xzaver, Xzavion, Xzavior, Xzvaier

Yadid (Hebrew) friend; beloved.
Yedid

Yadon (Hebrew) he will judge.
Yadean, Yadin, Yadun

Yael (Hebrew) a form of Jael.

Yafeu (Ibo) bold.

Yagil (Hebrew) he will rejoice.

Yago (Spanish) a form of James.

Yahto (Lakota) blue.

Yahya (Arabic) living.
Yahye

Yair (Hebrew) he will enlighten.
Yahir

Yakecen (Dene) sky song.

Yakez (Carrier) heaven.

Yakov (Russian) a form of Jacob.
Yaacob, Yaacov, Yaakov, Yachov, Yacoub, Yacov, Yakob, Yashko

Yale (German) productive. (English) old.

Yan, Yann (Russian) forms of John.
Yanichek, Yanick, Yanka, Yannick

Yana (Native American) bear.

Yancy (Native American) Englishman, Yankee.
Yan, Yance, Yancey, Yanci, Yansey, Yansy, Yantsey, Yauncey, Yauncy, Yency

Yanick, Yannick (Russian) familiar forms of Yan.
Yanic, Yanik, Yannic, Yannik, Yonic, Yonnik

Yanka (Russian) a familiar form of John.
Yanikm

Yanni (Greek) a form of John.
Ioannis, Yani, Yannakis, Yannis, Yanny, Yiannis, Yoni

Yanton (Hebrew) a form of Johnathon, Jonathon.

Yao (Ewe) born on Thursday.

Yaphet (Hebrew) a form of Japheth.
Yapheth, Yefat, Yephat

Yarb (Gypsy) herb.

Yardan (Arabic) king.

Yarden (Hebrew) a form of Jordan.

Yardley (English) enclosed meadow.
Lee, Yard, Yardlea, Yardlee, Yardleigh, Yardly

Yarom (Hebrew) he will raise up.
Yarum

Yaron (Hebrew) he will sing; he will cry out.
Jaron, Yairon

Yasashiku (Japanese) gentle; polite.

Yash (Hindi) victorious; glory.

Yasha (Russian) a form of Jacob, James.
Yascha, Yashka, Yashko

Yashwant (Hindi) glorious.

Yasin (Arabic) prophet.
Yasine, Yasseen, Yassin, Yassine, Yazen

Yasir (Afghan) humble; takes it easy. (Arabic) wealthy.
Yasar, Yaser, Yashar, Yasser

Yasuo (Japanese) restful.

Yates (English) gates.
Yeats

Yatin (Hindi) ascetic.

Yavin (Hebrew) he will understand.
Jabin

Yawo (Akan) born on Thursday.

Yazid (Arabic) his power will increase.
Yazeed, Yazide

Yechiel (Hebrew) God lives.

Yedidya (Hebrew) a form of Jedidiah. See also Didi.
Yadai, Yedidia, Yedidiah, Yido

Yegor (Russian) a form of George. See also Egor, Igor.
Ygor

Yehoshua (Hebrew) a form of Joshua.
Yeshua, Yeshuah, Yoshua, Y'shua, Yushua

Yehoyakem (Hebrew) a form of Joachim, Joaquín.
Yakim, Yehayakim, Yokim, Yoyakim

Yehudi (Hebrew) a form of Judah.
Yechudi, Yechudit, Yehuda, Yehudah, Yehudit

Yelutci (Moquelumnan) bear walking silently.

Yeoman (English) attendant; retainer.
Yoeman, Youman

Yeremey (Russian) a form of Jeremiah.
Yarema, Yaremka, Yeremy, Yerik

Yervant (Armenian) king, ruler. History: an Armenian king.

Yeshaya (Hebrew) gift. See also Shai.

Yeshurun (Hebrew) right way.

Yeska (Russian) a form of Joseph.
Yesya

Yestin (Welsh) just.

Yevgenyi (Russian) a form of Eugene.
Gena, Yevgeni, Yevgenij, Yevgeniy

Yigal (Hebrew) he will redeem.
Yagel, Yigael

Yirmaya (Hebrew) a form of Jeremiah.
Yirmayahu

Yishai (Hebrew) a form of Jesse.

Yisrael (Hebrew) a form of Israel.
Yesarel, Yisroel

Yitro (Hebrew) a form of Jethro.

Yitzchak (Hebrew) a form of Isaac. See also Itzak.
Yitzak, Yitzchok, Yitzhak

Yngve (Swedish) ancestor; lord, master.

Yo (Cambodian) honest.

Yoakim (Slavic) a form of Jacob.
Yoackim

Yoan (German) a form of Johan, Johann.
Yoann

Yoav (Hebrew) a form of Joab.

Yochanan (Hebrew) a form of John.
Yohanan

Yoel (Hebrew) a form of Joel.

Yogesh (Hindi) ascetic. Religion: another name for the Hindu god Shiva.

Yohance (Hausa) a form of John.

Yohan, Yohann (German) forms of Johan, Johann.
Yohane, Yohanes, Yohanne, Yohannes, Yohans, Yohn

Yonah (Hebrew) a form of Jonah.
Yona, Yonas

Yonatan (Hebrew) a form of Jonathan.
Yonathan, Yonathon, Yonaton, Yonattan

Yong (Chinese) courageous.
Yonge

Yong-Sun (Korean) dragon in the first position; courageous.

Yoni (Greek) a form of Yanni.
Yonis, Yonnas, Yonny, Yony

Yoofi (Akan) born on Friday.

Yooku (Fante) born on Wednesday.

Yoram (Hebrew) God is high.
Joram

Yorgos (Greek) a form of George.
Yiorgos, Yorgo

York (English) boar estate; yew-tree estate.
Yorick, Yorke, Yorker, Yorkie, Yorrick

Yorkoo (Fante) born on Thursday.

Yosef (Hebrew) a form of Joseph. See also Osip.
Yoceph, Yoosuf, Yoseff, Yoseph, Yosief, Yosif, Yosuf, Yosyf, Yousef, Yusif

Yóshi (Japanese) adopted son.
Yoshiki, Yoshiuki

Yoshiyahu (Hebrew) a form of Josiah.
Yoshia, Yoshiah, Yoshiya, Yoshiyah, Yosiah

Yoskolo (Moquelumnan) breaking off pine cones.

Yosu (Hebrew) a form of Jesus.

Yotimo (Moquelumnan) yellow jacket carrying food to its hive.

Yottoko (Native American) mud at the water's edge.

Young (English) young.
Yung

Young-Jae (Korean) pile of prosperity.

Young-Soo (Korean) keeping the prosperity.

Youri (Russian) a form of Yuri.

Yousef (Yiddish) a form of Joseph.
Yousaf, Youseef, Yousef, Youseph, Yousif, Youssef, Yousseff, Yousuf

Youssel (Yiddish) a familiar form of Joseph.
Yussel

Yov (Russian) a short form of Yoakim.

Yovani (Slavic) a form of Jovan.
Yovan, Yovanni, Yovanny, Yovany, Yovni

Yoyi (Hebrew) a form of George.

Yrjo (Finnish) a form of George.

Ysidro (Greek) a short form of Isidore.

Yu (Chinese) universe.
Yue

Yudell (English) a form of Udell.
Yudale, Yudel

Yuki (Japanese) snow.
Yukiko, Yukio, Yuuki

Yul (Mongolian) beyond the horizon.

Yule (English) born at Christmas.

Yuli (Basque) youthful.

Yuma (Native American) son of a chief.

Yunus (Turkish) a form of Jonah.

Yurcel (Turkish) sublime.

Yuri (Russian, Ukrainian) a form of George. (Hebrew) a familiar form of Uriah.
Yehor, Youri, Yura, Yure, Yuric, Yurii, Yurij, Yurik, Yurko, Yurri, Yury, Yusha

Yusif (Russian) a form of Joseph.
Yuseph, Yusof, Yussof, Yusup, Yuzef, Yuzep

Yustyn (Russian) a form of Justin.
Yusts

Yusuf (Arabic, Swahili) a form of Joseph.
Yusef, Yusuff

Yutu (Moquelumnan) coyote out hunting.

Yuval (Hebrew) rejoicing.

Yves (French) a form of Ivar, Ives.
Yvens, Yvon, Yyves

Yvon (French) a form of Ivar, Yves.
Ivon, Yuvon, Yvan, Yvonne

Zac (Hebrew) a short form of
Zachariah, Zachary.
Zacc

Zacarias (Portuguese, Spanish) a form
of Zachariah.
Zacaria, Zacariah

Zacary (Hebrew) a form of Zachary.
*Zac, Zacaras, Zacari, Zacariah, Zacarias,
Zacarie, Zacarious, Zacery, Zacory,
Zacrye*

Zaccary (Hebrew) a form of Zachary.
*Zac, Zaccaeus, Zaccari, Zaccaria,
Zaccariah, Zaccary, Zaccea, Zaccharie,
Zacchary, Zacchery, Zaccury*

Zaccheus (Hebrew) innocent, pure.
Zacceus, Zacchaeus, Zacchious

Zach (Hebrew) a short form of
Zachariah, Zachary.

Zachari (Hebrew) a form of Zachary.
Zacheri

Zacharia (Hebrew) a form of
Zachary.
Zacharya

Zachariah (Hebrew) God
remembered.
Zac, Zacarias, Zacarius, Zacary, Zaccary,
Zach, Zacharias, Zachary, Zacharyah,
Zachory, Zachury, Zack, Zakaria, Zako,
Zaquero, Zecharia, Zechariah, Zecharya,
Zeggery, Zeke, Zhachory

Zacharias (German) a form of
Zachariah.
*Zacarías, Zacharais, Zachariaus,
Zacharius, Zackarias, Zakarias,
Zecharias, Zekarias*

Zacharie (Hebrew) a form of
Zachary.
Zachare, Zacharee, Zachurie, Zecharie

Zachary (Hebrew) a familiar form of
Zachariah. History: Zachary Taylor
was the twelfth U.S. president. See
also Sachar, Sakeri.
*Xachary, Zac, Zacary, Zaccary, Zach,
Zacha, Zachaery, Zachaios, Zacharay,
Zacharey, Zachari, Zacharia, Zacharias,
Zacharie, Zacharry, Zachaury, Zachery,
Zachory, Zachrey, Zachry, Zachuery,
Zachury, Zack, Zackary, Zackery,
Zackory, Zakaria, Zakary, Zakery,
Zakkary, Zechary, Zechery, Zeke*

Zachery (Hebrew) a form of Zachary.
*Zacheray, Zacherey, Zacheria, Zacherias,
Zacheriah, Zacherie, Zacherius, Zackery*

Zachory (Hebrew) a form of Zachary.

Zachry (Hebrew) a form of Zachary.
Zachre, Zachrey, Zachri

Zack (Hebrew) a short form of
Zachariah, Zachary.
Zach, Zak, Zaks

Zackary (Hebrew) a form of Zachary.
*Zack, Zackari, Zacharia, Zackare,
Zackaree, Zackariah, Zackarie, Zackery,*
Zackhary, Zackie, Zackree, Zackrey,
Zackry

Zackery (Hebrew) a form of Zachery.
*Zackere, Zackeree, Zackerey, Zackeri,
Zackeria, Zackeriah, Zackerie, Zackerry*

Zackory (Hebrew) a form of Zachary.
*Zackoriah, Zackorie, Zacorey, Zacori,
Zacory, Zacry, Zakory*

Zadok (Hebrew) a short form of
Tzadok.
Zaddik, Zadik, Zadoc, Zaydok

Zadornin (Basque) Saturn.

Zafir (Arabic) victorious.
Zafar, Zafeer, Zafer, Zaffar

Zahid (Arabic) self-denying, ascetic.
Zaheed

Zahir (Arabic) shining, bright.
*Zahair, Zahar, Zaheer, Zahi, Zair, Zaire,
Zayyir*

Zahur (Swahili) flower.

Zaid (Arabic) increase, growth.
Zaied, Zaiid, Zayd

Zaide (Hebrew) older.

Zaim (Arabic) brigadier general.

Zain (English) a form of Zane.
Zaine

Zakaria (Hebrew) a form of
Zachariah.
*Zakaraiya, Zakareeya, Zakareeyah,
Zakariah, Zakariya, Zakeria, Zakeriah*

Zakariyya (Arabic) prophet. Religion:
an Islamic prophet.

Zakary (Hebrew) a form of Zachery.
*Zak, Zakarai, Zakare, Zakaree, Zakari,
Zakarias, Zakarie, Zakarius, Zakariye,
Zake, Zakhar, Zaki, Zakir, Zakkai,
Zako, Zakqary, Zakree, Zakri, Zakris,
Zakry*

Zakery (Hebrew) a form of Zachary.
Zakeri, Zakerie, Zakiry

Zaki (Arabic) bright; pure. (Hausa)
lion.
Zakee, Zakia, Zakie, Zakiy, Zakki

Zakia (Swahili) intelligent.

Zakkary (Hebrew) a form of Zachary.
Zakk, Zakkari, Zakkery, Zakkyre

Zako (Hungarian) a form of
Zachariah.

Zale (Greek) sea strength.
Zayle

Zalmai (Afghan) young.

Zalman (Yiddish) a form of Solomon.
Zaloman

Zamiel (German) a form of Samuel.
Zamal, Zamuel

Zamir (Hebrew) song; bird.
Zameer

Zan (Italian) clown.
Zann, Zanni, Zannie, Zanny, Zhan

Zander (Greek) a short form of
Alexander.
Zandore, Zandra, Zandrae, Zandy

Zane (English) a form of John.
Zain, Zayne, Zhane

Zanis (Latvian) a form of Janis.
Zannis

Zanvil (Hebrew) a form of Samuel.
Zanwill

Zaquan (American) a combination of
the prefix Za + Quan.
Zaquain, Zaquon, Zaqwan

Zareb (African) protector.

Zared (Hebrew) ambush.
Zaryd

Zarek (Polish) may God protect the
king.
*Zarik, Zarrick, Zerek, Zerick, Zerric,
Zerrick*

Zavier (Arabic) a form of Xavier.
*Zavair, Zaverie, Zavery, Zavierre, Zavior,
Zavyr, Zayvius, Zxavian*

Zayit (Hebrew) olive.

Zayne (English) a form of Zane.
Zayan, Zayin, Zayn

Zdenek (Czech) follower of Saint
Denis.

Zeb (Hebrew) a short form of
Zebediah, Zebulon.
Zev

Zebediah (Hebrew) God's gift.
*Zeb, Zebadia, Zebadiah, Zebedee,
Zebedia, Zebidiah, Zedidiah*

Zebedee (Hebrew) a familiar form of
Zebediah.
Zebadee

Zebulon (Hebrew) exalted, honored;
lofty house.
Zabulan, Zeb, Zebulan, Zebulen,
*Zebulin, Zebulun, Zebulyn, Zev,
Zevulon, Zevulun, Zhebulen, Zubin*

Zechariah (Hebrew) a form of
Zachariah.
*Zecharia, Zecharian, Zecheriah,
Zechuriah, Zekariah, Zekarias, Zeke,
Zekeria, Zekeriah, Zekerya*

Zed (Hebrew) a short form of
Zedekiah.

Zedekiah (Hebrew) God is mighty
and just.
Zed, Zedechiah, Zedekias, Zedikiah

Zedidiah (Hebrew) a form of
Zebediah.

Zeeman (Dutch) seaman.

Zeév (Hebrew) wolf.
Zeévi, Zeff, Zif

Zeheb (Turkish) gold.

Zeke (Hebrew) a short form of
Ezekiel, Zachariah, Zachary,
Zechariah.

Zeki (Turkish) clever, intelligent.
Zeky

Zelgai (Afghan) heart.

Zelig (Yiddish) a form of Selig.
Zeligman, Zelik

Zelimir (Slavic) wishes for peace.

Zemar (Afghan) lion.

Zen (Japanese) religious. Religion: a
form of Buddhism.

Zenda (Czech) a form of Eugene.
Zhek

Zeno (Greek) cart; harness. History: a Greek philosopher.
Zenan, Zenas, Zenon, Zino, Zinon

Zephaniah (Hebrew) treasured by God.
Zaph, Zaphania, Zeph, Zephan

Zephyr (Greek) west wind.
Zeferino, Zeffrey, Zephery, Zephire, Zephram, Zephran, Zephrin

Zero (Arabic) empty, void.

Zeroun (Armenian) wise and respected.

Zeshawn (American) a combination of the prefix Ze + Shawn.
Zeshan, Zeshaun, Zeshon, Zishaan, Zishan, Zshawn

Zesiro (Luganda) older of twins.

Zeus (Greek) living. Mythology: chief god of the Greek pantheon.

Zeusef (Portuguese) a form of Joseph.

Zev (Hebrew) a short form of Zebulon.

Zevi (Hebrew) a form of Tzvi.
Zhvie, Zhvy, Zvi

Zhek (Russian) a short form of Evgeny.
Zhenechka, Zhenka, Zhenya

Zhìxin (Chinese) ambitious.
Zhi, Zhìhuán, Zhipeng, Zhi-yang, Zhìyuan

Zhuàng (Chinese) strong.

Zhora (Russian) a form of George.
Zhorik. Zhorka, Zhorz, Zhurka

Zia (Hebrew) trembling; moving. (Arabic) light.
Ziah

Zigfrid (Latvian, Russian) a form of Siegfried.
Zegfrido, Zigfrids, Ziggy, Zygfryd, Zygi

Ziggy (American) a familiar form of Siegfried, Sigmund.
Ziggie

Zigor (Basque) punishment.

Zikomo (Nguni) thank-you.

Zilaba (Luganda) born while sick.
Zilabamuzale

Zimra (Hebrew) song of praise.
Zemora, Zimrat, Zimri, Zimria, Zimriah, Zimriya

Zimraan (Arabic) praise.

Zinan (Japanese) second son.

Zindel (Yiddish) a form of Alexander.
Zindil, Zunde

Zion (Hebrew) sign, omen; excellent. Bible: the name used to refer to Israel and to the Jewish people.
Tzion, Zyon

Ziskind (Yiddish) sweet child.

Ziv (Hebrew) shining brightly. (Slavic) a short form of Ziven.

Ziven (Slavic) vigorous, lively.
Zev, Ziv, Zivka, Zivon

Ziyad (Arabic) increase.
Zayd, Ziyaad

Zlatan (Czech) gold.
Zlatek, Zlatko

Zohar (Hebrew) bright light.
Zohair

Zollie, Zolly (Hebrew) forms of Solly.
Zoilo

Zoltán (Hungarian) life.

Zorba (Greek) live each day.

Zorion (Basque) a form of Orion.
Zoran, Zoren, Zorian, Zoron, Zorrine, Zorrion

Zorya (Slavic) star; dawn.

Zotikos (Greek) saintly, holy. Religion: a saint in the Eastern Orthodox Church.

Zotom (Kiowa) a biter.

Zsigmond (Hungarian) a form of Sigmund.
Ziggy, Zigmund, Zsiga

Zuberi (Swahili) strong.

Zubin (Hebrew) a short form of Zebulon.
Zubeen

Zuhayr (Arabic) brilliant, shining.
Zyhair, Zuheer

Zuka (Shona) sixpence.

Zuriel (Hebrew) God is my rock.

Zygmunt (Polish) a form of Sigmund.

Very Best Baby Name Worksheet

| **Mom's Favorite Names** | | | | | **Dad's Favorite Names** | | | |
Rating	Girls	Rating	Boys	Rating	Girls	Rating	Boys
____	_____	____	_____	____	_____	____	_____
____	_____	____	_____	____	_____	____	_____
____	_____	____	_____	____	_____	____	_____
____	_____	____	_____	____	_____	____	_____
____	_____	____	_____	____	_____	____	_____
____	_____	____	_____	____	_____	____	_____
____	_____	____	_____	____	_____	____	_____
____	_____	____	_____	____	_____	____	_____
____	_____	____	_____	____	_____	____	_____
____	_____	____	_____	____	_____	____	_____
____	_____	____	_____	____	_____	____	_____
____	_____	____	_____	____	_____	____	_____
____	_____	____	_____	____	_____	____	_____
____	_____	____	_____	____	_____	____	_____
____	_____	____	_____	____	_____	____	_____
____	_____	____	_____	____	_____	____	_____
____	_____	____	_____	____	_____	____	_____
____	_____	____	_____	____	_____	____	_____
____	_____	____	_____	____	_____	____	_____
____	_____	____	_____	____	_____	____	_____
____	_____	____	_____	____	_____	____	_____
____	_____	____	_____	____	_____	____	_____
____	_____	____	_____	____	_____	____	_____

Final Choice Worksheet

Girl's Names

Rating	First	Middle	Last
_____	_____	_____	_____
_____	_____	_____	_____
_____	_____	_____	_____
_____	_____	_____	_____
_____	_____	_____	_____
_____	_____	_____	_____
_____	_____	_____	_____
_____	_____	_____	_____
_____	_____	_____	_____

Boy's Names

Rating	First	Middle	Last
_____	_____	_____	_____
_____	_____	_____	_____
_____	_____	_____	_____
_____	_____	_____	_____
_____	_____	_____	_____
_____	_____	_____	_____
_____	_____	_____	_____
_____	_____	_____	_____

The 15 things to consider: namesakes, nationality, religion, gender, number of names, sounds, rhythms, pronunciation, spelling, popularity, uniqueness, stereotypes, initials, nicknames, meanings.

Also from Meadowbrook Press

✦ *Pregnancy, Childbirth, and the Newborn*
More complete and up-to-date than any other pregnancy guide, this remarkable book is the "bible" for child-birth educators. Now revised with a greatly expanded treatment of pregnancy tests, complications, and infections; an expanded list of drugs and medications (plus advice for uses); and a brand-new chapter on creating a detailed birth plan.

✦ *Eating Expectantly*
Dietitian Bridget Swinney offers a practical and tasty approach to prenatal nutrition, combining nutrition guidelines for each trimester with 200 complete menus, 85 tasty recipes, plus cooking and shopping tips. Cited by *Child* magazine as one of the "10 best parenting books of 1993," *Eating Expectantly* is newly revised with the most current nutrition information.

✦ *Feed Me! I'm Yours*
Parents love this easy-to-use, economical guide to making baby food at home. More than 200 recipes cover everything a parent needs to know about teething foods, nutritious snacks, and quick, pleasing lunches.

✦ *First-Year Baby Care*
This is one of the leading baby-care books to guide you through your baby's first year. It contains complete information on the basics of baby care, including bathing, diapering, medical facts, and feeding your baby. Includes step-by-step illustrated instructions to make finding information easy, newborn screening and immunization schedules, breastfeeding information for working mothers, expanded information on child care options, reference guides to common illnesses, and environmental and safety tips.

We offer many more titles written to delight, inform, and entertain.

To order books with a credit card or browse our full

selection of titles, visit our web site at:

www.meadowbrookpress.com

or call toll-free to place an order, request a free catalog, or ask a question:

1-800-338-2232

Meadowbrook Press • 5451 Smetana Drive • Minnetonka, MN • 55343